OMNIBUS 7

I AM A HERO

Art and story
KENGO HANAZAWA
花沢健吾

This Dark Horse Manga omnibus
collects *I Am a Hero* chapters 144
to 167, first appearing in Japan as
I Am a Hero Volumes 13 and 14.

Translation
KUMAR SIVASUBRAMANIAN

English Adaptation
PHILIP R. SIMON

Lettering
STEVE DUTRO

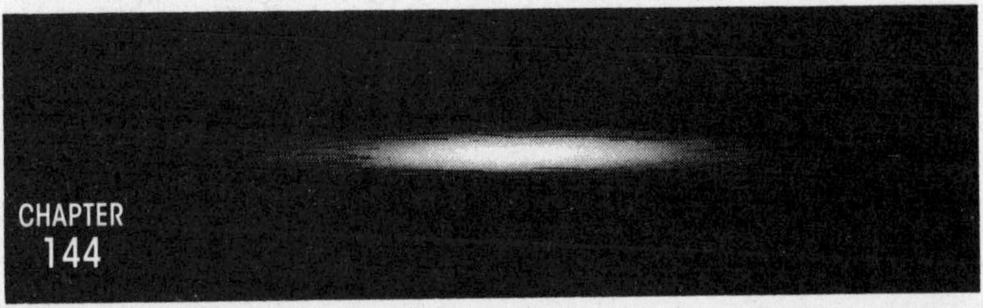
CHAPTER
144

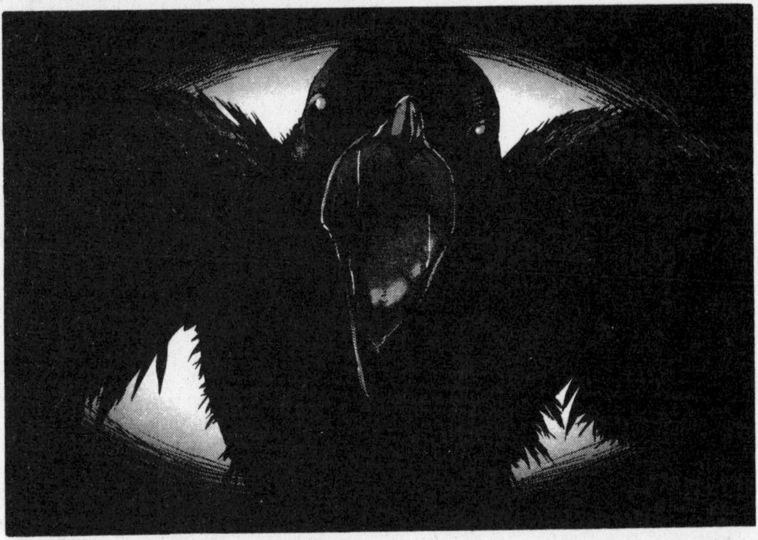

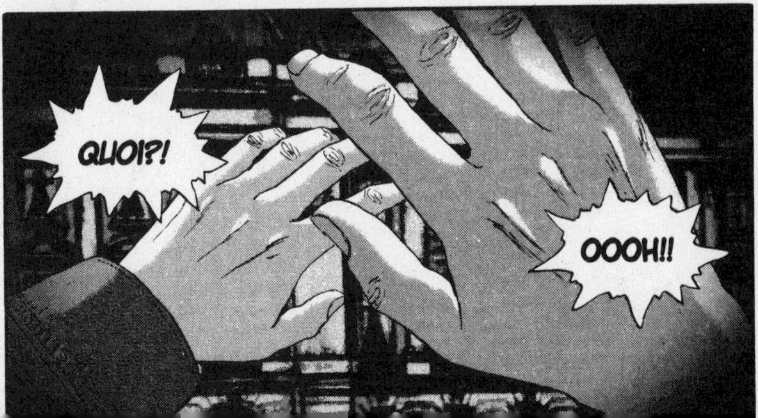
OOOH!!
QUOI?!

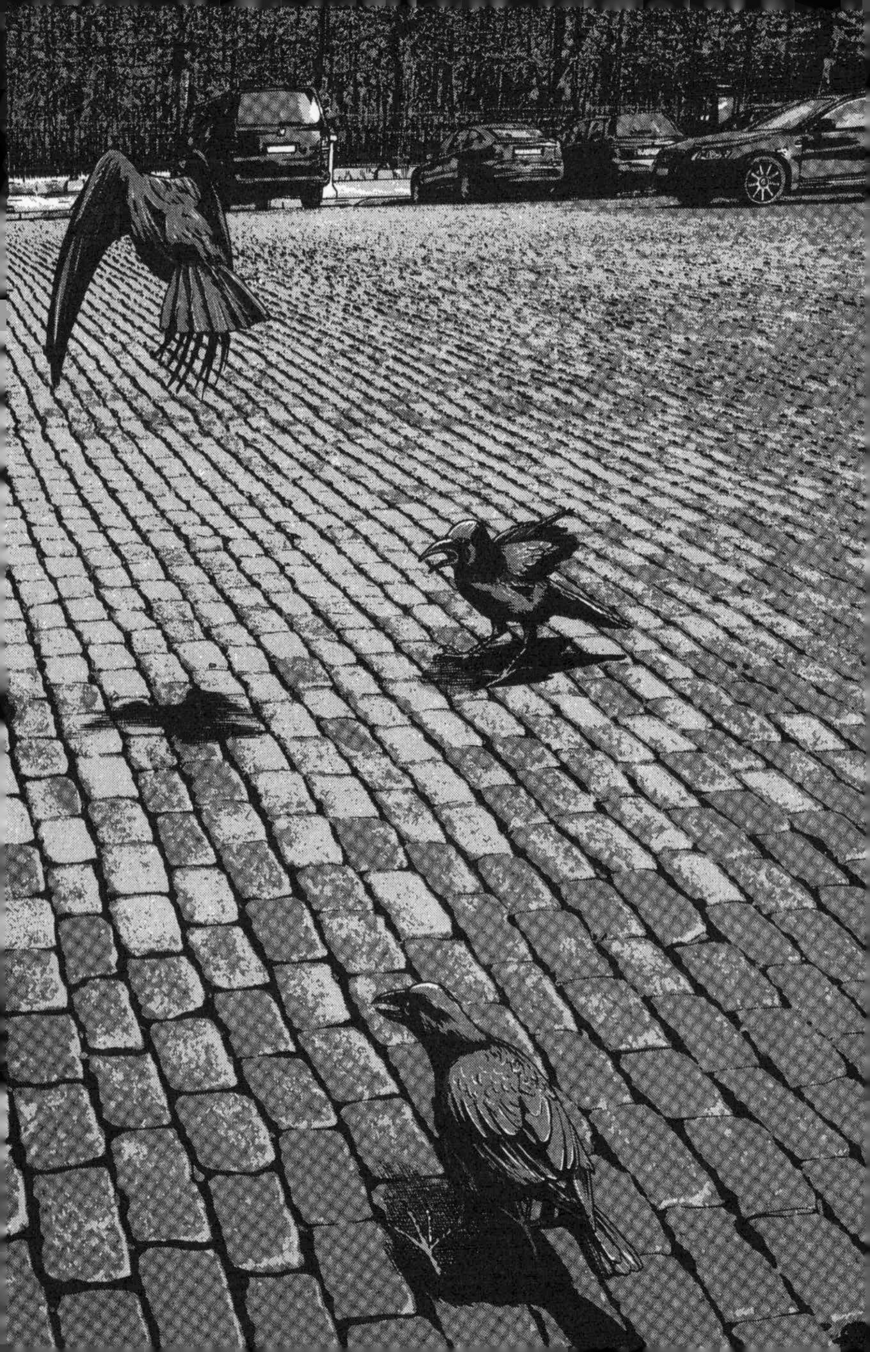

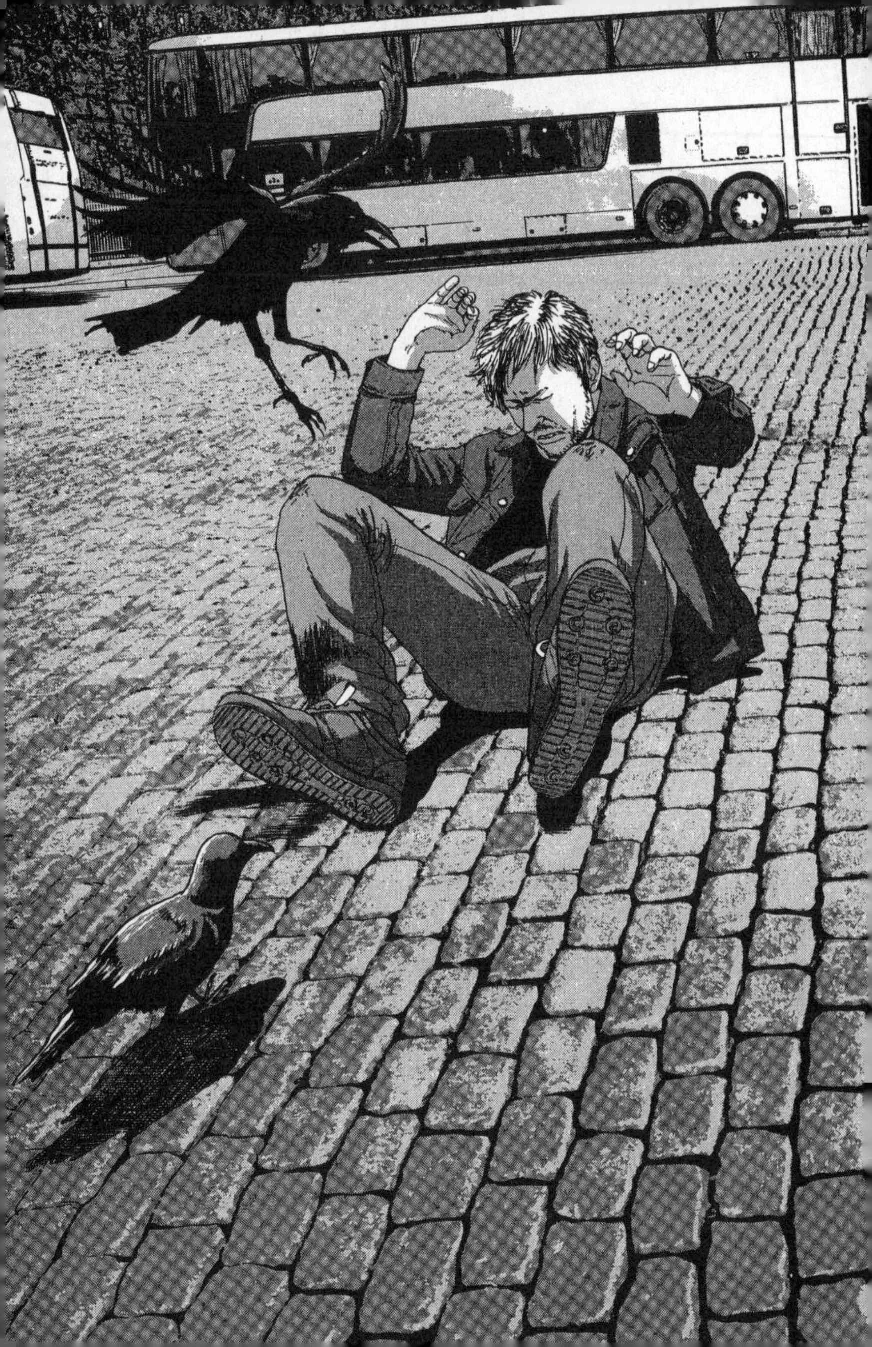

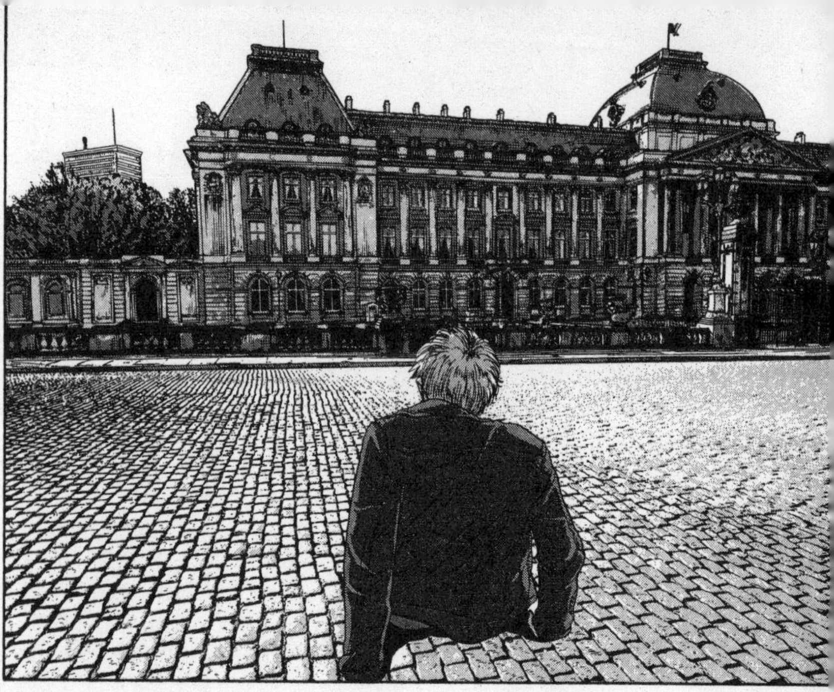
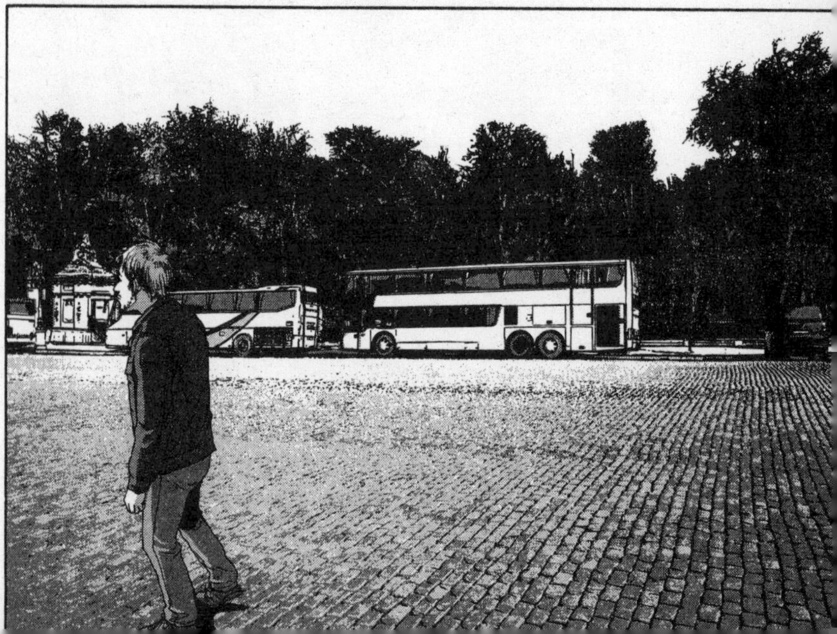

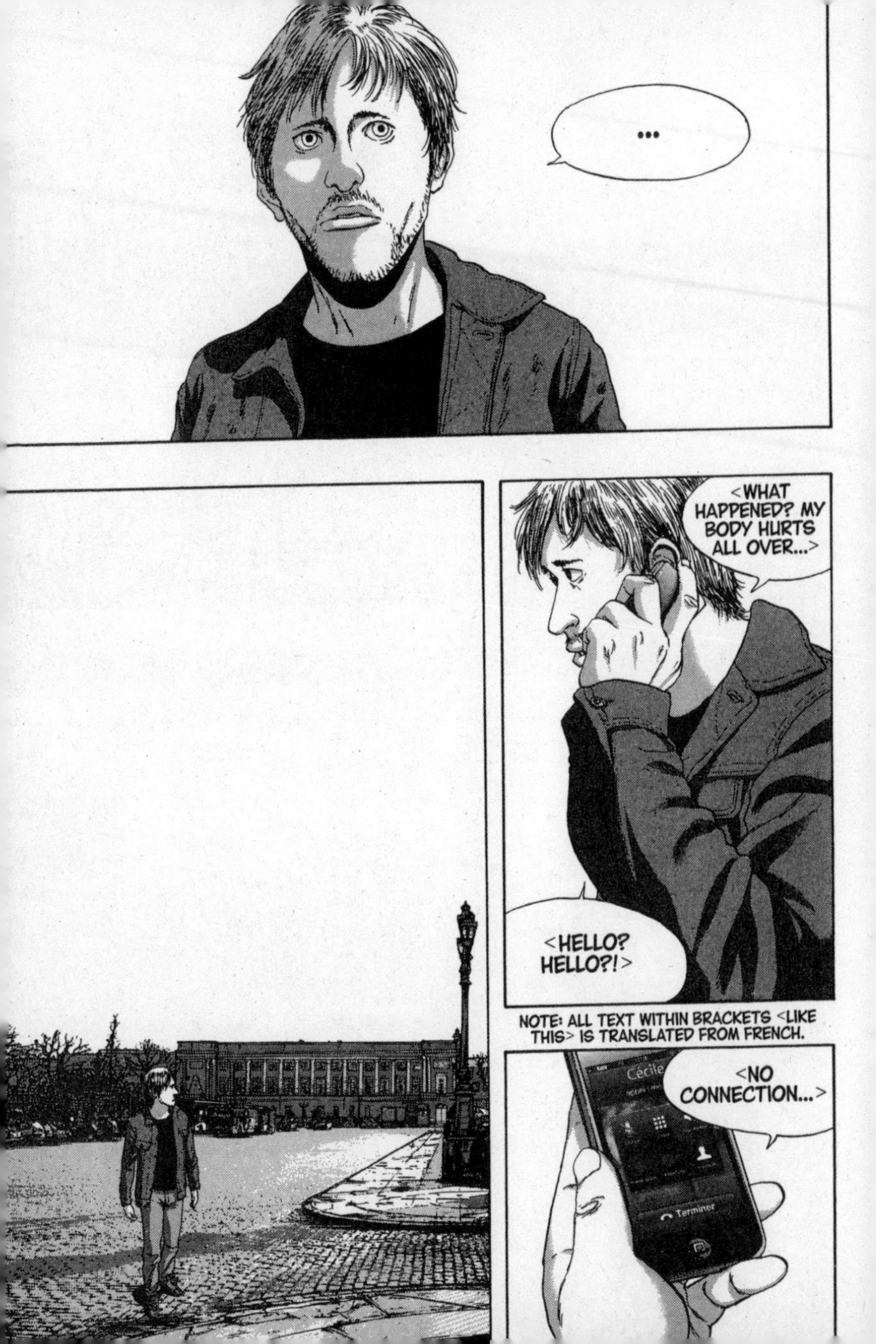
...
<WHAT HAPPENED? MY BODY HURTS ALL OVER...>
<HELLO? HELLO?!>
NOTE: ALL TEXT WITHIN BRACKETS <LIKE THIS> IS TRANSLATED FROM FRENCH.
<NO CONNECTION...>
Terminer

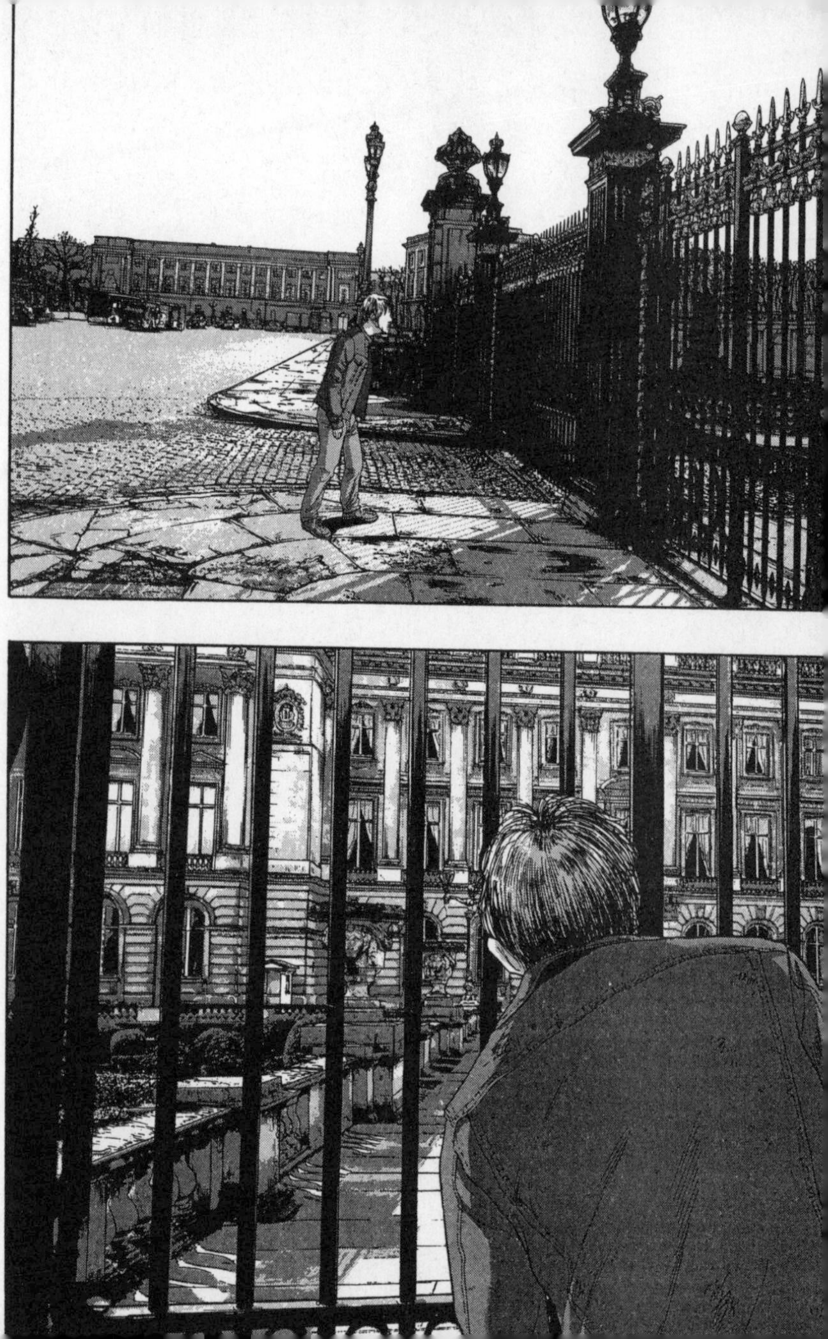

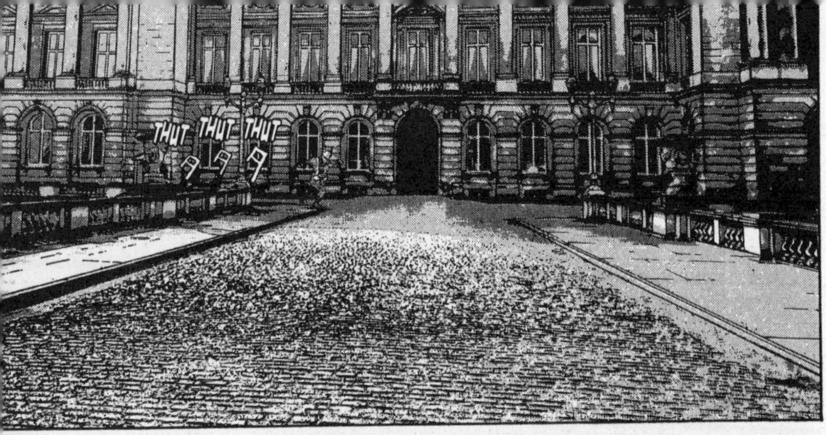
THUT THUT THUT

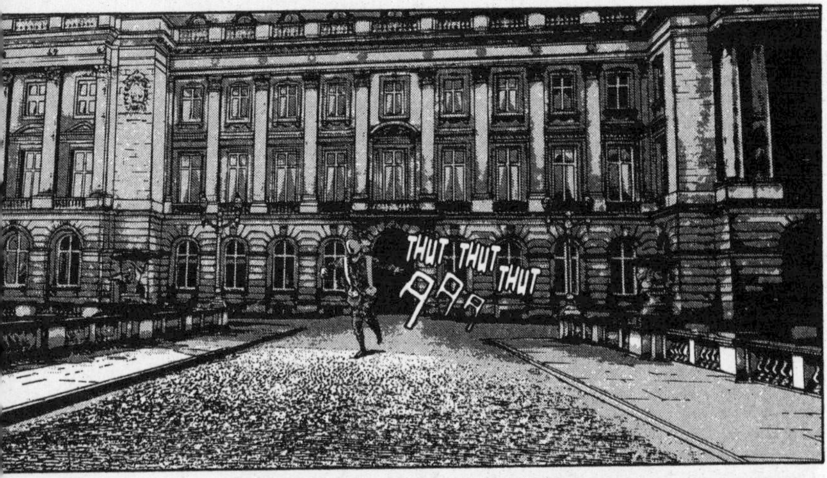
THUT THUT THUT

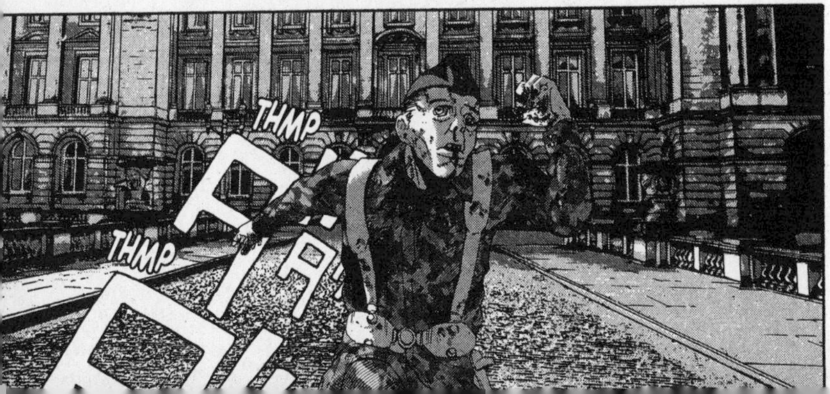
THMP
THMP

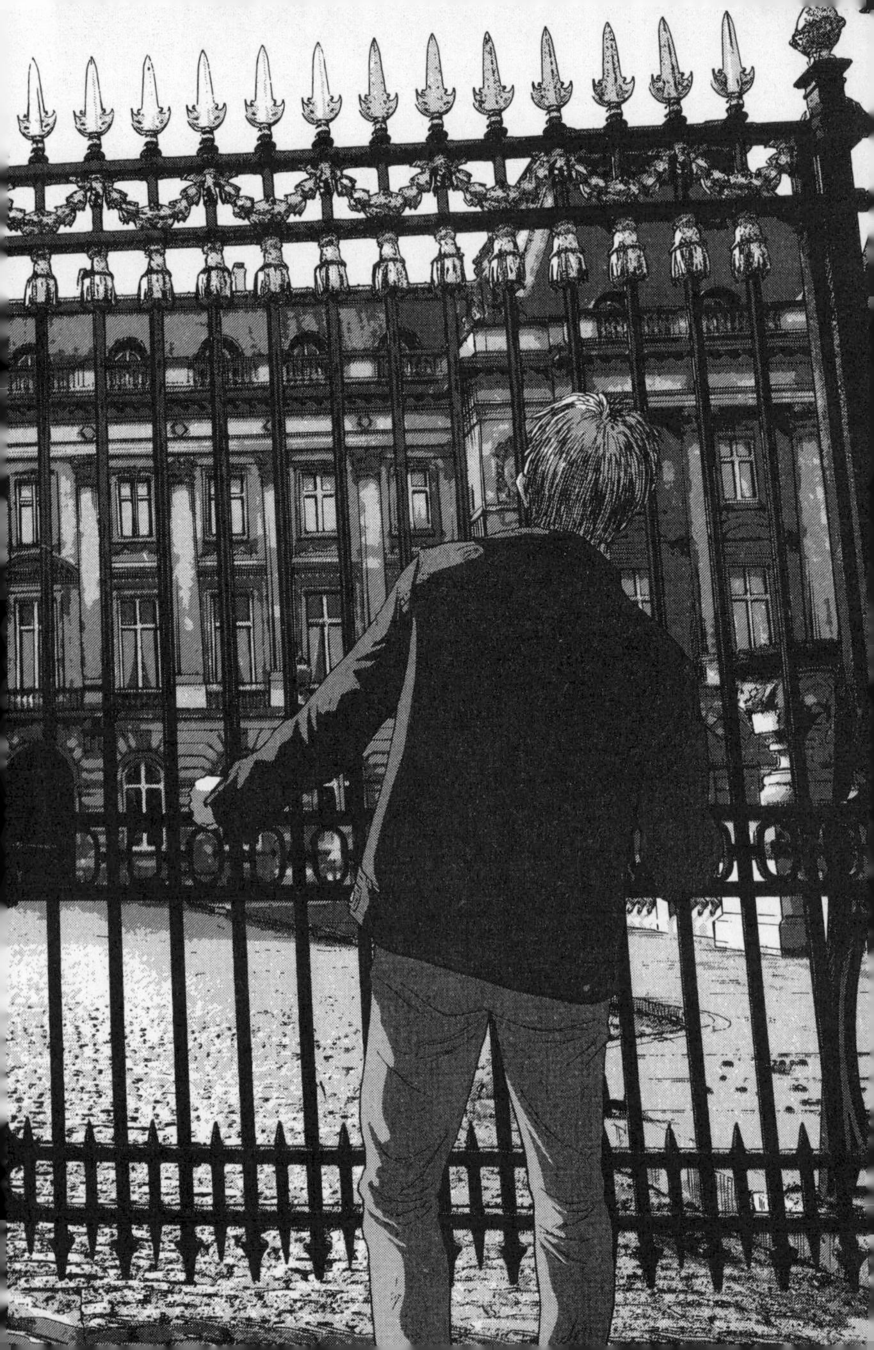

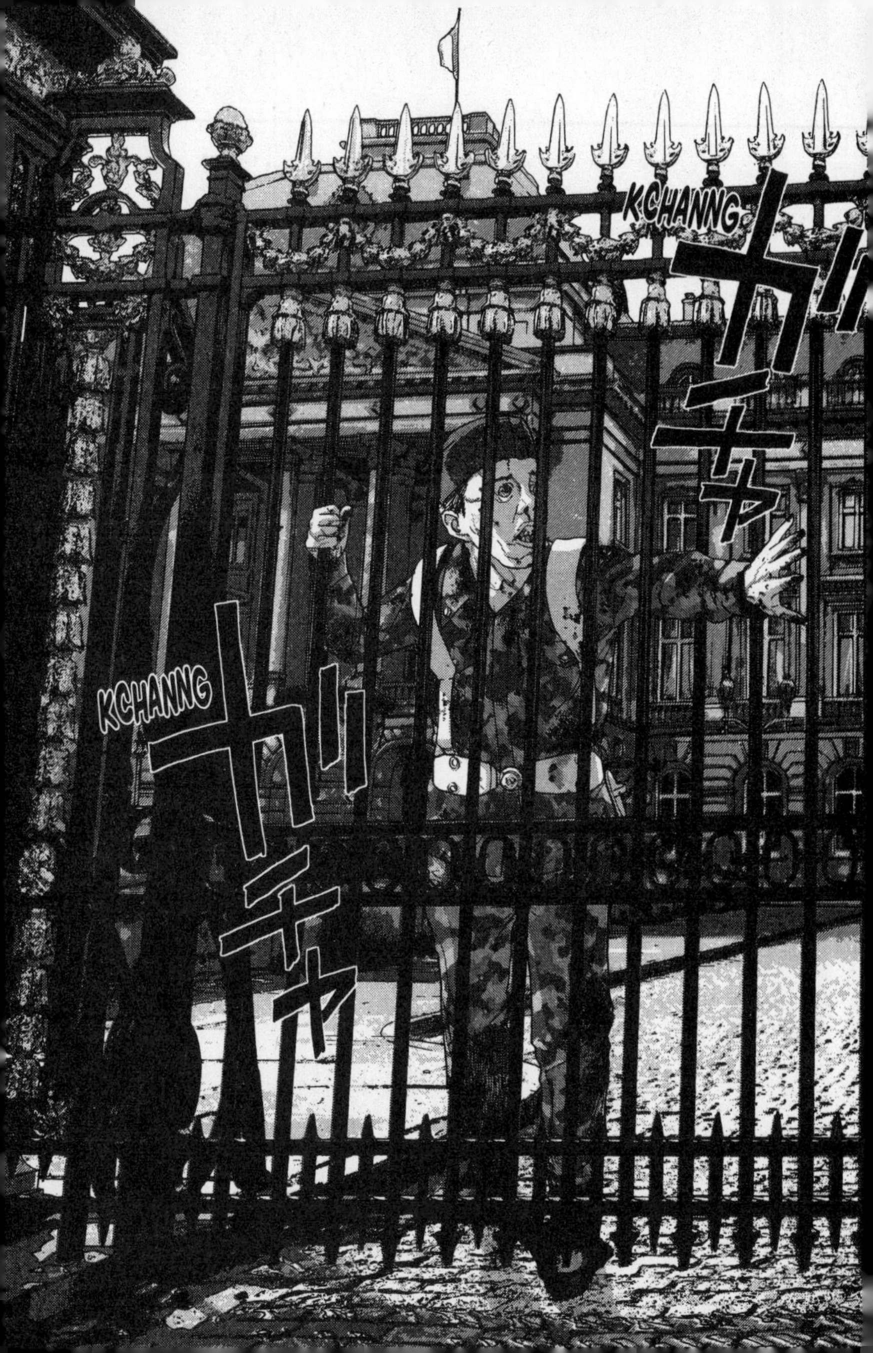
KCHANNG
KCHANNG

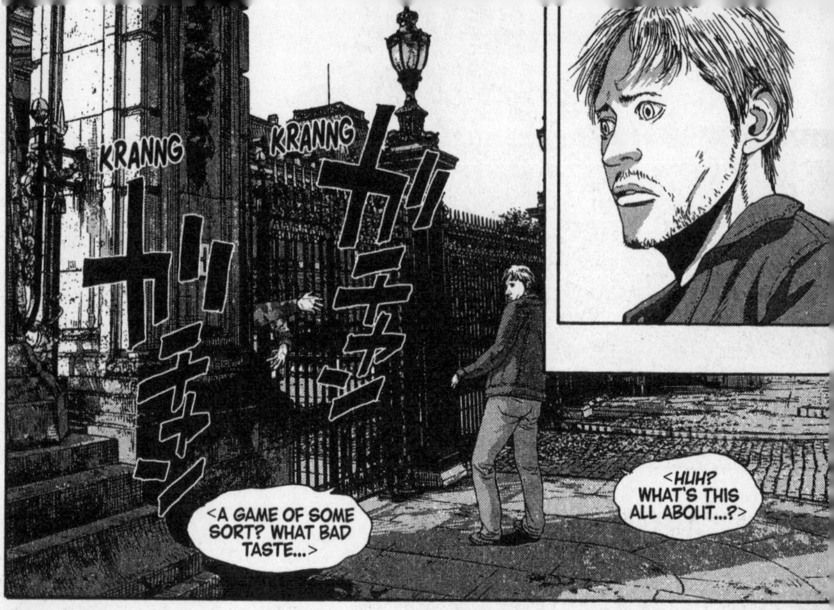
KRANNG
KRANNG
<HUH? WHAT'S THIS ALL ABOUT...?>
<A GAME OF SOME SORT? WHAT BAD TASTE...>

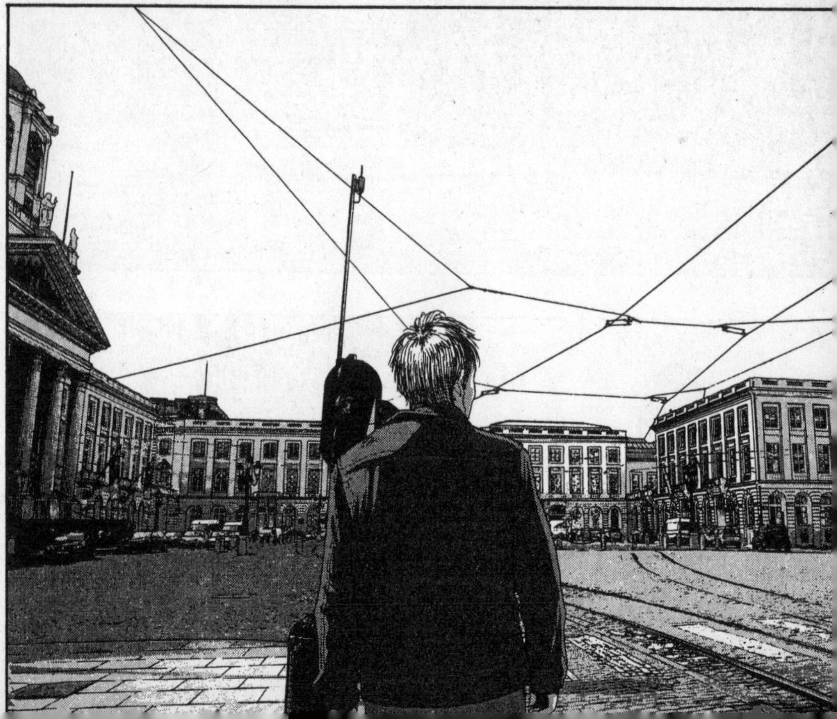

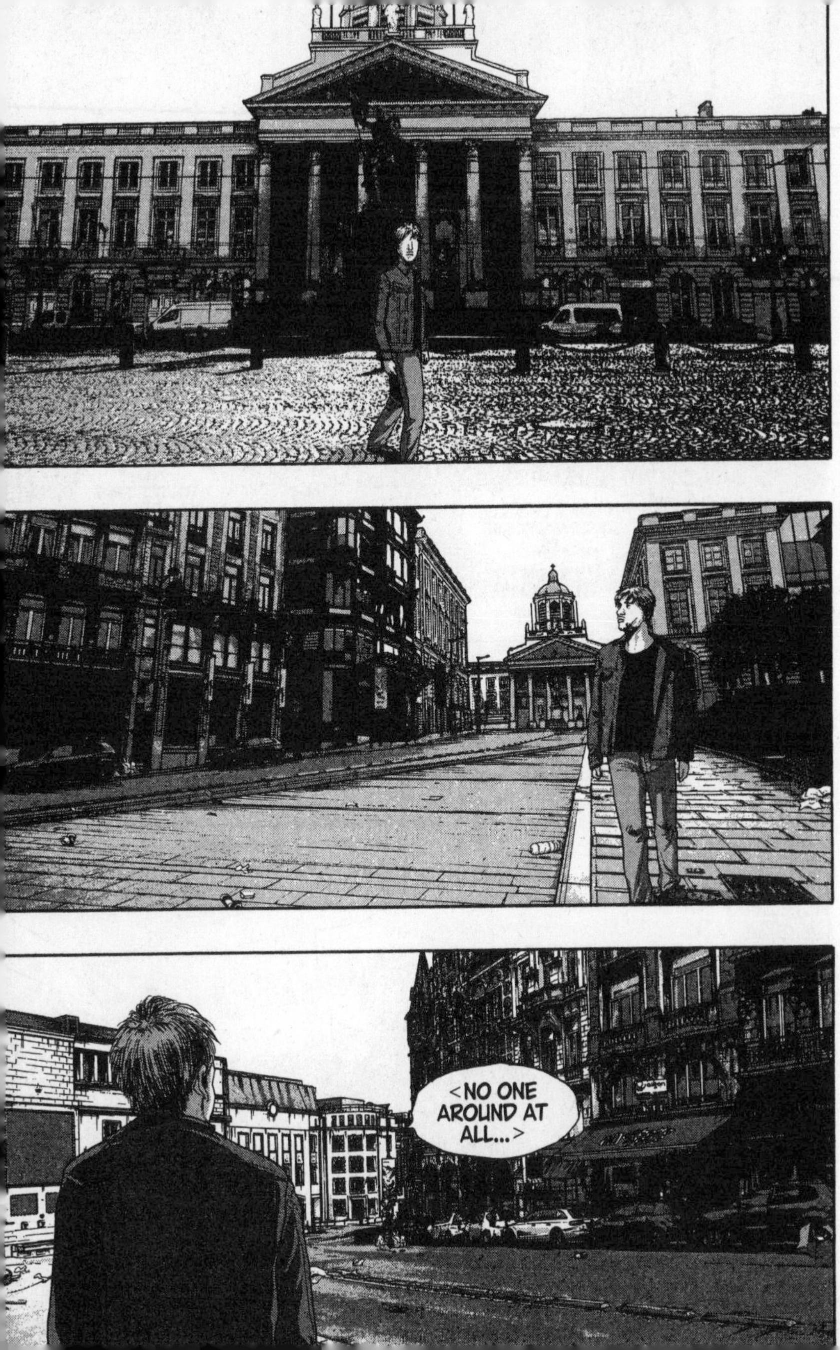
<NO ONE AROUND AT ALL...>

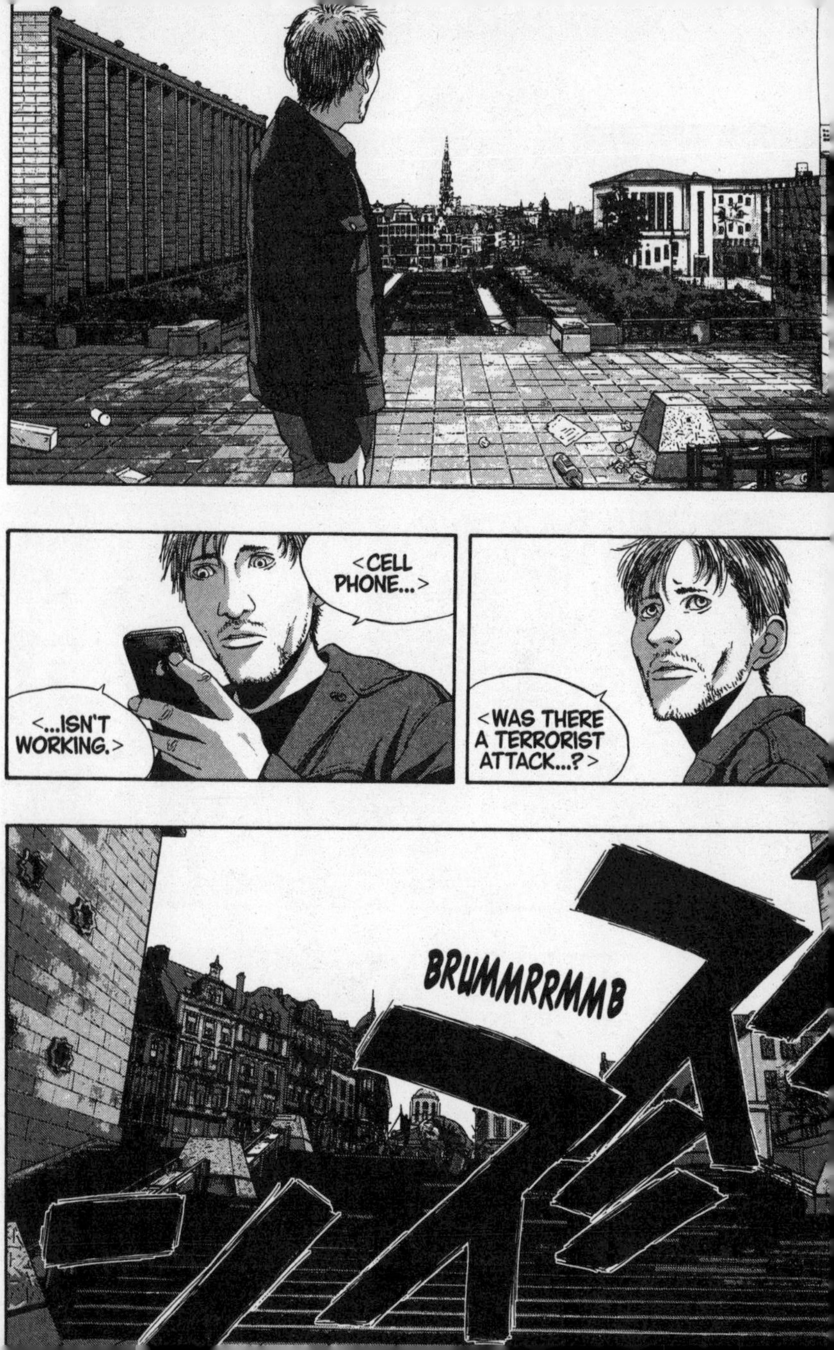
<WAS THERE A TERRORIST ATTACK...?>
<CELL PHONE...>
<...ISN'T WORKING.>
BRUMMRRMMB

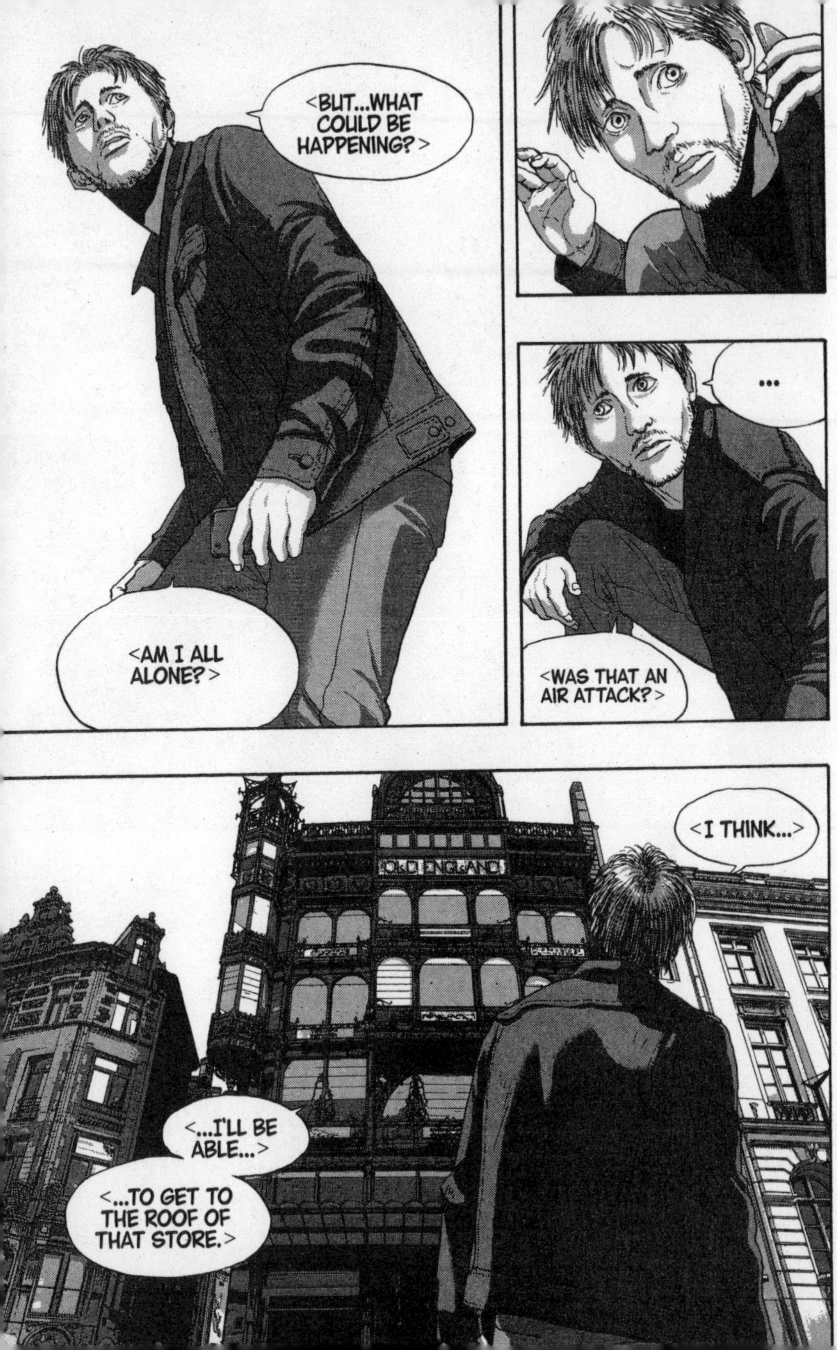
...
<WAS THAT AN AIR ATTACK?>
<BUT...WHAT COULD BE HAPPENING?>
<AM I ALL ALONE?>
<I THINK...>
OLD ENGLAND
<...I'LL BE ABLE...>
<...TO GET TO THE ROOF OF THAT STORE.>

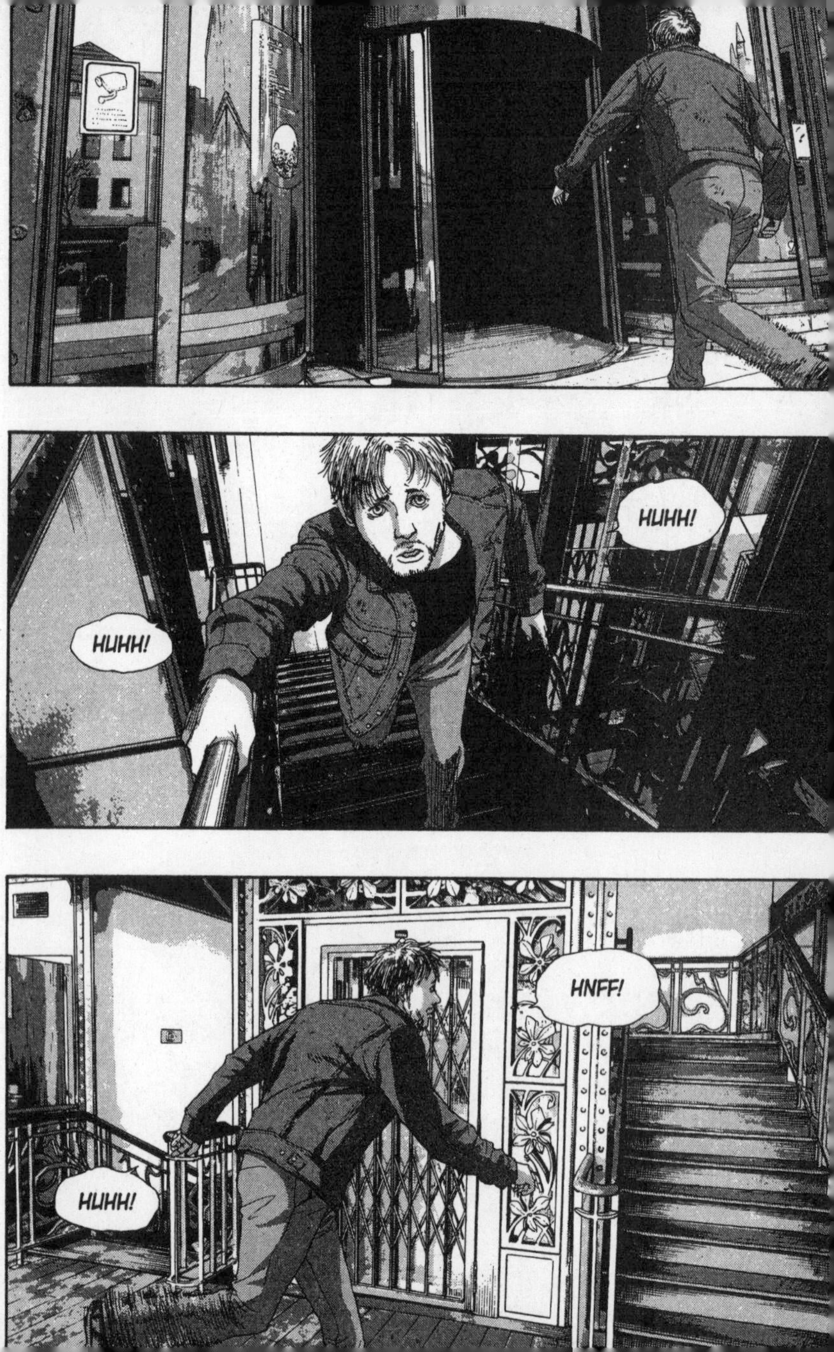
HUHH!
HUHH!
HNFF!
HUHH!

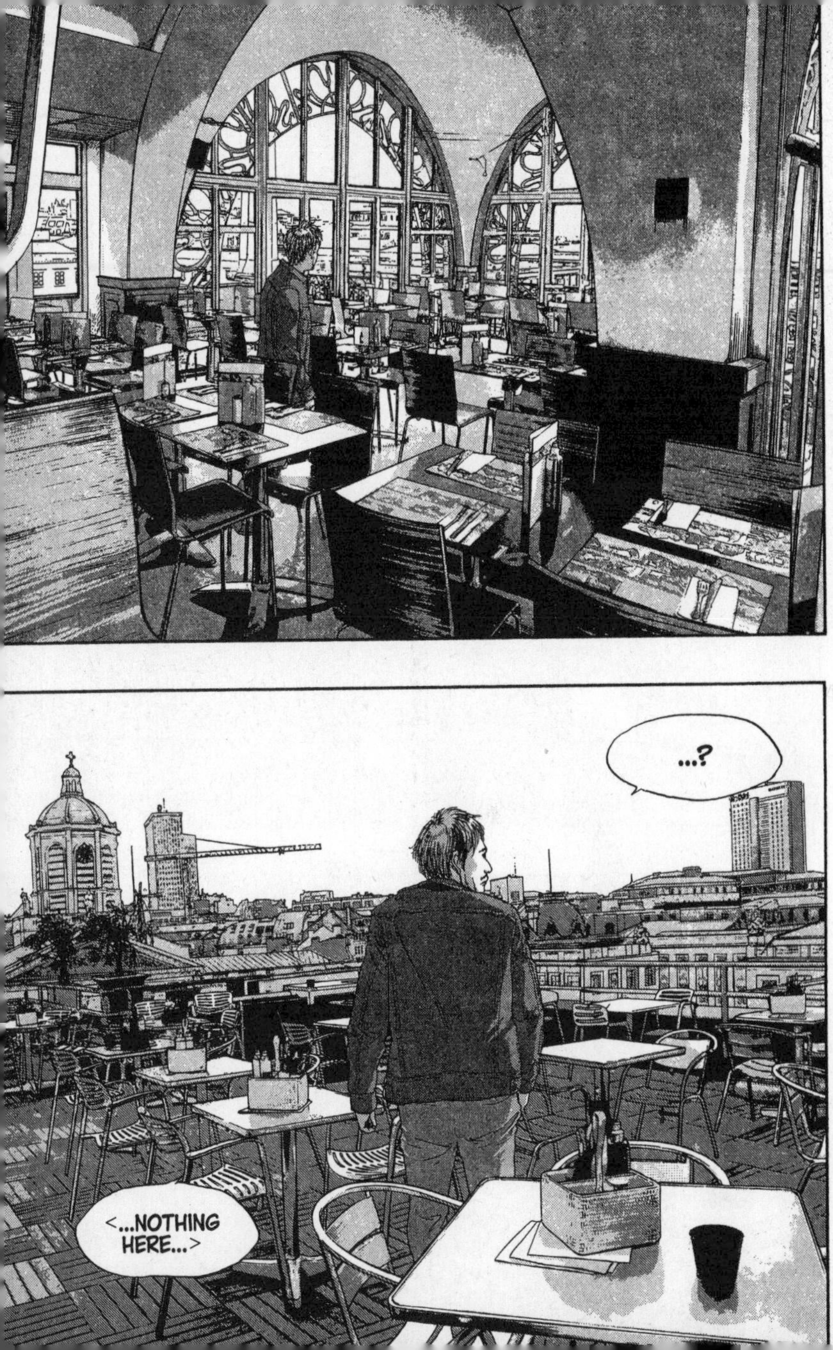
...?
<...NOTHING HERE...>

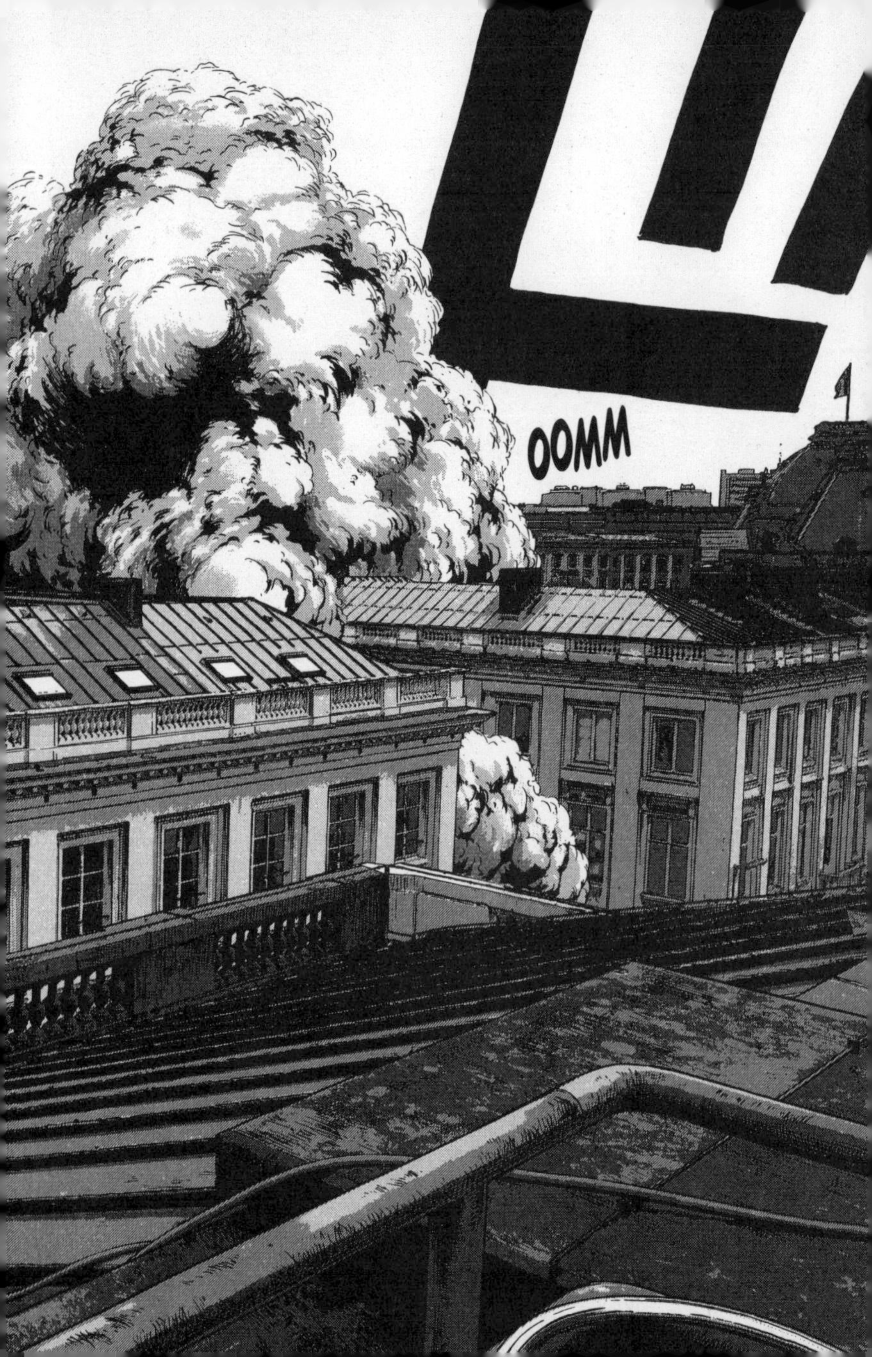
OOMM

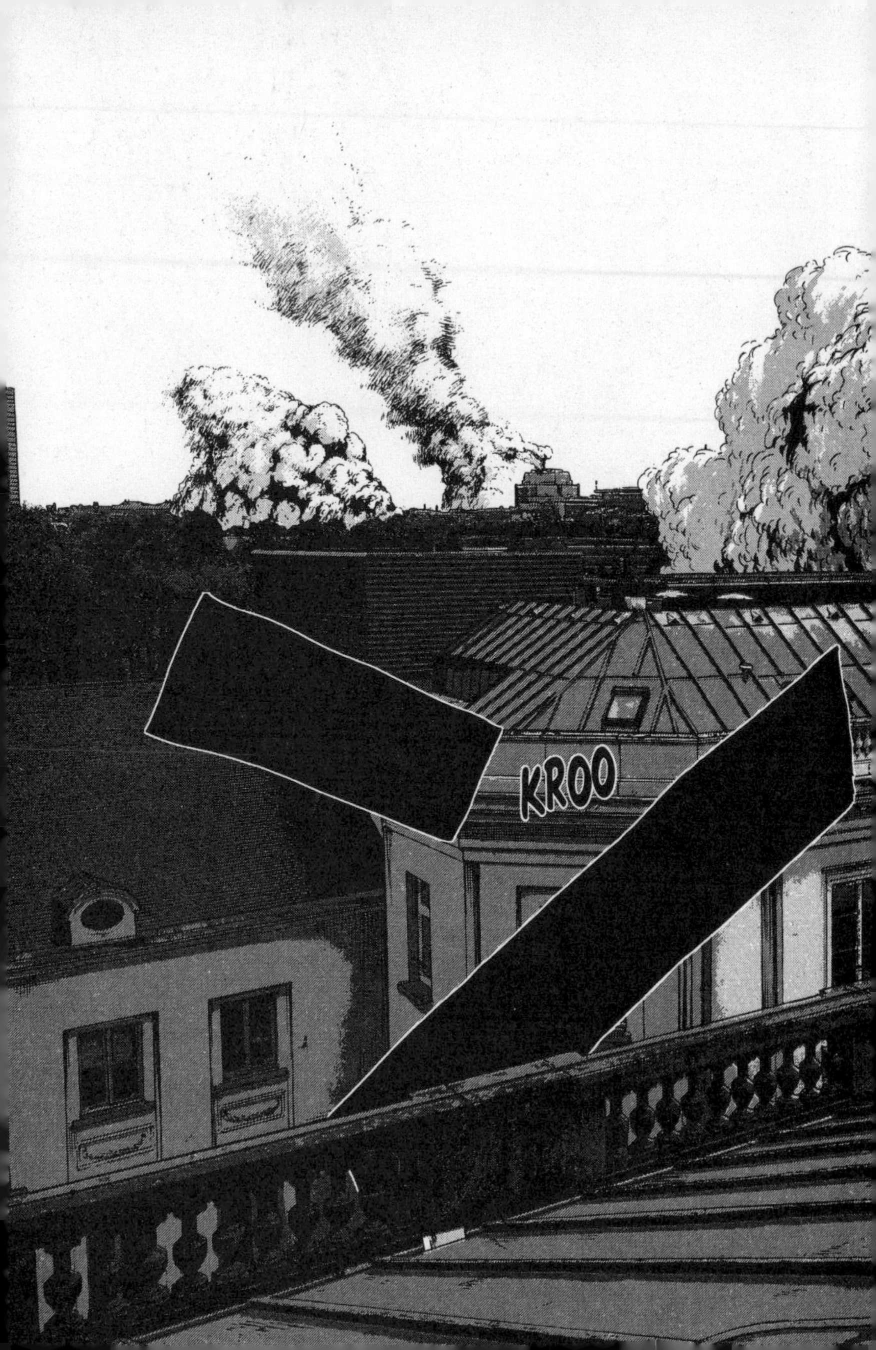
KROO

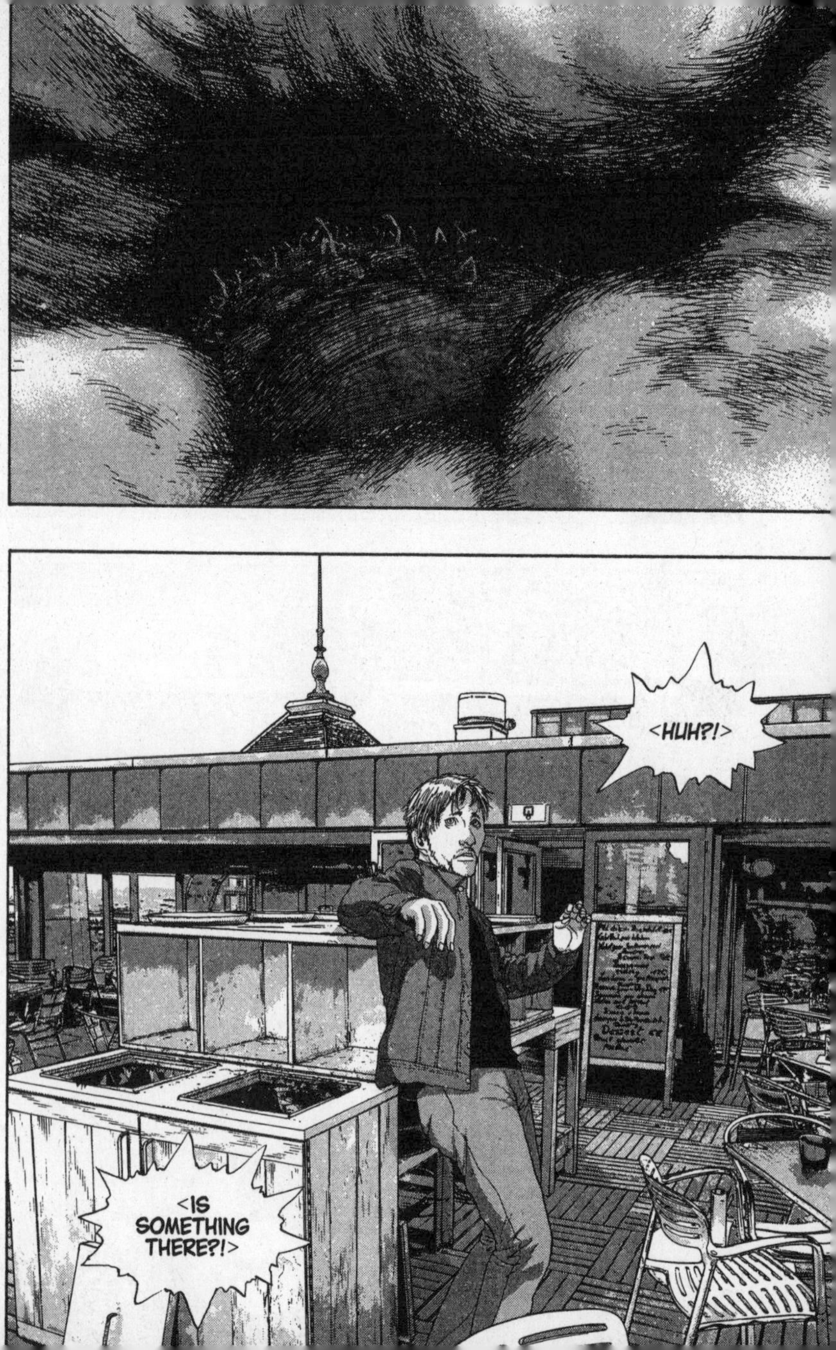
<HUH?!>
<IS SOMETHING THERE?!>

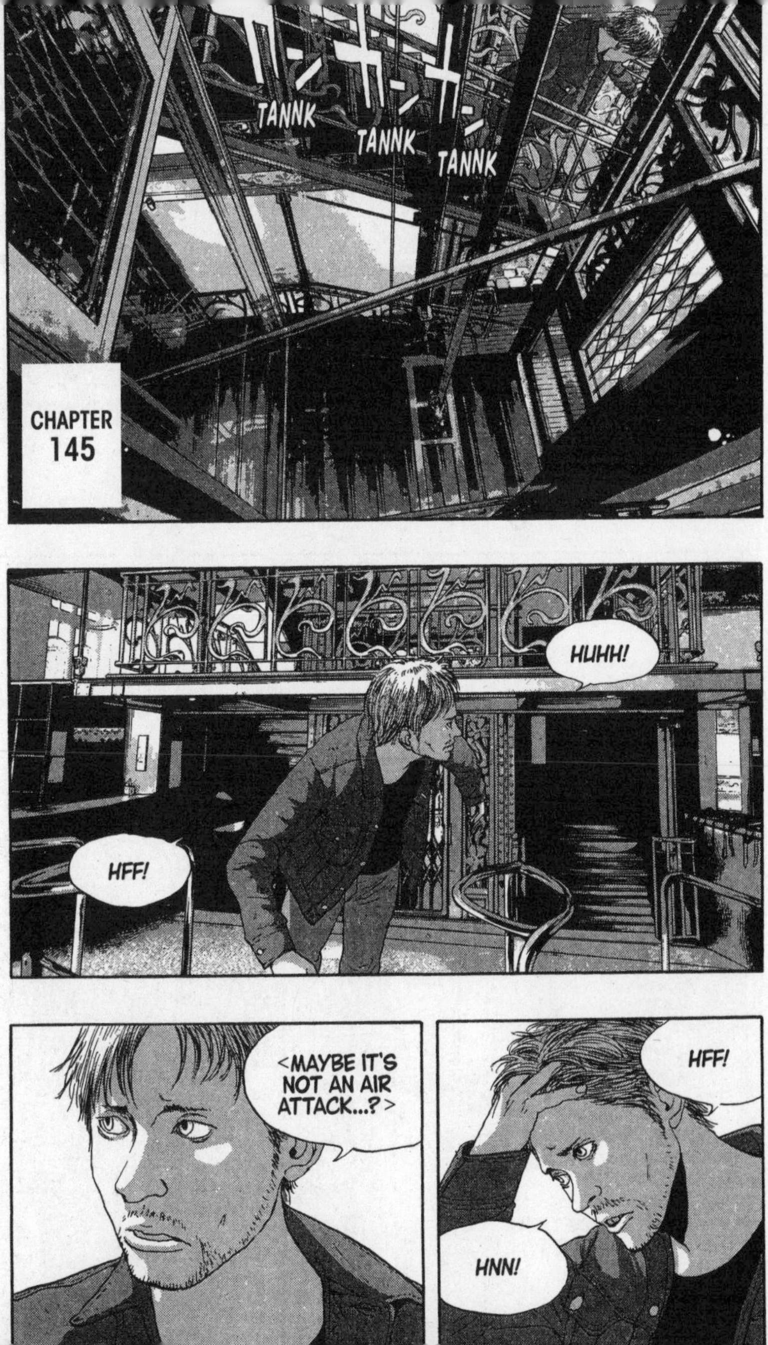
TANNK
TANNK
TANNK
CHAPTER 145
HUHH!
HFF!
HFF!
HNN!
<MAYBE IT'S NOT AN AIR ATTACK...?>

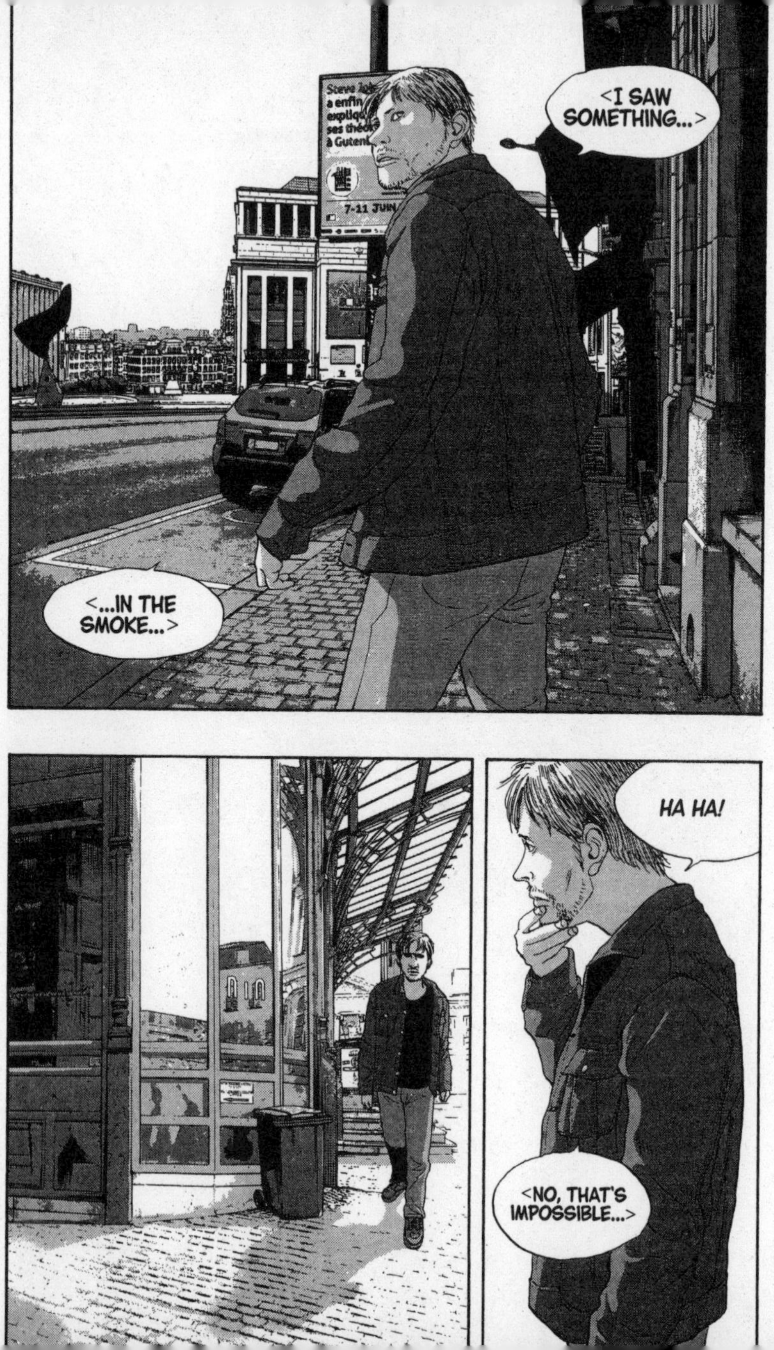
<I SAW SOMETHING...>
<...IN THE SMOKE...>
HA HA!
<NO, THAT'S IMPOSSIBLE...>

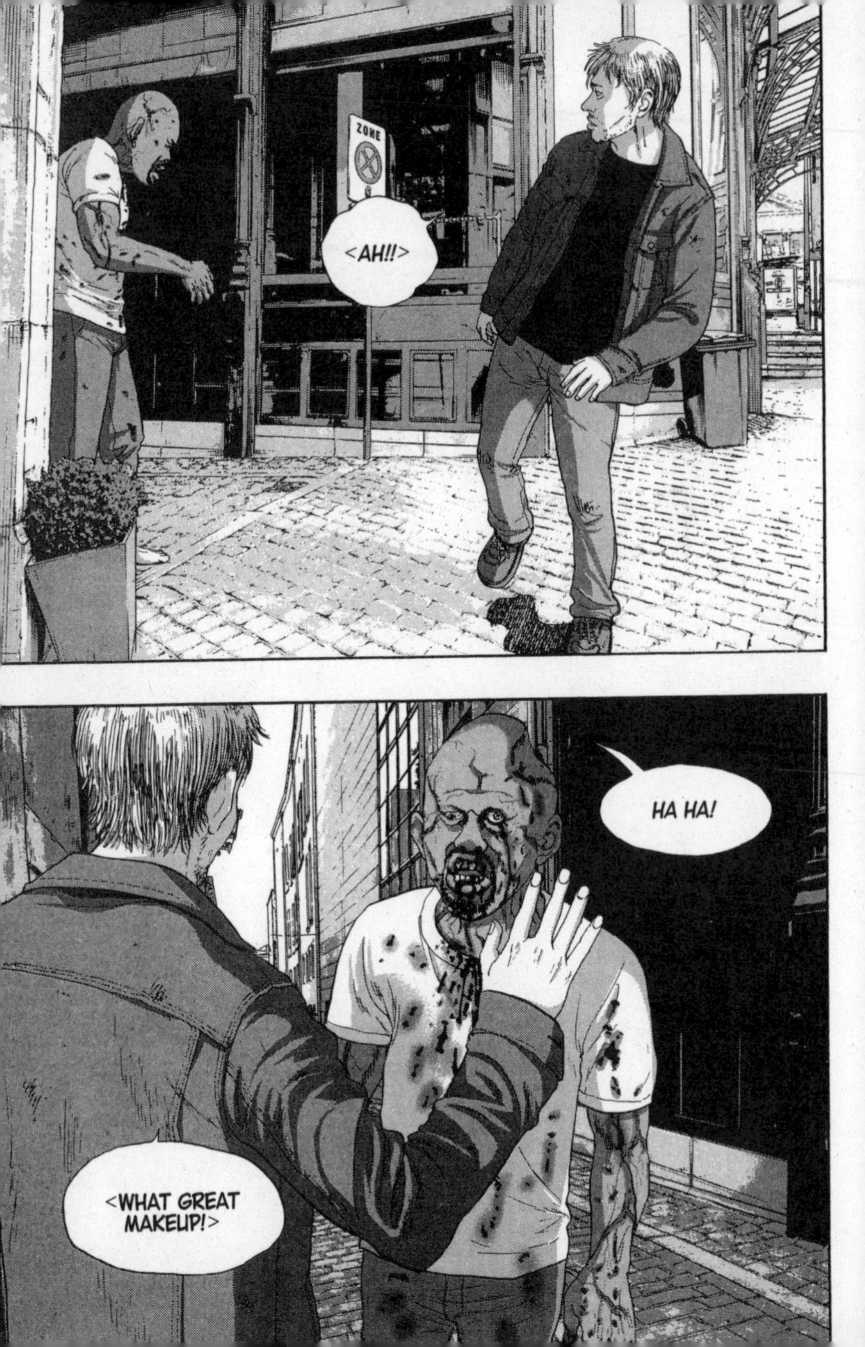
ZONE
<AH!!>
HA HA!
<WHAT GREAT MAKEUP!>

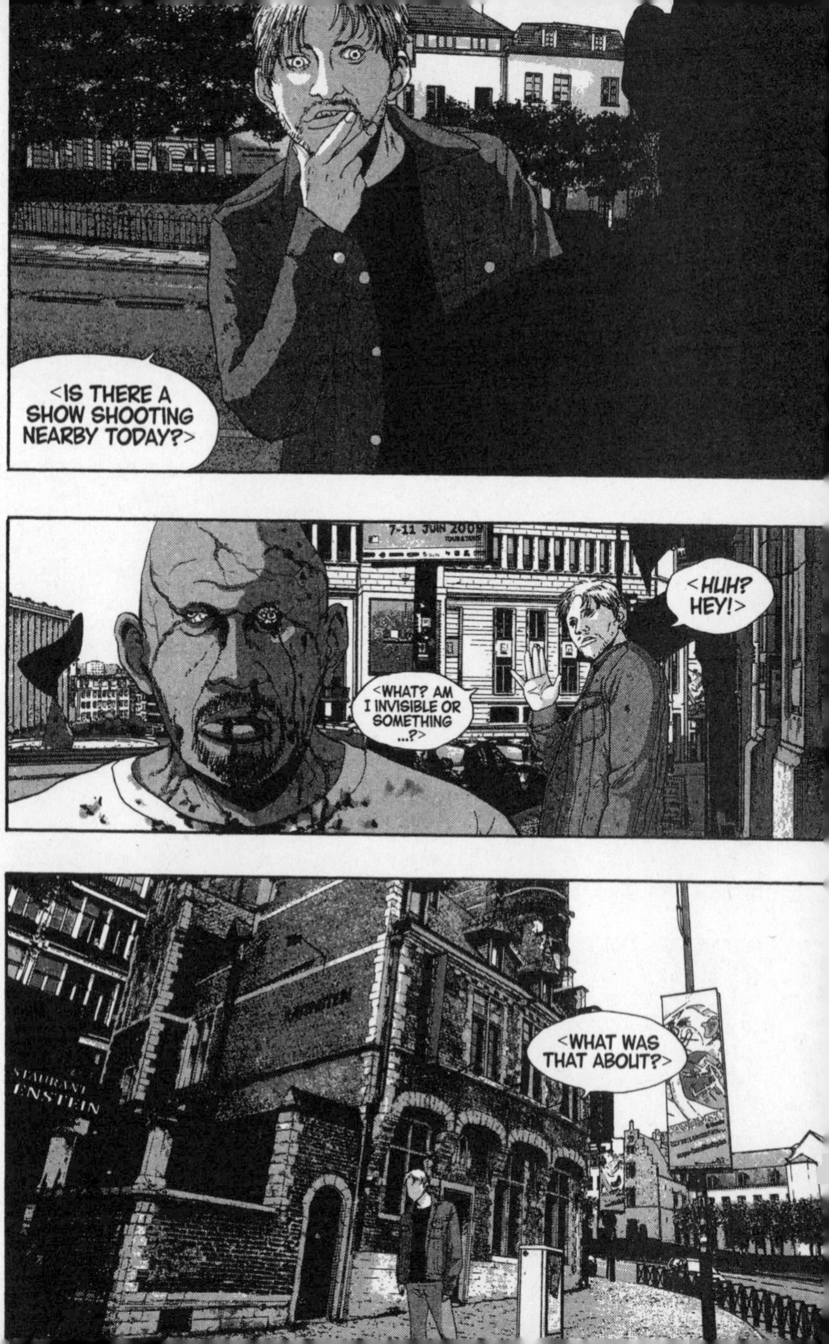
<IS THERE A SHOW SHOOTING NEARBY TODAY?>
<HUH? HEY!>
<WHAT? AM I INVISIBLE OR SOMETHING ...?>
<WHAT WAS THAT ABOUT?>

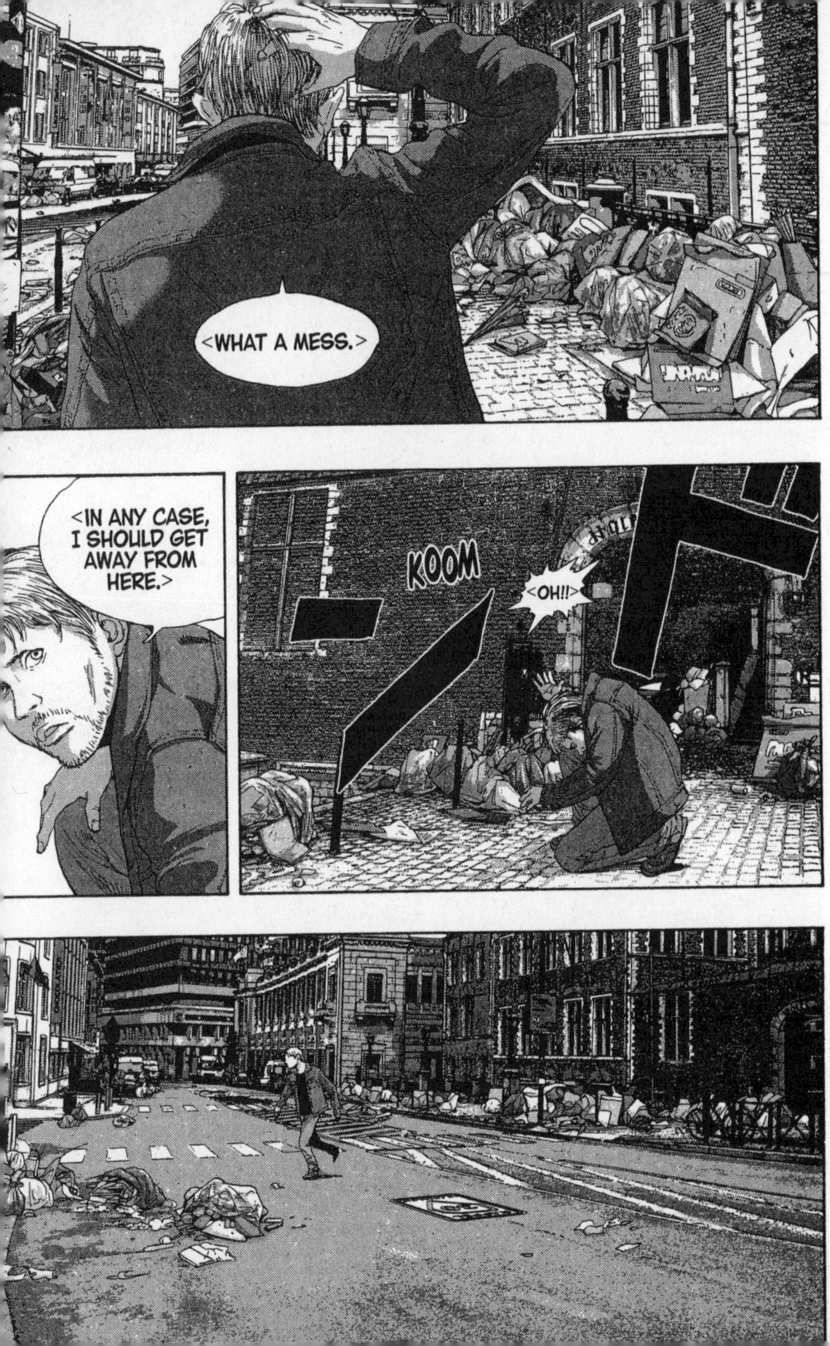

<WHAT A MESS.>
KOOM
<OH!!>
<IN ANY CASE, I SHOULD GET AWAY FROM HERE.>

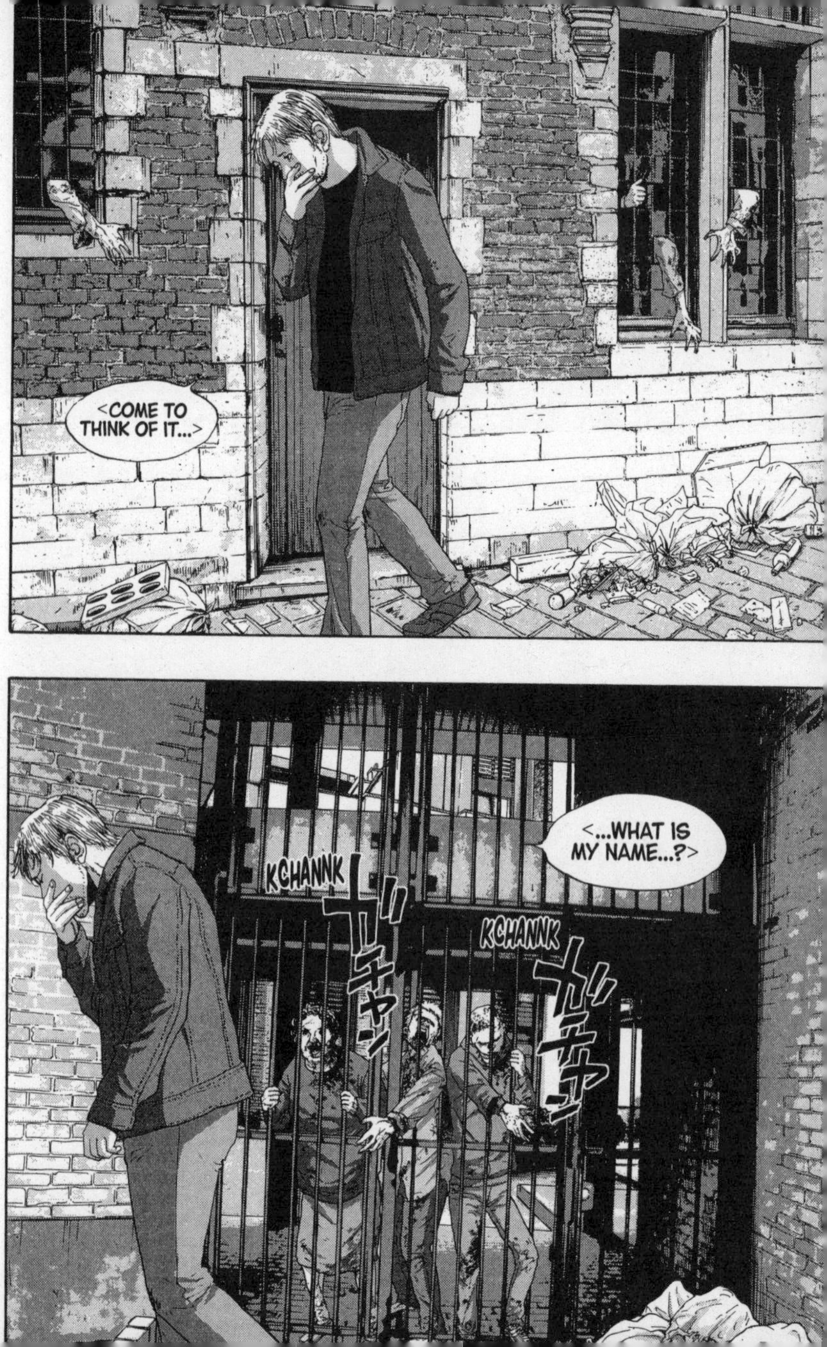
<COME TO THINK OF IT...>
<...WHAT IS MY NAME...?>
KCHANNK
KCHANNK

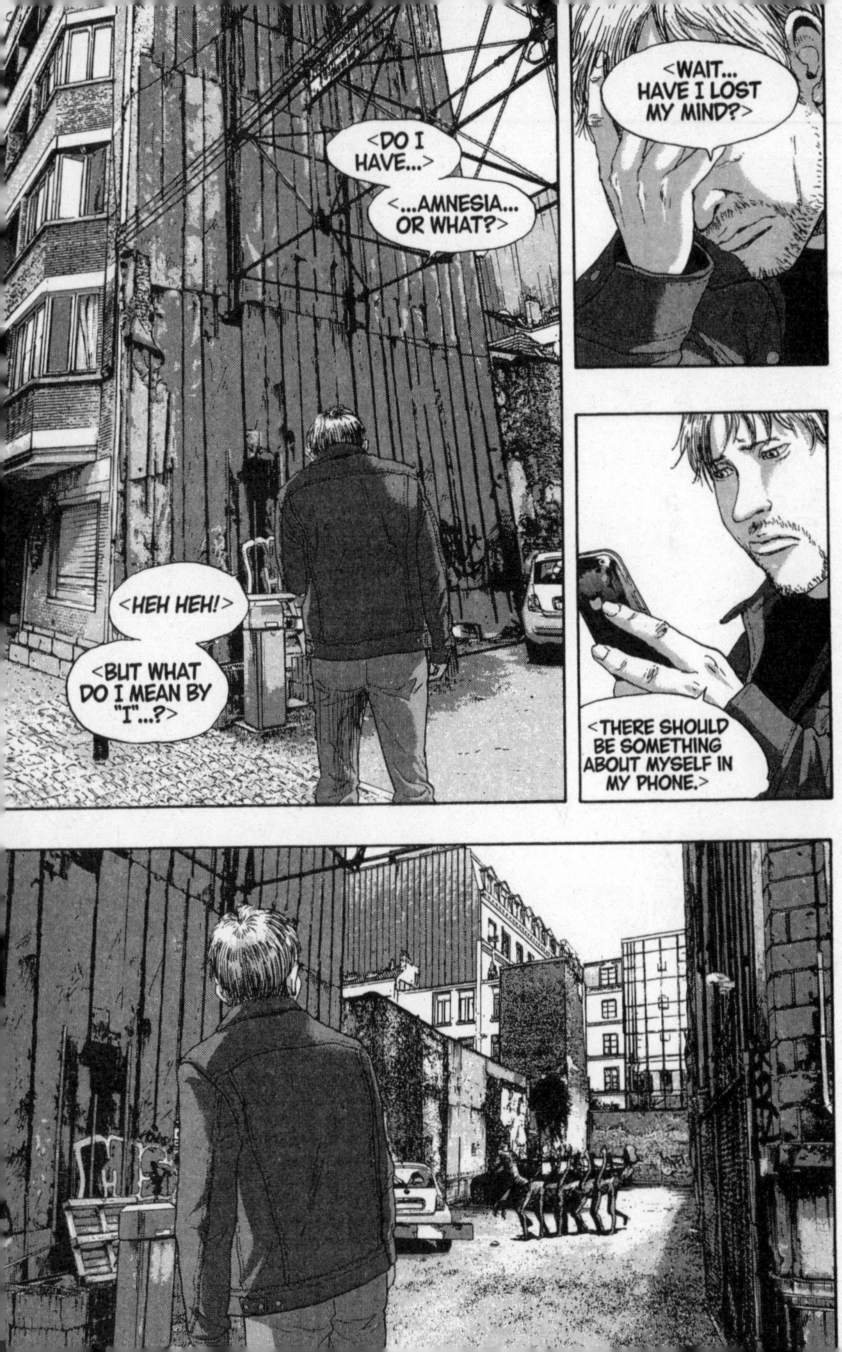
<WAIT... HAVE I LOST MY MIND?>
<THERE SHOULD BE SOMETHING ABOUT MYSELF IN MY PHONE.>
<DO I HAVE...>
<...AMNESIA... OR WHAT?>
<HEH HEH!>
<BUT WHAT DO I MEAN BY "I"...?>

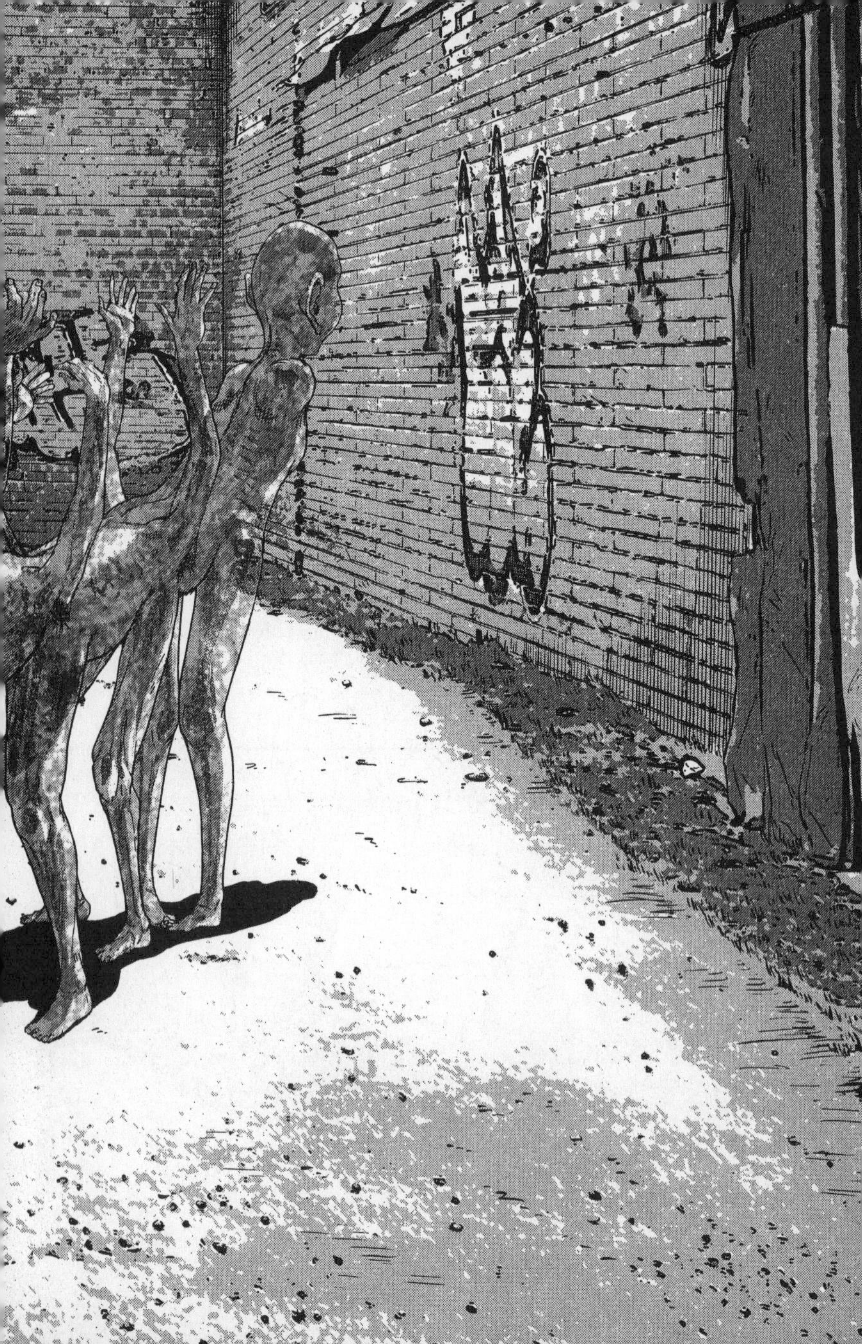

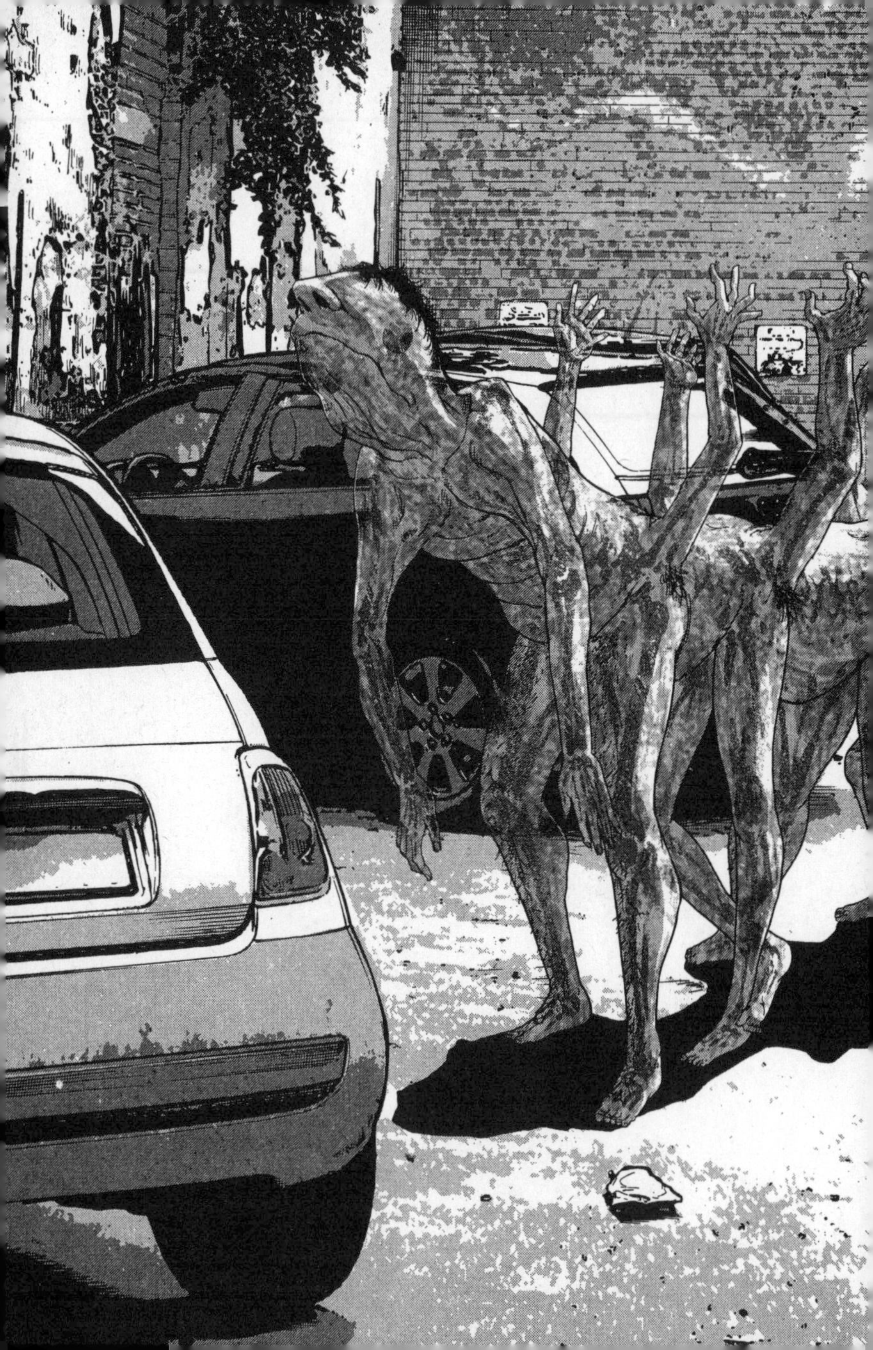

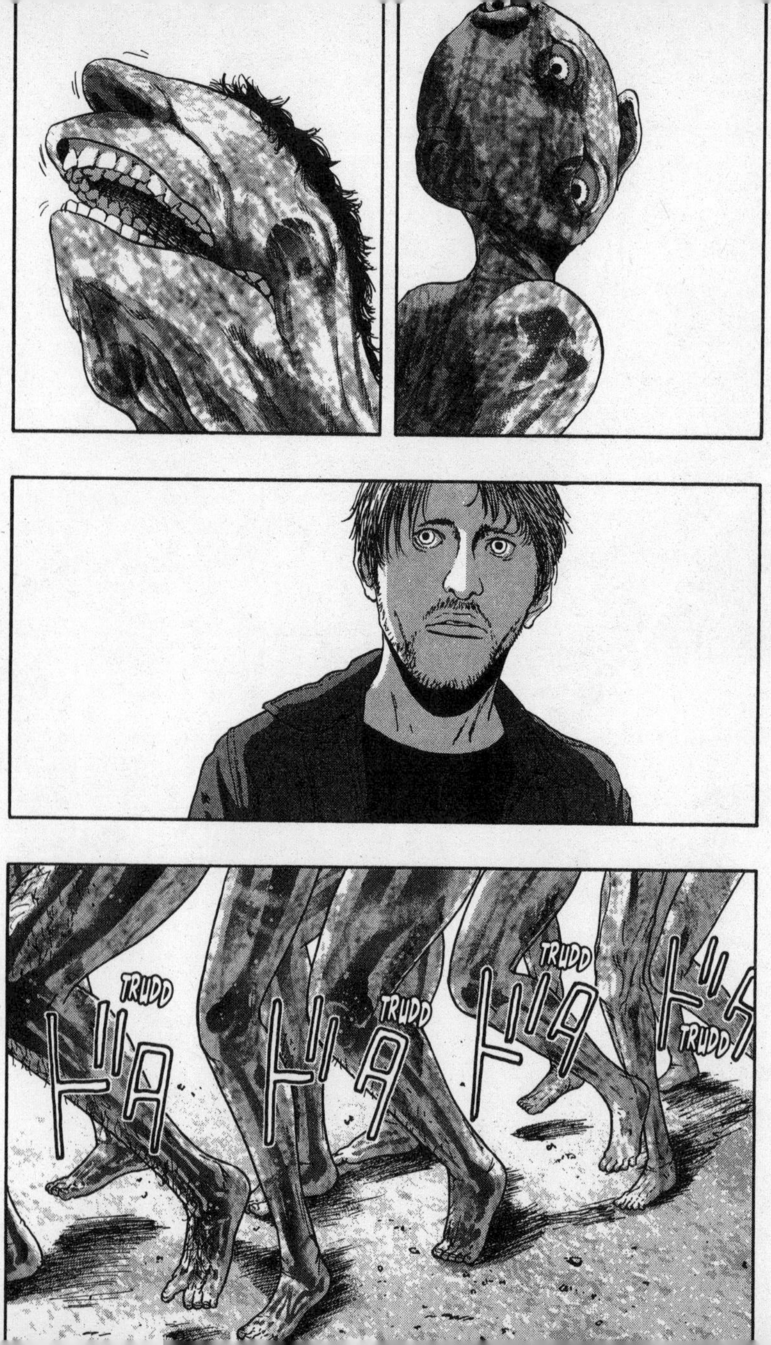
TRUDD
TRUDD
TRUDD
TRUDD

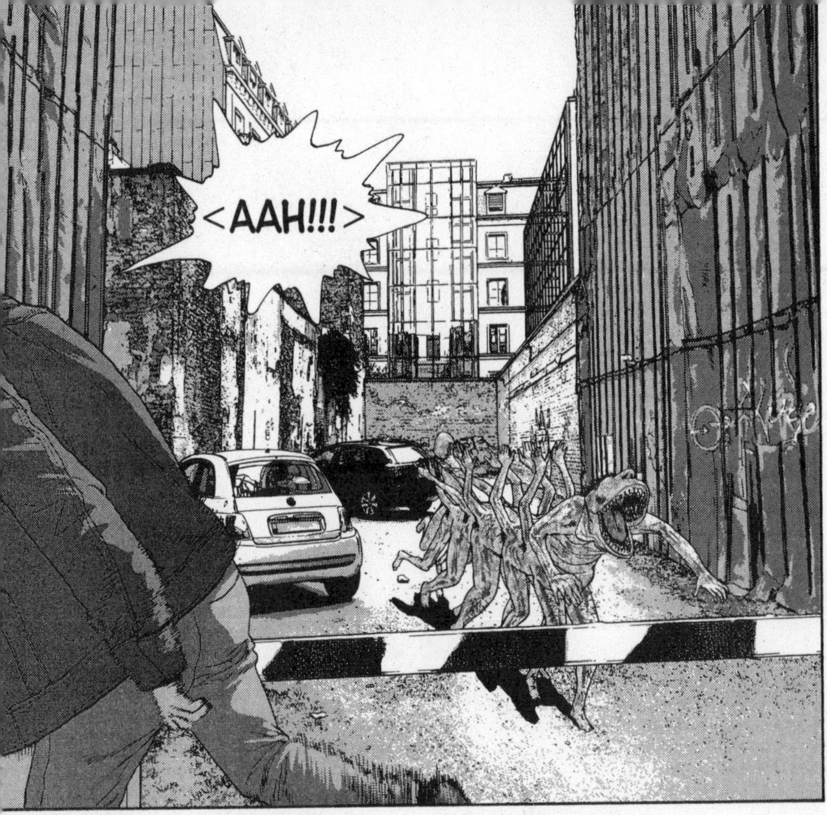
<AAH!!!>
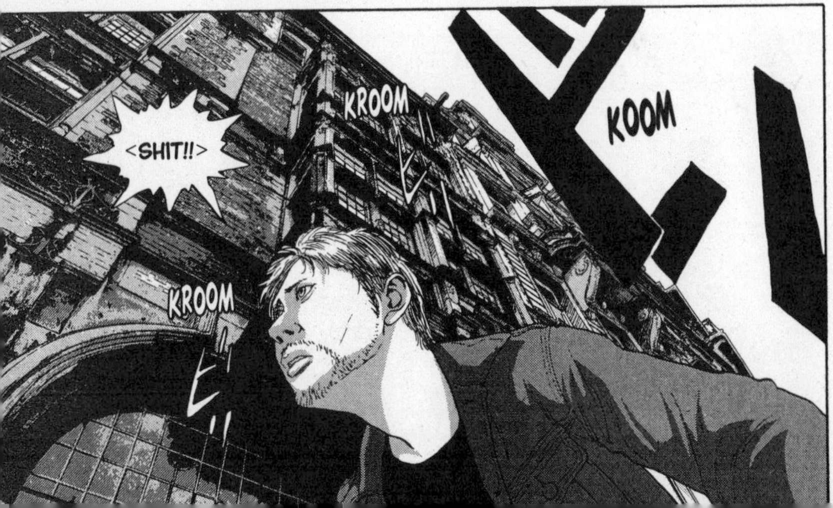
KOOM
KROOM
<SHIT!!>
KROOM

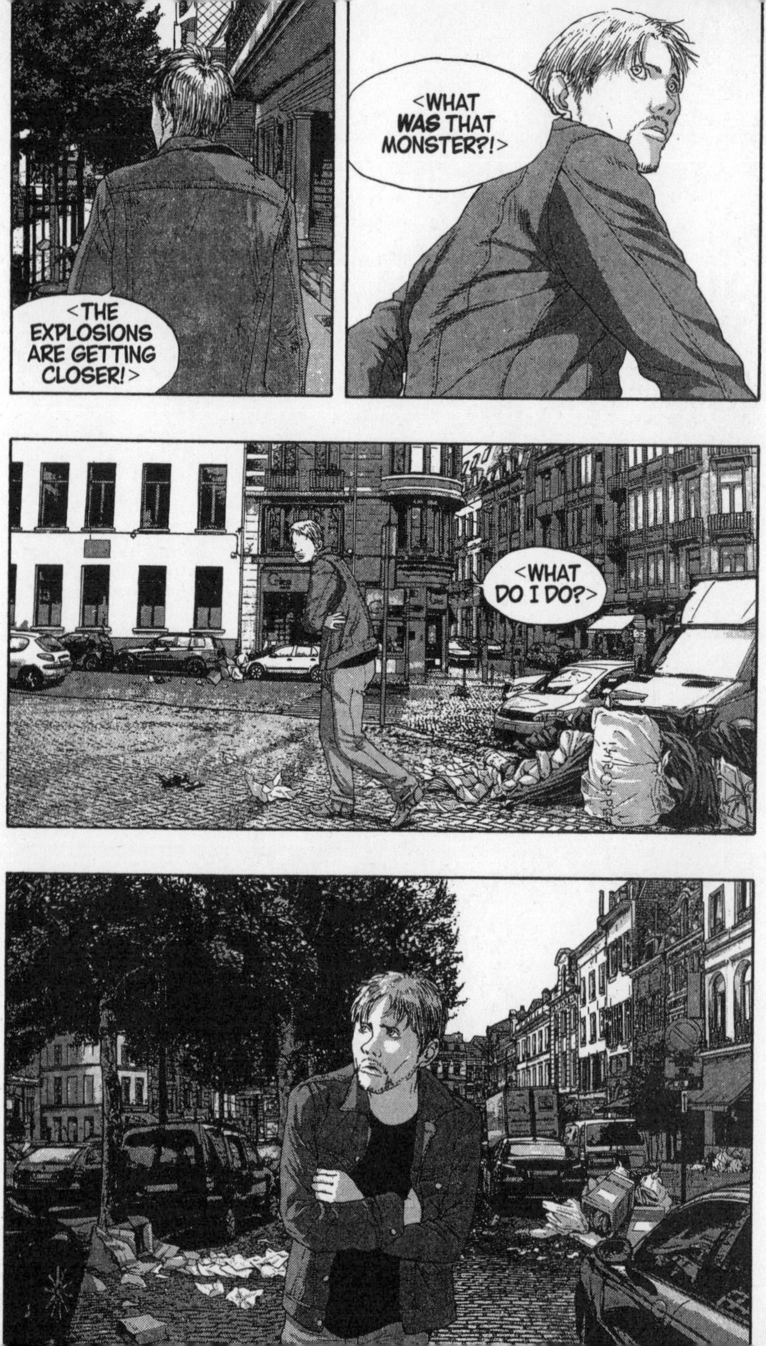
<WHAT WAS THAT MONSTER?!>
<THE EXPLOSIONS ARE GETTING CLOSER!>
<WHAT DO I DO?>

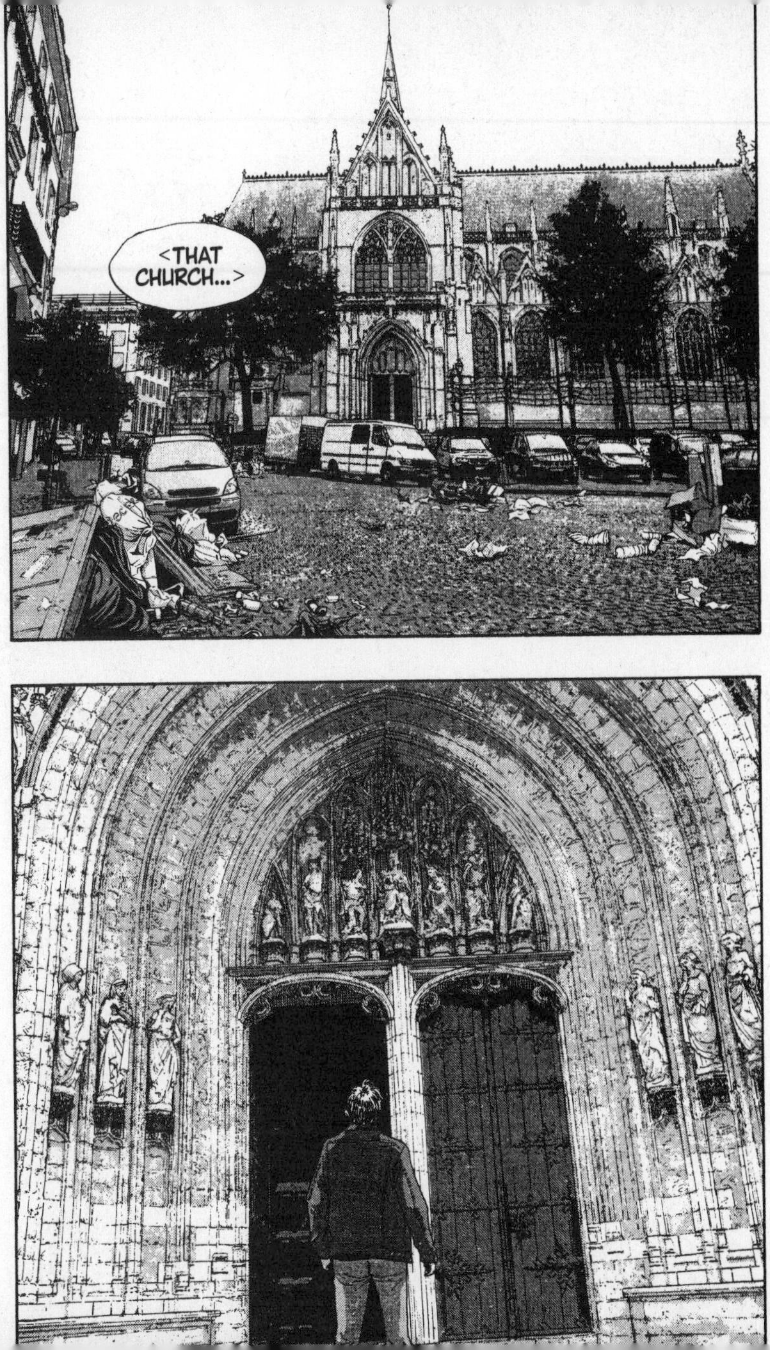
<THAT CHURCH...>

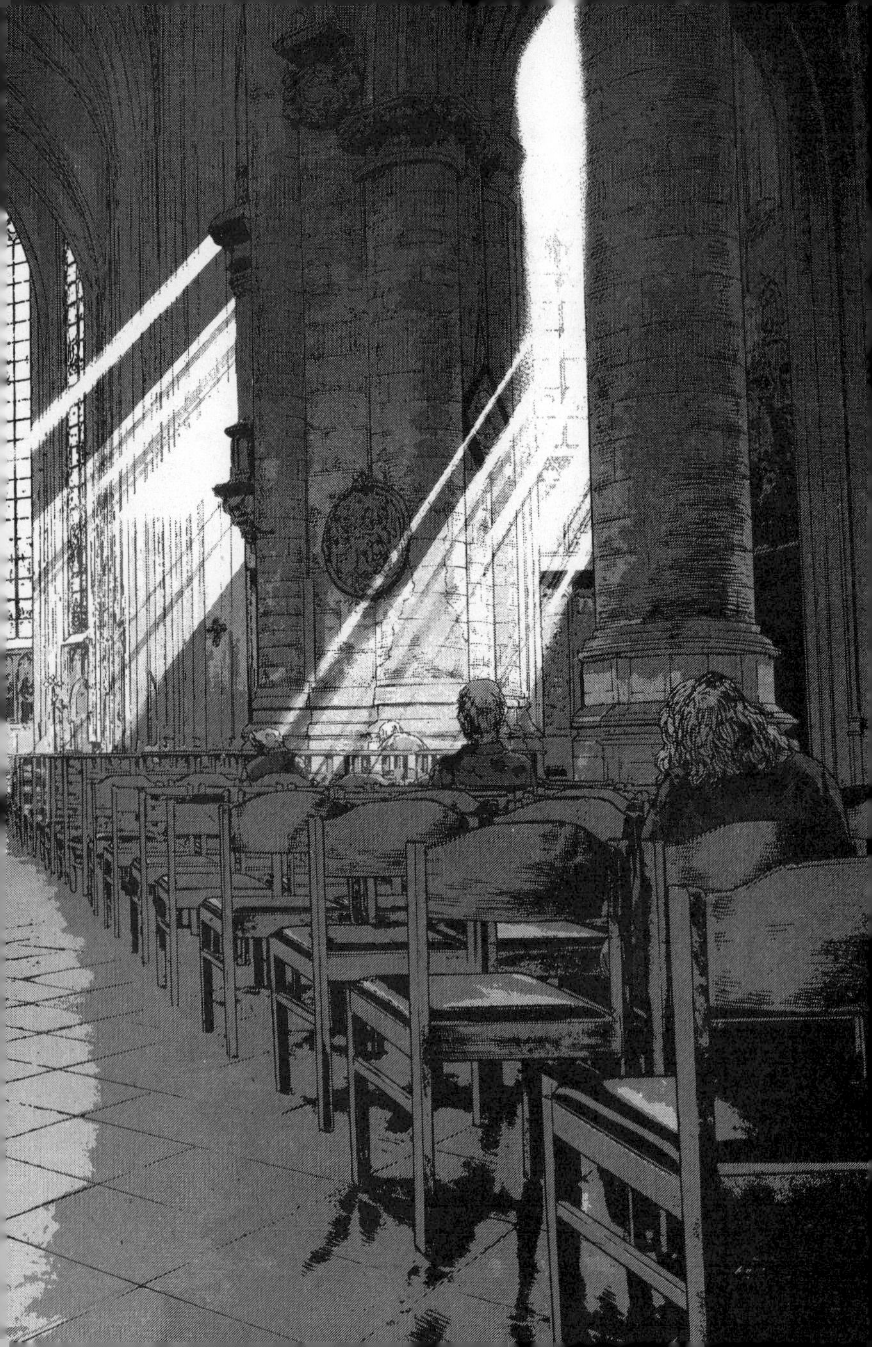

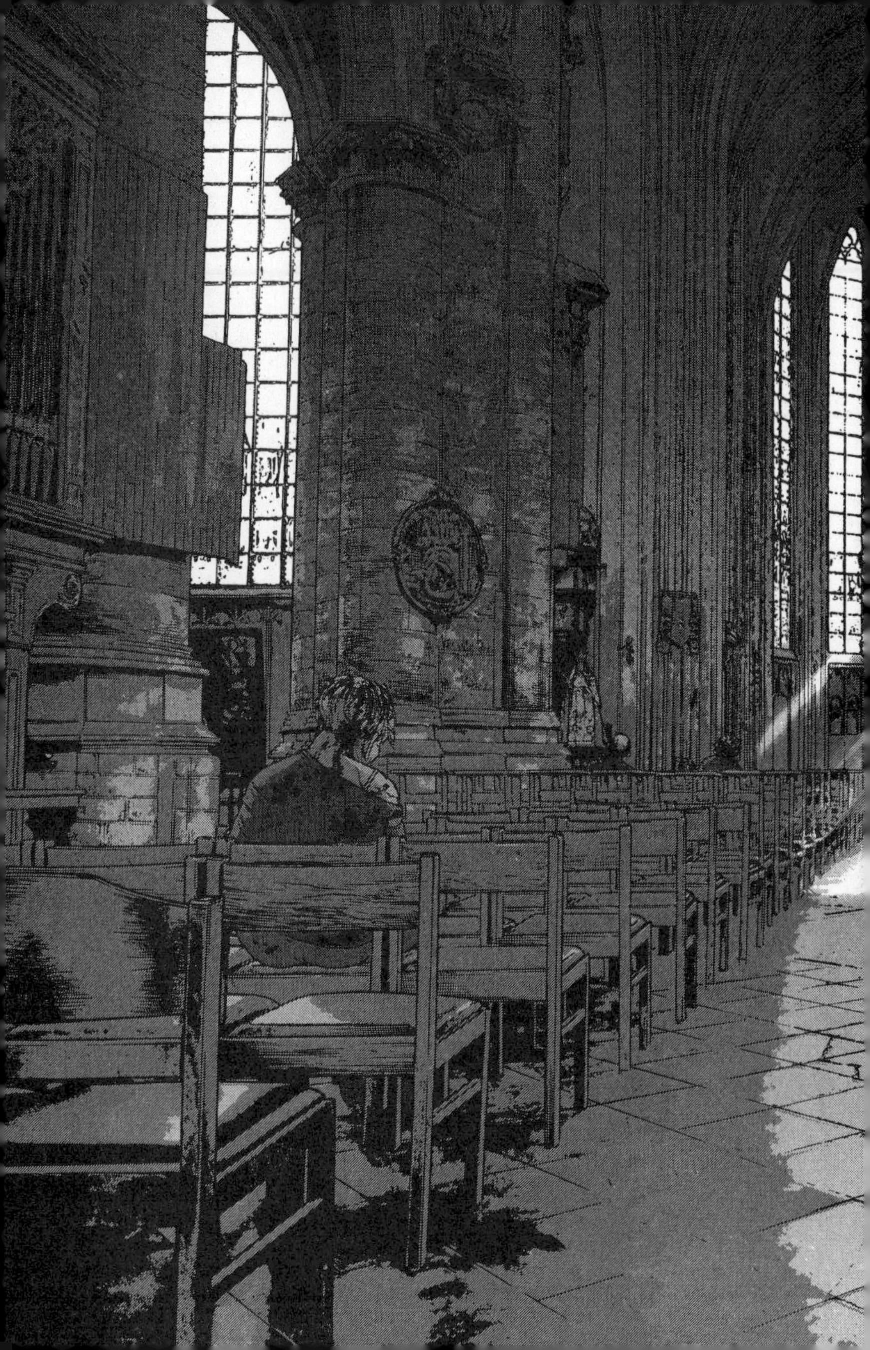

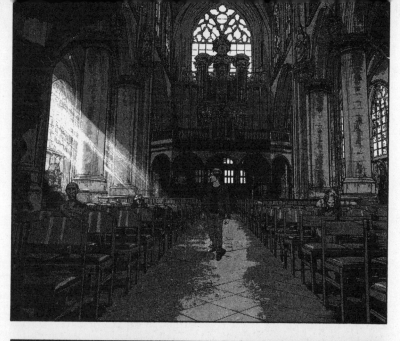

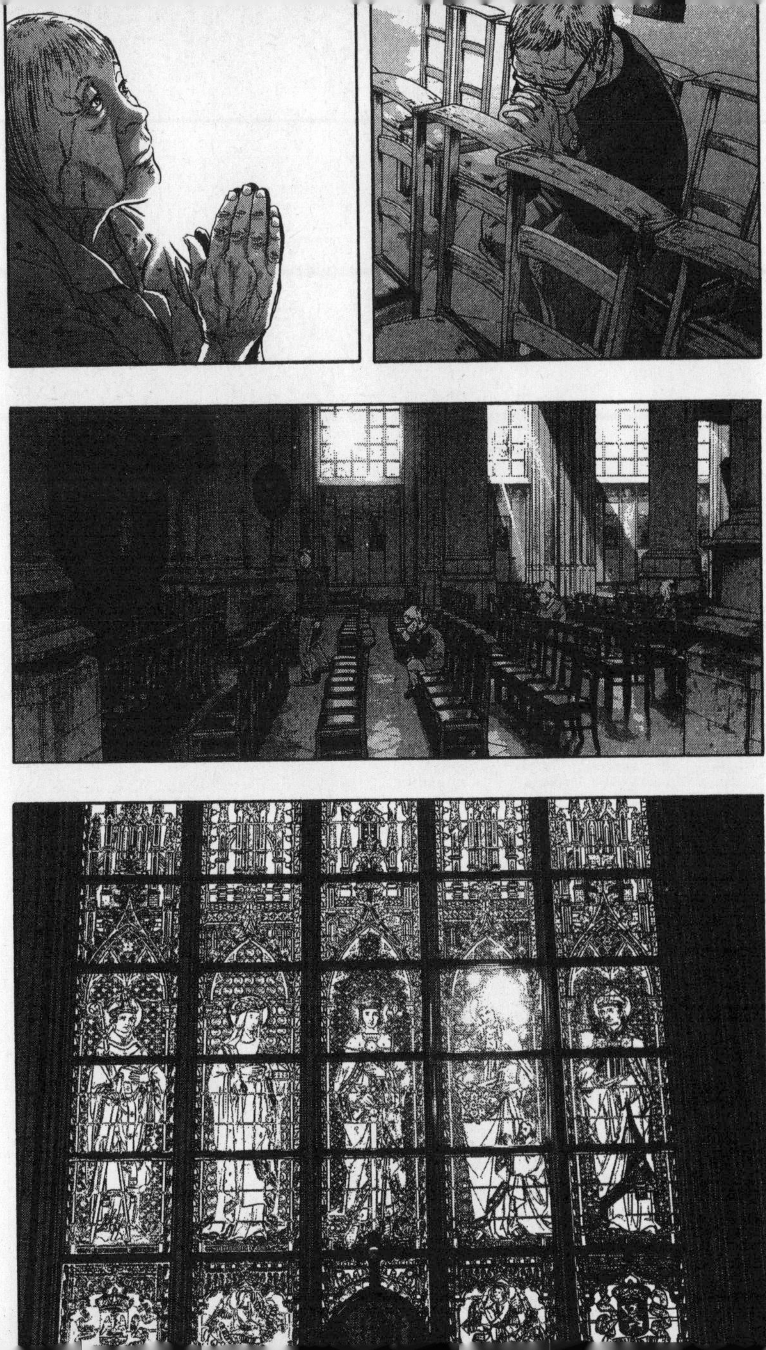

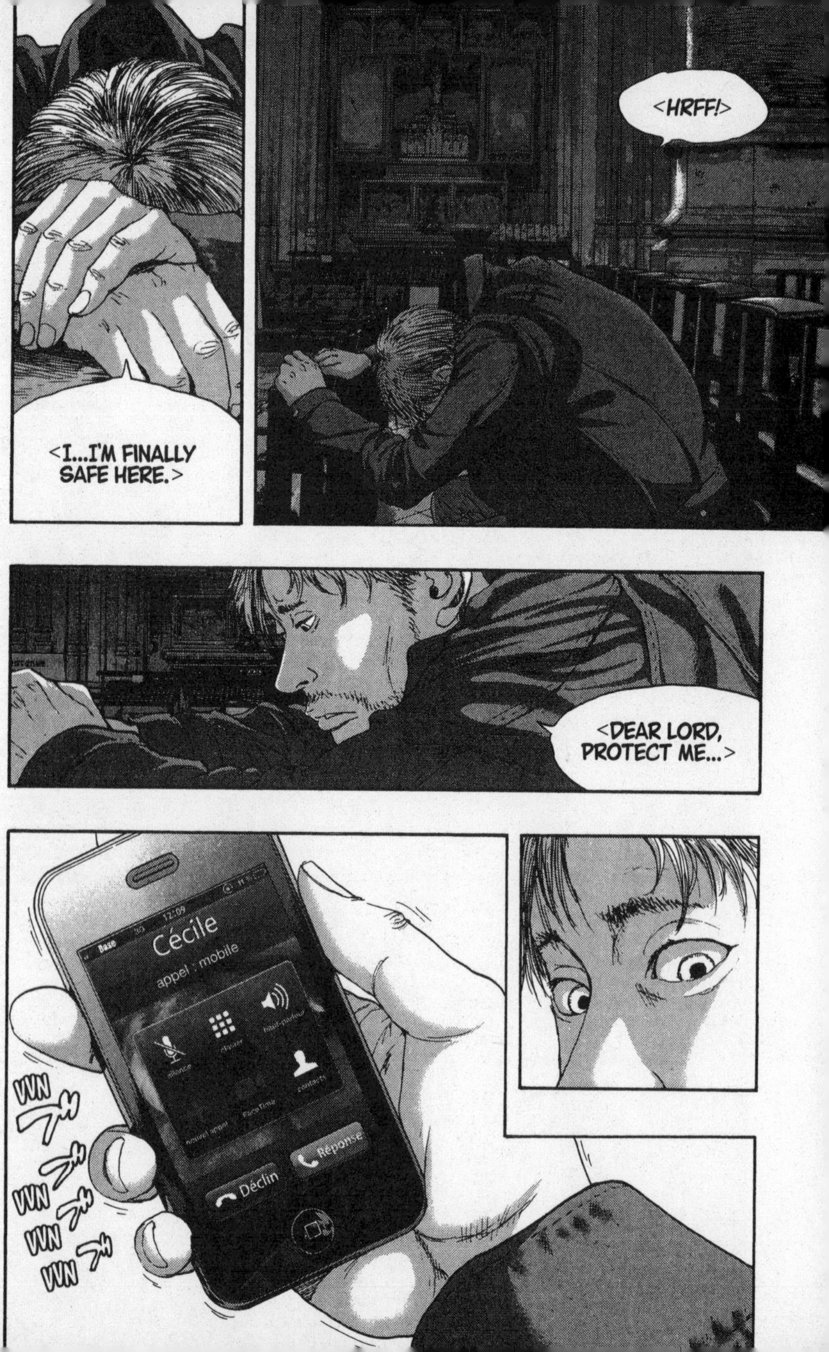
<HRFF!>
<I...I'M FINALLY SAFE HERE.>
<DEAR LORD, PROTECT ME...>
12:09
Cécile
appel : mobile
Réponse
Déclin
VVN
VVN
VVN
VVN

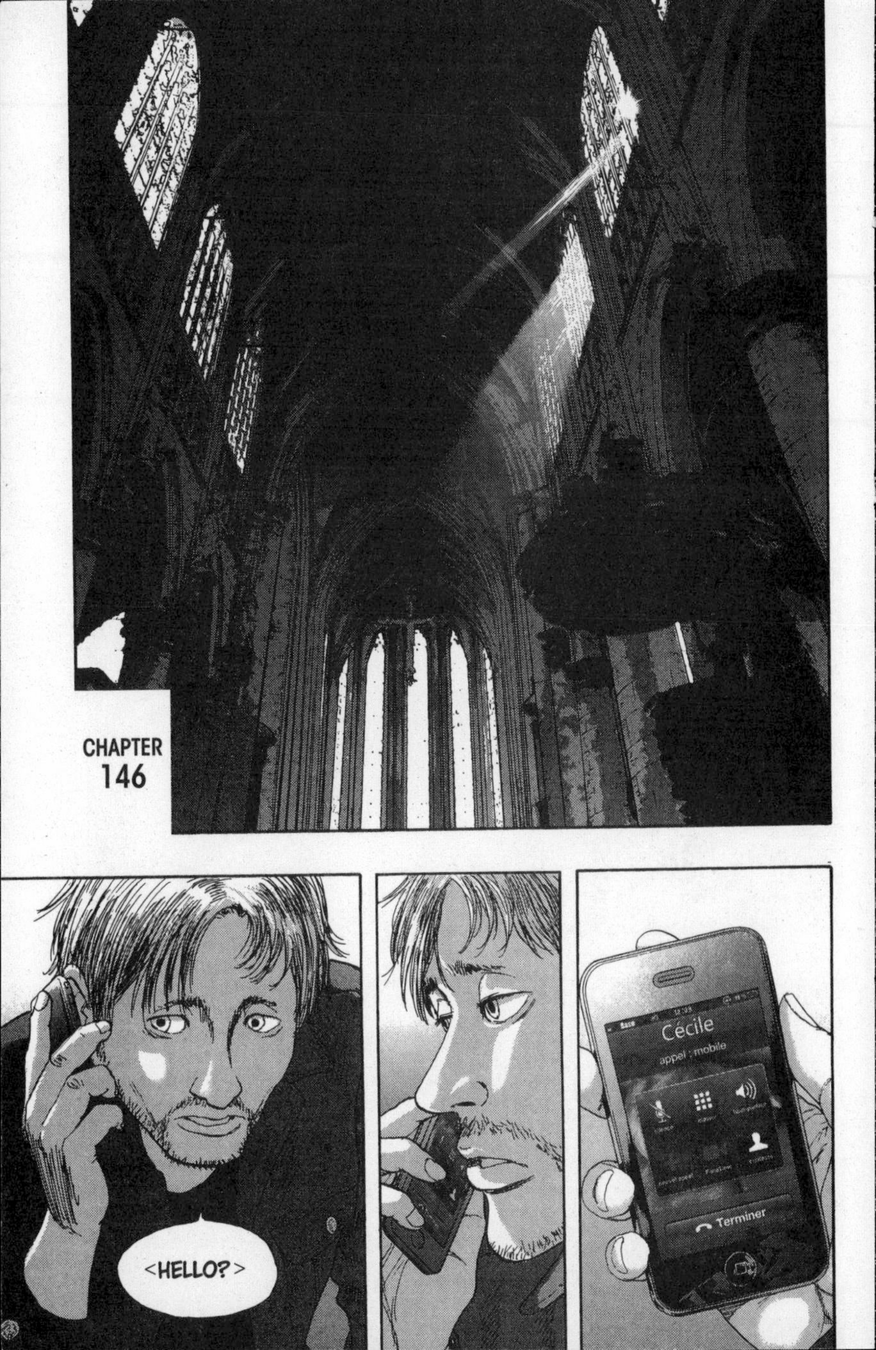
CHAPTER
146
Cécile
appel : mobile
Terminer
<HELLO?>

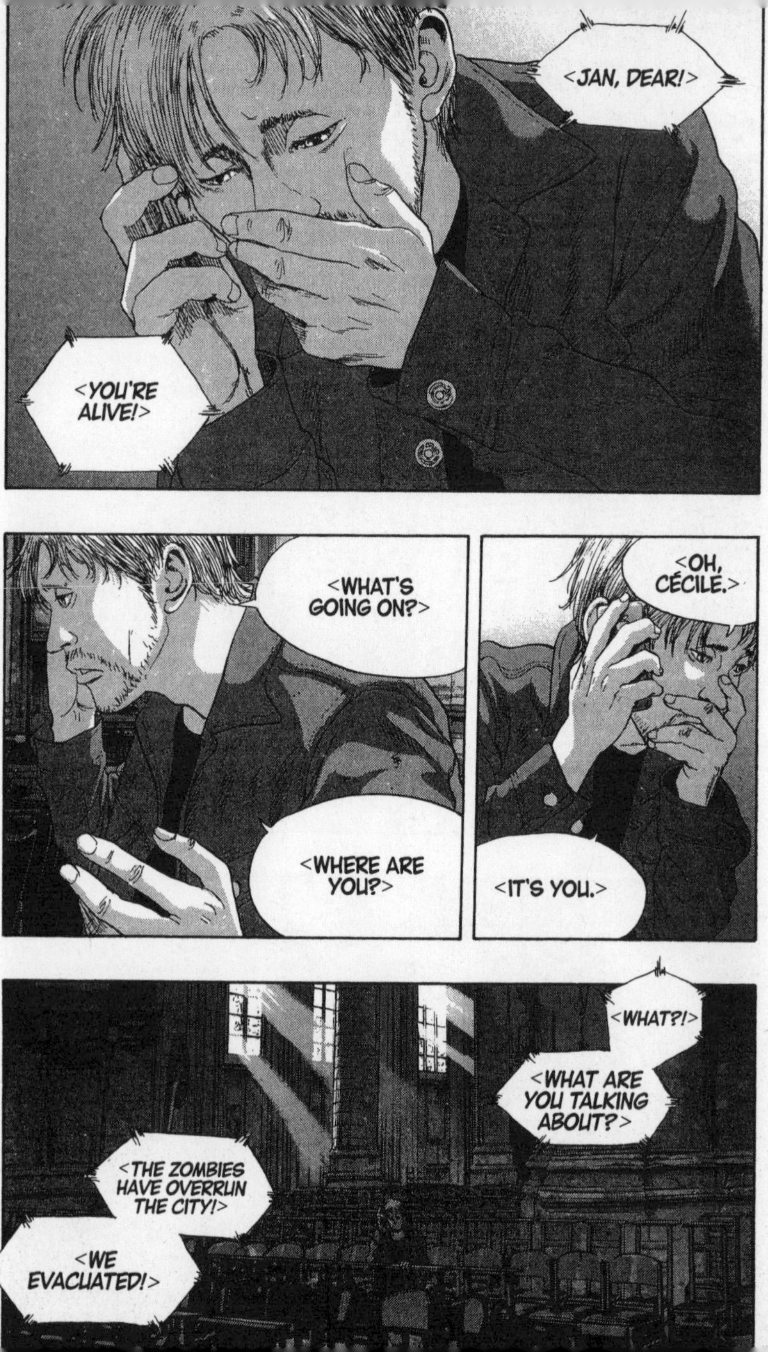
<JAN, DEAR!>
<YOU'RE ALIVE!>
<OH, CÉCILE.>
<IT'S YOU.>
<WHAT'S GOING ON?>
<WHERE ARE YOU?>
<WHAT?!>
<WHAT ARE YOU TALKING ABOUT?>
<THE ZOMBIES HAVE OVERRUN THE CITY!>
<WE EVACUATED!>

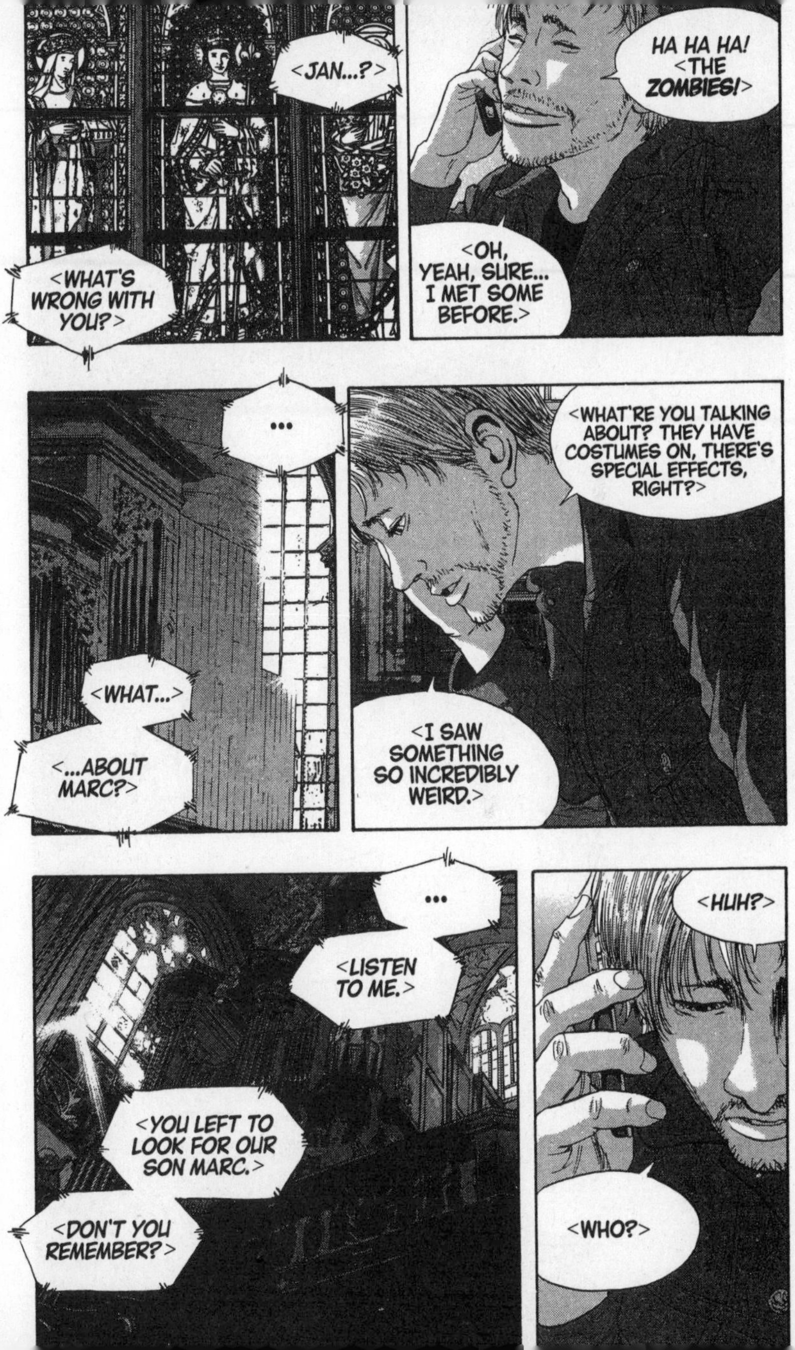
HA HA HA! <THE ZOMBIES!>
<OH, YEAH, SURE... I MET SOME BEFORE.>
<JAN...?>
<WHAT'S WRONG WITH YOU?>
<WHAT'RE YOU TALKING ABOUT? THEY HAVE COSTUMES ON, THERE'S SPECIAL EFFECTS, RIGHT?>
<I SAW SOMETHING SO INCREDIBLY WEIRD.>
...
<WHAT...>
<...ABOUT MARC?>
<HUH?>
<WHO?>
...
<LISTEN TO ME.>
<YOU LEFT TO LOOK FOR OUR SON MARC.>
<DON'T YOU REMEMBER?>

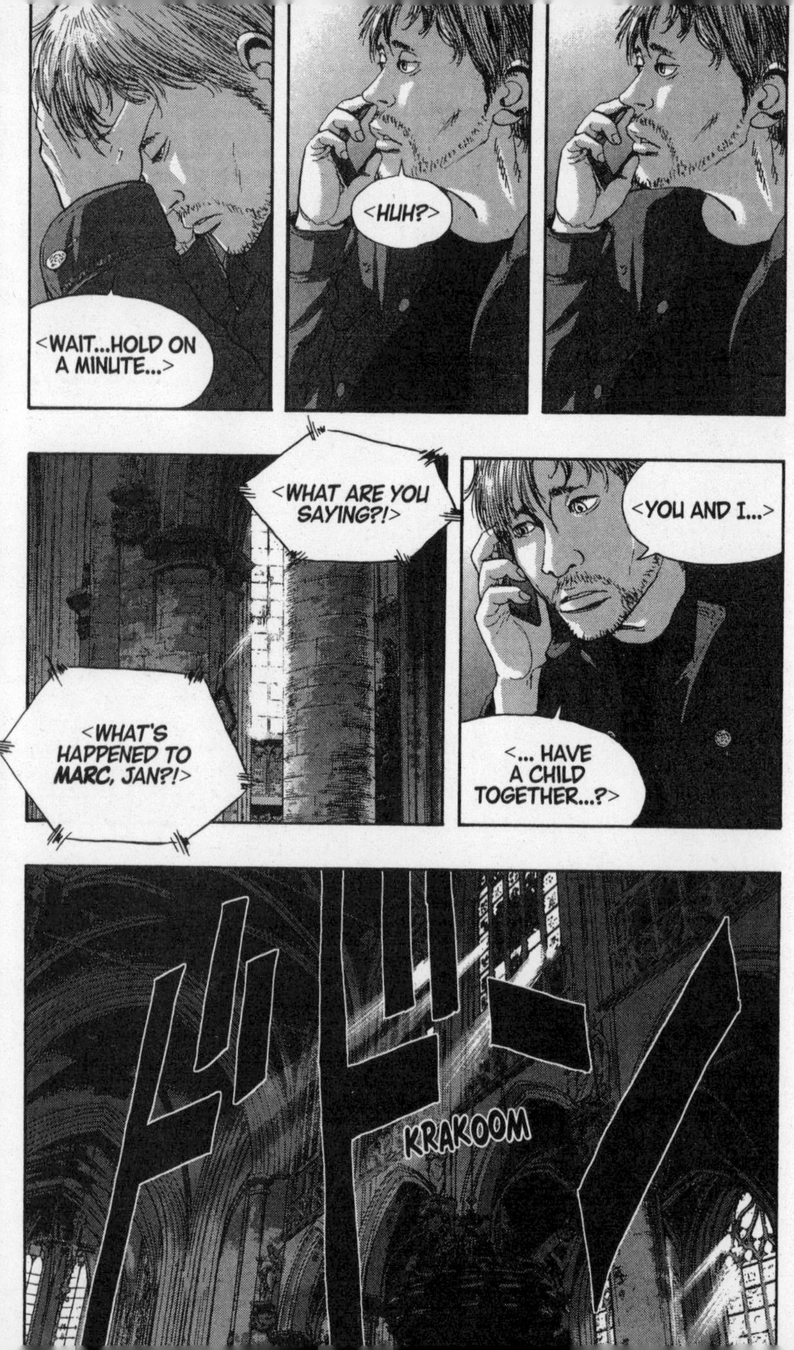
<HUH?>
<WAIT...HOLD ON A MINUTE...>
<YOU AND I...>
<... HAVE A CHILD TOGETHER...?>
<WHAT ARE YOU SAYING?!>
<WHAT'S HAPPENED TO MARC, JAN?!>
KRAKOOM

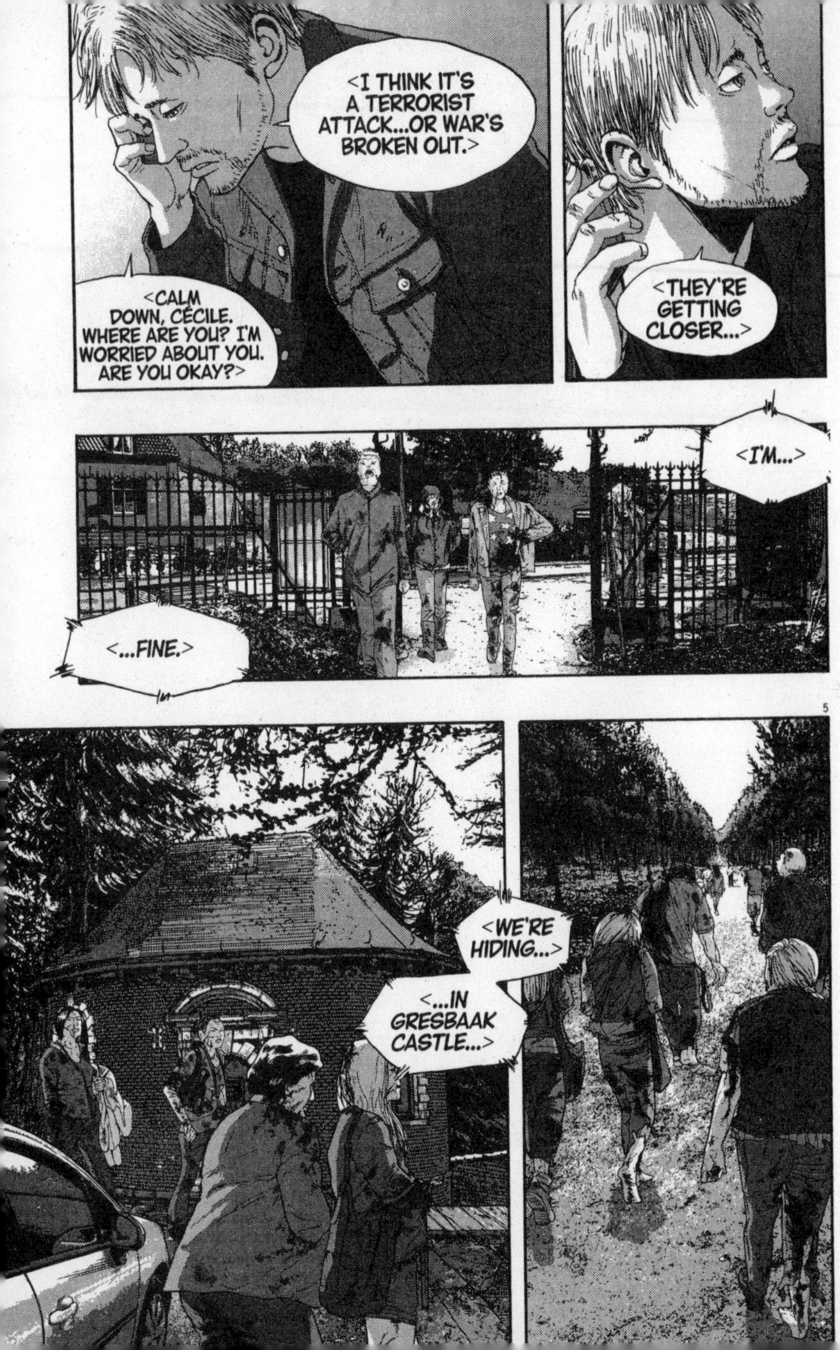
<THEY'RE GETTING CLOSER...>
<I THINK IT'S A TERRORIST ATTACK...OR WAR'S BROKEN OUT.>
<CALM DOWN, CÉCILE. WHERE ARE YOU? I'M WORRIED ABOUT YOU. ARE YOU OKAY?>
<I'M...>
<...FINE.>
<WE'RE HIDING...>
<...IN GRESBAAK CASTLE...>

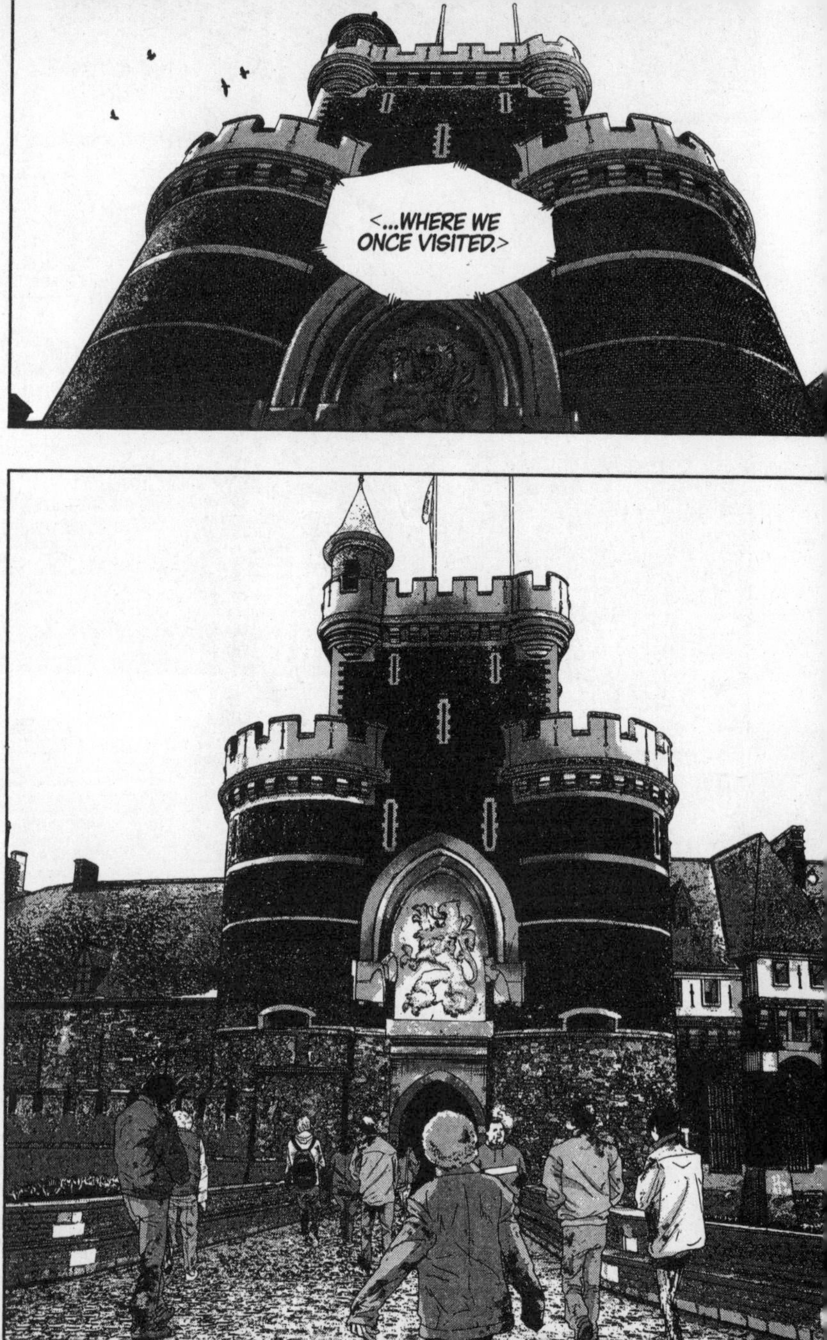
<...WHERE WE ONCE VISITED.>

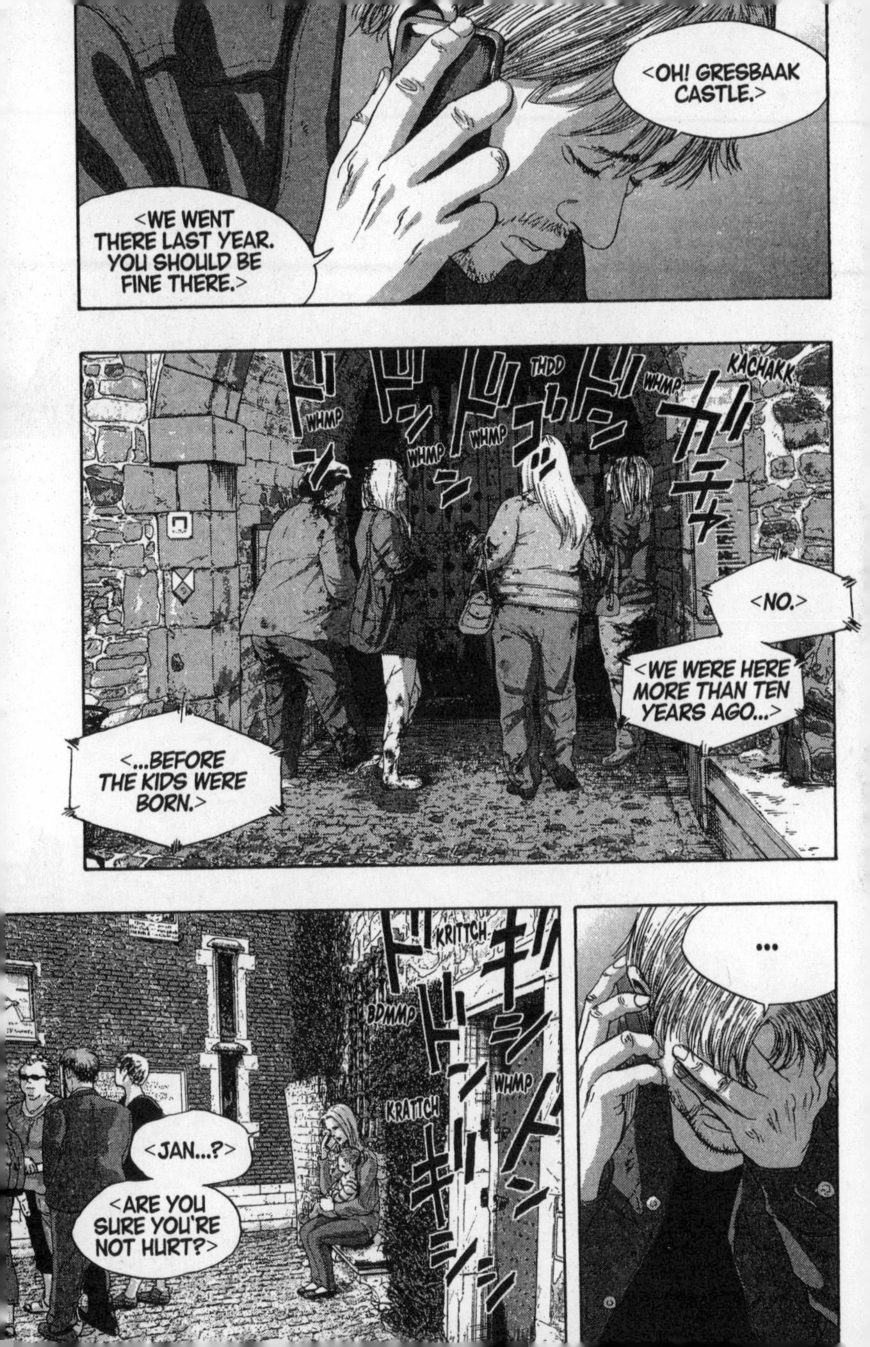
<OH! GRESBAAK CASTLE.>
<WE WENT THERE LAST YEAR. YOU SHOULD BE FINE THERE.>
KACHAKK
WHMP
THDD
WHMP
WHMP
WHMP
<NO.>
<WE WERE HERE MORE THAN TEN YEARS AGO...>
<...BEFORE THE KIDS WERE BORN.>
...
KRITTCH
BDMMP
WHMP
KRATTCH
<JAN...?>
<ARE YOU SURE YOU'RE NOT HURT?>

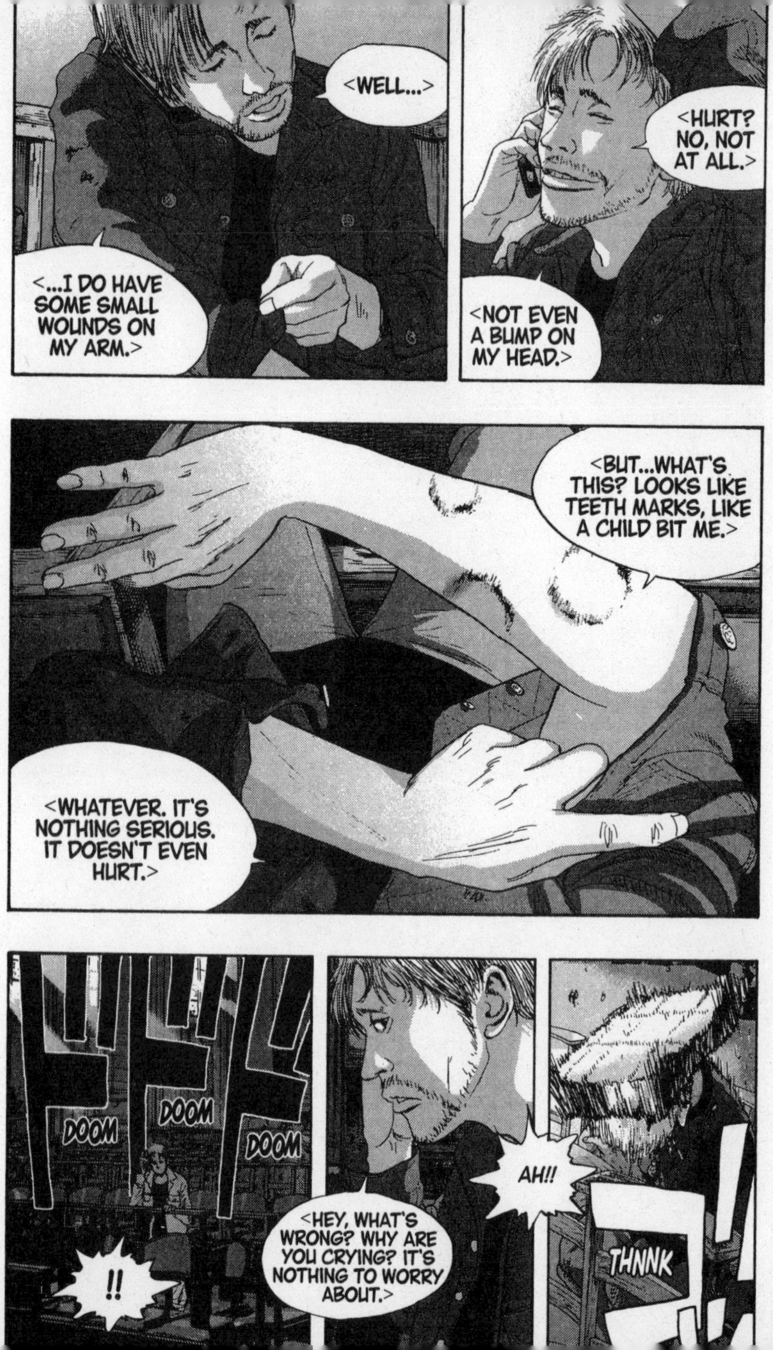
<HURT? NO, NOT AT ALL.>
<NOT EVEN A BUMP ON MY HEAD.>
<WELL...>
<...I DO HAVE SOME SMALL WOUNDS ON MY ARM.>
<BUT...WHAT'S THIS? LOOKS LIKE TEETH MARKS, LIKE A CHILD BIT ME.>
<WHATEVER. IT'S NOTHING SERIOUS. IT DOESN'T EVEN HURT.>
AH!!
THNNK
<HEY, WHAT'S WRONG? WHY ARE YOU CRYING? IT'S NOTHING TO WORRY ABOUT.>
DOOM
DOOM
DOOM
!!

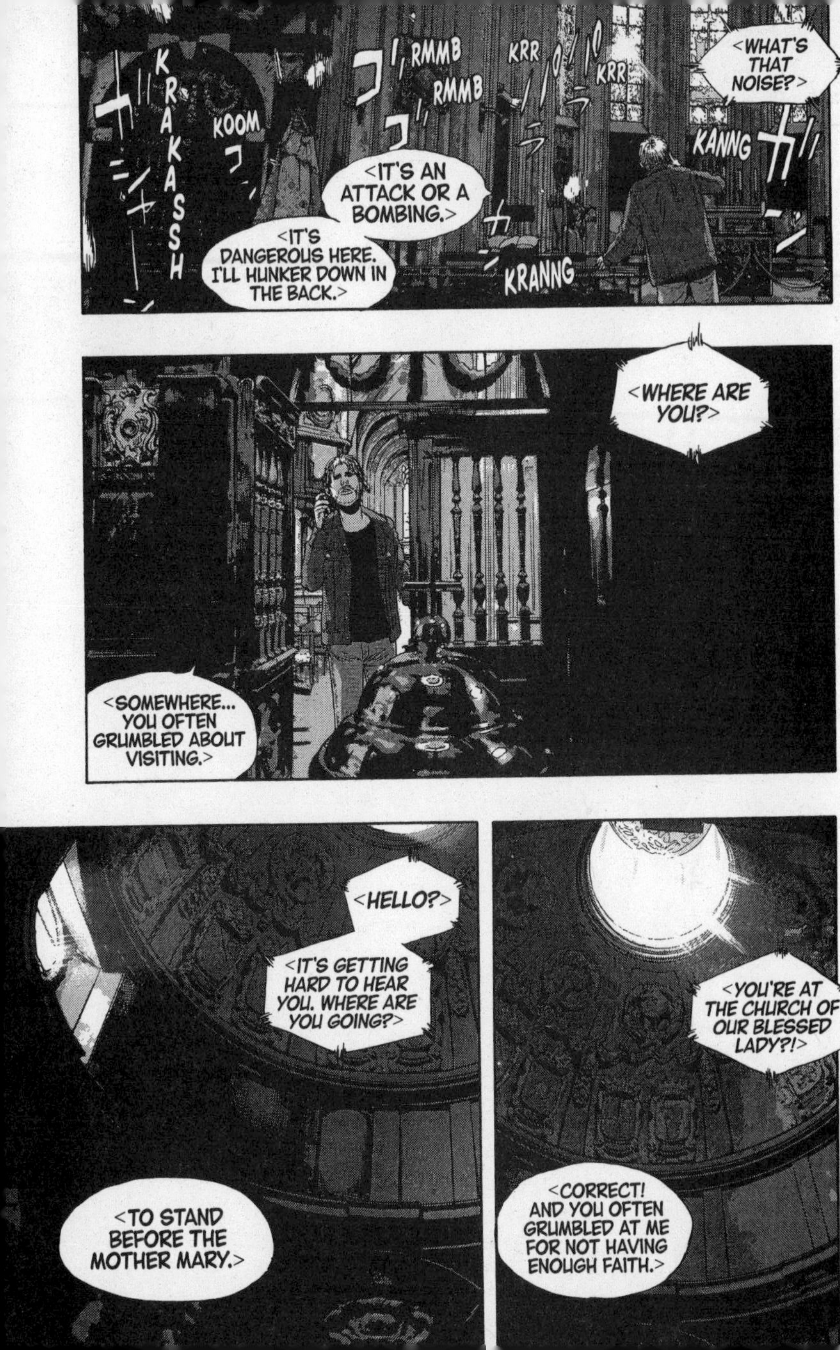
<WHAT'S THAT NOISE?>
KANNG
KRR
KRR
RMMB
RMMB
KRANNG
<IT'S AN ATTACK OR A BOMBING.>
<IT'S DANGEROUS HERE. I'LL HUNKER DOWN IN THE BACK.>
KOOM
KRAKASSH
<WHERE ARE YOU?>
<SOMEWHERE... YOU OFTEN GRUMBLED ABOUT VISITING.>
<YOU'RE AT THE CHURCH OF OUR BLESSED LADY?!>
<CORRECT! AND YOU OFTEN GRUMBLED AT ME FOR NOT HAVING ENOUGH FAITH.>
<HELLO?>
<IT'S GETTING HARD TO HEAR YOU. WHERE ARE YOU GOING?>
<TO STAND BEFORE THE MOTHER MARY.>

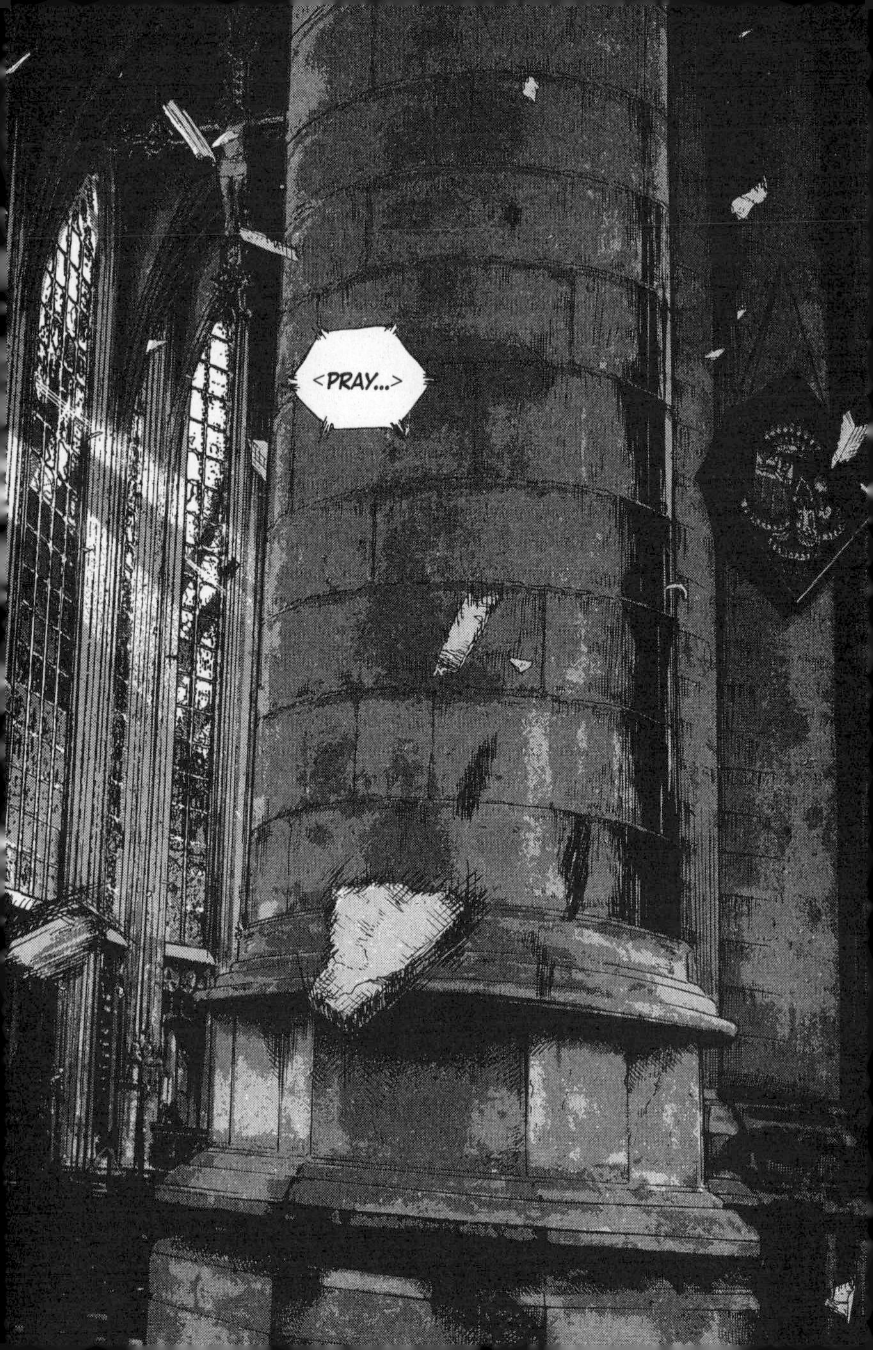
<PRAY...>

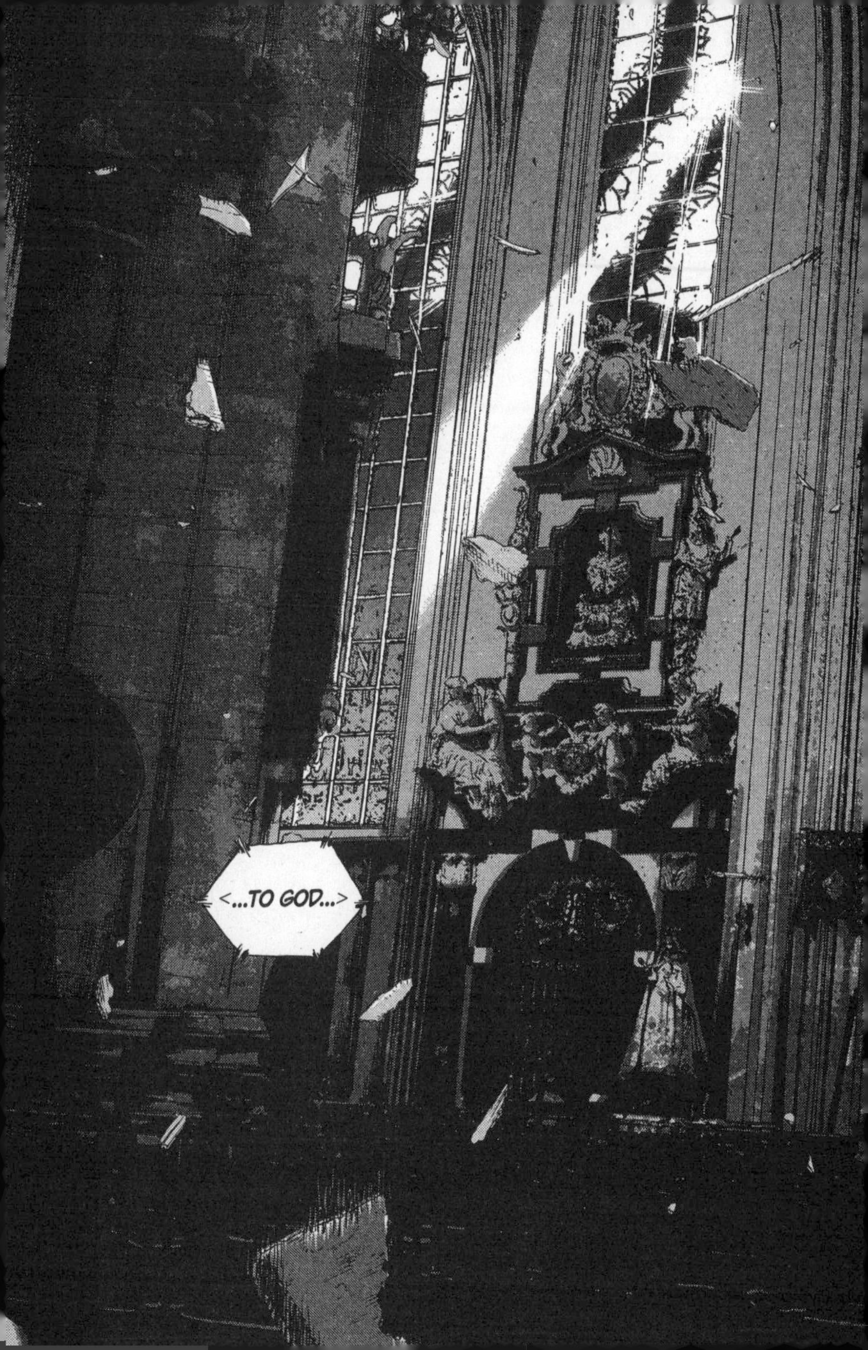
<...TO GOD...>

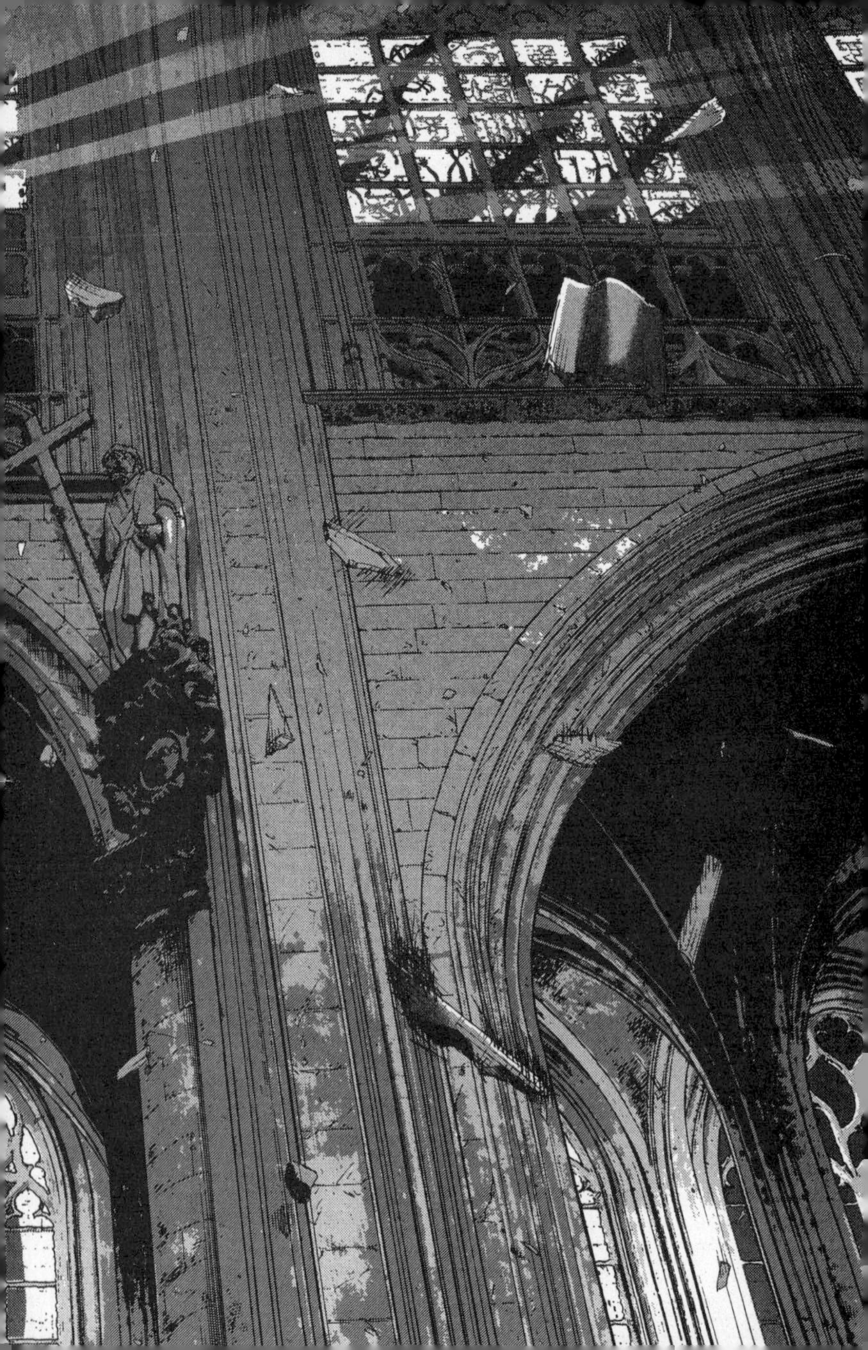

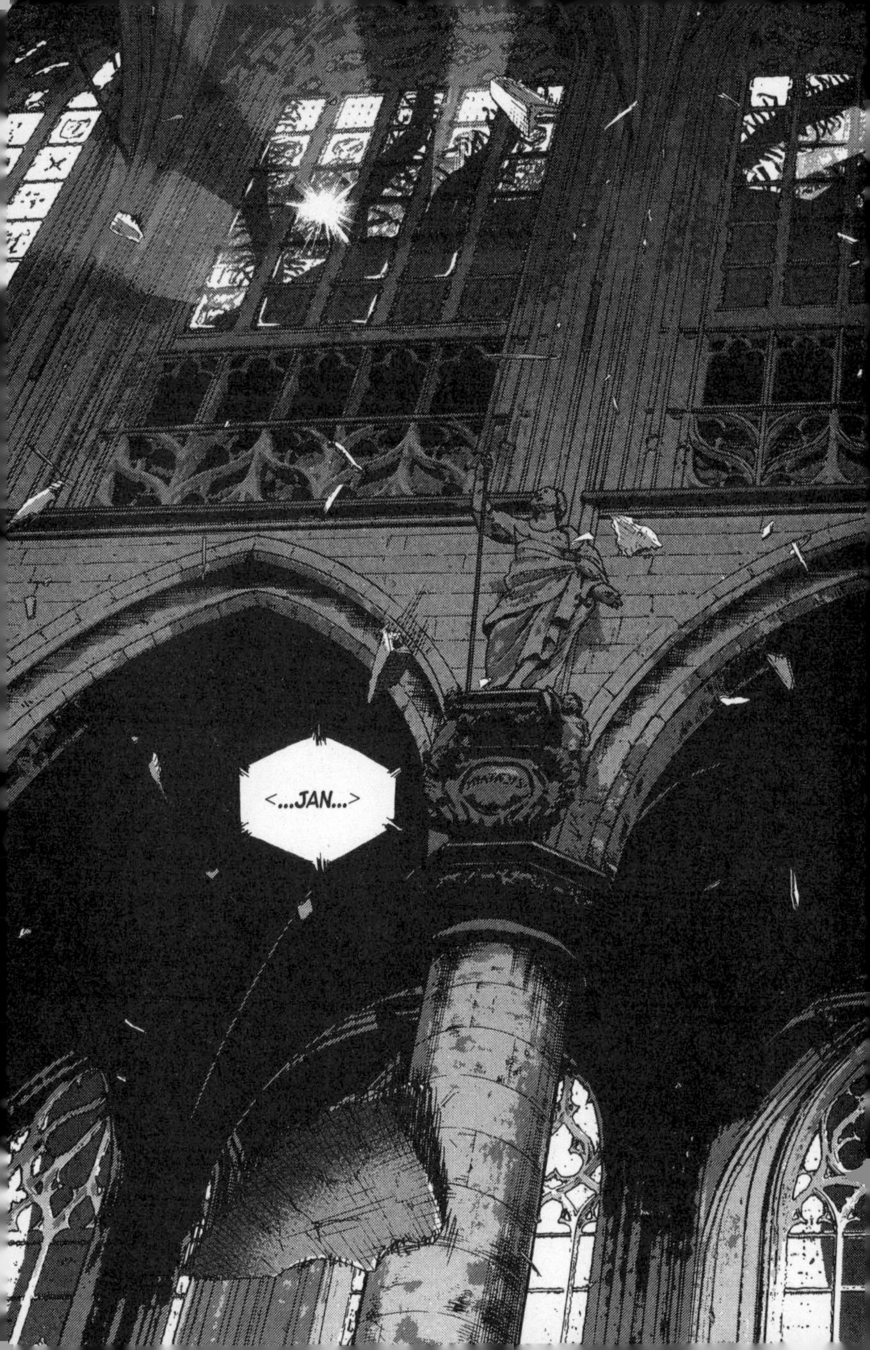
<...JAN...>

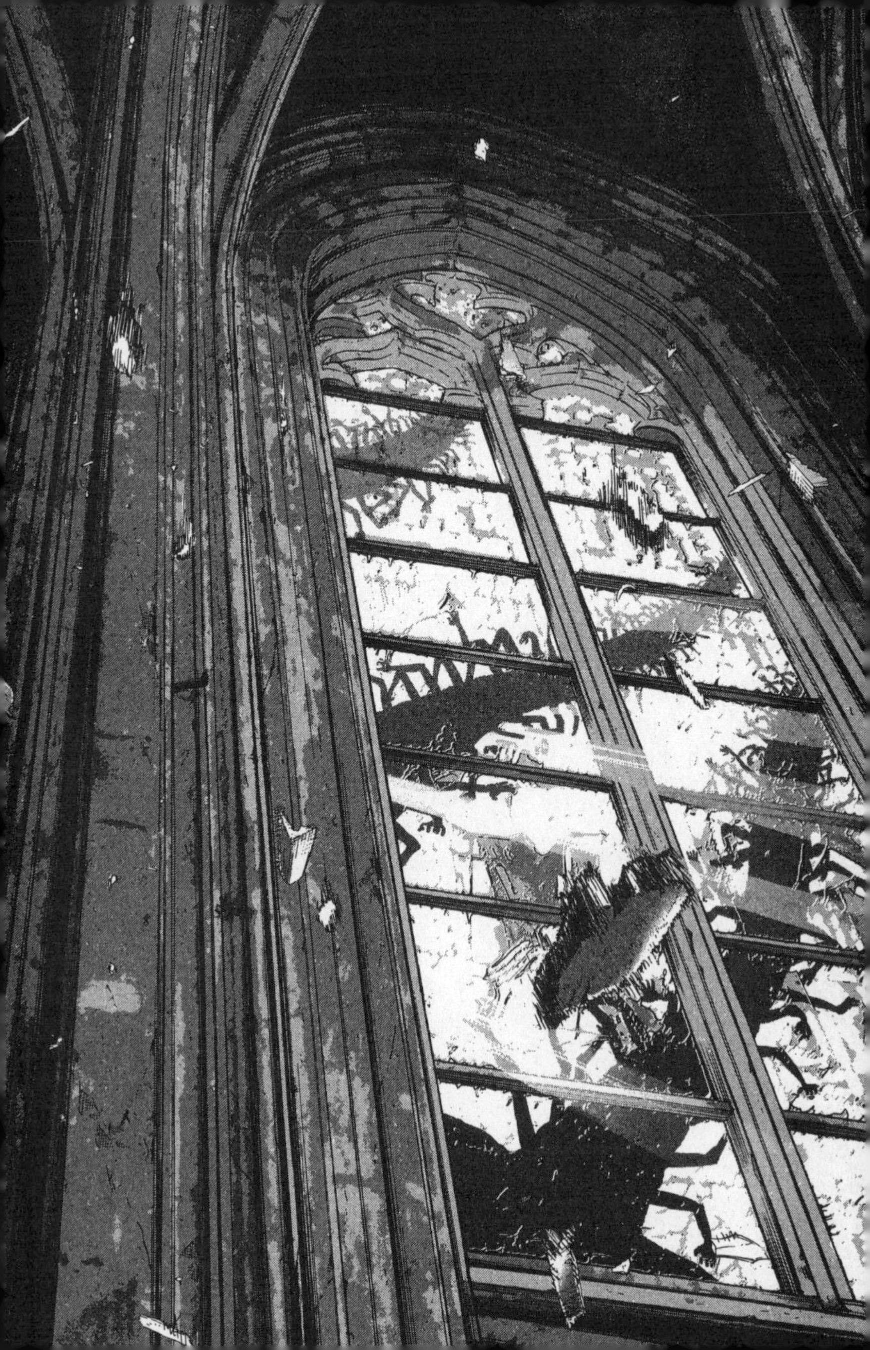

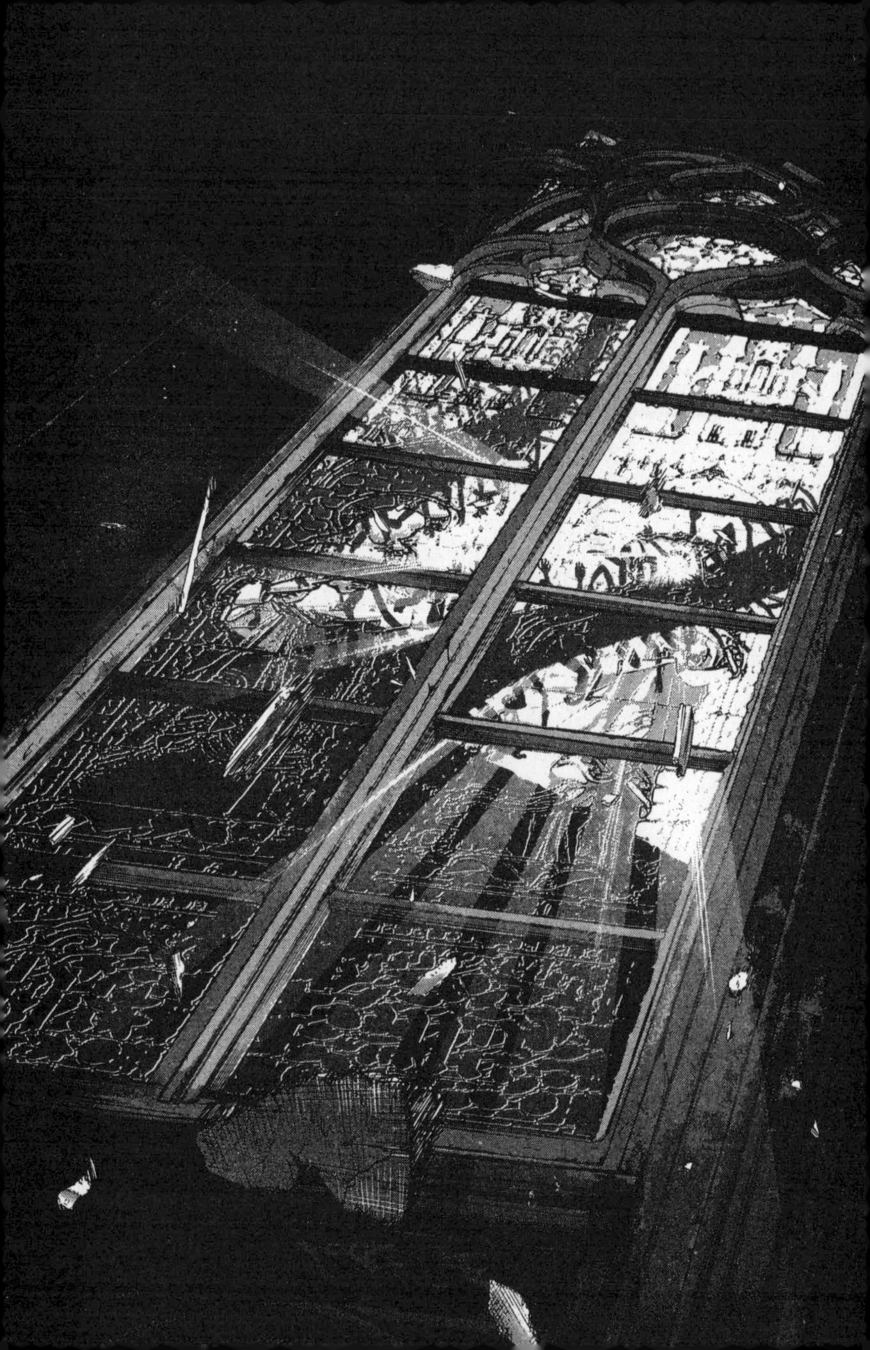

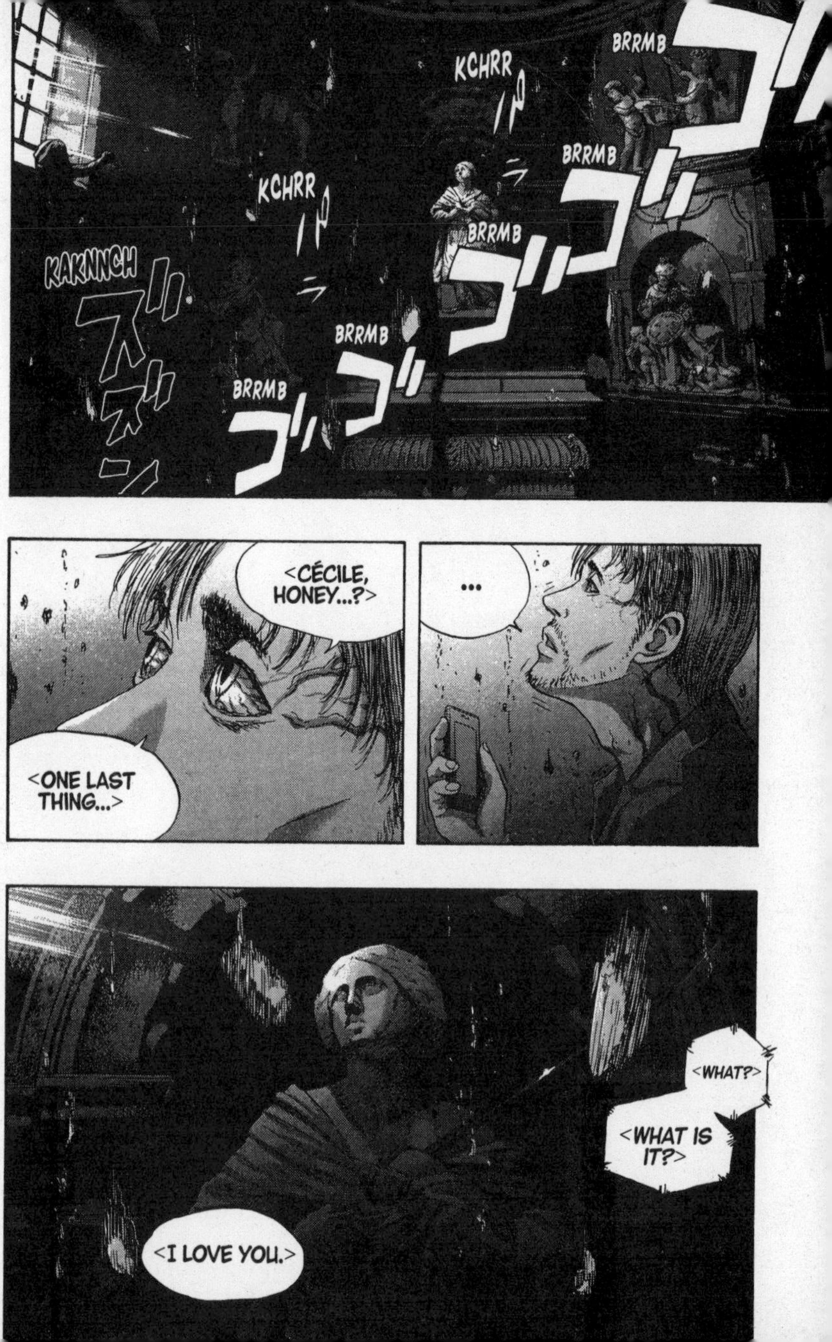
BRRMB
KCHRR
BRRMB
BRRMB
KCHRR
BRRMB
BRRMB
KAKNNCH
...
<CÉCILE, HONEY...?>
<ONE LAST THING...>
<WHAT?>
<WHAT IS IT?>
<I LOVE YOU.>

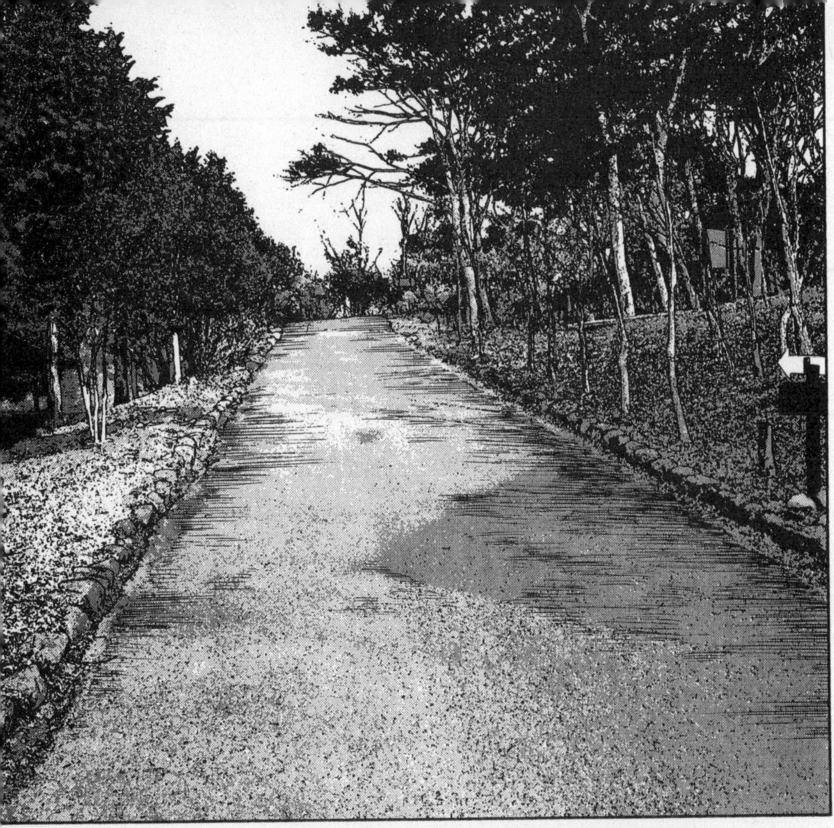

SIGNS: ASHINOKO / TENT VILLAGE

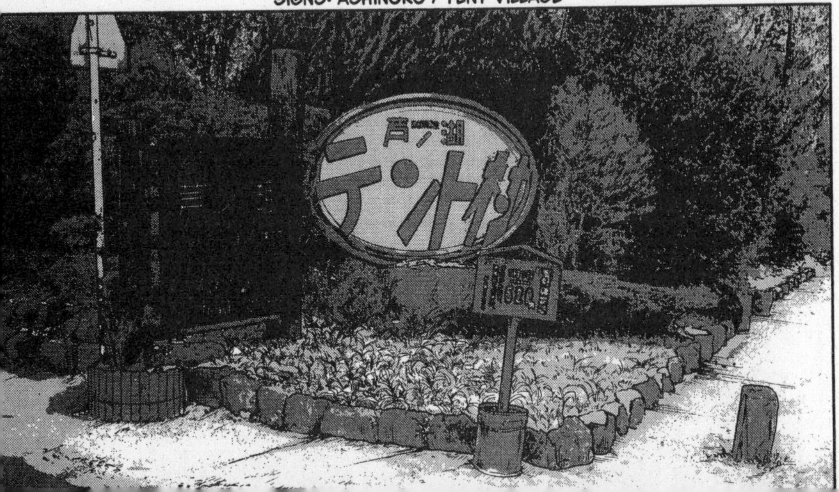

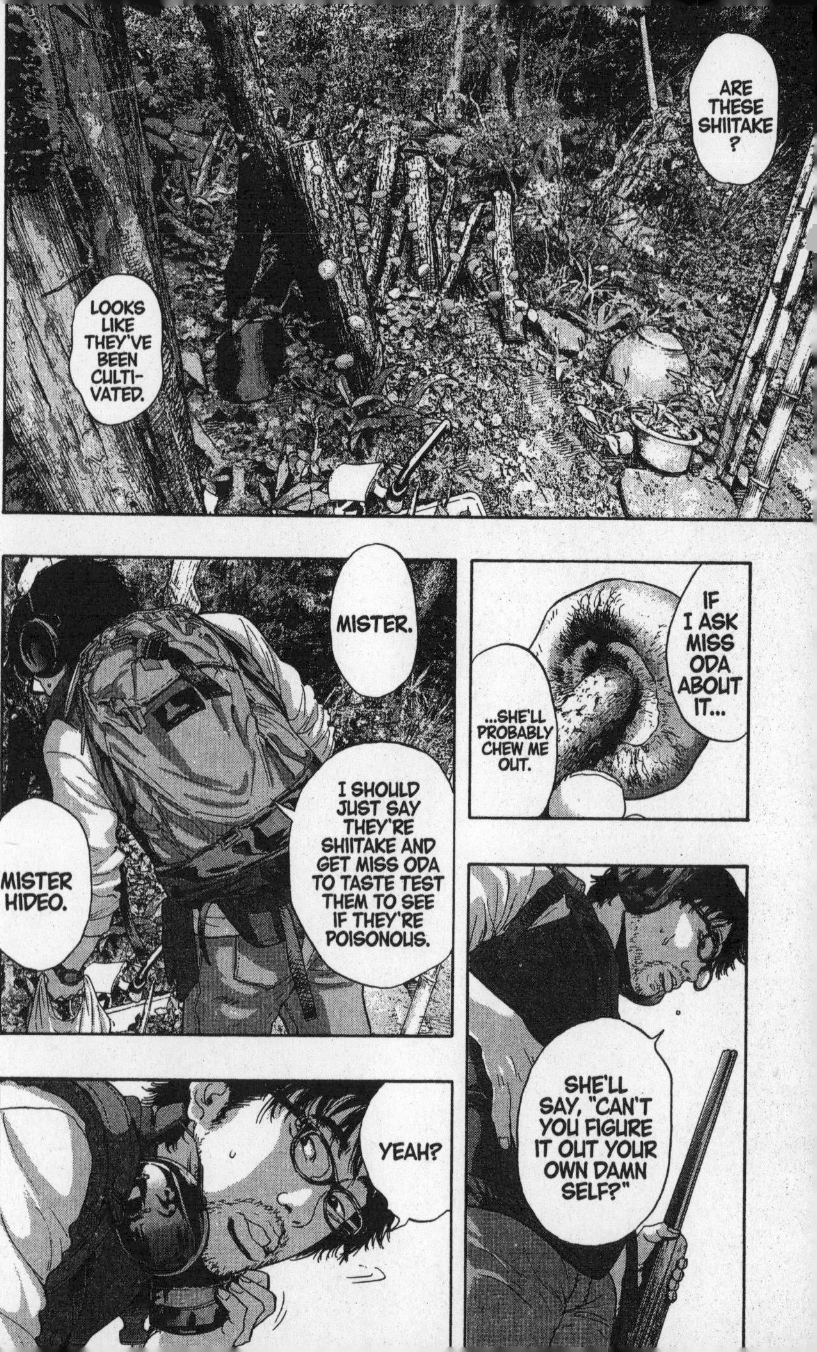
ARE THESE SHIITAKE?
LOOKS LIKE THEY'VE BEEN CULTI-VATED.
IF I ASK MISS ODA ABOUT IT...
...SHE'LL PROBABLY CHEW ME OUT.
SHE'LL SAY, "CAN'T YOU FIGURE IT OUT YOUR OWN DAMN SELF?"
MISTER.
I SHOULD JUST SAY THEY'RE SHIITAKE AND GET MISS ODA TO TASTE TEST THEM TO SEE IF THEY'RE POISONOUS.
MISTER HIDEO.
YEAH?

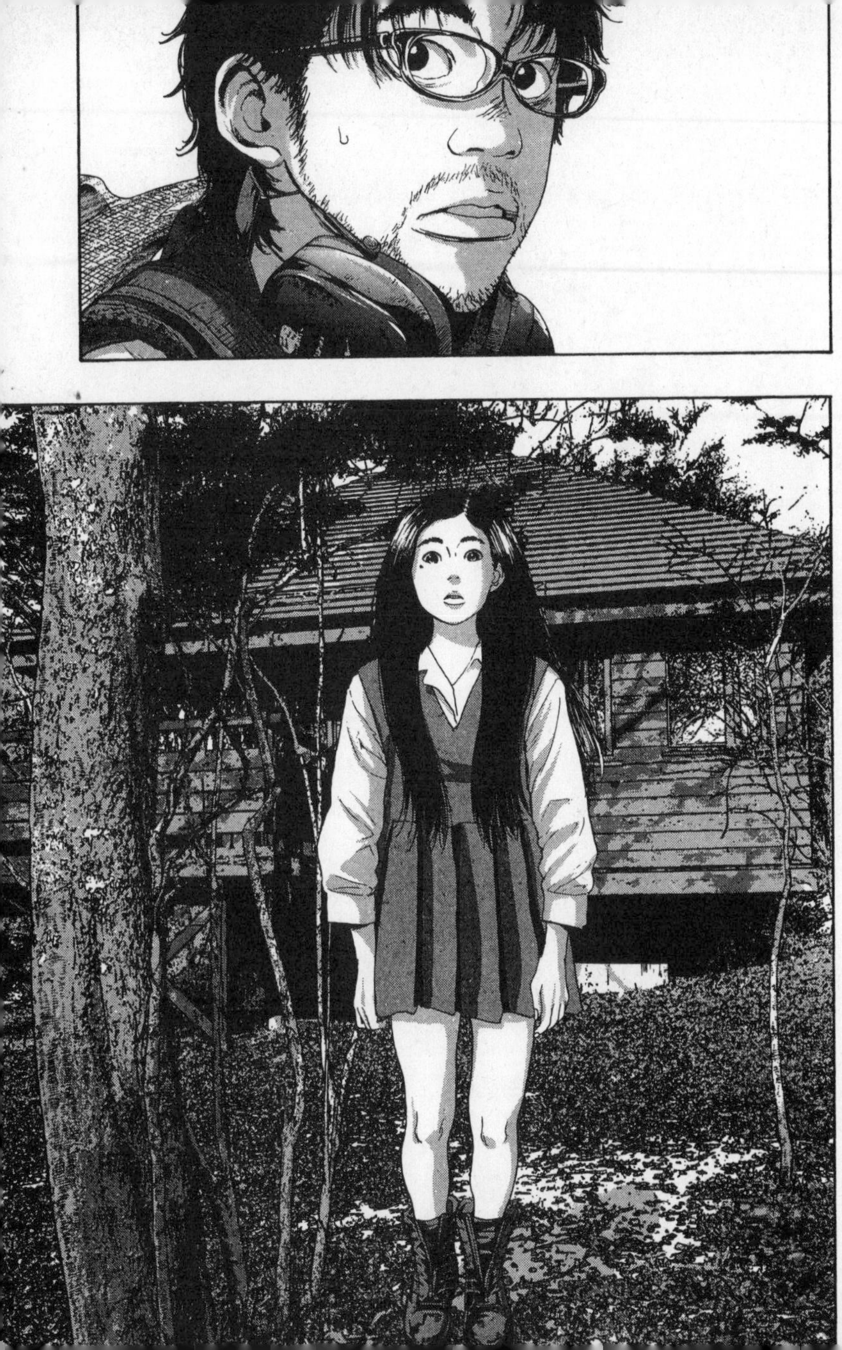

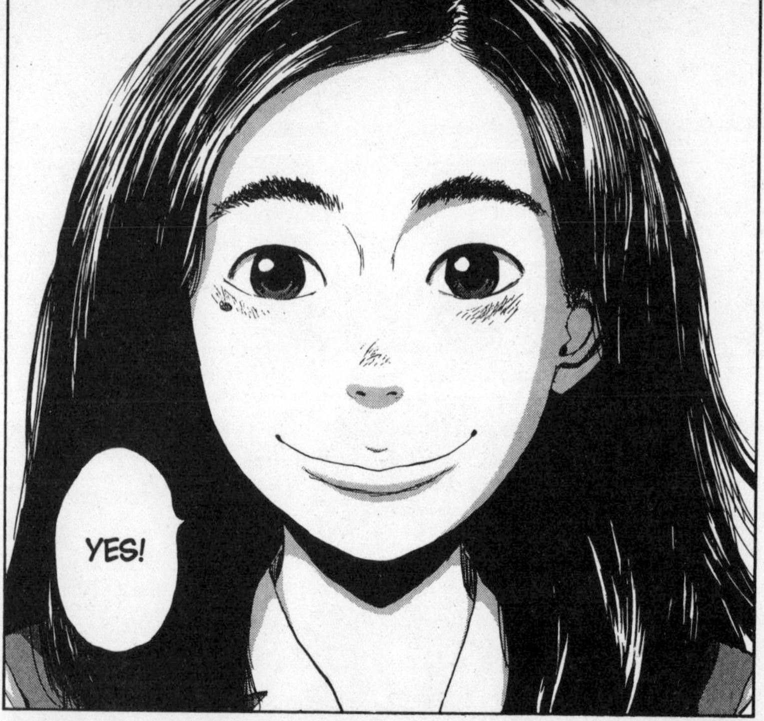
YES!
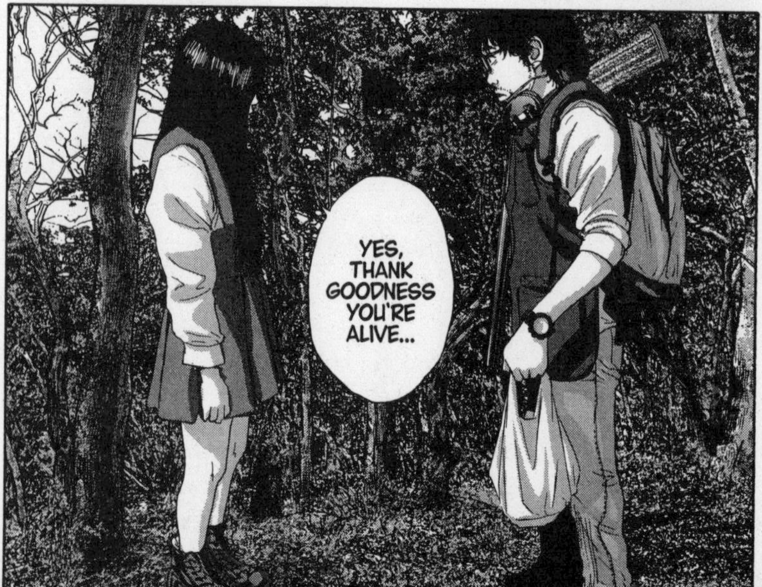
YES, THANK GOODNESS YOU'RE ALIVE...

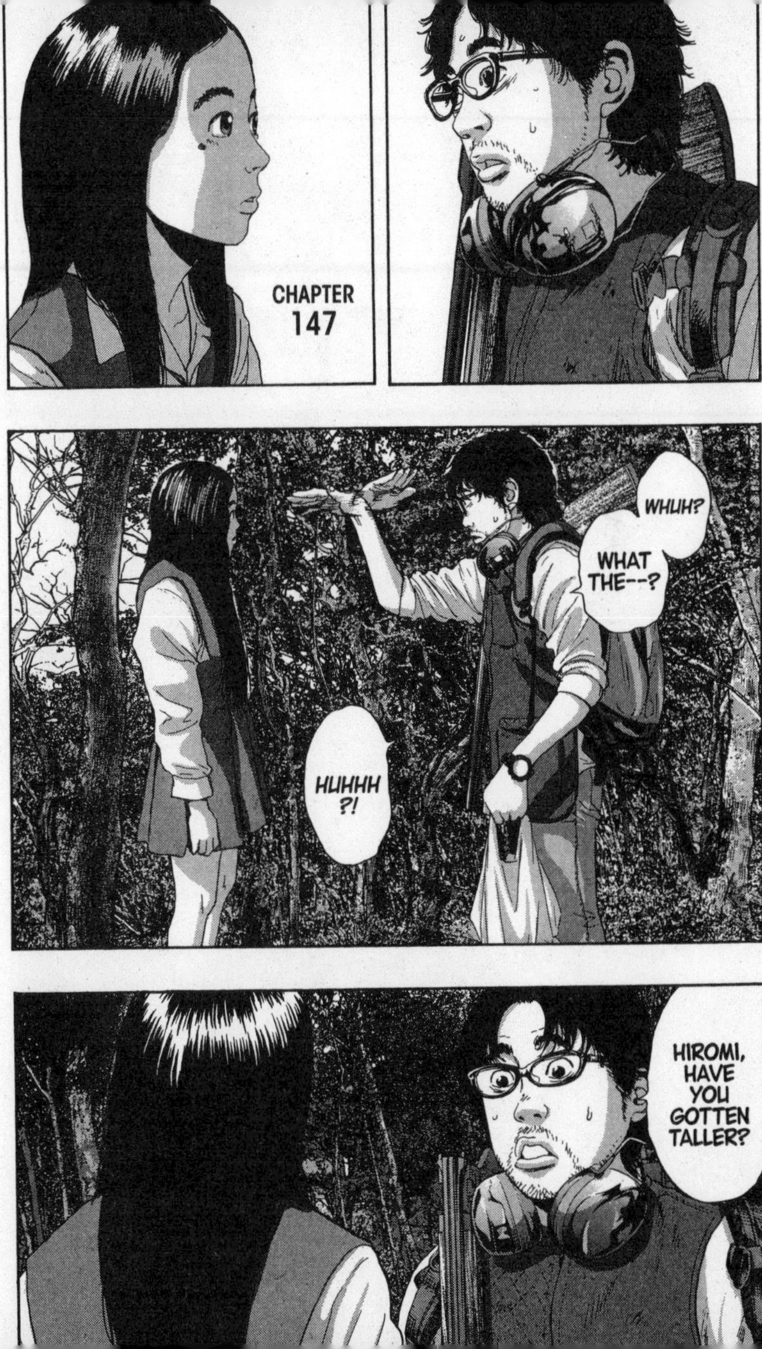
CHAPTER
147
WHUH?
WHAT THE--?
HUHHH?!
HIROMI, HAVE YOU GOTTEN TALLER?

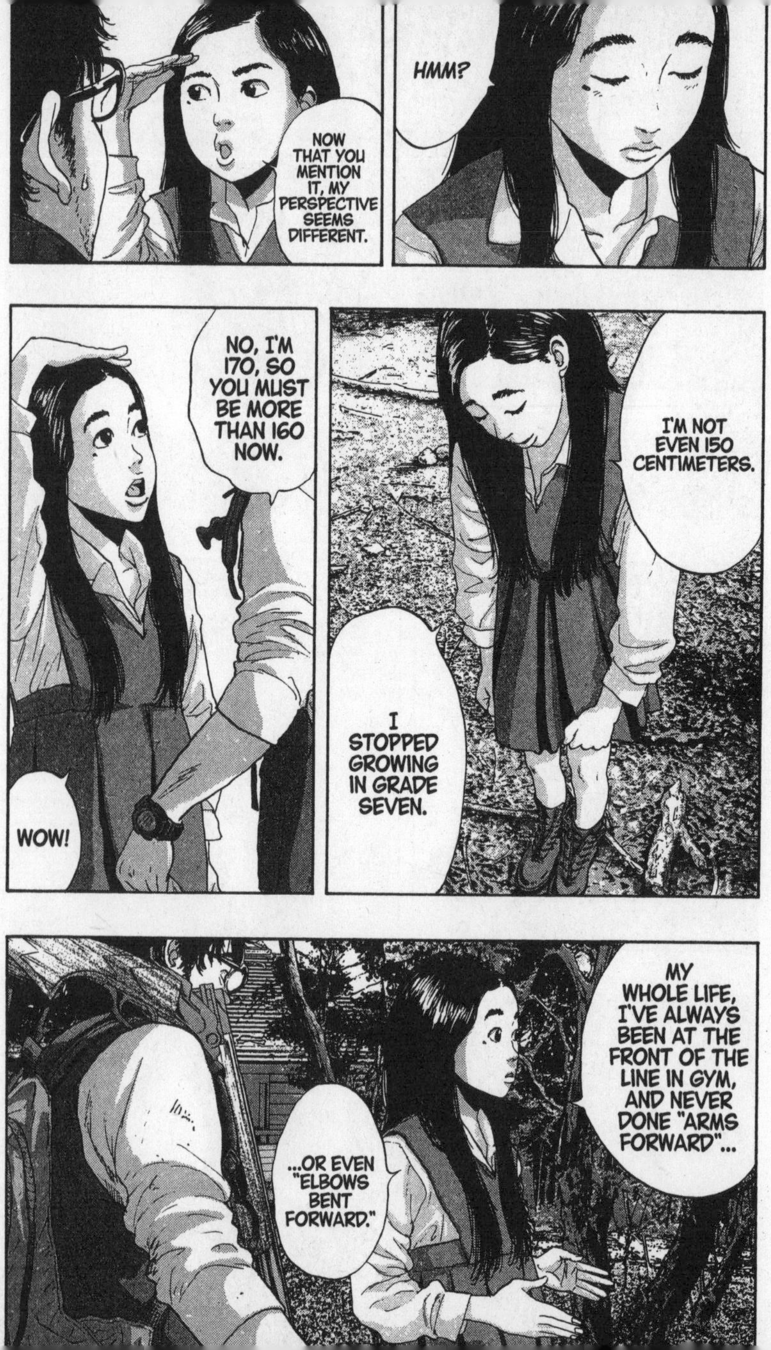
HMM?
NOW THAT YOU MENTION IT, MY PERSPECTIVE SEEMS DIFFERENT.
I'M NOT EVEN 150 CENTIMETERS.
I STOPPED GROWING IN GRADE SEVEN.
NO, I'M 170, SO YOU MUST BE MORE THAN 160 NOW.
WOW!
MY WHOLE LIFE, I'VE ALWAYS BEEN AT THE FRONT OF THE LINE IN GYM, AND NEVER DONE "ARMS FORWARD"...
...OR EVEN "ELBOWS BENT FORWARD."

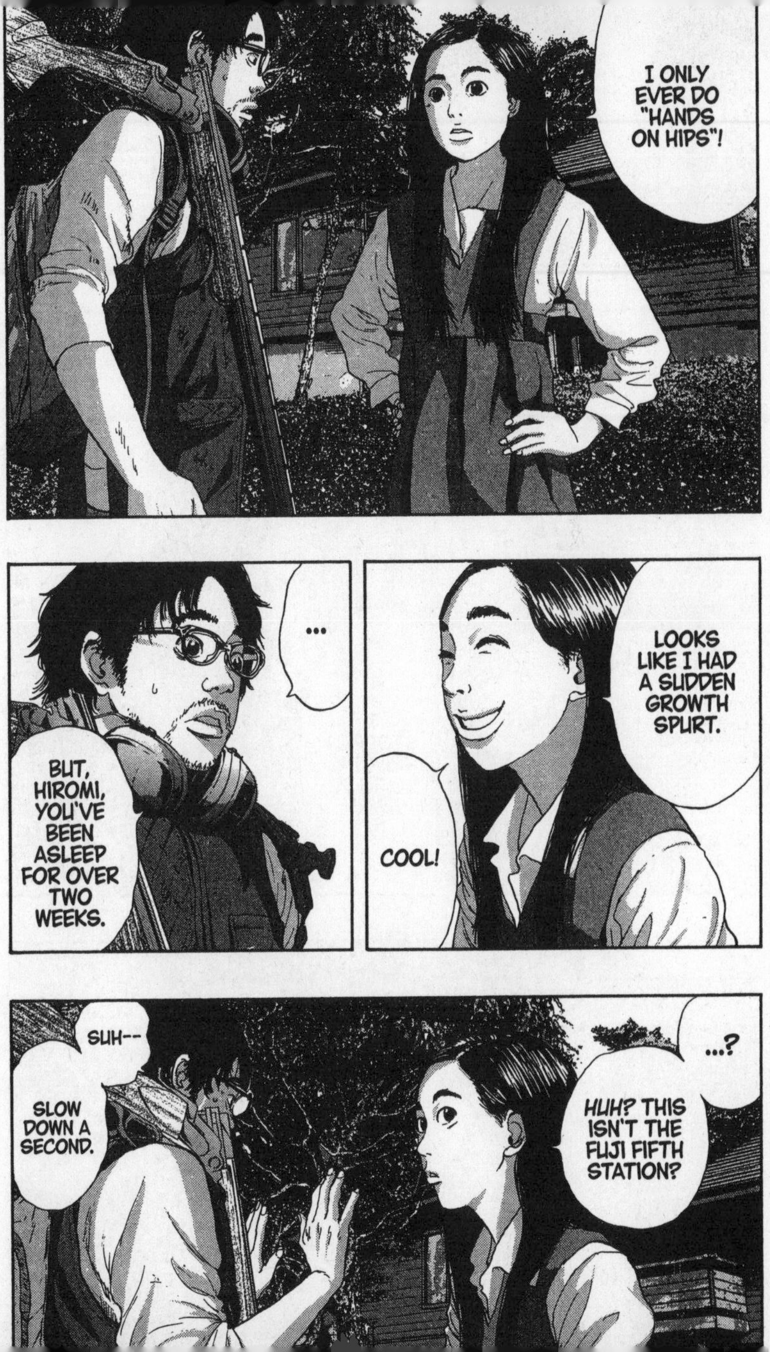
I ONLY EVER DO "HANDS ON HIPS"!
LOOKS LIKE I HAD A SUDDEN GROWTH SPURT.
COOL!
...
BUT, HIROMI, YOU'VE BEEN ASLEEP FOR OVER TWO WEEKS.
...?
HUH? THIS ISN'T THE FUJI FIFTH STATION?
SUH--
SLOW DOWN A SECOND.

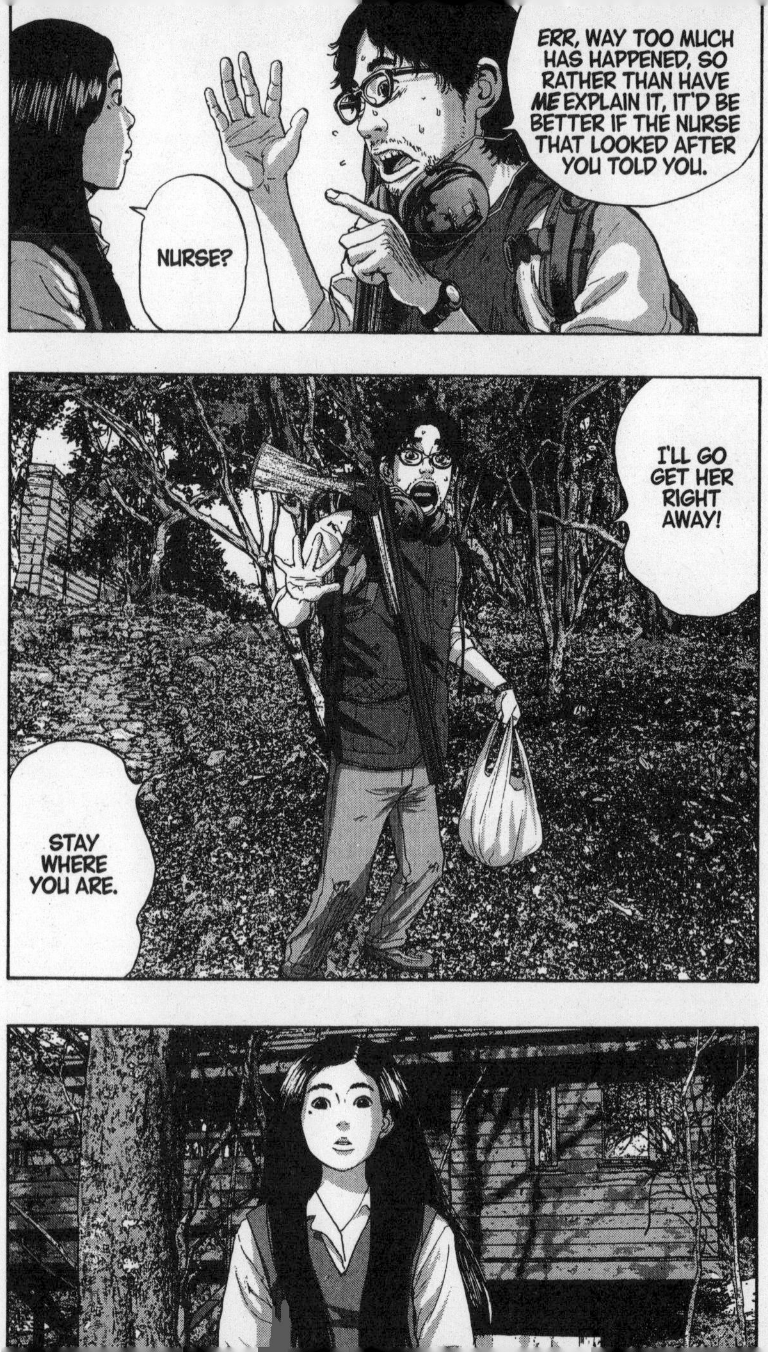
ERR, WAY TOO MUCH HAS HAPPENED, SO RATHER THAN HAVE ME EXPLAIN IT, IT'D BE BETTER IF THE NURSE THAT LOOKED AFTER YOU TOLD YOU.
NURSE?
I'LL GO GET HER RIGHT AWAY!
STAY WHERE YOU ARE.

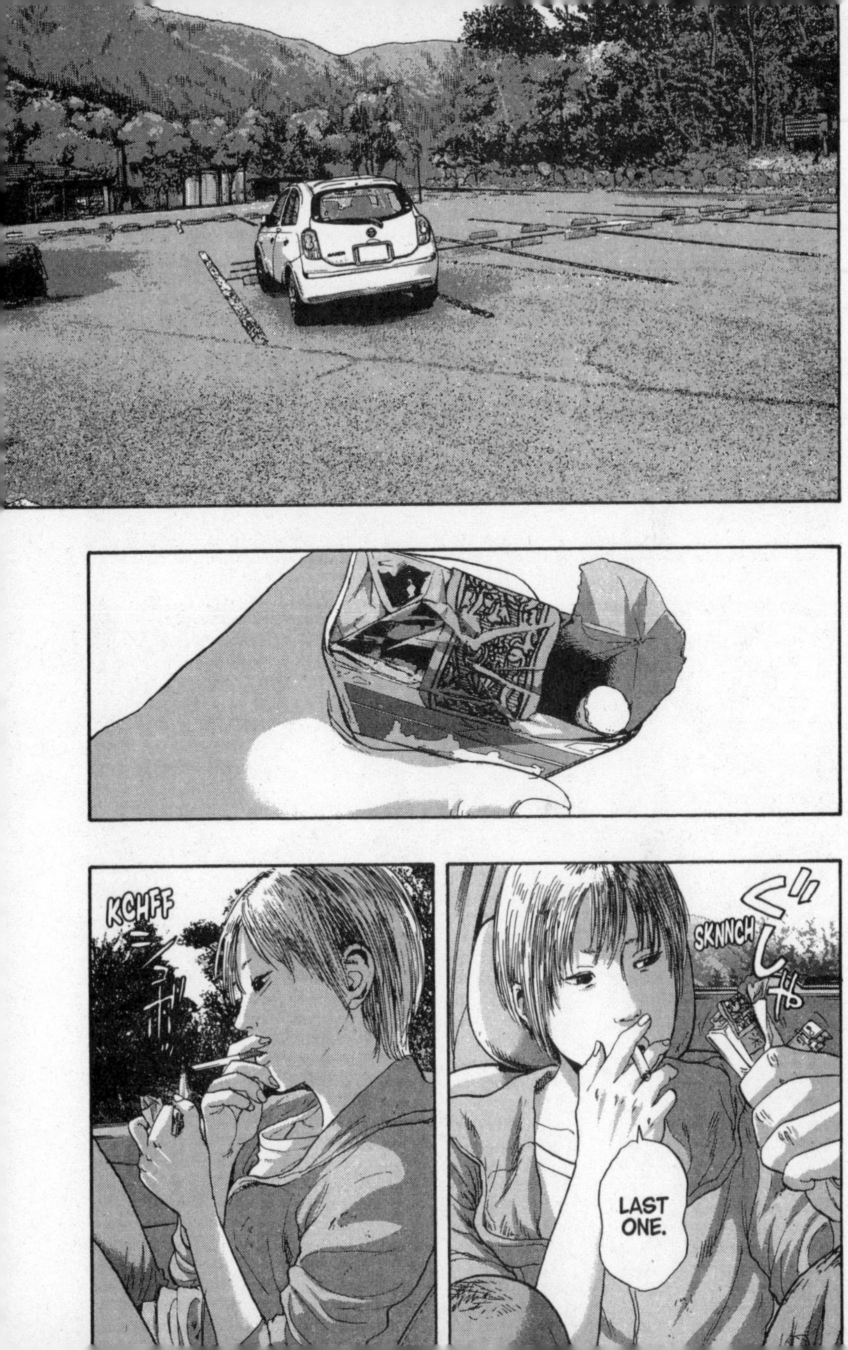
SKNNCH
ぐしゃ
LAST ONE.
KCHFF

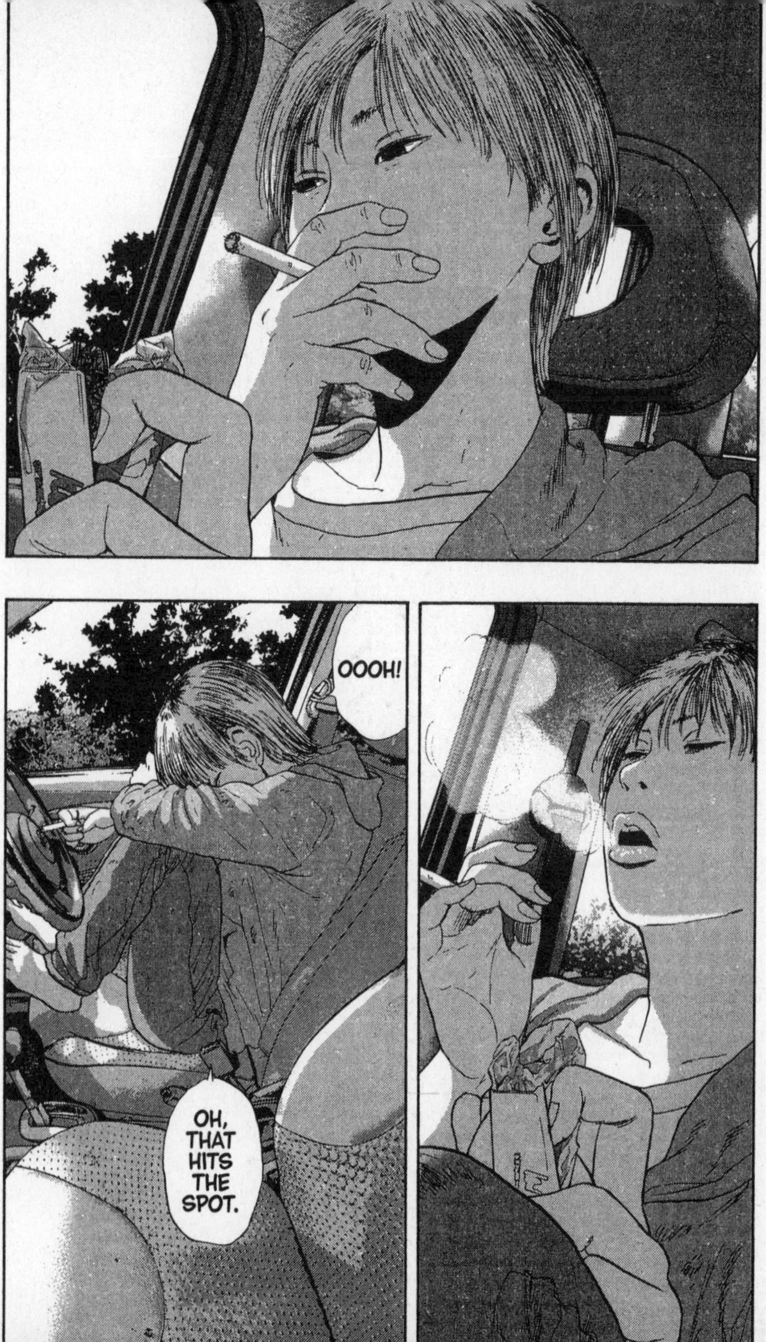
OOOH!
OH, THAT HITS THE SPOT.

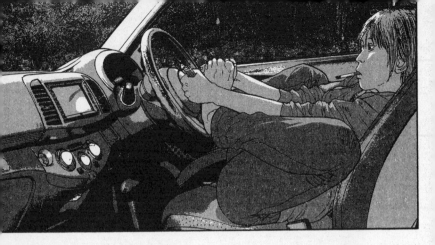

VRUMM

RUNNING OUT OF GAS...

WHAT DO WE DO?

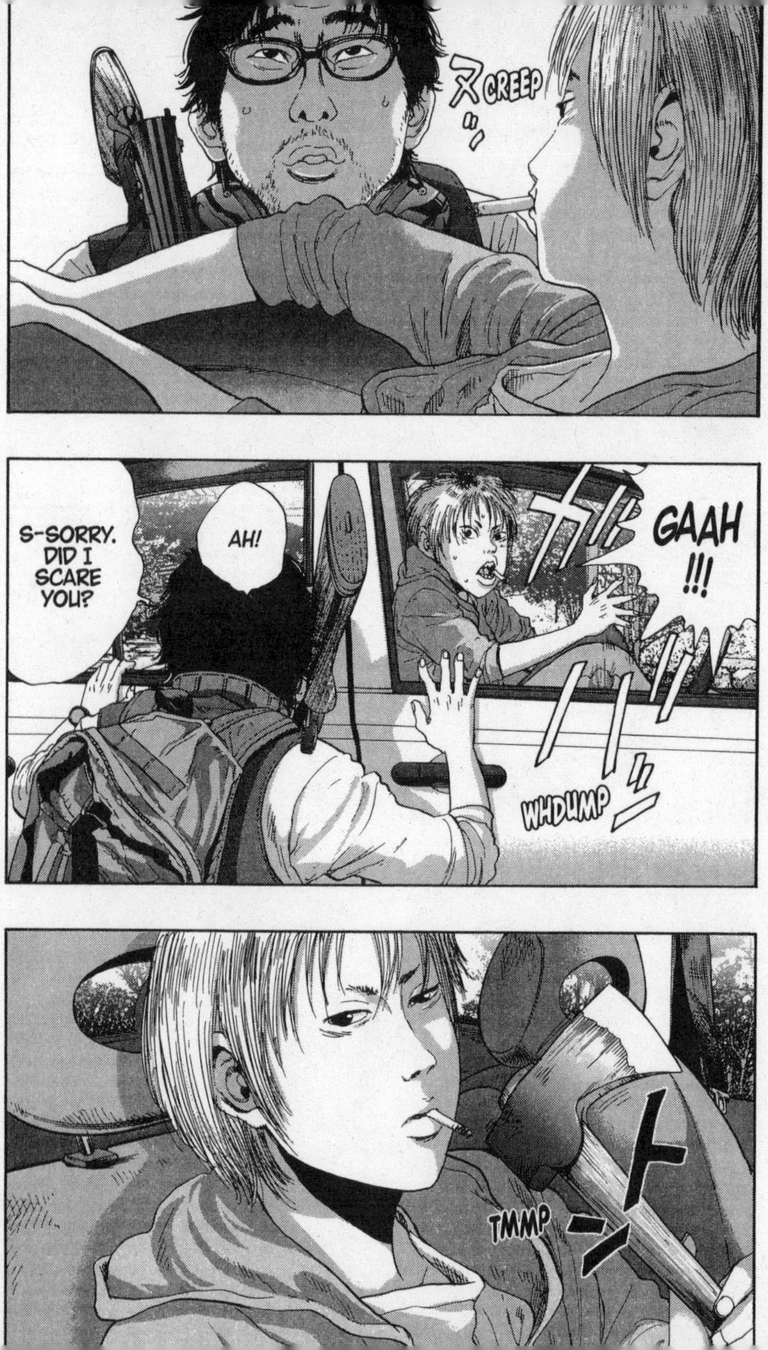
ヌ CREEP
GAAH !!!
AH!
S-SORRY. DID I SCARE YOU?
WHDUMP
TMMP

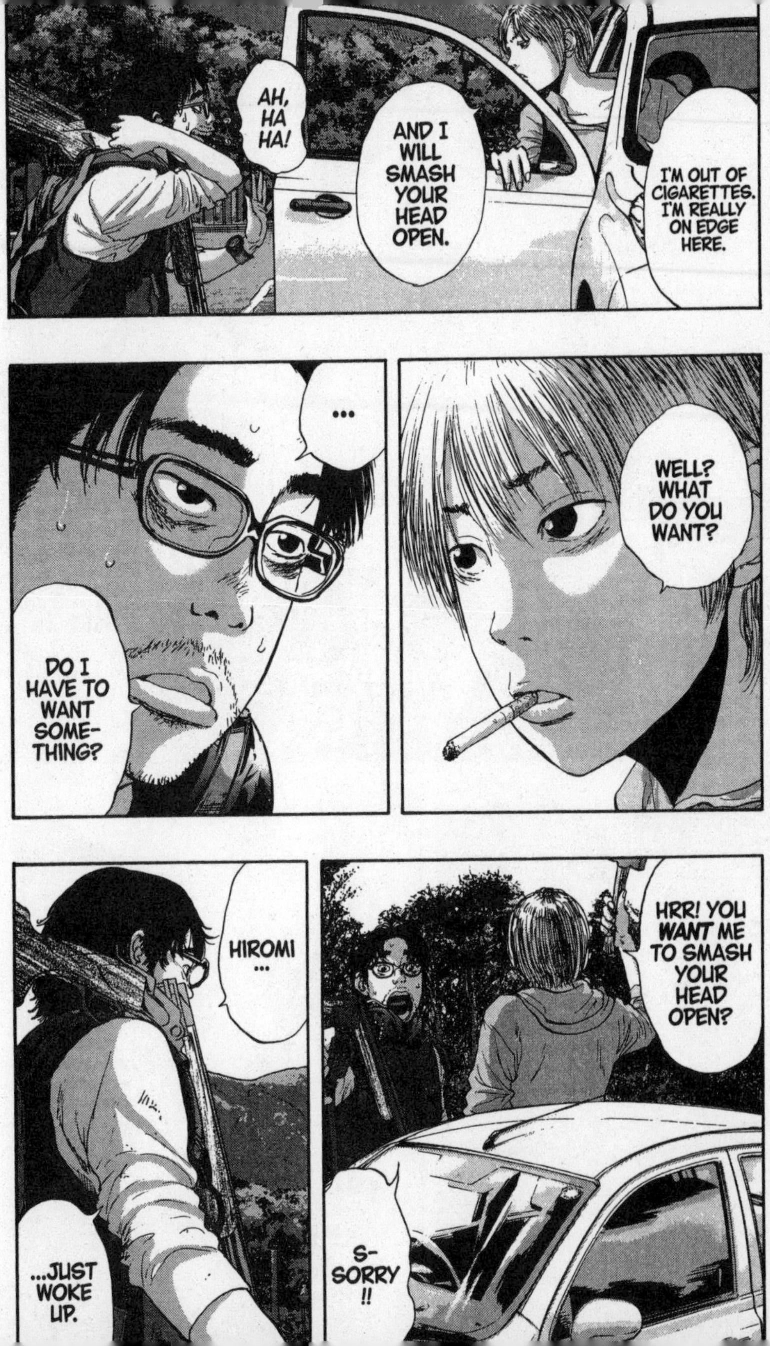
I'M OUT OF CIGARETTES. I'M REALLY ON EDGE HERE.
AND I WILL SMASH YOUR HEAD OPEN.
AH, HA HA!
WELL? WHAT DO YOU WANT?
...
DO I HAVE TO WANT SOME-THING?
HRR! YOU *WANT* ME TO SMASH YOUR HEAD OPEN?
S-SORRY!!
HIROMI...
...JUST WOKE UP.

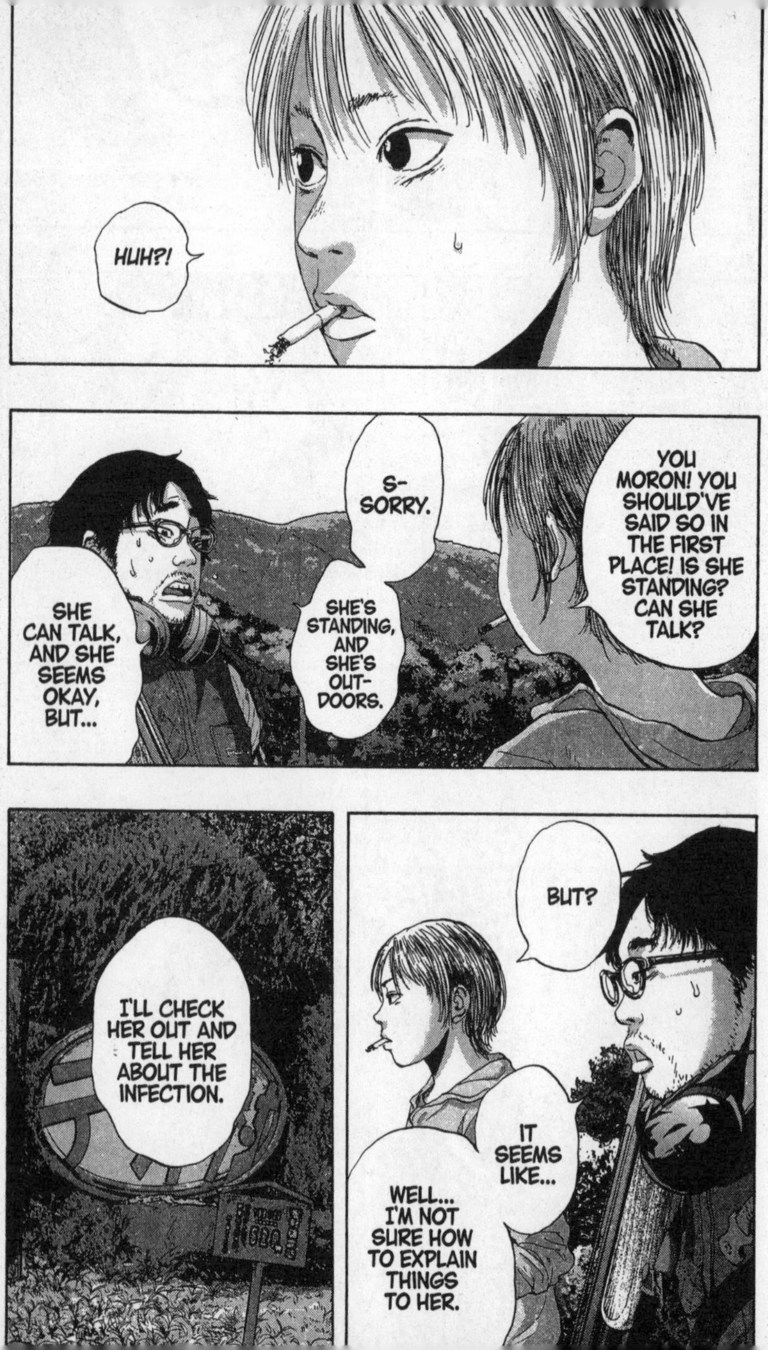
HUH?!
YOU MORON! YOU SHOULD'VE SAID SO IN THE FIRST PLACE! IS SHE STANDING? CAN SHE TALK?
S-SORRY.
SHE'S STANDING, AND SHE'S OUT-DOORS.
SHE CAN TALK, AND SHE SEEMS OKAY, BUT...
BUT?
IT SEEMS LIKE...
WELL... I'M NOT SURE HOW TO EXPLAIN THINGS TO HER.
I'LL CHECK HER OUT AND TELL HER ABOUT THE INFECTION.

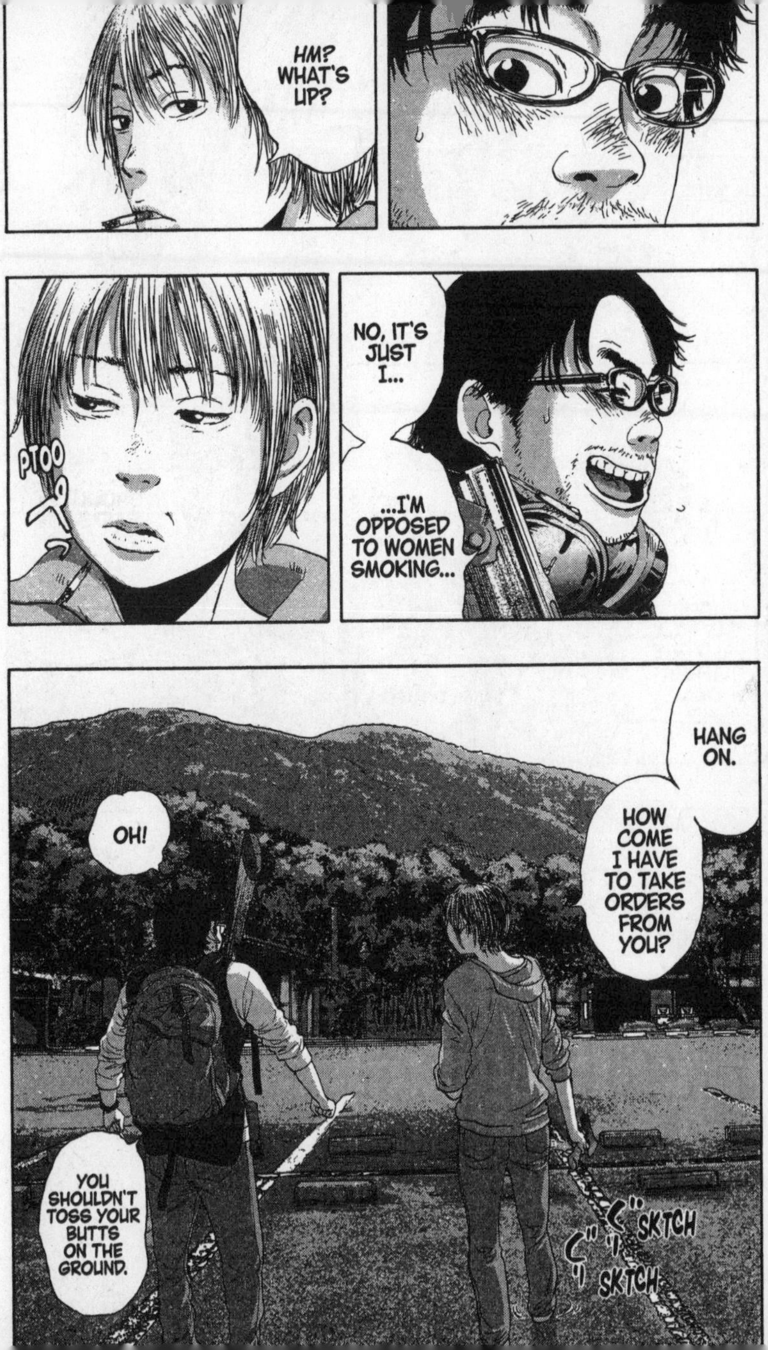
HM? WHAT'S UP?
NO, IT'S JUST I...
...I'M OPPOSED TO WOMEN SMOKING...
PTOO
HANG ON.
HOW COME I HAVE TO TAKE ORDERS FROM YOU?
OH!
SKTCH
SKTCH
YOU SHOULDN'T TOSS YOUR BUTTS ON THE GROUND.

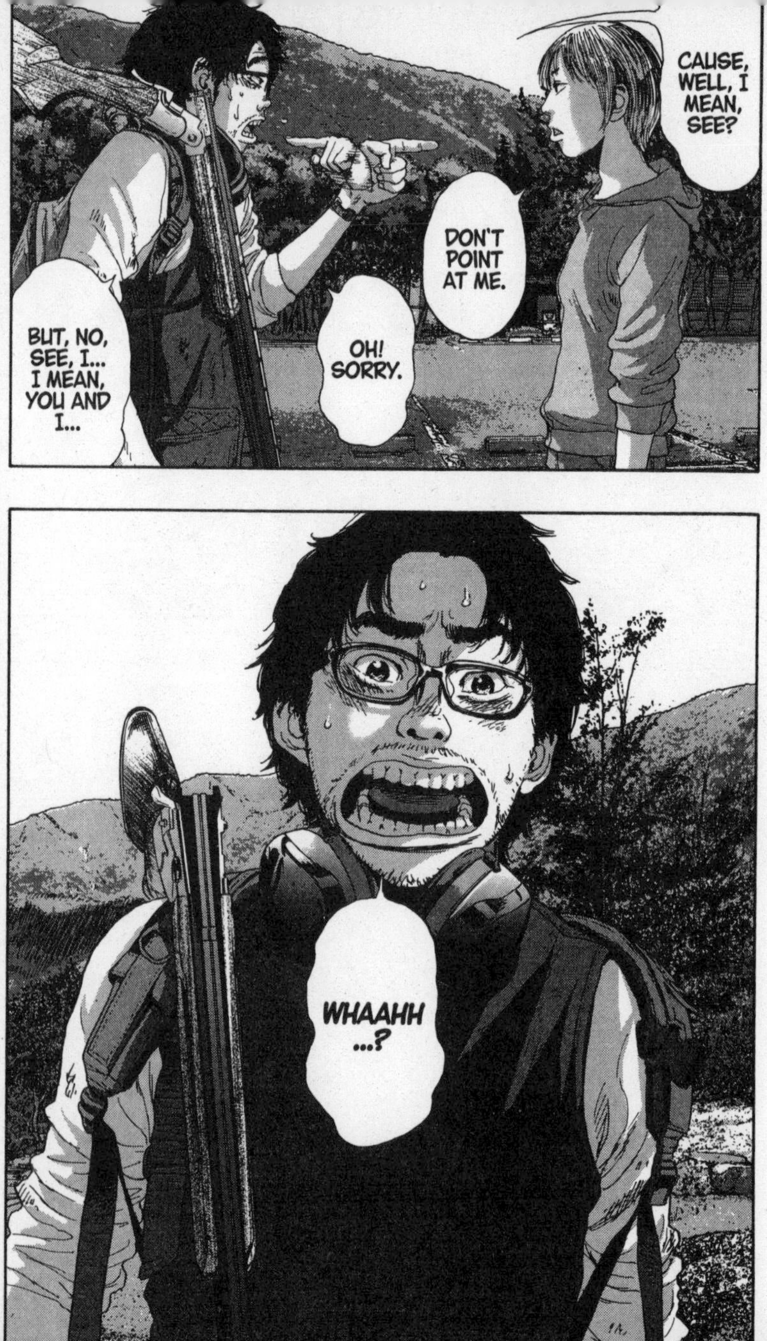
CAUSE, WELL, I MEAN, SEE?
DON'T POINT AT ME.
OH! SORRY.
BUT, NO, SEE, I... I MEAN, YOU AND I...
WHAAHH ...?

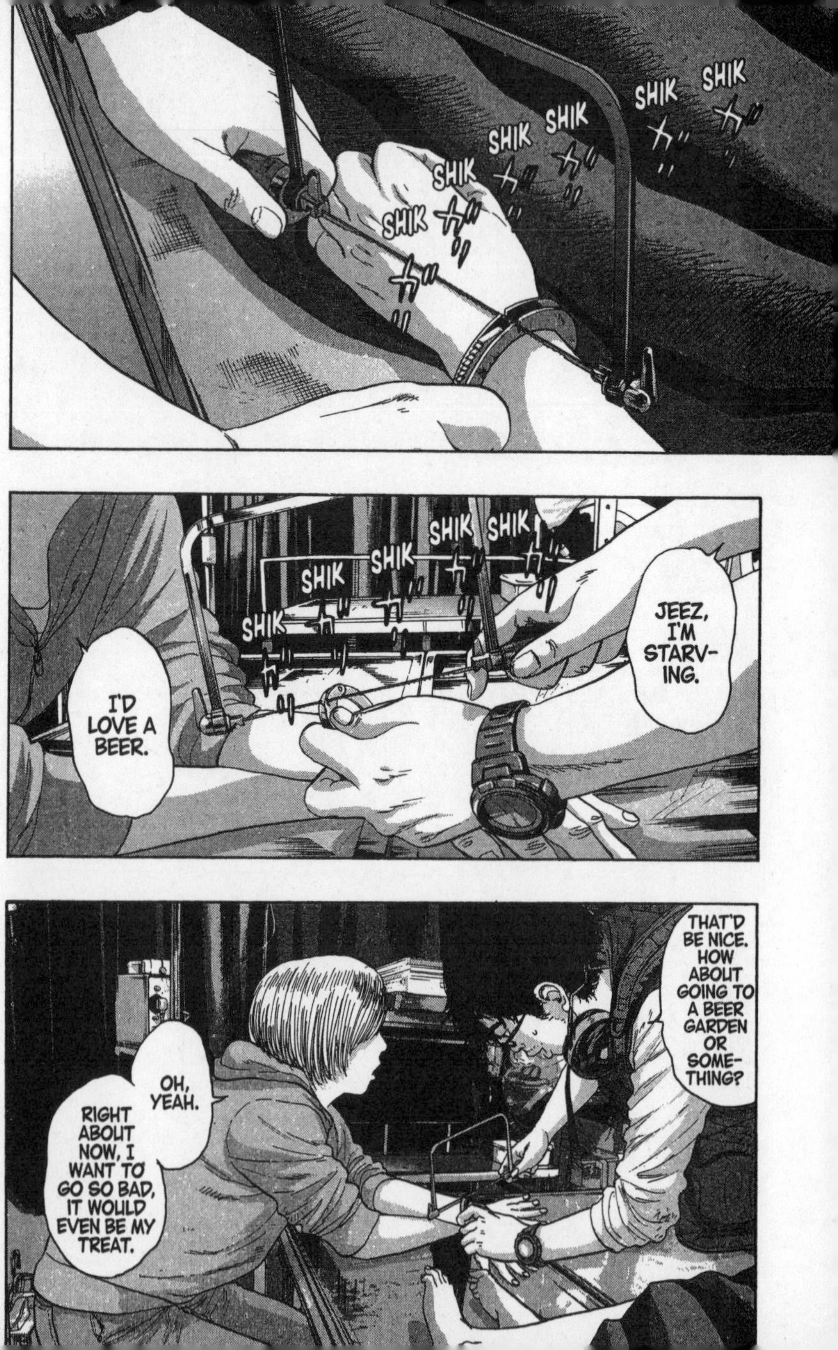
SHIK SHIK SHIK SHIK SHIK SHIK
SHIK SHIK SHIK SHIK SHIK
JEEZ, I'M STARV-ING.
I'D LOVE A BEER.
THAT'D BE NICE. HOW ABOUT GOING TO A BEER GARDEN OR SOME-THING?
OH, YEAH.
RIGHT ABOUT NOW, I WANT TO GO SO BAD, IT WOULD EVEN BE MY TREAT.

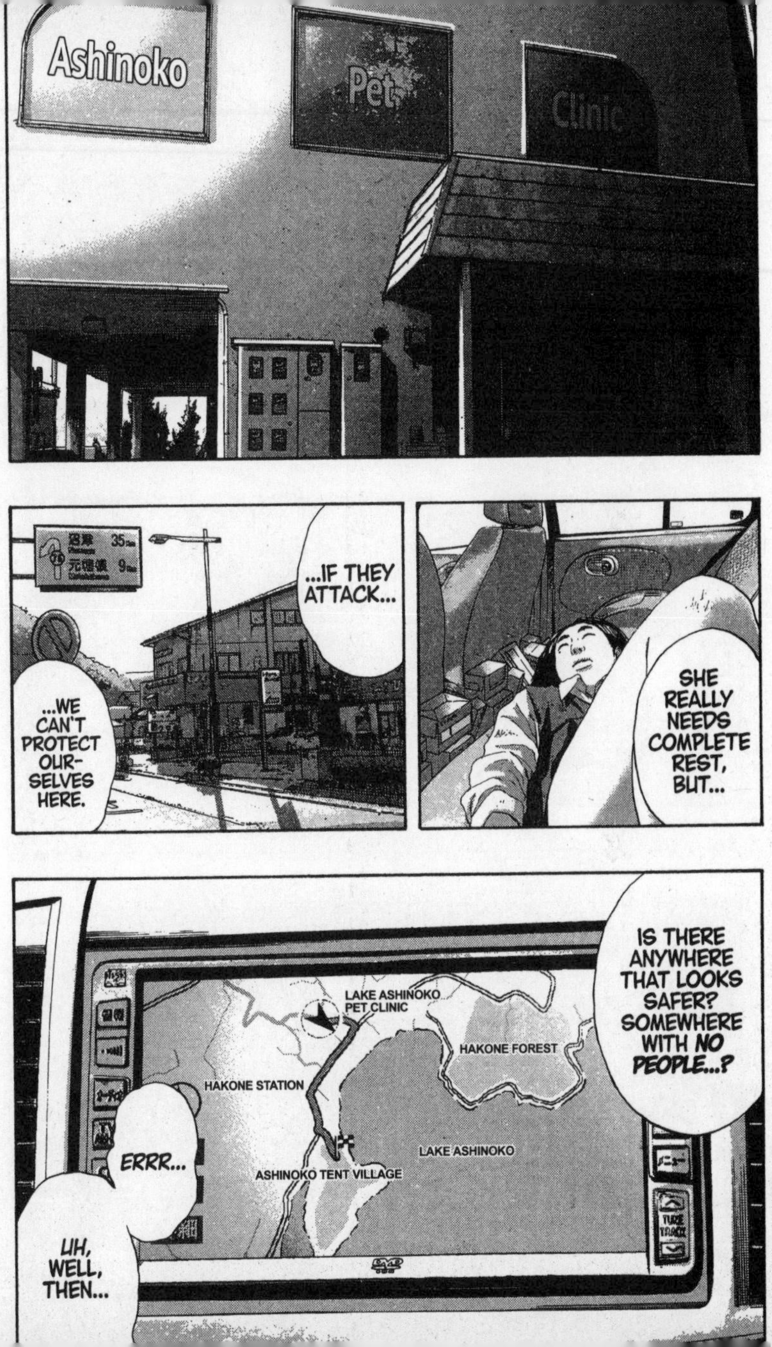
Ashinoko
Pet
Clinic
SHE REALLY NEEDS COMPLETE REST, BUT...
...IF THEY ATTACK...
...WE CAN'T PROTECT OUR-SELVES HERE.
IS THERE ANYWHERE THAT LOOKS SAFER? SOMEWHERE WITH *NO PEOPLE...?*
LAKE ASHINOKO PET CLINIC
HAKONE FOREST
HAKONE STATION
LAKE ASHINOKO
ASHINOKO TENT VILLAGE
ERRR...
UH, WELL, THEN...

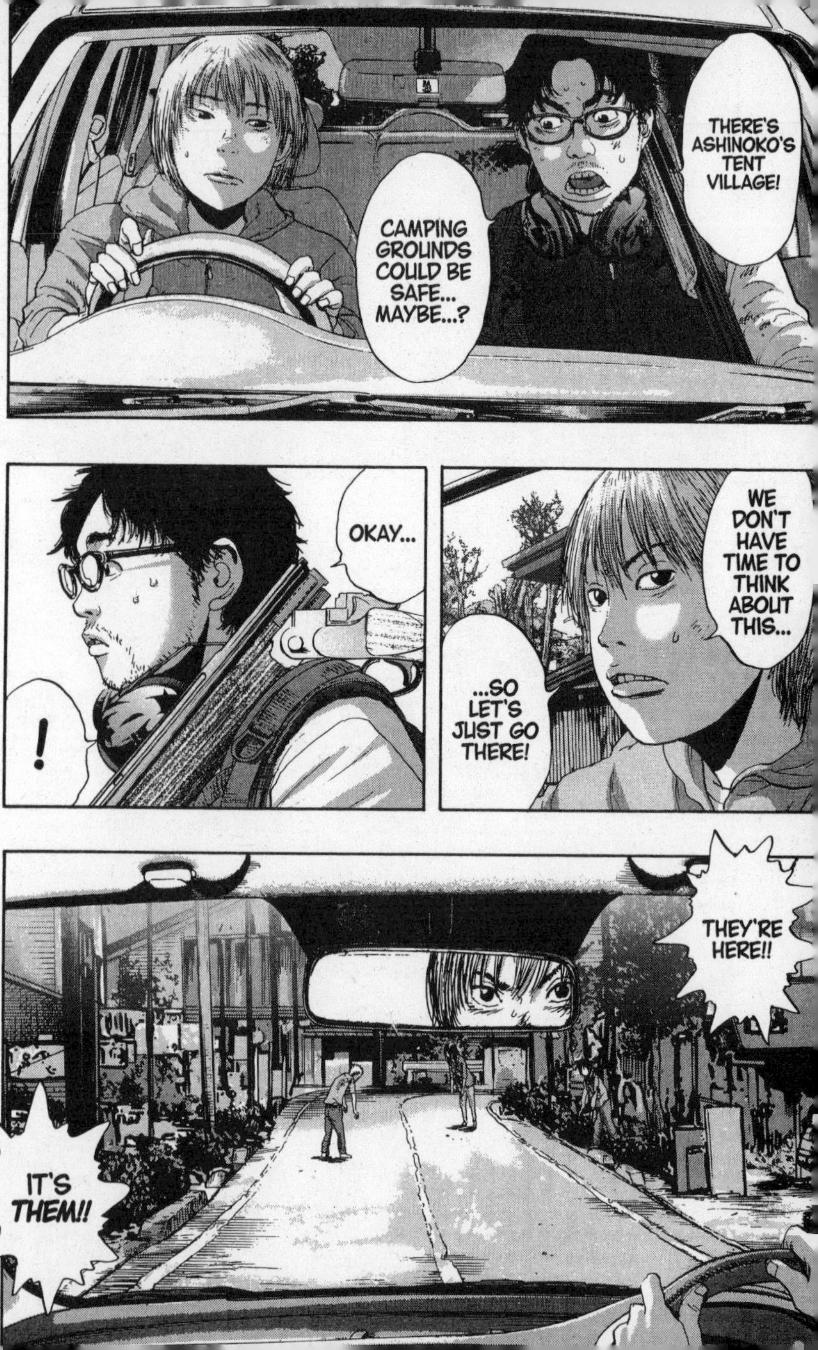
THERE'S ASHINOKO'S TENT VILLAGE!
CAMPING GROUNDS COULD BE SAFE... MAYBE...?
WE DON'T HAVE TIME TO THINK ABOUT THIS...
...SO LET'S JUST GO THERE!
OKAY...
!
THEY'RE HERE!!
IT'S *THEM!!*

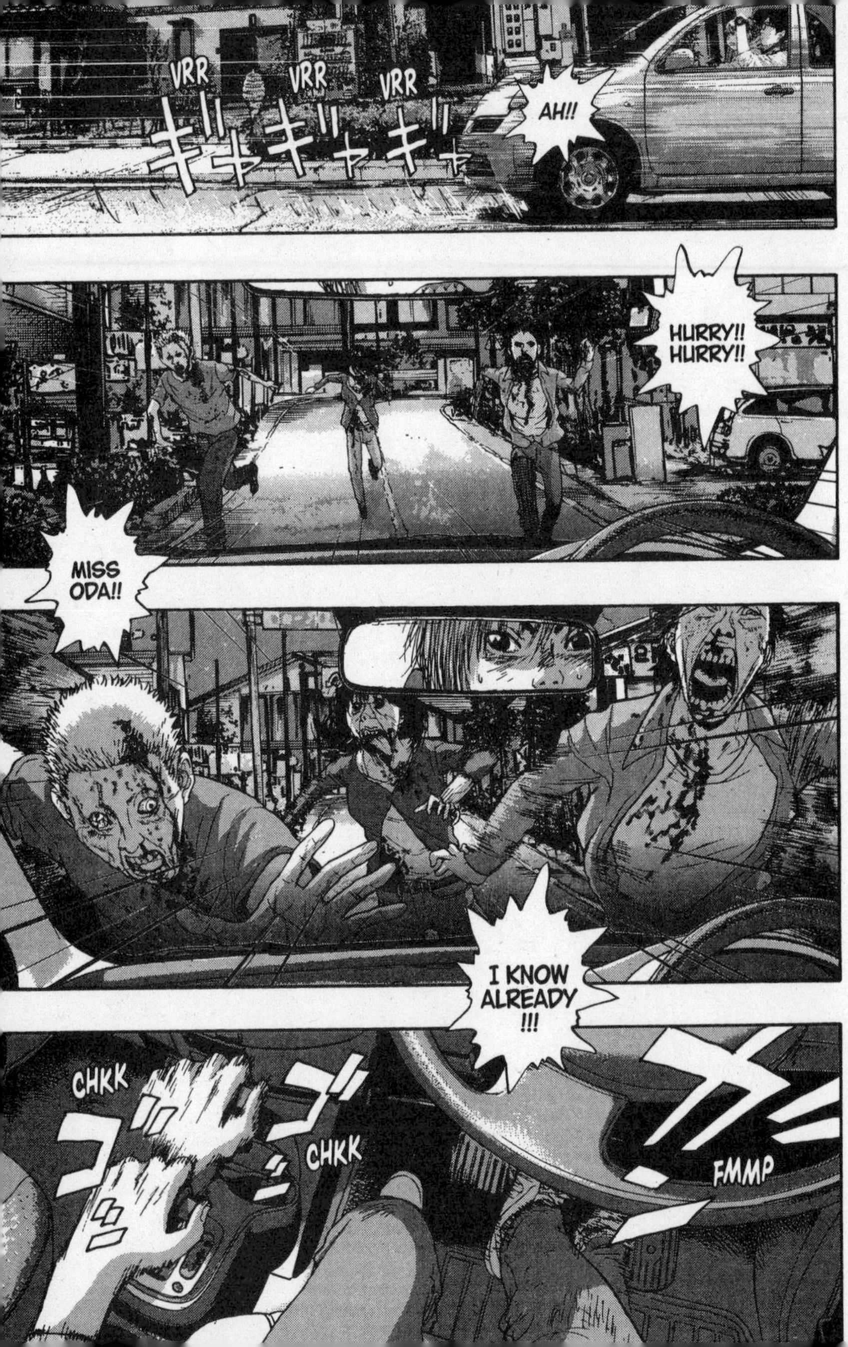
AH!!
VRR
VRR
VRR
HURRY!! HURRY!!
MISS ODA!!
I KNOW ALREADY !!!
FMMP
CHKK
CHKK

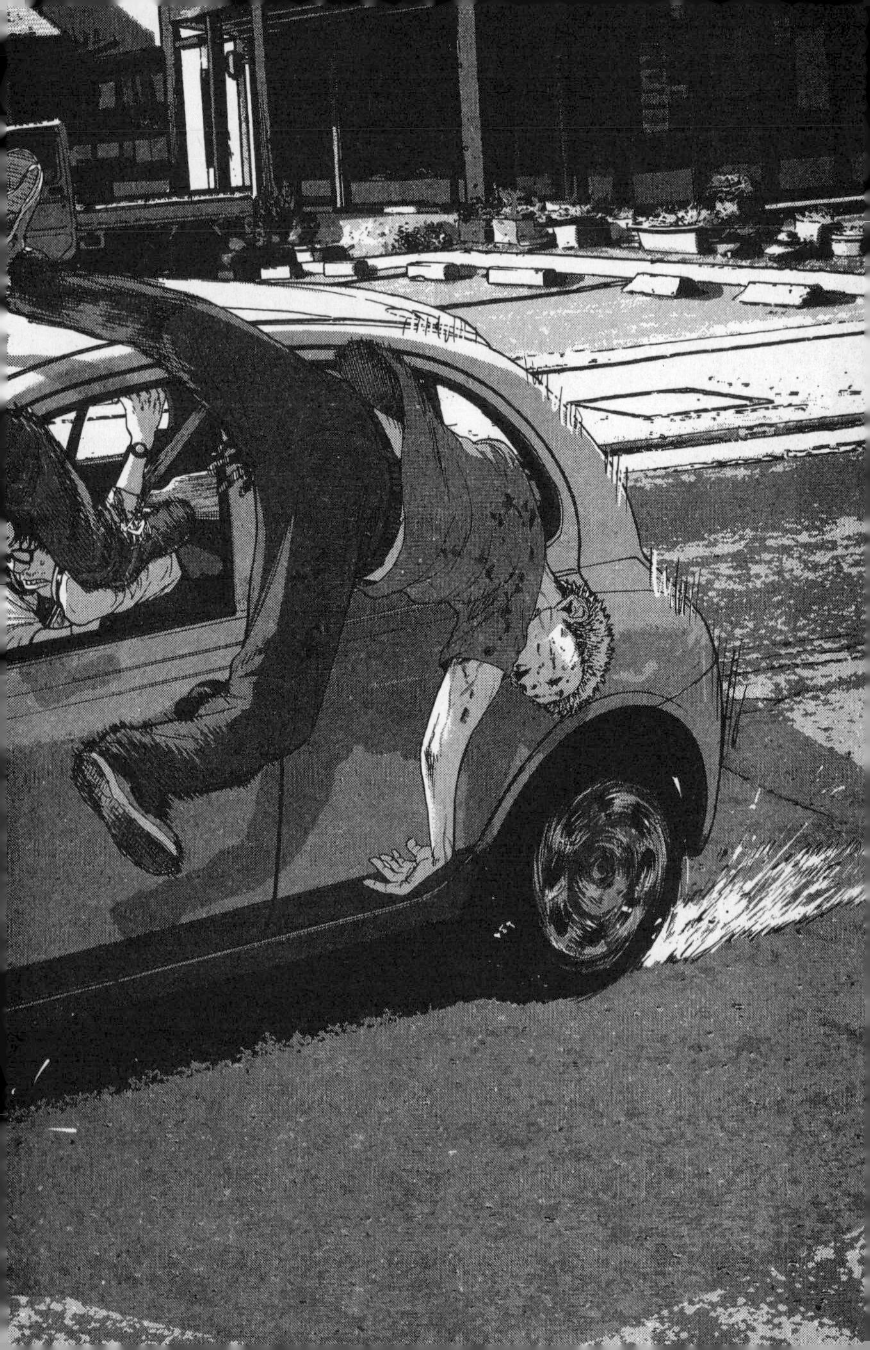

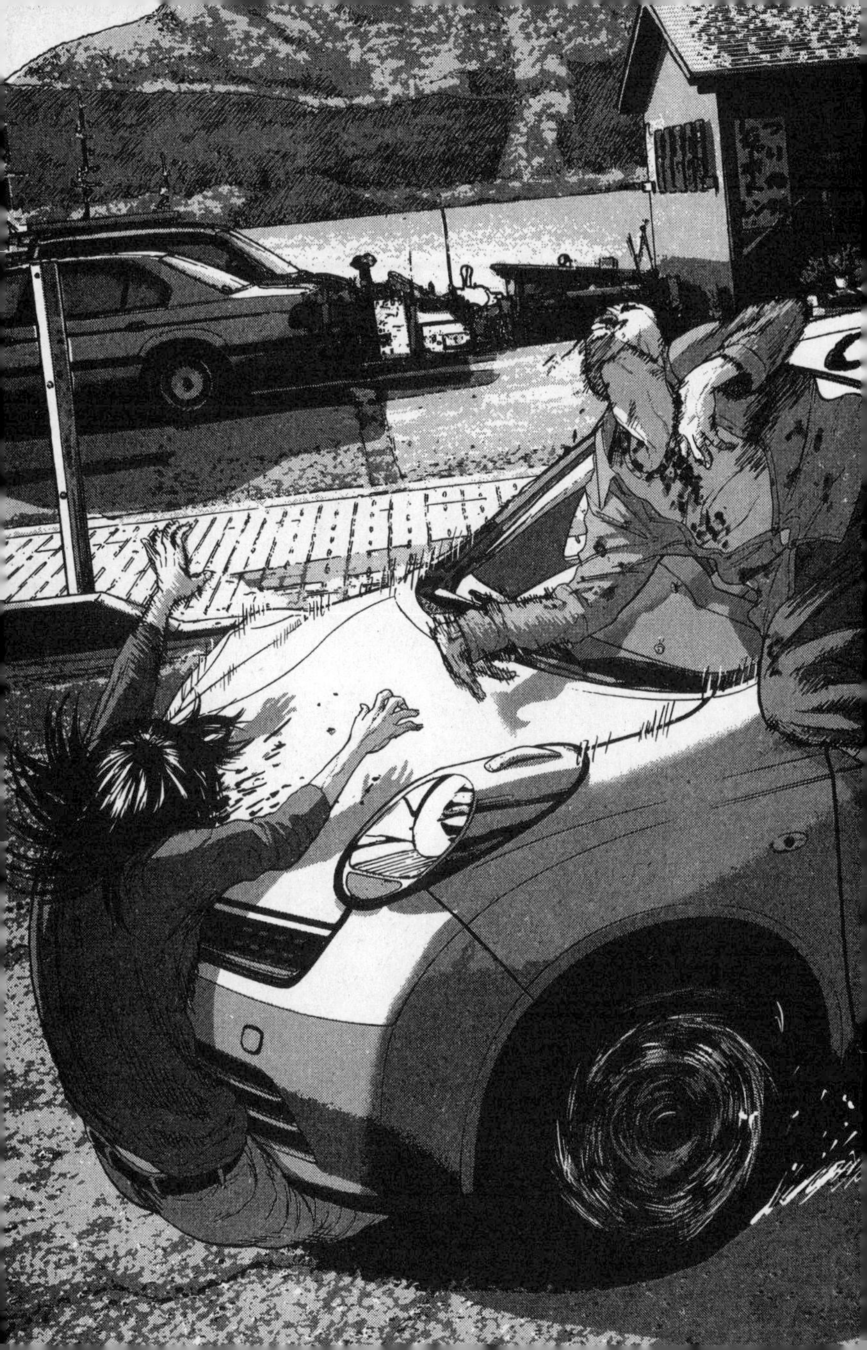

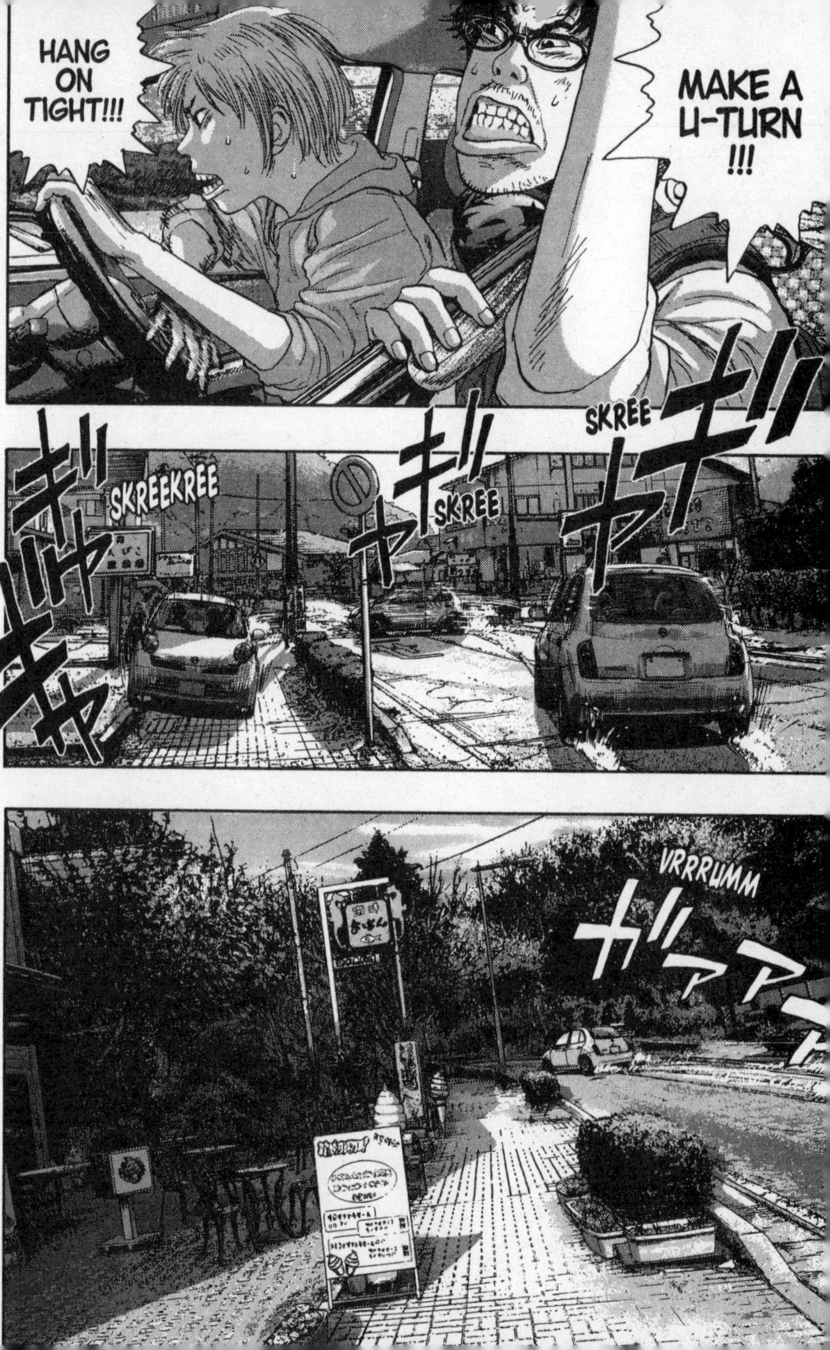
MAKE A U-TURN !!!
HANG ON TIGHT!!!
SKREE
SKREE
SKREEKREE
VRRRUMM

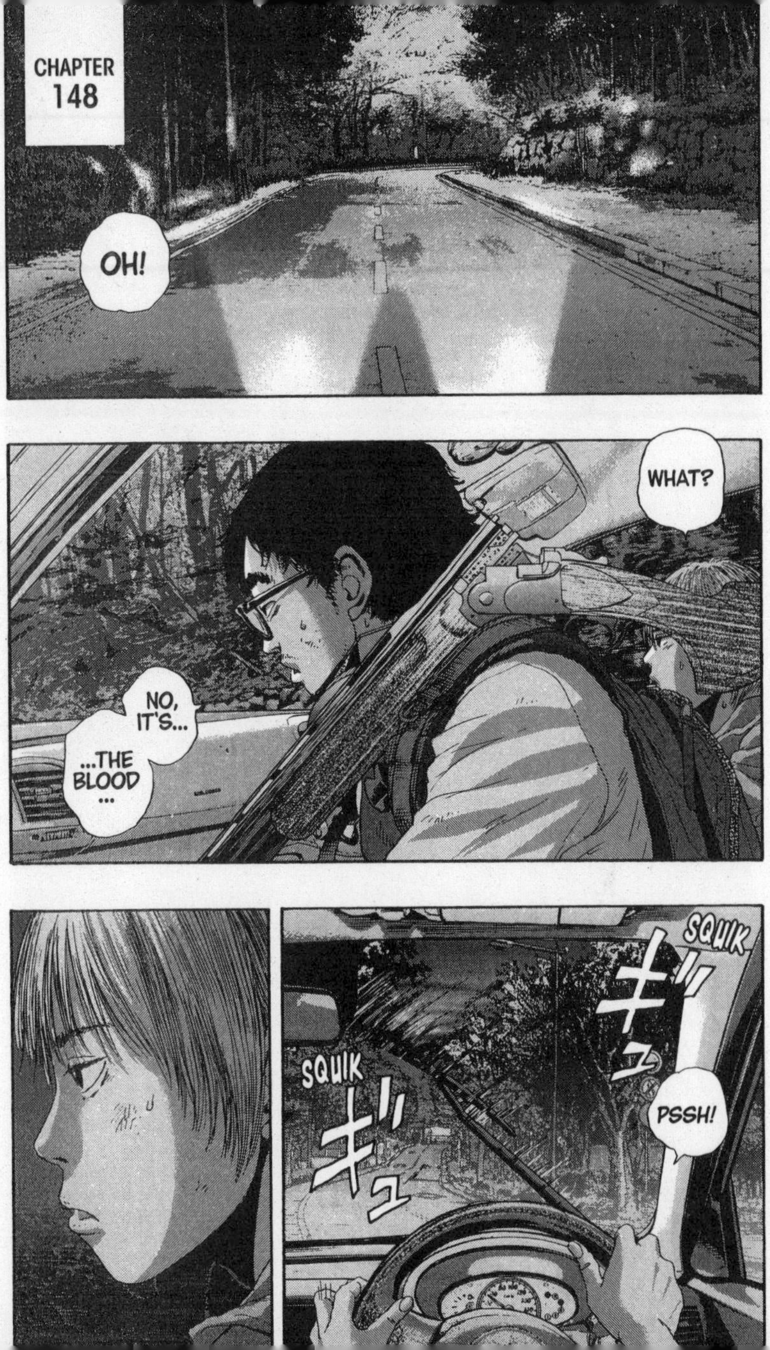
CHAPTER 148
OH!
WHAT?
NO, IT'S...
...THE BLOOD ...
SQUIK
ギュ
SQUIK
ギュ
PSSH!

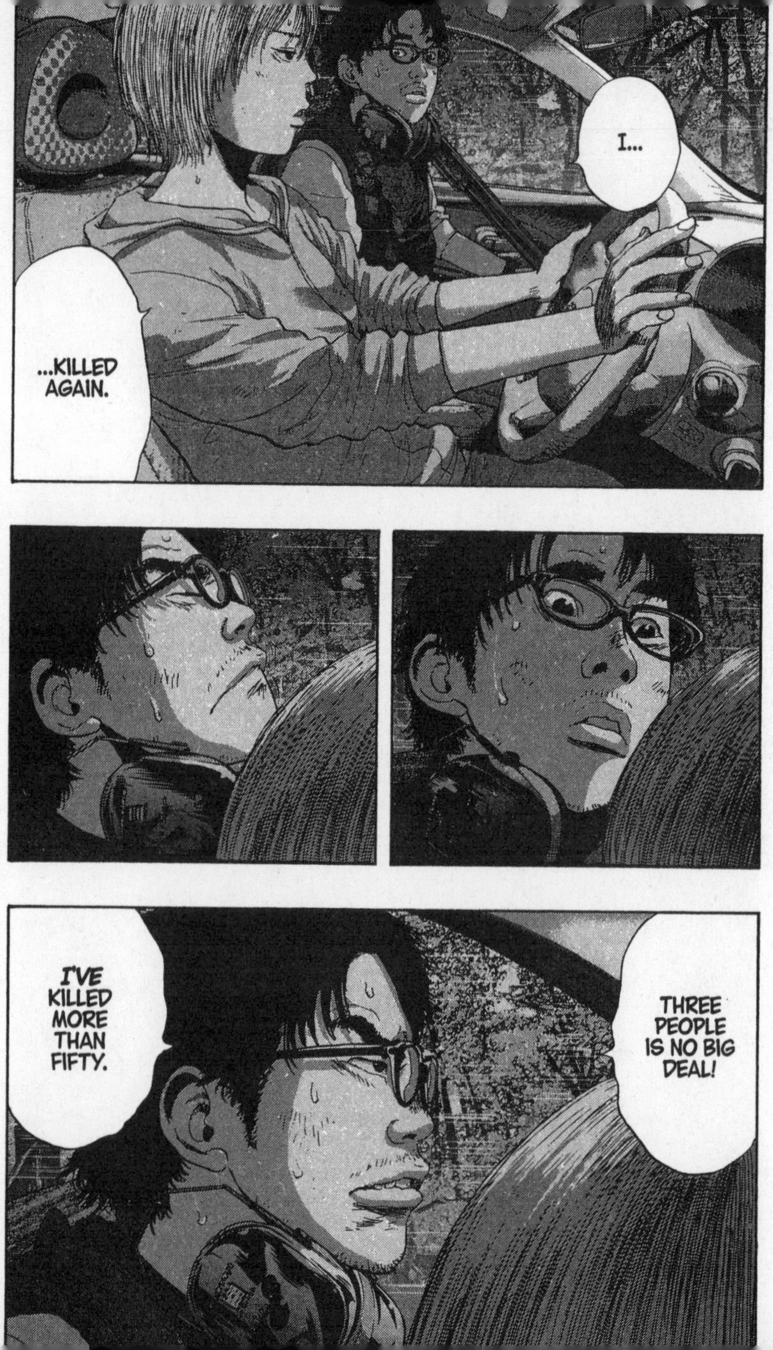
I...
...KILLED AGAIN.
THREE PEOPLE IS NO BIG DEAL!
I'VE KILLED MORE THAN FIFTY.

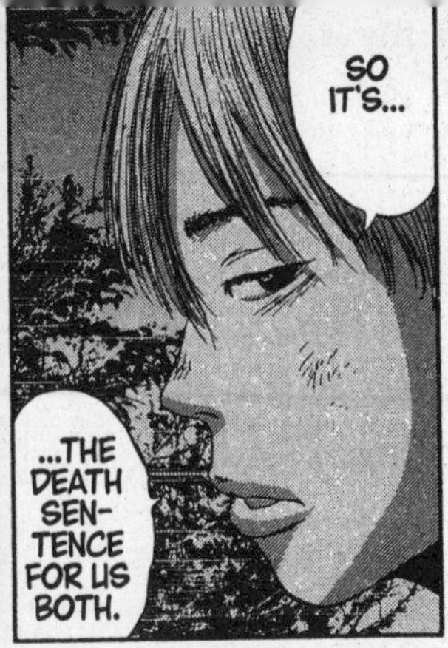
SO IT'S...
...THE DEATH SEN-TENCE FOR US BOTH.

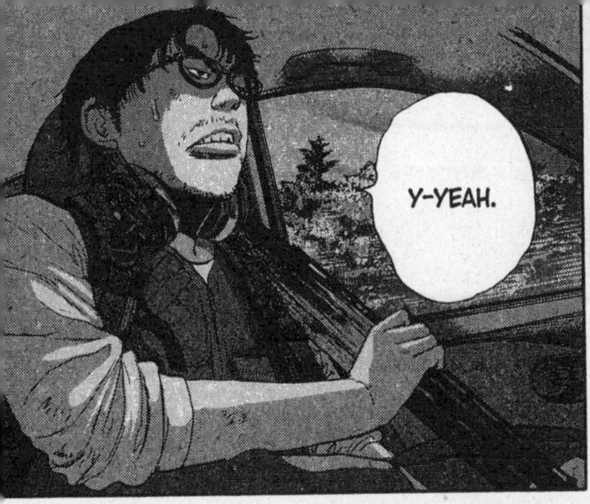
Y-YEAH.

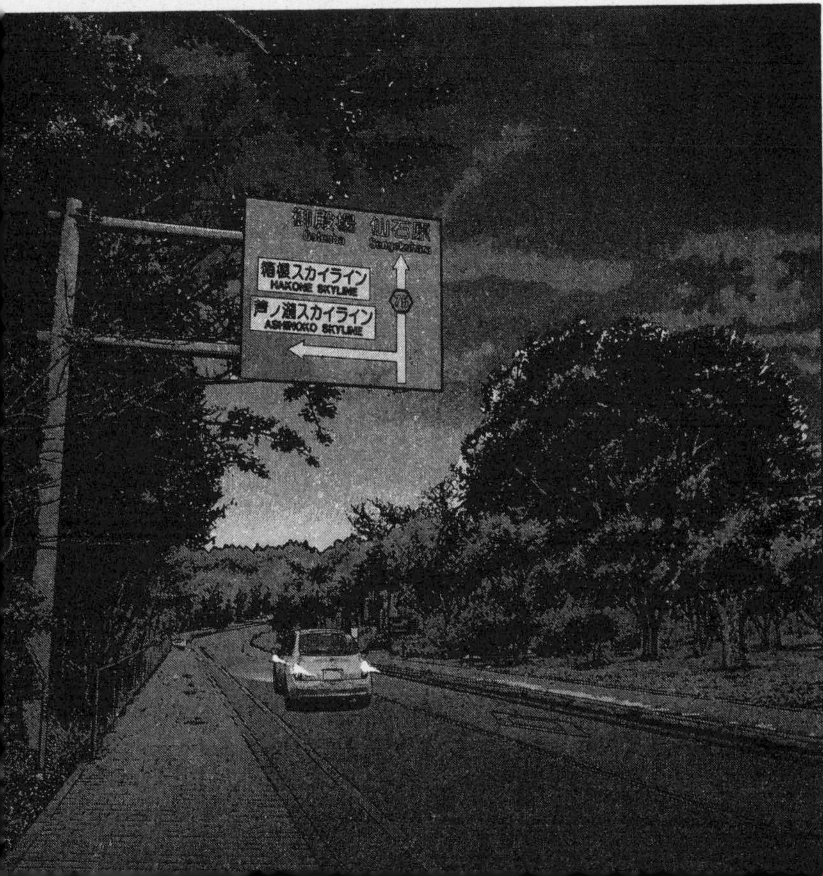
御殿場
仙石原
箱根スカイライン
HAKONE SKYLINE
芦ノ湖スカイライン
ASHINOKO SKYLINE
75

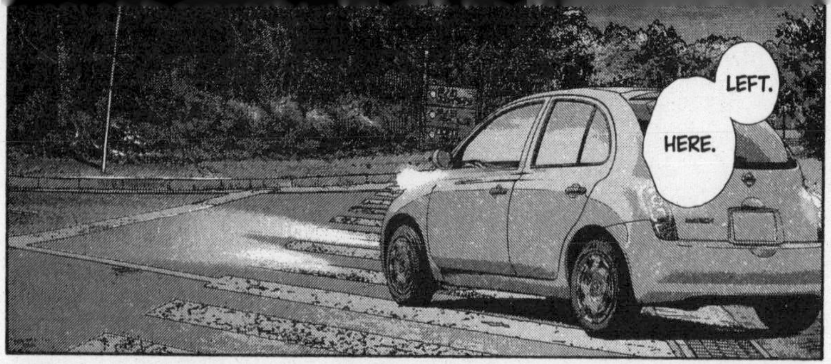
LEFT.
HERE.

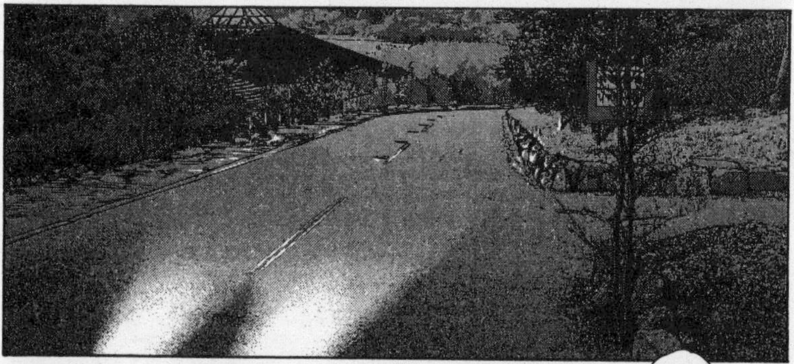

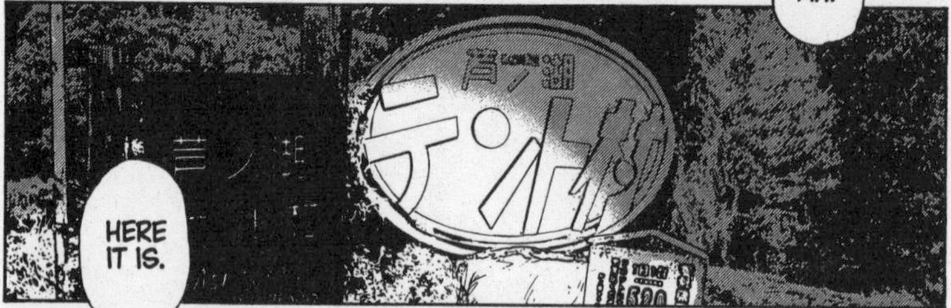
AH!
SIGN: ASHINOKO / TENT VILLAGE
HERE IT IS.

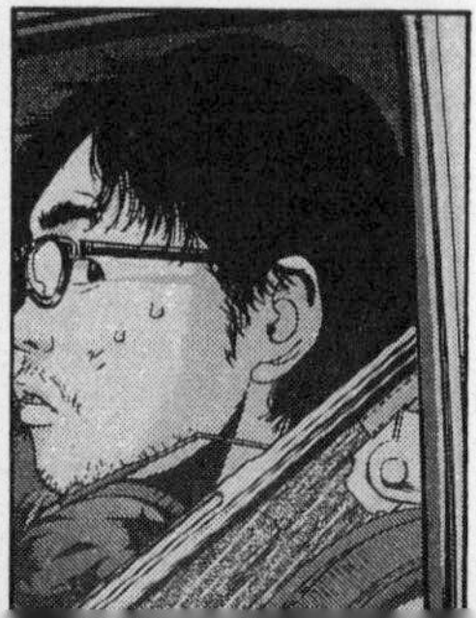

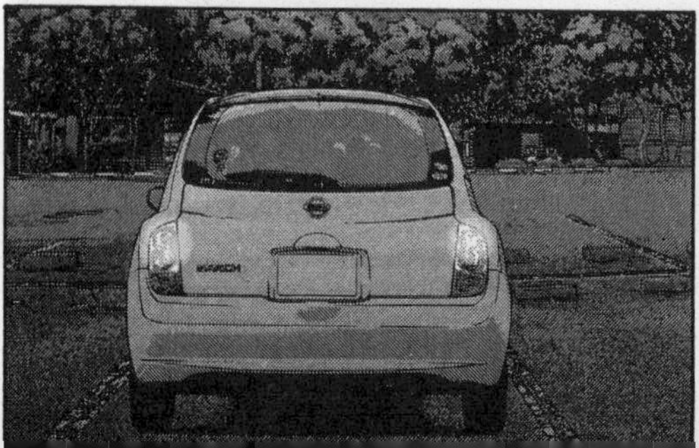

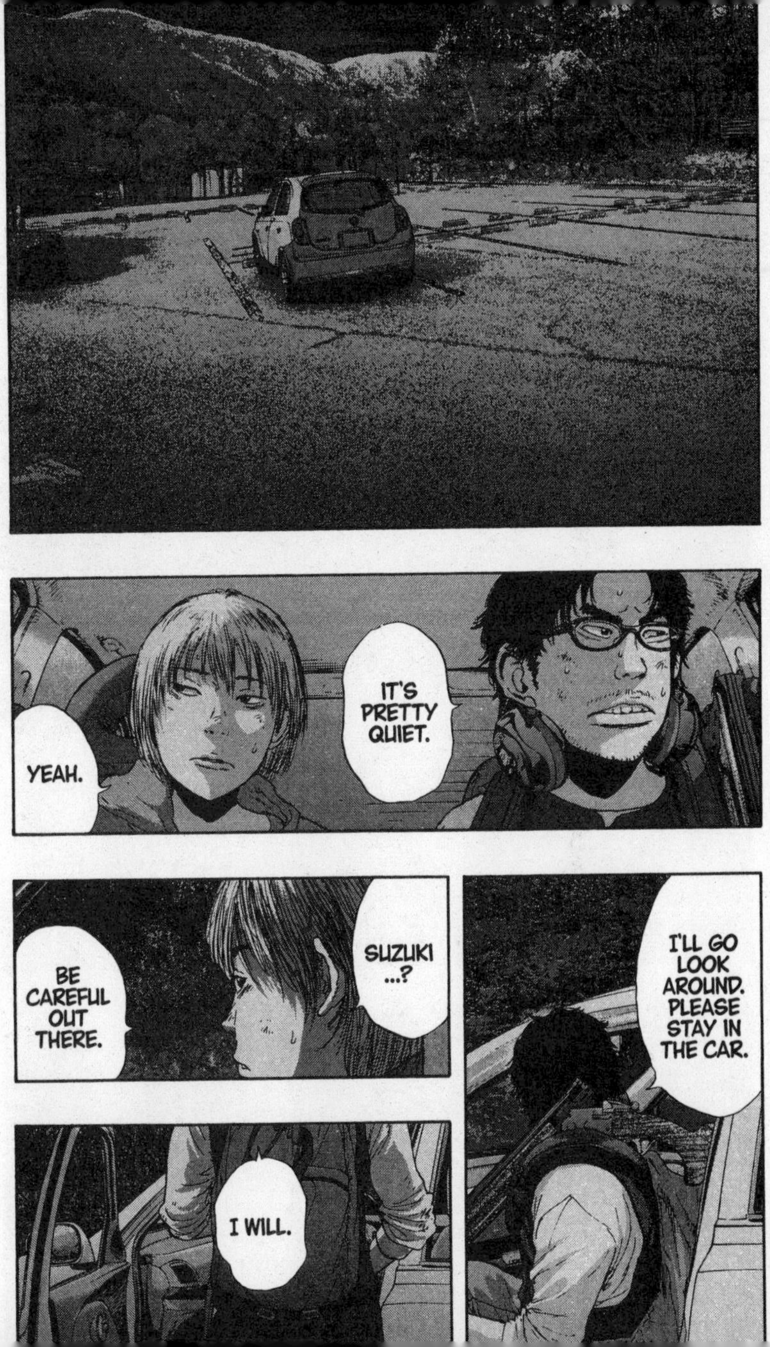
IT'S PRETTY QUIET.
YEAH.
I'LL GO LOOK AROUND. PLEASE STAY IN THE CAR.
SUZUKI ...?
BE CAREFUL OUT THERE.
I WILL.

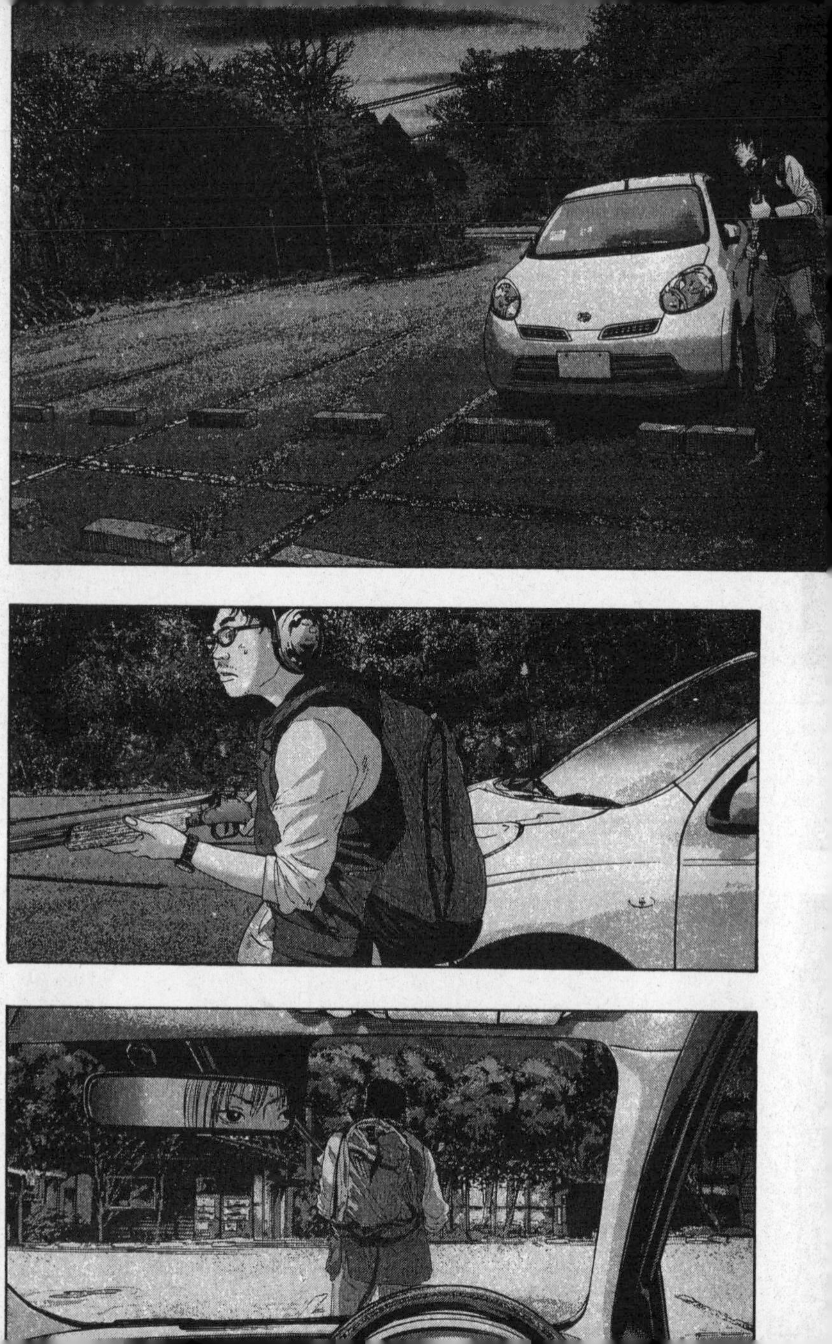

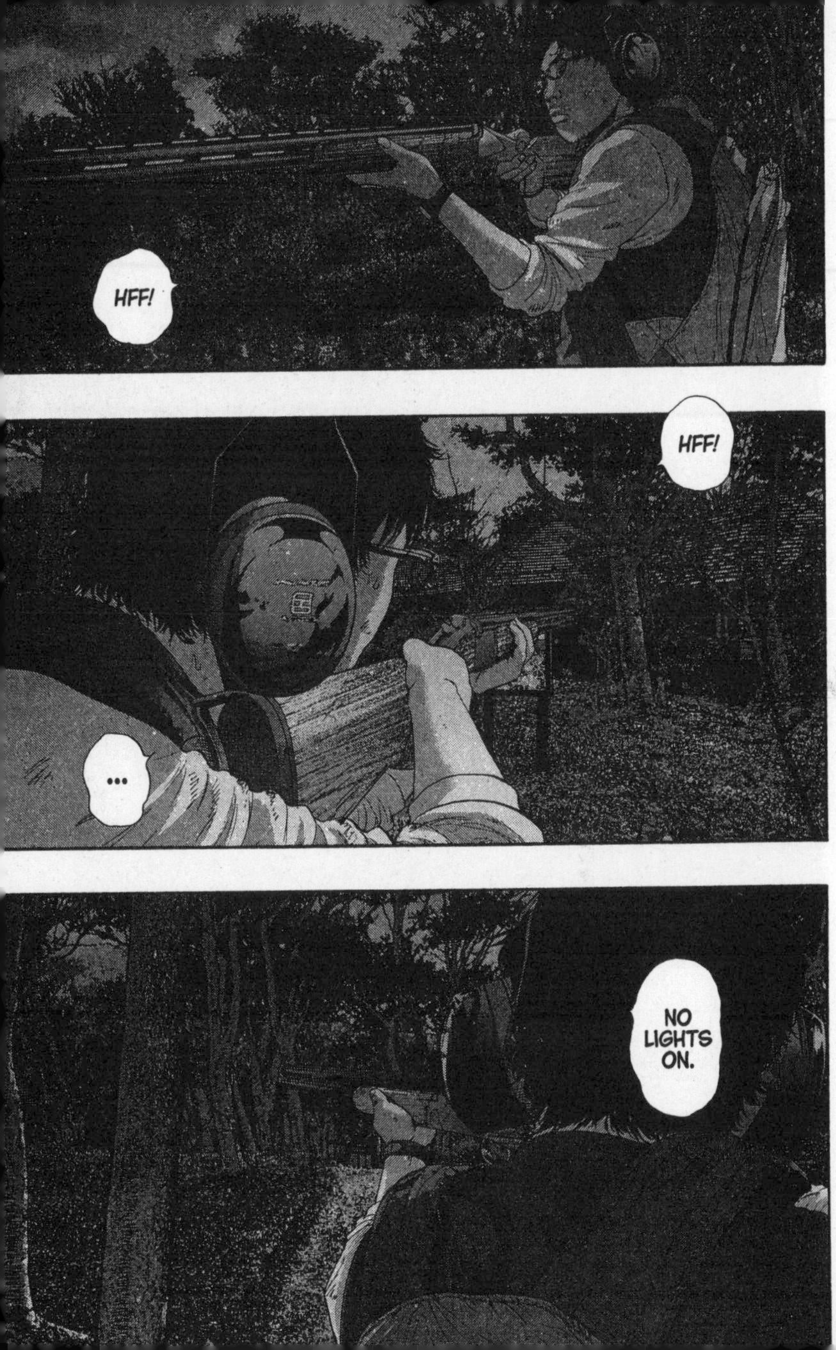
HFF!
HFF!
...
NO LIGHTS ON.

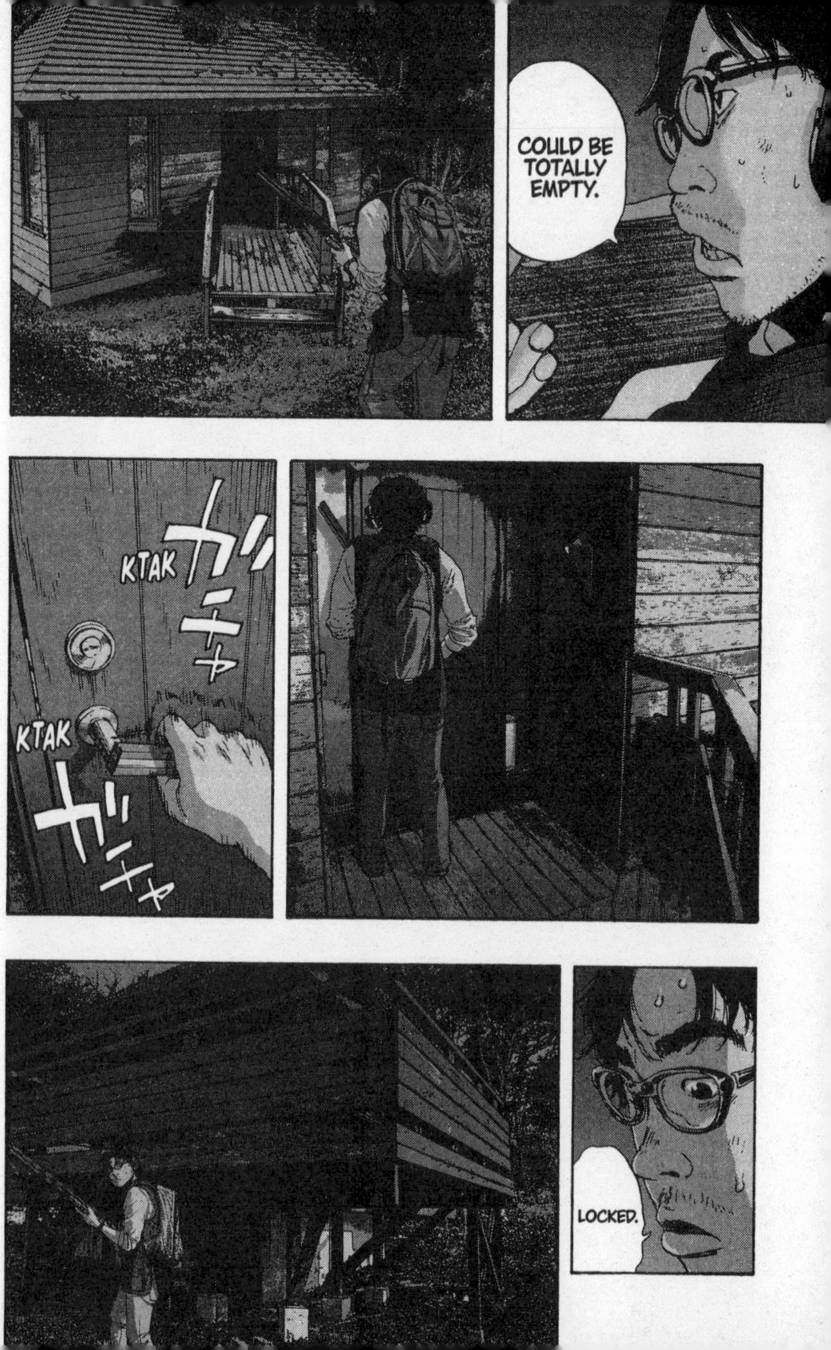
COULD BE TOTALLY EMPTY.
KTAK
ガチャ
KTAK
ガチャ
LOCKED.

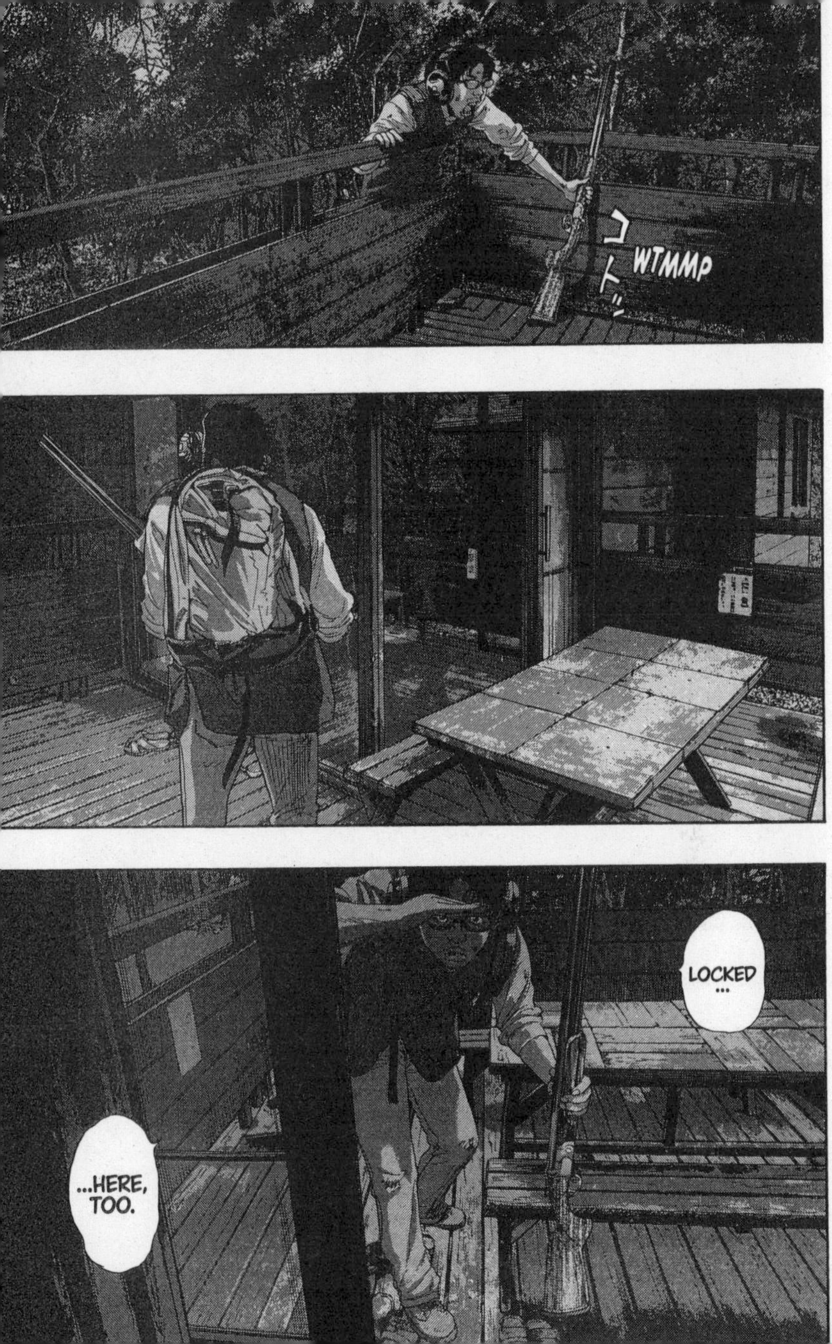
コトッ
WTMMP
LOCKED ...
...HERE, TOO.

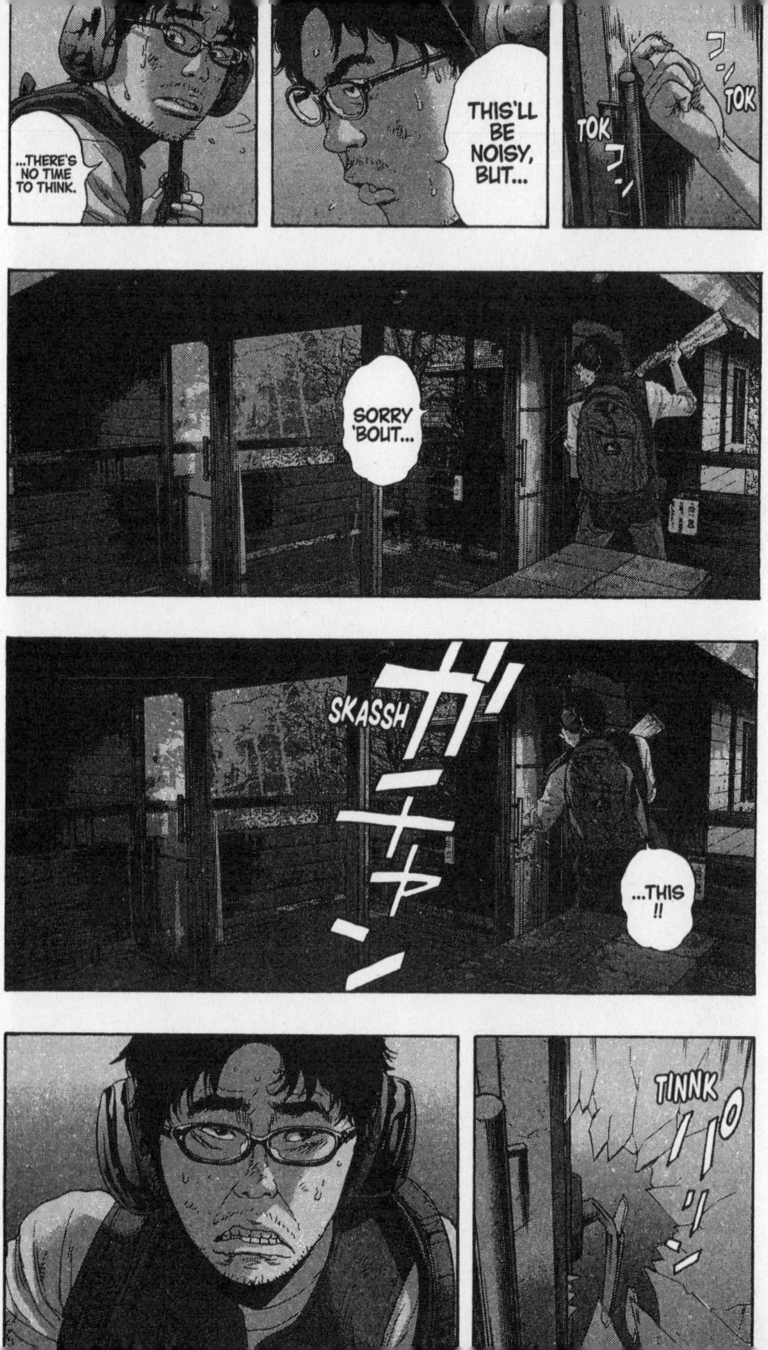
TOK
TOK
THIS'LL BE NOISY, BUT...
...THERE'S NO TIME TO THINK.
SORRY 'BOUT...
SKASSH
...THIS !!
TINNK

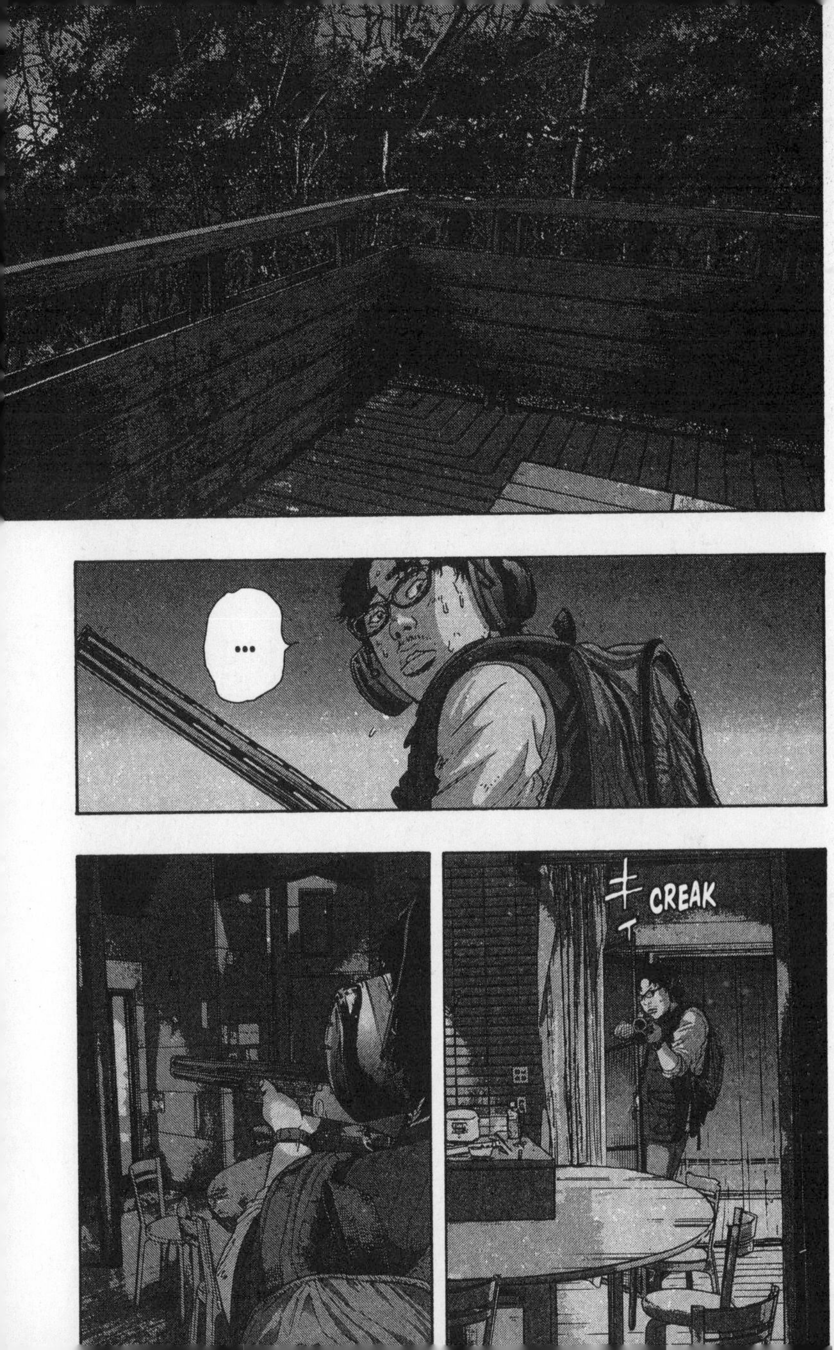
...
キィ
CREAK

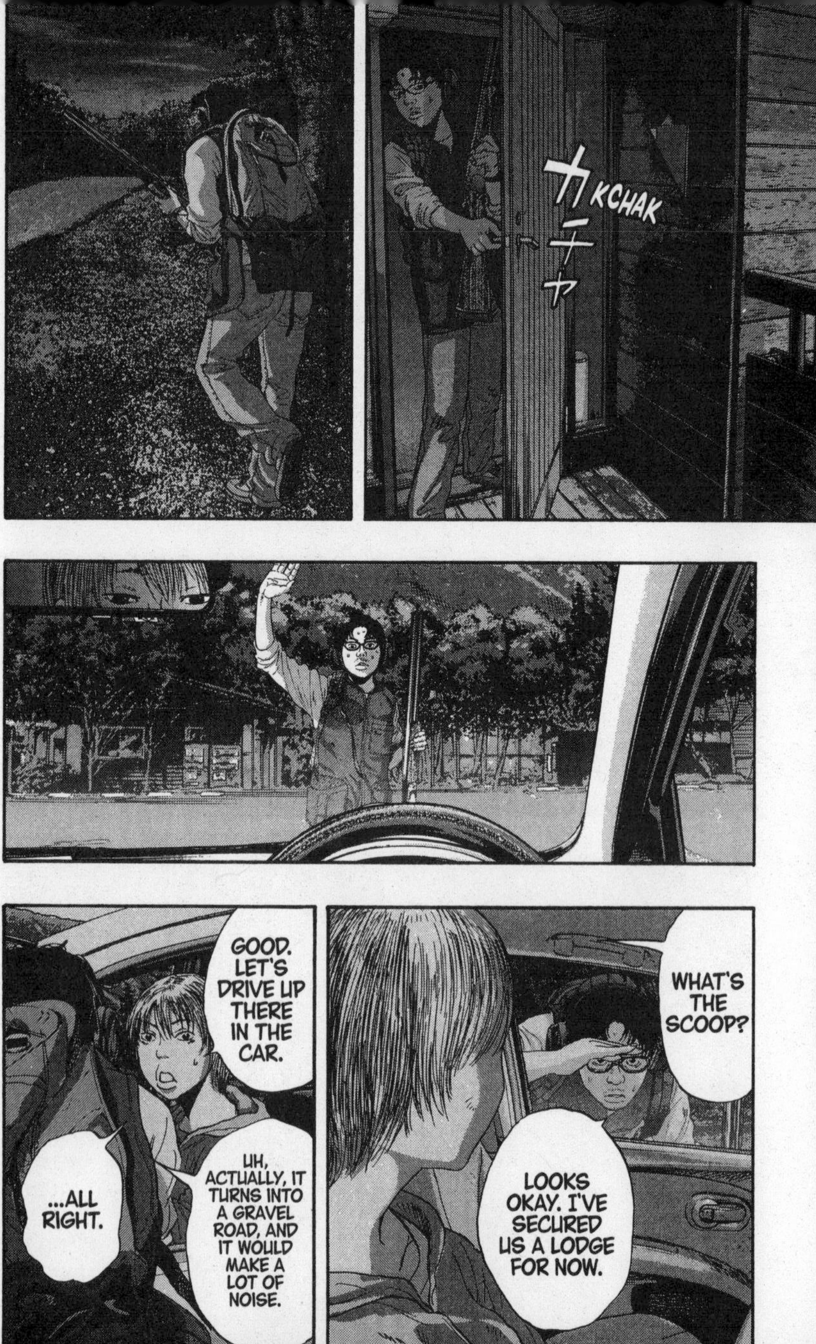
カチャ
KCHAK
WHAT'S THE SCOOP?
LOOKS OKAY. I'VE SECURED US A LODGE FOR NOW.
GOOD. LET'S DRIVE UP THERE IN THE CAR.
UH, ACTUALLY, IT TURNS INTO A GRAVEL ROAD, AND IT WOULD MAKE A LOT OF NOISE.
...ALL RIGHT.

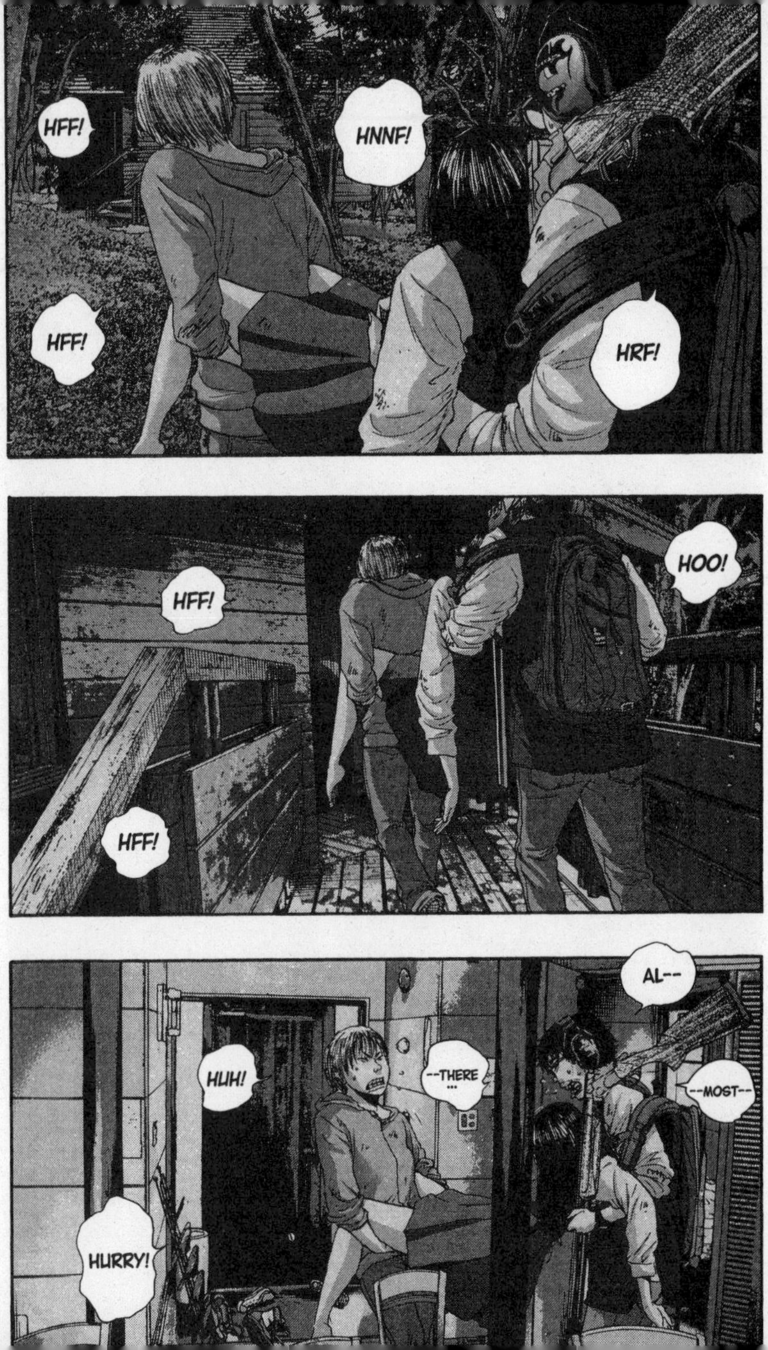
HNNF!
HRF!
HFF!
HFF!
HOO!
HFF!
HFF!
AL--
--MOST--
--THERE ...
HUH!
HURRY!

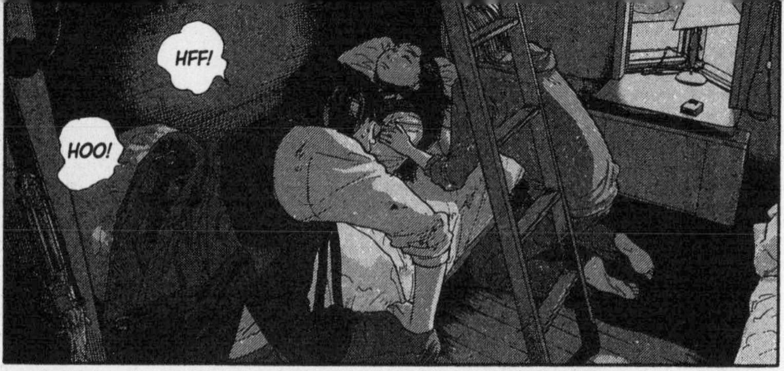
HFF!
HOO!

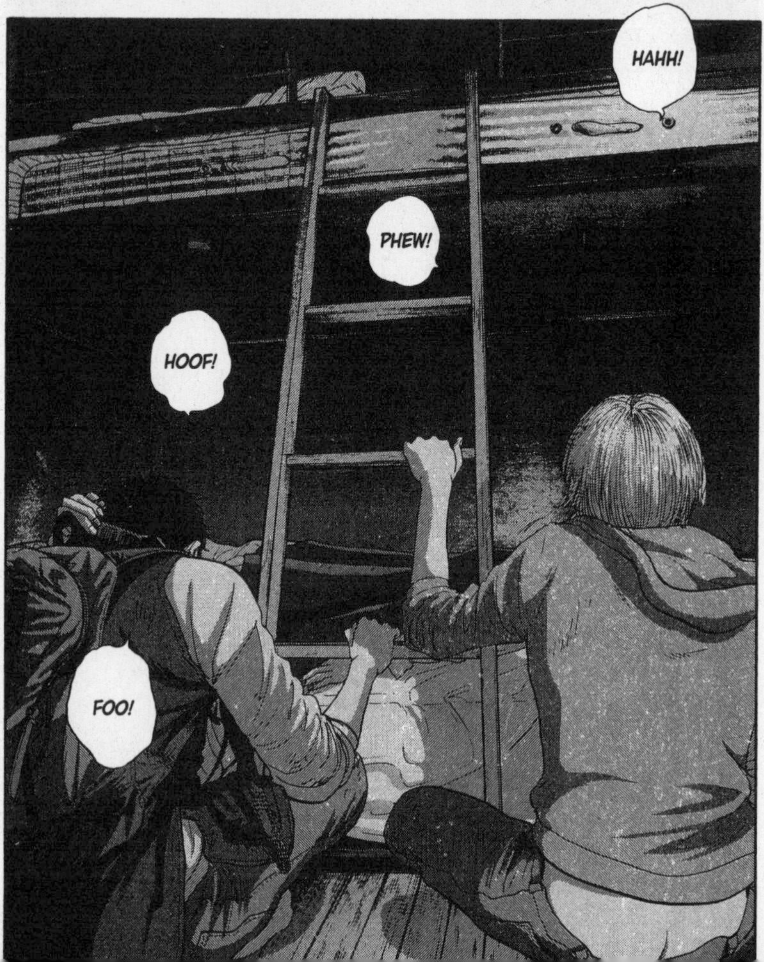
HAHH!
PHEW!
HOOF!
FOO!

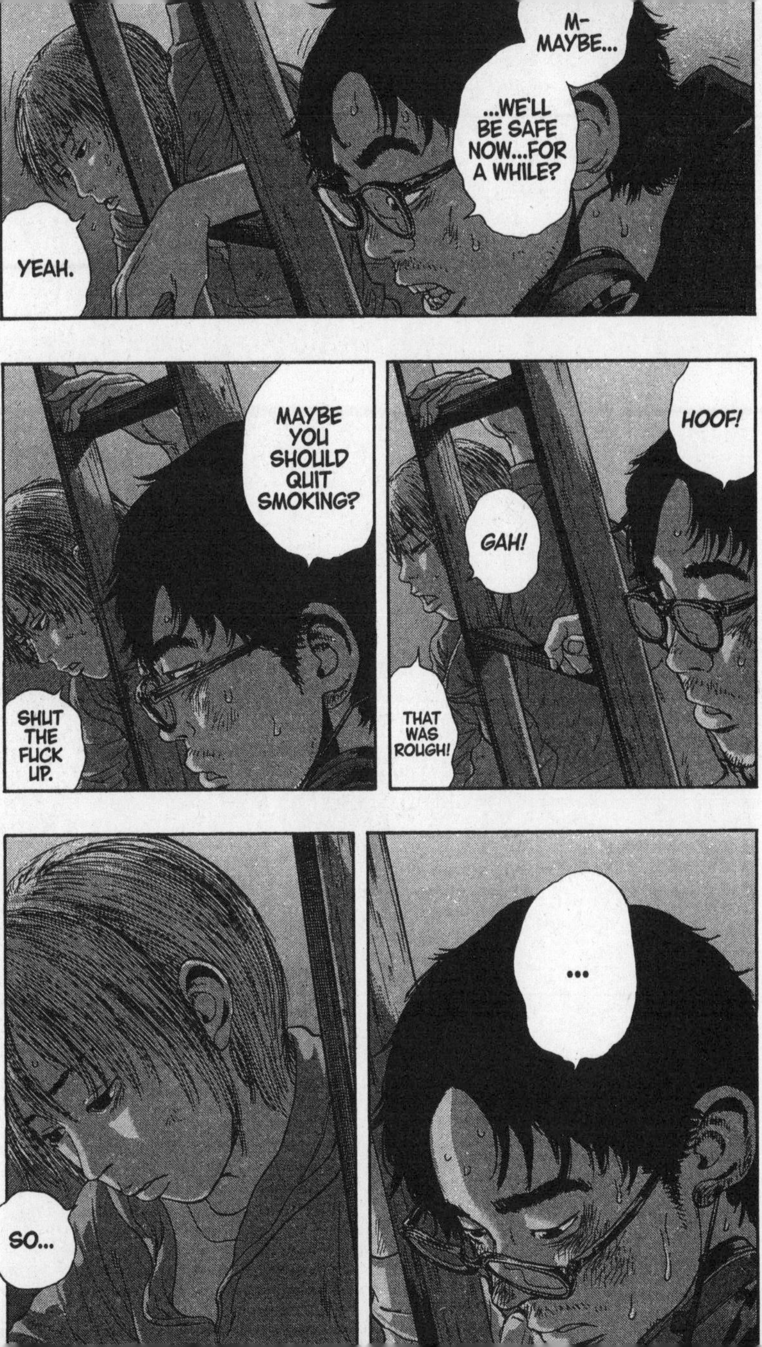
M-MAYBE...
...WE'LL BE SAFE NOW...FOR A WHILE?
YEAH.
HOOF!
GAH!
THAT WAS ROUGH!
MAYBE YOU SHOULD QUIT SMOKING?
SHUT THE FUCK UP.
...
SO...

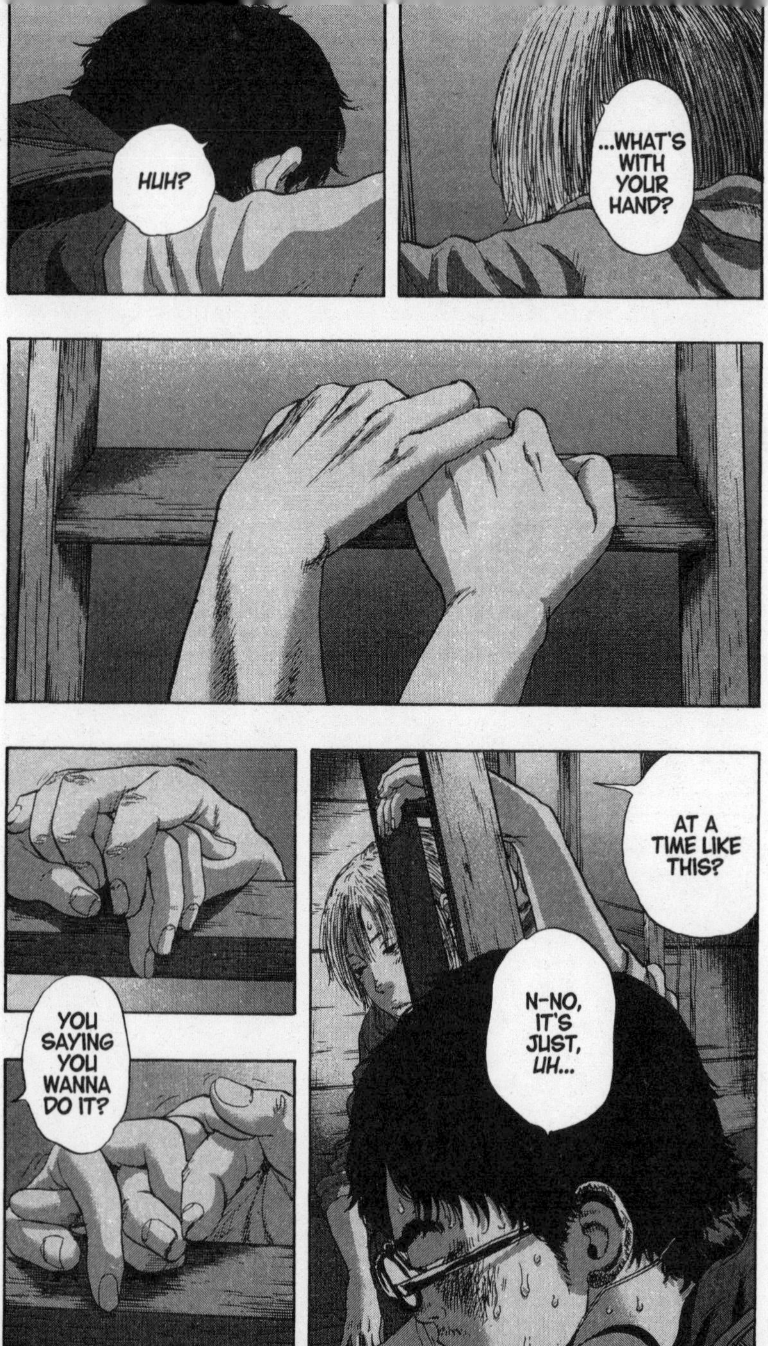
...WHAT'S WITH YOUR HAND?
HUH?
YOU SAYING YOU WANNA DO IT?
AT A TIME LIKE THIS?
N-NO, IT'S JUST, UH...

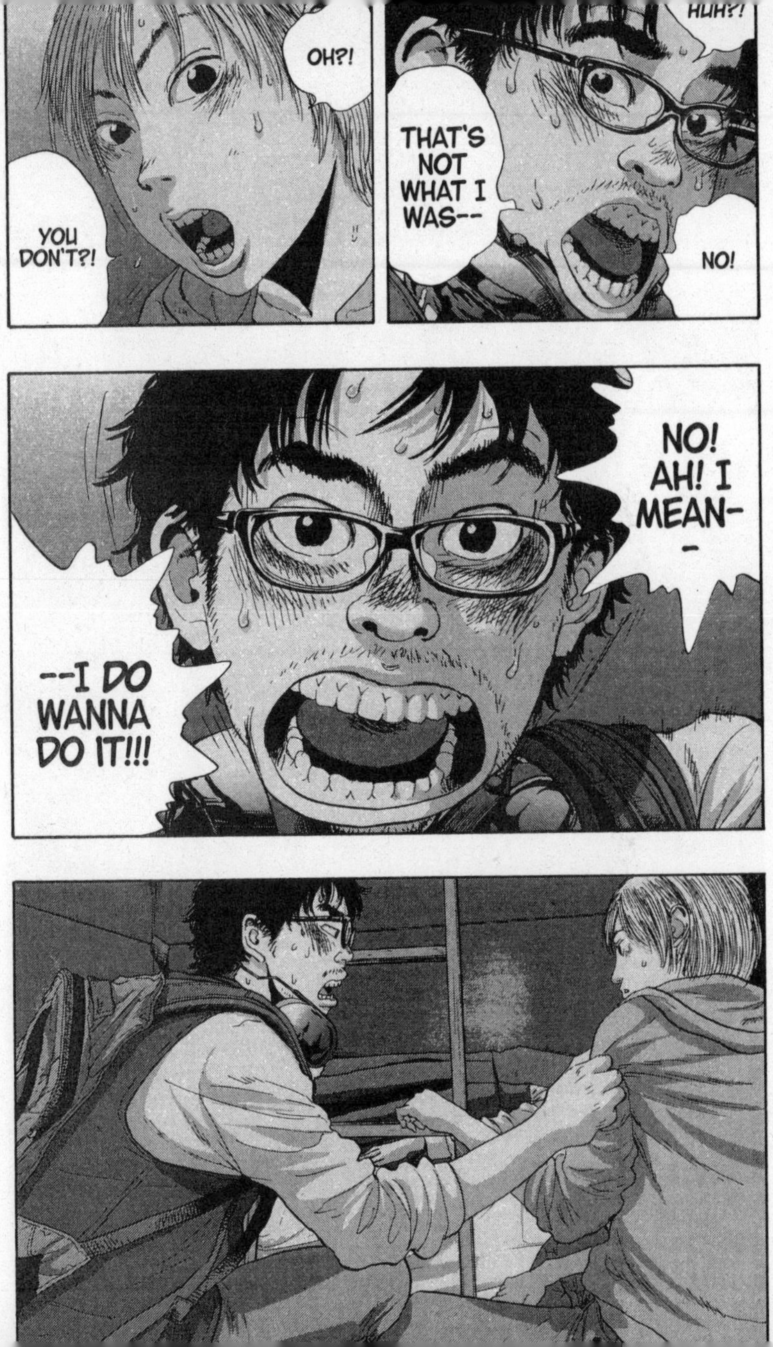
HUH?!
THAT'S NOT WHAT I WAS--
NO!
OH?!
YOU DON'T?!
NO! AH! I MEAN--
--I DO WANNA DO IT!!!

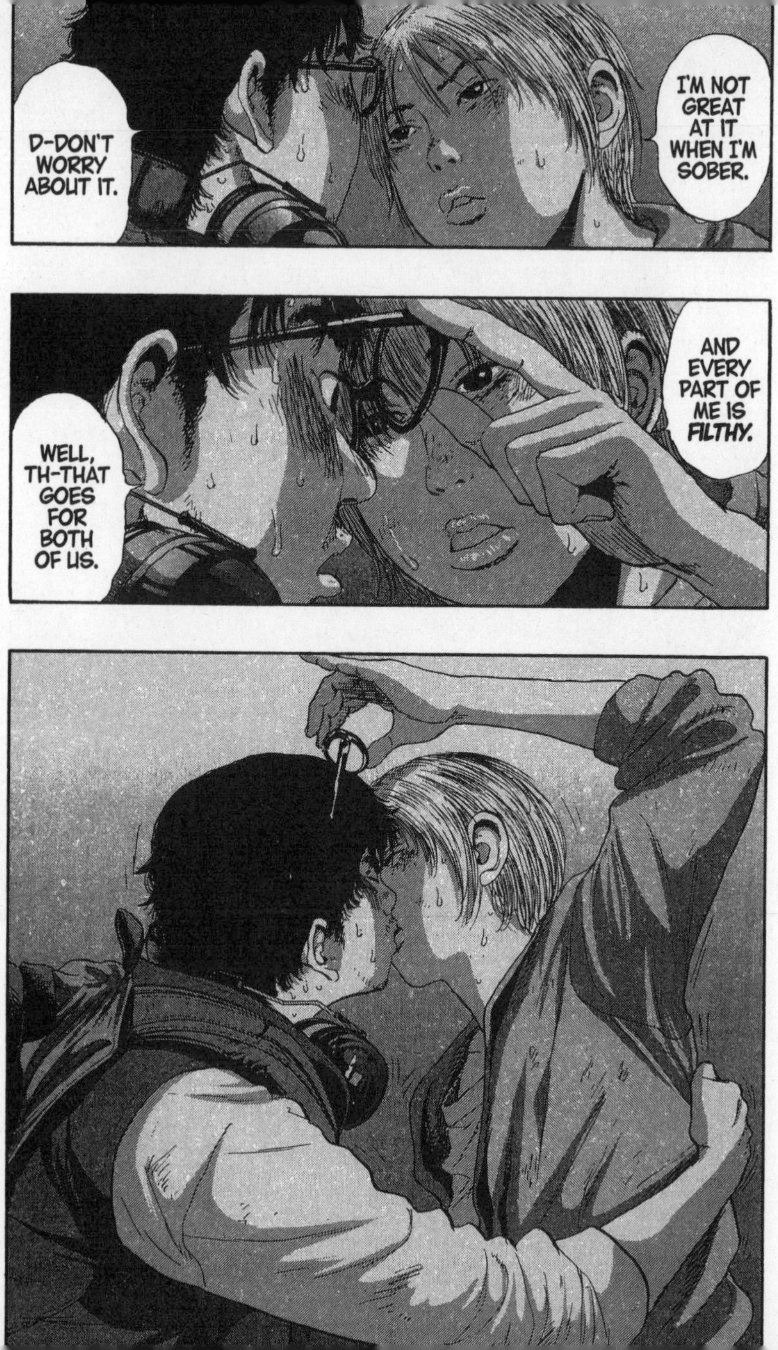
I'M NOT GREAT AT IT WHEN I'M SOBER.
D-DON'T WORRY ABOUT IT.
AND EVERY PART OF ME IS FILTHY.
WELL, TH-THAT GOES FOR BOTH OF US.

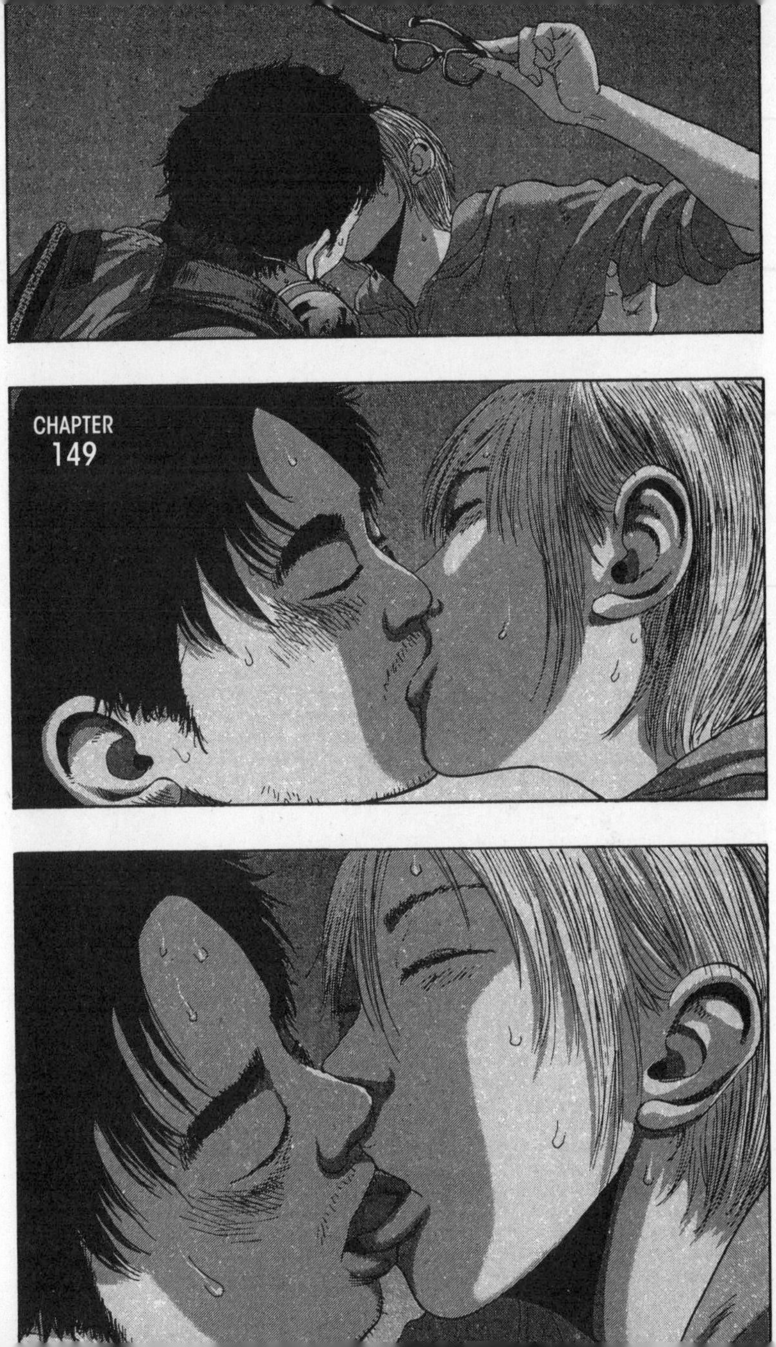
CHAPTER
149

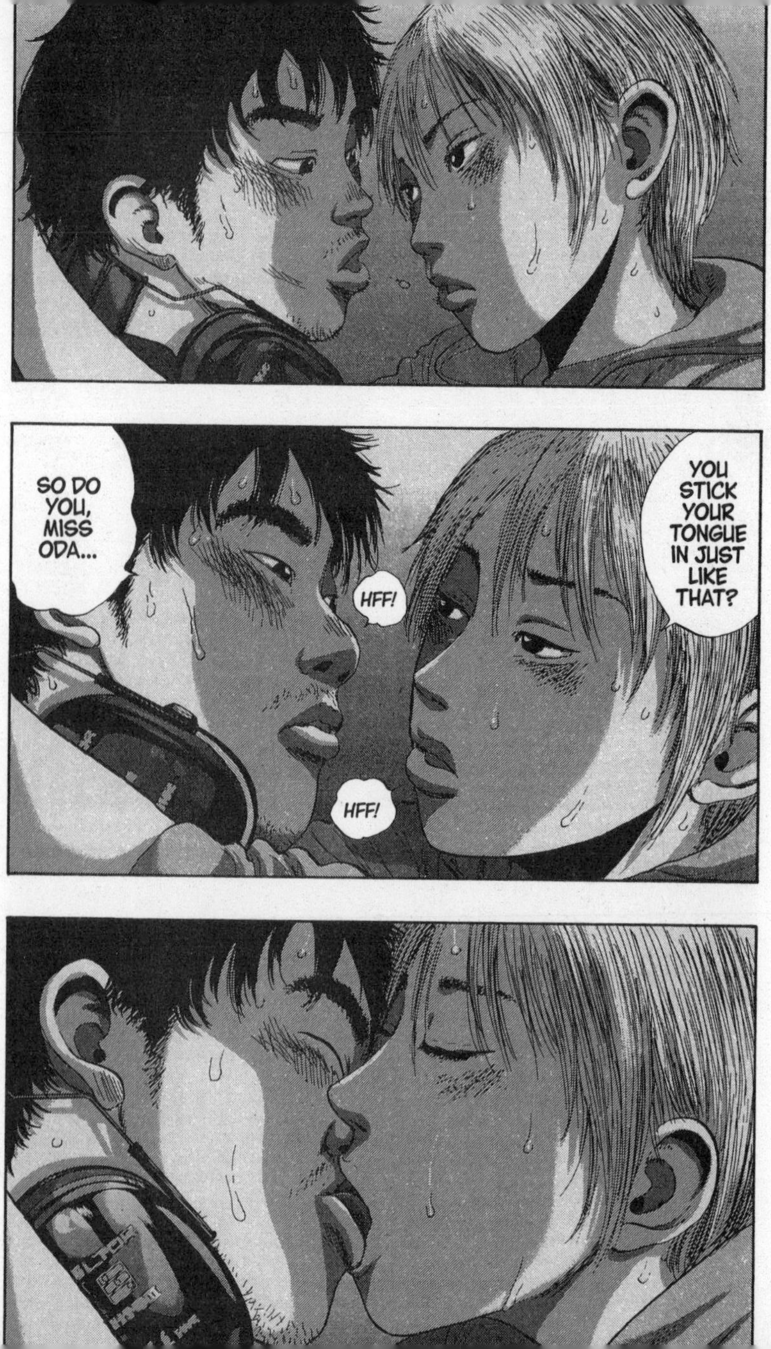
YOU STICK YOUR TONGUE IN JUST LIKE THAT?
SO DO YOU, MISS ODA...
HFF!
HFF!

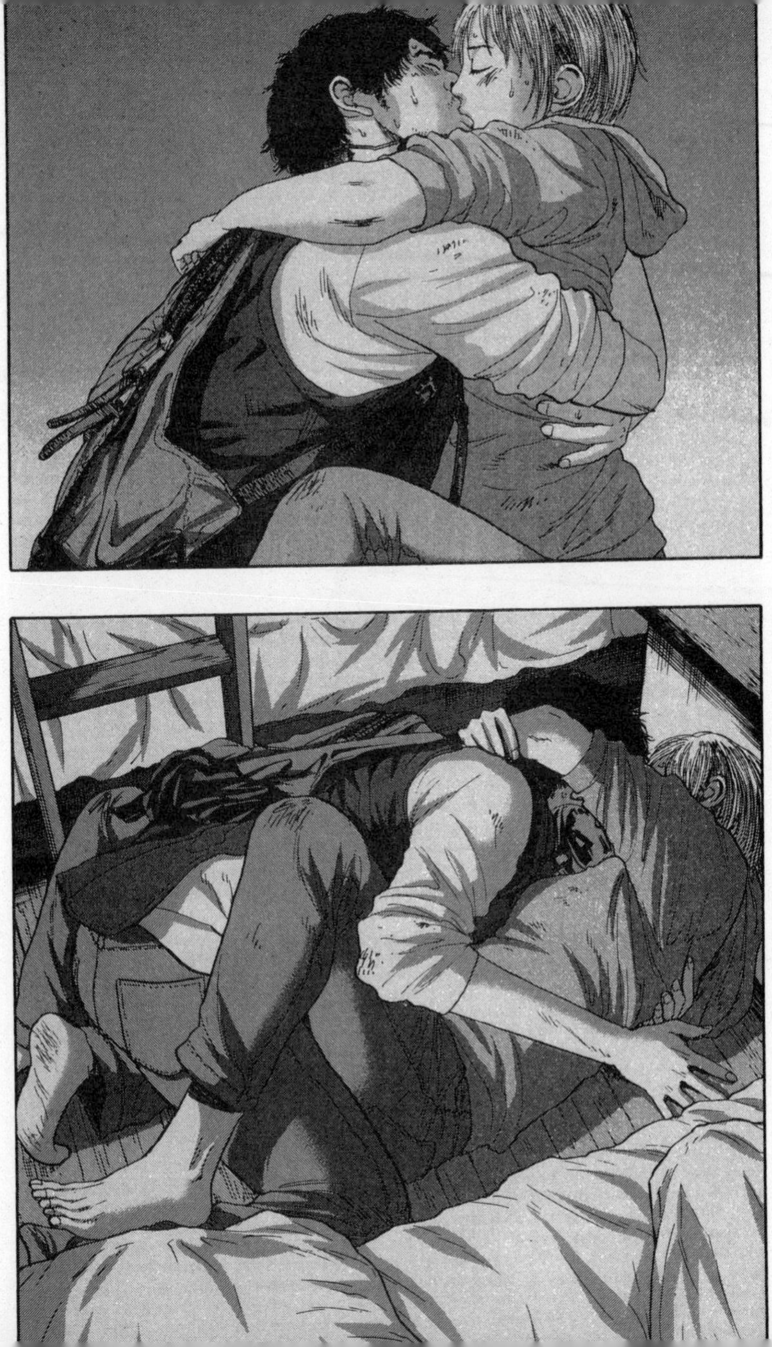

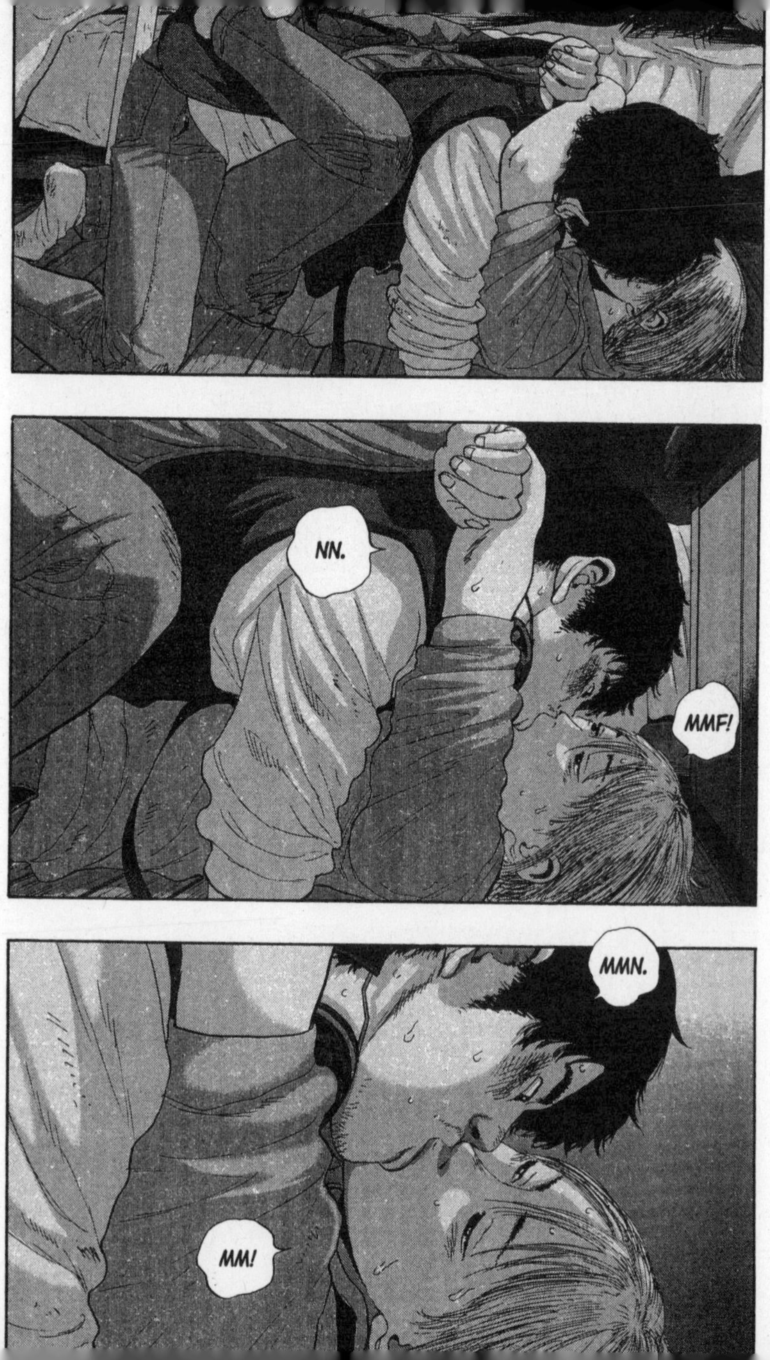
MMF!
NN.
MMN.
MM!

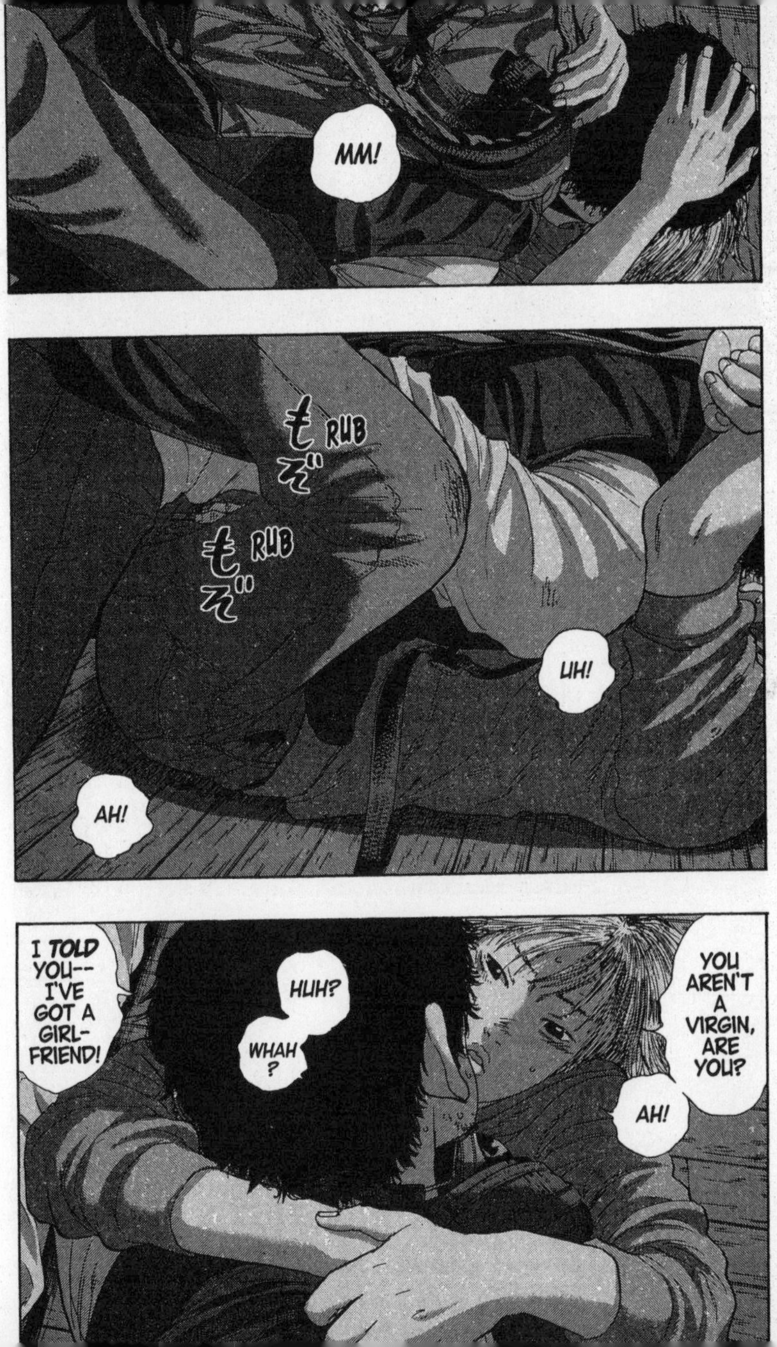
MM!
もぞ RUB
もぞ RUB
UH!
AH!
YOU AREN'T A VIRGIN, ARE YOU?
AH!
HUH?
WHAH?
I TOLD YOU-- I'VE GOT A GIRL-FRIEND!

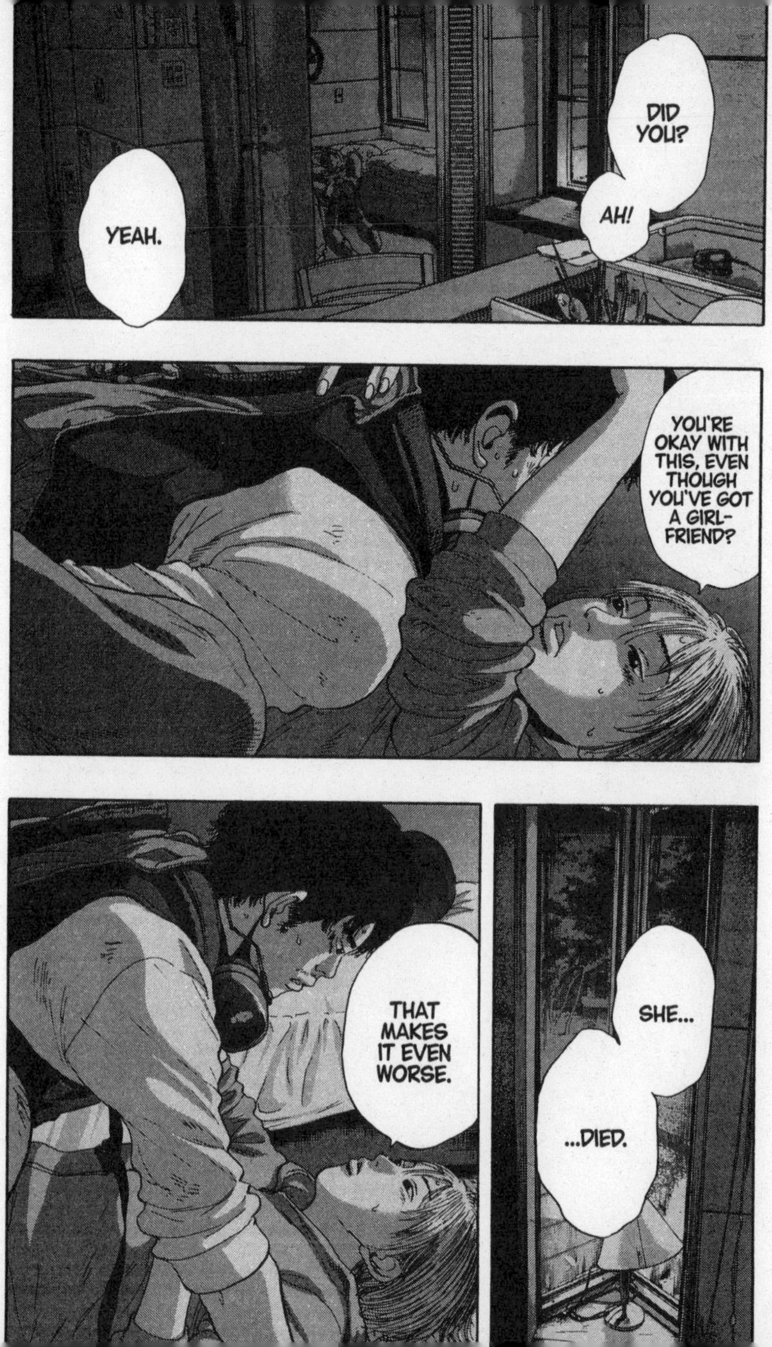
DID YOU?
AH!
YEAH.
YOU'RE OKAY WITH THIS, EVEN THOUGH YOU'VE GOT A GIRL-FRIEND?
SHE...
...DIED.
THAT MAKES IT EVEN WORSE.

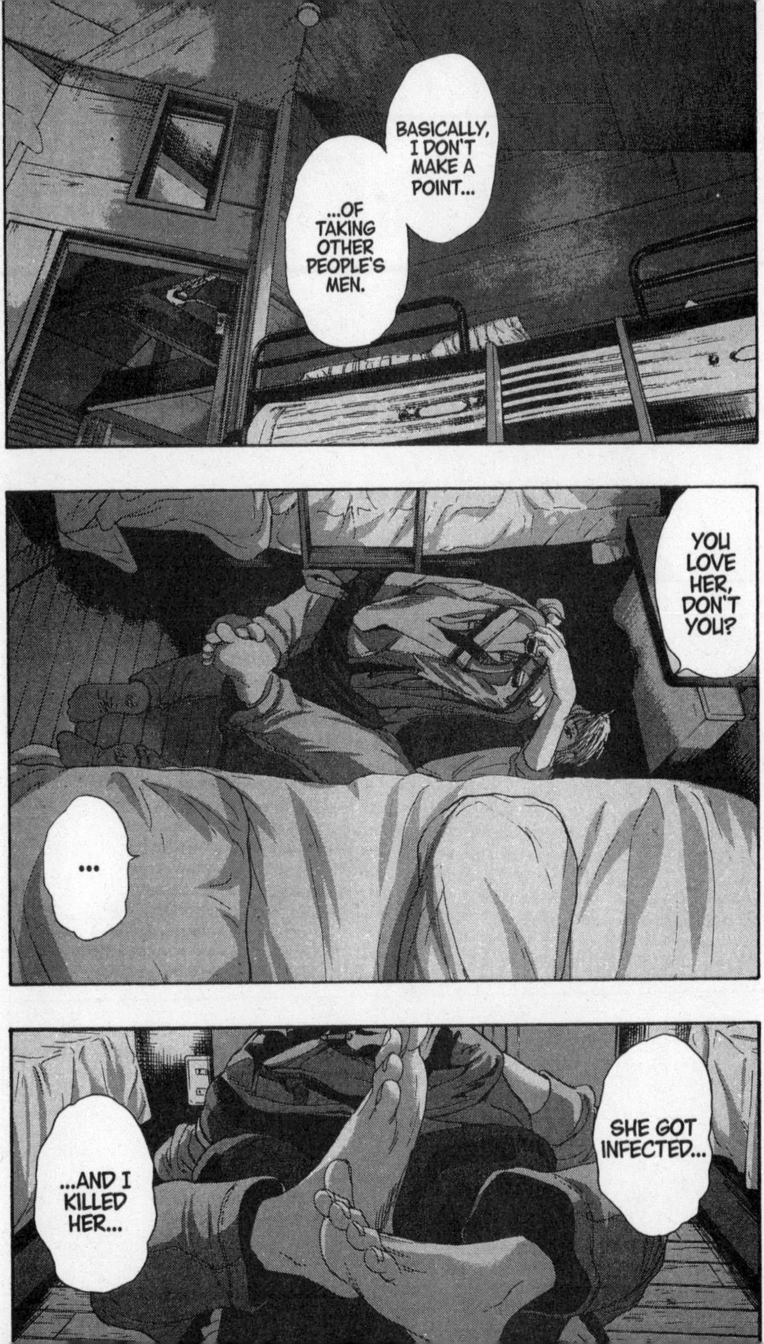
BASICALLY, I DON'T MAKE A POINT...
...OF TAKING OTHER PEOPLE'S MEN.
YOU LOVE HER, DON'T YOU?
...
SHE GOT INFECTED...
...AND I KILLED HER...

WHILE SHE WAS INFECTED, IN HER DELIRIUM...

...SHE MUMBLED... THE NAME OF HER EX.

S-SO...

...I....

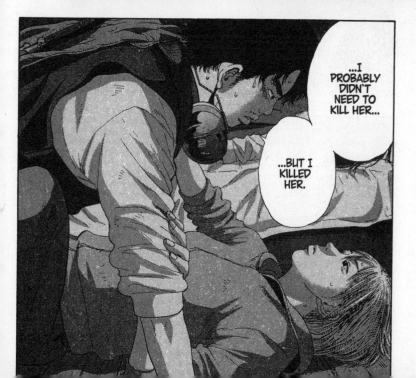

...I PROBABLY DIDN'T NEED TO KILL HER...

...BUT I KILLED HER.

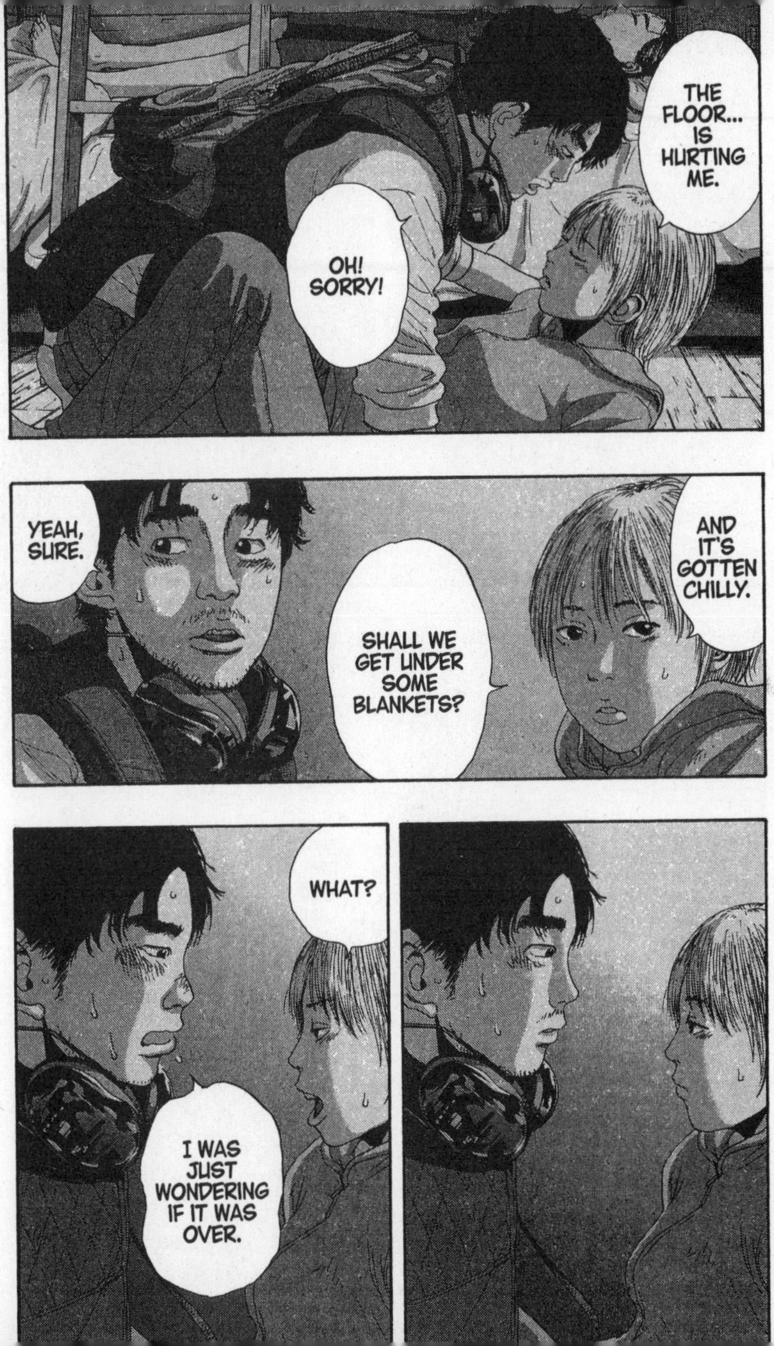
THE FLOOR... IS HURTING ME.
OH! SORRY!
AND IT'S GOTTEN CHILLY.
SHALL WE GET UNDER SOME BLANKETS?
YEAH, SURE.
WHAT?
I WAS JUST WONDERING IF IT WAS OVER.

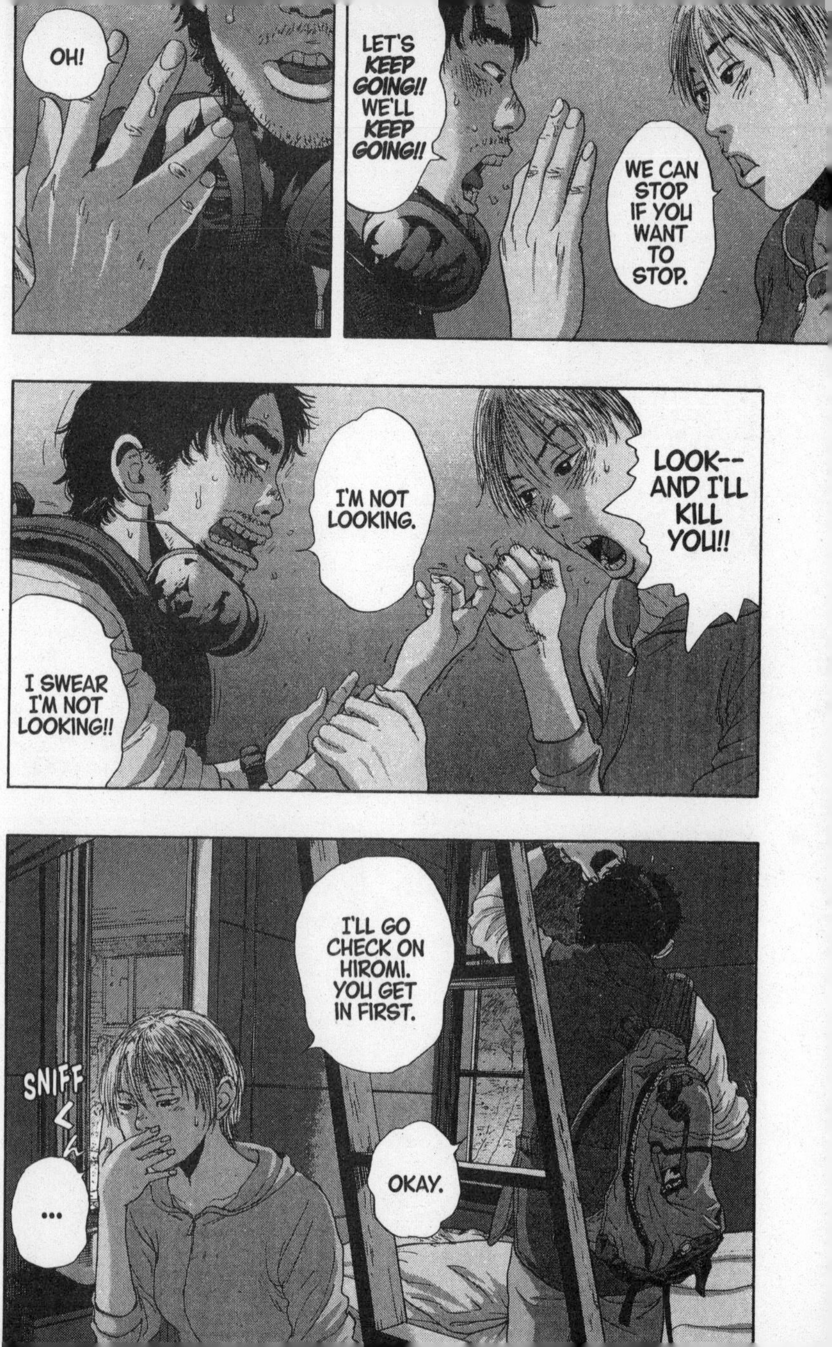
WE CAN STOP IF YOU WANT TO STOP.
LET'S KEEP GOING!! WE'LL KEEP GOING!!
OH!
LOOK-- AND I'LL KILL YOU!!
I'M NOT LOOKING.
I SWEAR I'M NOT LOOKING!!
I'LL GO CHECK ON HIROMI. YOU GET IN FIRST.
OKAY.
SNIFF
くん
...

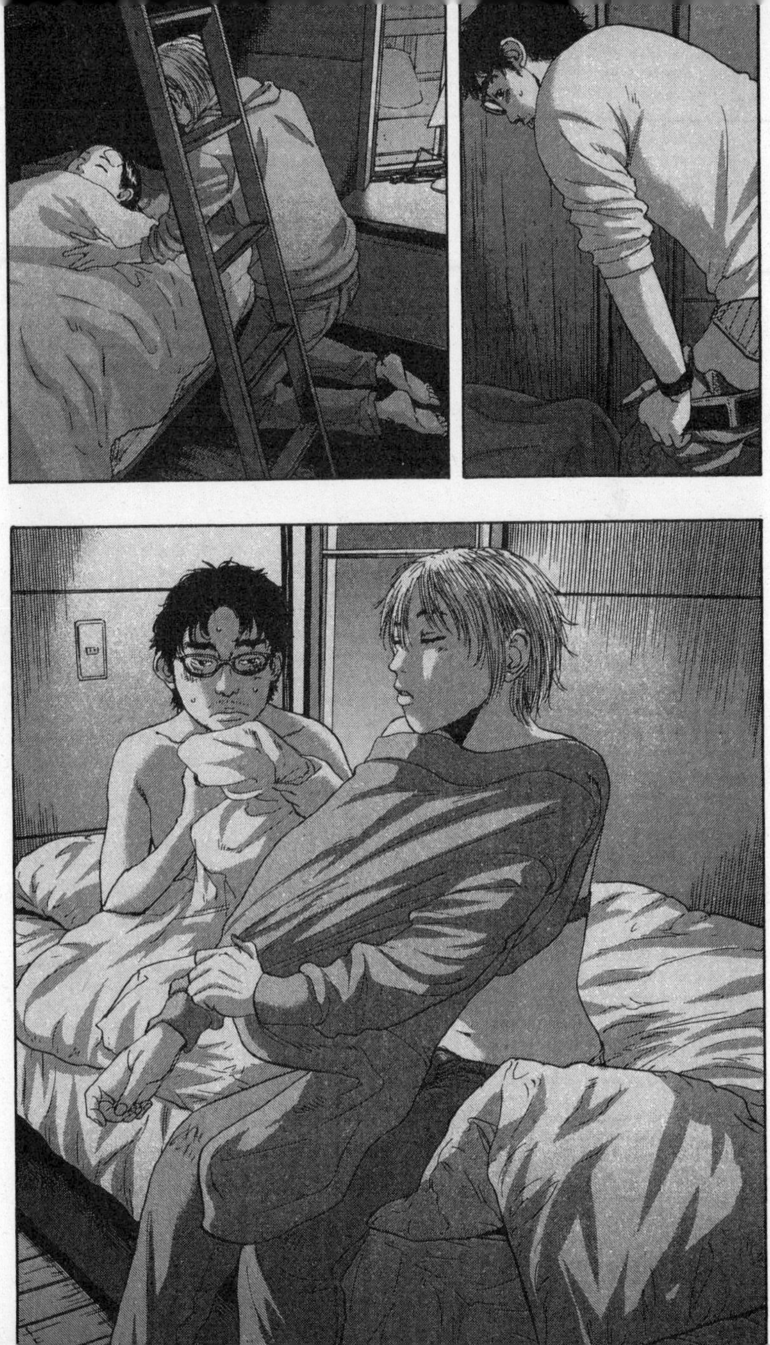

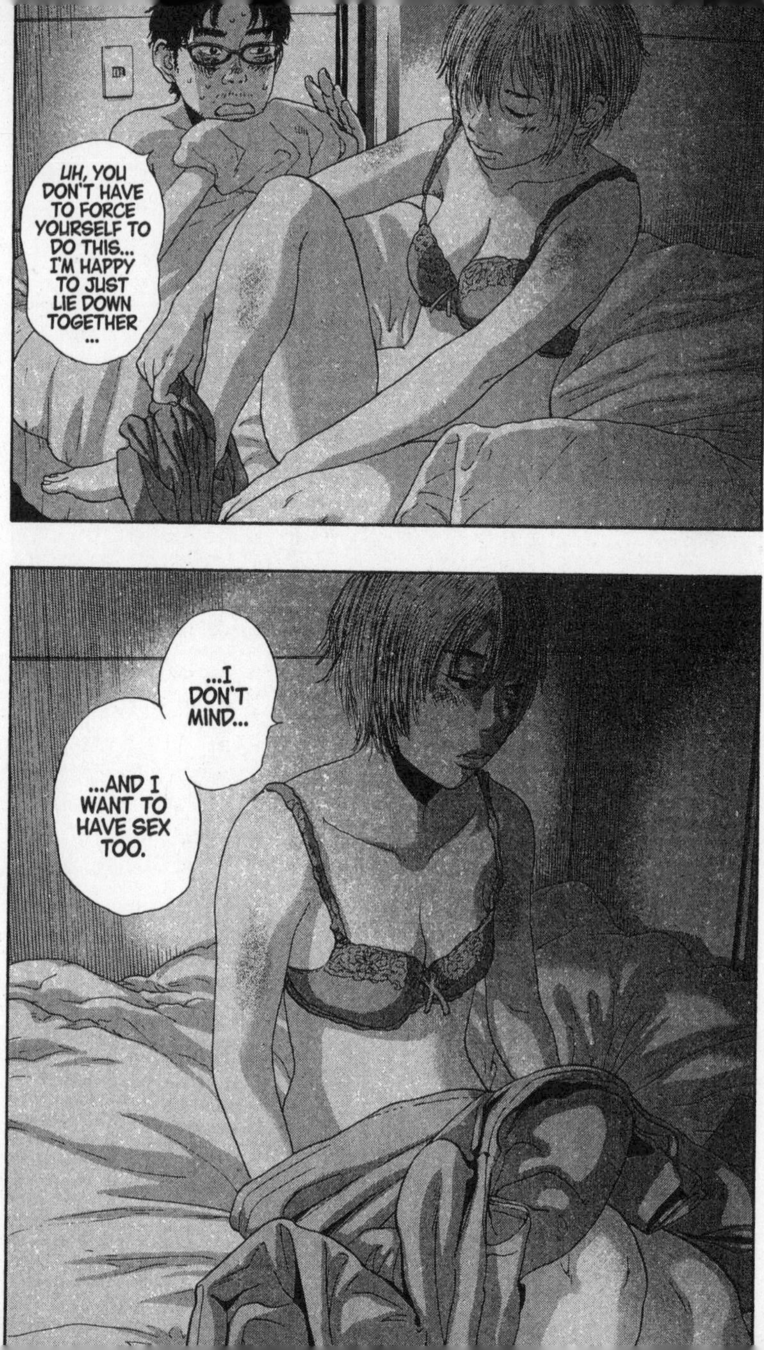
UH, YOU DON'T HAVE TO FORCE YOURSELF TO DO THIS... I'M HAPPY TO JUST LIE DOWN TOGETHER ...
...I DON'T MIND...
...AND I WANT TO HAVE SEX TOO.

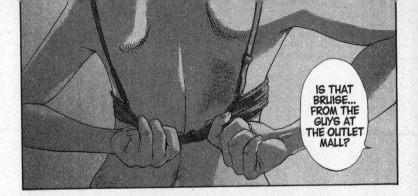

IS THAT BRUISE... FROM THE GUYS AT THE OUTLET MALL?

YEP. I WAS DIS- OBEDIENT, SO THEY BEAT ME OFTEN.

BUT AT THE START, THEY WERE ALL TIMID LIKE YOU, TOO.

THAT'S *TERRIBLE!*

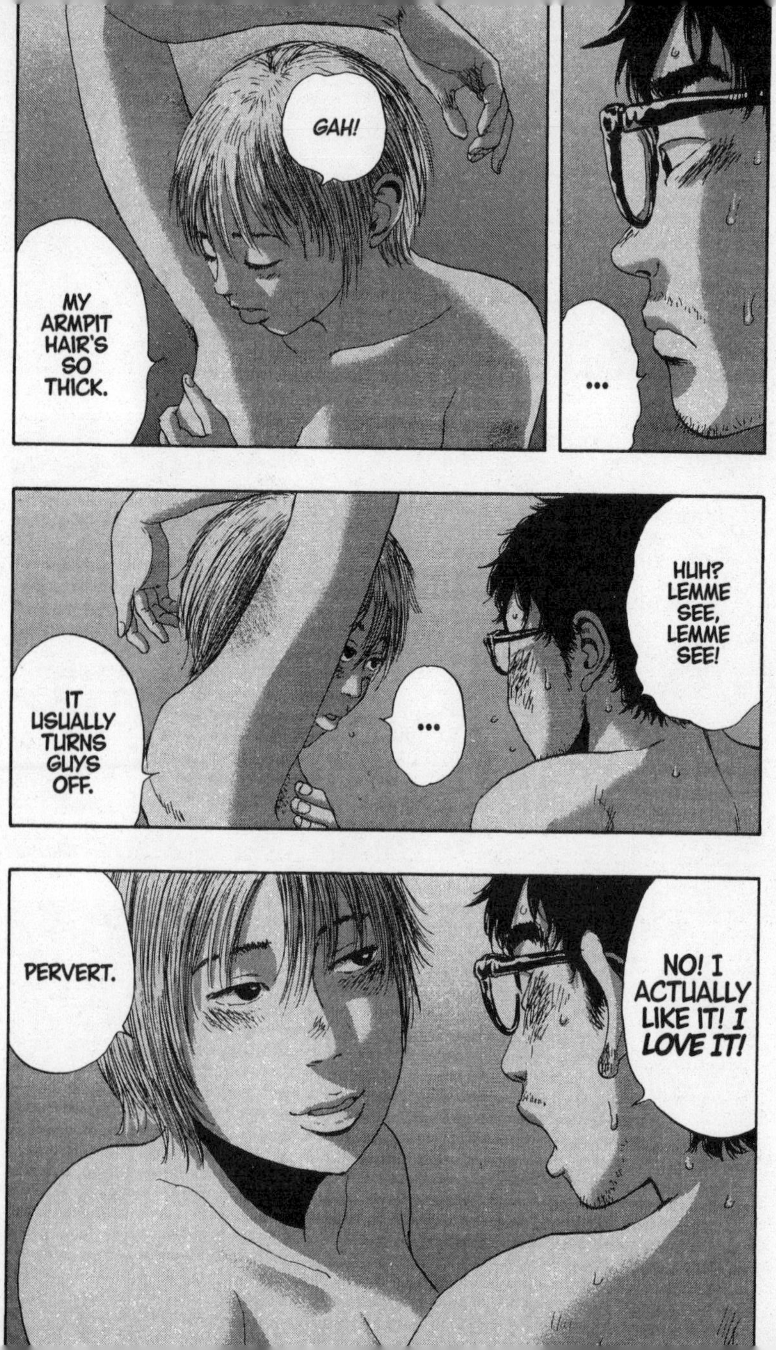
...
GAH!
MY ARMPIT HAIR'S SO THICK.
HUH? LEMME SEE, LEMME SEE!
...
IT USUALLY TURNS GUYS OFF.
NO! I ACTUALLY LIKE IT! I *LOVE IT!*
PERVERT.

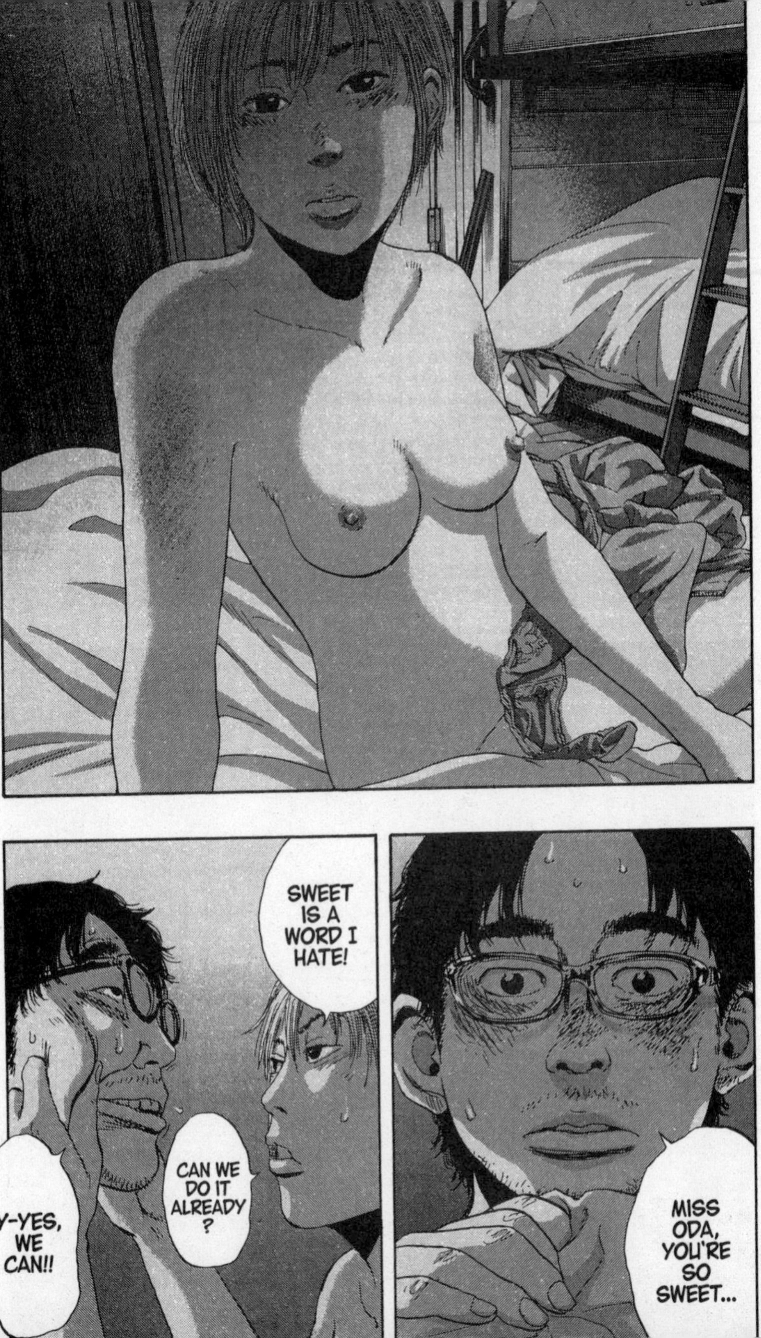
MISS ODA, YOU'RE SO SWEET...
SWEET IS A WORD I HATE!
CAN WE DO IT ALREADY?
Y-YES, WE CAN!!

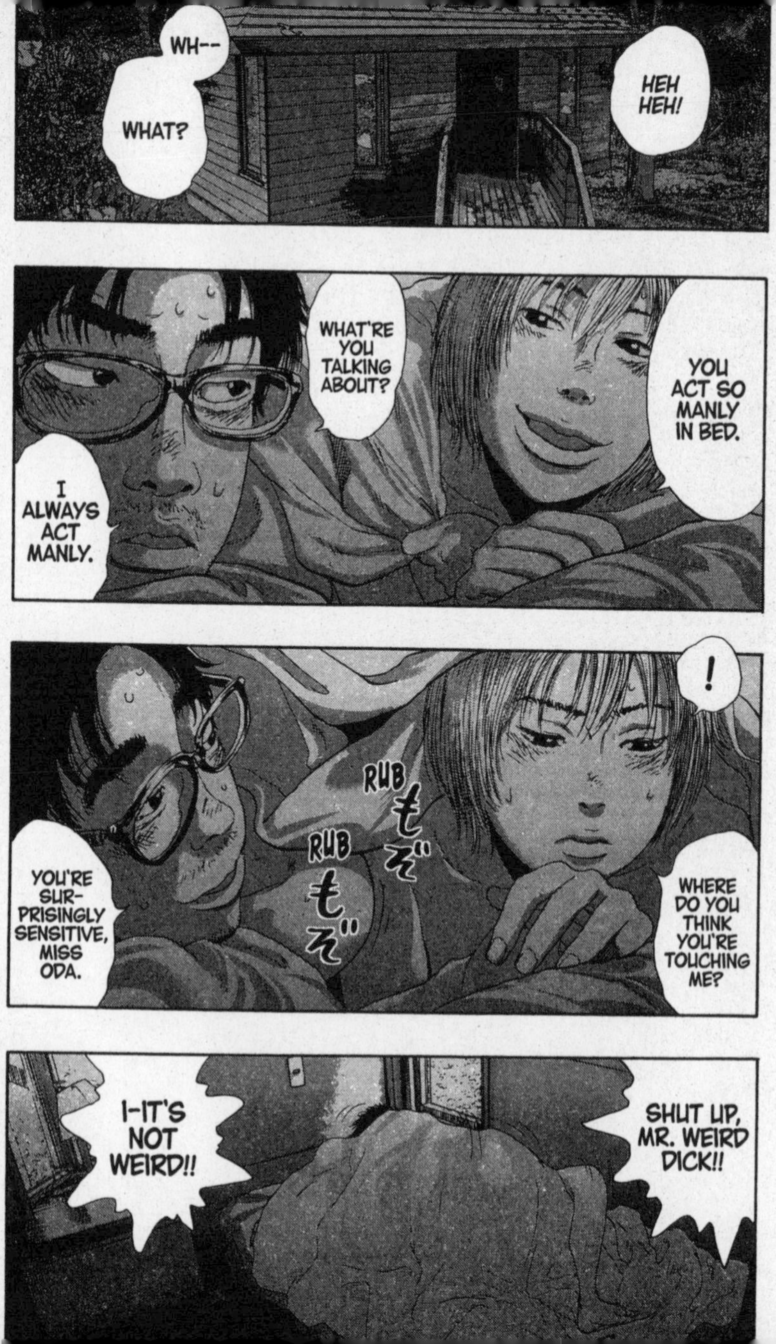
HEH HEH!
WH-- WHAT?
YOU ACT SO MANLY IN BED.
WHAT'RE YOU TALKING ABOUT?
I ALWAYS ACT MANLY.
!
RUB
RUB
WHERE DO YOU THINK YOU'RE TOUCHING ME?
YOU'RE SUR-PRISINGLY SENSITIVE, MISS ODA.
SHUT UP, MR. WEIRD DICK!!
I-IT'S NOT WEIRD!!

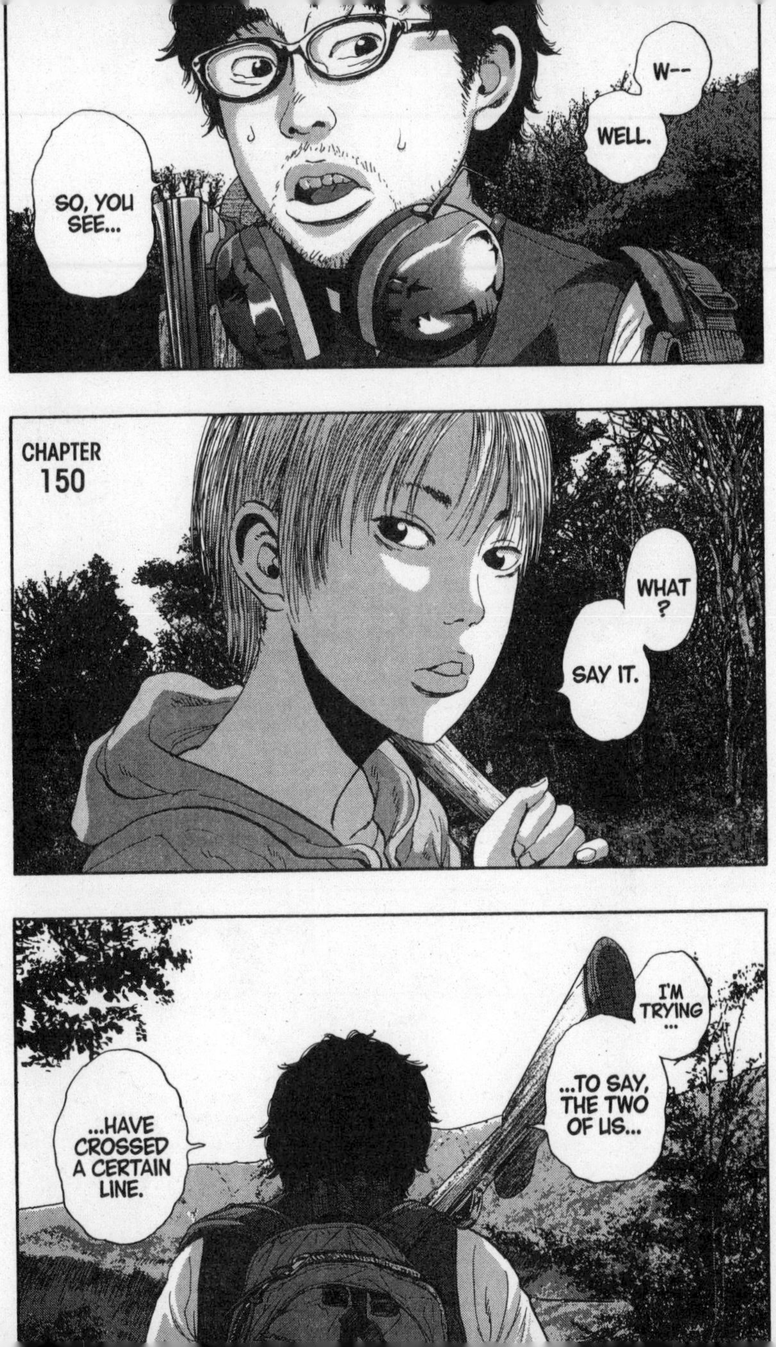
W--
WELL.
SO, YOU SEE...
CHAPTER 150
WHAT?
SAY IT.
I'M TRYING...
...TO SAY, THE TWO OF US...
...HAVE CROSSED A CERTAIN LINE.

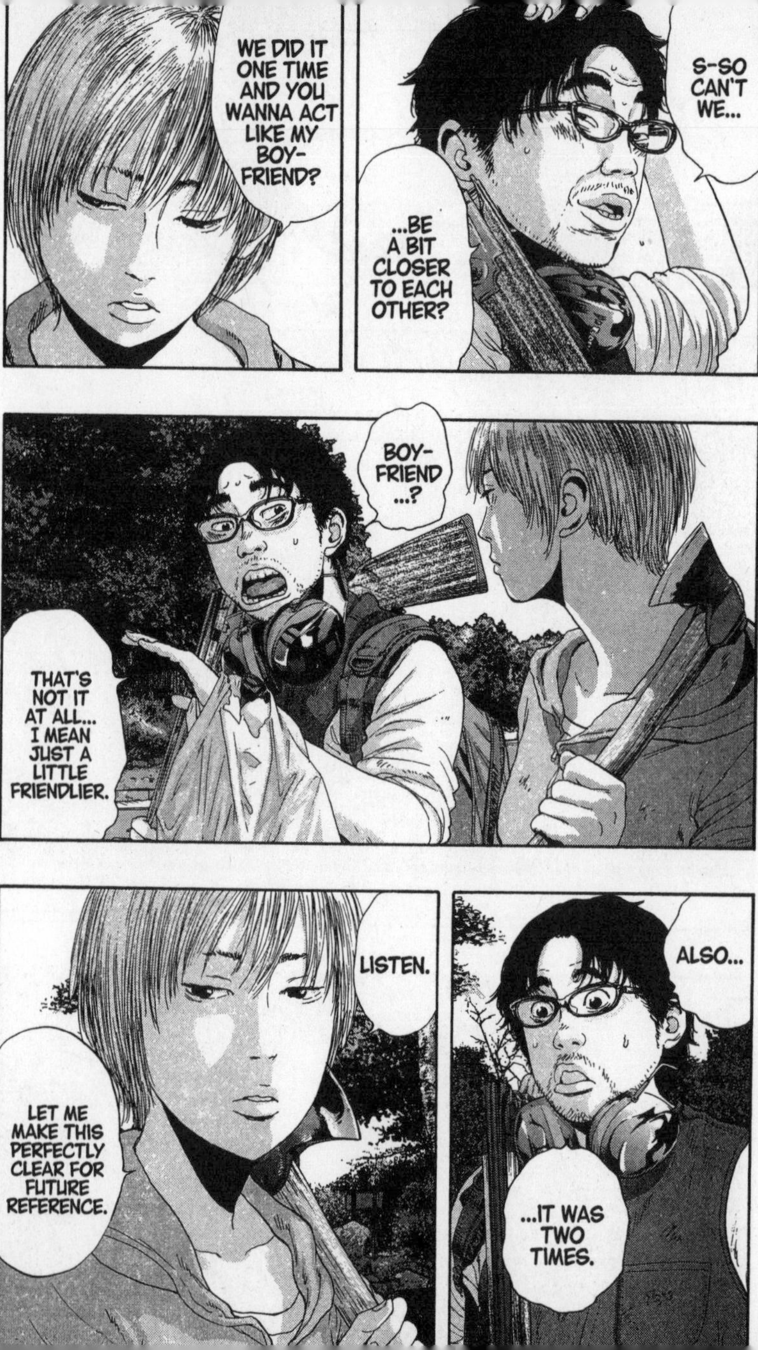
S-SO CAN'T WE...
...BE A BIT CLOSER TO EACH OTHER?
WE DID IT ONE TIME AND YOU WANNA ACT LIKE MY BOY-FRIEND?
BOY-FRIEND ...?
THAT'S NOT IT AT ALL... I MEAN JUST A LITTLE FRIENDLIER.
ALSO...
...IT WAS TWO TIMES.
LISTEN.
LET ME MAKE THIS PERFECTLY CLEAR FOR FUTURE REFERENCE.

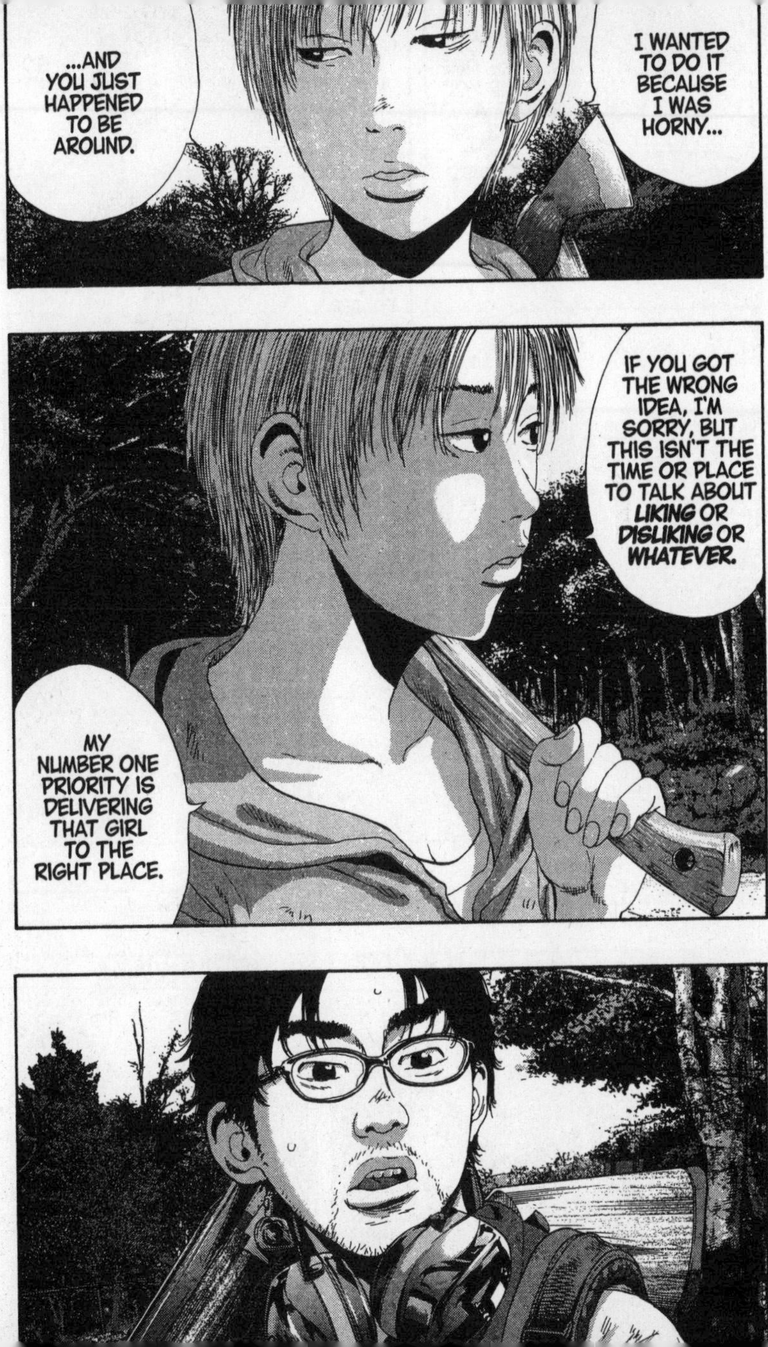
I WANTED TO DO IT BECAUSE I WAS HORNY...
...AND YOU JUST HAPPENED TO BE AROUND.
IF YOU GOT THE WRONG IDEA, I'M SORRY, BUT THIS ISN'T THE TIME OR PLACE TO TALK ABOUT LIKING OR DISLIKING OR WHATEVER.
MY NUMBER ONE PRIORITY IS DELIVERING THAT GIRL TO THE RIGHT PLACE.

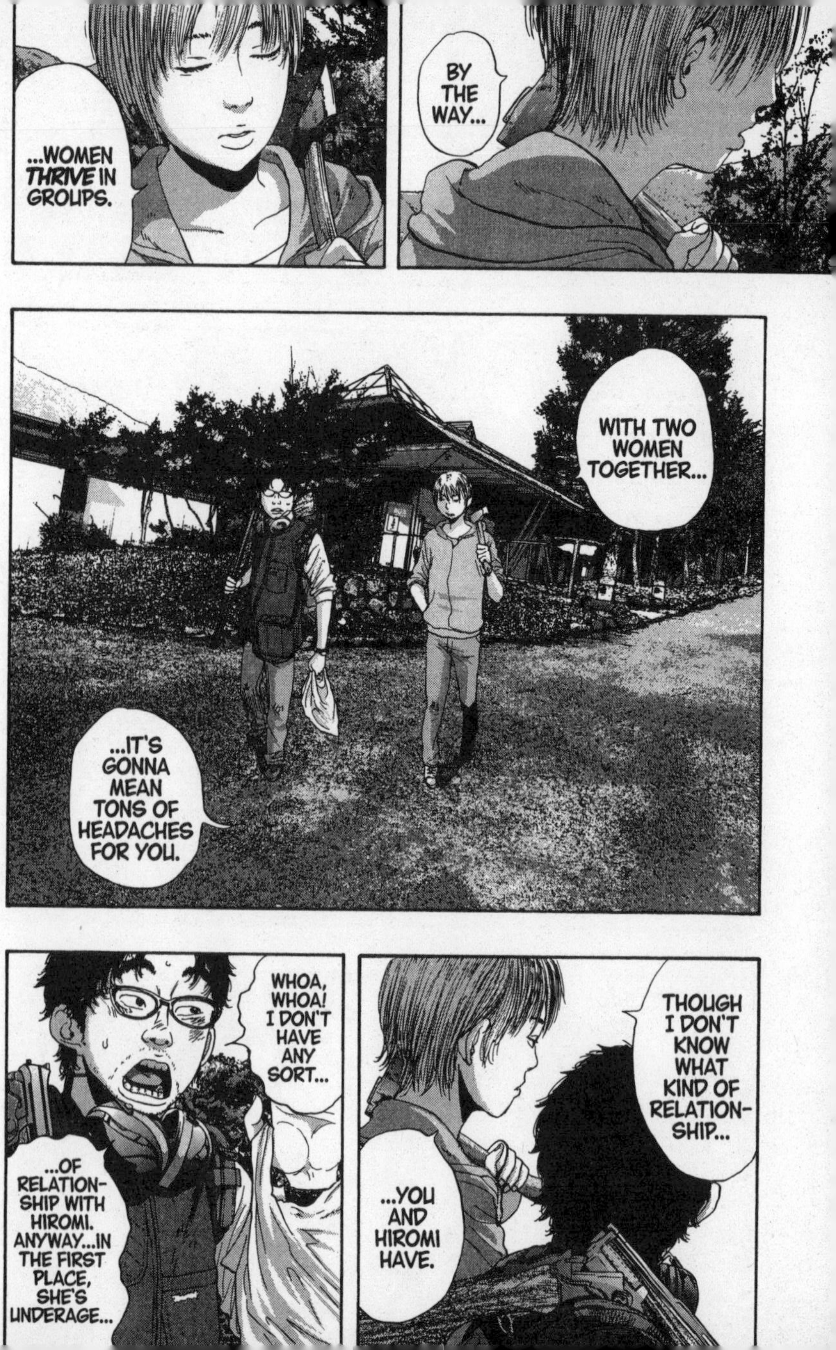
BY THE WAY...
...WOMEN THRIVE IN GROUPS.
WITH TWO WOMEN TOGETHER...
...IT'S GONNA MEAN TONS OF HEADACHES FOR YOU.
THOUGH I DON'T KNOW WHAT KIND OF RELATIONSHIP...
...YOU AND HIROMI HAVE.
WHOA, WHOA! I DON'T HAVE ANY SORT...
...OF RELATION-SHIP WITH HIROMI. ANYWAY...IN THE FIRST PLACE, SHE'S UNDERAGE...

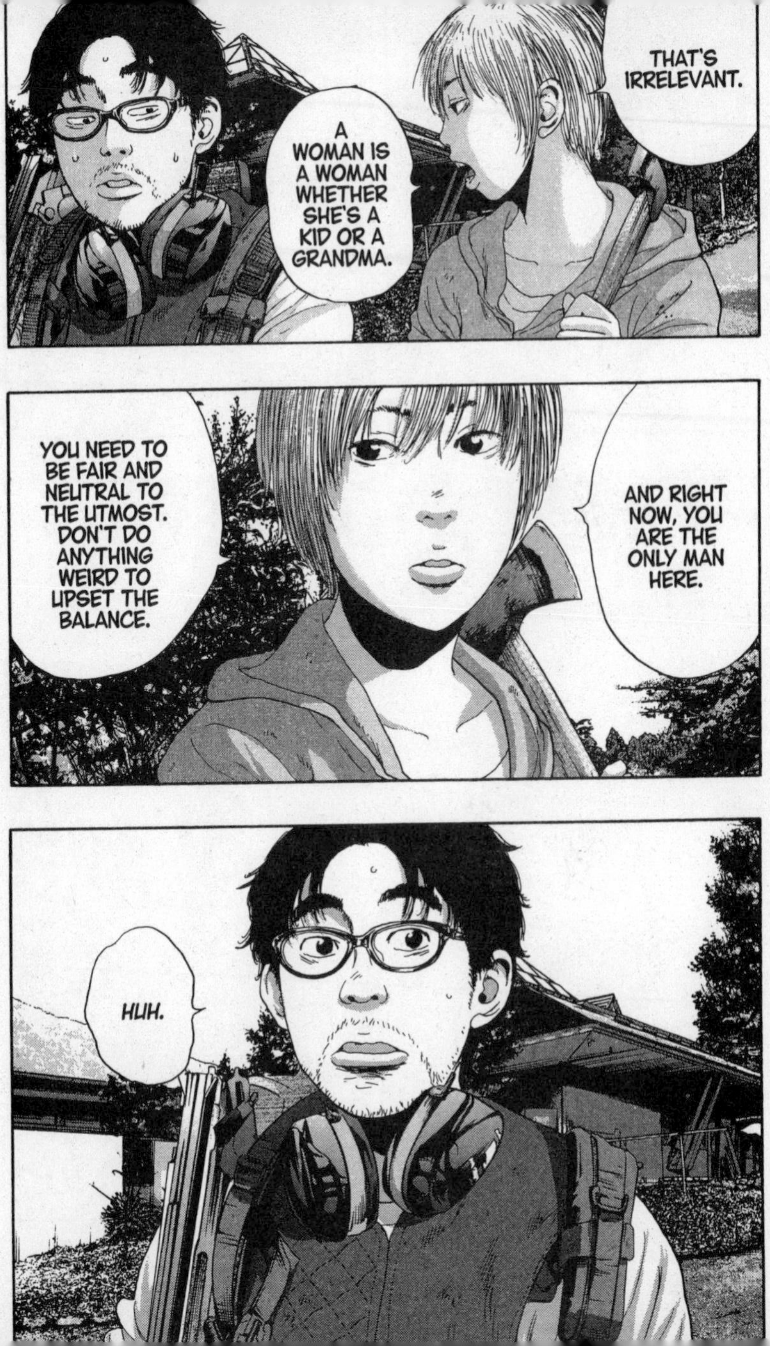
THAT'S IRRELEVANT.
A WOMAN IS A WOMAN WHETHER SHE'S A KID OR A GRANDMA.
AND RIGHT NOW, YOU ARE THE ONLY MAN HERE.
YOU NEED TO BE FAIR AND NEUTRAL TO THE UTMOST. DON'T DO ANYTHING WEIRD TO UPSET THE BALANCE.
HUH.

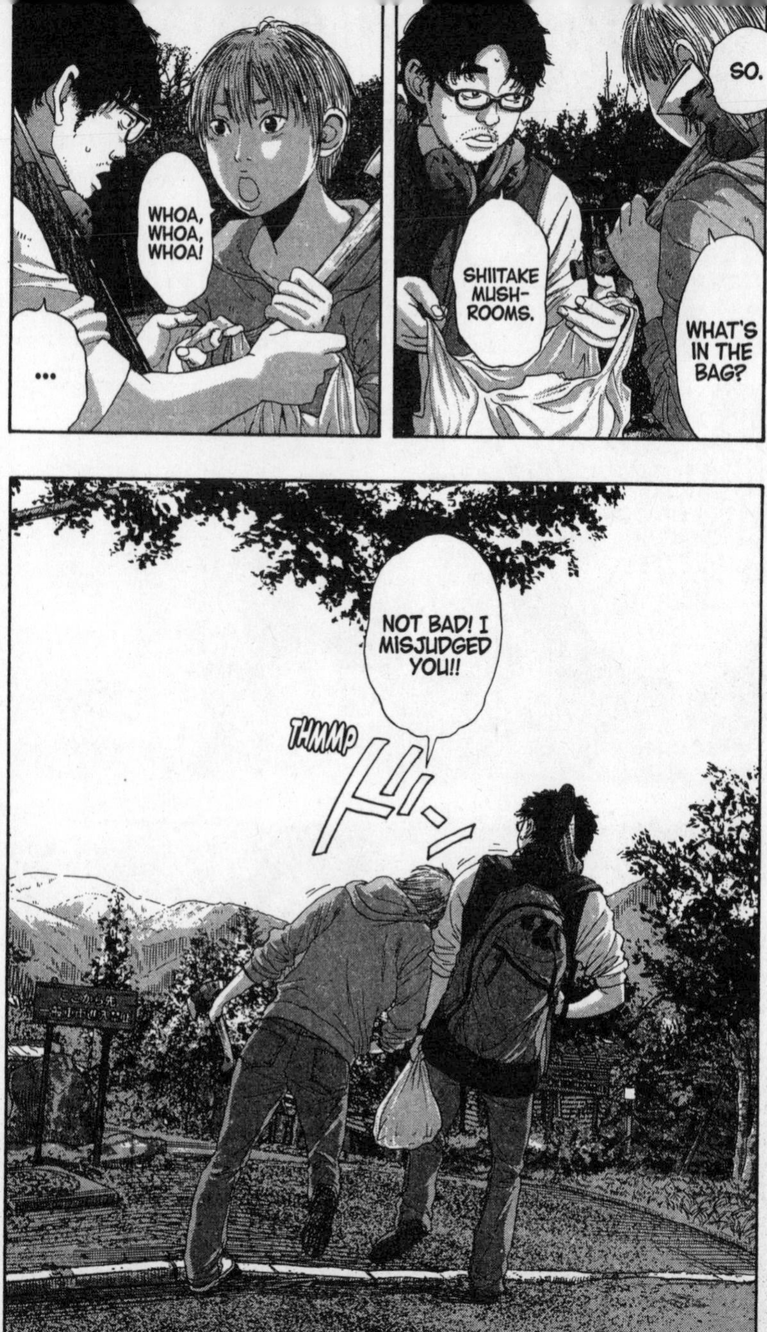
SO.
WHAT'S IN THE BAG?
SHIITAKE MUSH-ROOMS.
WHOA, WHOA, WHOA!
...
NOT BAD! I MISJUDGED YOU!!
THMMP

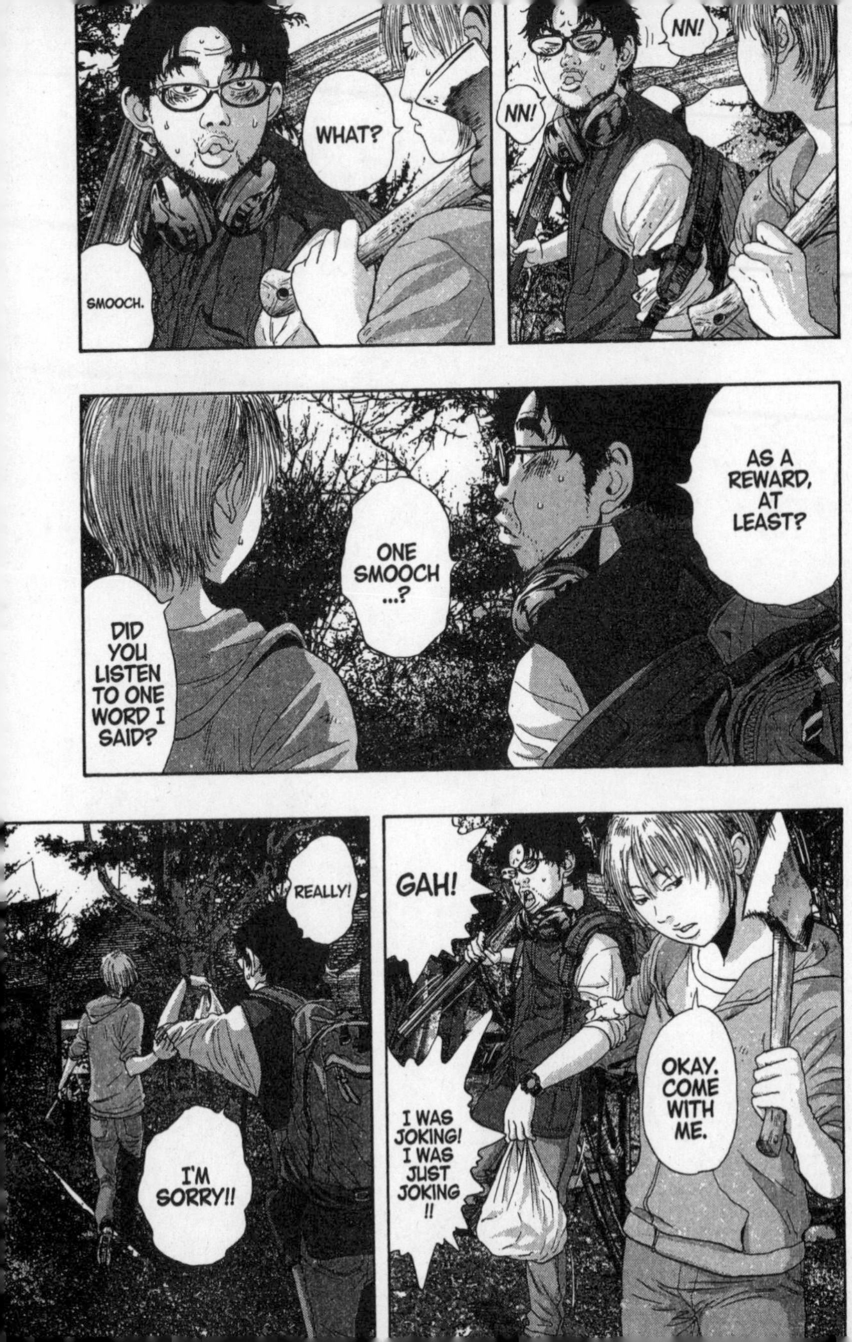
NN!
NN!
WHAT?
SMOOCH.
AS A REWARD, AT LEAST?
ONE SMOOCH ...?
DID YOU LISTEN TO ONE WORD I SAID?
OKAY. COME WITH ME.
GAH!
I WAS JOKING! I WAS JUST JOKING !!
REALLY!
I'M SORRY!!

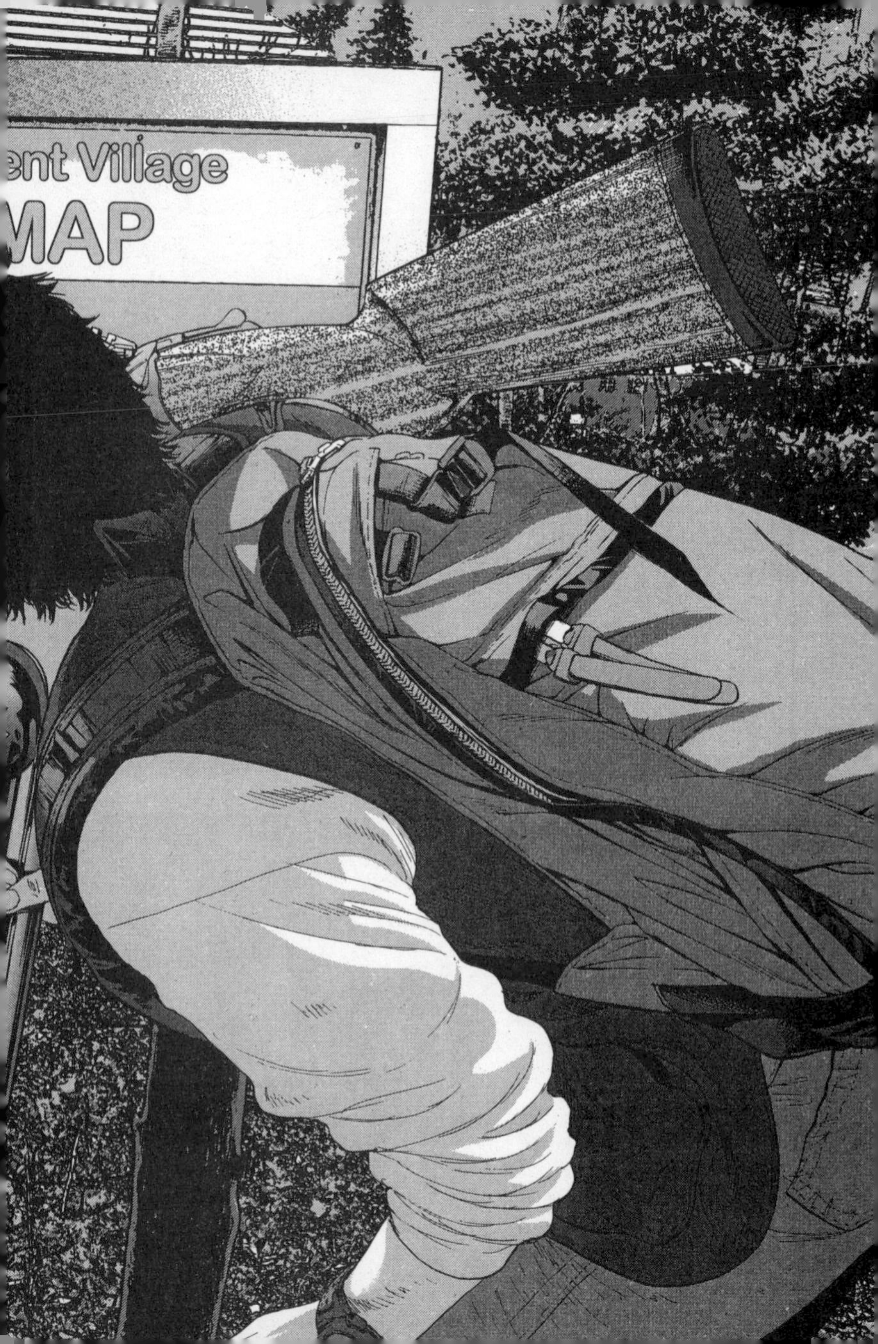
ent Village
MAP

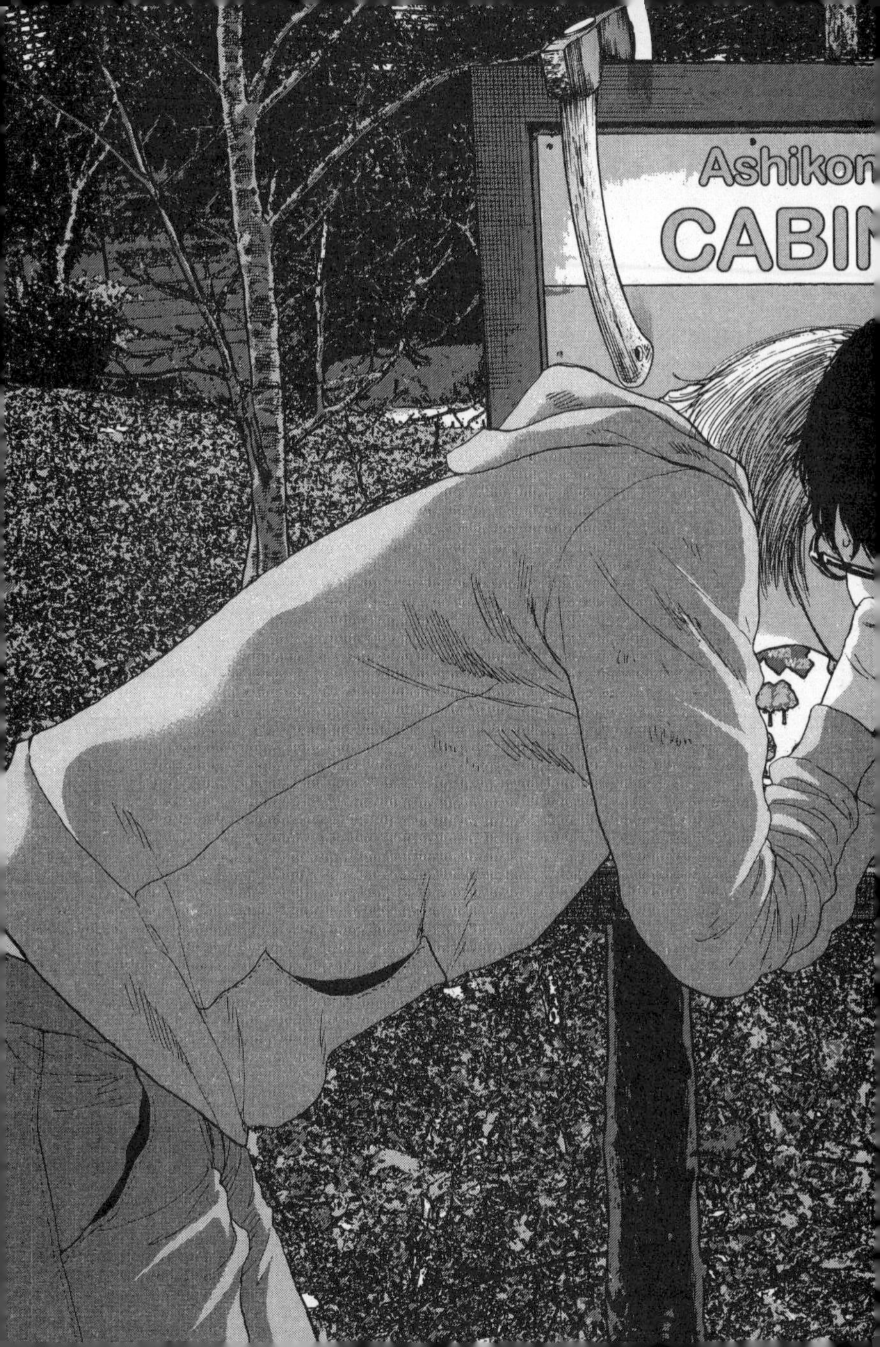
Ashikon
CABIN

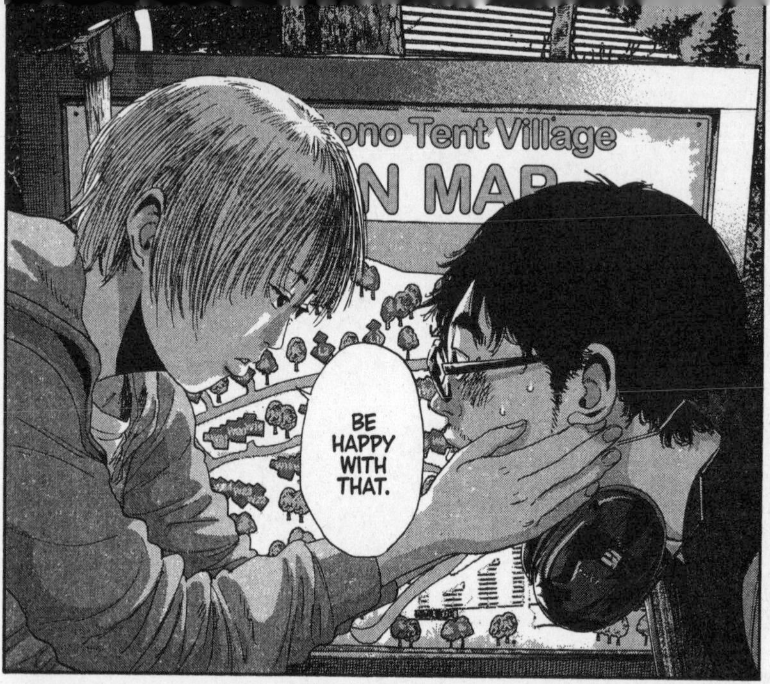
Tent Village
BE HAPPY WITH THAT.

10

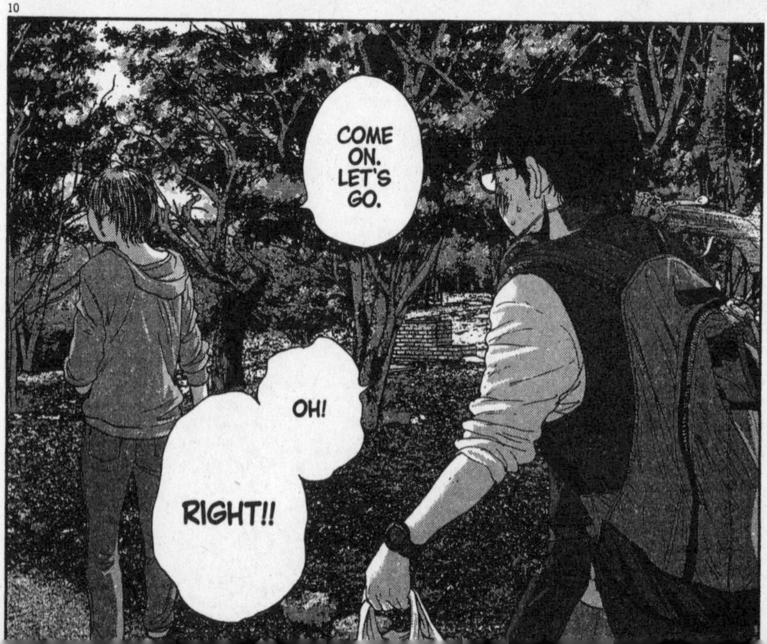
COME ON. LET'S GO.
OH!
RIGHT!!

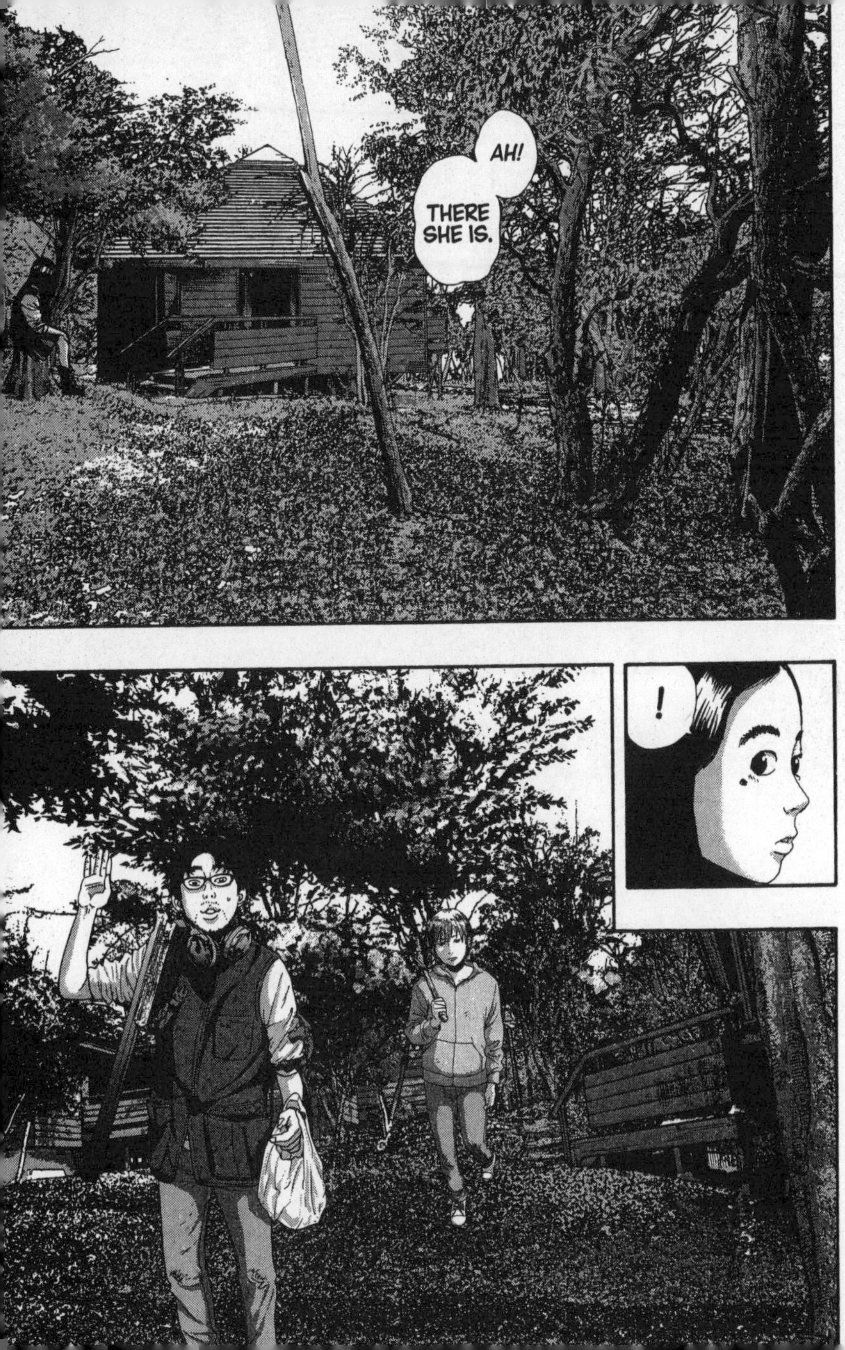
AH!
THERE SHE IS.
!

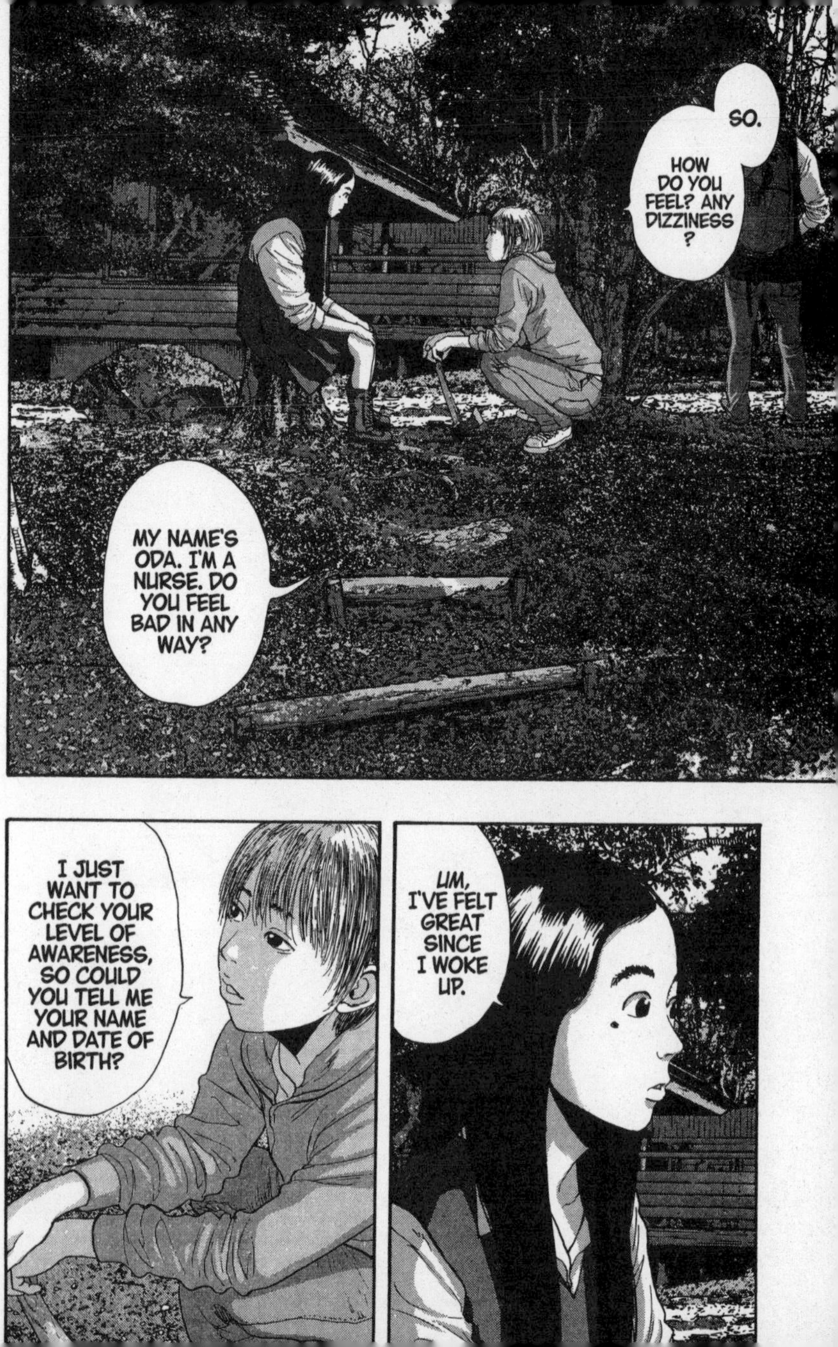
SO.
HOW DO YOU FEEL? ANY DIZZINESS?
MY NAME'S ODA. I'M A NURSE. DO YOU FEEL BAD IN ANY WAY?
UM, I'VE FELT GREAT SINCE I WOKE UP.
I JUST WANT TO CHECK YOUR LEVEL OF AWARENESS, SO COULD YOU TELL ME YOUR NAME AND DATE OF BIRTH?

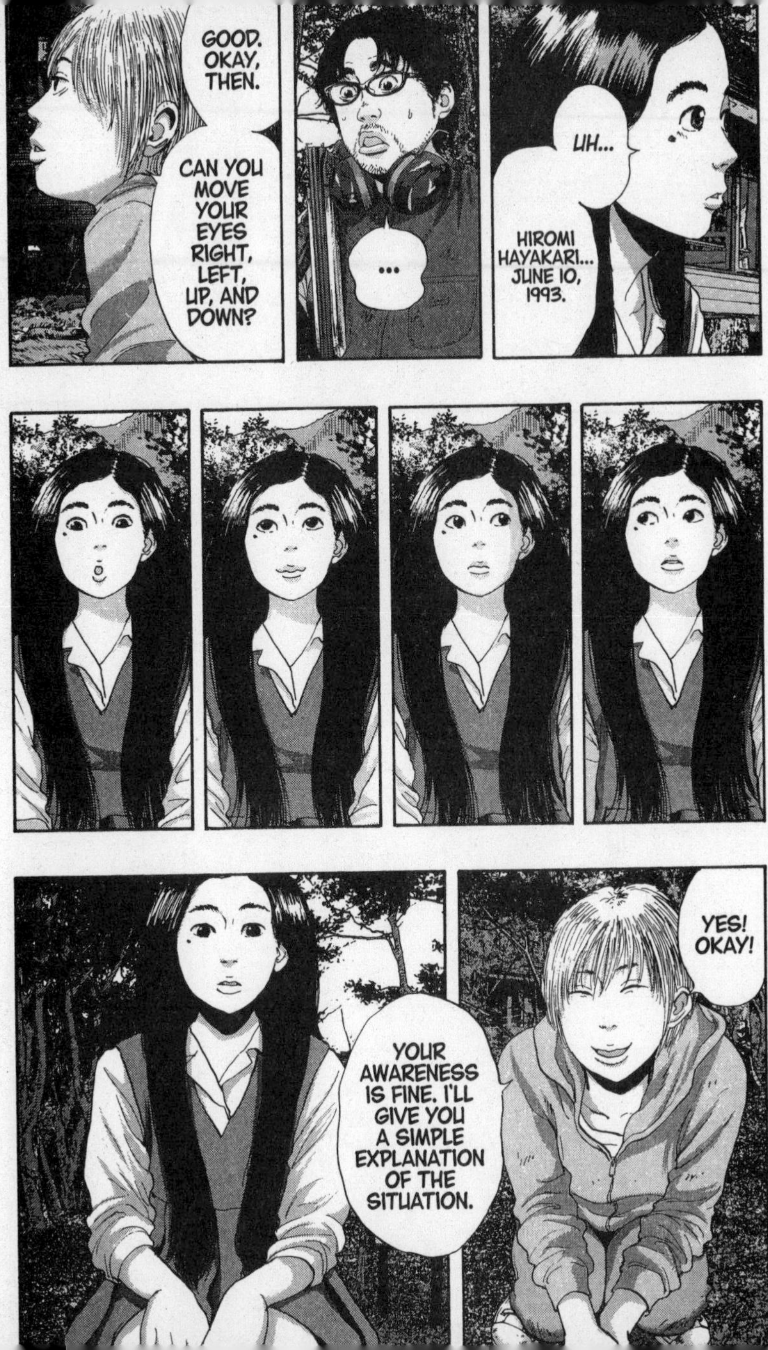
UH...
HIROMI HAYAKARI... JUNE 10, 1993.
...
GOOD. OKAY, THEN.
CAN YOU MOVE YOUR EYES RIGHT, LEFT, UP, AND DOWN?
YES! OKAY!
YOUR AWARENESS IS FINE. I'LL GIVE YOU A SIMPLE EXPLANATION OF THE SITUATION.

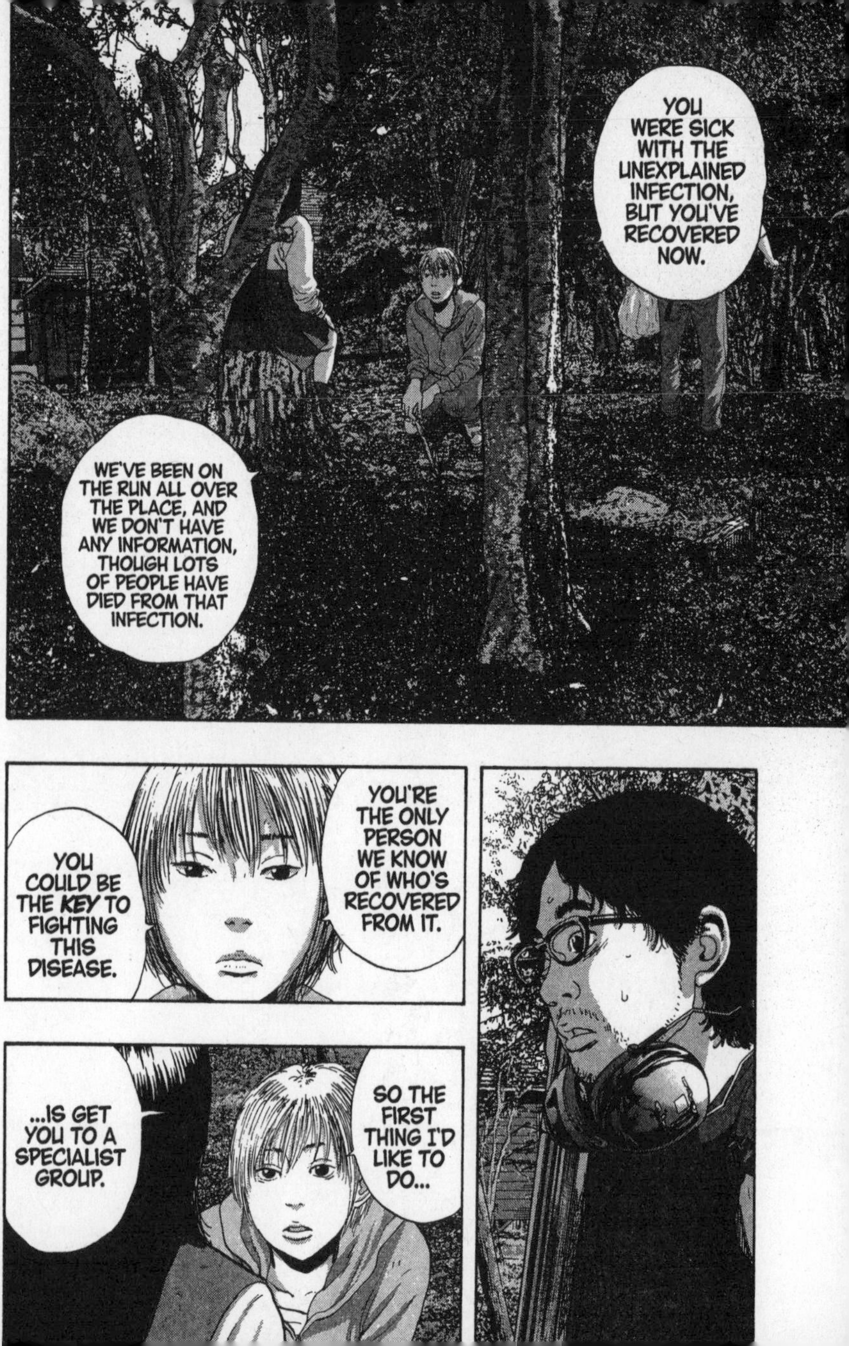
YOU WERE SICK WITH THE UNEXPLAINED INFECTION, BUT YOU'VE RECOVERED NOW.
WE'VE BEEN ON THE RUN ALL OVER THE PLACE, AND WE DON'T HAVE ANY INFORMATION, THOUGH LOTS OF PEOPLE HAVE DIED FROM THAT INFECTION.
YOU'RE THE ONLY PERSON WE KNOW OF WHO'S RECOVERED FROM IT.
YOU COULD BE THE *KEY* TO FIGHTING THIS DISEASE.
SO THE FIRST THING I'D LIKE TO DO...
...IS GET YOU TO A SPECIALIST GROUP.

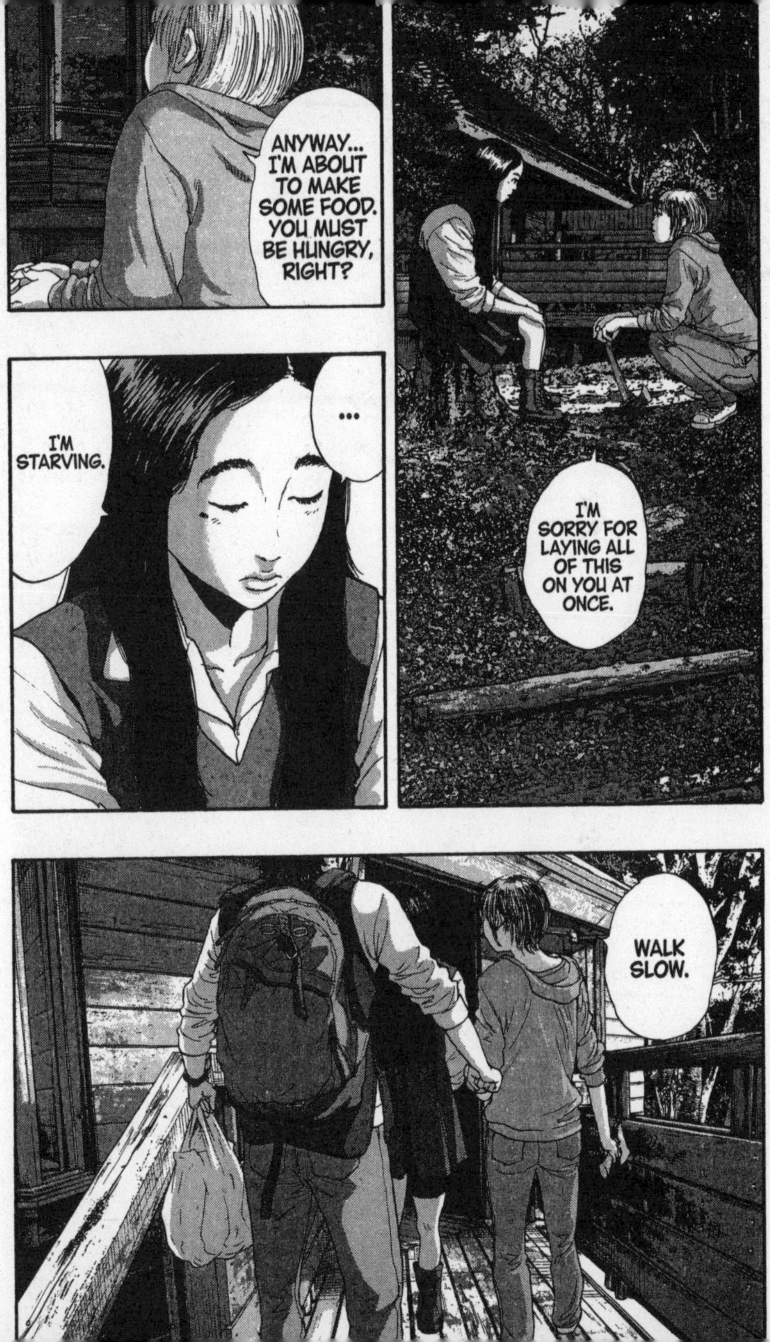
I'M SORRY FOR LAYING ALL OF THIS ON YOU AT ONCE.
ANYWAY... I'M ABOUT TO MAKE SOME FOOD. YOU MUST BE HUNGRY, RIGHT?
...
I'M STARVING.
WALK SLOW.

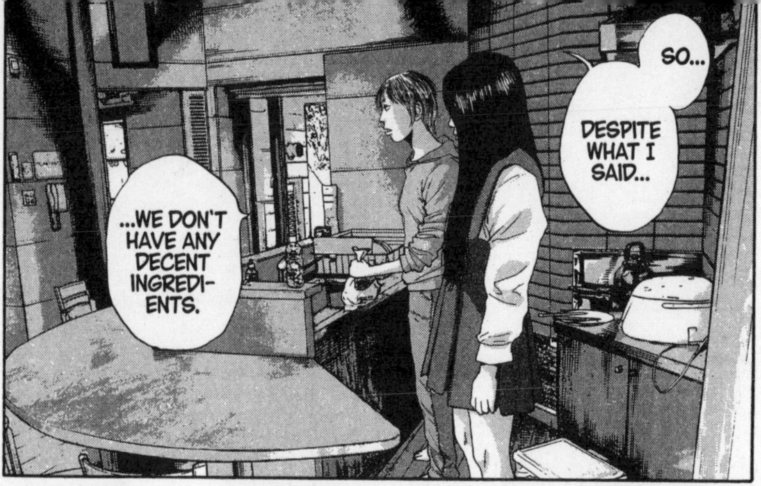
SO...
DESPITE WHAT I SAID...
...WE DON'T HAVE ANY DECENT INGREDI-ENTS.

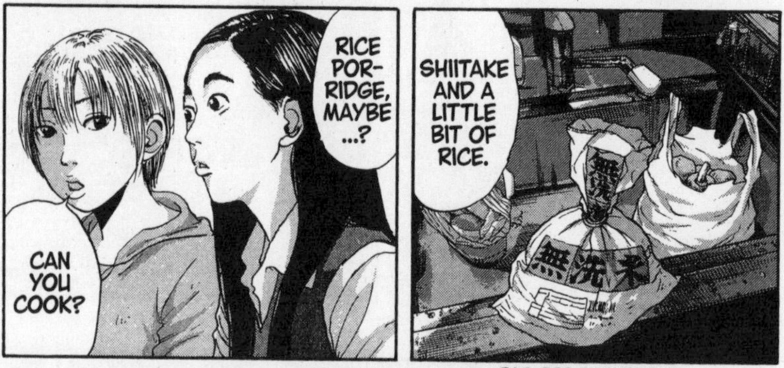
SHIITAKE AND A LITTLE BIT OF RICE.
無洗米
RICE POR-RIDGE, MAYBE ...?
CAN YOU COOK?

BAG: PRE-WASHED RICE

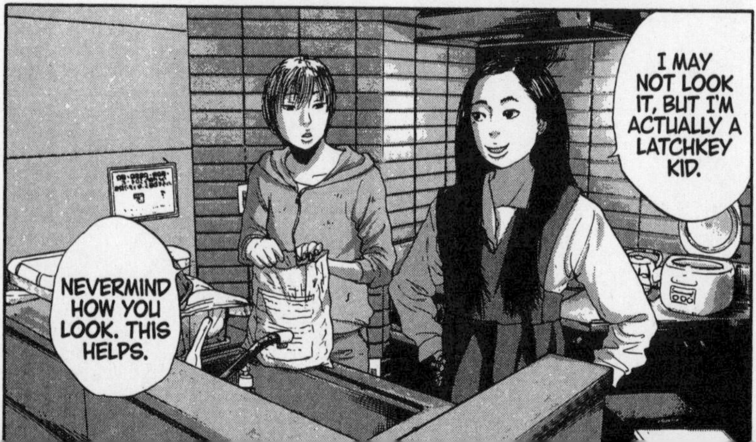
I MAY NOT LOOK IT, BUT I'M ACTUALLY A LATCHKEY KID.
NEVERMIND HOW YOU LOOK. THIS HELPS.

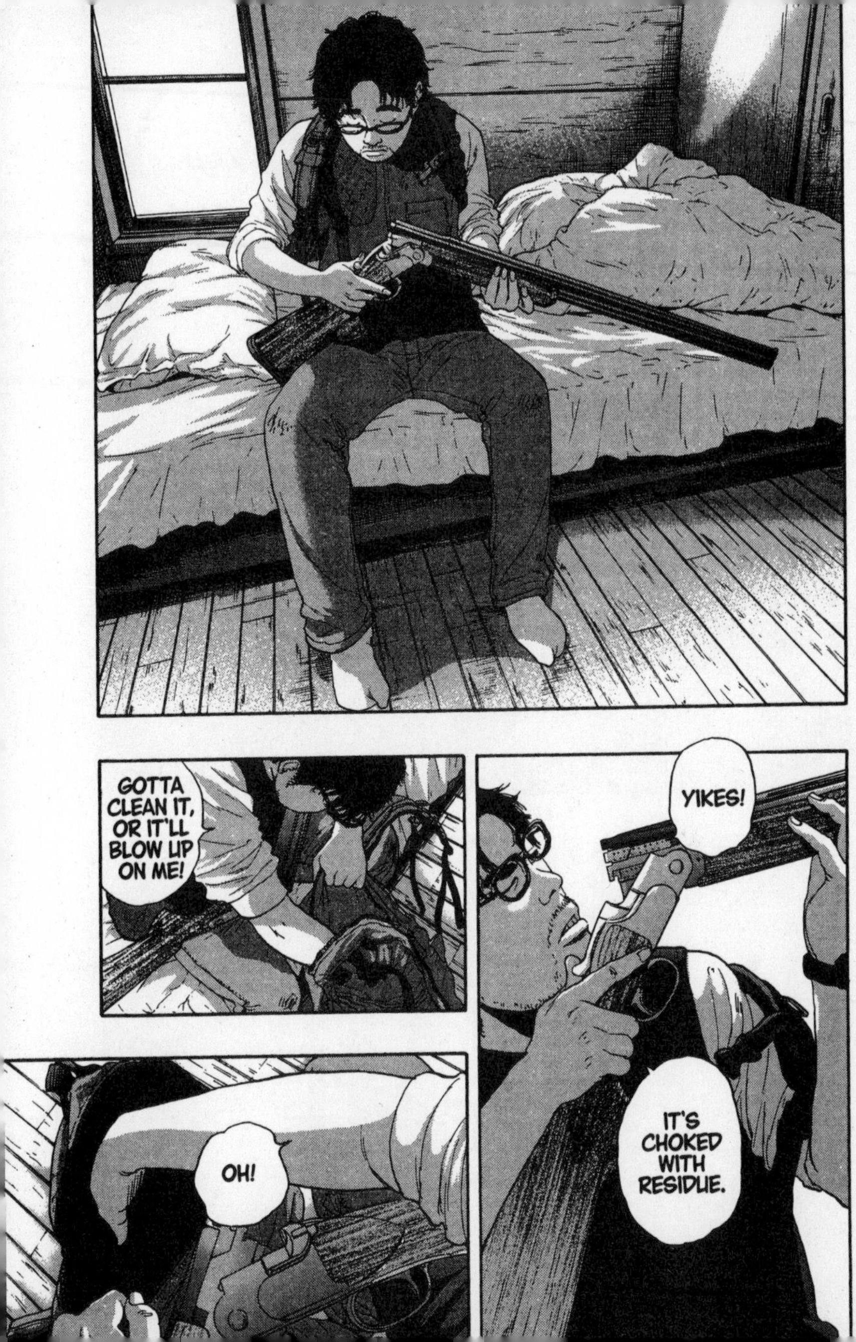
YIKES!
IT'S CHOKED WITH RESIDUE.
GOTTA CLEAN IT, OR IT'LL BLOW UP ON ME!
OH!

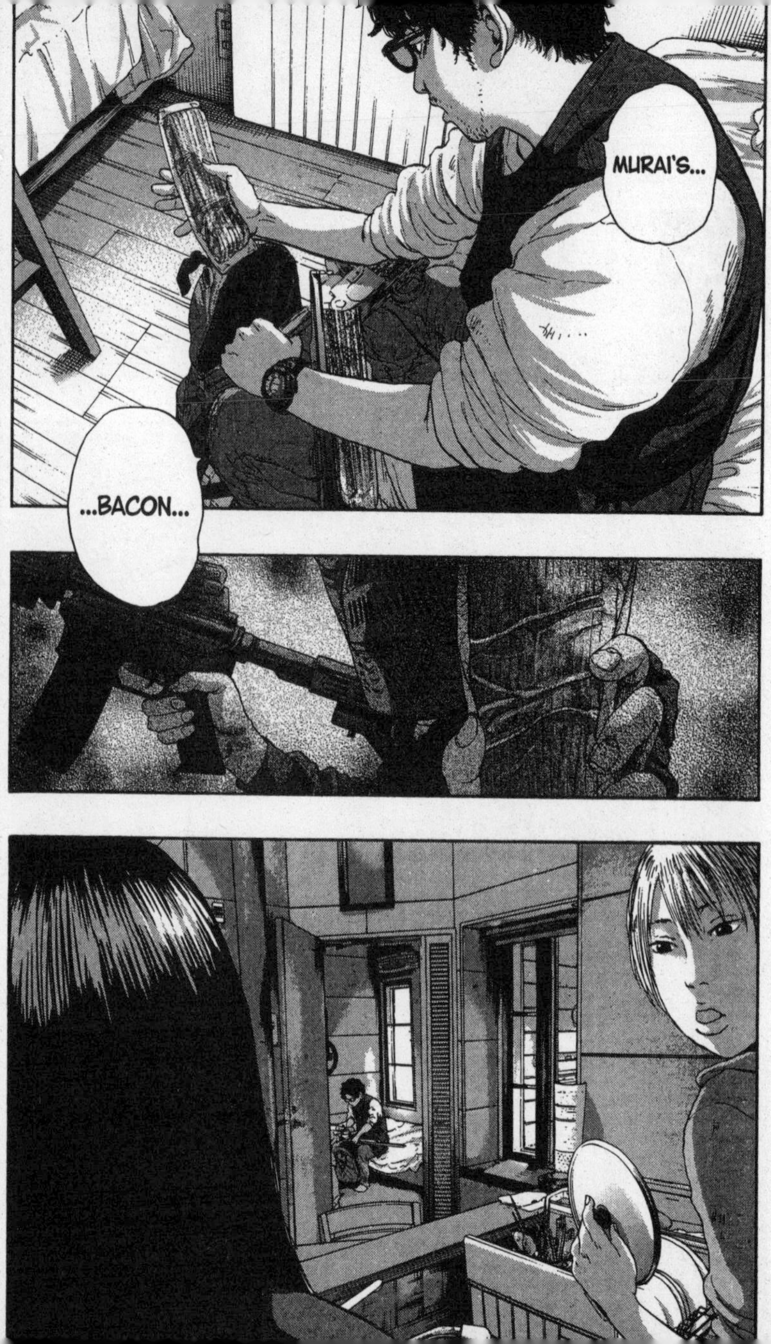
MURAI'S...
...BACON...

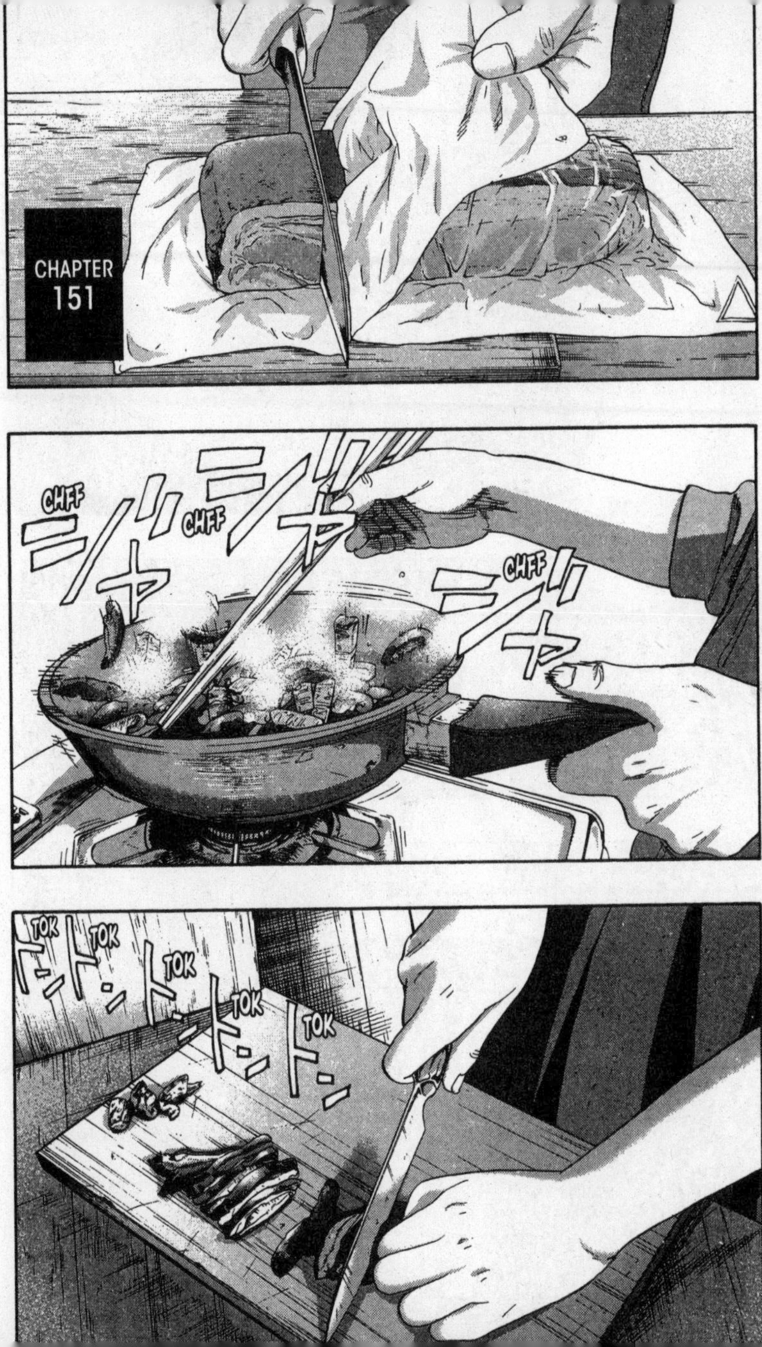
CHAPTER
151
CHFF
CHFF
CHFF
TOK
TOK
TOK
TOK
TOK

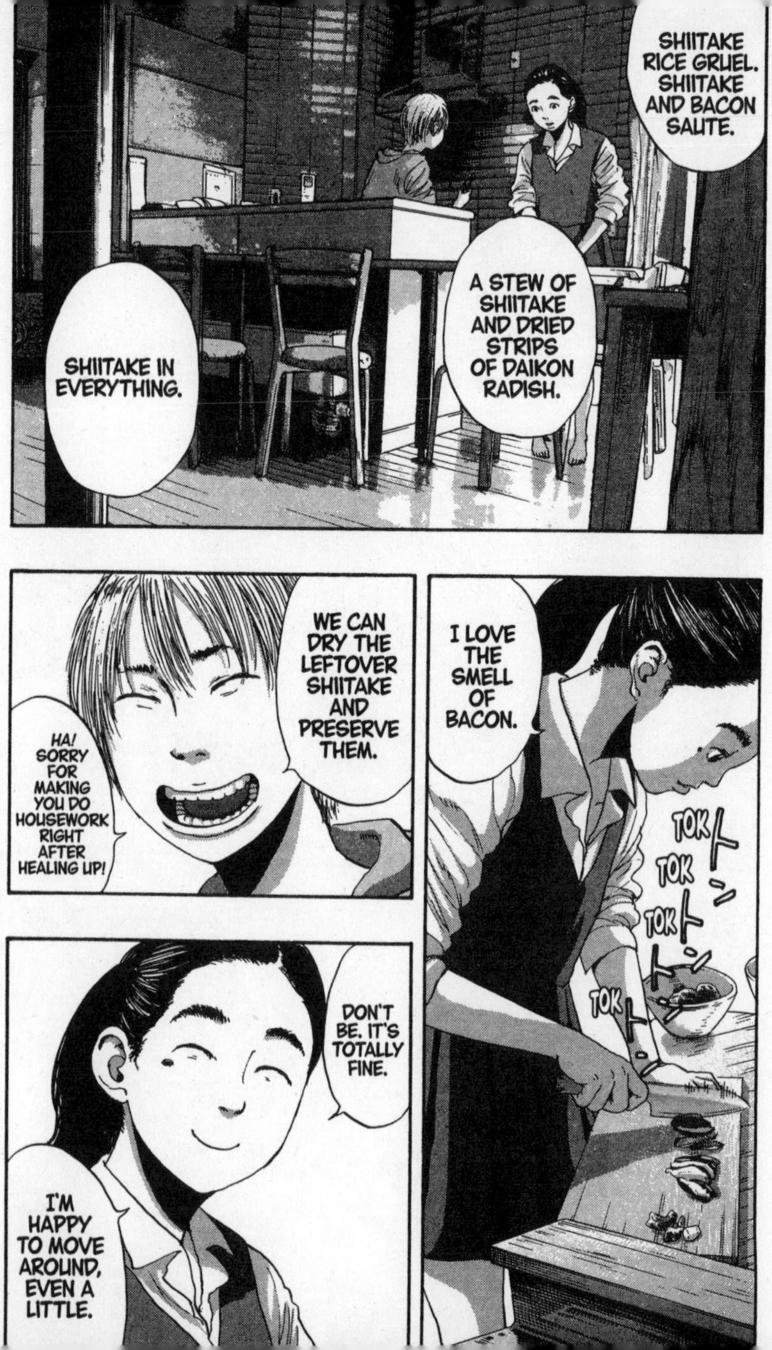
SHIITAKE RICE GRUEL. SHIITAKE AND BACON SAUTE.
A STEW OF SHIITAKE AND DRIED STRIPS OF DAIKON RADISH.
SHIITAKE IN EVERYTHING.
I LOVE THE SMELL OF BACON.
TOK
TOK
TOK
TOK
WE CAN DRY THE LEFTOVER SHIITAKE AND PRESERVE THEM.
HA! SORRY FOR MAKING YOU DO HOUSEWORK RIGHT AFTER HEALING UP!
DON'T BE. IT'S TOTALLY FINE.
I'M HAPPY TO MOVE AROUND, EVEN A LITTLE.

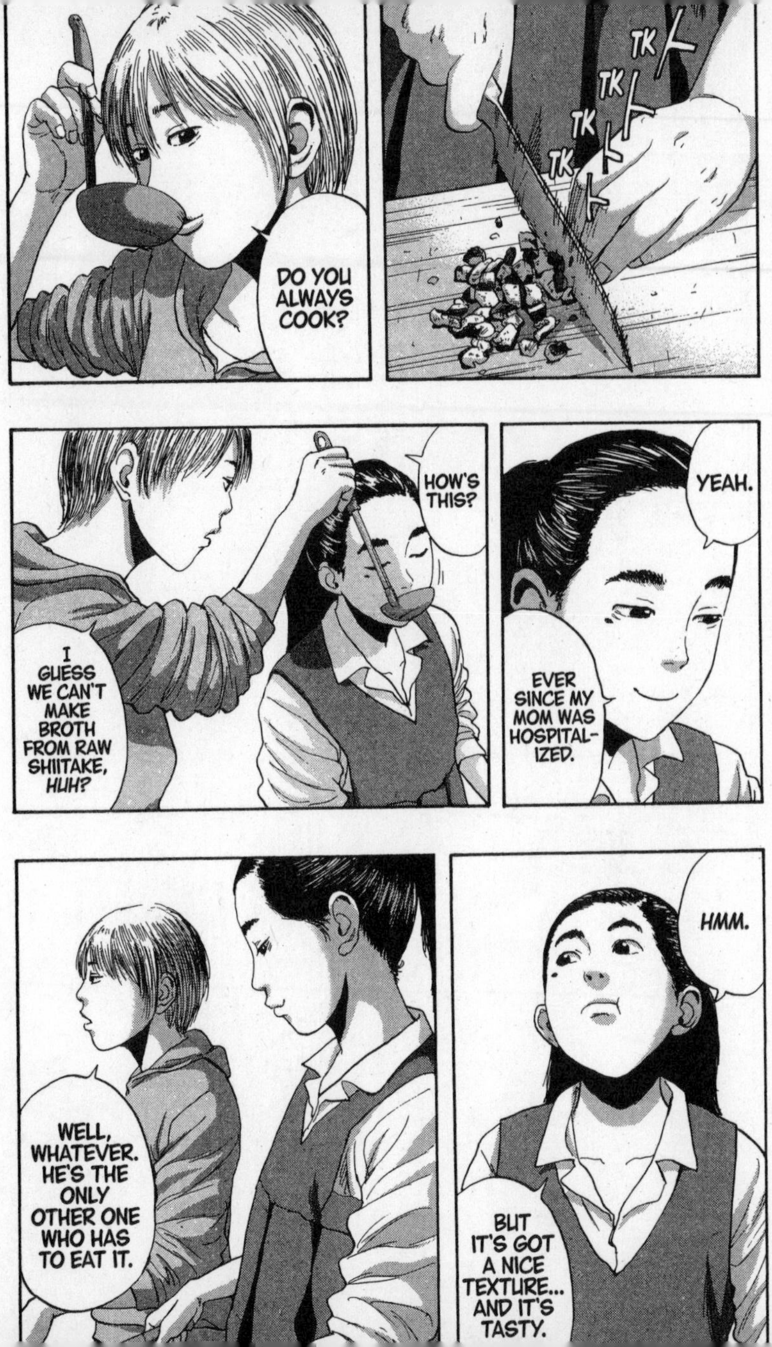
TK TK TK TK
DO YOU ALWAYS COOK?
YEAH.
EVER SINCE MY MOM WAS HOSPITAL-IZED.
HOW'S THIS?
I GUESS WE CAN'T MAKE BROTH FROM RAW SHIITAKE, HUH?
HMM.
BUT IT'S GOT A NICE TEXTURE... AND IT'S TASTY.
WELL, WHATEVER. HE'S THE ONLY OTHER ONE WHO HAS TO EAT IT.

WHPP

KCHIK

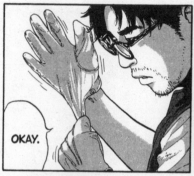

OKAY.

WHK
WHK
WHK

FWSH

FWSH

SQUICK

SQUICK

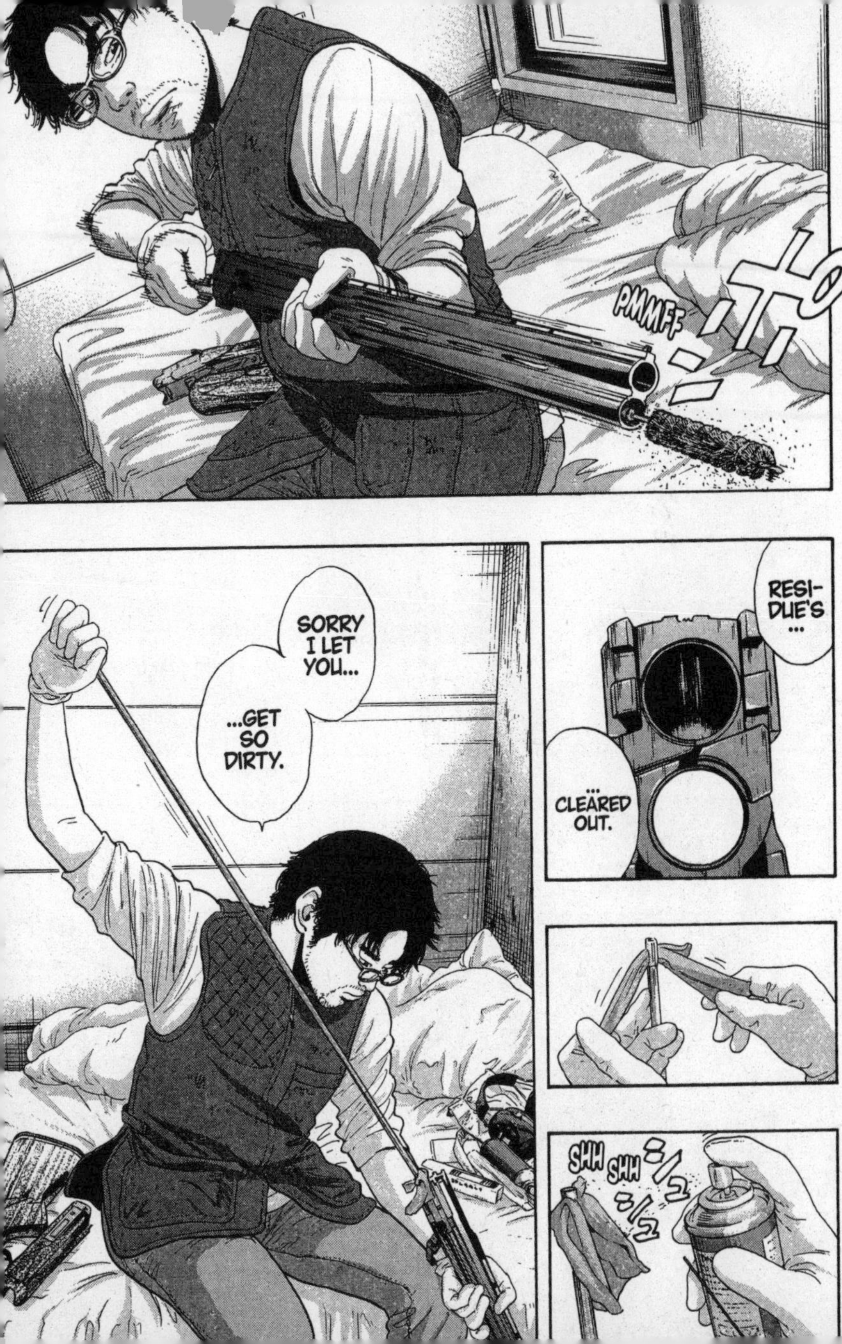
PMMFF
RESI-
DUE'S
...
...
CLEARED
OUT.
SHH SHH
SORRY
I LET
YOU...
...GET
SO
DIRTY.

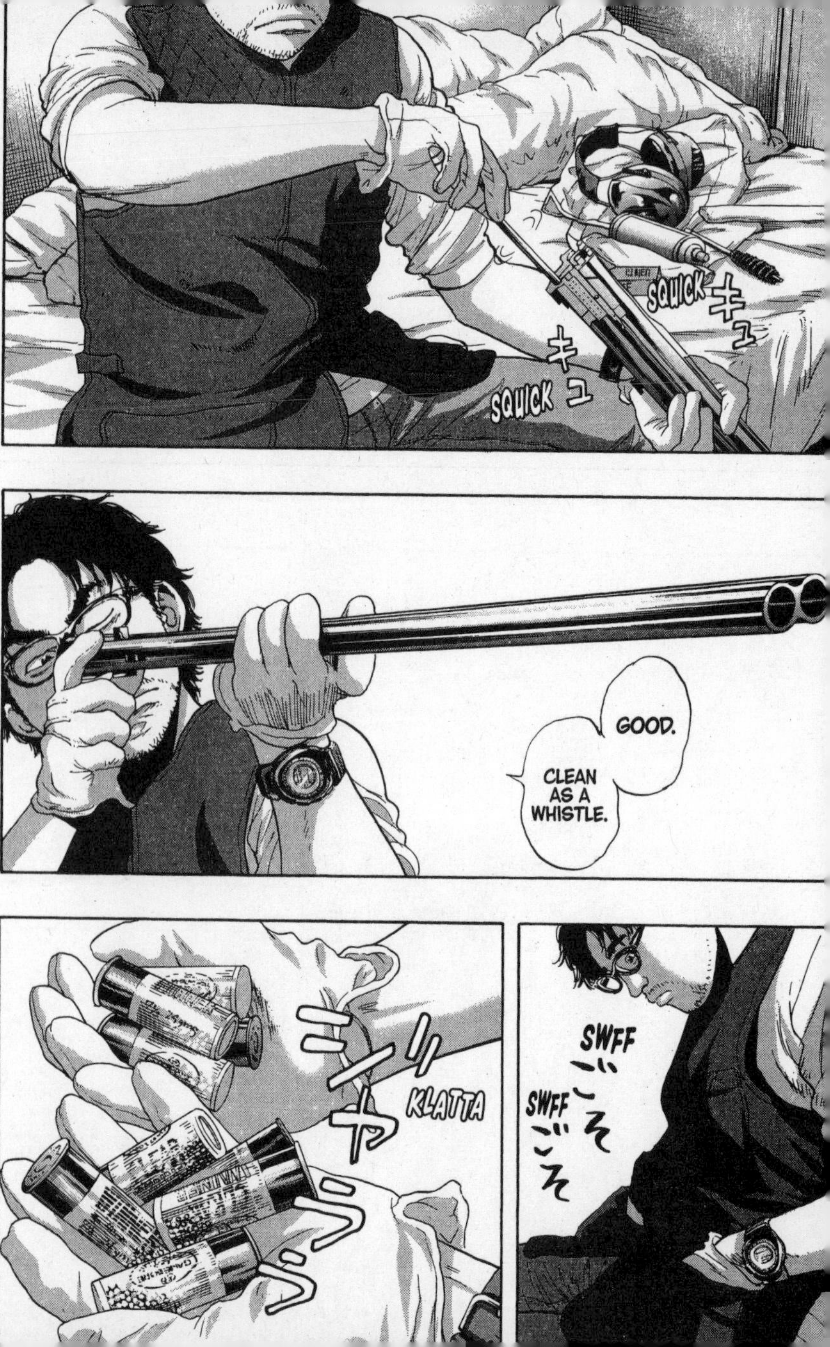

SQUICK
キュ
キュ
SQUICK
GOOD.
CLEAN AS A WHISTLE.
SWFF
ごそ
SWFF
ごそ
KLATTA

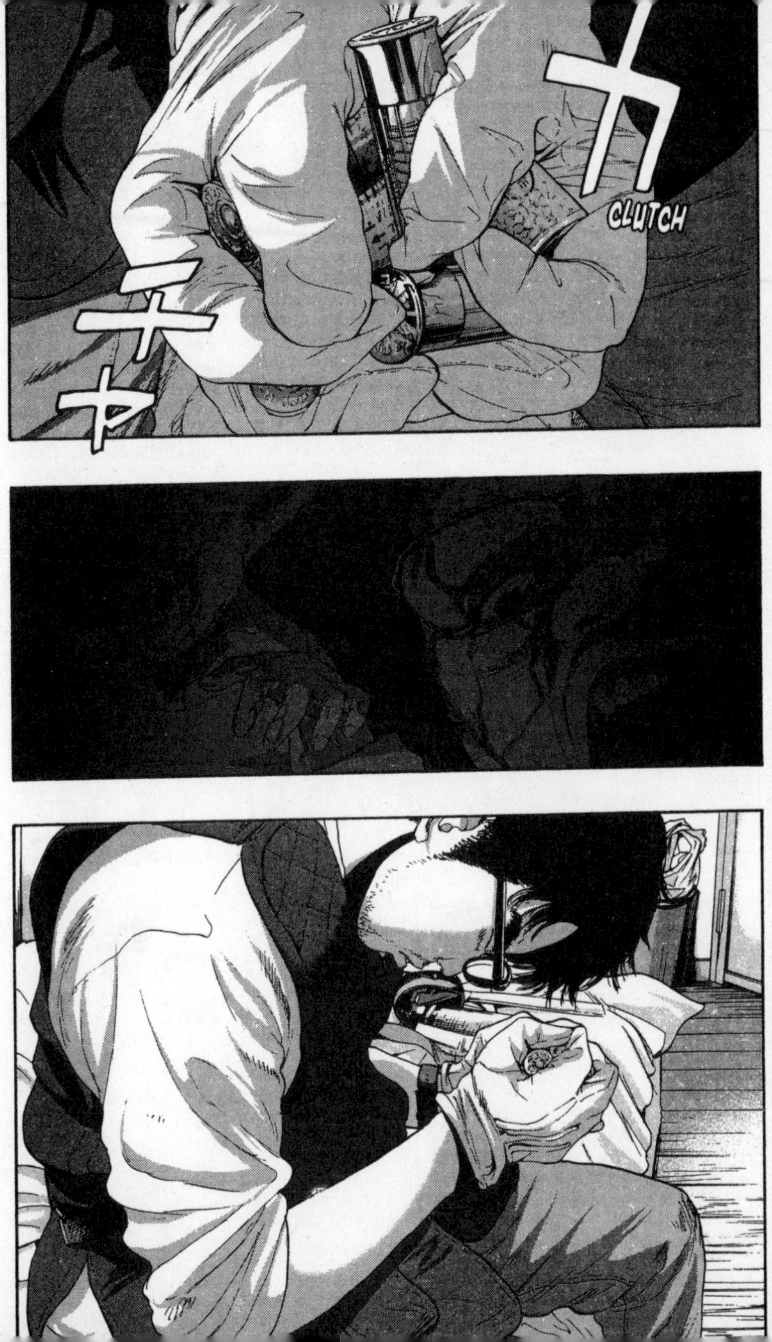
CLUTCH

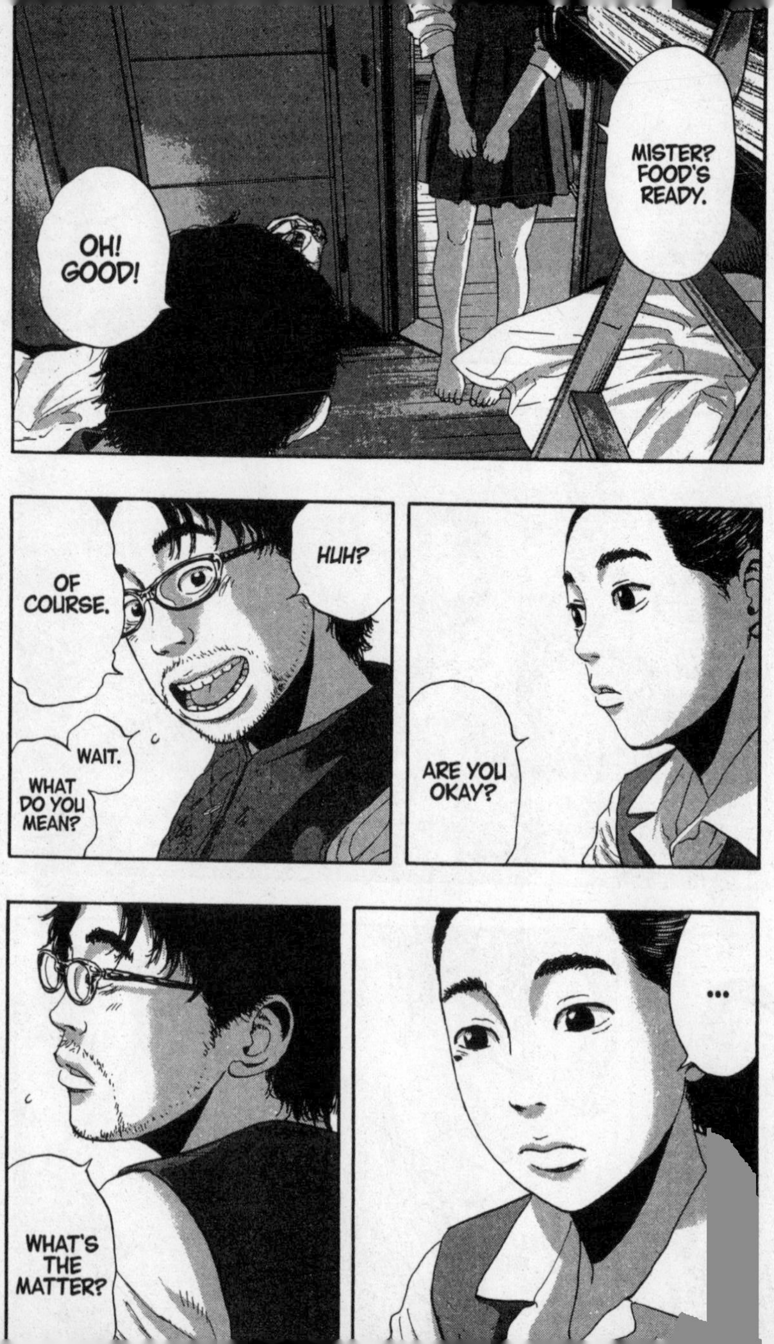
MISTER? FOOD'S READY.
OH! GOOD!
ARE YOU OKAY?
HUH?
OF COURSE.
WAIT.
WHAT DO YOU MEAN?
...
WHAT'S THE MATTER?

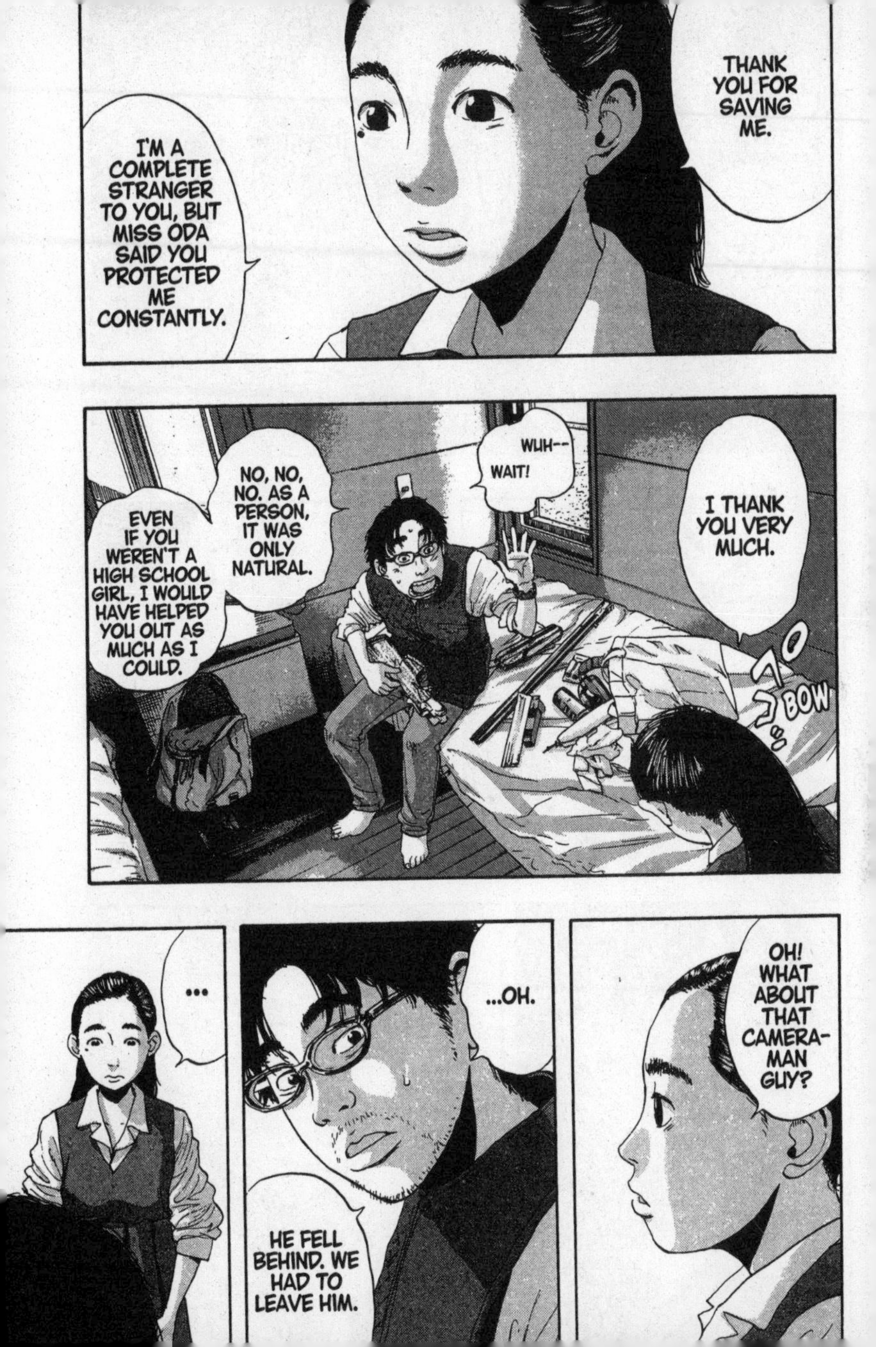
THANK YOU FOR SAVING ME.
I'M A COMPLETE STRANGER TO YOU, BUT MISS ODA SAID YOU PROTECTED ME CONSTANTLY.
I THANK YOU VERY MUCH.
BOW
WUH-- WAIT!
NO, NO, NO. AS A PERSON, IT WAS ONLY NATURAL.
EVEN IF YOU WEREN'T A HIGH SCHOOL GIRL, I WOULD HAVE HELPED YOU OUT AS MUCH AS I COULD.
OH! WHAT ABOUT THAT CAMERA-MAN GUY?
...OH.
HE FELL BEHIND. WE HAD TO LEAVE HIM.
...

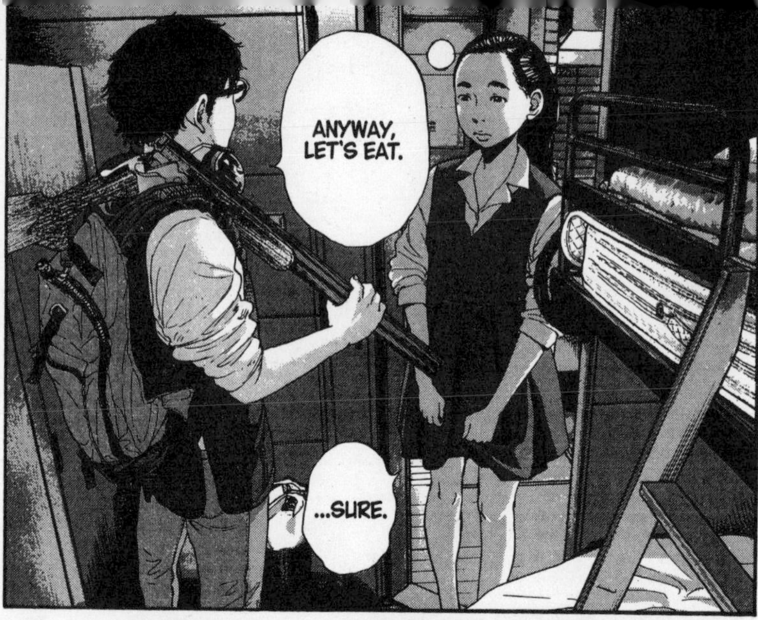
ANYWAY, LET'S EAT.
...SURE.

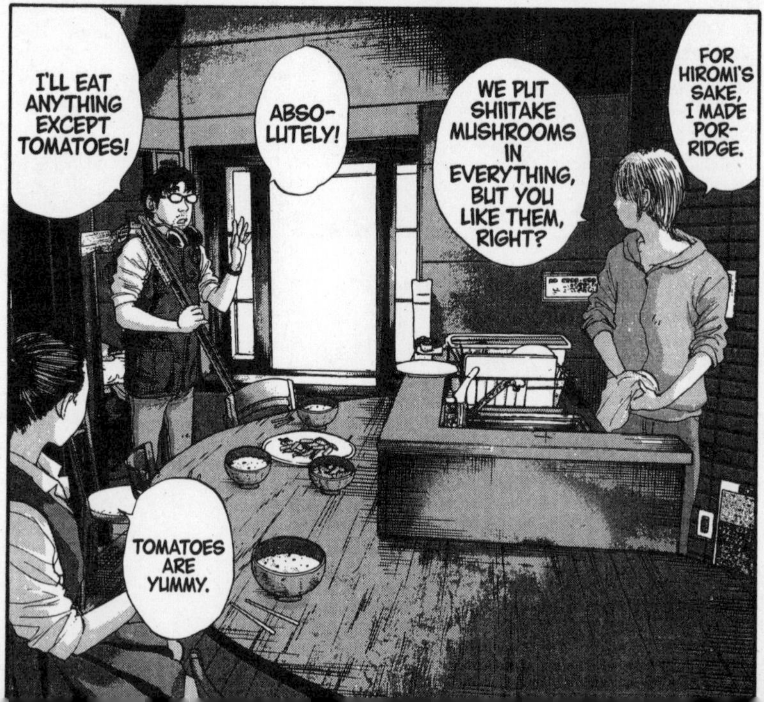
FOR HIROMI'S SAKE, I MADE POR-RIDGE.
WE PUT SHIITAKE MUSHROOMS IN EVERYTHING, BUT YOU LIKE THEM, RIGHT?
ABSO-LUTELY!
I'LL EAT ANYTHING EXCEPT TOMATOES!
TOMATOES ARE YUMMY.

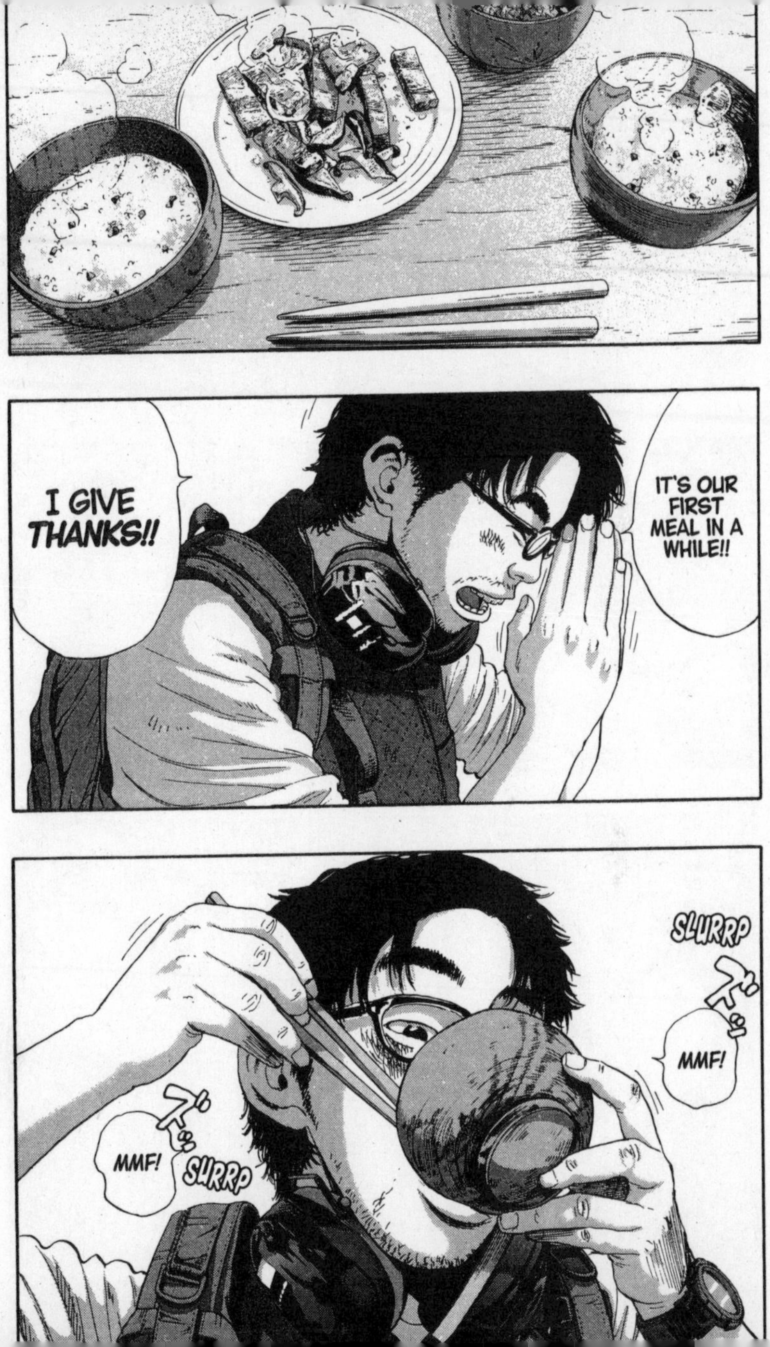
IT'S OUR FIRST MEAL IN A WHILE!!
I GIVE THANKS!!
SLURRP
ズッ
MMF!
ズッ
MMF!
SLURRP

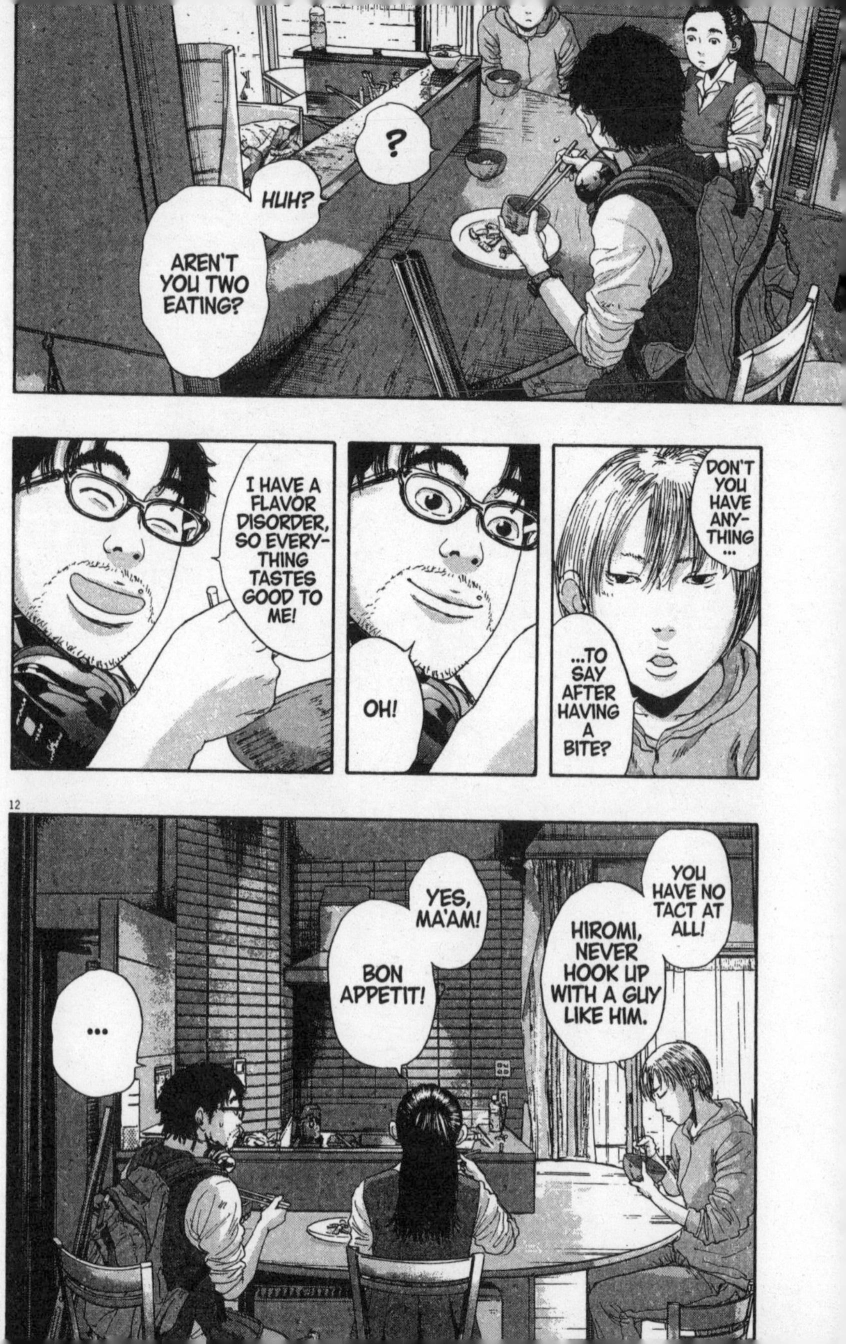
?
HUH?
AREN'T YOU TWO EATING?
DON'T YOU HAVE ANYTHING...
...TO SAY AFTER HAVING A BITE?
OH!
I HAVE A FLAVOR DISORDER, SO EVERYTHING TASTES GOOD TO ME!
YOU HAVE NO TACT AT ALL!
HIROMI, NEVER HOOK UP WITH A GUY LIKE HIM.
YES, MA'AM!
BON APPETIT!
...

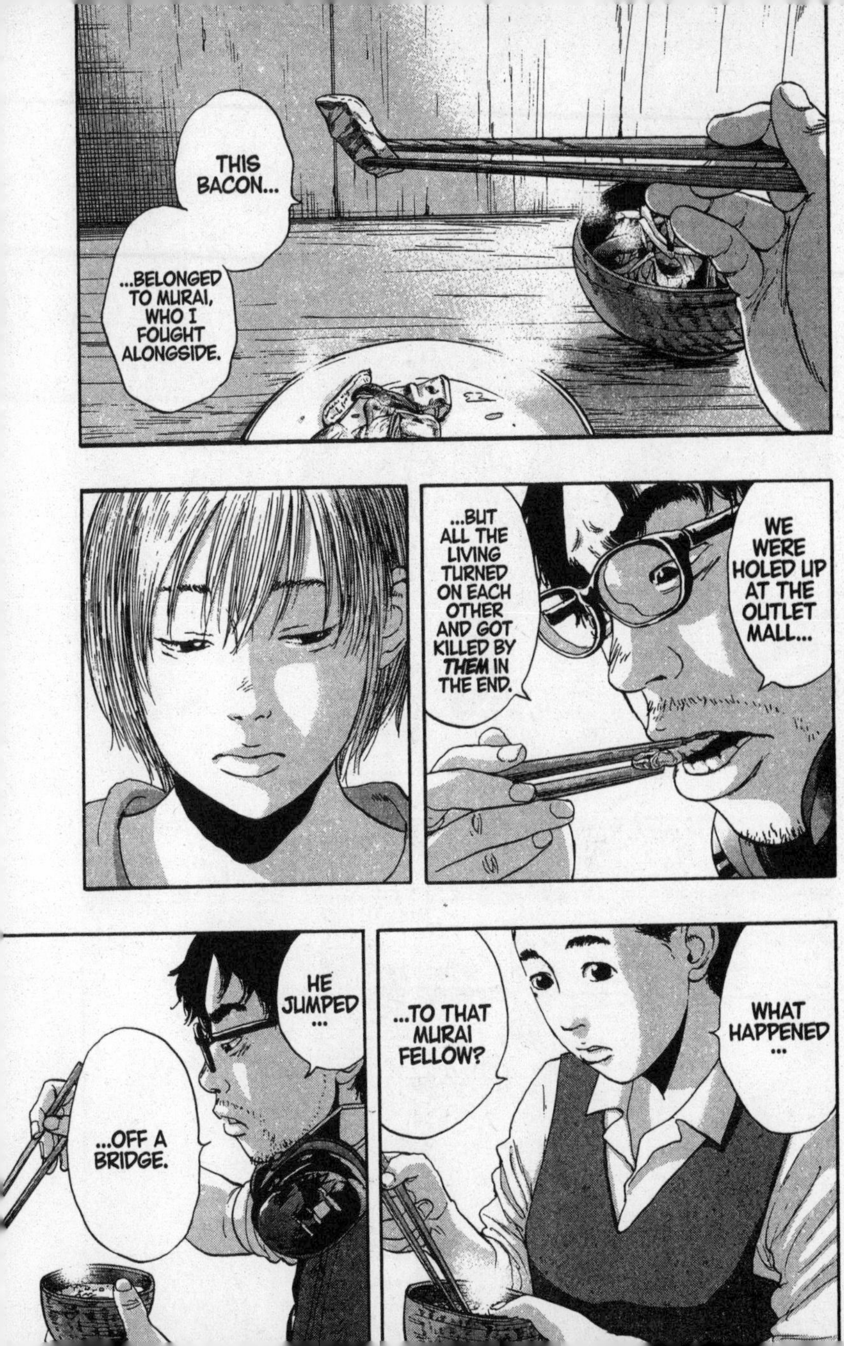
THIS BACON...
...BELONGED TO MURAI, WHO I FOUGHT ALONGSIDE.
WE WERE HOLED UP AT THE OUTLET MALL...
...BUT ALL THE LIVING TURNED ON EACH OTHER AND GOT KILLED BY *THEM* IN THE END.
WHAT HAPPENED...
...TO THAT MURAI FELLOW?
HE JUMPED...
...OFF A BRIDGE.

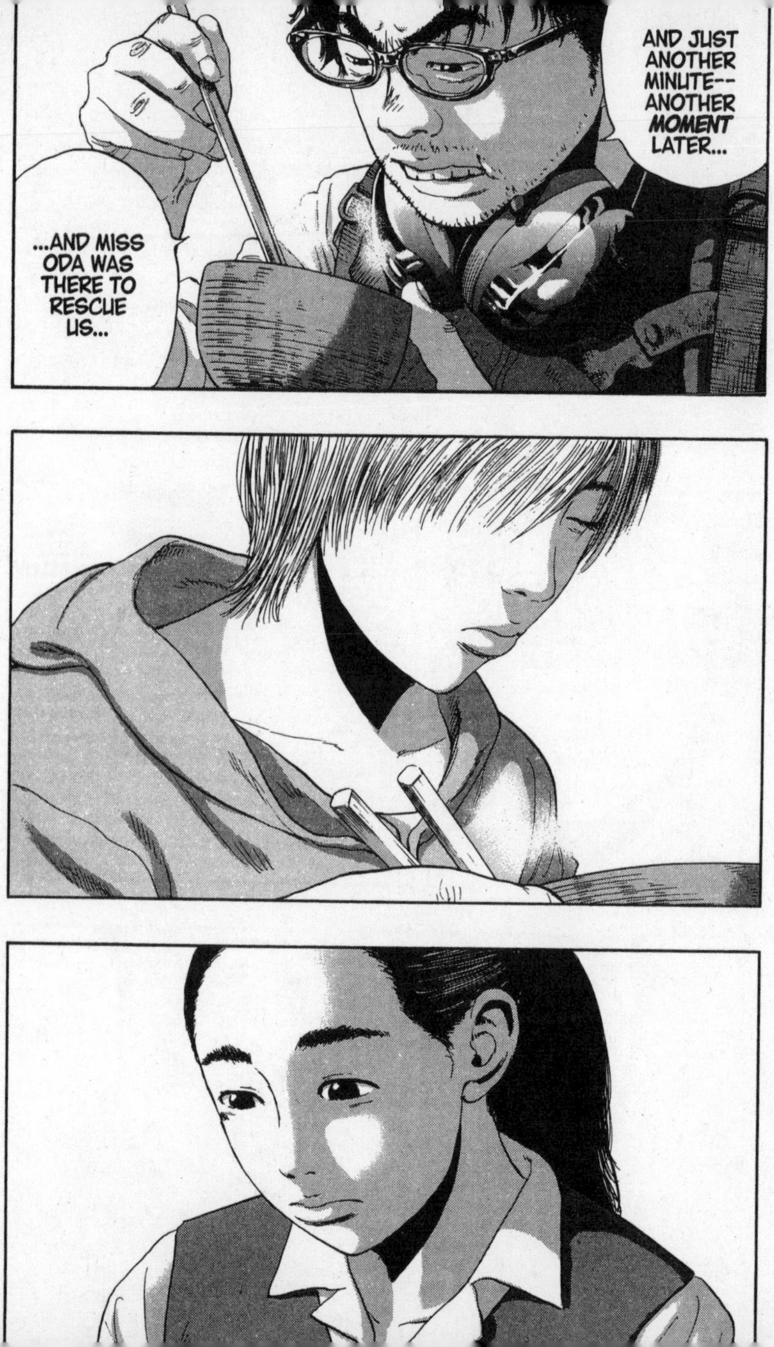
AND JUST ANOTHER MINUTE-- ANOTHER *MOMENT* LATER...
...AND MISS ODA WAS THERE TO RESCUE US...

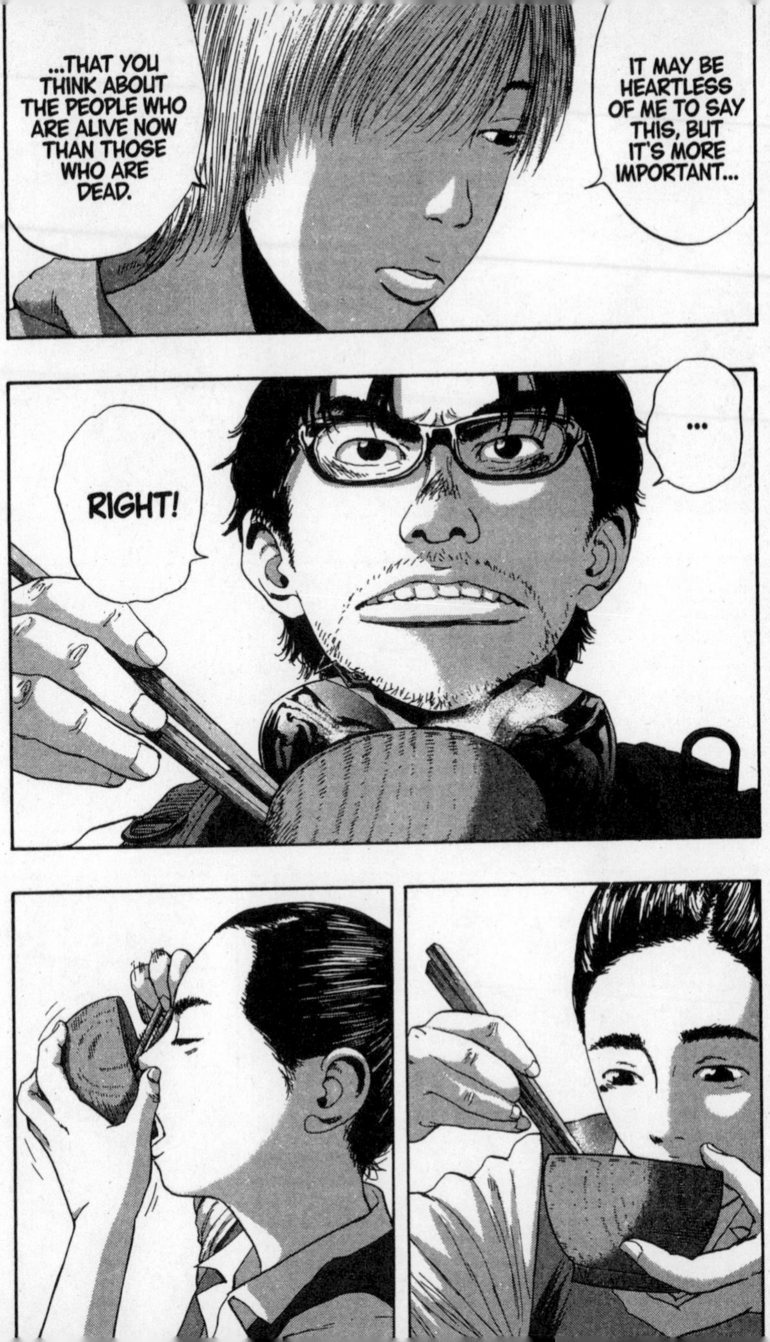
IT MAY BE HEARTLESS OF ME TO SAY THIS, BUT IT'S MORE IMPORTANT...
...THAT YOU THINK ABOUT THE PEOPLE WHO ARE ALIVE NOW THAN THOSE WHO ARE DEAD.
...
RIGHT!

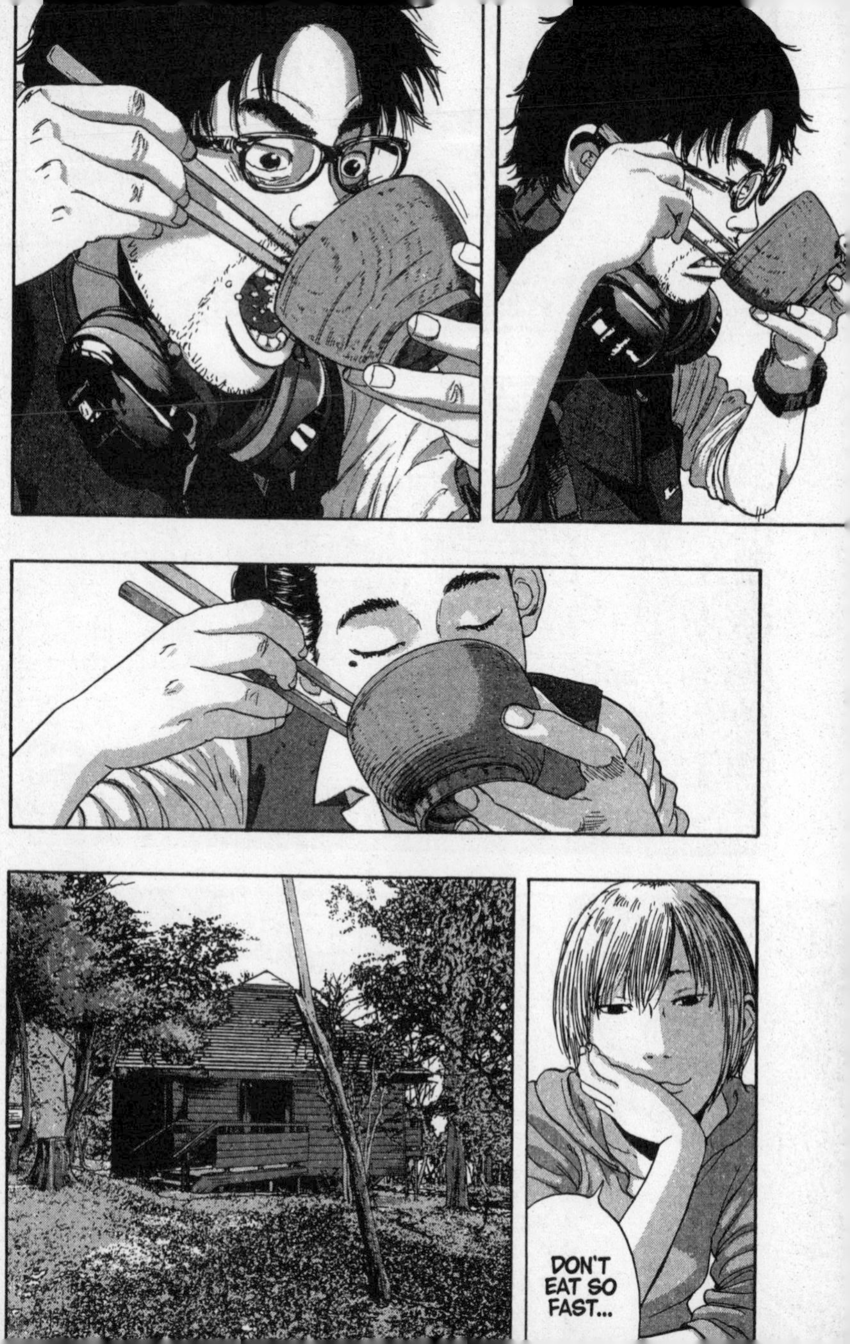
DON'T EAT SO FAST...

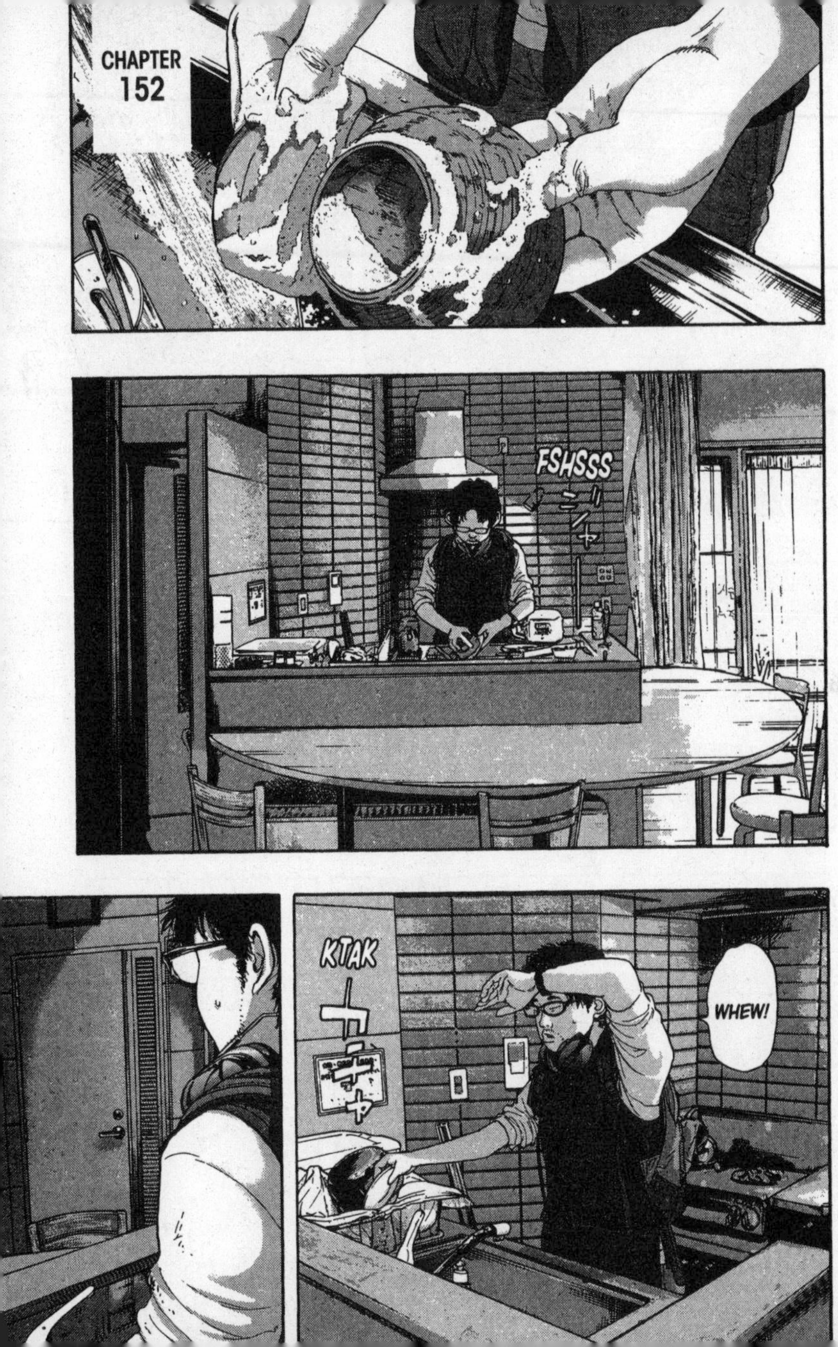
CHAPTER 152
FSHSSS
KTAK
WHEW!

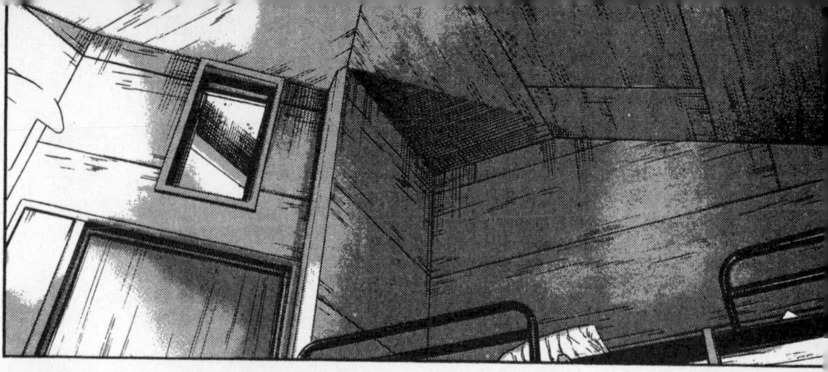

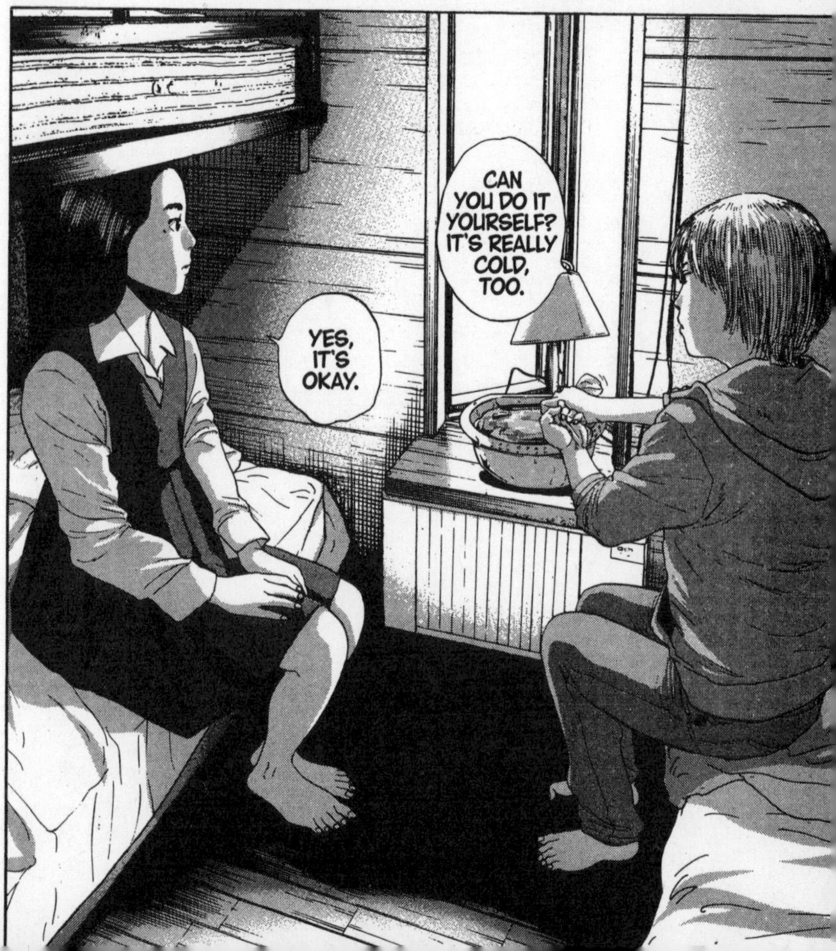
CAN YOU DO IT YOURSELF? IT'S REALLY COLD, TOO.
YES, IT'S OKAY.

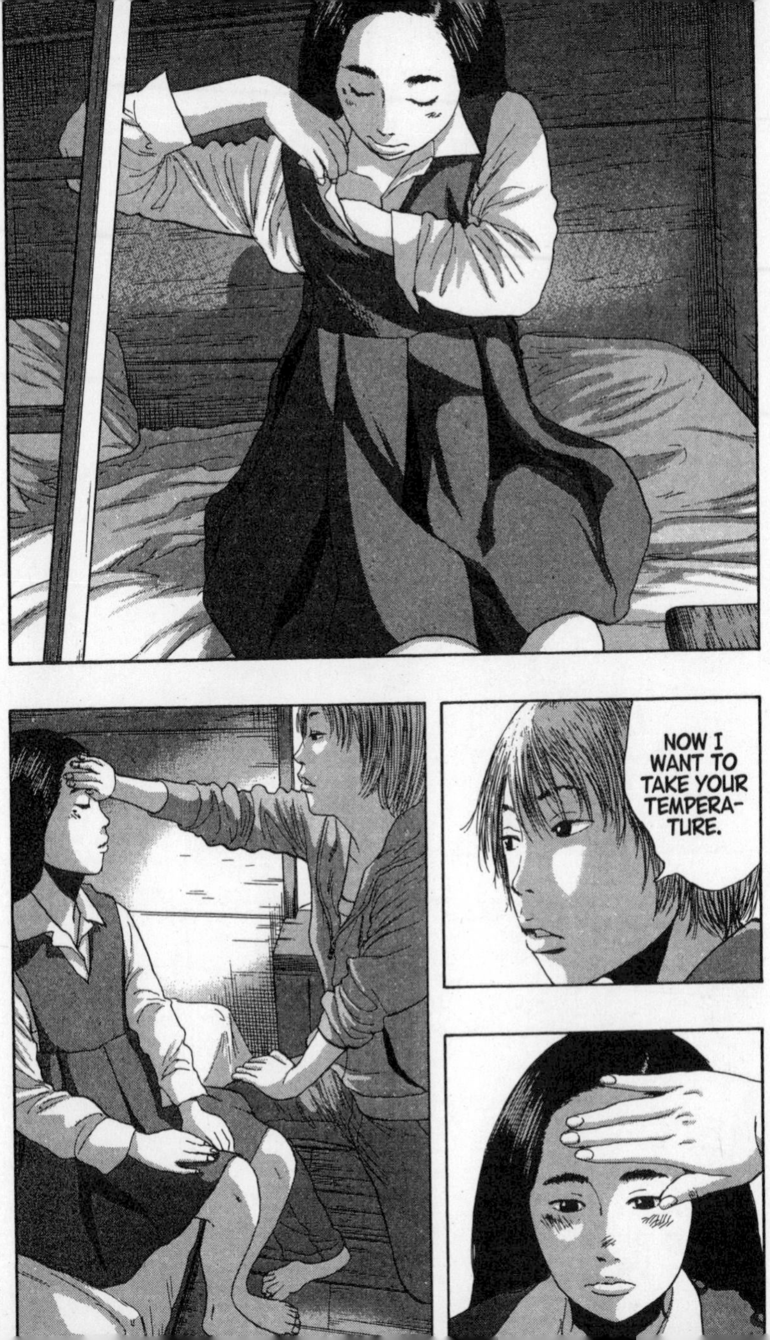
NOW I WANT TO TAKE YOUR TEMPERA-TURE.

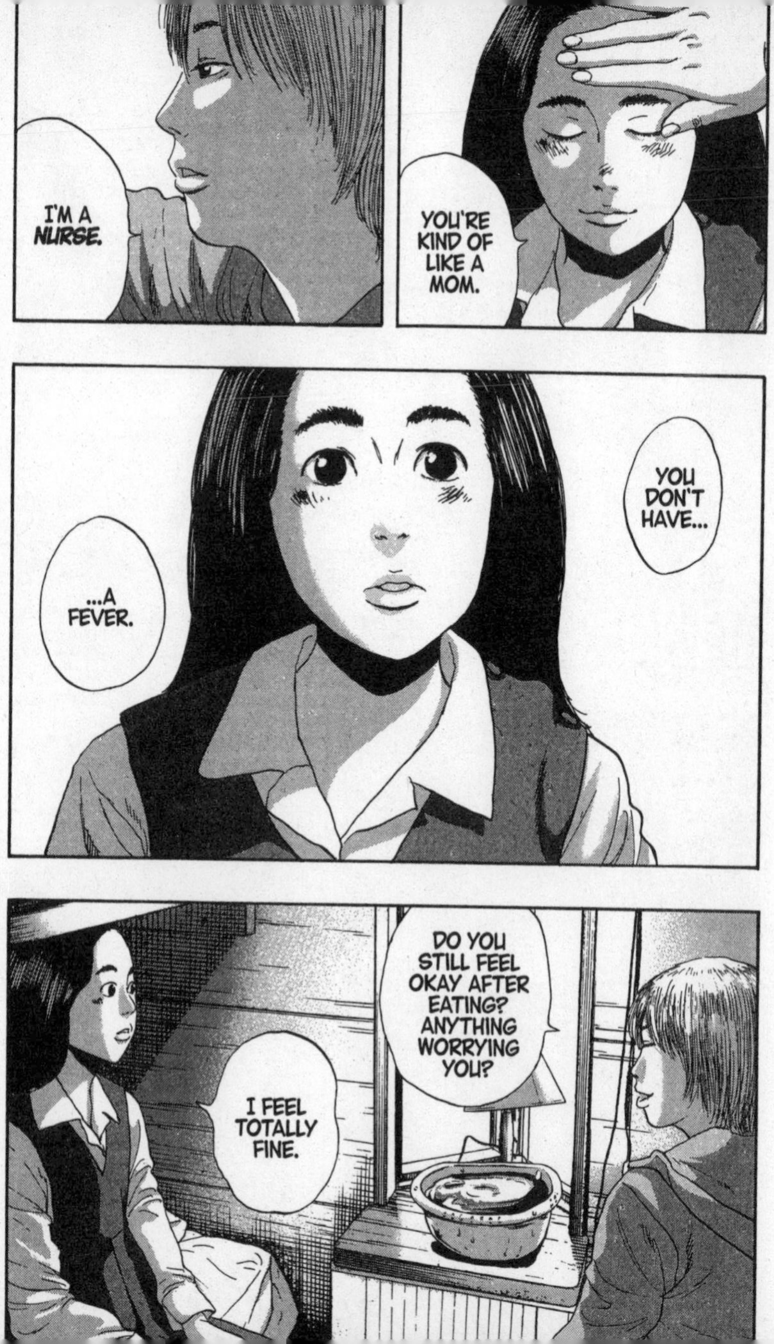
YOU'RE KIND OF LIKE A MOM.
I'M A NURSE.
YOU DON'T HAVE...
...A FEVER.
DO YOU STILL FEEL OKAY AFTER EATING? ANYTHING WORRYING YOU?
I FEEL TOTALLY FINE.

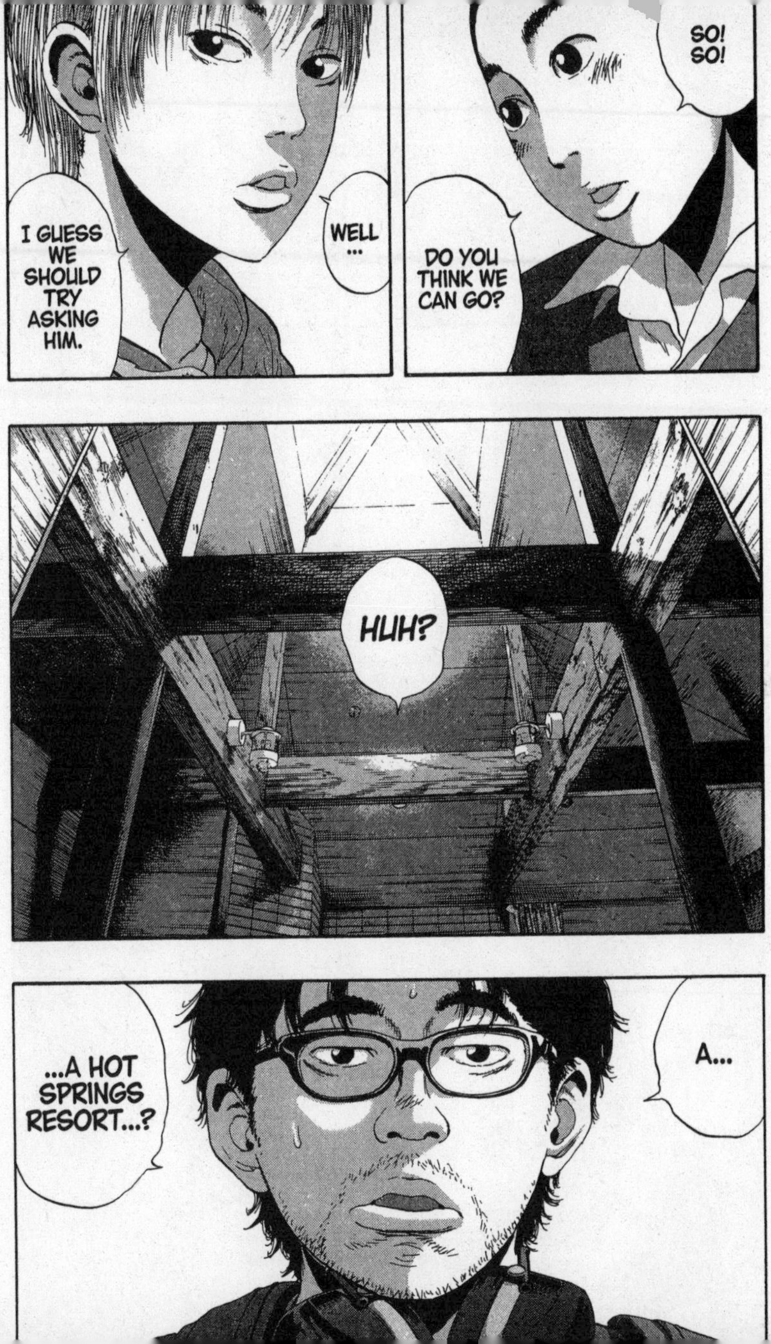
SO! SO!
DO YOU THINK WE CAN GO?
WELL ...
I GUESS WE SHOULD TRY ASKING HIM.
HUH?
A...
...A HOT SPRINGS RESORT...?

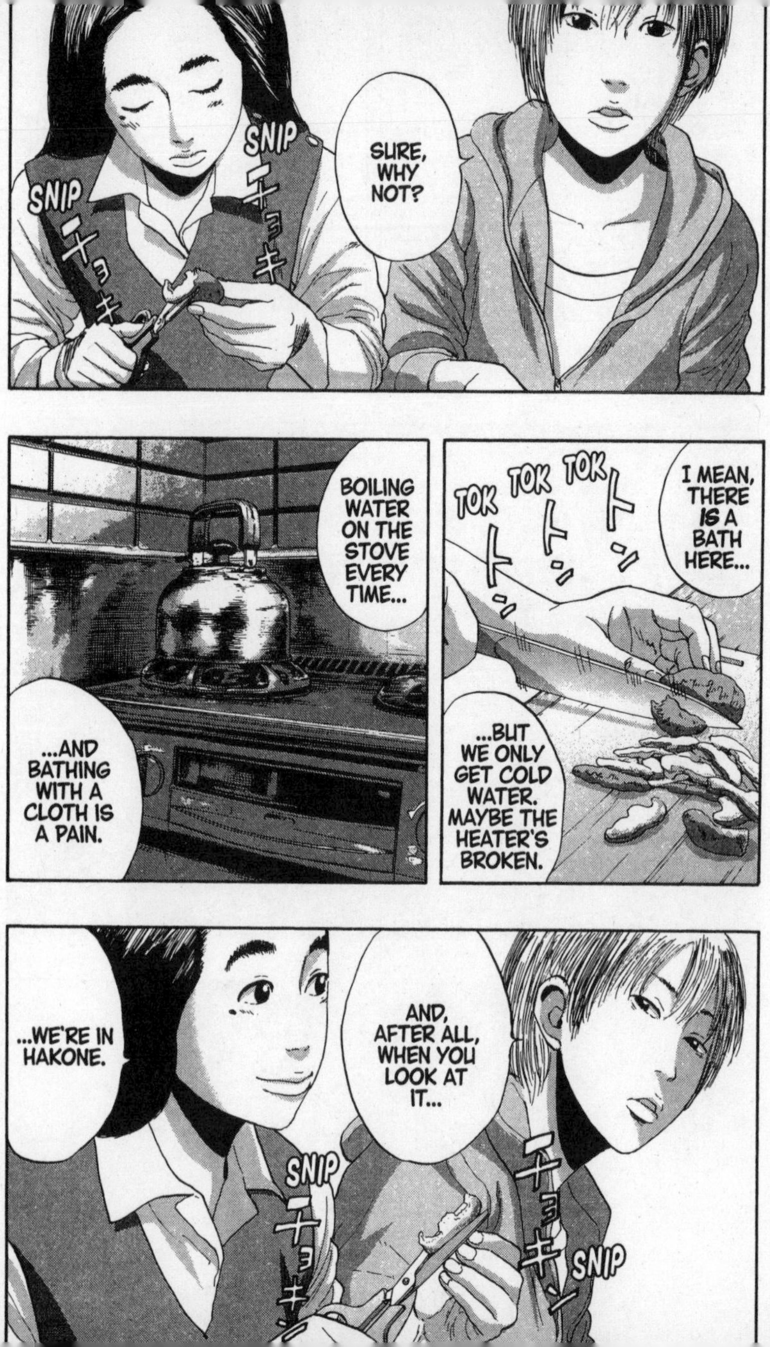
SURE, WHY NOT?
SNIP
チョキ
SNIP
チョキ
I MEAN, THERE IS A BATH HERE...
TOK TOK TOK
トッ
トッ
トッ
...BUT WE ONLY GET COLD WATER. MAYBE THE HEATER'S BROKEN.
BOILING WATER ON THE STOVE EVERY TIME...
...AND BATHING WITH A CLOTH IS A PAIN.
AND, AFTER ALL, WHEN YOU LOOK AT IT...
SNIP
チョキン
...WE'RE IN HAKONE.
SNIP
チョキン

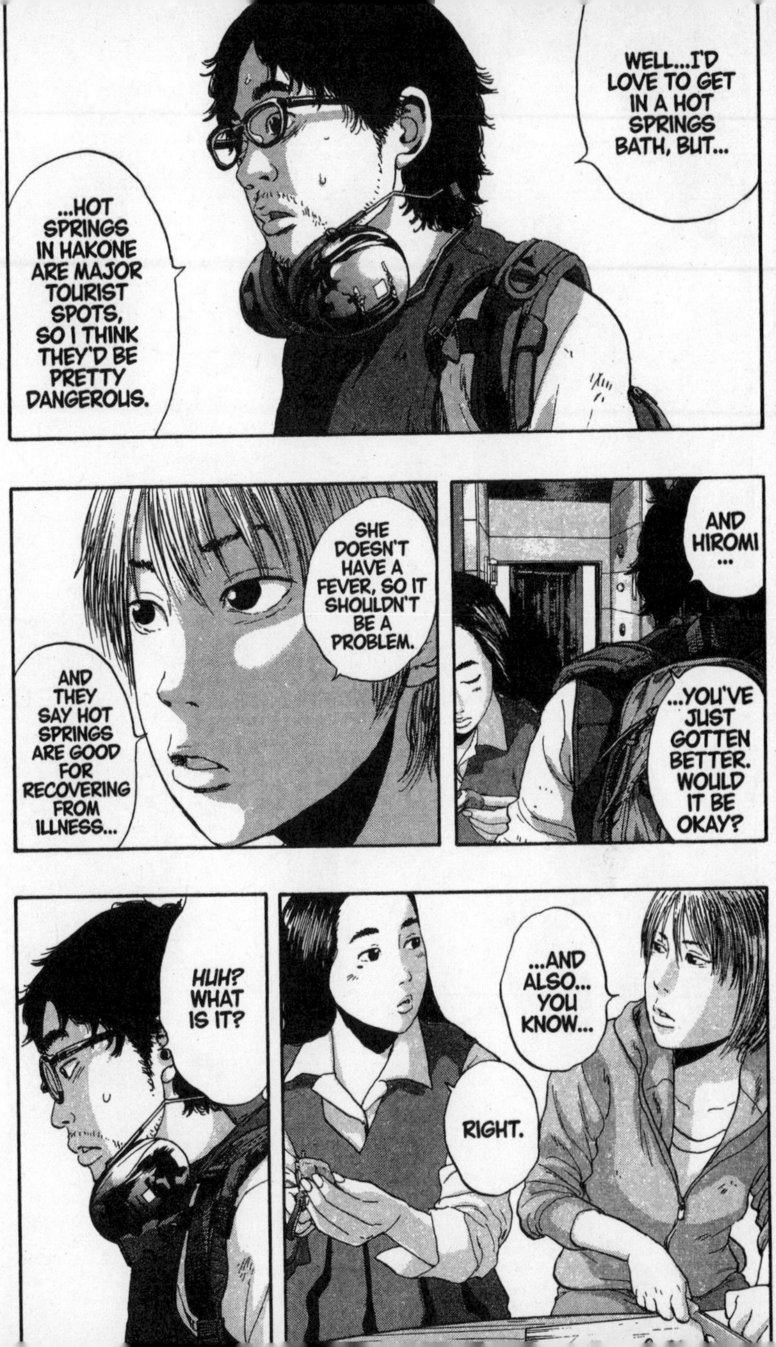
WELL...I'D LOVE TO GET IN A HOT SPRINGS BATH, BUT...
...HOT SPRINGS IN HAKONE ARE MAJOR TOURIST SPOTS, SO I THINK THEY'D BE PRETTY DANGEROUS.
AND HIROMI...
...YOU'VE JUST GOTTEN BETTER. WOULD IT BE OKAY?
SHE DOESN'T HAVE A FEVER, SO IT SHOULDN'T BE A PROBLEM.
AND THEY SAY HOT SPRINGS ARE GOOD FOR RECOVERING FROM ILLNESS...
...AND ALSO... YOU KNOW...
RIGHT.
HUH? WHAT IS IT?

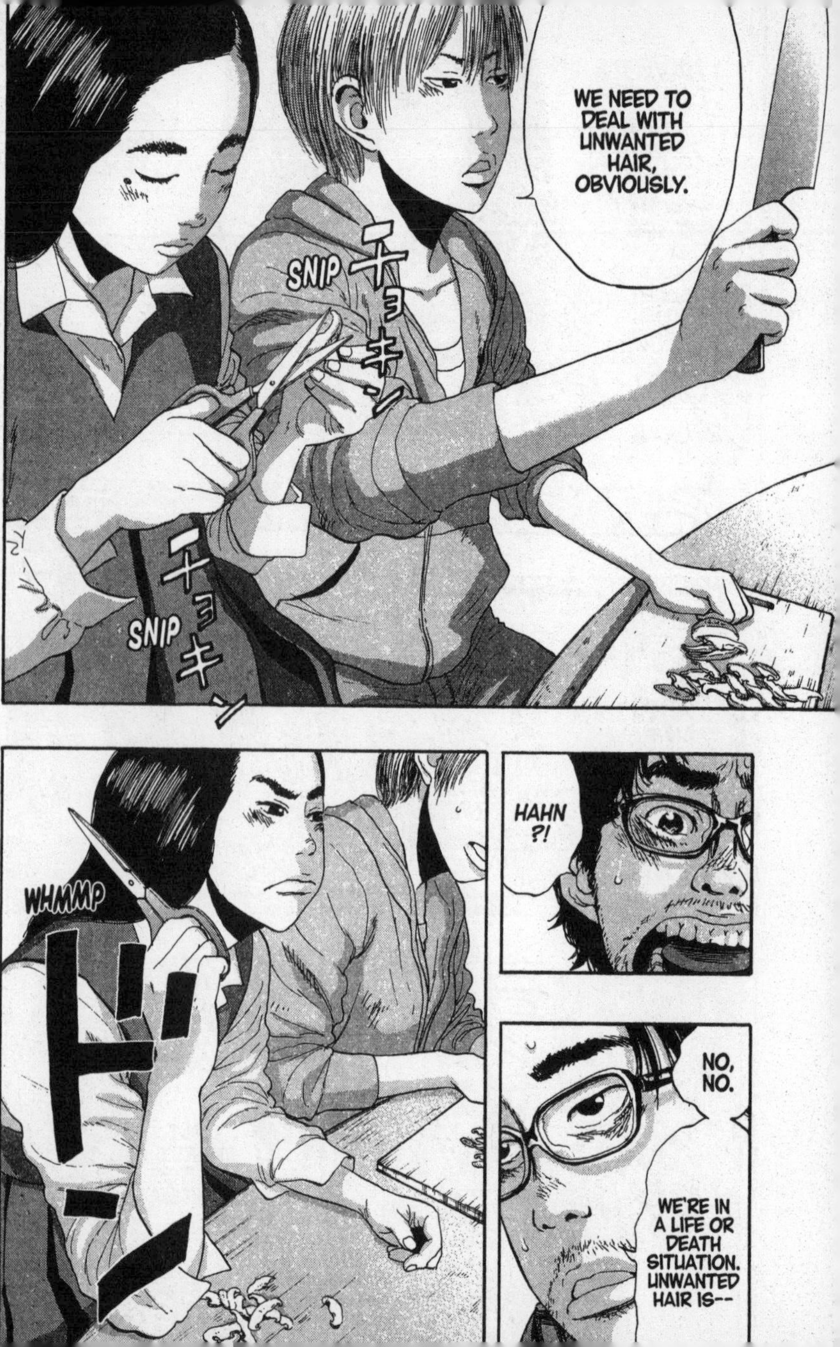

WE NEED TO DEAL WITH UNWANTED HAIR, OBVIOUSLY.
SNIP
チョキン
SNIP
チョキン
HAHN ?!
NO, NO.
WE'RE IN A LIFE OR DEATH SITUATION. UNWANTED HAIR IS--
WHMMP
ド

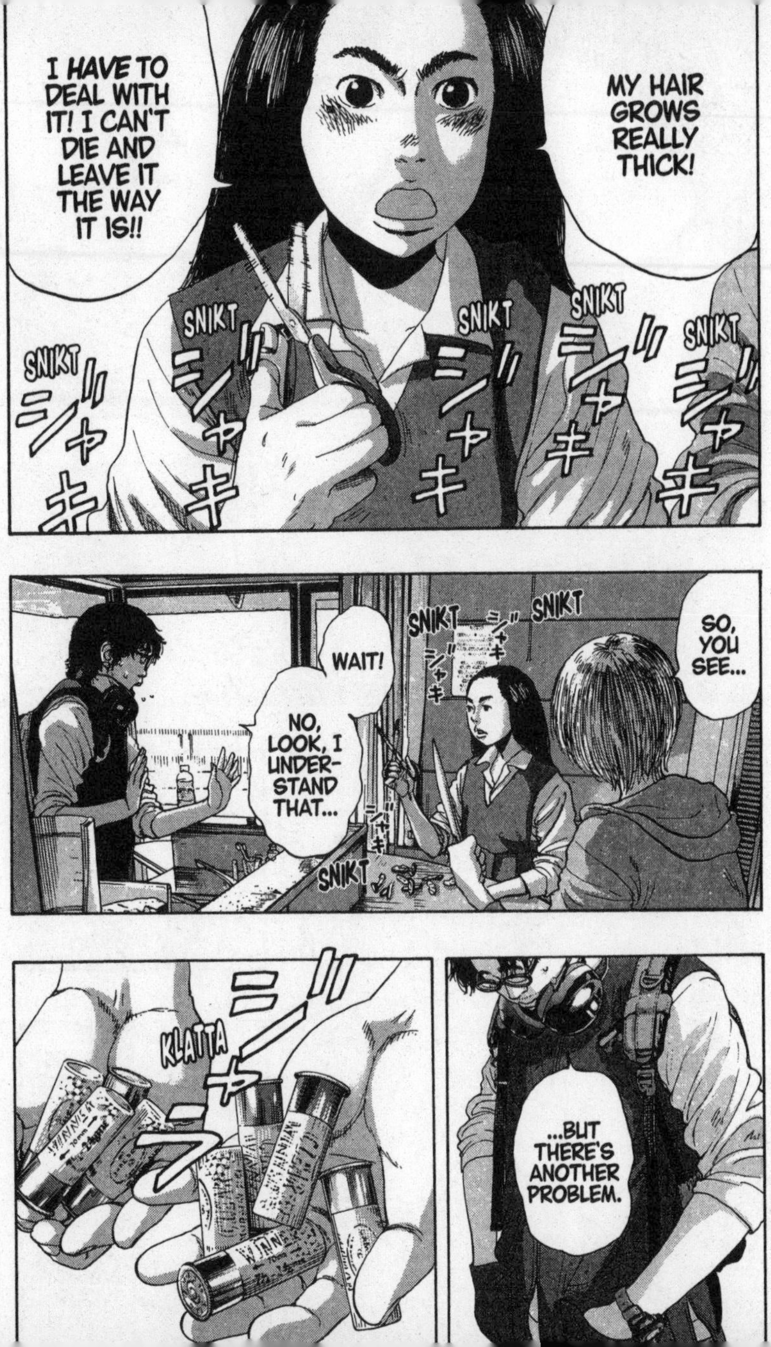
MY HAIR GROWS REALLY THICK!
I HAVE TO DEAL WITH IT! I CAN'T DIE AND LEAVE IT THE WAY IT IS!!
SNIKT
SNIKT
SNIKT
SNIKT
SNIKT
SO, YOU SEE...
SNIKT
SNIKT
WAIT!
NO, LOOK, I UNDERSTAND THAT...
SNIKT
...BUT THERE'S ANOTHER PROBLEM.
KLATTA

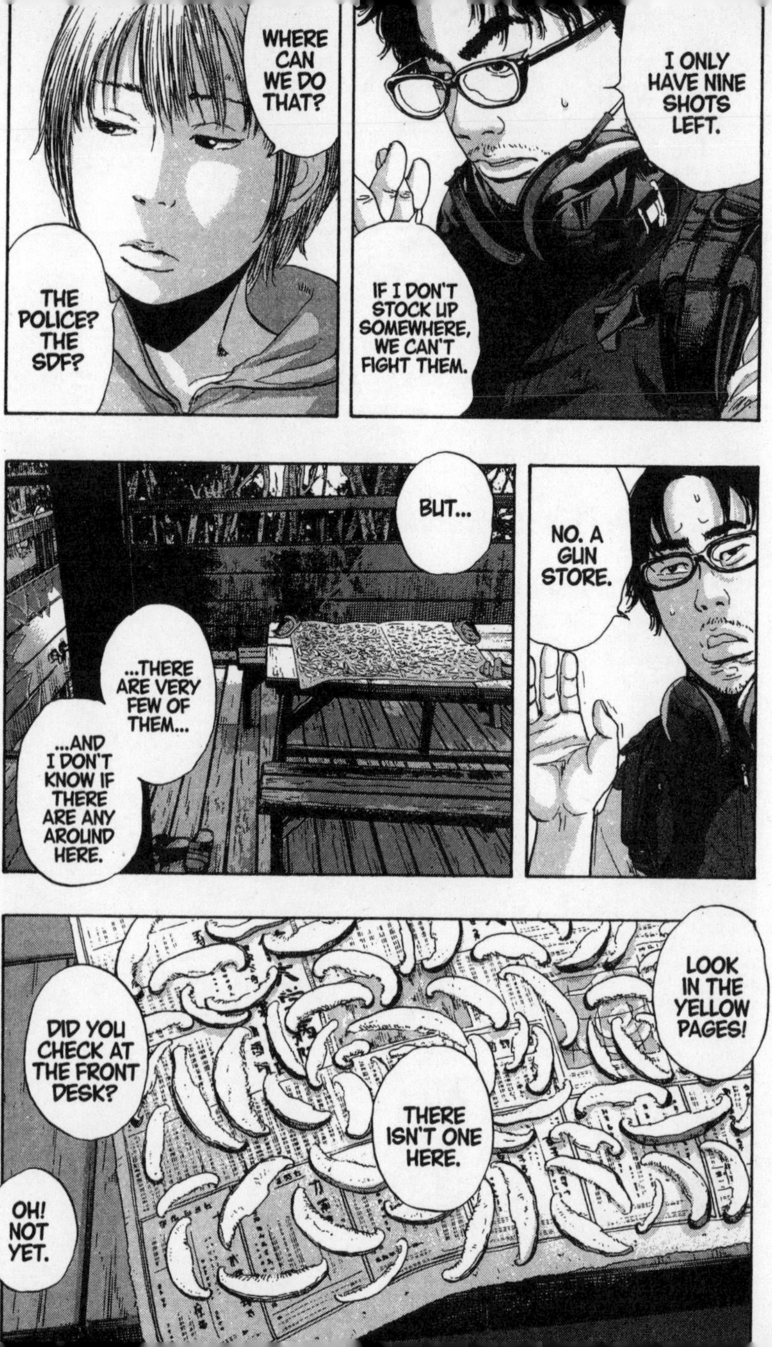
I ONLY HAVE NINE SHOTS LEFT.
IF I DON'T STOCK UP SOMEWHERE, WE CAN'T FIGHT THEM.
WHERE CAN WE DO THAT?
THE POLICE? THE SDF?
NO. A GUN STORE.
BUT...
...THERE ARE VERY FEW OF THEM...
...AND I DON'T KNOW IF THERE ARE ANY AROUND HERE.
LOOK IN THE YELLOW PAGES!
THERE ISN'T ONE HERE.
DID YOU CHECK AT THE FRONT DESK?
OH! NOT YET.

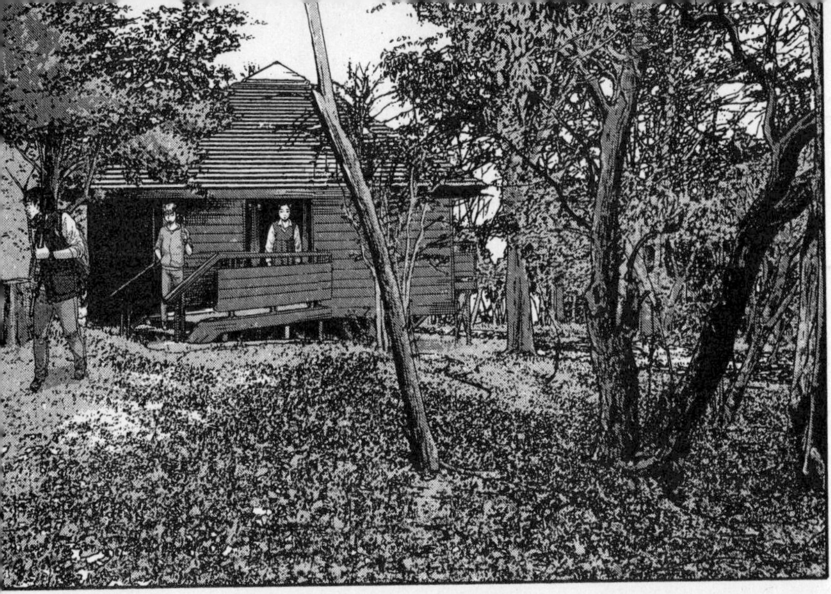
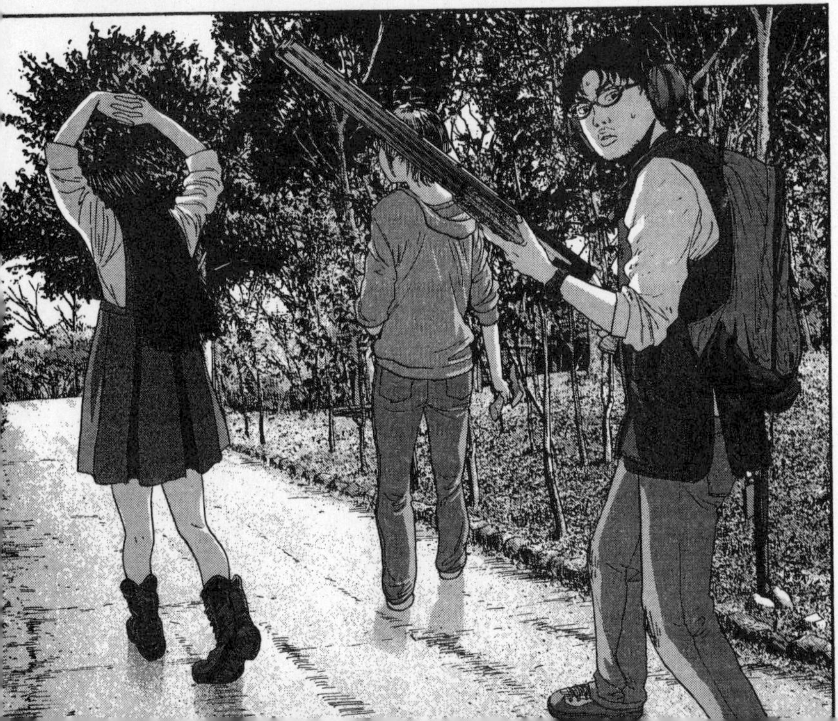

STAY SHARP.

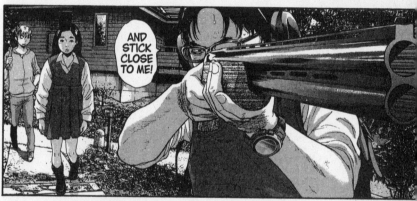

AND STICK CLOSE TO ME!

BE CARE-FUL.

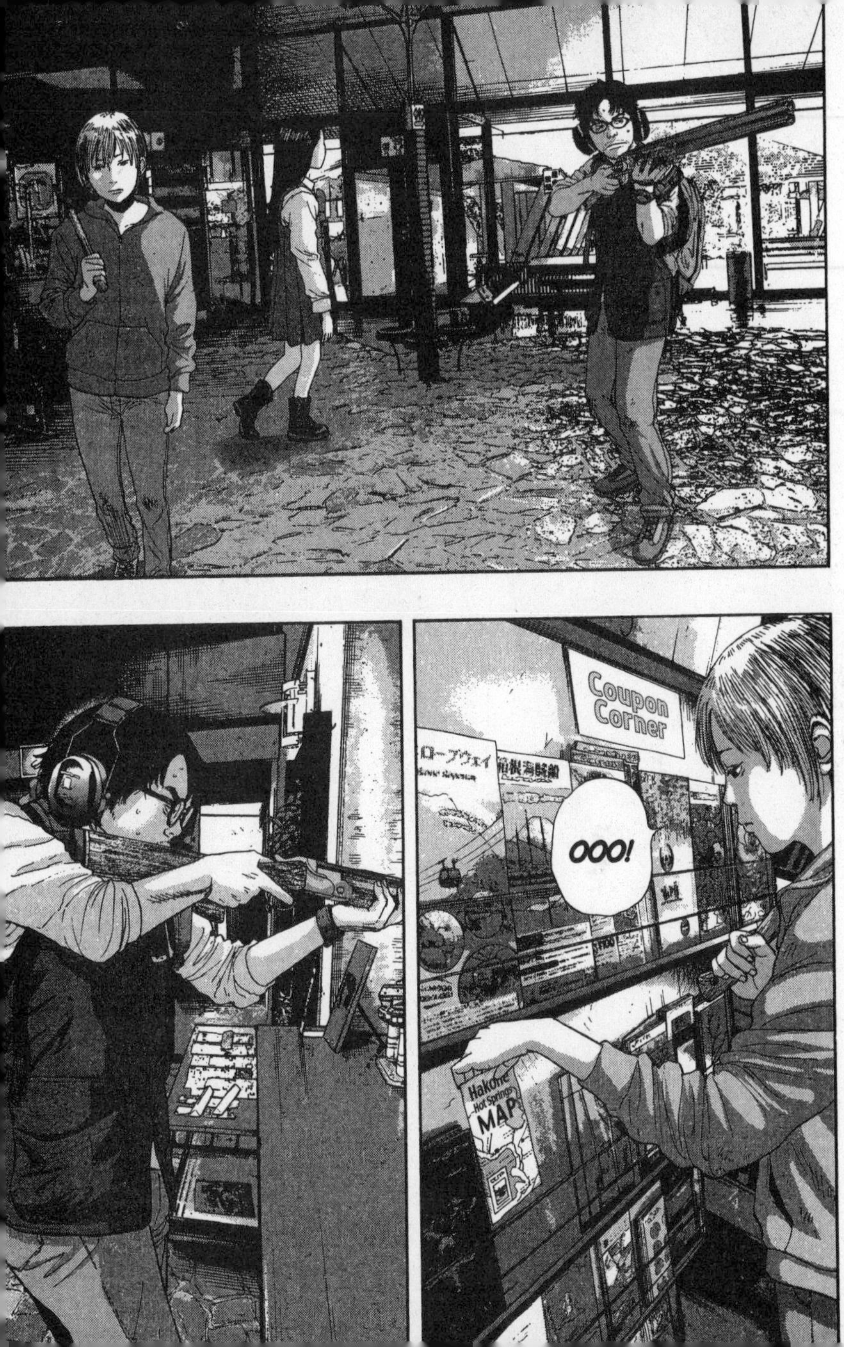
Coupon Corner
ロープウェイ
箱根海賊船
OOO!
Hakone Hot Springs MAP

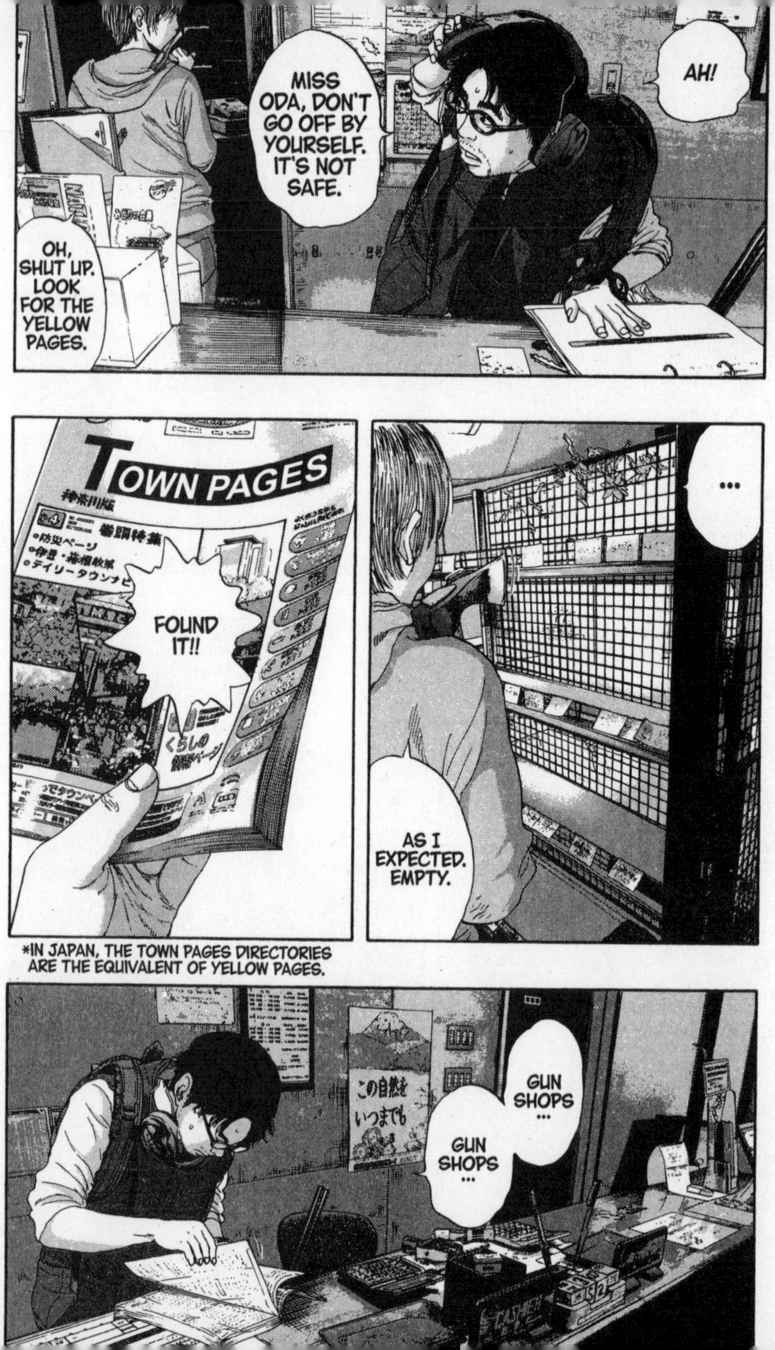
AH!
MISS ODA, DON'T GO OFF BY YOURSELF. IT'S NOT SAFE.
OH, SHUT UP. LOOK FOR THE YELLOW PAGES.
...
AS I EXPECTED. EMPTY.
TOWN PAGES
FOUND IT!!
GUN SHOPS ...
GUN SHOPS ...
この自然をいつまでも

*IN JAPAN, THE TOWN PAGES DIRECTORIES ARE THE EQUIVALENT OF YELLOW PAGES.

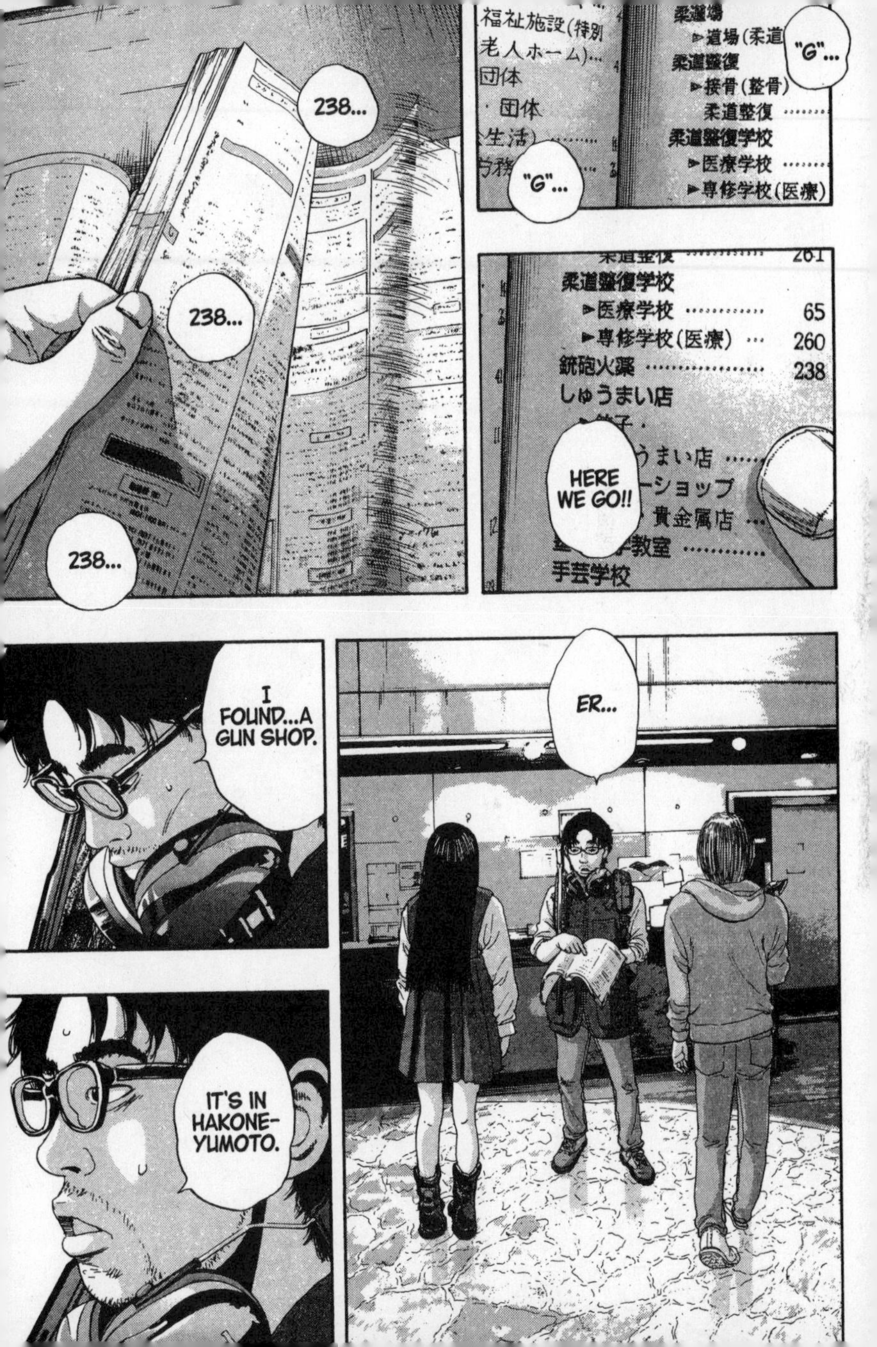

"G"...
"G"...
柔道場
▶道場(柔道
柔道整復
▶接骨(整骨)
柔道整復
柔道整復学校
▶医療学校
▶専修学校(医療)
福祉施設(特別
老人ホーム)
団体
・団体
生活)
柔道整復学校
▶医療学校 65
▶専修学校(医療) ... 260
銃砲火薬 238
しゅうまい店
HERE WE GO!!
238...
238...
238...
ER...
I FOUND...A GUN SHOP.
IT'S IN HAKONE-YUMOTO.

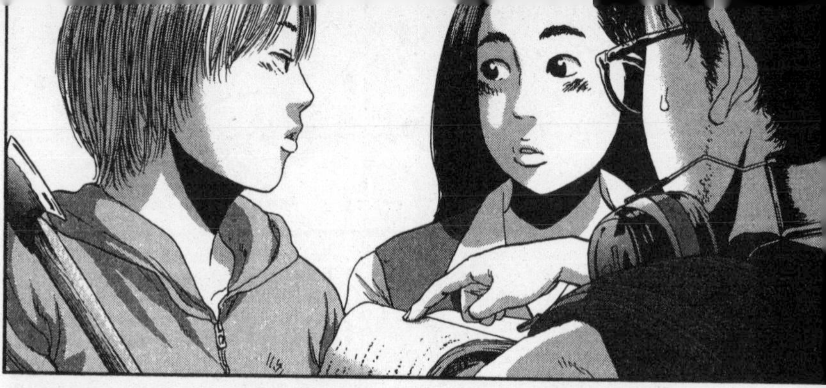
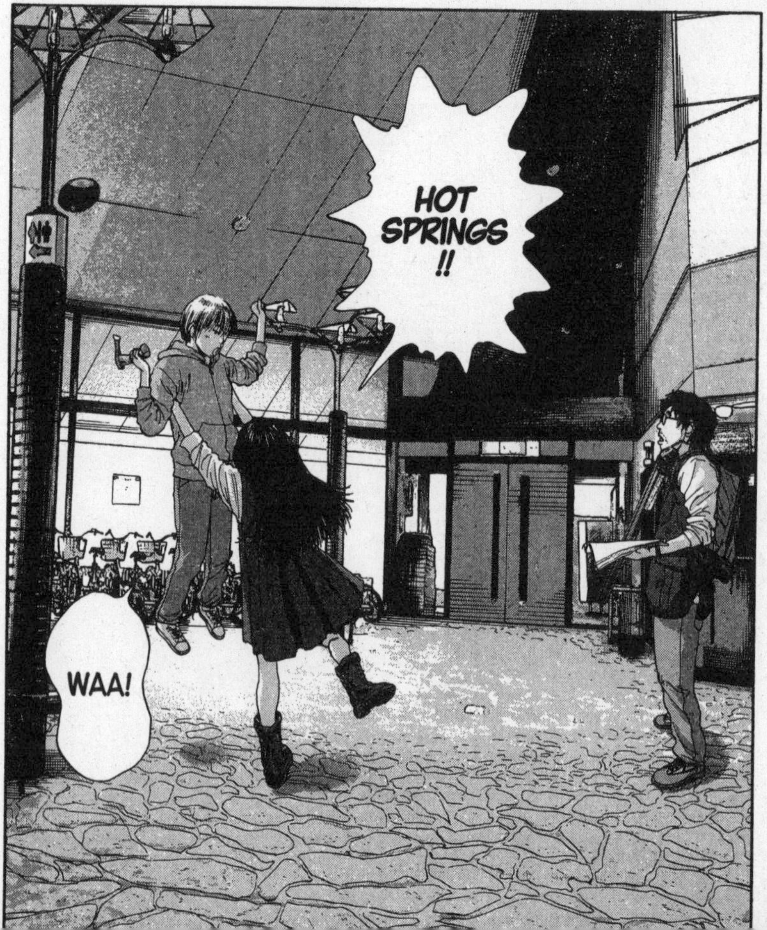
HOT SPRINGS !!
WAA!

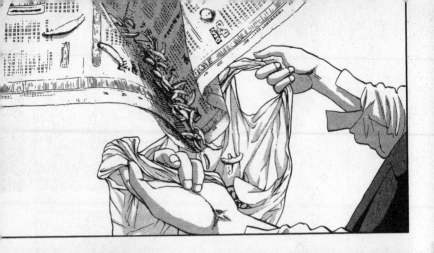

CHAPTER
153

WE MANAGED TO MAKE TONS OF DRIED SHIITAKE, HUH?

I WANTED TO DRY THEM A BIT MORE, THOUGH.

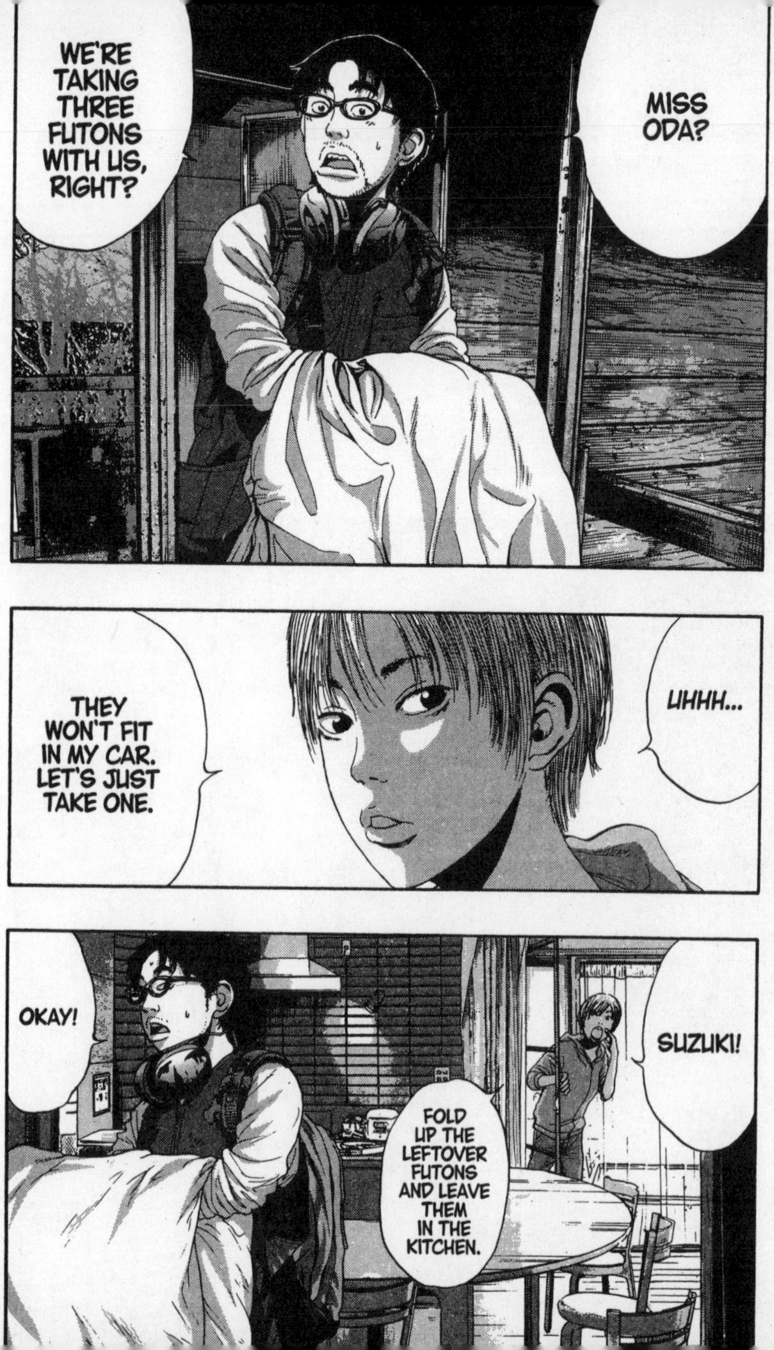
MISS ODA?
WE'RE TAKING THREE FUTONS WITH US, RIGHT?
UHHH...
THEY WON'T FIT IN MY CAR. LET'S JUST TAKE ONE.
SUZUKI!
FOLD UP THE LEFTOVER FUTONS AND LEAVE THEM IN THE KITCHEN.
OKAY!

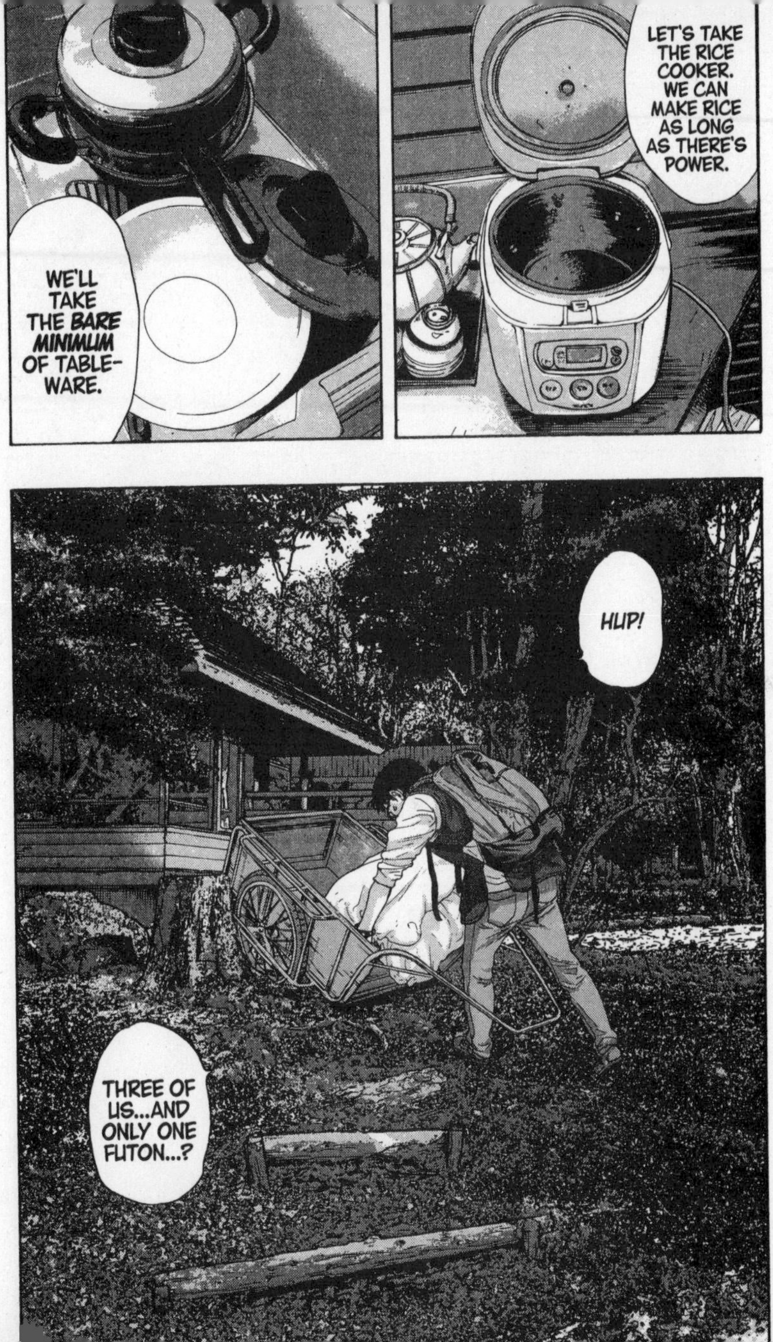
LET'S TAKE THE RICE COOKER. WE CAN MAKE RICE AS LONG AS THERE'S POWER.
WE'LL TAKE THE *BARE MINIMUM* OF TABLE-WARE.
HUP!
THREE OF US...AND ONLY ONE FUTON...?

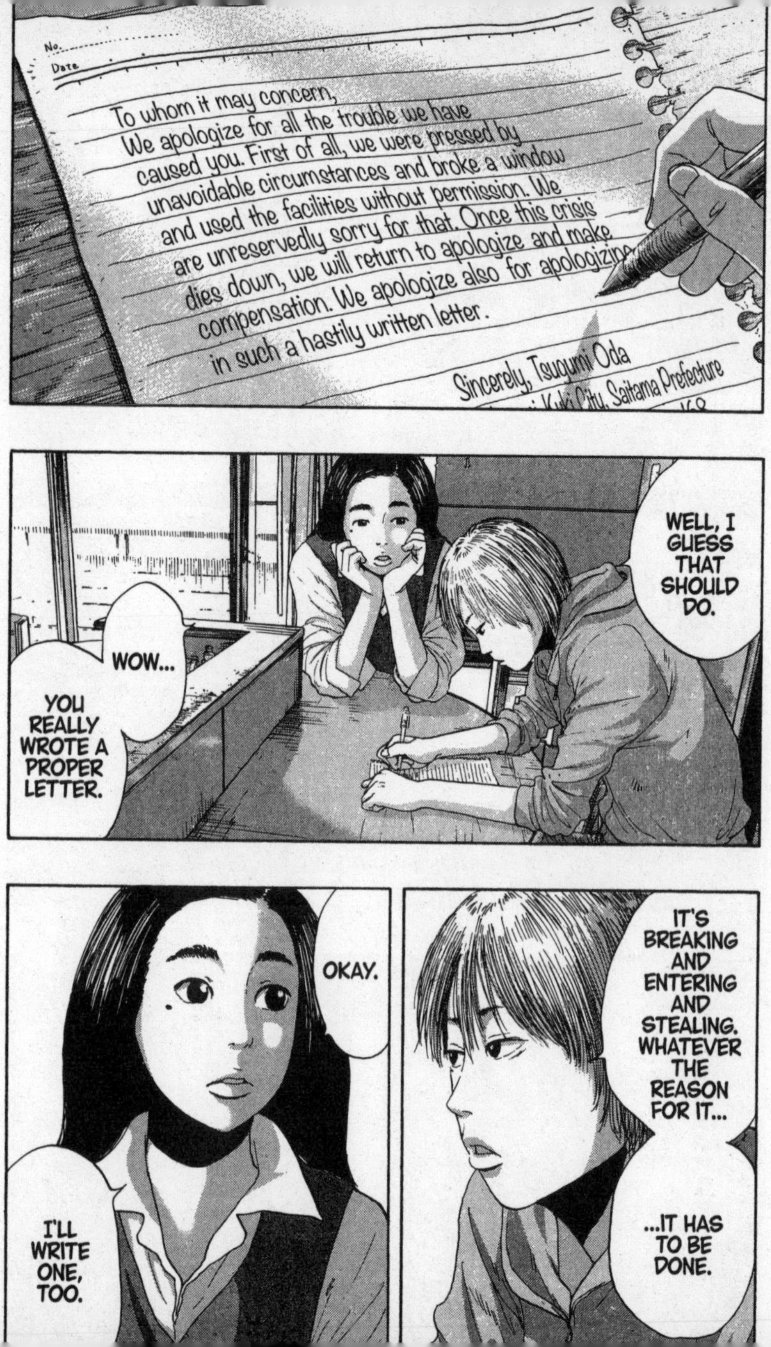
No.
Date
To whom it may concern,
We apologize for all the trouble we have caused you. First of all, we were pressed by unavoidable circumstances and broke a window and used the facilities without permission. We are unreservedly sorry for that. Once this crisis dies down, we will return to apologize and make compensation. We apologize also for apologizing in such a hastily written letter.
Sincerely, Tsugumi Oda
Kuki City, Saitama Prefecture
WELL, I GUESS THAT SHOULD DO.
WOW...
YOU REALLY WROTE A PROPER LETTER.
IT'S BREAKING AND ENTERING AND STEALING. WHATEVER THE REASON FOR IT...
...IT HAS TO BE DONE.
OKAY.
I'LL WRITE ONE, TOO.

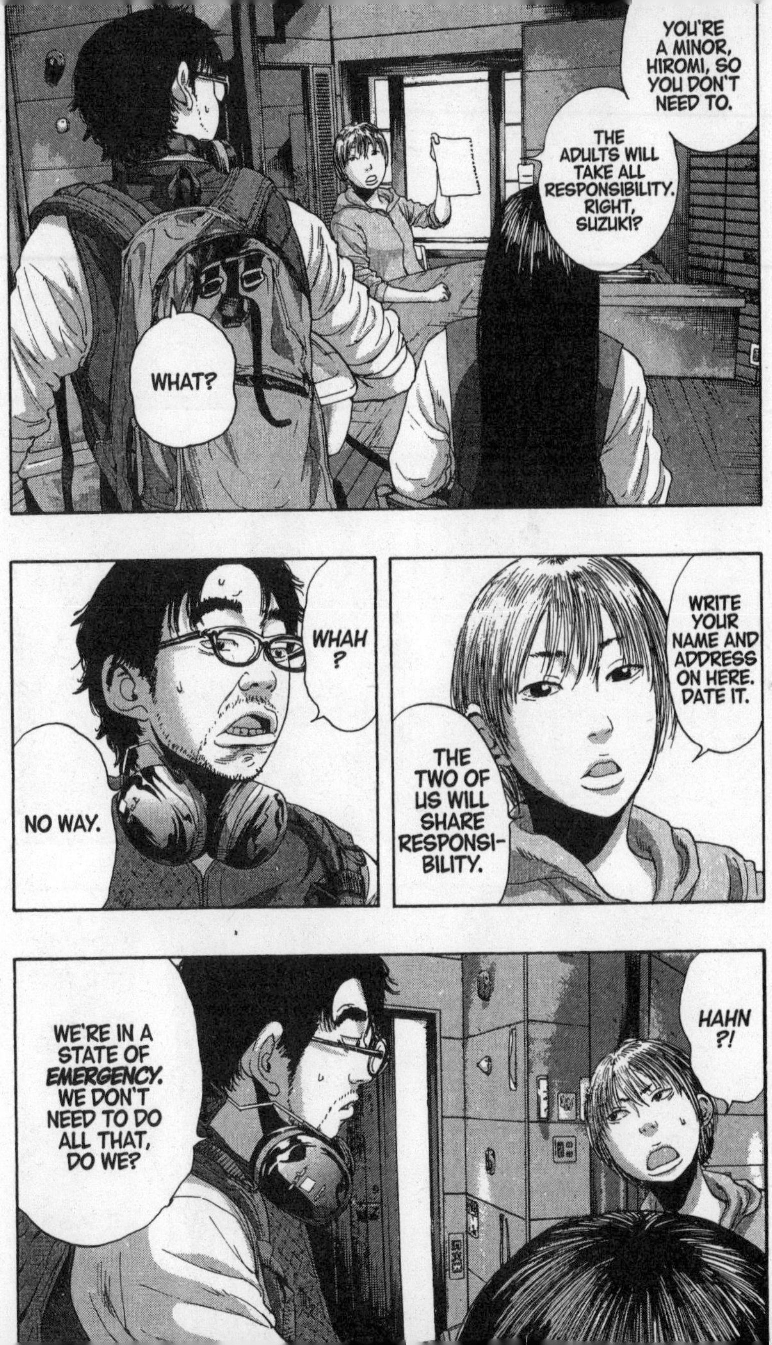
YOU'RE A MINOR, HIROMI, SO YOU DON'T NEED TO.
THE ADULTS WILL TAKE ALL RESPONSIBILITY. RIGHT, SUZUKI?
WHAT?
WRITE YOUR NAME AND ADDRESS ON HERE. DATE IT.
THE TWO OF US WILL SHARE RESPONSIBILITY.
WHAH?
NO WAY.
HAHN?!
WE'RE IN A STATE OF *EMERGENCY.* WE DON'T NEED TO DO ALL THAT, DO WE?

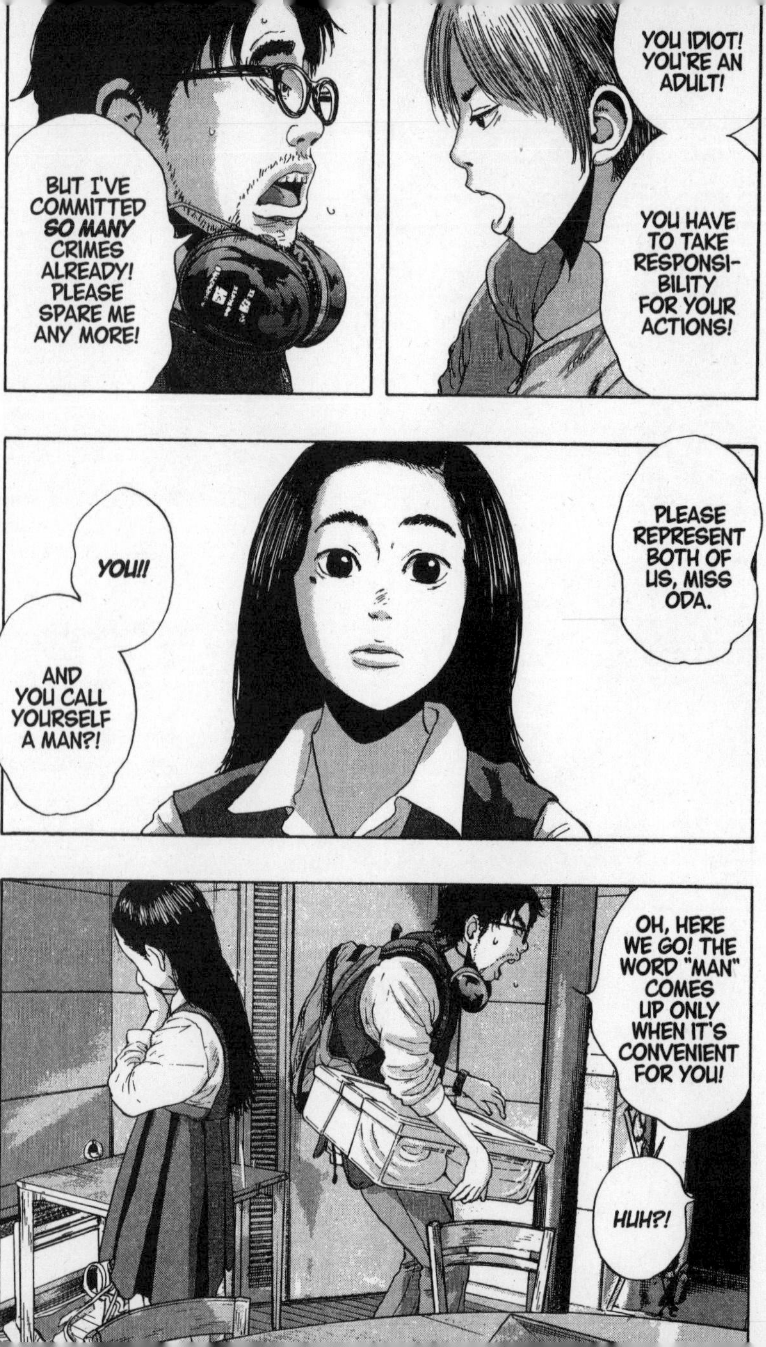
YOU IDIOT! YOU'RE AN ADULT!
YOU HAVE TO TAKE RESPONSI-BILITY FOR YOUR ACTIONS!
BUT I'VE COMMITTED SO MANY CRIMES ALREADY! PLEASE SPARE ME ANY MORE!
PLEASE REPRESENT BOTH OF US, MISS ODA.
YOU!!
AND YOU CALL YOURSELF A MAN?!
OH, HERE WE GO! THE WORD "MAN" COMES UP ONLY WHEN IT'S CONVENIENT FOR YOU!
HUH?!

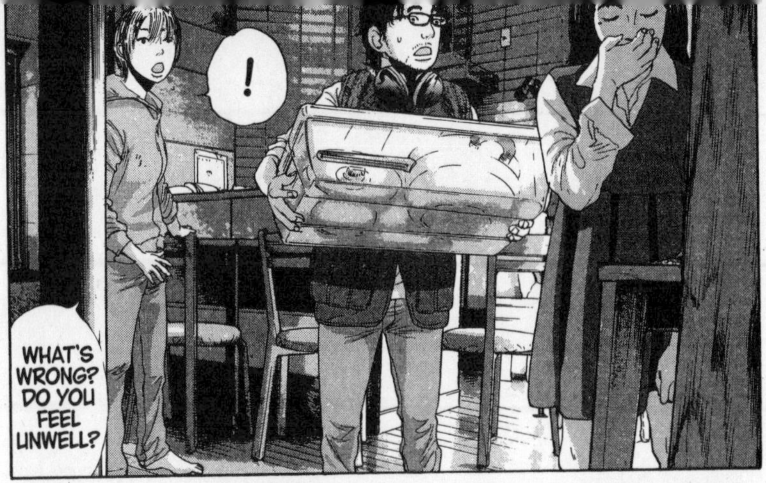
!
WHAT'S WRONG? DO YOU FEEL UNWELL?

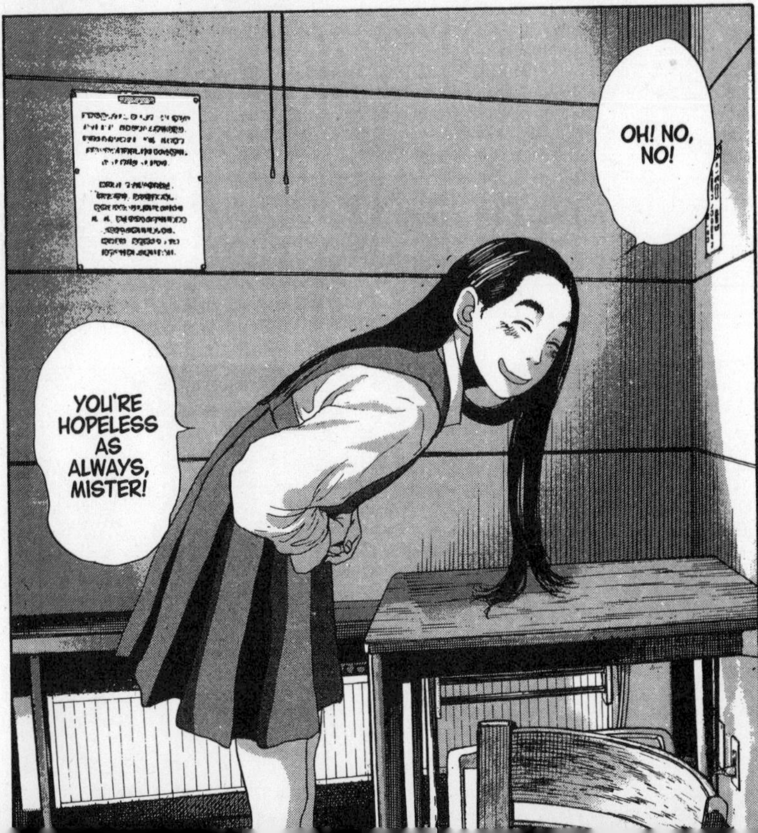
OH! NO, NO!
YOU'RE HOPELESS AS ALWAYS, MISTER!

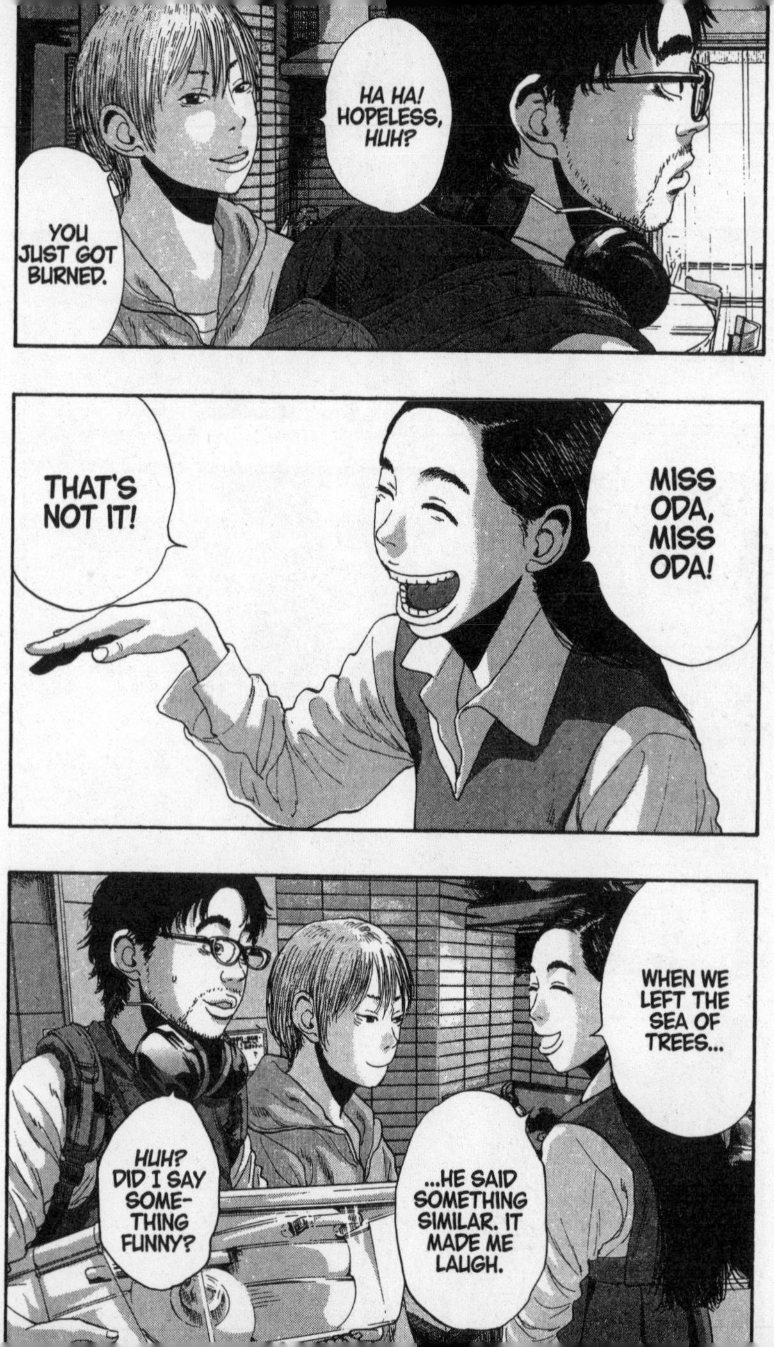
HA HA! HOPELESS, HUH?
YOU JUST GOT BURNED.
MISS ODA, MISS ODA!
THAT'S NOT IT!
WHEN WE LEFT THE SEA OF TREES...
...HE SAID SOMETHING SIMILAR. IT MADE ME LAUGH.
HUH? DID I SAY SOME-THING FUNNY?

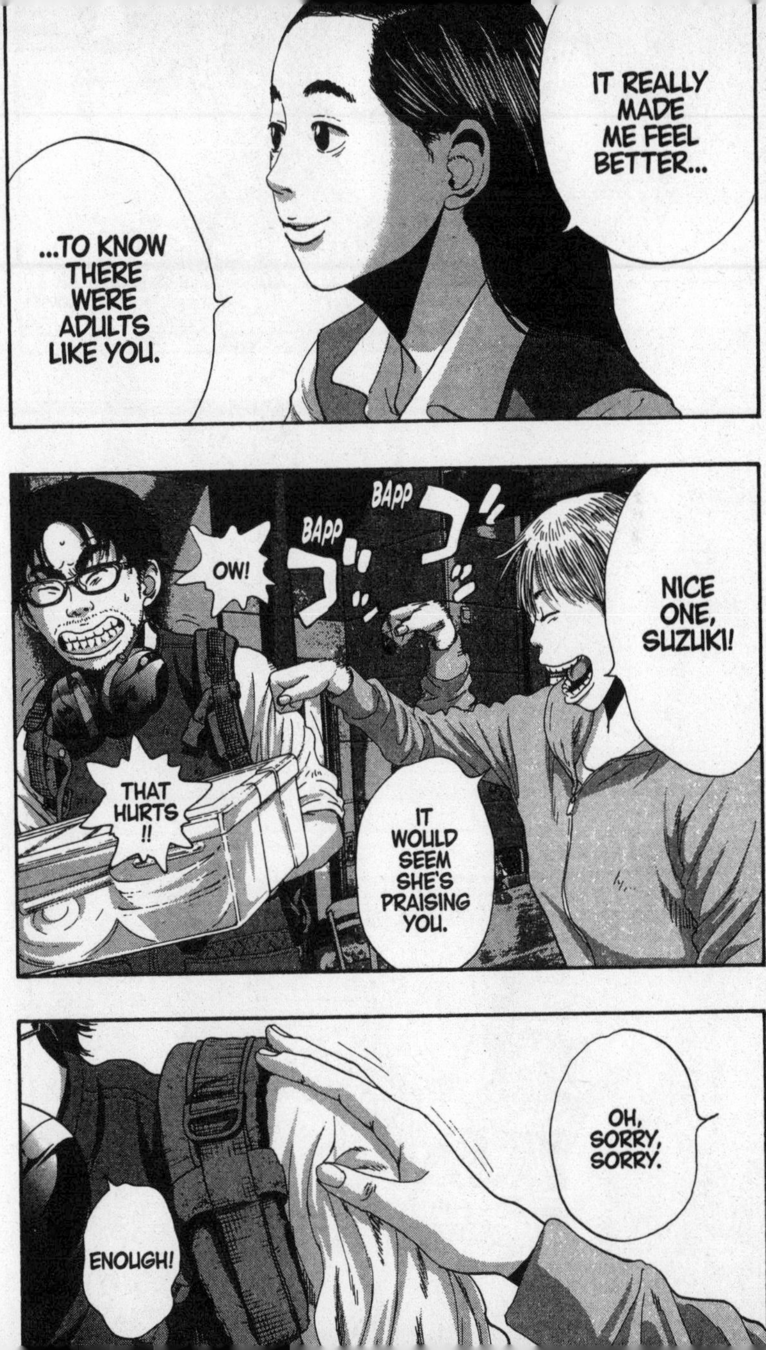
IT REALLY MADE ME FEEL BETTER...
...TO KNOW THERE WERE ADULTS LIKE YOU.
NICE ONE, SUZUKI!
BAPP
BAPP
OW!
IT WOULD SEEM SHE'S PRAISING YOU.
THAT HURTS !!
OH, SORRY, SORRY.
ENOUGH!

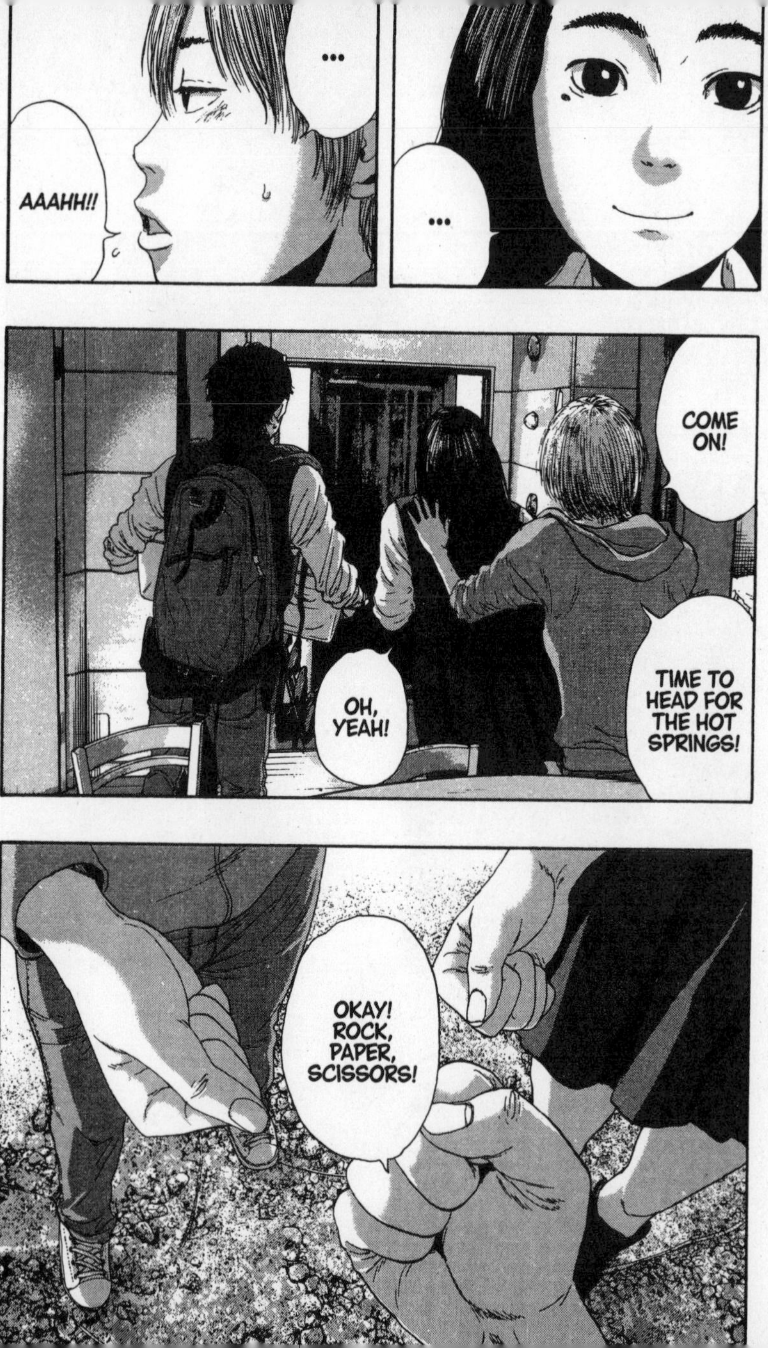
...
...
AAAHH!!
COME ON!
TIME TO HEAD FOR THE HOT SPRINGS!
OH, YEAH!
OKAY! ROCK, PAPER, SCISSORS!

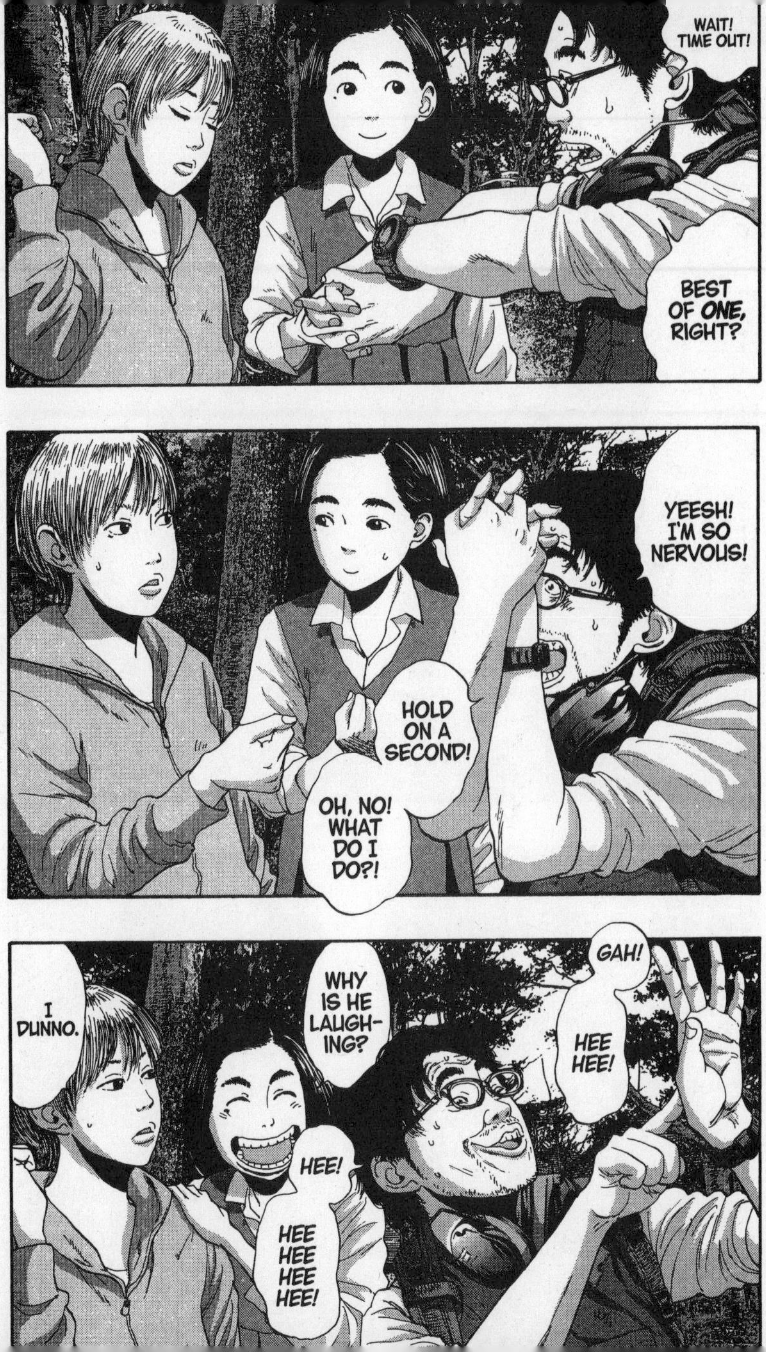
WAIT! TIME OUT!
BEST OF ONE, RIGHT?
YEESH! I'M SO NERVOUS!
HOLD ON A SECOND!
OH, NO! WHAT DO I DO?!
GAH!
HEE HEE!
WHY IS HE LAUGHING?
I DUNNO.
HEE!
HEE HEE HEE HEE!

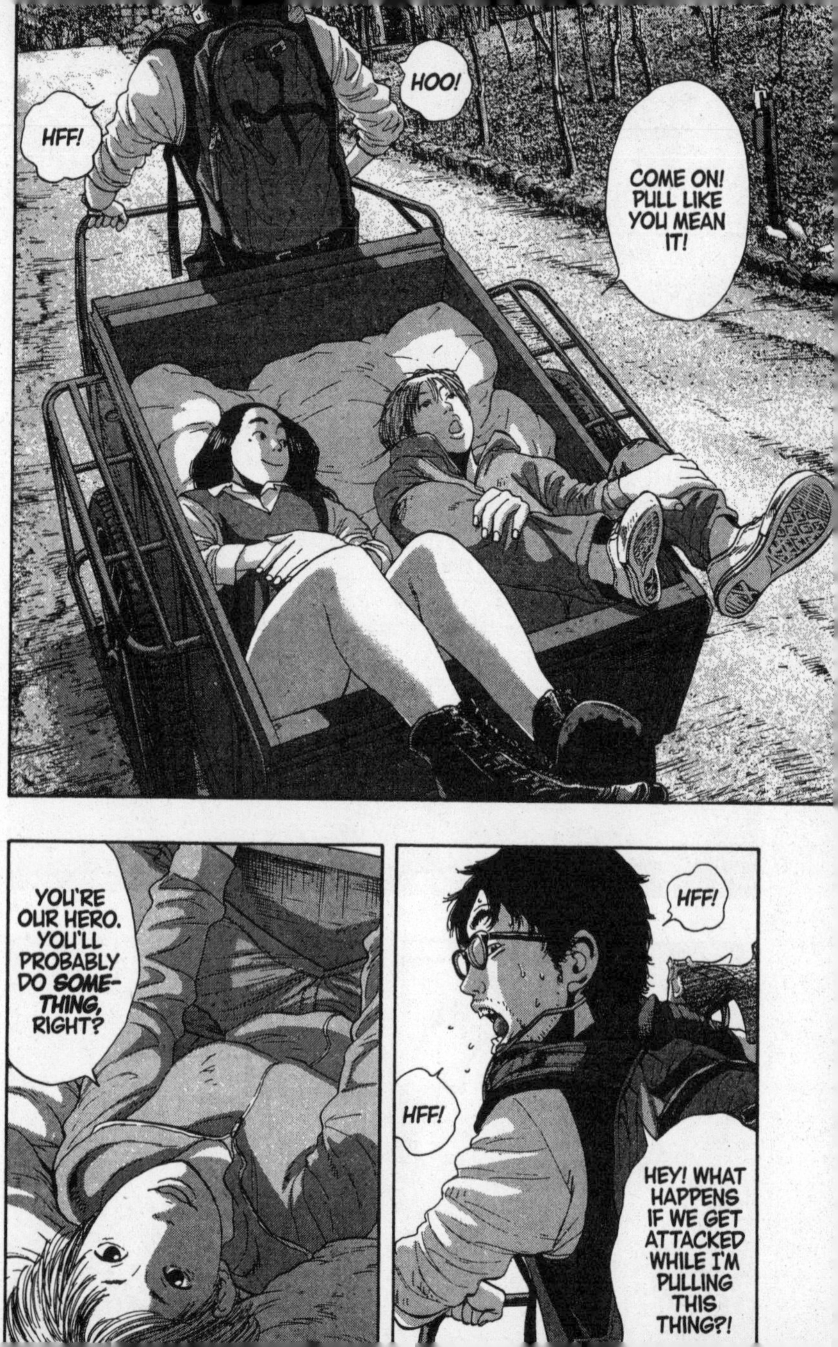
COME ON! PULL LIKE YOU MEAN IT!
HOO!
HFF!
HFF!
HFF!
HEY! WHAT HAPPENS IF WE GET ATTACKED WHILE I'M PULLING THIS THING?!
YOU'RE OUR HERO. YOU'LL PROBABLY DO SOME-THING, RIGHT?

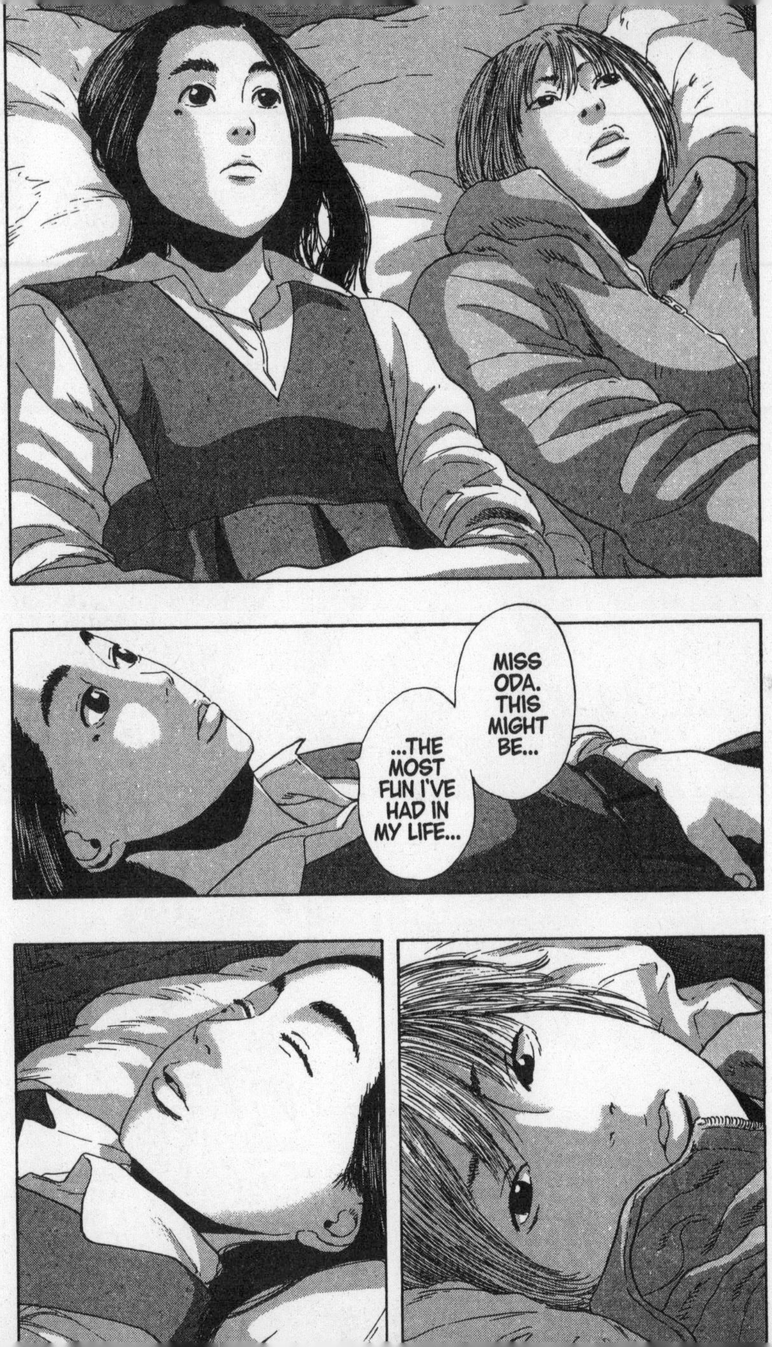
MISS ODA. THIS MIGHT BE...
...THE MOST FUN I'VE HAD IN MY LIFE...

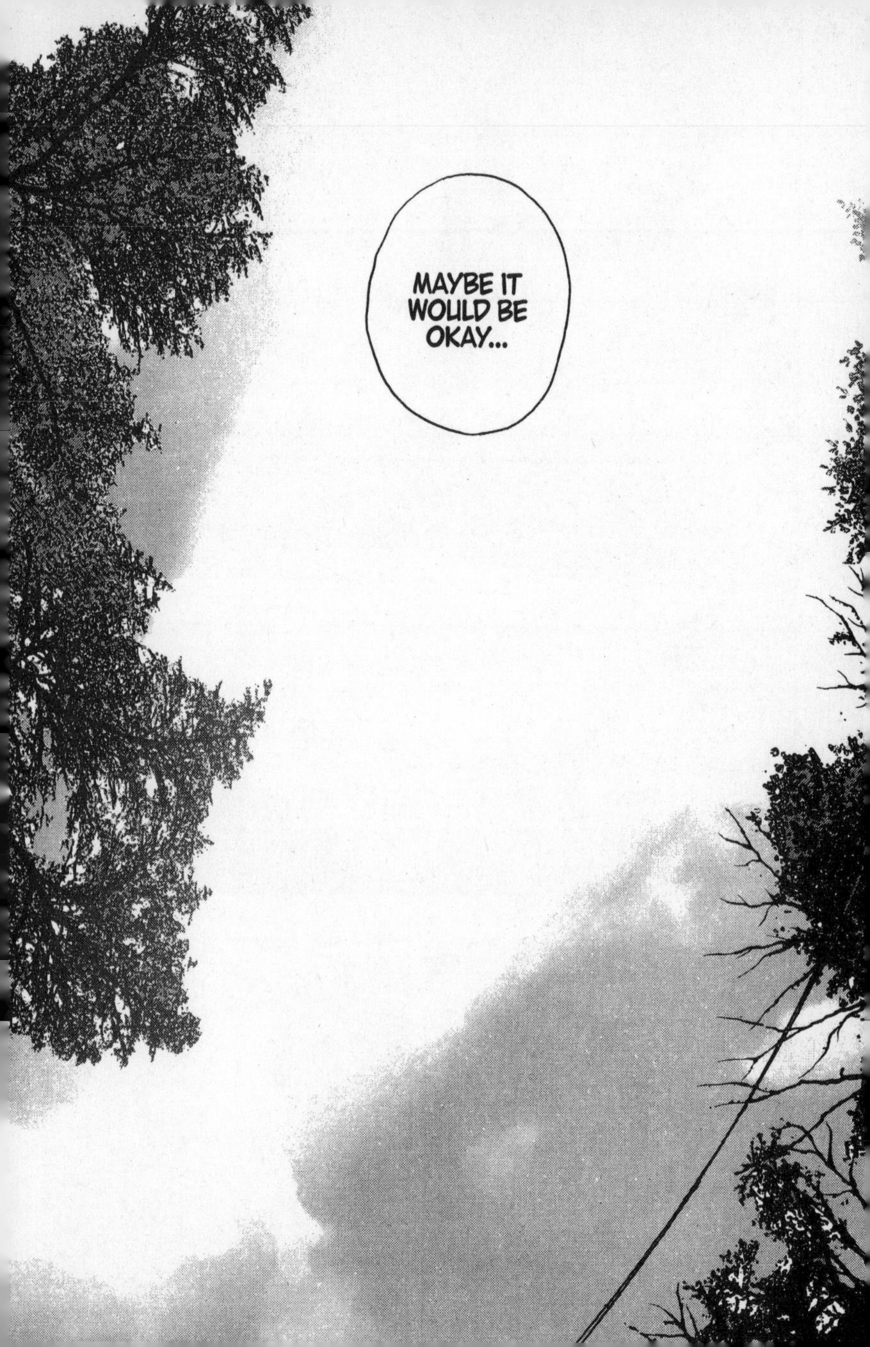
MAYBE IT WOULD BE OKAY...

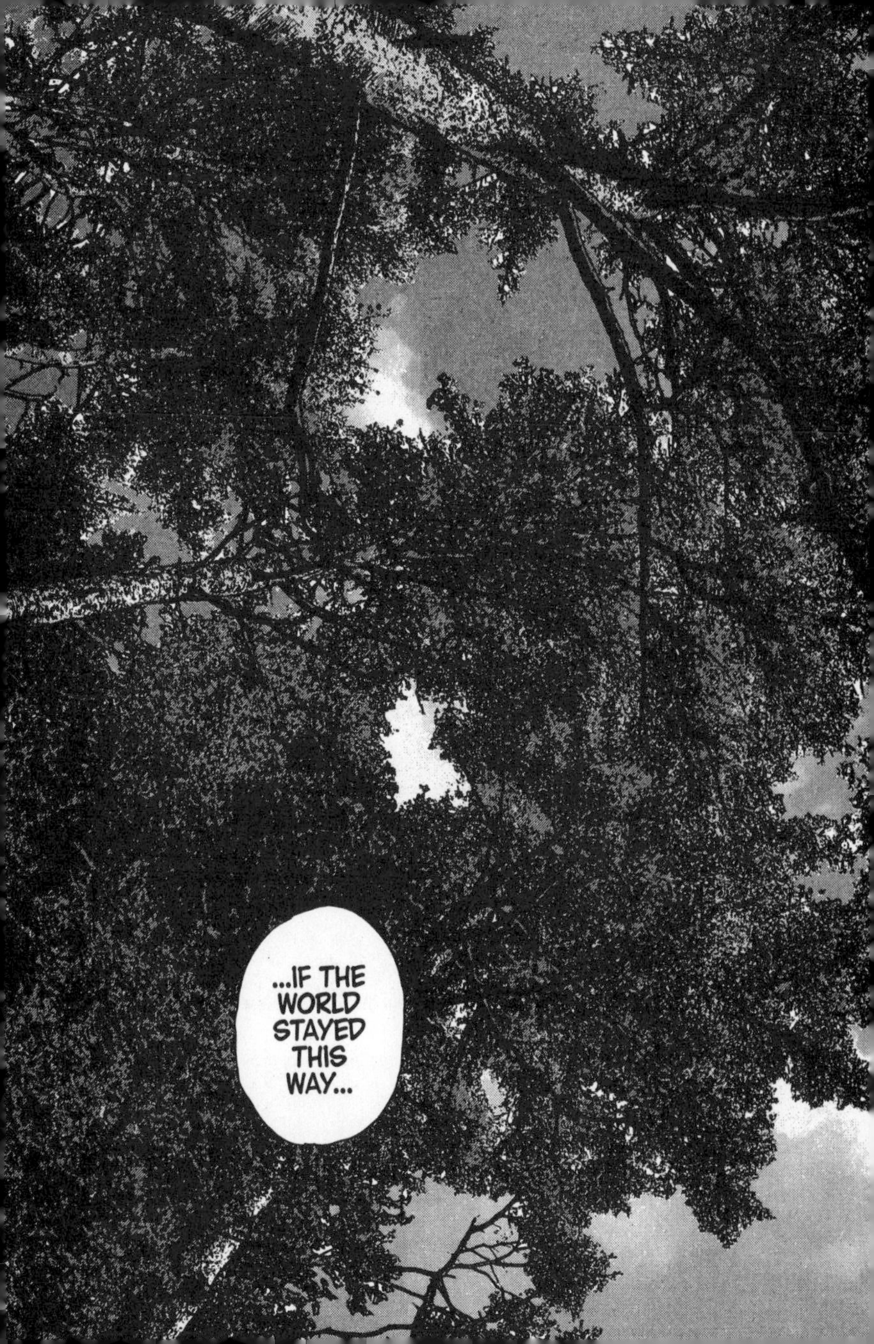
...IF THE WORLD STAYED THIS WAY...

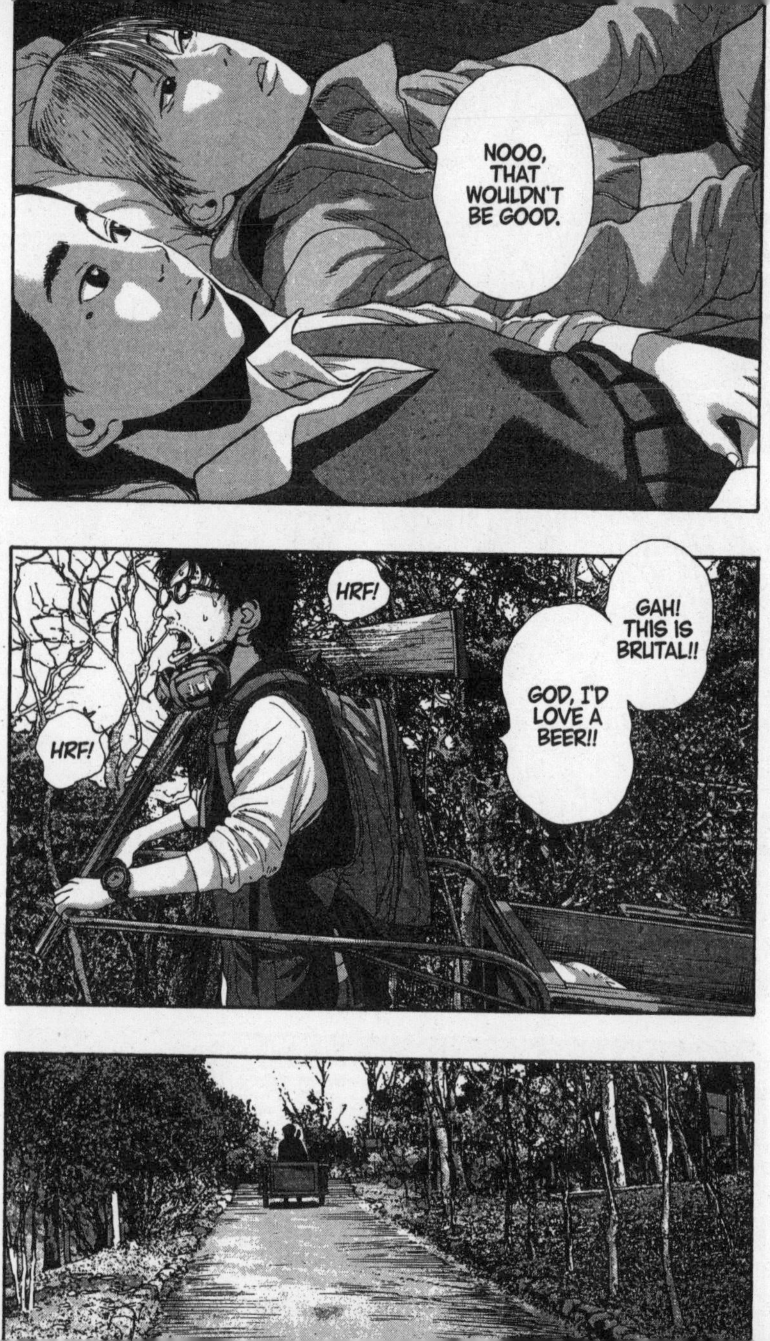
NOOO, THAT WOULDN'T BE GOOD.
GAH! THIS IS BRUTAL!!
GOD, I'D LOVE A BEER!!
HRF!
HRF!

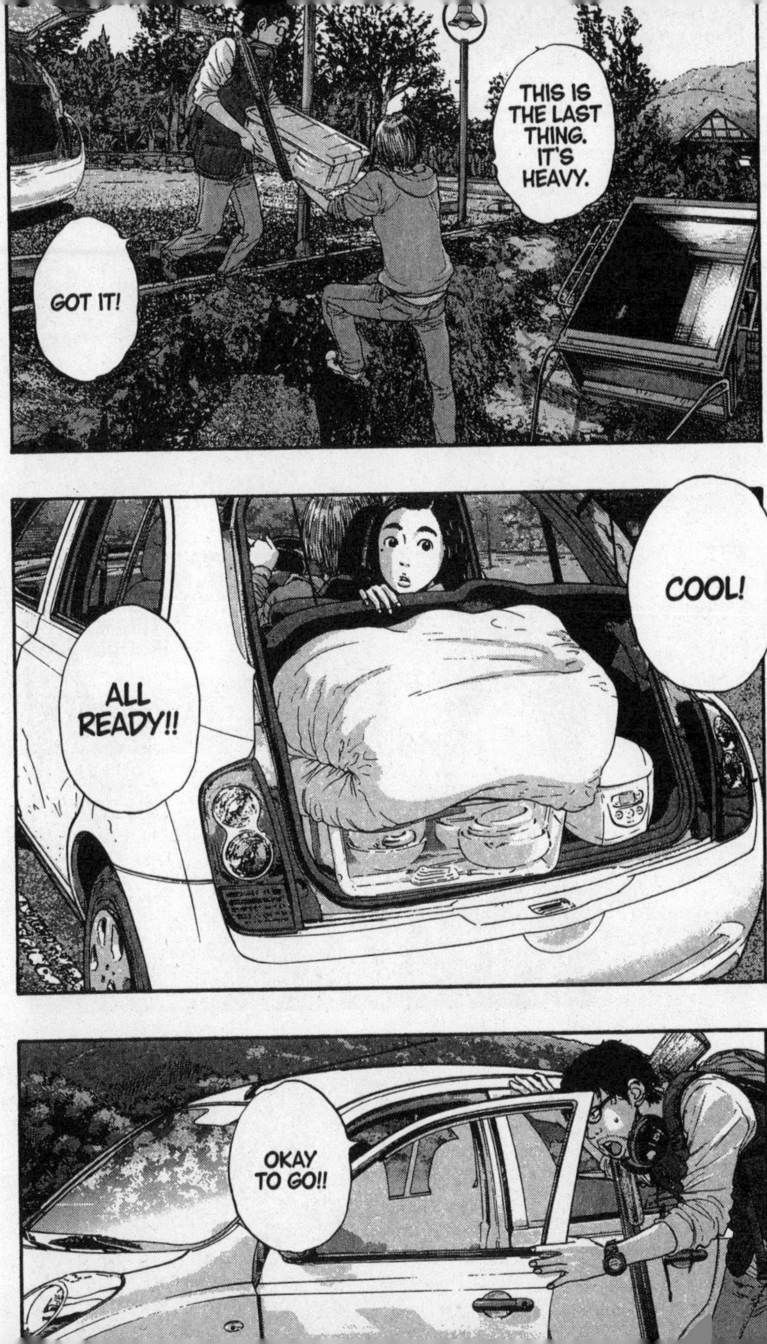
THIS IS THE LAST THING. IT'S HEAVY.
GOT IT!
COOL!
ALL READY!!
OKAY TO GO!!

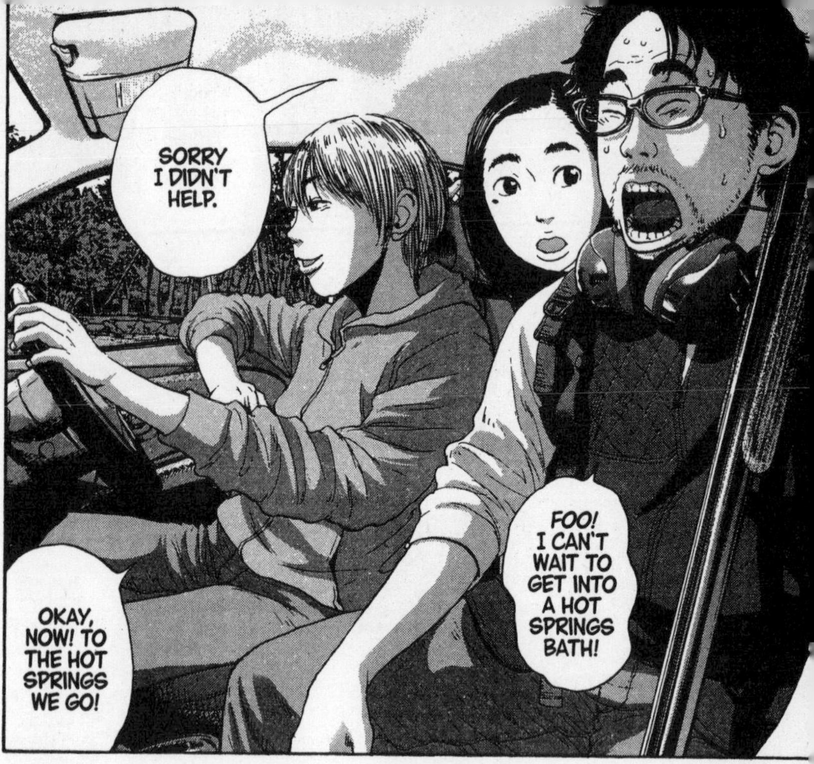
SORRY I DIDN'T HELP.
FOO! I CAN'T WAIT TO GET INTO A HOT SPRINGS BATH!
OKAY, NOW! TO THE HOT SPRINGS WE GO!

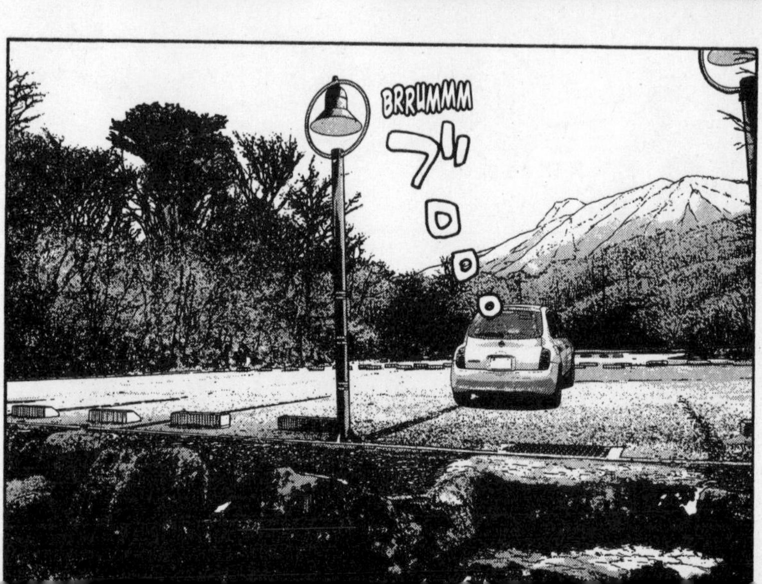
BRRUMMM

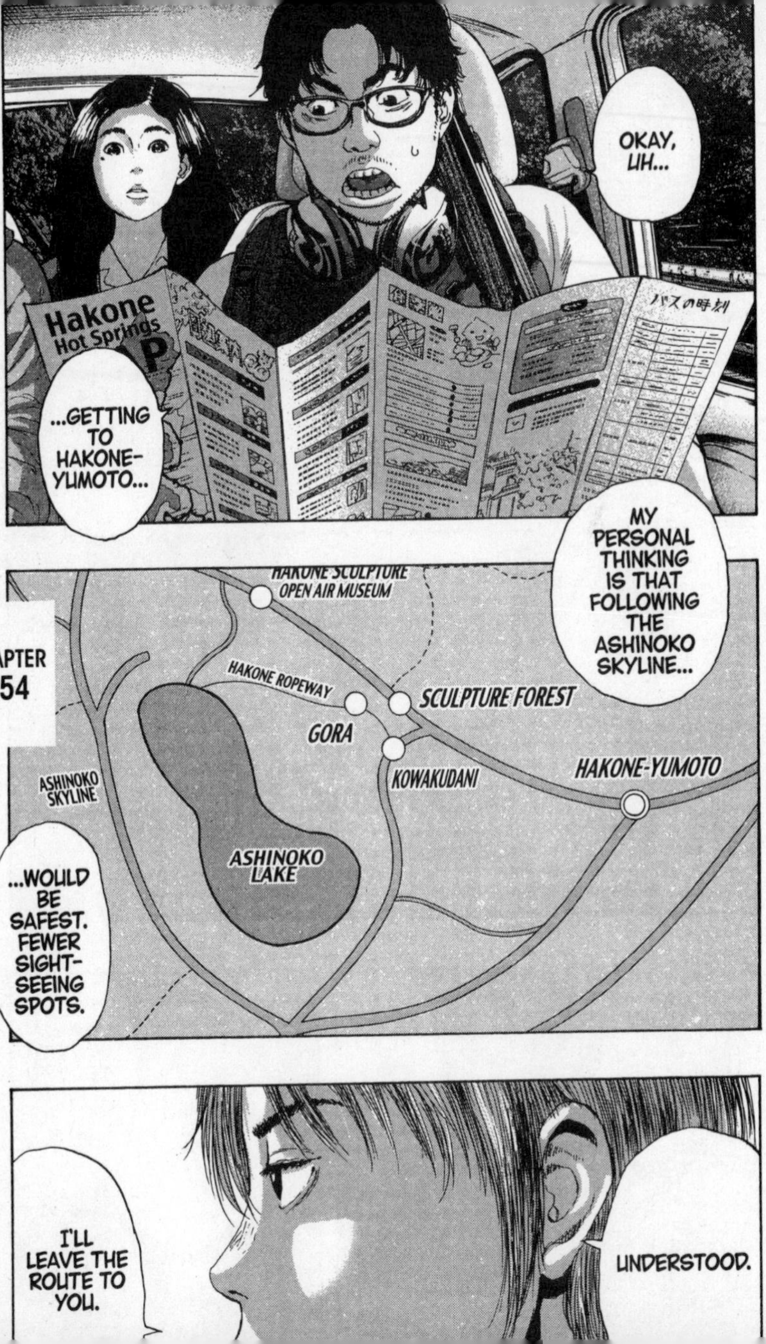
OKAY, UH...
Hakone Hot Springs MAP
バスの時刻
...GETTING TO HAKONE-YUMOTO...
MY PERSONAL THINKING IS THAT FOLLOWING THE ASHINOKO SKYLINE...
HAKONE SCULPTURE OPEN AIR MUSEUM
CHAPTER 154
HAKONE ROPEWAY
SCULPTURE FOREST
GORA
KOWAKUDANI
HAKONE-YUMOTO
ASHINOKO SKYLINE
ASHINOKO LAKE
...WOULD BE SAFEST. FEWER SIGHT-SEEING SPOTS.
UNDERSTOOD.
I'LL LEAVE THE ROUTE TO YOU.

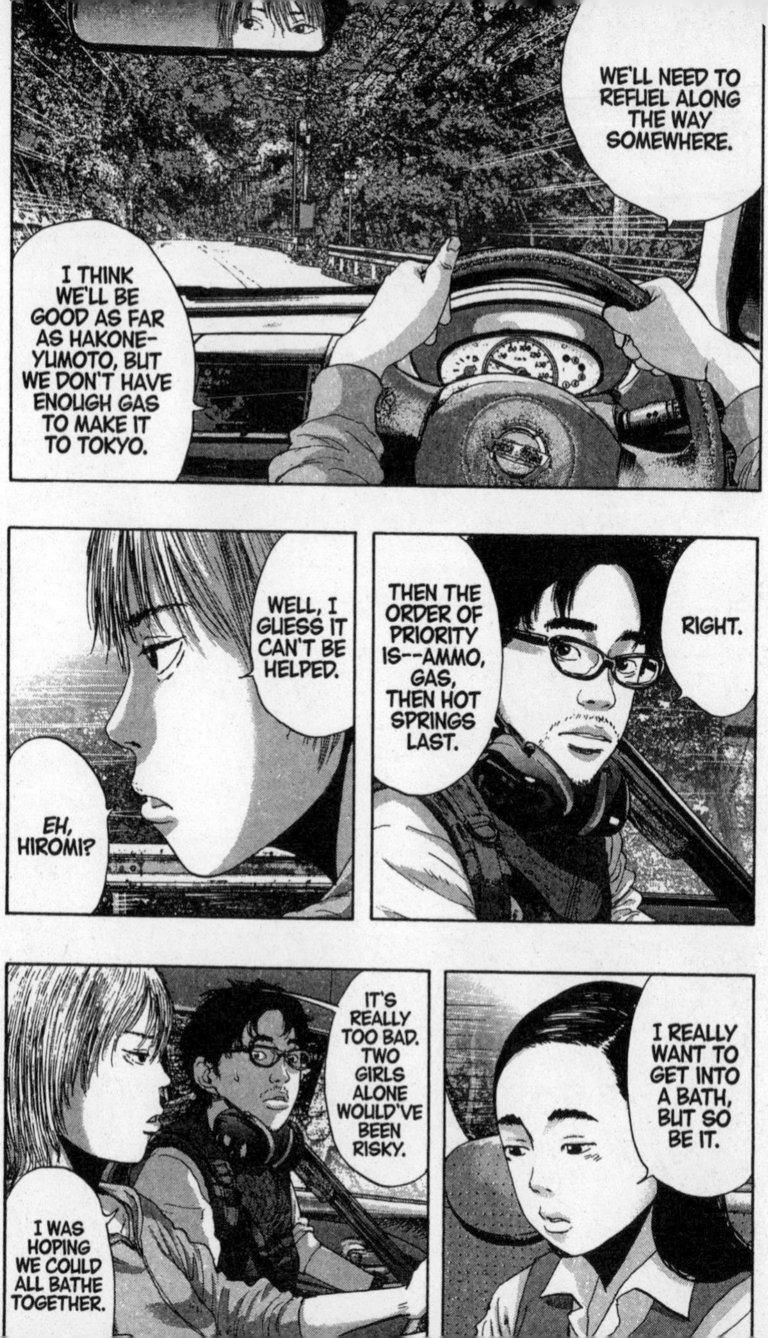
WE'LL NEED TO REFUEL ALONG THE WAY SOMEWHERE.
I THINK WE'LL BE GOOD AS FAR AS HAKONE-YUMOTO, BUT WE DON'T HAVE ENOUGH GAS TO MAKE IT TO TOKYO.
RIGHT.
THEN THE ORDER OF PRIORITY IS--AMMO, GAS, THEN HOT SPRINGS LAST.
WELL, I GUESS IT CAN'T BE HELPED.
EH, HIROMI?
I REALLY WANT TO GET INTO A BATH, BUT SO BE IT.
IT'S REALLY TOO BAD. TWO GIRLS ALONE WOULD'VE BEEN RISKY.
I WAS HOPING WE COULD ALL BATHE TOGETHER.

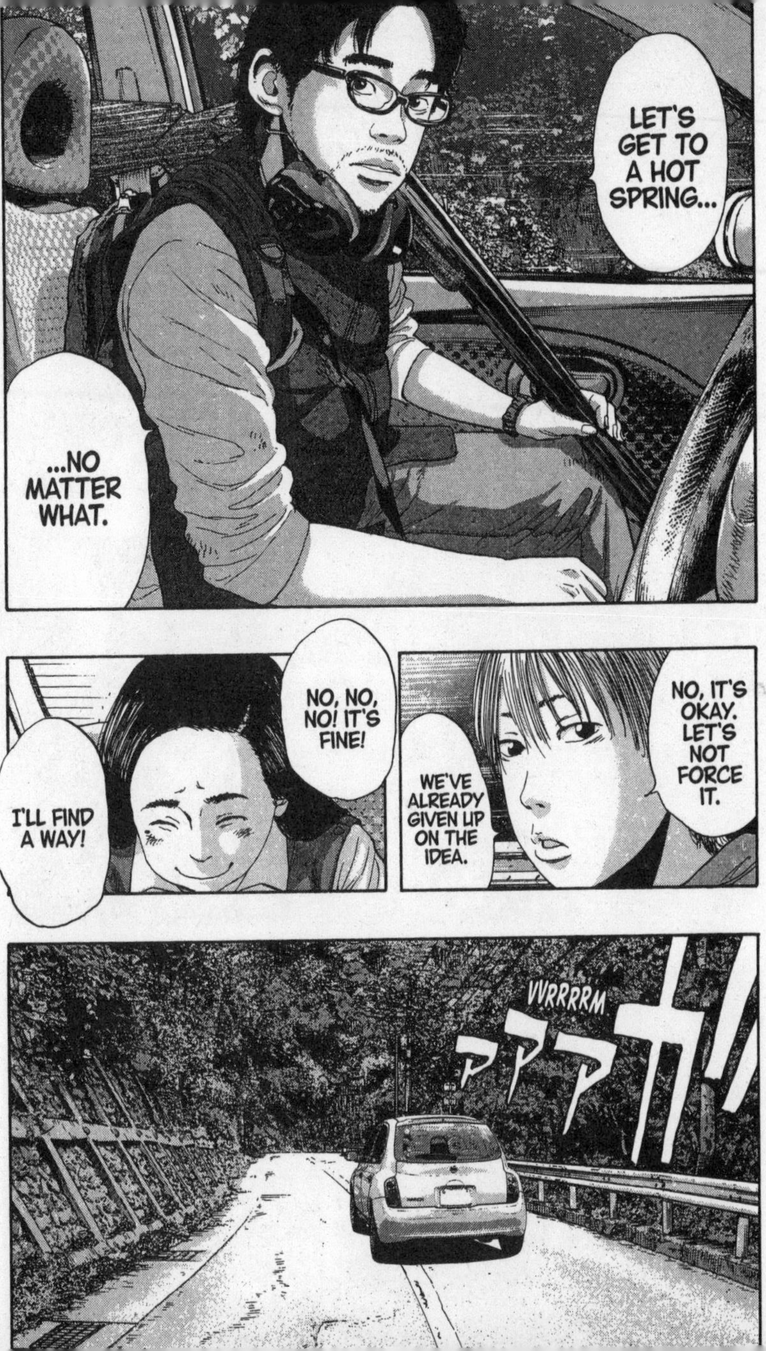
LET'S GET TO A HOT SPRING...
...NO MATTER WHAT.
NO, IT'S OKAY. LET'S NOT FORCE IT.
WE'VE ALREADY GIVEN UP ON THE IDEA.
NO, NO, NO! IT'S FINE!
I'LL FIND A WAY!
VVRRRRM

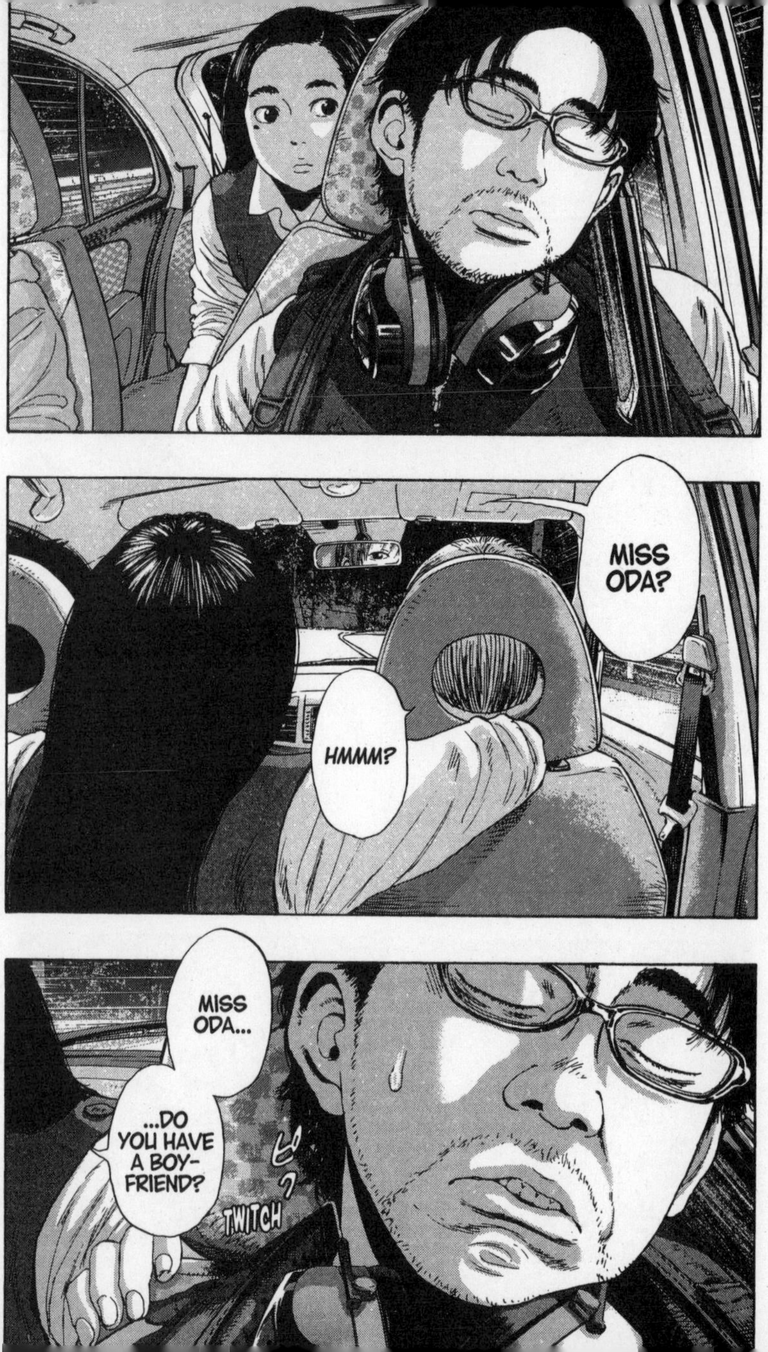
MISS ODA?
HMMM?
MISS ODA...
...DO YOU HAVE A BOY-FRIEND?
ピクッ
TWITCH

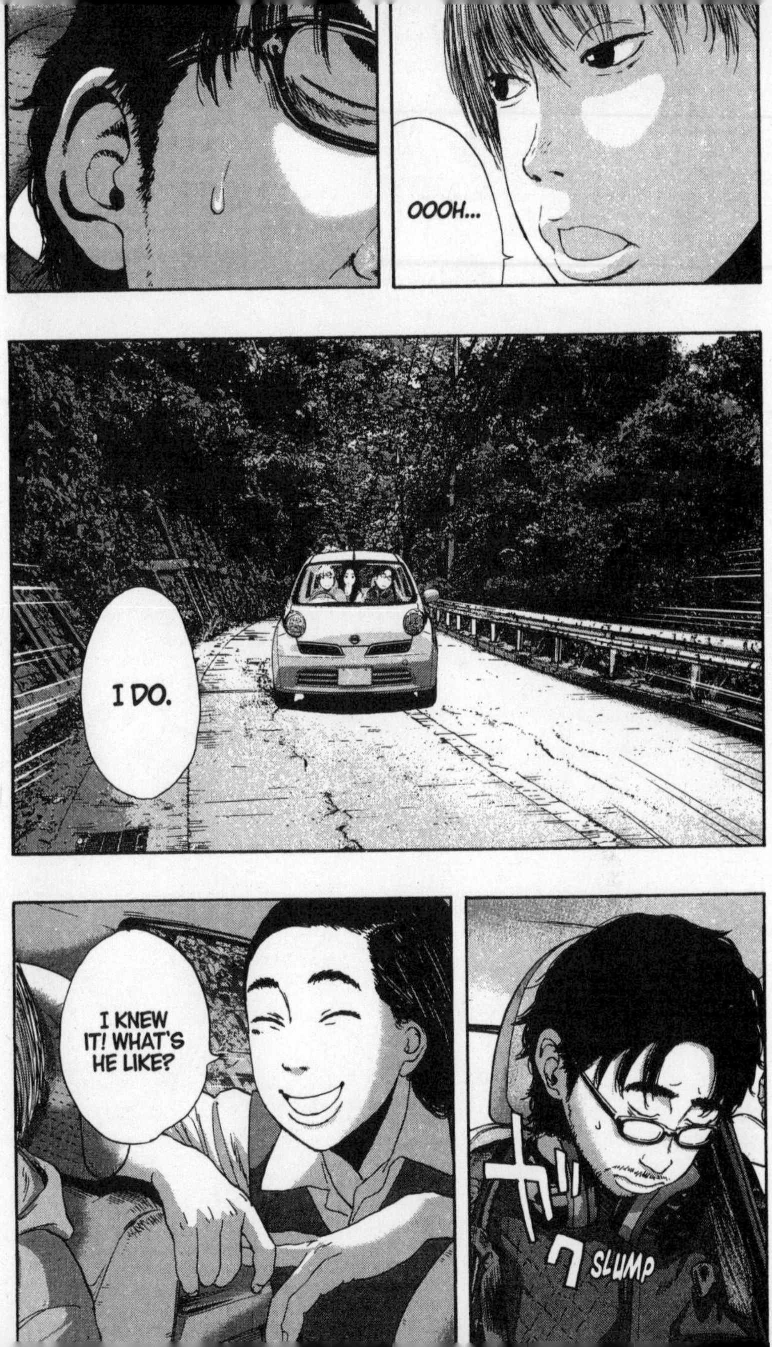
OOOH...
I DO.
SLUMP
I KNEW IT! WHAT'S HE LIKE?

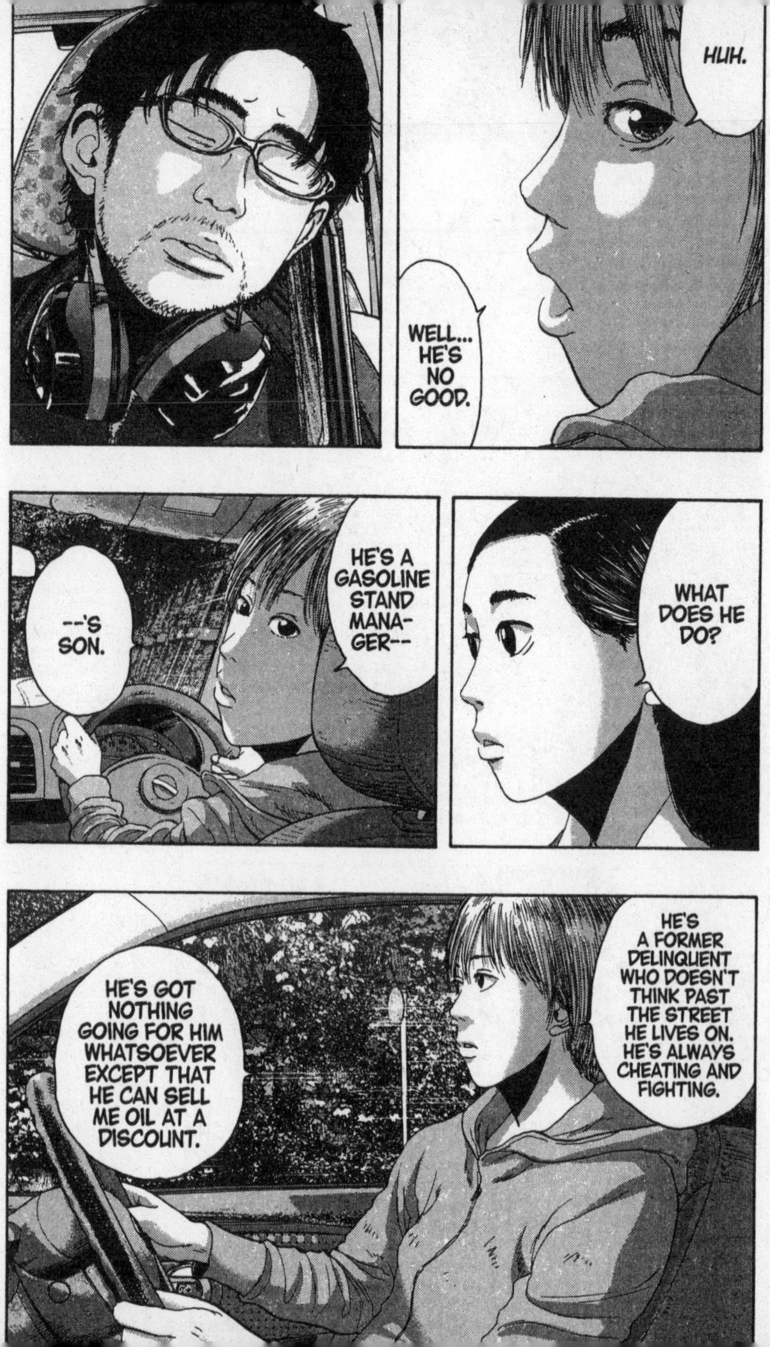
HUH.
WELL... HE'S NO GOOD.
WHAT DOES HE DO?
HE'S A GASOLINE STAND MANAGER--
--'S SON.
HE'S A FORMER DELINQUENT WHO DOESN'T THINK PAST THE STREET HE LIVES ON. HE'S ALWAYS CHEATING AND FIGHTING.
HE'S GOT NOTHING GOING FOR HIM WHATSOEVER EXCEPT THAT HE CAN SELL ME OIL AT A DISCOUNT.

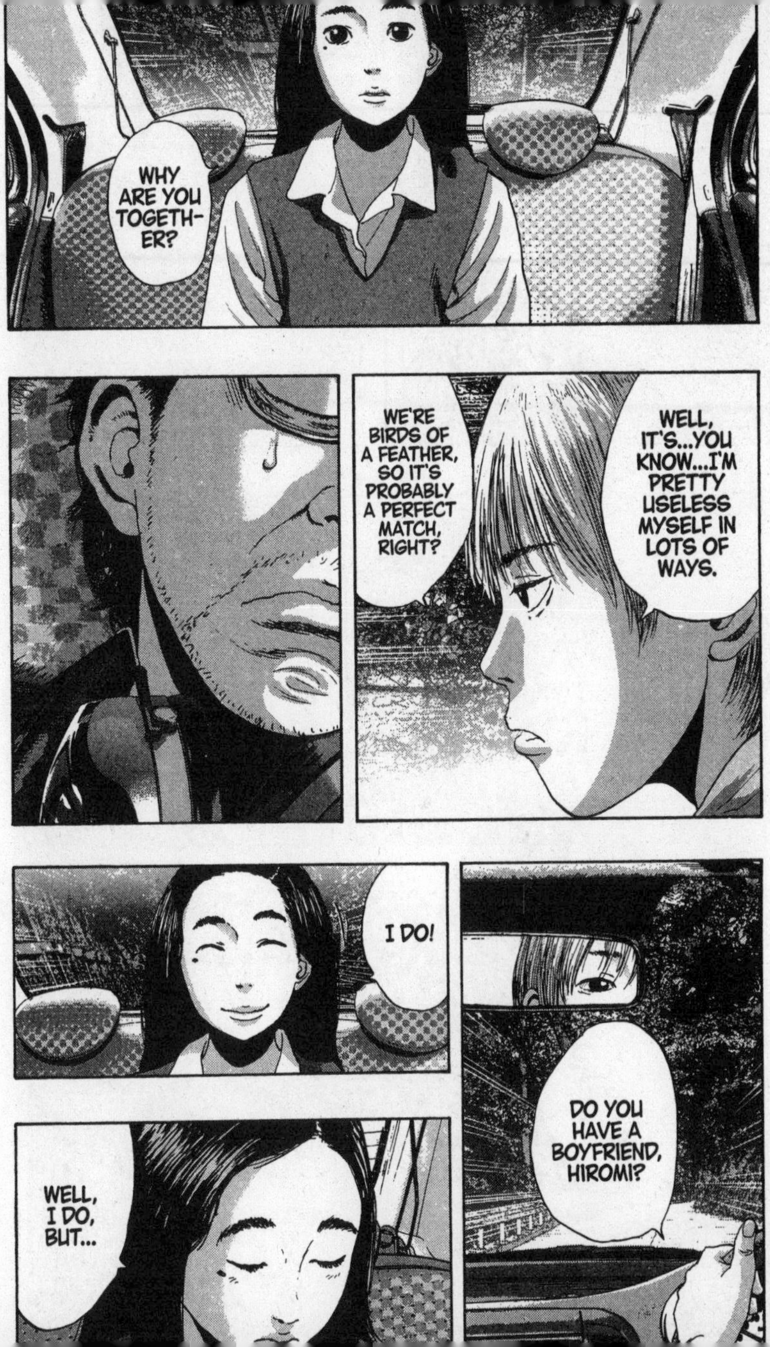
WHY ARE YOU TOGETH-ER?
WELL, IT'S...YOU KNOW...I'M PRETTY USELESS MYSELF IN LOTS OF WAYS.
WE'RE BIRDS OF A FEATHER, SO IT'S PROBABLY A PERFECT MATCH, RIGHT?
DO YOU HAVE A BOYFRIEND, HIROMI?
I DO!
WELL, I DO, BUT...

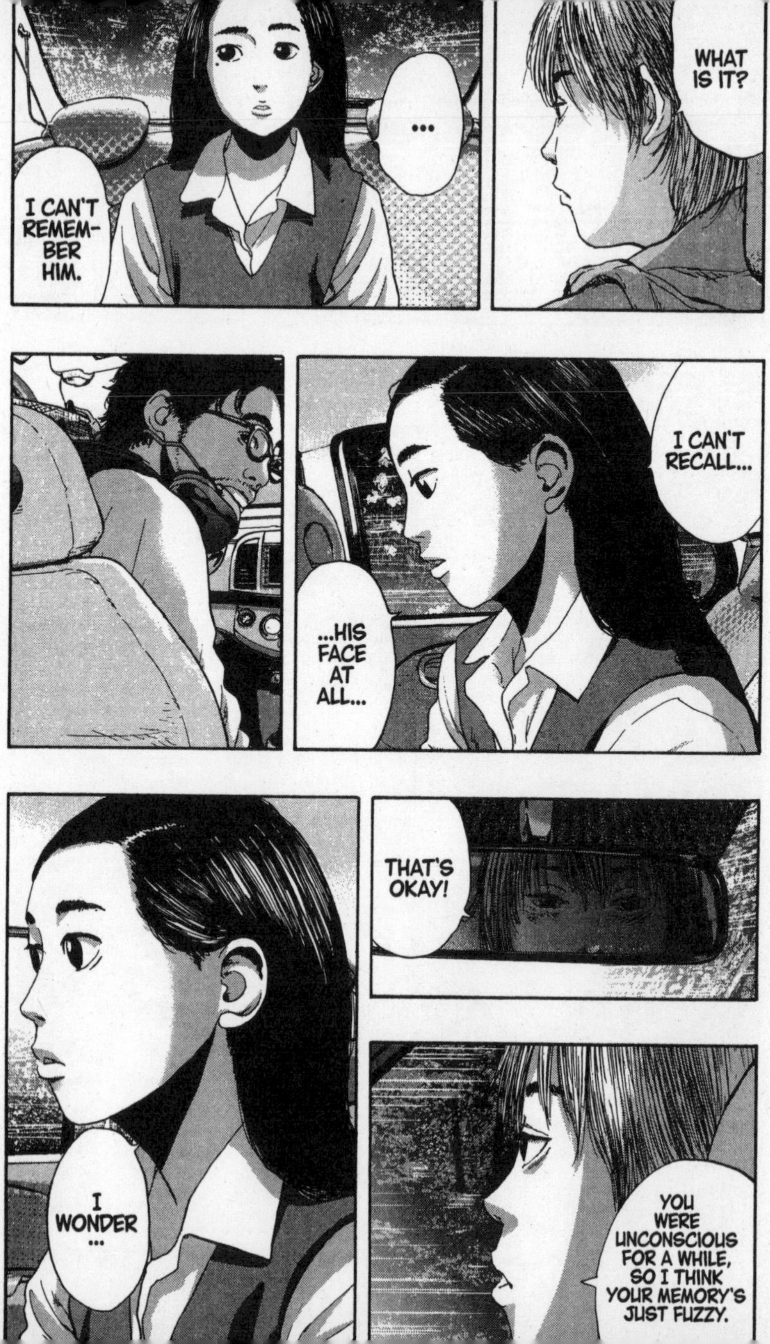
WHAT IS IT?
...
I CAN'T REMEMBER HIM.
I CAN'T RECALL...
...HIS FACE AT ALL...
THAT'S OKAY!
YOU WERE UNCONSCIOUS FOR A WHILE, SO I THINK YOUR MEMORY'S JUST FUZZY.
I WONDER ...

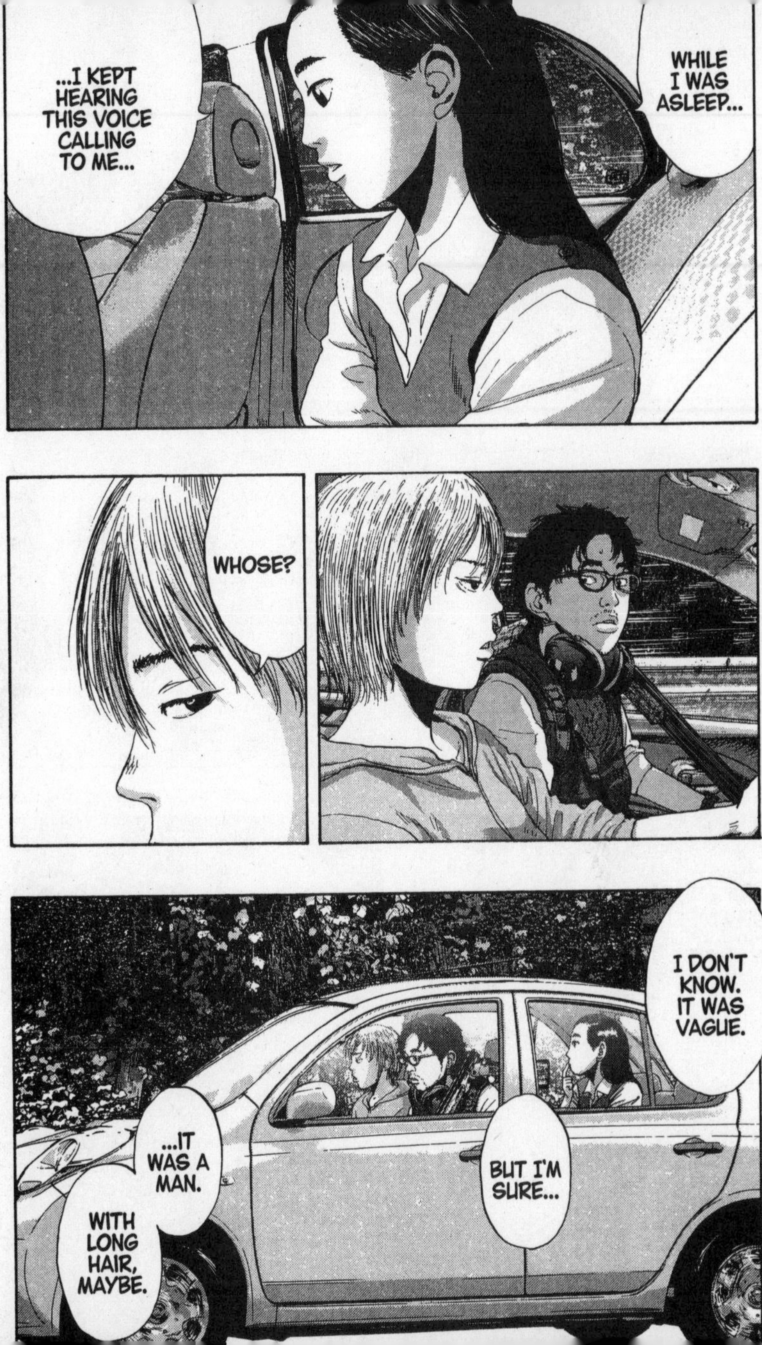
WHILE I WAS ASLEEP...
...I KEPT HEARING THIS VOICE CALLING TO ME...
WHOSE?
I DON'T KNOW. IT WAS VAGUE.
BUT I'M SURE...
...IT WAS A MAN.
WITH LONG HAIR, MAYBE.

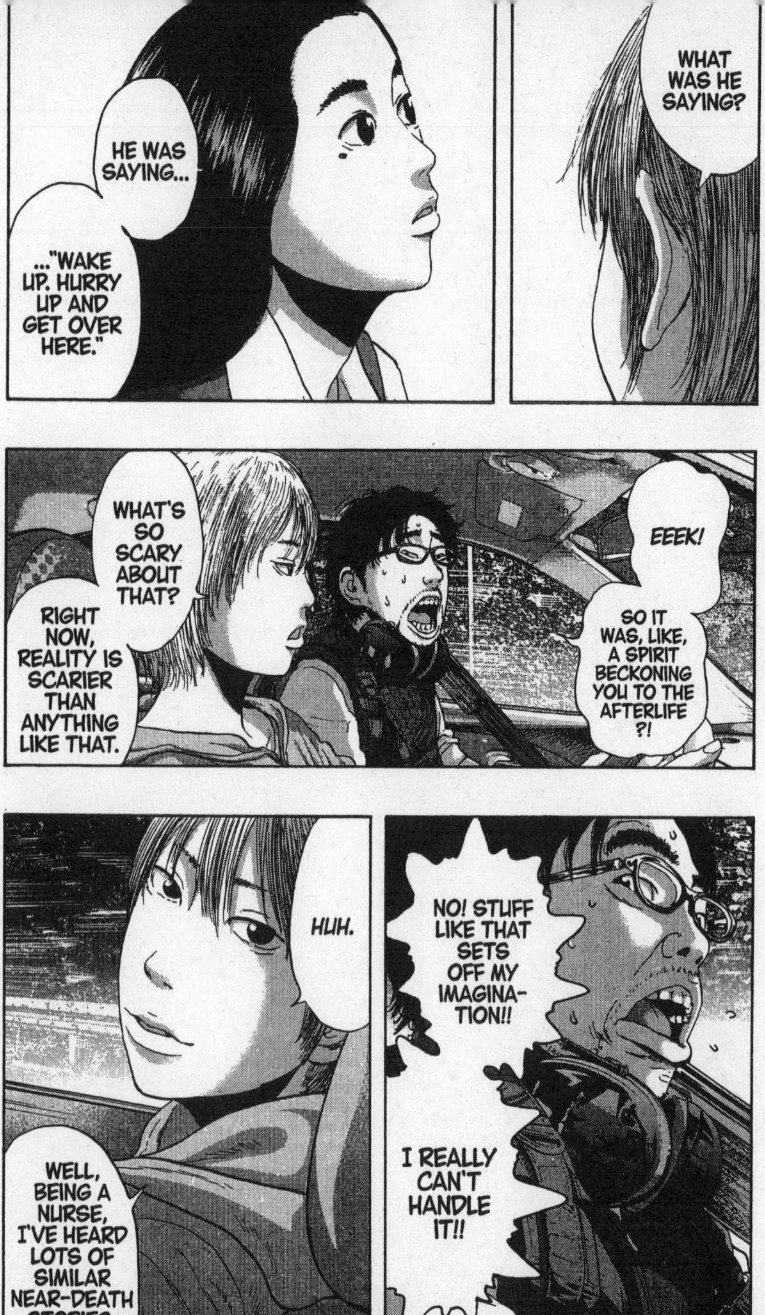
WHAT WAS HE SAYING?
HE WAS SAYING...
..."WAKE UP. HURRY UP AND GET OVER HERE."
EEEK!
SO IT WAS, LIKE, A SPIRIT BECKONING YOU TO THE AFTERLIFE?!
WHAT'S SO SCARY ABOUT THAT?
RIGHT NOW, REALITY IS SCARIER THAN ANYTHING LIKE THAT.
NO! STUFF LIKE THAT SETS OFF MY IMAGINATION!!
I REALLY CAN'T HANDLE IT!!
HUH.
WELL, BEING A NURSE, I'VE HEARD LOTS OF SIMILAR NEAR-DEATH STORIES.

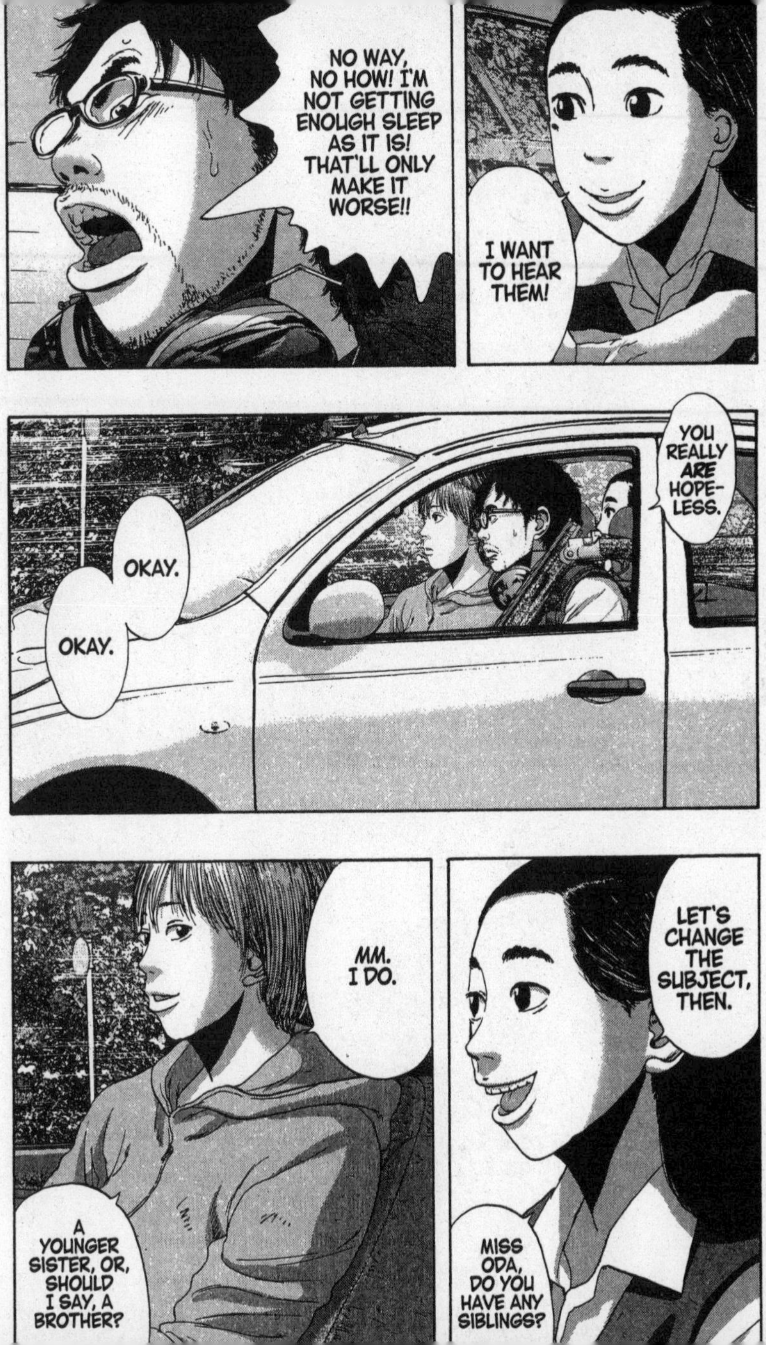
I WANT TO HEAR THEM!
NO WAY, NO HOW! I'M NOT GETTING ENOUGH SLEEP AS IT IS! THAT'LL ONLY MAKE IT WORSE!!
YOU REALLY ARE HOPELESS.
OKAY.
OKAY.
LET'S CHANGE THE SUBJECT, THEN.
MISS ODA, DO YOU HAVE ANY SIBLINGS?
MM. I DO.
A YOUNGER SISTER, OR, SHOULD I SAY, A BROTHER?

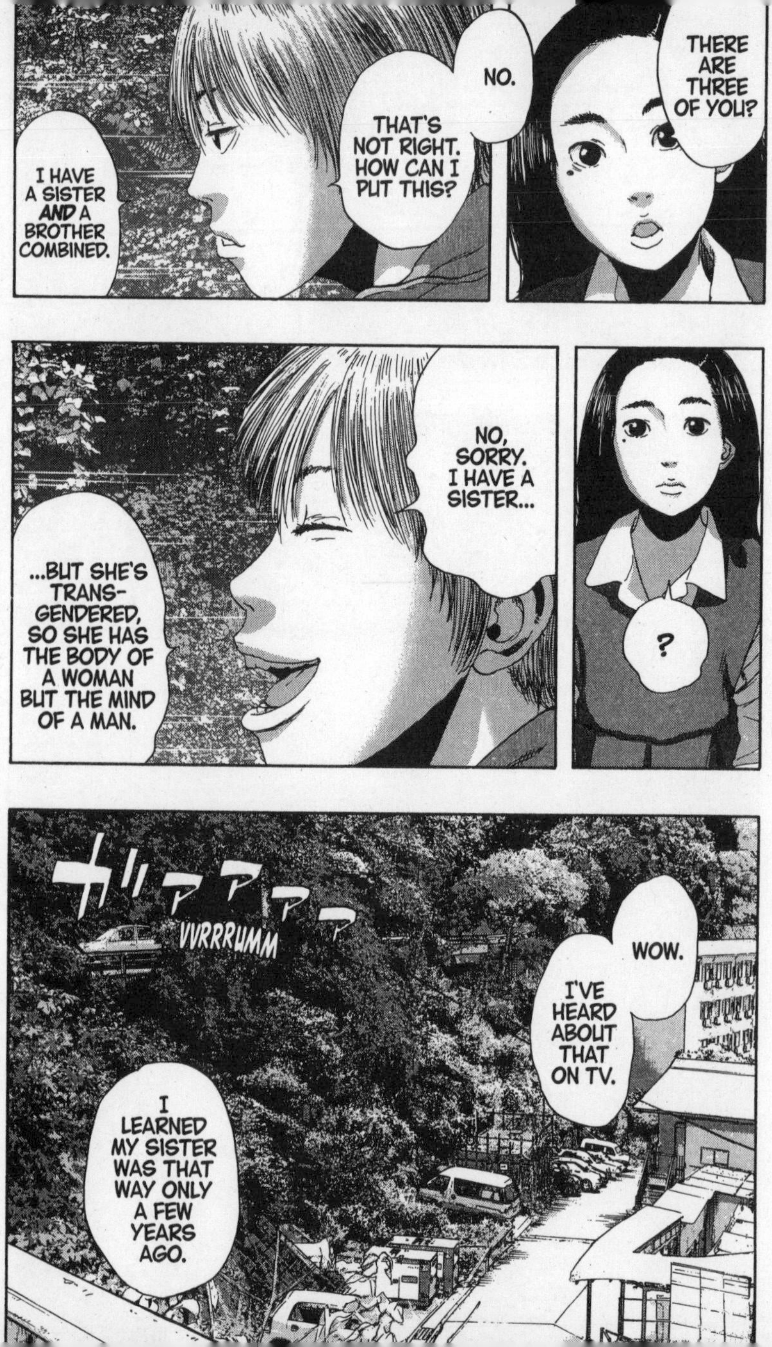

THERE ARE THREE OF YOU?
NO.
THAT'S NOT RIGHT. HOW CAN I PUT THIS?
I HAVE A SISTER AND A BROTHER COMBINED.
?
NO, SORRY. I HAVE A SISTER...
...BUT SHE'S TRANS-GENDERED, SO SHE HAS THE BODY OF A WOMAN BUT THE MIND OF A MAN.
VVRRRUMM
WOW.
I'VE HEARD ABOUT THAT ON TV.
I LEARNED MY SISTER WAS THAT WAY ONLY A FEW YEARS AGO.

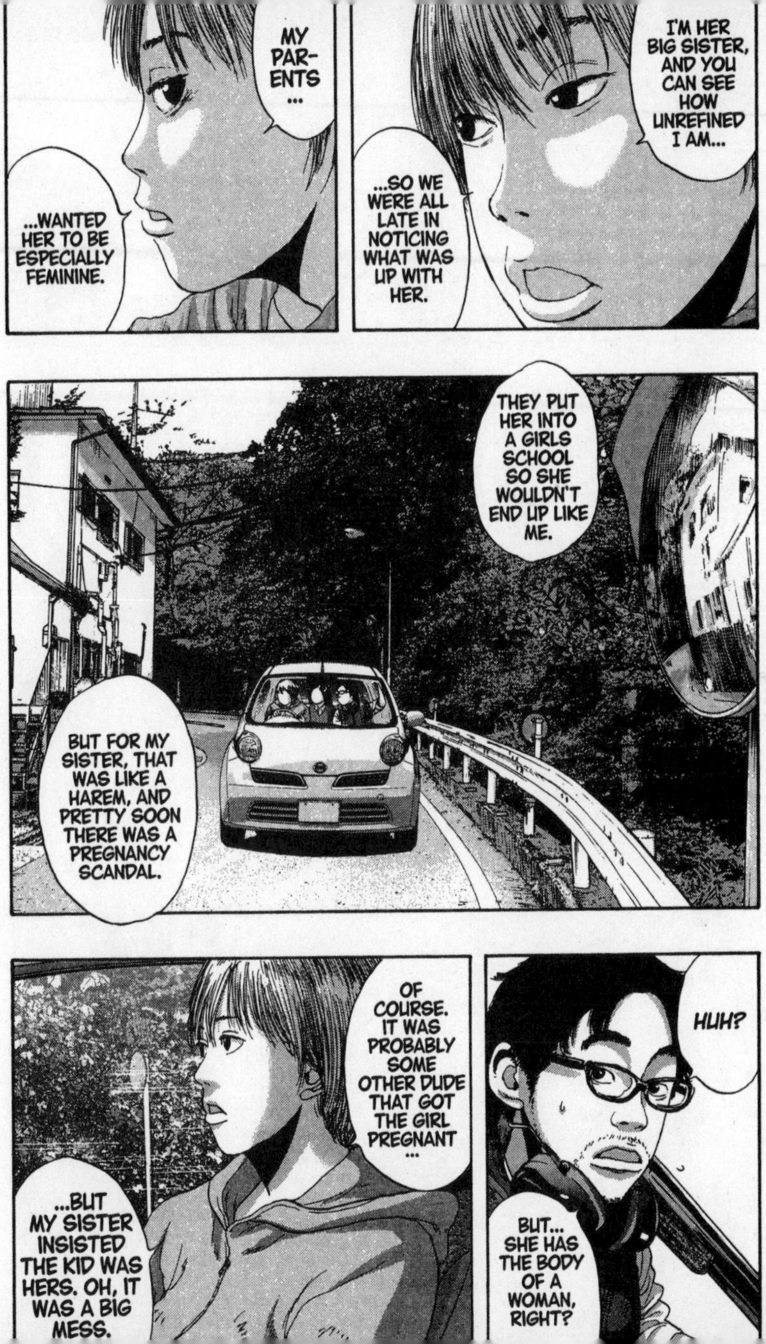
I'M HER BIG SISTER, AND YOU CAN SEE HOW UNREFINED I AM...
...SO WE WERE ALL LATE IN NOTICING WHAT WAS UP WITH HER.
MY PARENTS...
...WANTED HER TO BE ESPECIALLY FEMININE.
THEY PUT HER INTO A GIRLS SCHOOL SO SHE WOULDN'T END UP LIKE ME.
BUT FOR MY SISTER, THAT WAS LIKE A HAREM, AND PRETTY SOON THERE WAS A PREGNANCY SCANDAL.
HUH?
BUT... SHE HAS THE BODY OF A WOMAN, RIGHT?
OF COURSE. IT WAS PROBABLY SOME OTHER DUDE THAT GOT THE GIRL PREGNANT...
...BUT MY SISTER INSISTED THE KID WAS HERS. OH, IT WAS A BIG MESS.

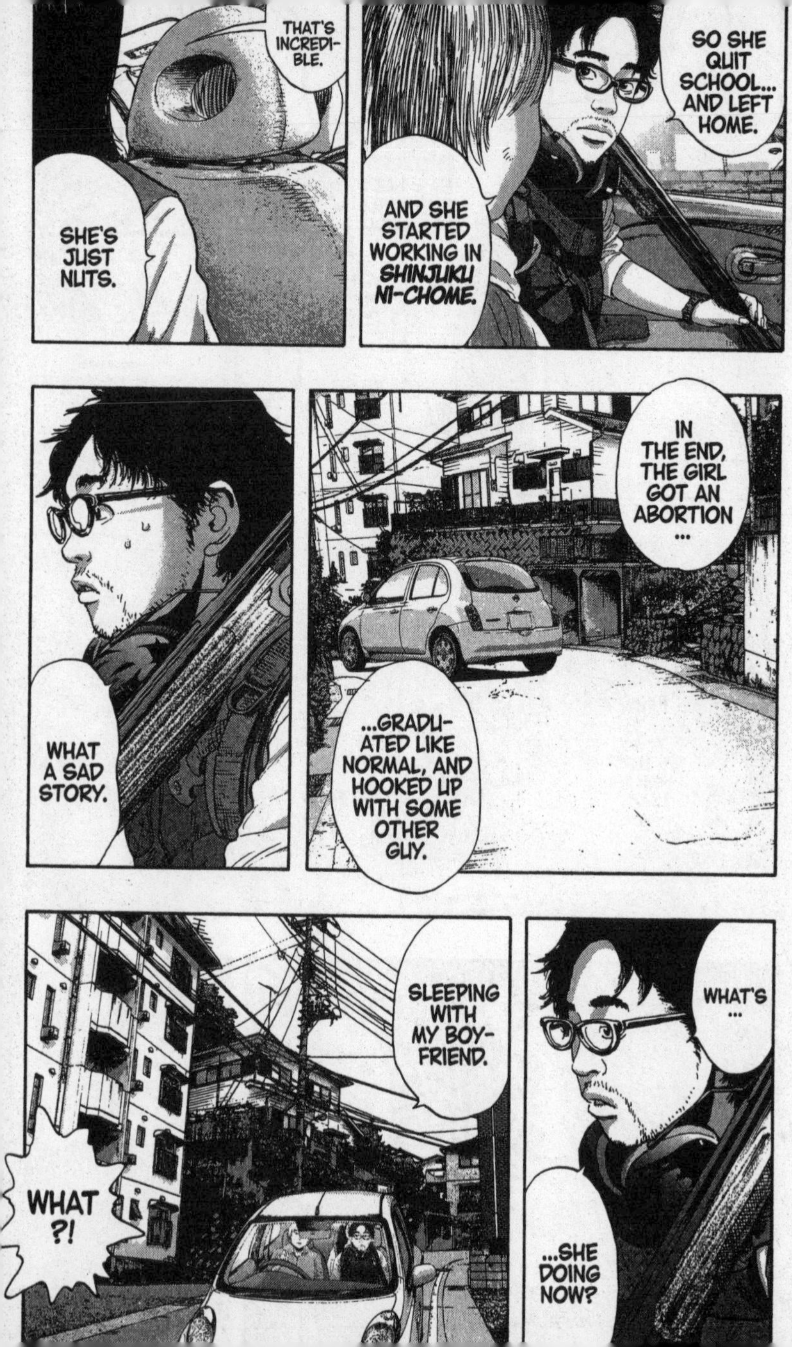
SO SHE QUIT SCHOOL... AND LEFT HOME.
AND SHE STARTED WORKING IN SHINJUKU NI-CHOME.
THAT'S INCREDIBLE.
SHE'S JUST NUTS.
IN THE END, THE GIRL GOT AN ABORTION ...
...GRADUATED LIKE NORMAL, AND HOOKED UP WITH SOME OTHER GUY.
WHAT A SAD STORY.
WHAT'S ...
...SHE DOING NOW?
SLEEPING WITH MY BOYFRIEND.
WHAT ?!

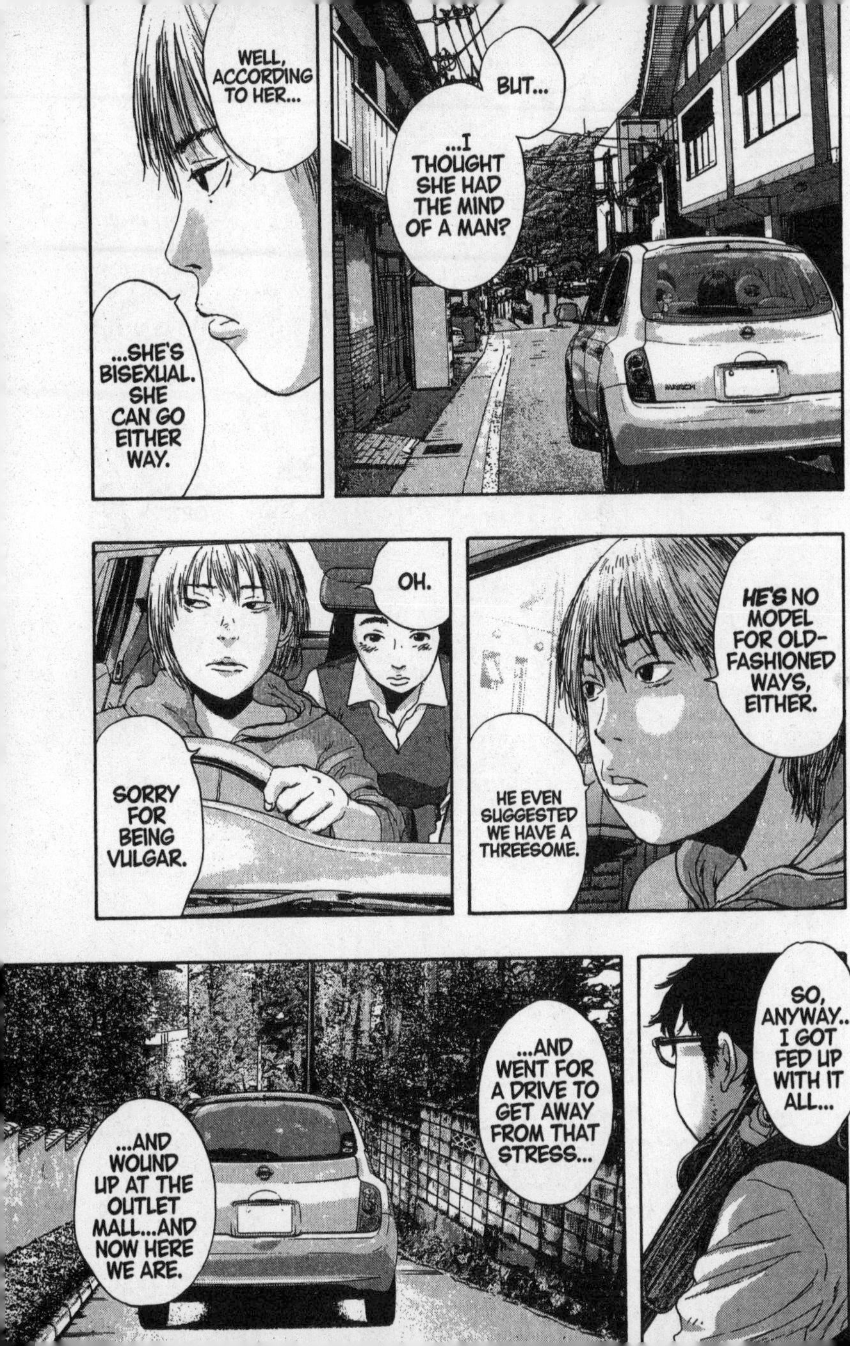
BUT...
...I THOUGHT SHE HAD THE MIND OF A MAN?
WELL, ACCORDING TO HER...
...SHE'S BISEXUAL. SHE CAN GO EITHER WAY.
HE'S NO MODEL FOR OLD-FASHIONED WAYS, EITHER.
HE EVEN SUGGESTED WE HAVE A THREESOME.
OH.
SORRY FOR BEING VULGAR.
SO, ANYWAY... I GOT FED UP WITH IT ALL...
...AND WENT FOR A DRIVE TO GET AWAY FROM THAT STRESS...
...AND WOUND UP AT THE OUTLET MALL...AND NOW HERE WE ARE.

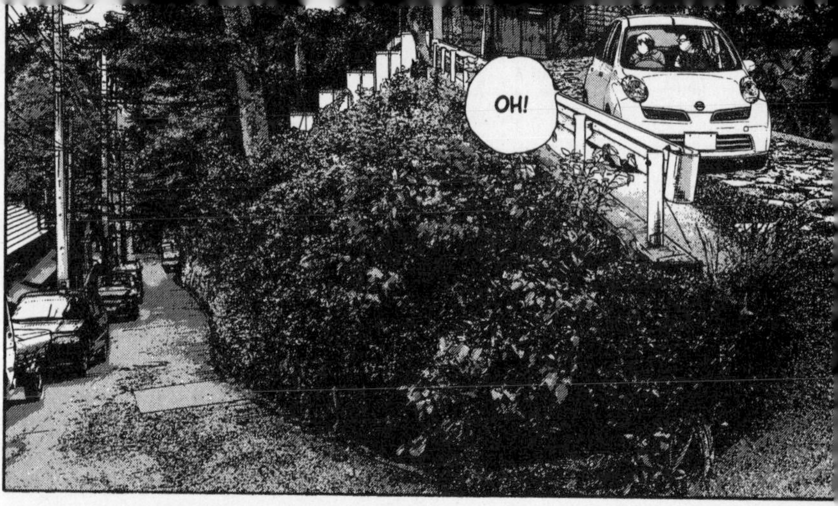
OH!
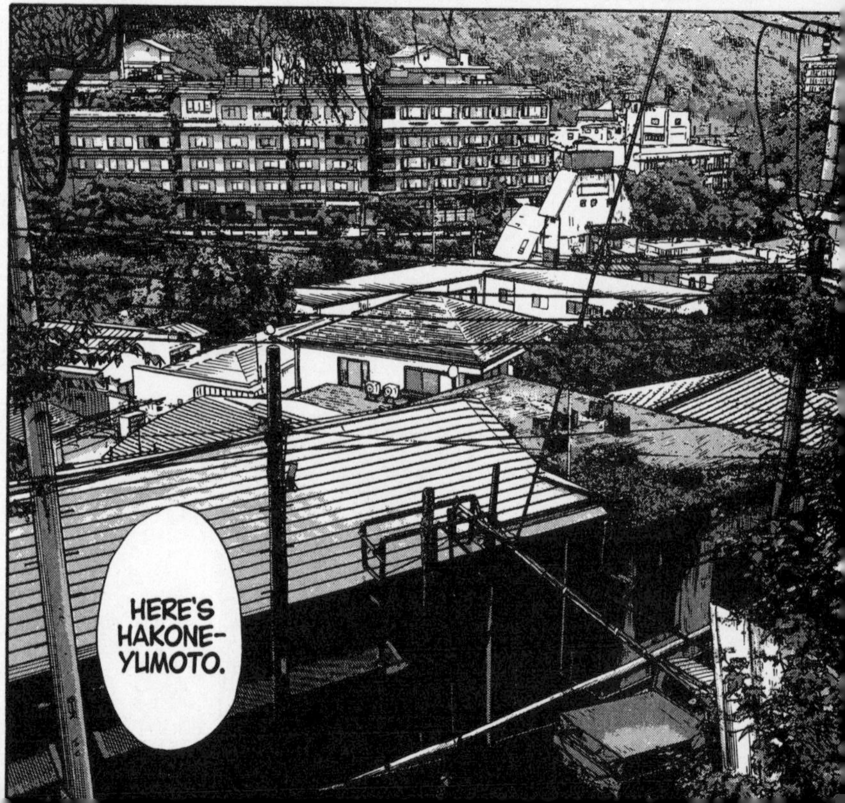
HERE'S HAKONE-YUMOTO.

CHAPTER 155

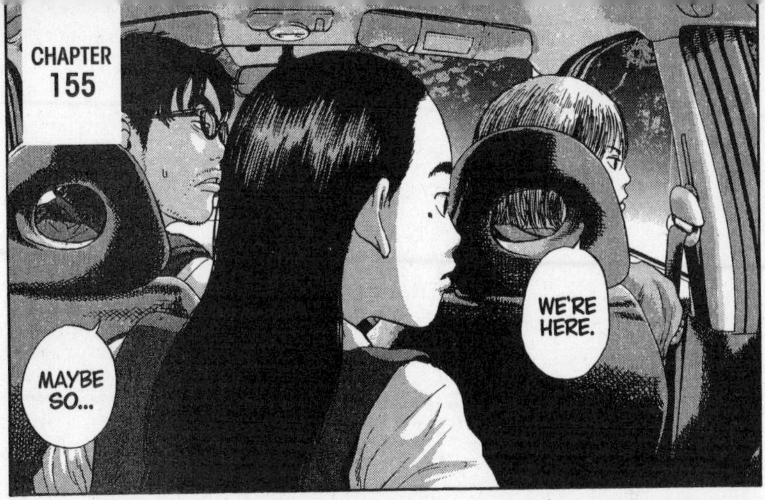
WE'RE HERE.
MAYBE SO...

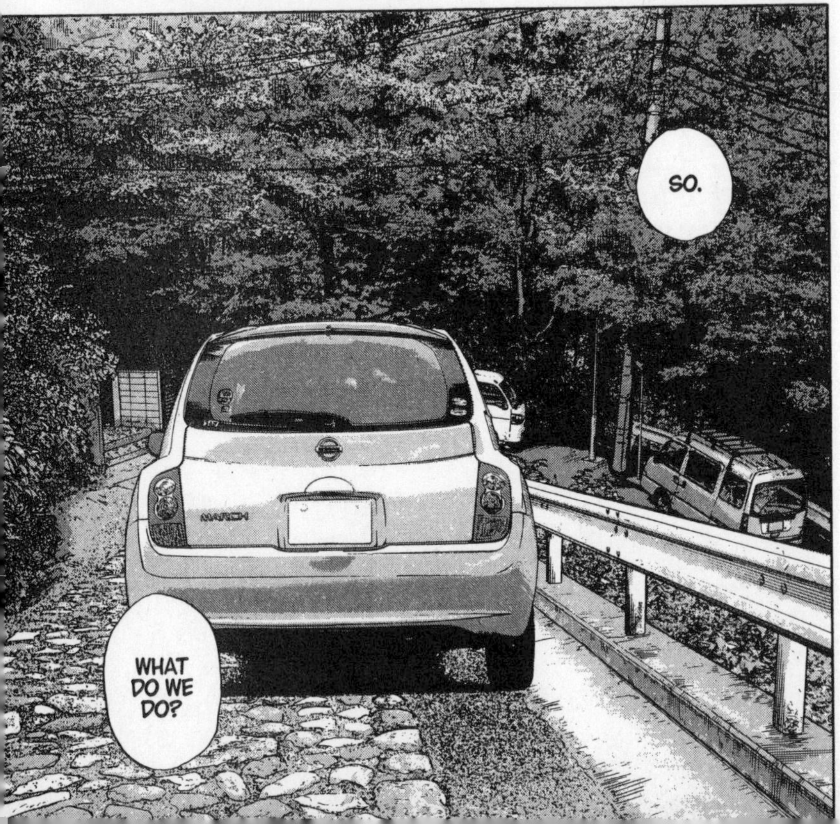
SO.
WHAT DO WE DO?

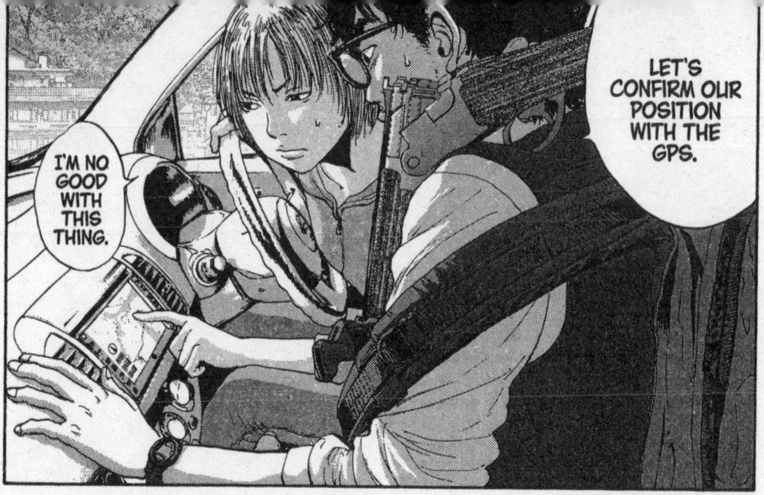
LET'S CONFIRM OUR POSITION WITH THE GPS.
I'M NO GOOD WITH THIS THING.

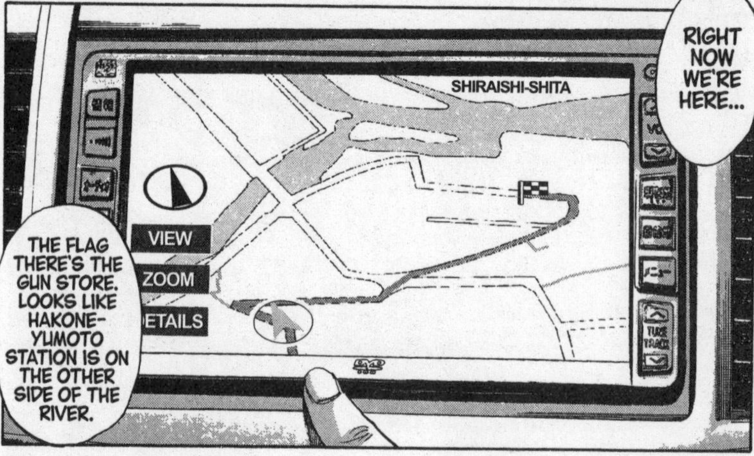
RIGHT NOW WE'RE HERE...
SHIRAISHI-SHITA
THE FLAG THERE'S THE GUN STORE. LOOKS LIKE HAKONE-YUMOTO STATION IS ON THE OTHER SIDE OF THE RIVER.
VIEW
ZOOM
ETAILS

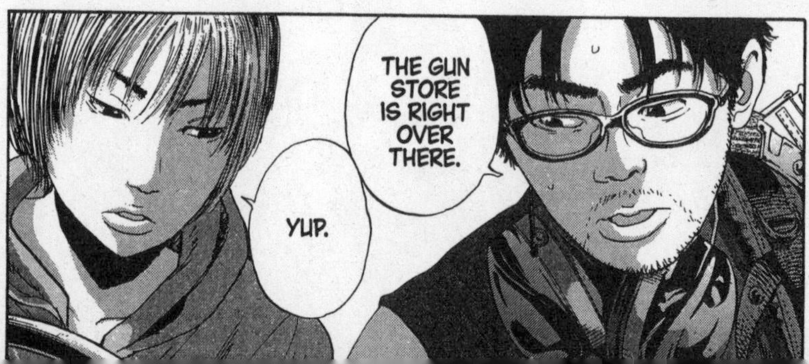
THE GUN STORE IS RIGHT OVER THERE.
YUP.

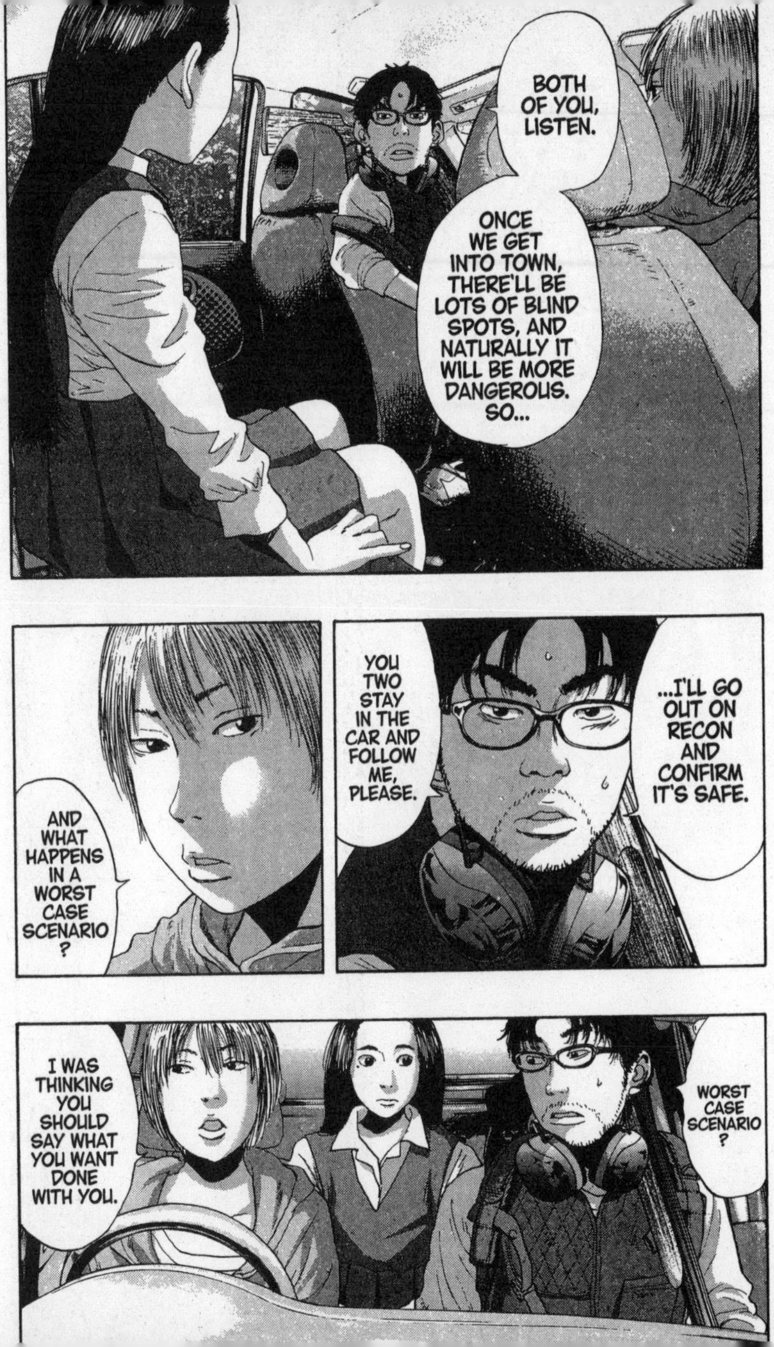
BOTH OF YOU, LISTEN.
ONCE WE GET INTO TOWN, THERE'LL BE LOTS OF BLIND SPOTS, AND NATURALLY IT WILL BE MORE DANGEROUS. SO...
...I'LL GO OUT ON RECON AND CONFIRM IT'S SAFE.
YOU TWO STAY IN THE CAR AND FOLLOW ME, PLEASE.
AND WHAT HAPPENS IN A WORST CASE SCENARIO ?
WORST CASE SCENARIO ?
I WAS THINKING YOU SHOULD SAY WHAT YOU WANT DONE WITH YOU.

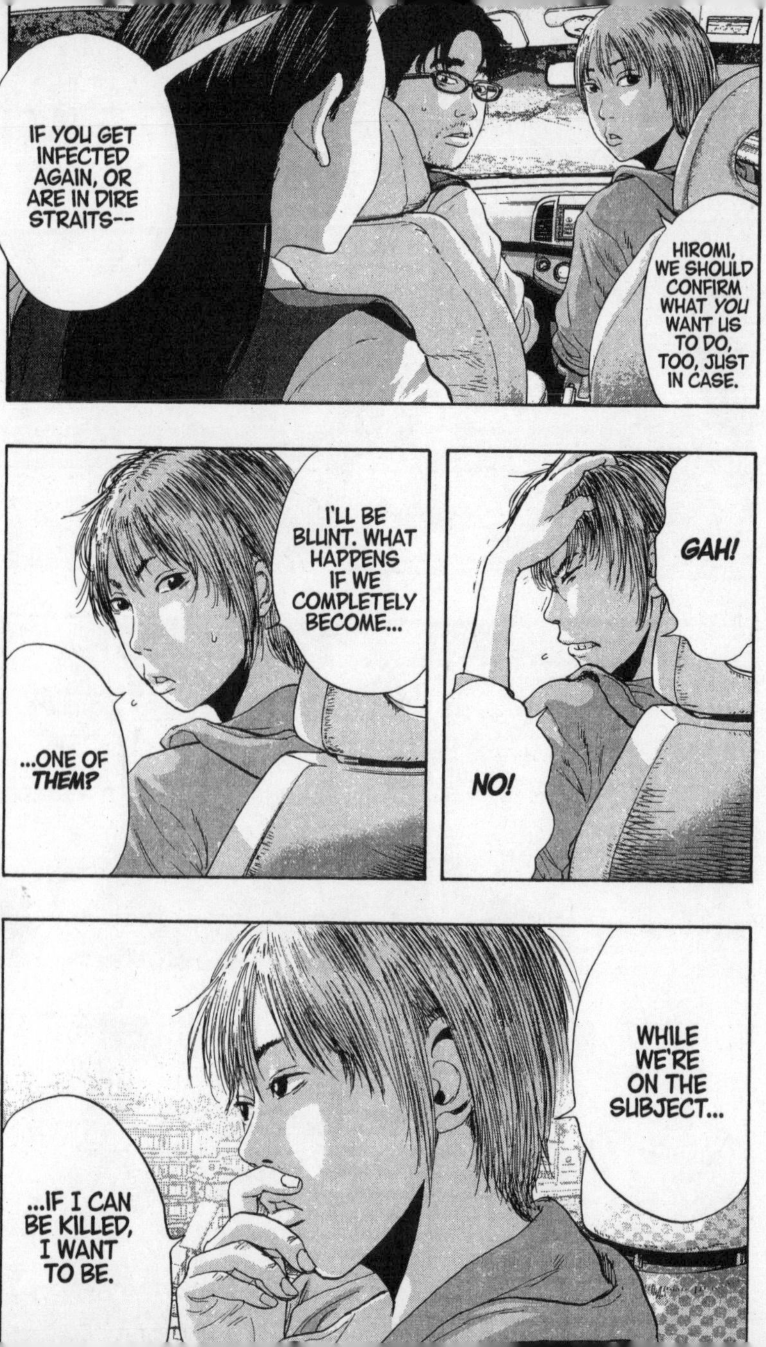
HIROMI, WE SHOULD CONFIRM WHAT YOU WANT US TO DO, TOO, JUST IN CASE.
IF YOU GET INFECTED AGAIN, OR ARE IN DIRE STRAITS--
GAH!
NO!
I'LL BE BLUNT. WHAT HAPPENS IF WE COMPLETELY BECOME...
...ONE OF THEM?
WHILE WE'RE ON THE SUBJECT...
...IF I CAN BE KILLED, I WANT TO BE.

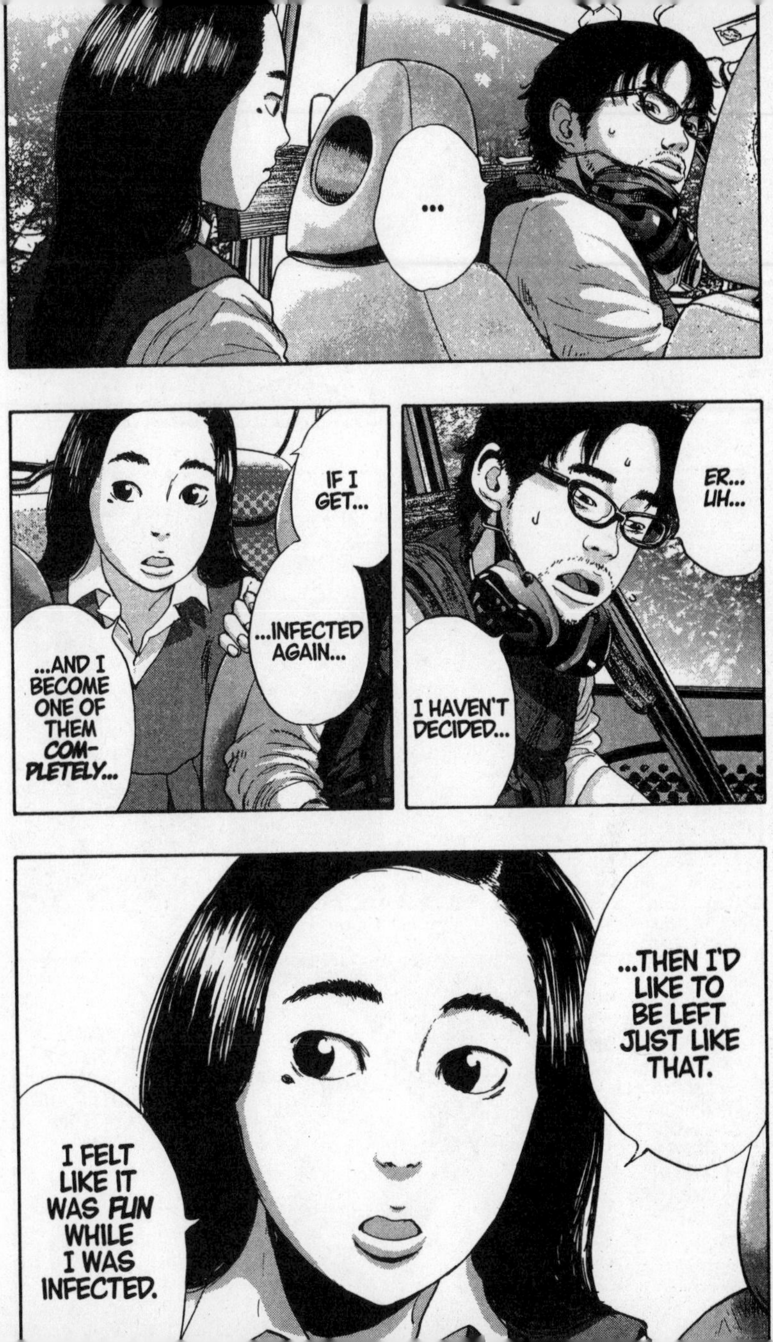
...
ER... UH...
I HAVEN'T DECIDED...
IF I GET...
...INFECTED AGAIN...
...AND I BECOME ONE OF THEM COMPLETELY...
...THEN I'D LIKE TO BE LEFT JUST LIKE THAT.
I FELT LIKE IT WAS *FUN* WHILE I WAS INFECTED.

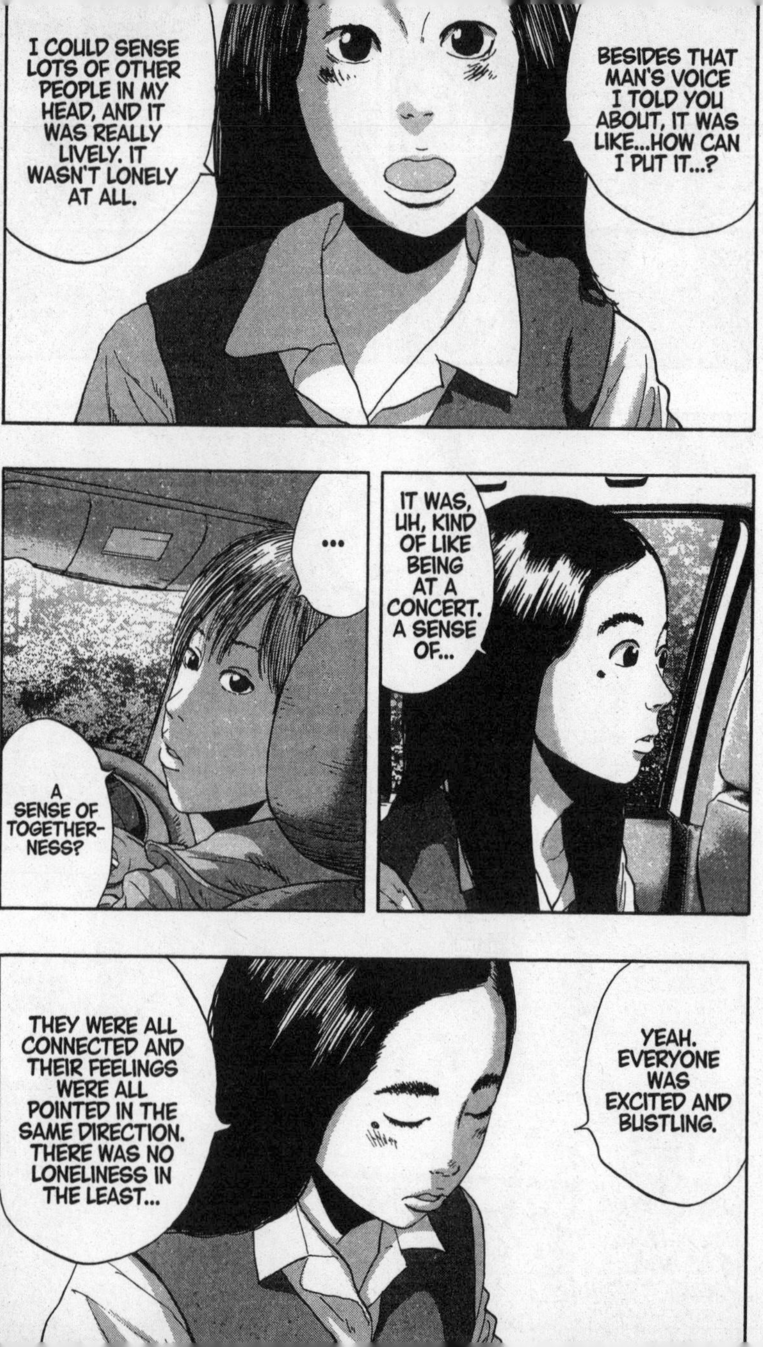
BESIDES THAT MAN'S VOICE I TOLD YOU ABOUT, IT WAS LIKE...HOW CAN I PUT IT...?
I COULD SENSE LOTS OF OTHER PEOPLE IN MY HEAD, AND IT WAS REALLY LIVELY. IT WASN'T LONELY AT ALL.
IT WAS, UH, KIND OF LIKE BEING AT A CONCERT. A SENSE OF...
...
A SENSE OF TOGETHER-NESS?
YEAH. EVERYONE WAS EXCITED AND BUSTLING.
THEY WERE ALL CONNECTED AND THEIR FEELINGS WERE ALL POINTED IN THE SAME DIRECTION. THERE WAS NO LONELINESS IN THE LEAST...

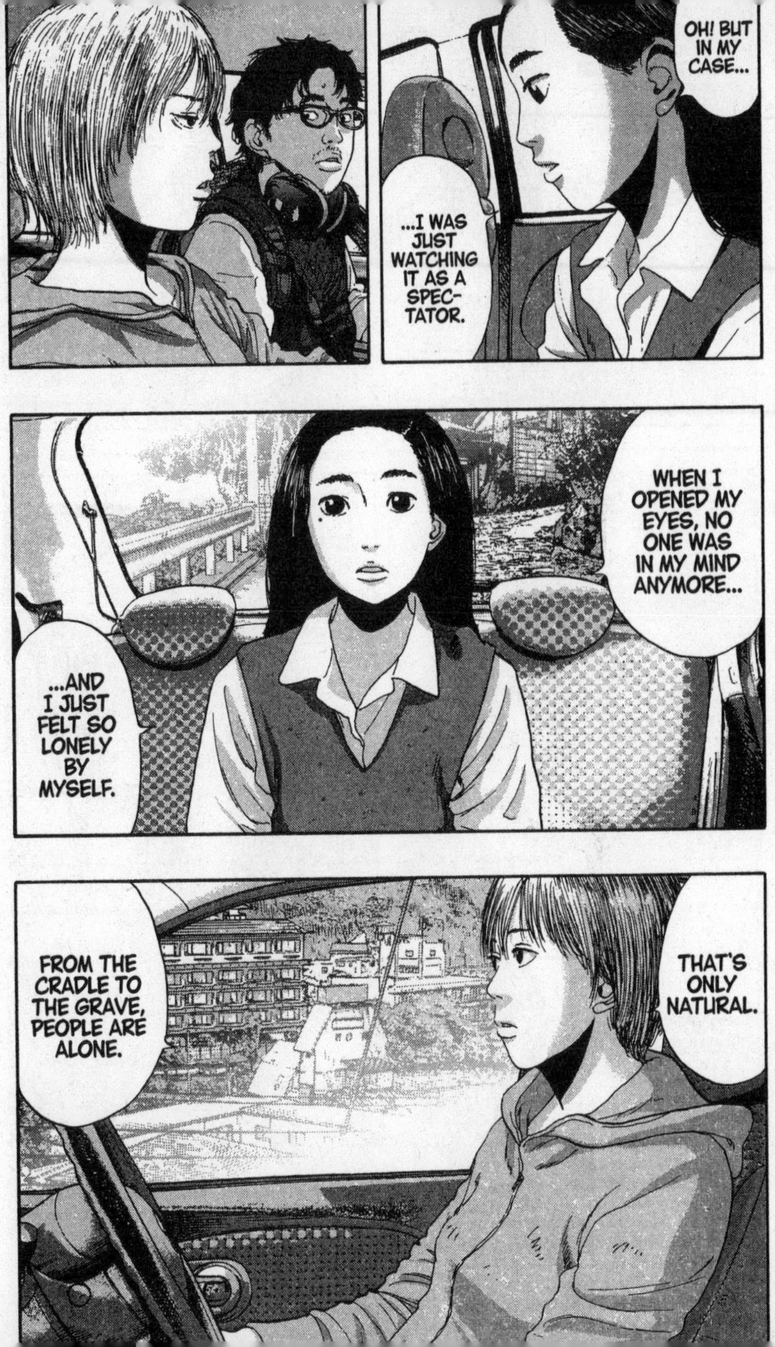
OH! BUT IN MY CASE...
...I WAS JUST WATCHING IT AS A SPEC-TATOR.
WHEN I OPENED MY EYES, NO ONE WAS IN MY MIND ANYMORE...
...AND I JUST FELT SO LONELY BY MYSELF.
THAT'S ONLY NATURAL.
FROM THE CRADLE TO THE GRAVE, PEOPLE ARE ALONE.

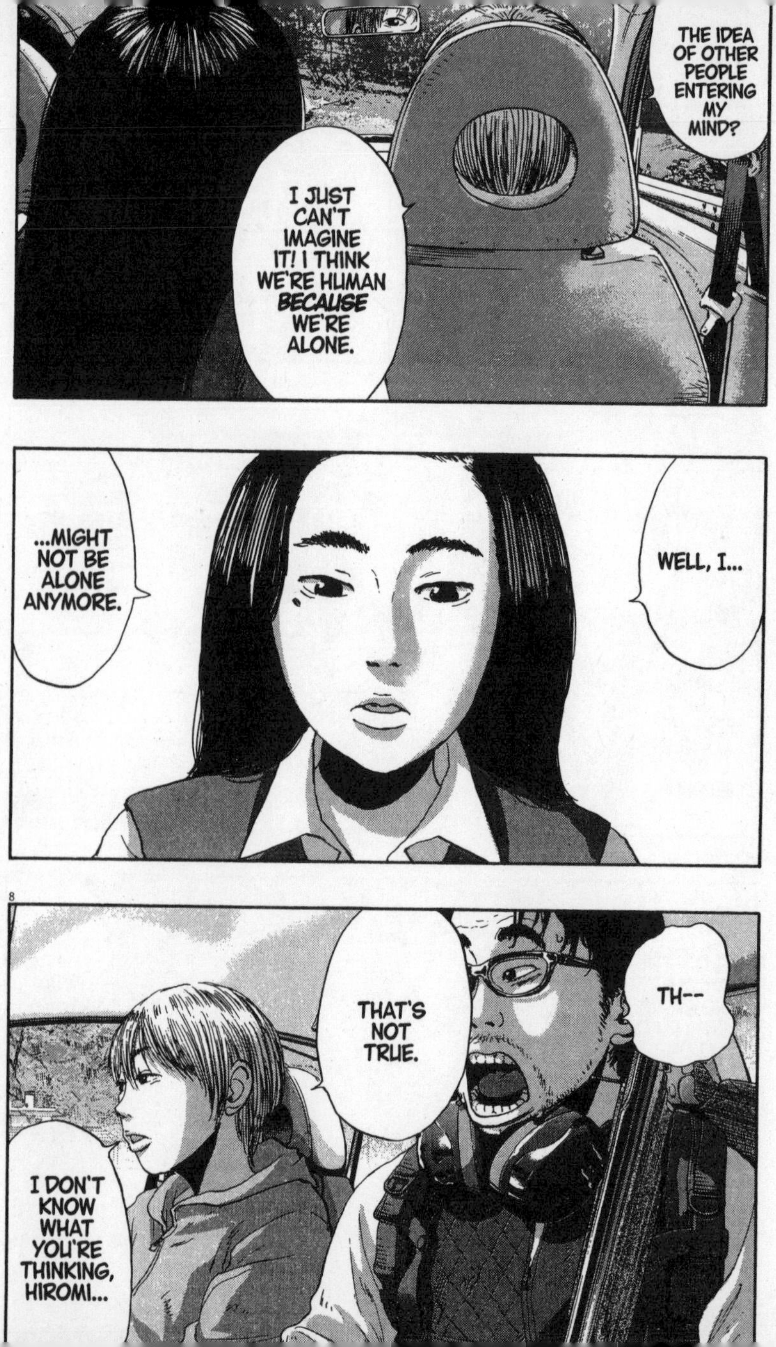
THE IDEA OF OTHER PEOPLE ENTERING MY MIND?
I JUST CAN'T IMAGINE IT! I THINK WE'RE HUMAN BECAUSE WE'RE ALONE.
WELL, I...
...MIGHT NOT BE ALONE ANYMORE.
TH--
THAT'S NOT TRUE.
I DON'T KNOW WHAT YOU'RE THINKING, HIROMI...

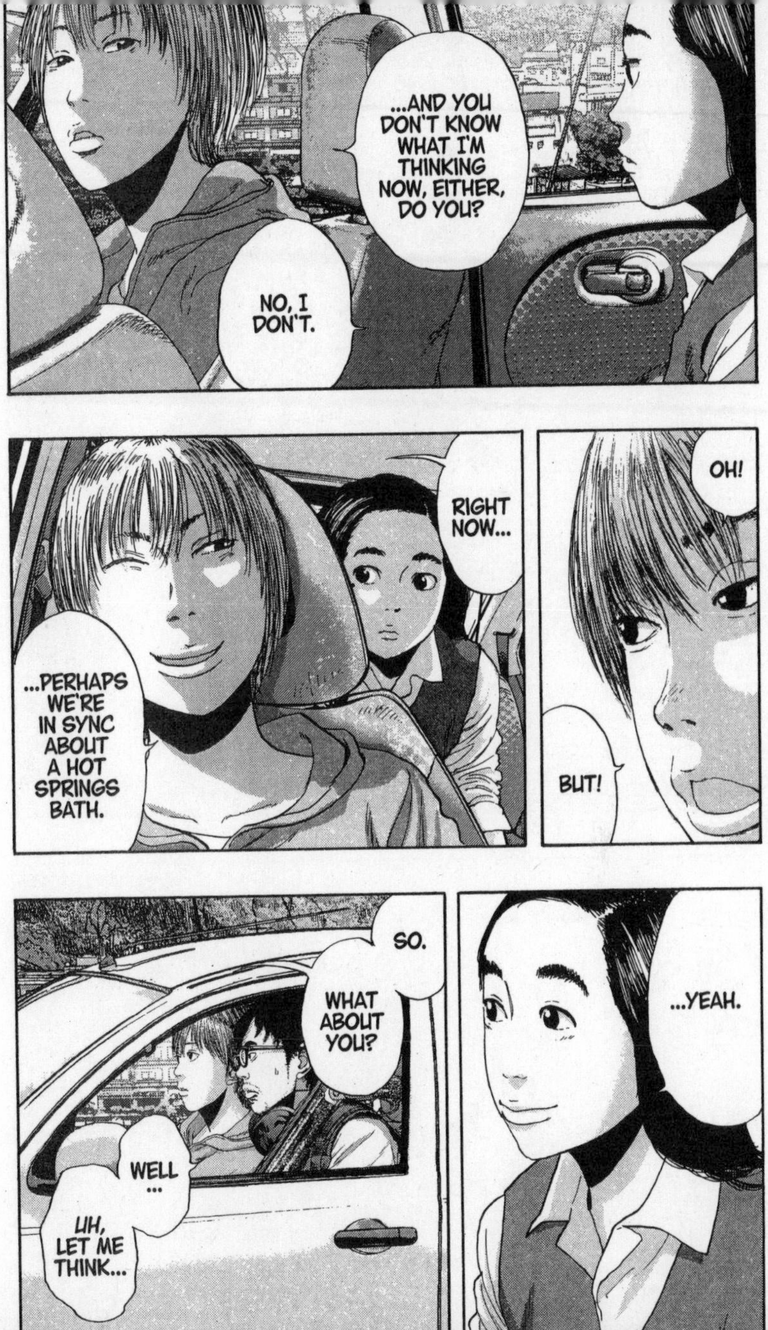
...AND YOU DON'T KNOW WHAT I'M THINKING NOW, EITHER, DO YOU?
NO, I DON'T.
OH!
BUT!
RIGHT NOW...
...PERHAPS WE'RE IN SYNC ABOUT A HOT SPRINGS BATH.
...YEAH.
SO.
WHAT ABOUT YOU?
WELL ...
UH, LET ME THINK...

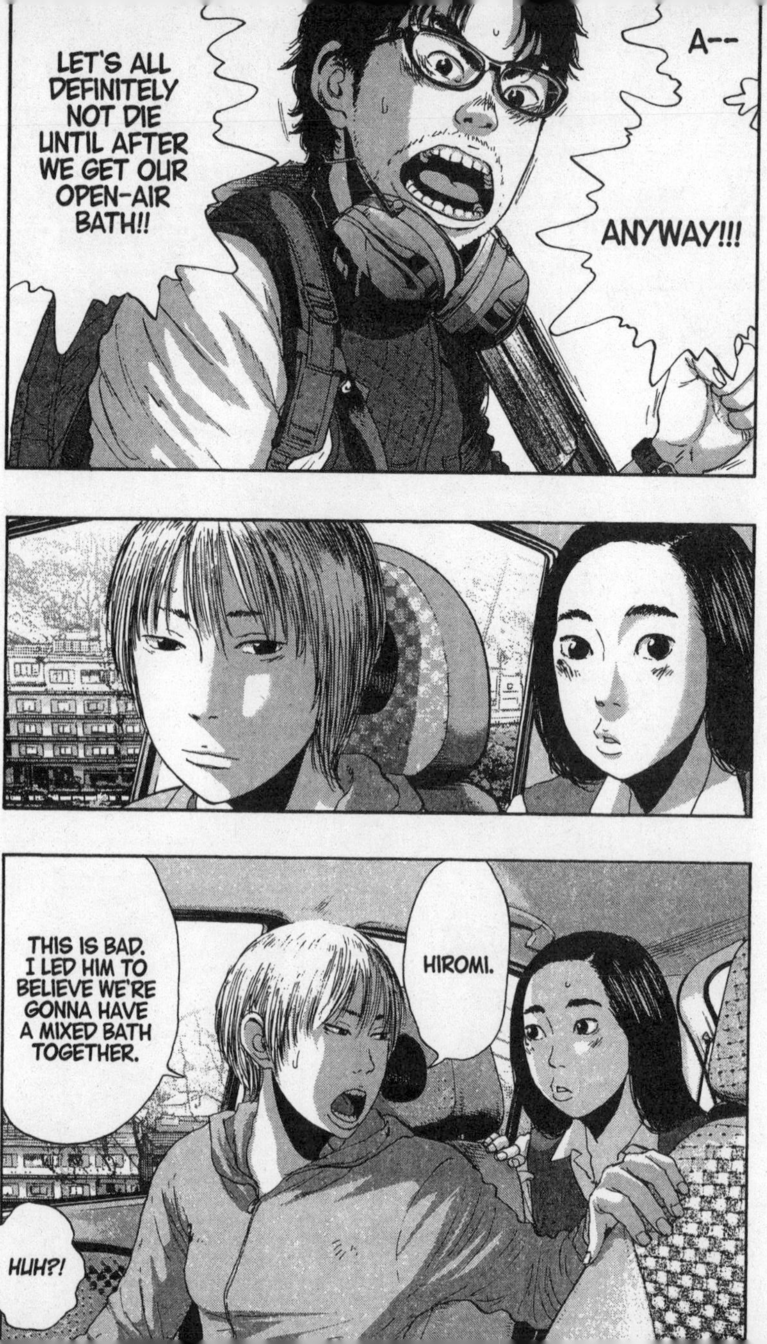
A--
ANYWAY!!!
LET'S ALL DEFINITELY NOT DIE UNTIL AFTER WE GET OUR OPEN-AIR BATH!!
HIROMI.
THIS IS BAD. I LED HIM TO BELIEVE WE'RE GONNA HAVE A MIXED BATH TOGETHER.
HUH?!

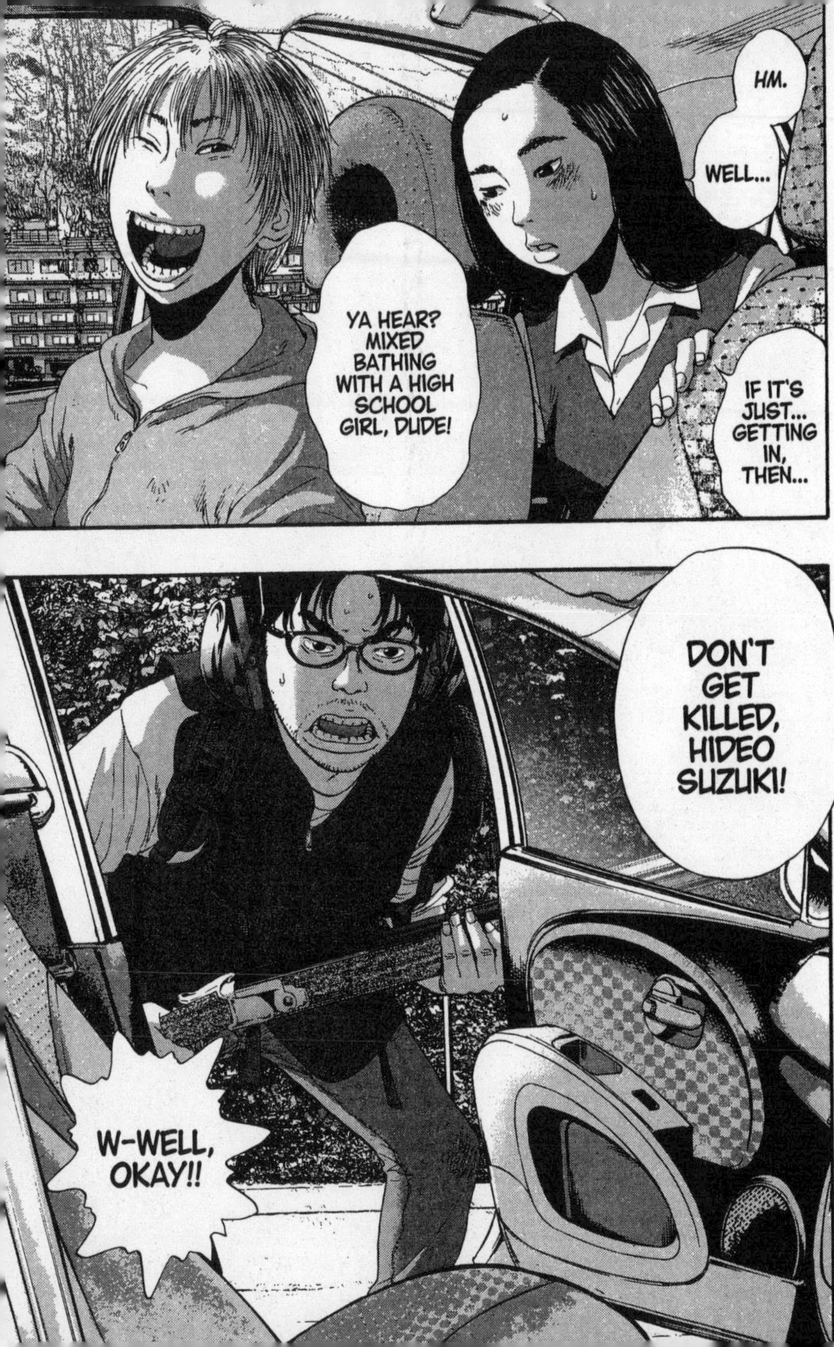
HM.
WELL...
IF IT'S JUST... GETTING IN, THEN...
YA HEAR? MIXED BATHING WITH A HIGH SCHOOL GIRL, DUDE!
DON'T GET KILLED, HIDEO SUZUKI!
W-WELL, OKAY!!

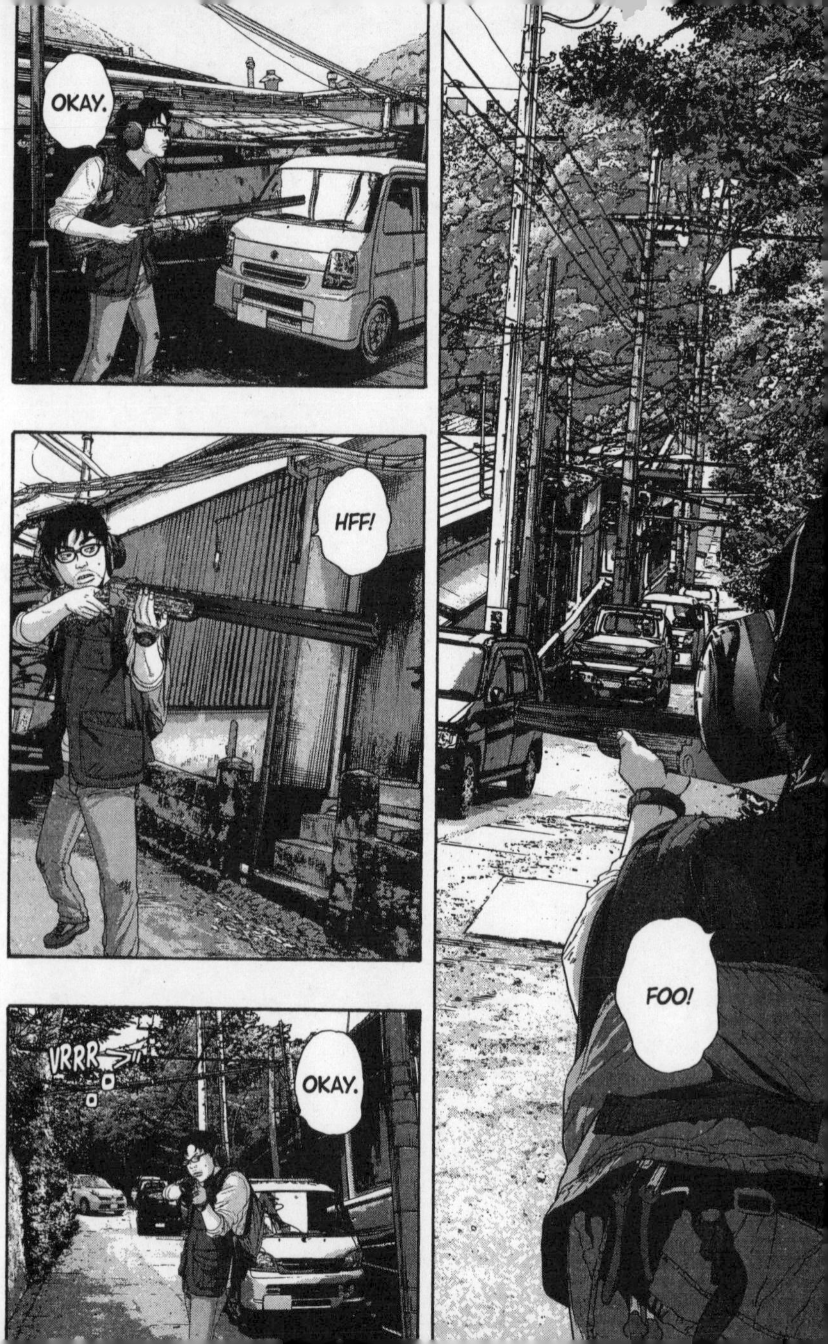
FOO!
OKAY.
HFF!
VRRR
OKAY.

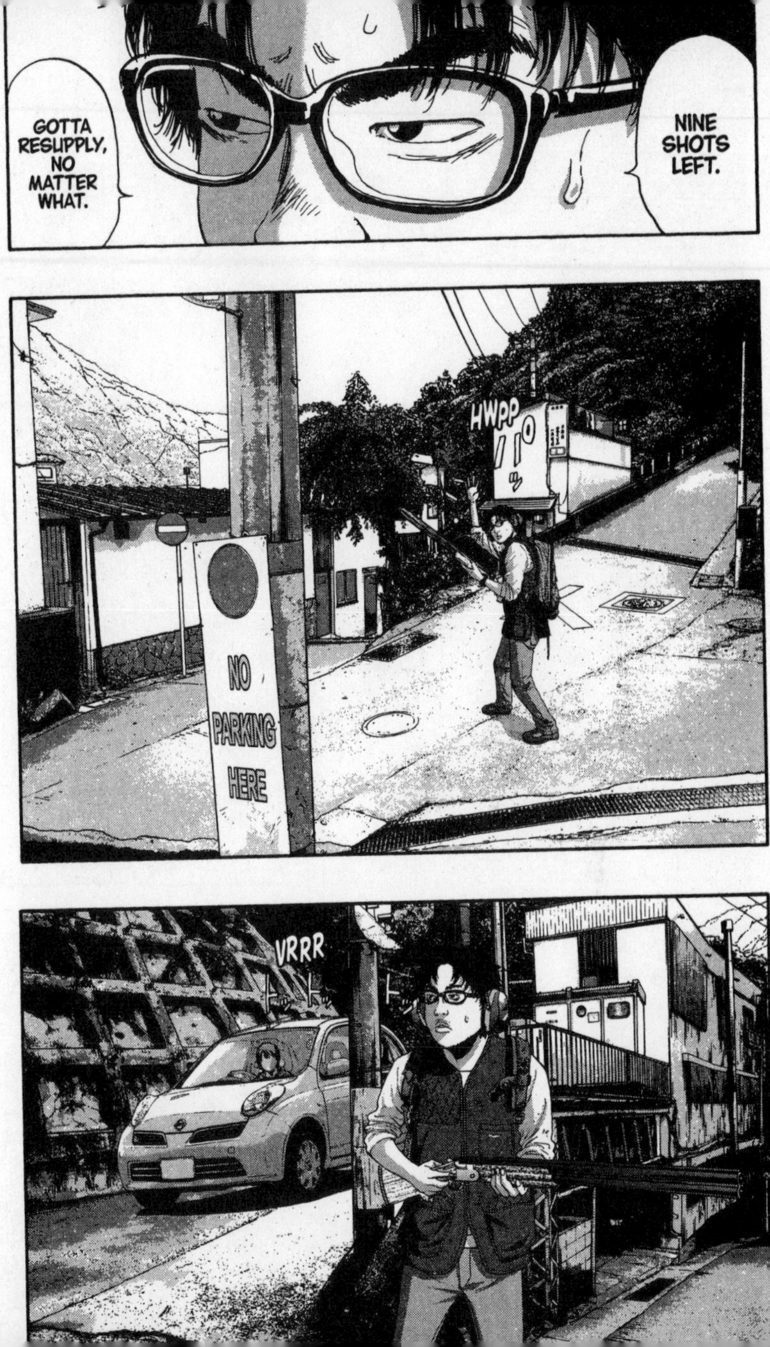
NINE SHOTS LEFT.
GOTTA RESUPPLY, NO MATTER WHAT.
HWPP
NO PARKING HERE
VRRR

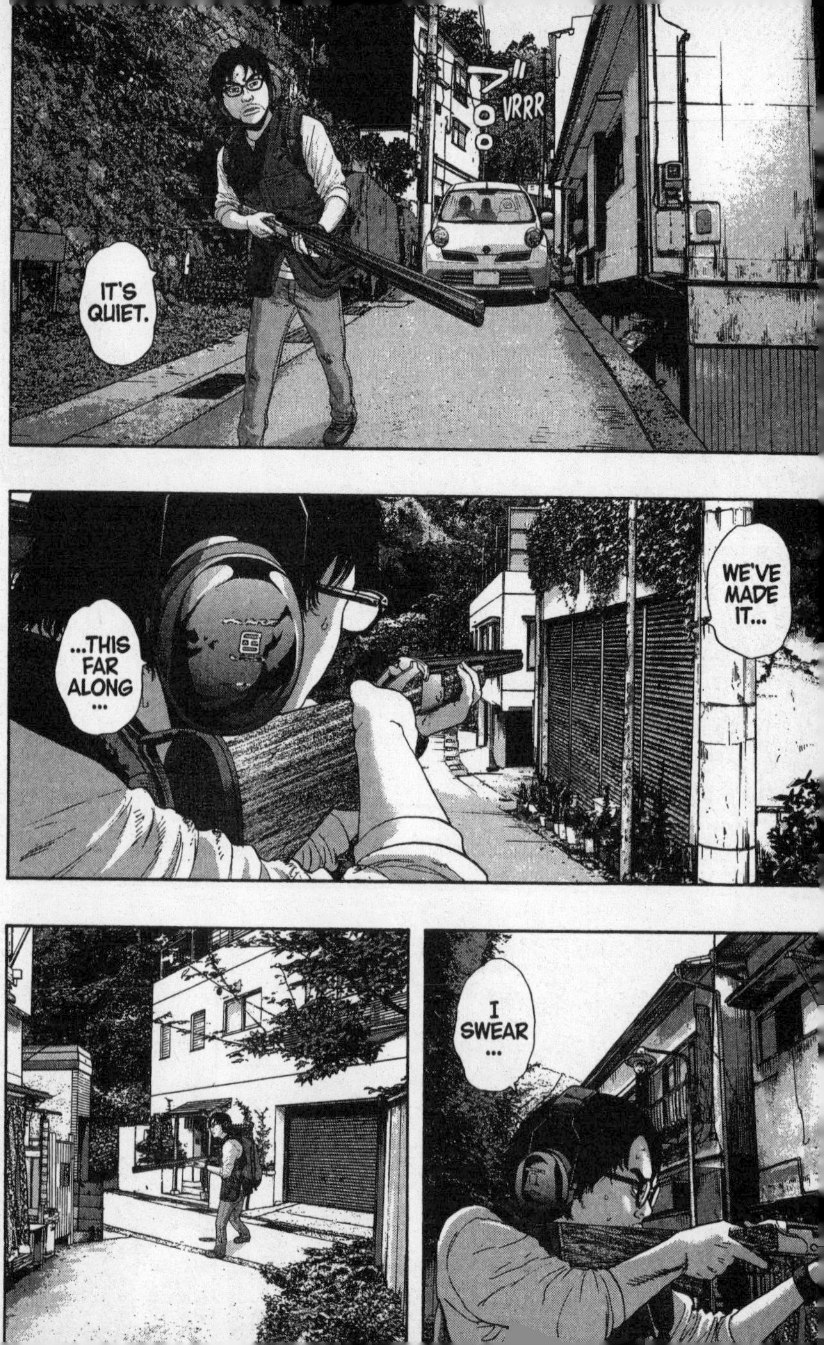
VRRR
IT'S QUIET.
WE'VE MADE IT...
...THIS FAR ALONG...
I SWEAR...

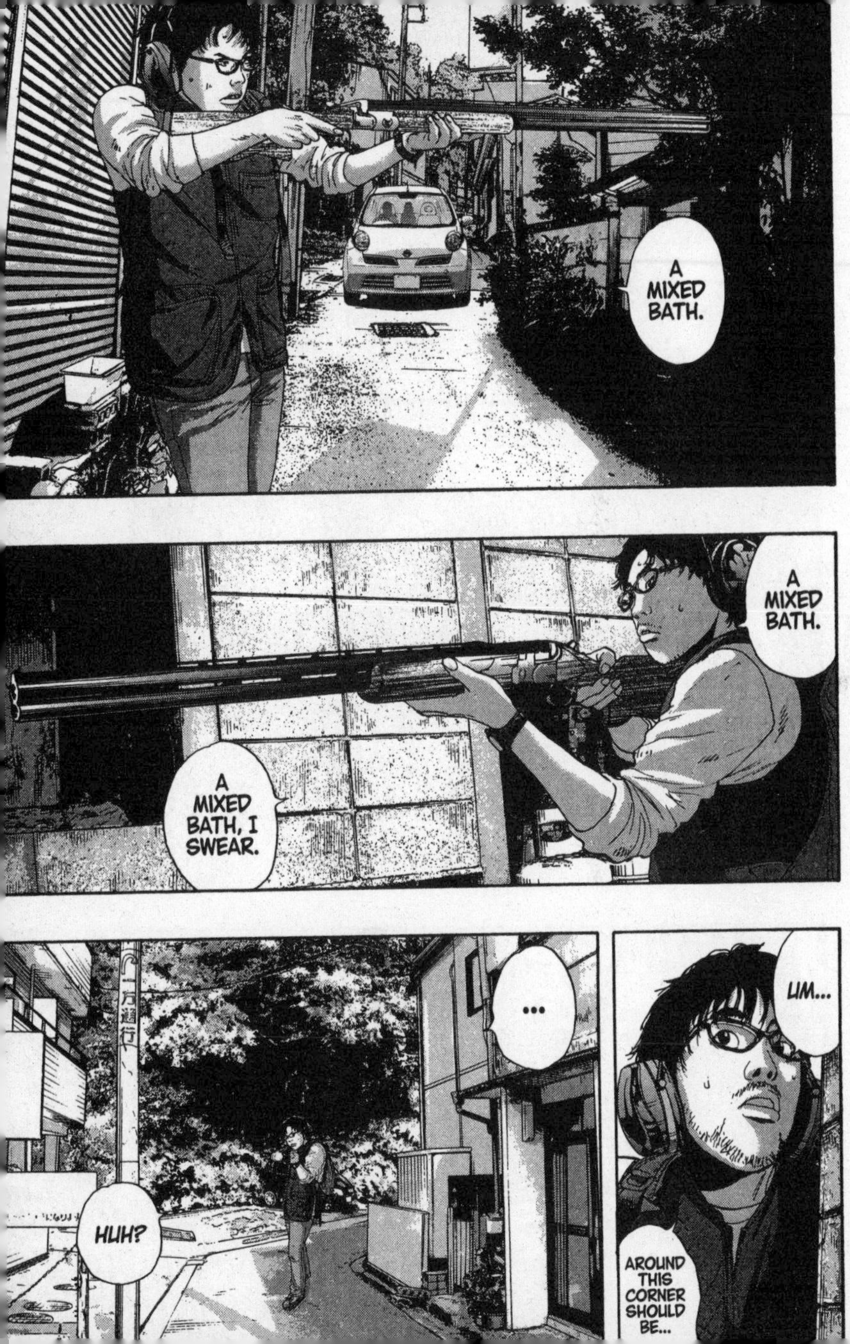
A MIXED BATH.
A MIXED BATH.
A MIXED BATH, I SWEAR.
UM...
AROUND THIS CORNER SHOULD BE...
...
HUH?

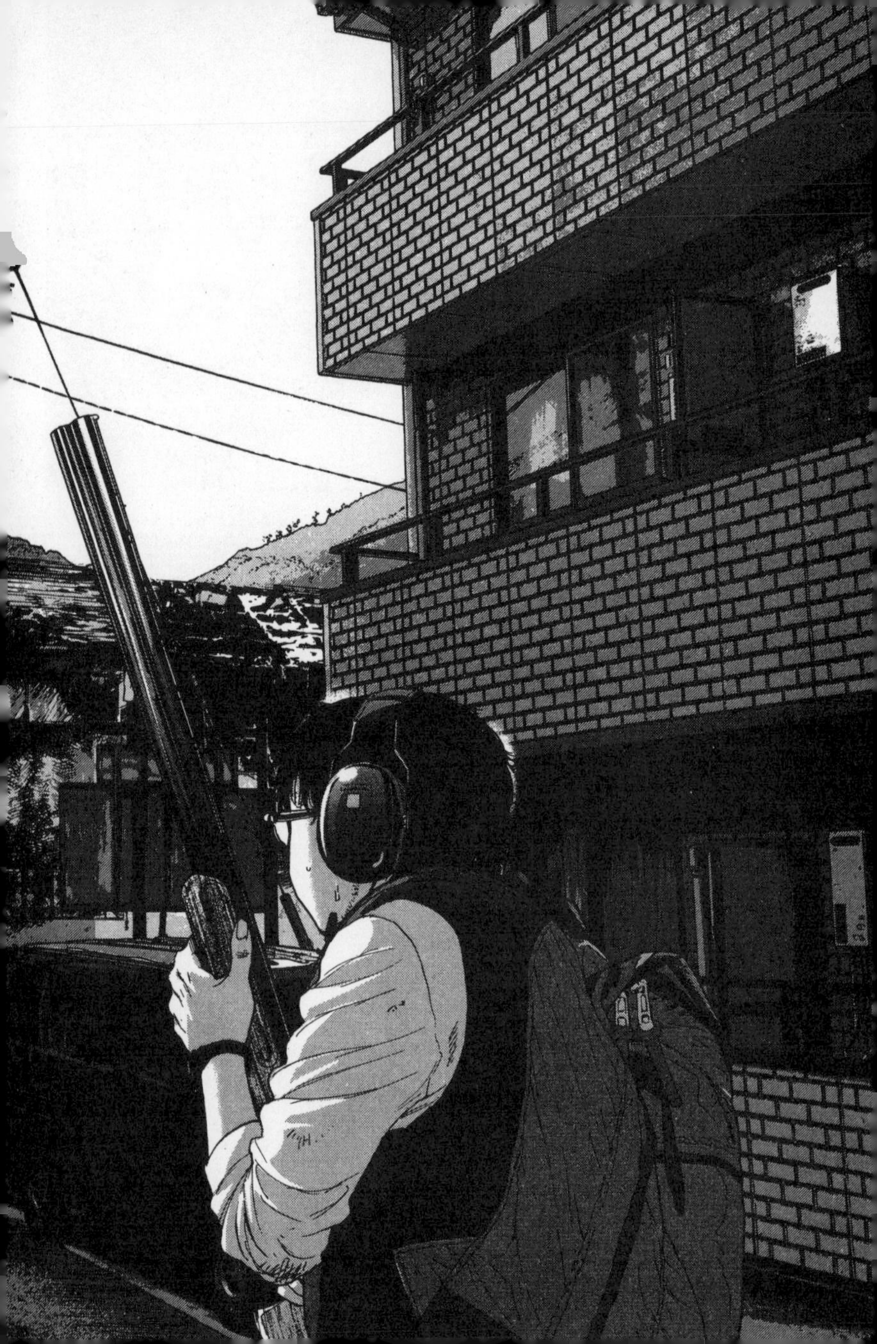

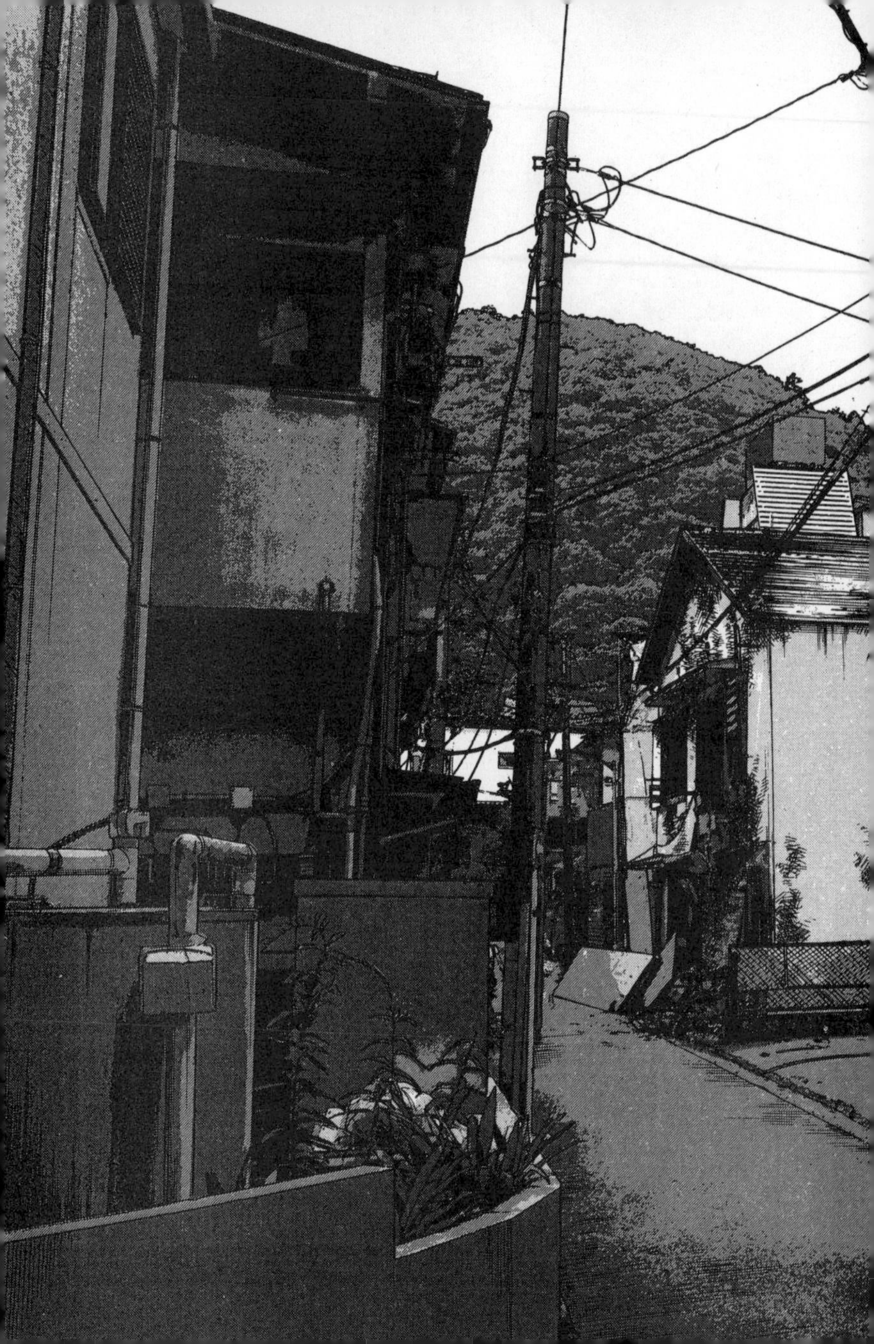

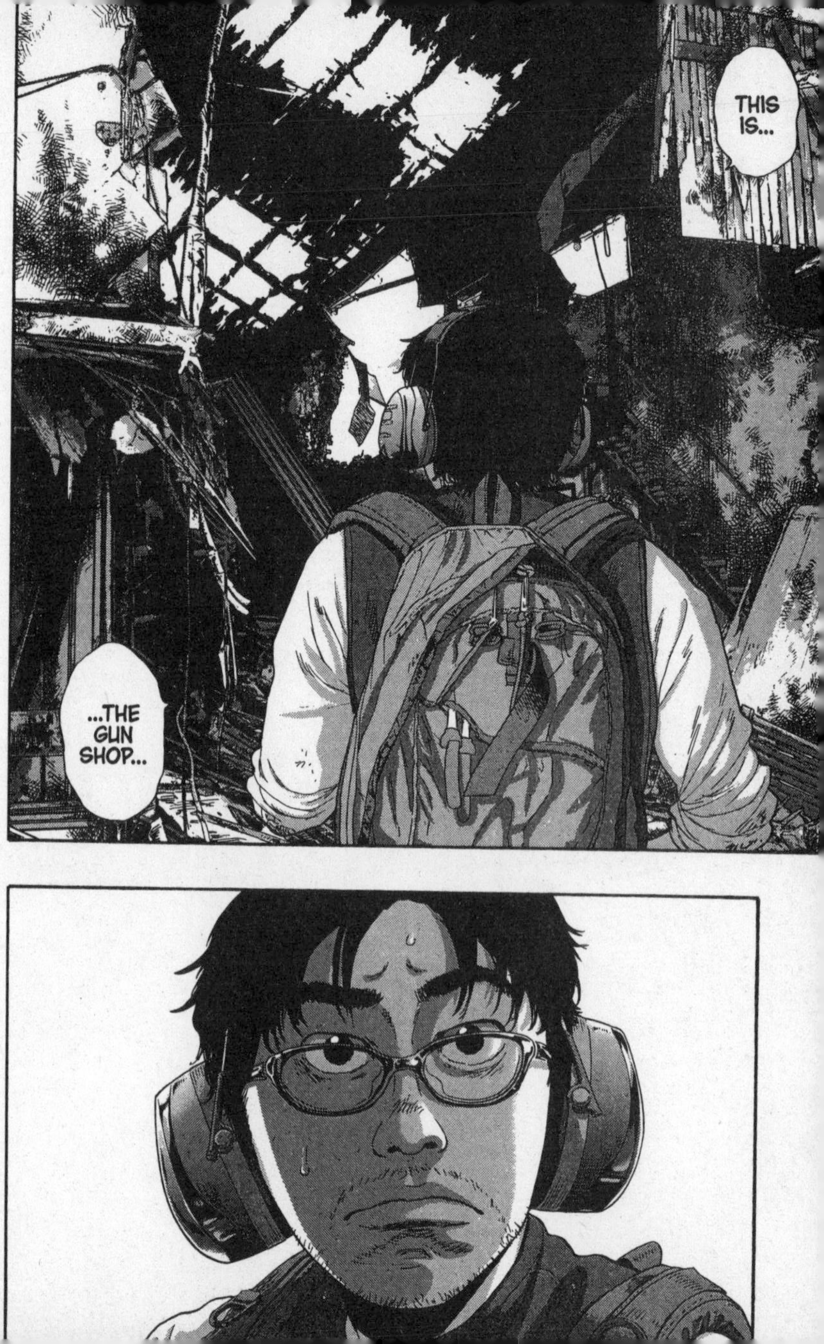
THIS IS...
...THE GUN SHOP...

I AM
A HERO

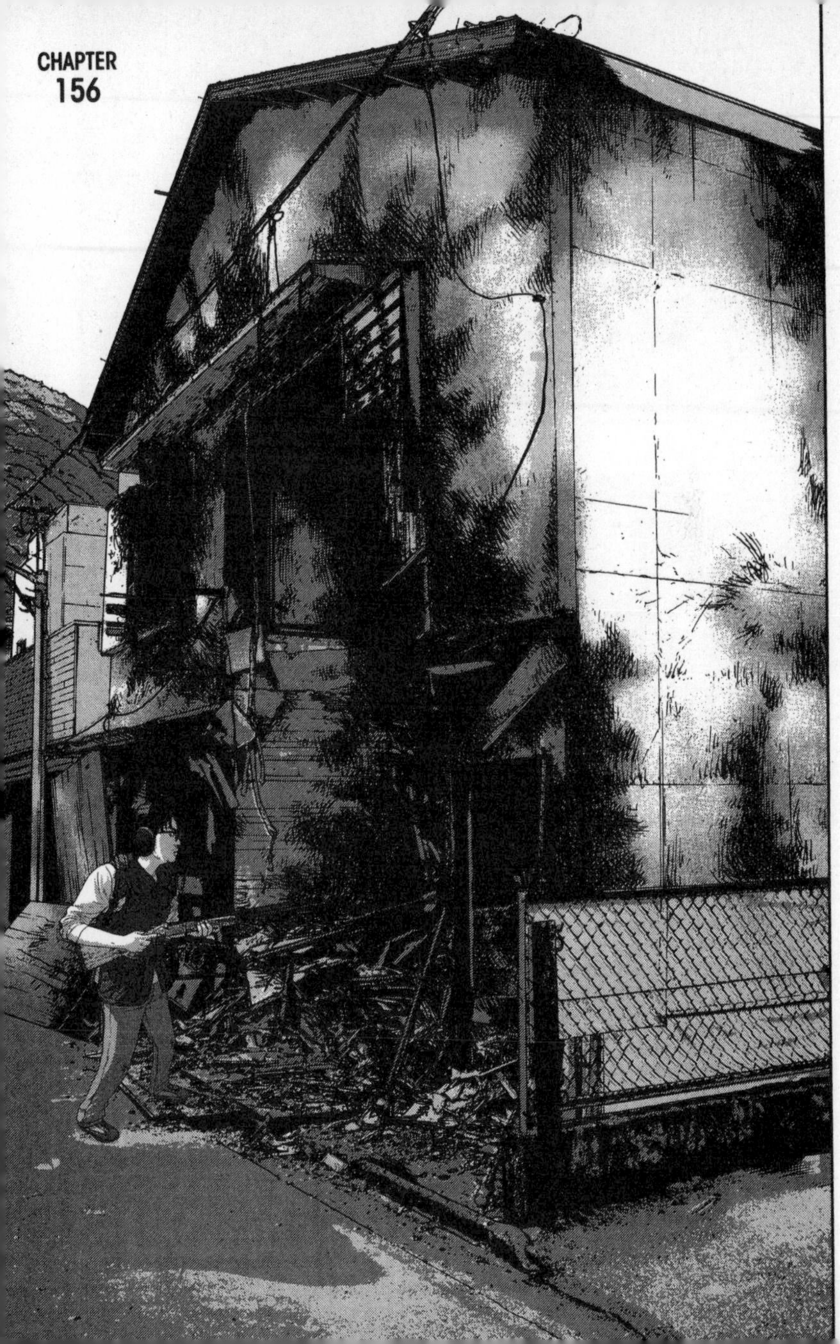
CHAPTER
156

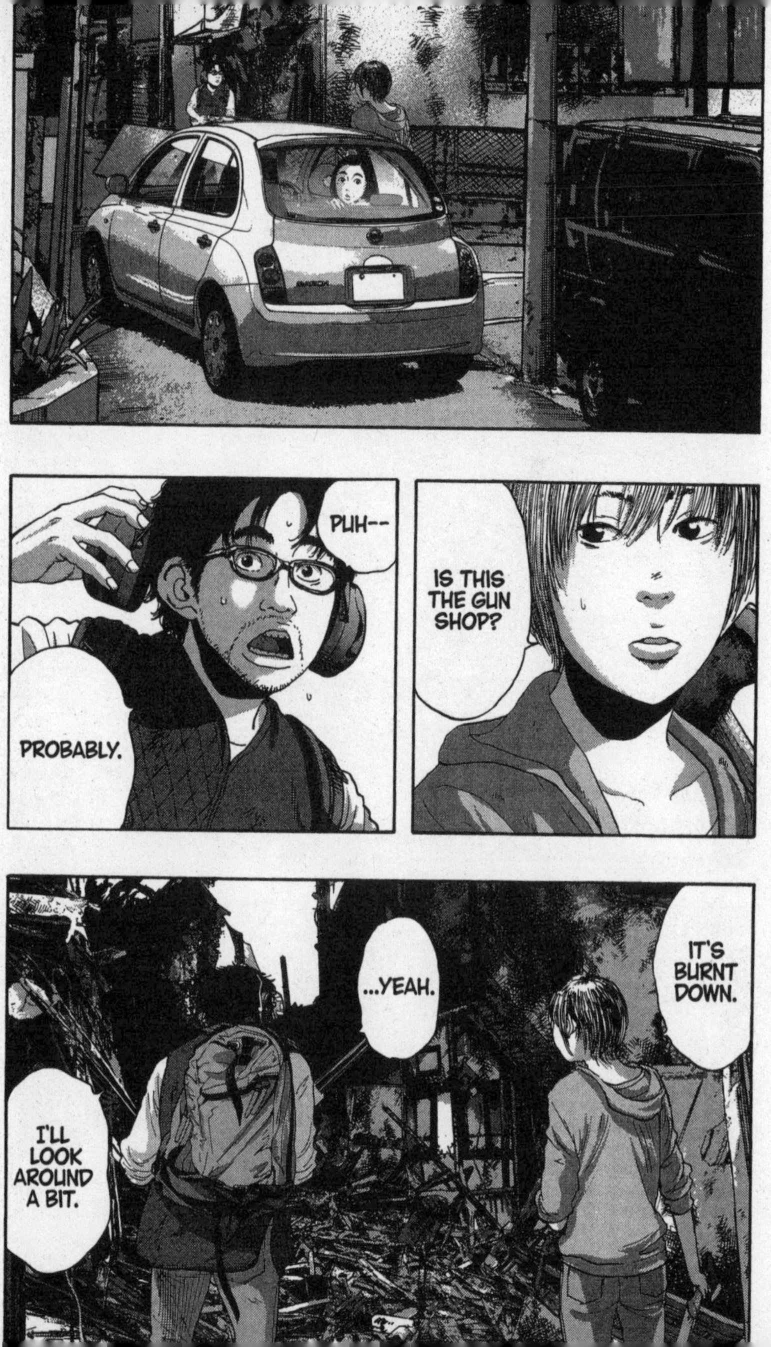
IS THIS THE GUN SHOP?
PUH--
PROBABLY.
IT'S BURNT DOWN.
...YEAH.
I'LL LOOK AROUND A BIT.

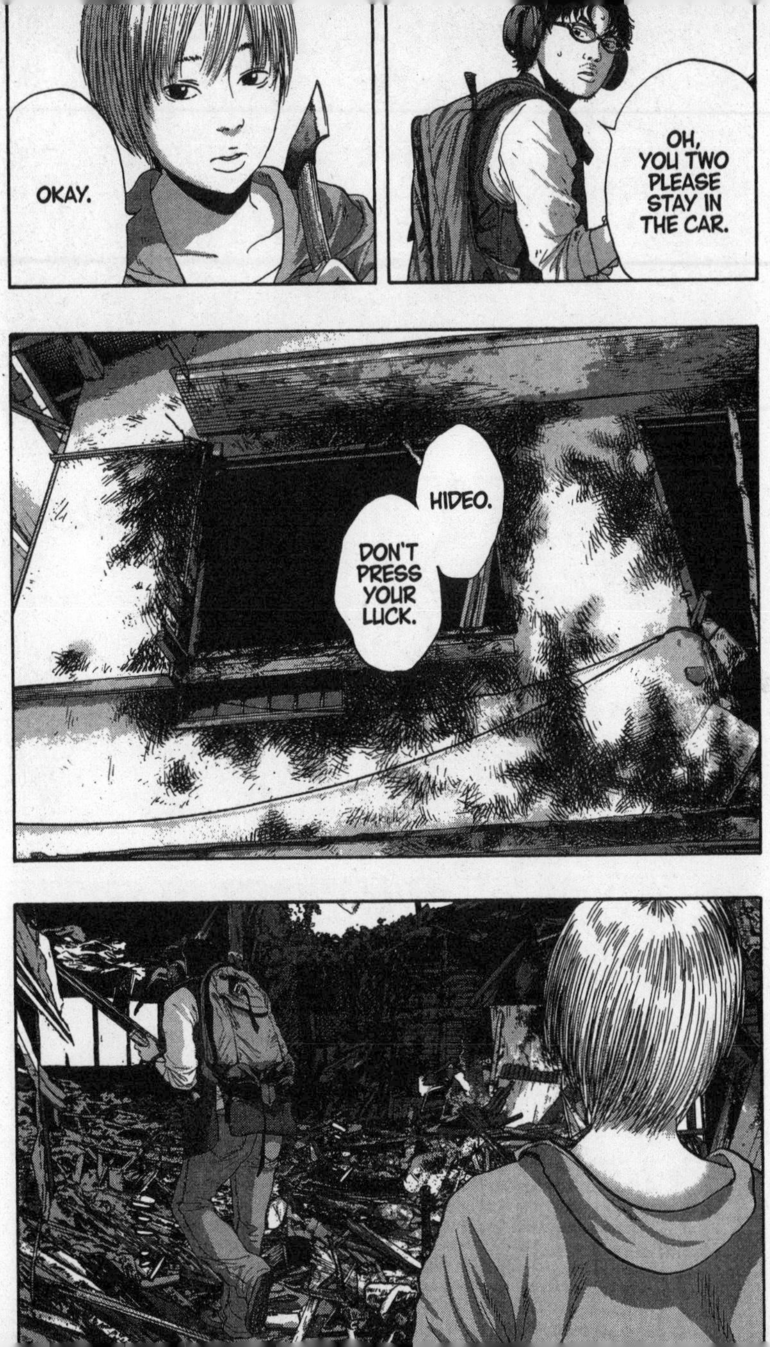
OH, YOU TWO PLEASE STAY IN THE CAR.
OKAY.
HIDEO.
DON'T PRESS YOUR LUCK.

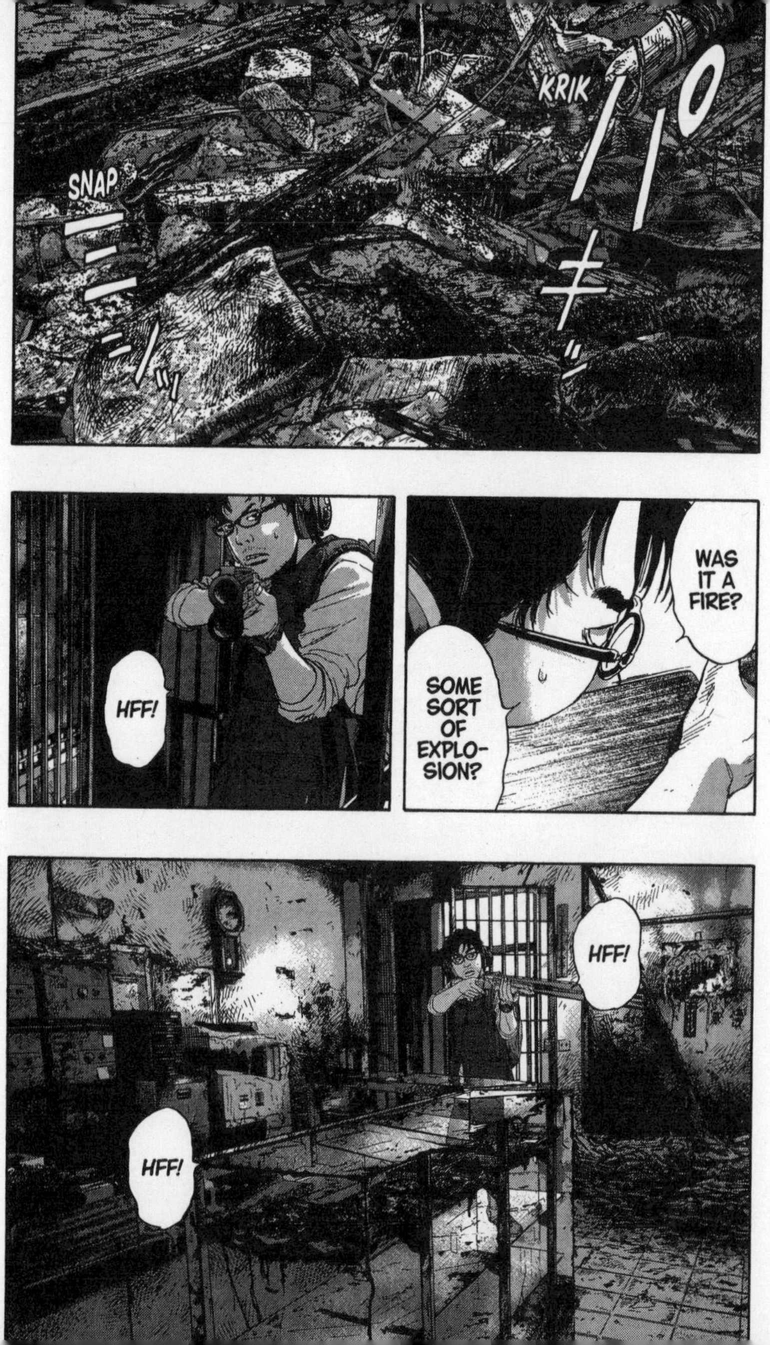
KRIK
SNAP
WAS IT A FIRE?
SOME SORT OF EXPLOSION?
HFF!
HFF!
HFF!

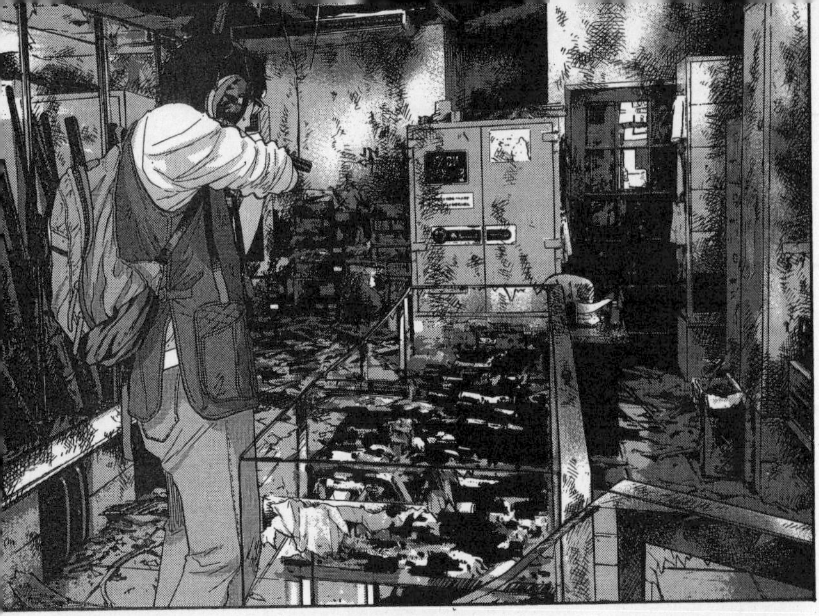

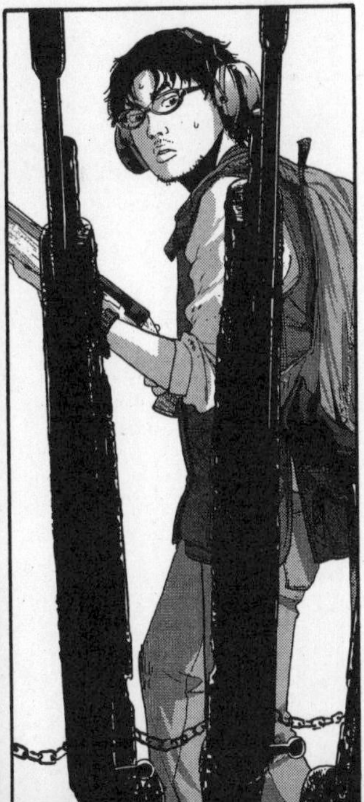

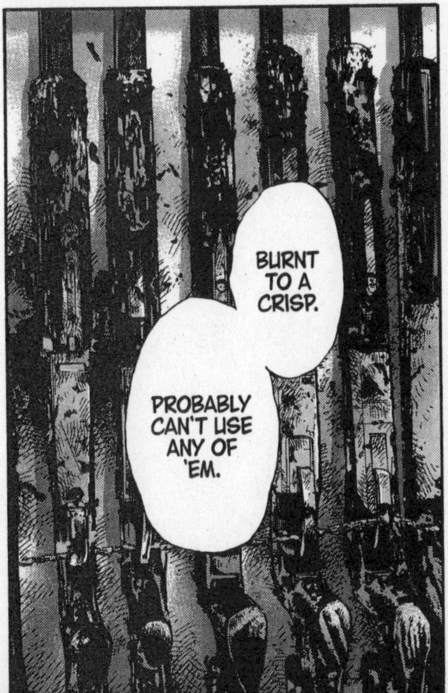
BURNT TO A CRISP.
PROBABLY CAN'T USE ANY OF 'EM.

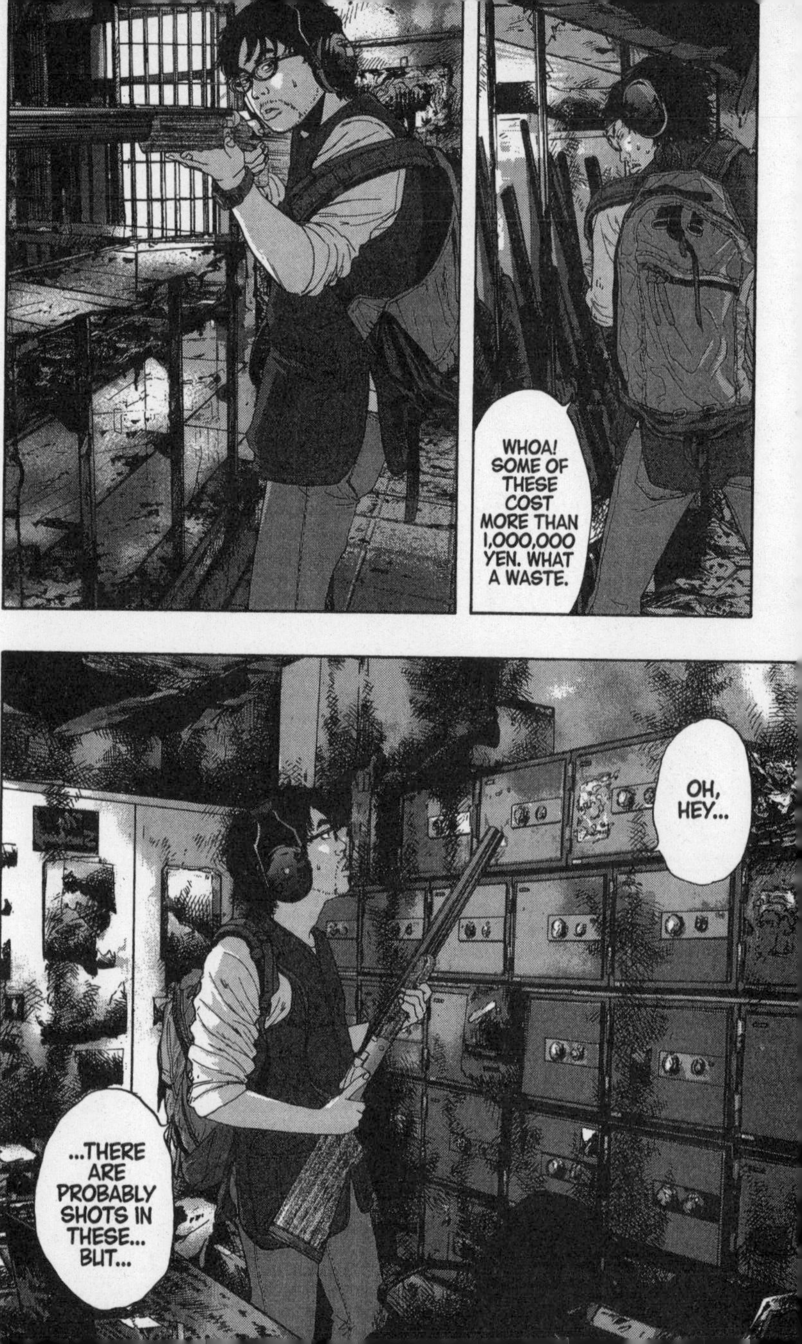
WHOA! SOME OF THESE COST MORE THAN 1,000,000 YEN. WHAT A WASTE.
OH, HEY...
...THERE ARE PROBABLY SHOTS IN THESE... BUT...

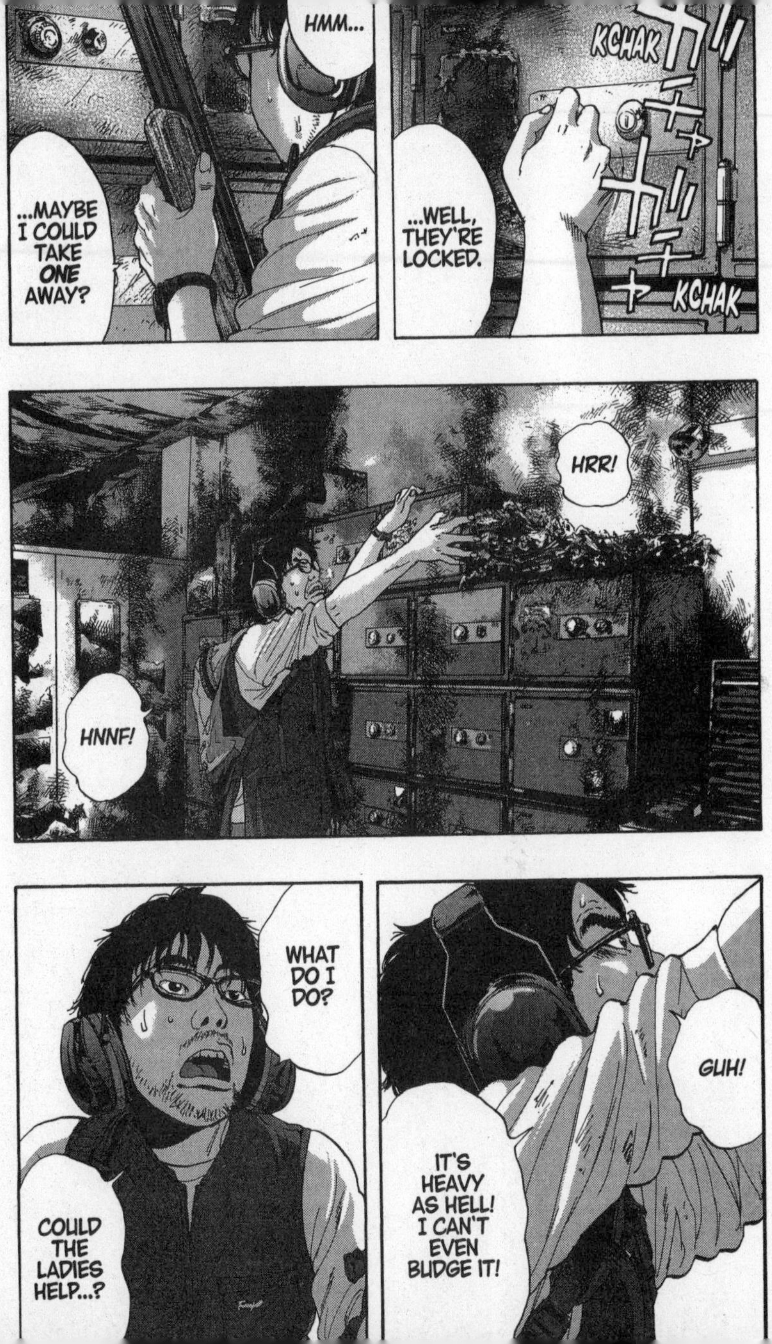
KCHAK
...WELL, THEY'RE LOCKED.
KCHAK
HMM...
...MAYBE I COULD TAKE ONE AWAY?
HRR!
HNNF!
GUH!
IT'S HEAVY AS HELL! I CAN'T EVEN BUDGE IT!
WHAT DO I DO?
COULD THE LADIES HELP...?

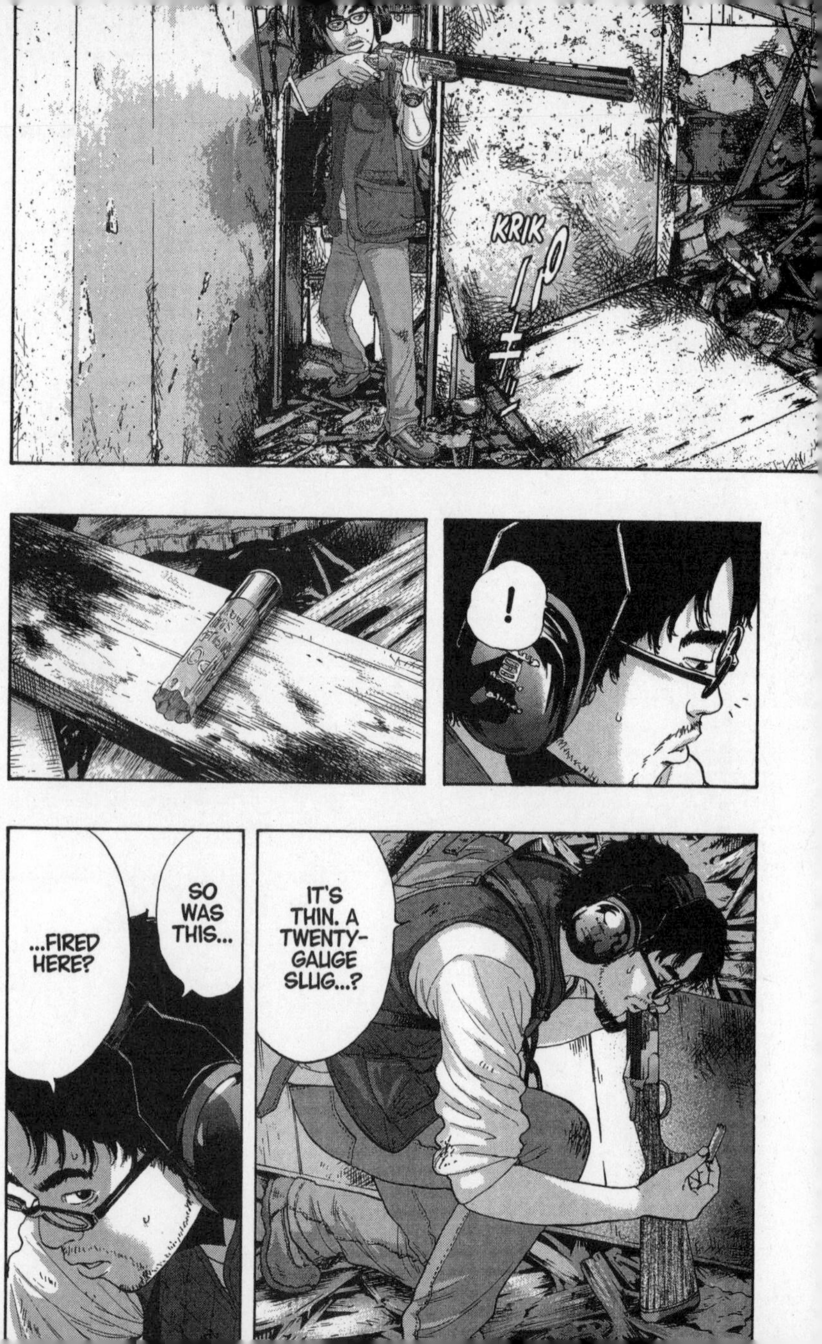
KRIK
!
IT'S THIN. A TWENTY-GAUGE SLUG...?
SO WAS THIS...
...FIRED HERE?

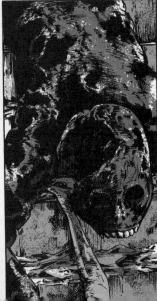

SHOT
IN THE
HEAD?

WERE YOU
HUMAN...
OR ONE
OF *THEM*?

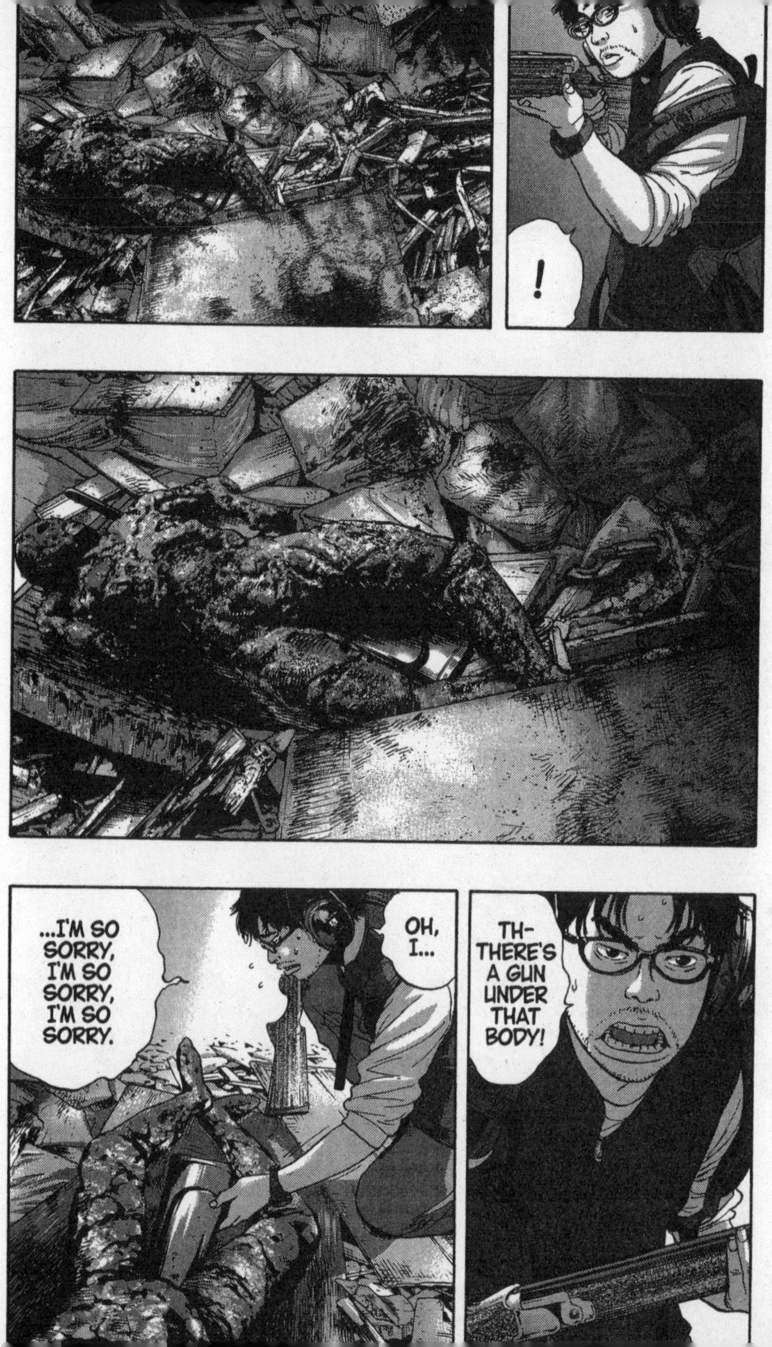
!
TH- THERE'S A GUN UNDER THAT BODY!
OH, I...
...I'M SO SORRY, I'M SO SORRY, I'M SO SORRY.

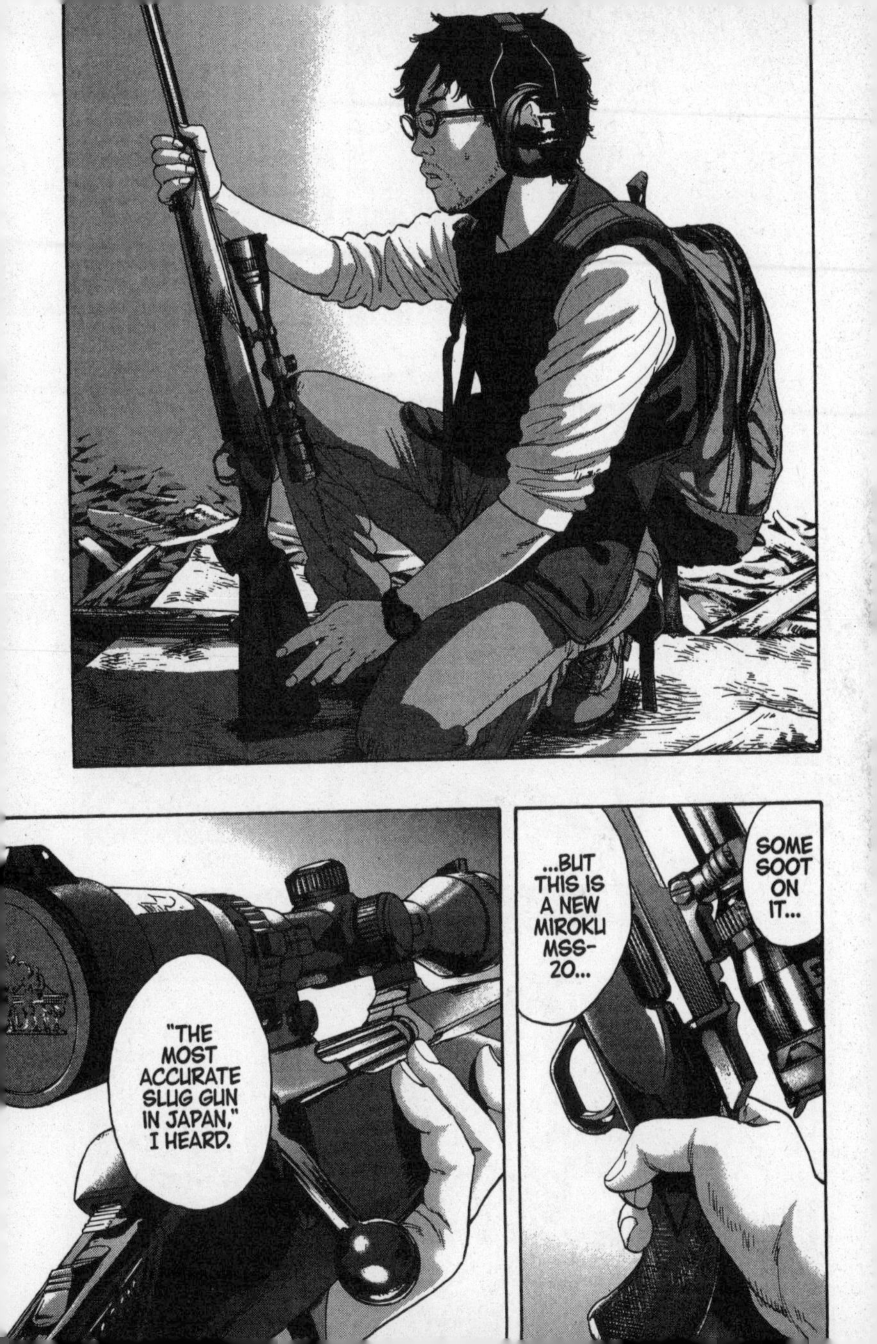
SOME SOOT ON IT...
...BUT THIS IS A NEW MIROKU MSS-20...
"THE MOST ACCURATE SLUG GUN IN JAPAN," I HEARD.

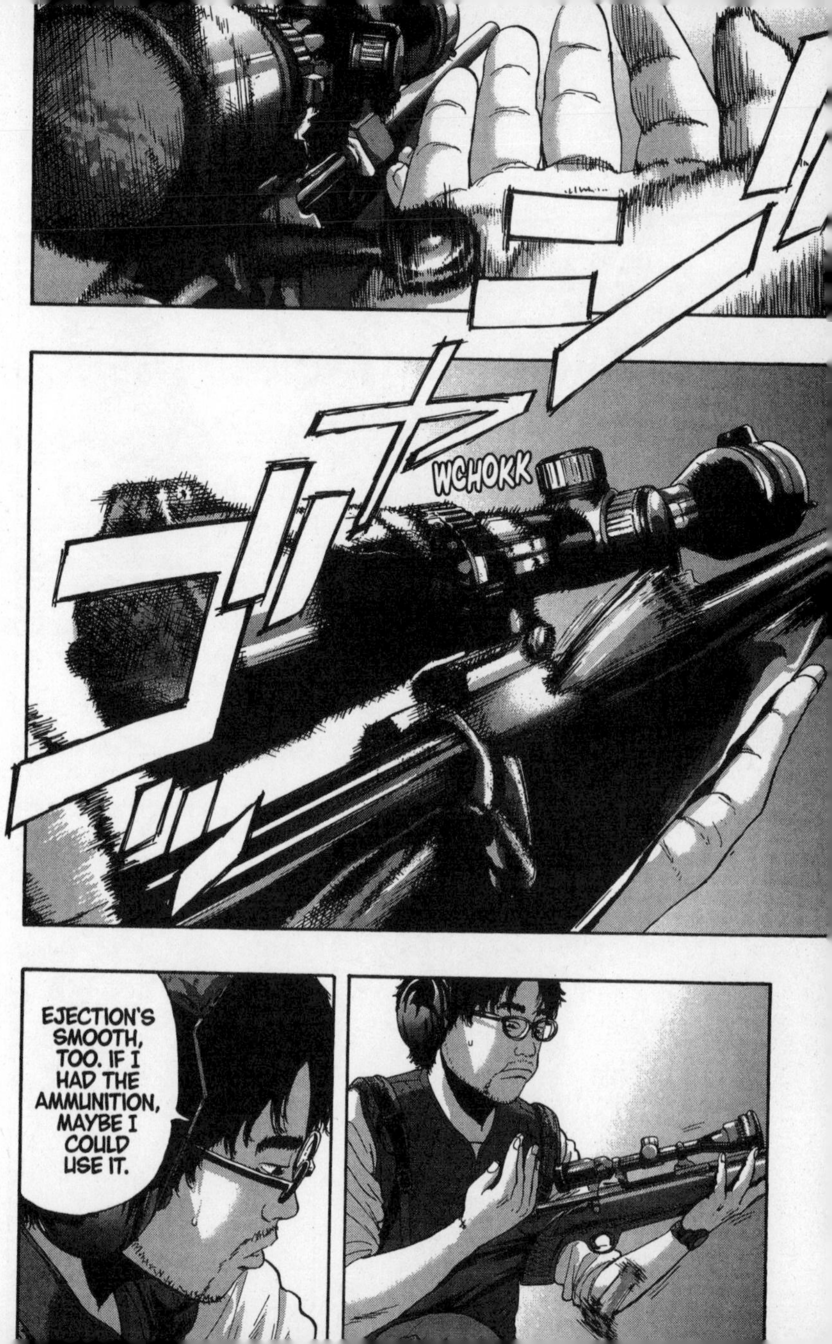
WCHOKK
EJECTION'S SMOOTH, TOO. IF I HAD THE AMMUNITION, MAYBE I COULD USE IT.

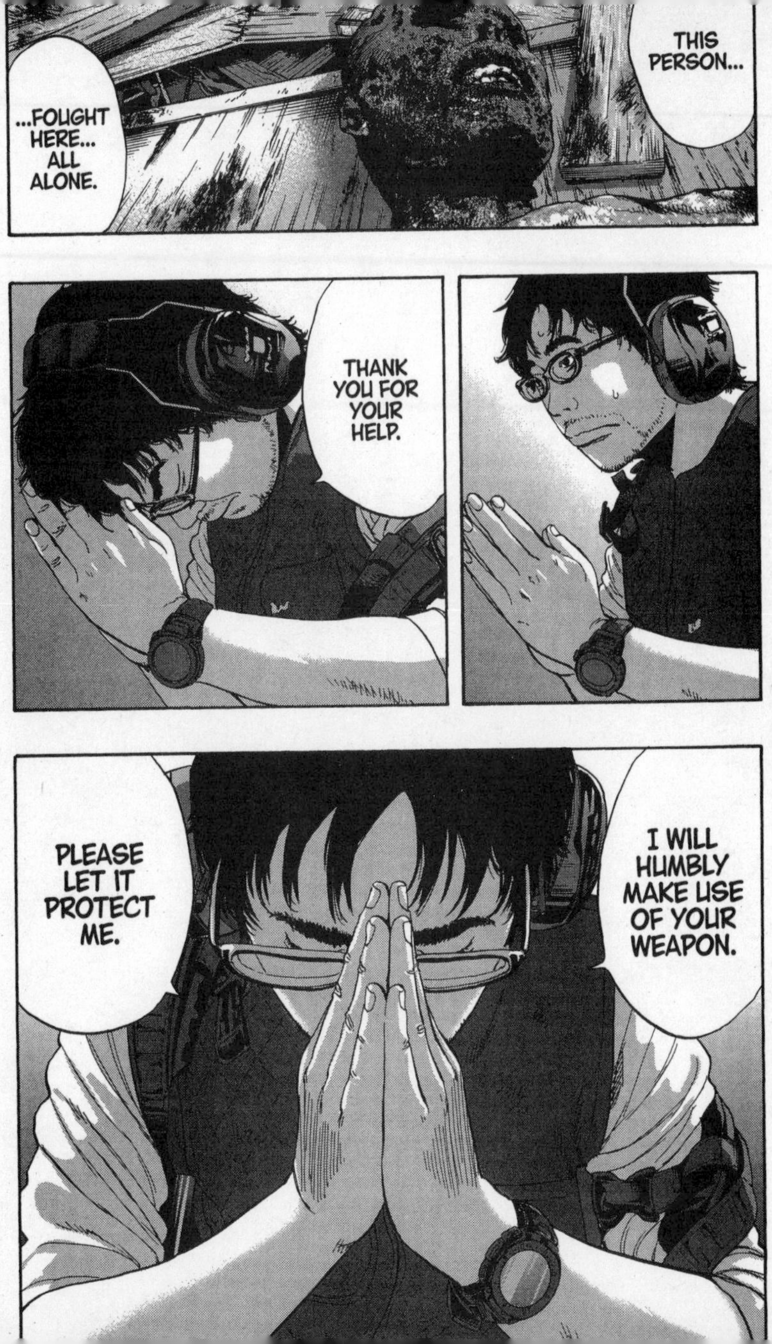
THIS PERSON...
...FOUGHT HERE... ALL ALONE.
THANK YOU FOR YOUR HELP.
I WILL HUMBLY MAKE USE OF YOUR WEAPON.
PLEASE LET IT PROTECT ME.

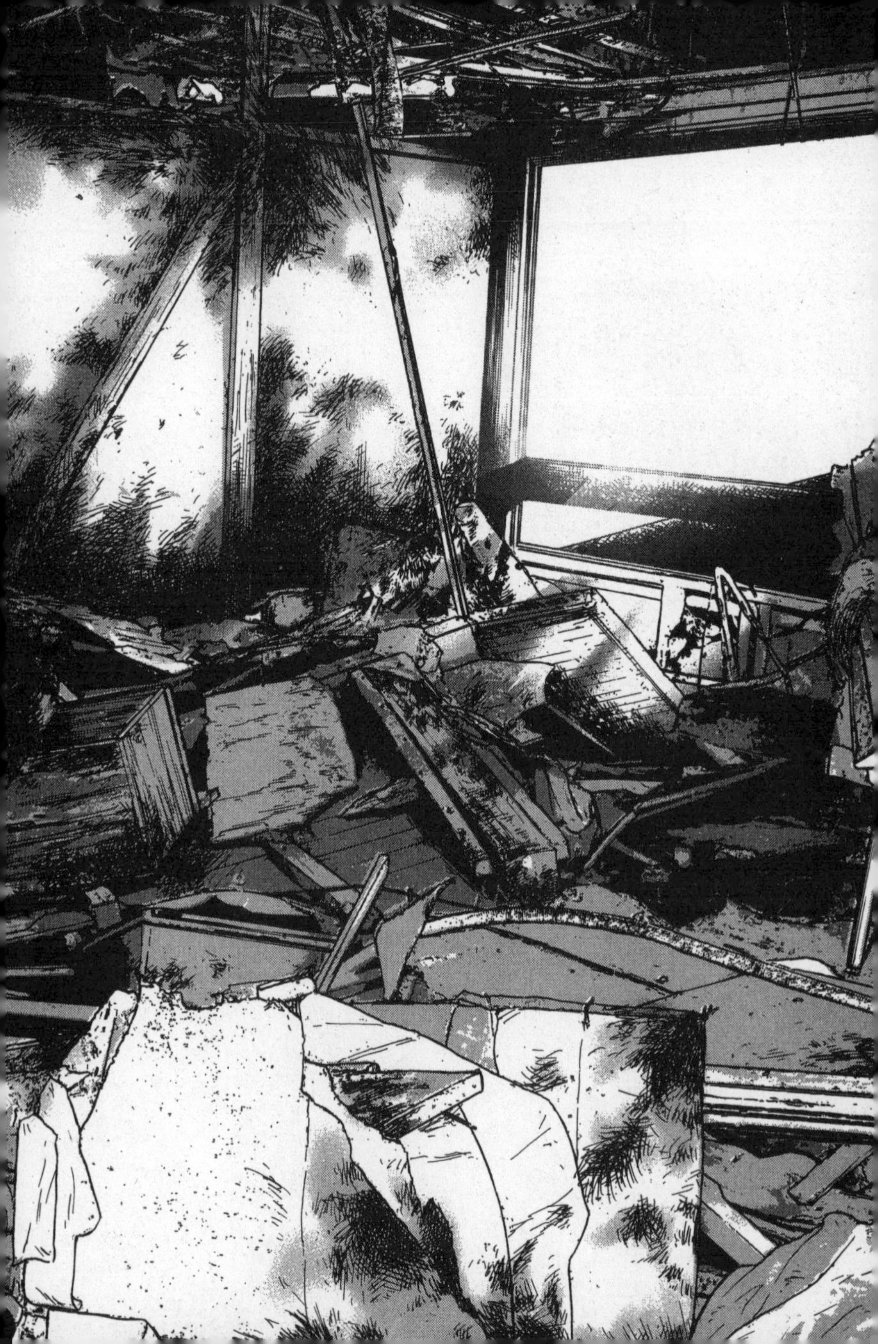

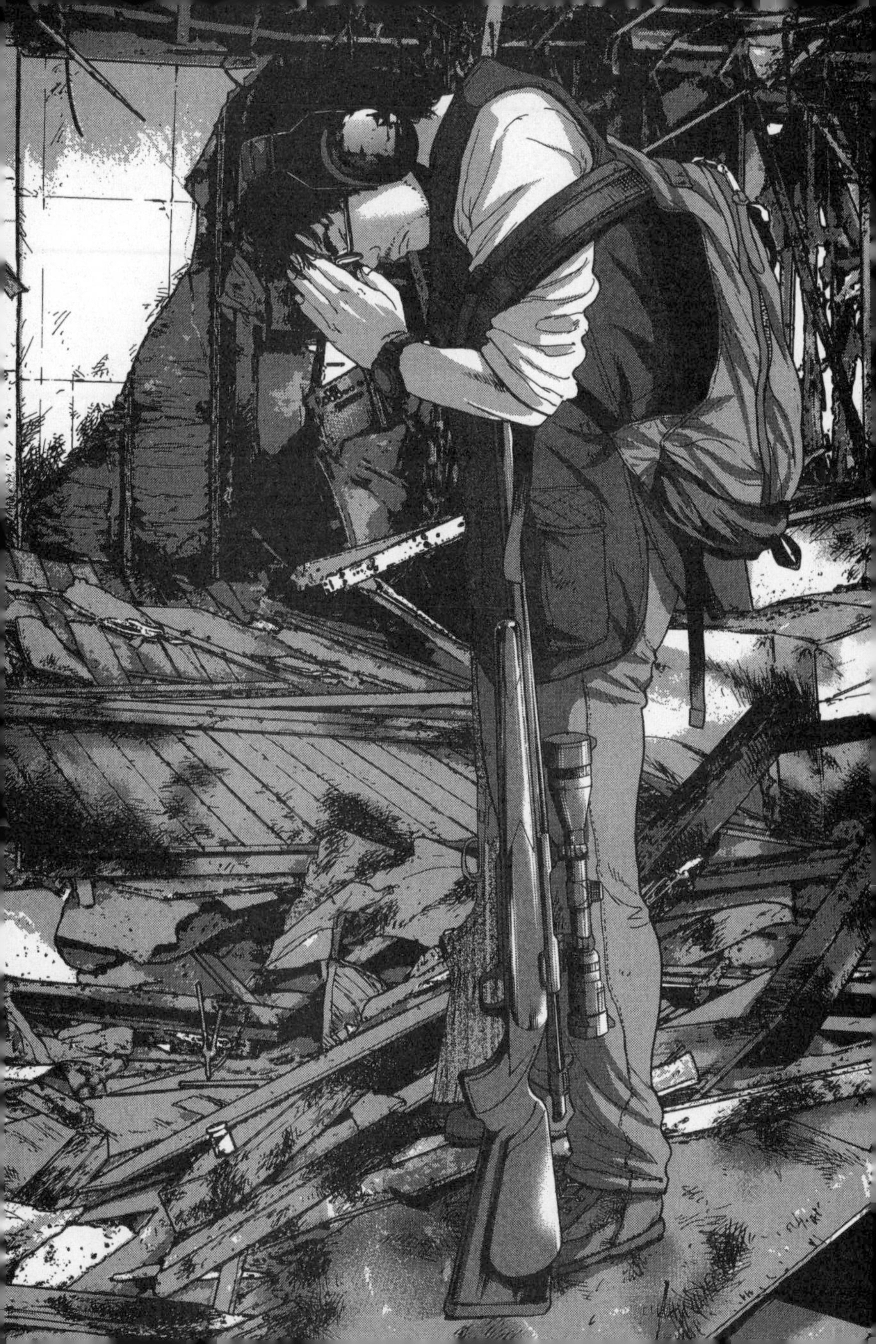

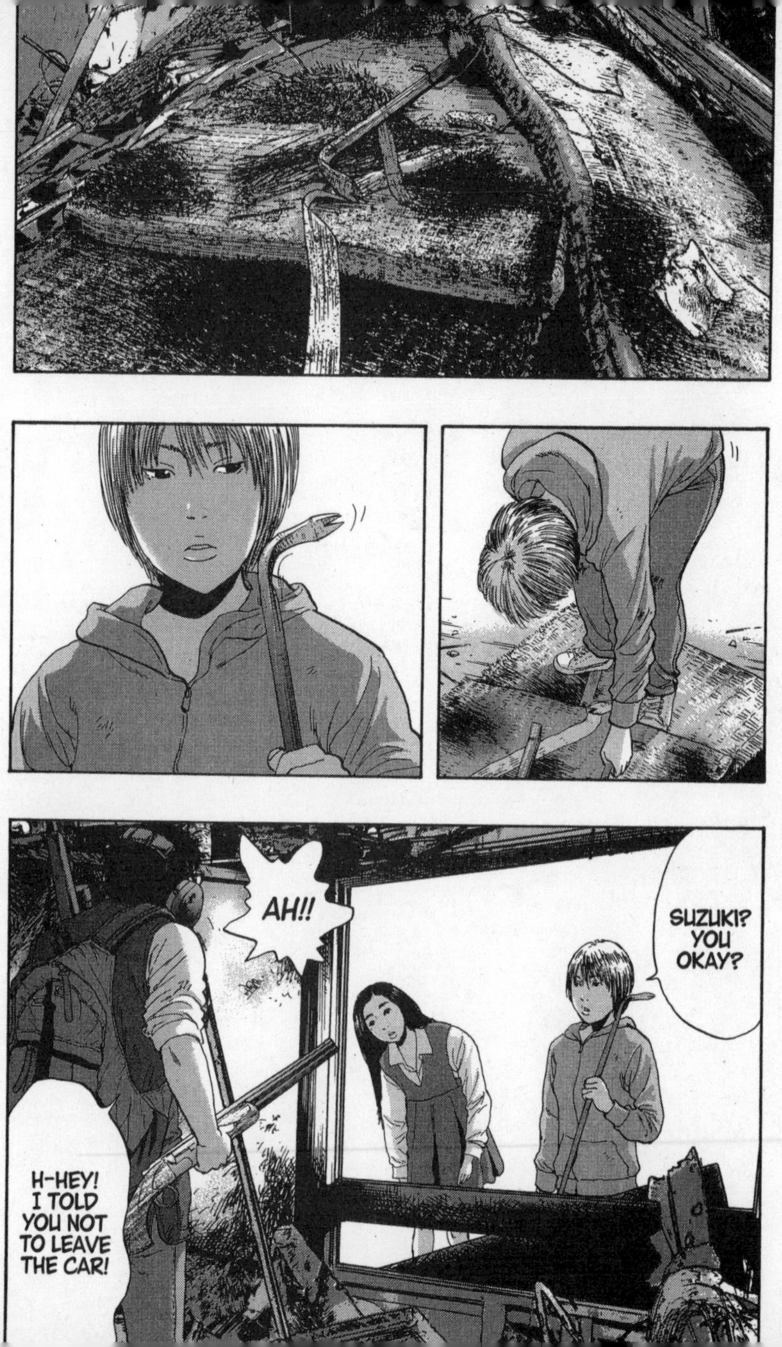
SUZUKI? YOU OKAY?
AH!!
H-HEY! I TOLD YOU NOT TO LEAVE THE CAR!

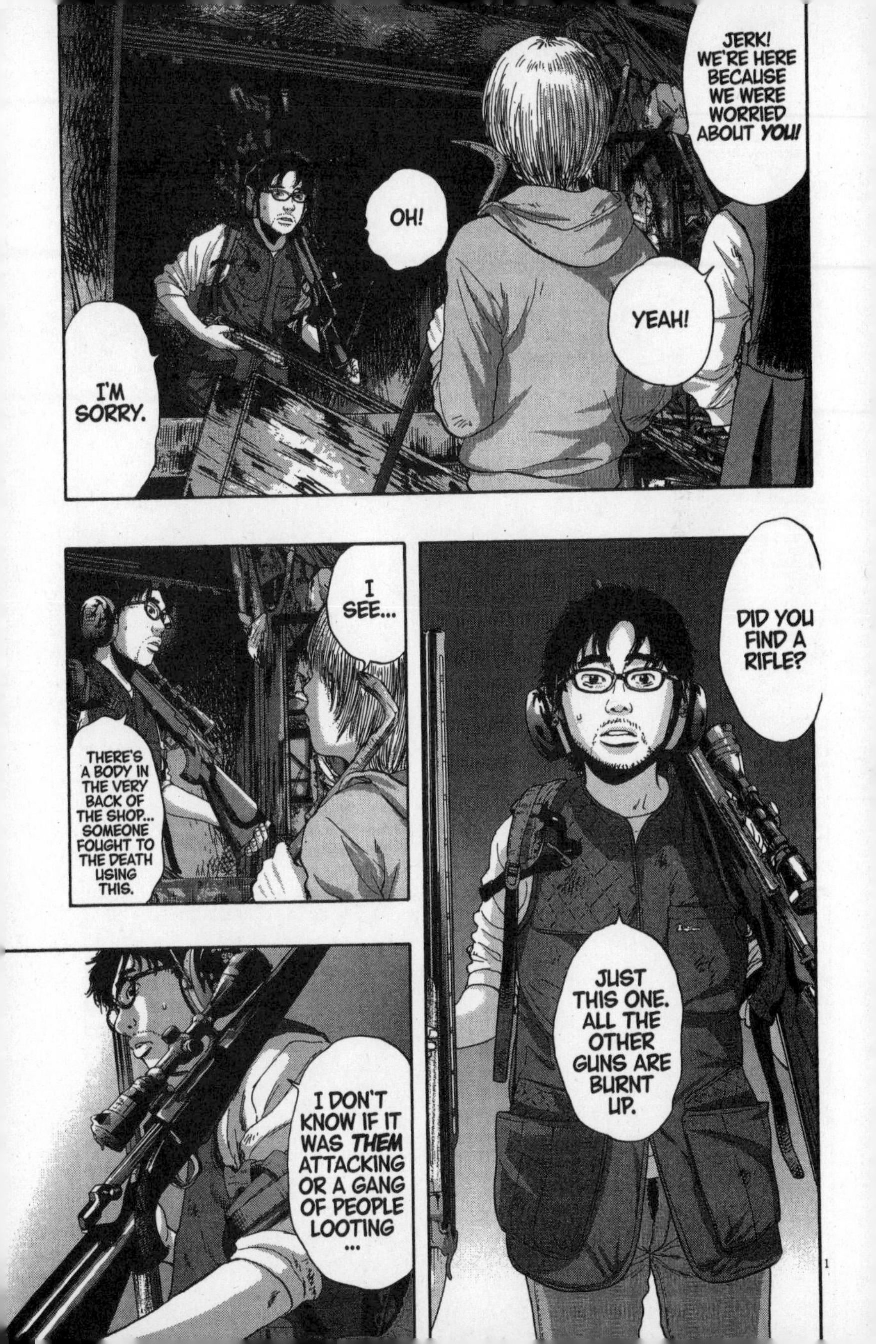
JERK! WE'RE HERE BECAUSE WE WERE WORRIED ABOUT *YOU!*
YEAH!
OH!
I'M SORRY.
DID YOU FIND A RIFLE?
JUST THIS ONE. ALL THE OTHER GUNS ARE BURNT UP.
I SEE...
THERE'S A BODY IN THE VERY BACK OF THE SHOP... SOMEONE FOUGHT TO THE DEATH USING THIS.
I DON'T KNOW IF IT WAS *THEM* ATTACKING OR A GANG OF PEOPLE LOOTING...

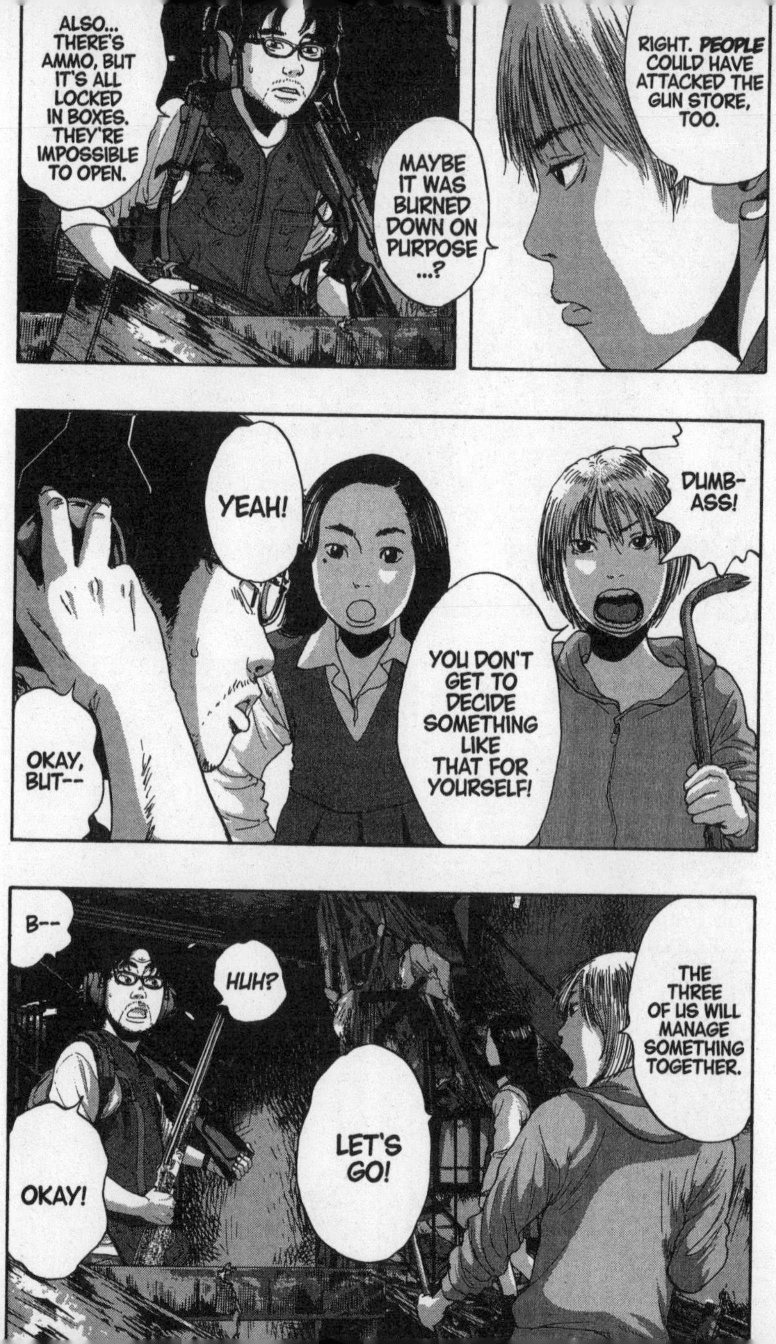
RIGHT. PEOPLE COULD HAVE ATTACKED THE GUN STORE, TOO.
MAYBE IT WAS BURNED DOWN ON PURPOSE ...?
ALSO... THERE'S AMMO, BUT IT'S ALL LOCKED IN BOXES. THEY'RE IMPOSSIBLE TO OPEN.
DUMB-ASS!
YOU DON'T GET TO DECIDE SOMETHING LIKE THAT FOR YOURSELF!
YEAH!
OKAY, BUT--
THE THREE OF US WILL MANAGE SOMETHING TOGETHER.
LET'S GO!
HUH?
B--
OKAY!

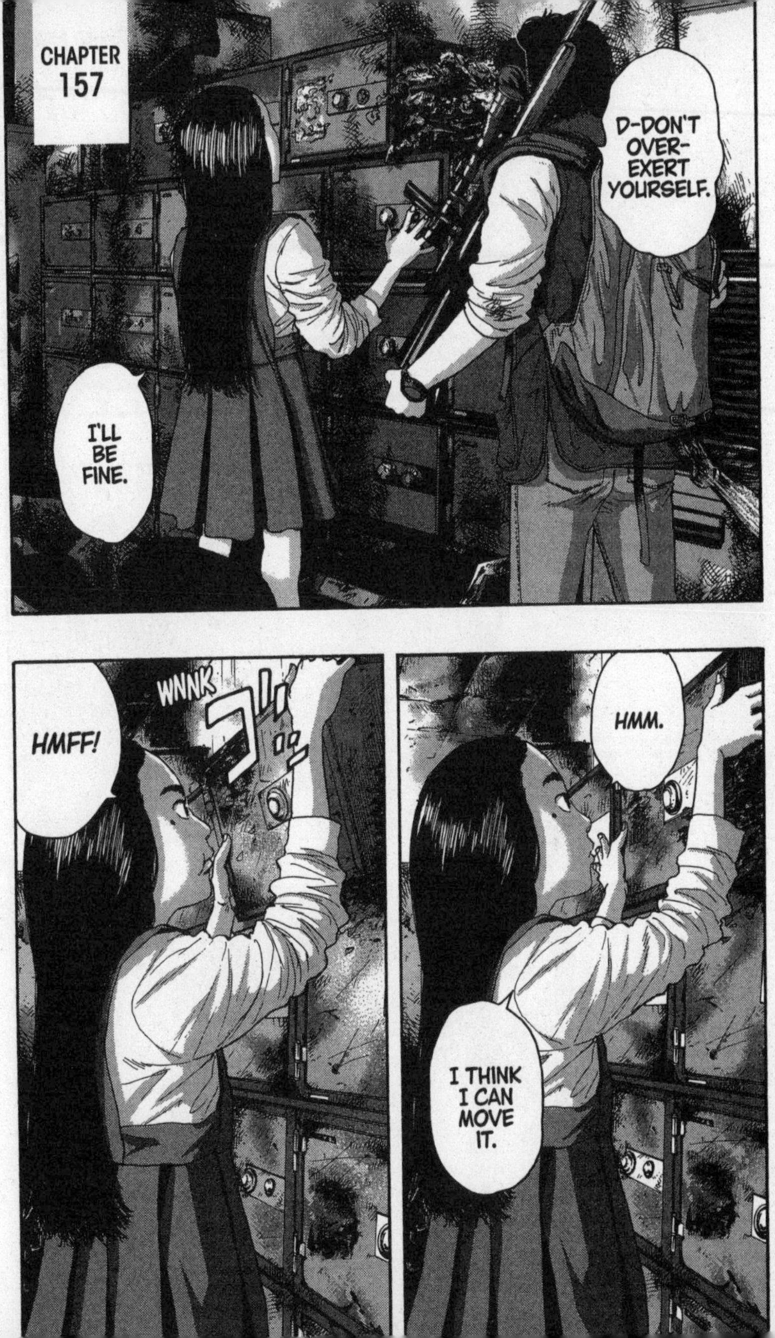
CHAPTER 157
D-DON'T OVER-EXERT YOURSELF.
I'LL BE FINE.
HMM.
I THINK I CAN MOVE IT.
WNNK
HMFF!

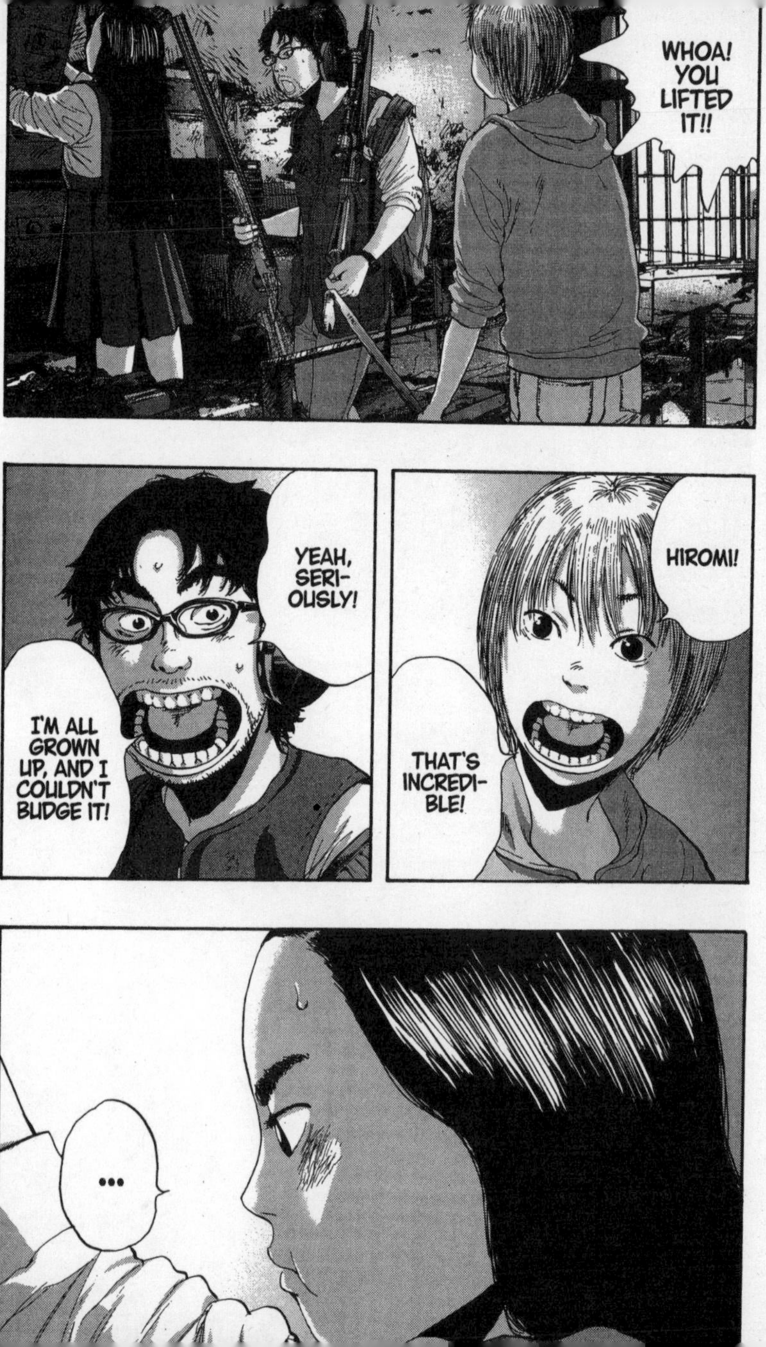
WHOA! YOU LIFTED IT!!
HIROMI!
THAT'S INCREDIBLE!
YEAH, SERIOUSLY!
I'M ALL GROWN UP, AND I COULDN'T BUDGE IT!
...

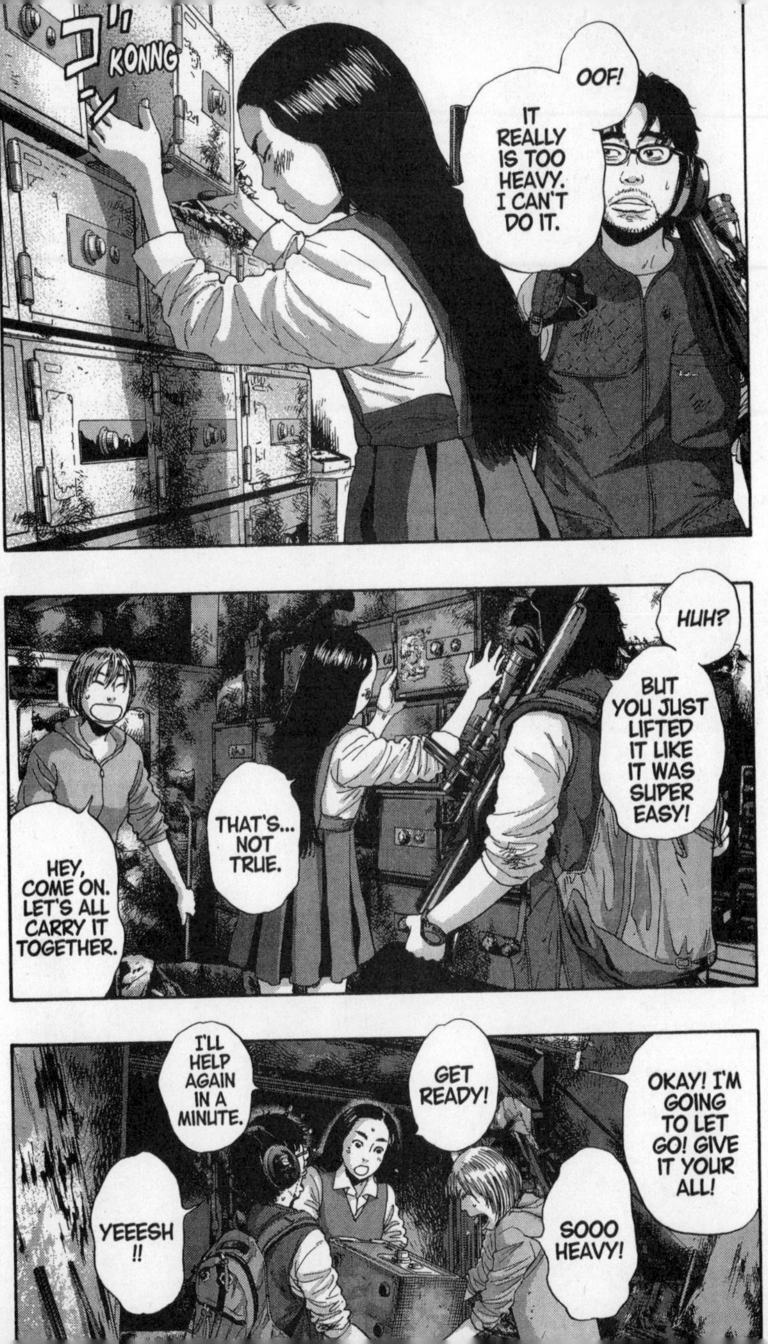
OOF!
IT REALLY IS TOO HEAVY. I CAN'T DO IT.
KONNG
HUH?
BUT YOU JUST LIFTED IT LIKE IT WAS SUPER EASY!
THAT'S... NOT TRUE.
HEY, COME ON. LET'S ALL CARRY IT TOGETHER.
OKAY! I'M GOING TO LET GO! GIVE IT YOUR ALL!
GET READY!
I'LL HELP AGAIN IN A MINUTE.
SOOO HEAVY!
YEEESH !!

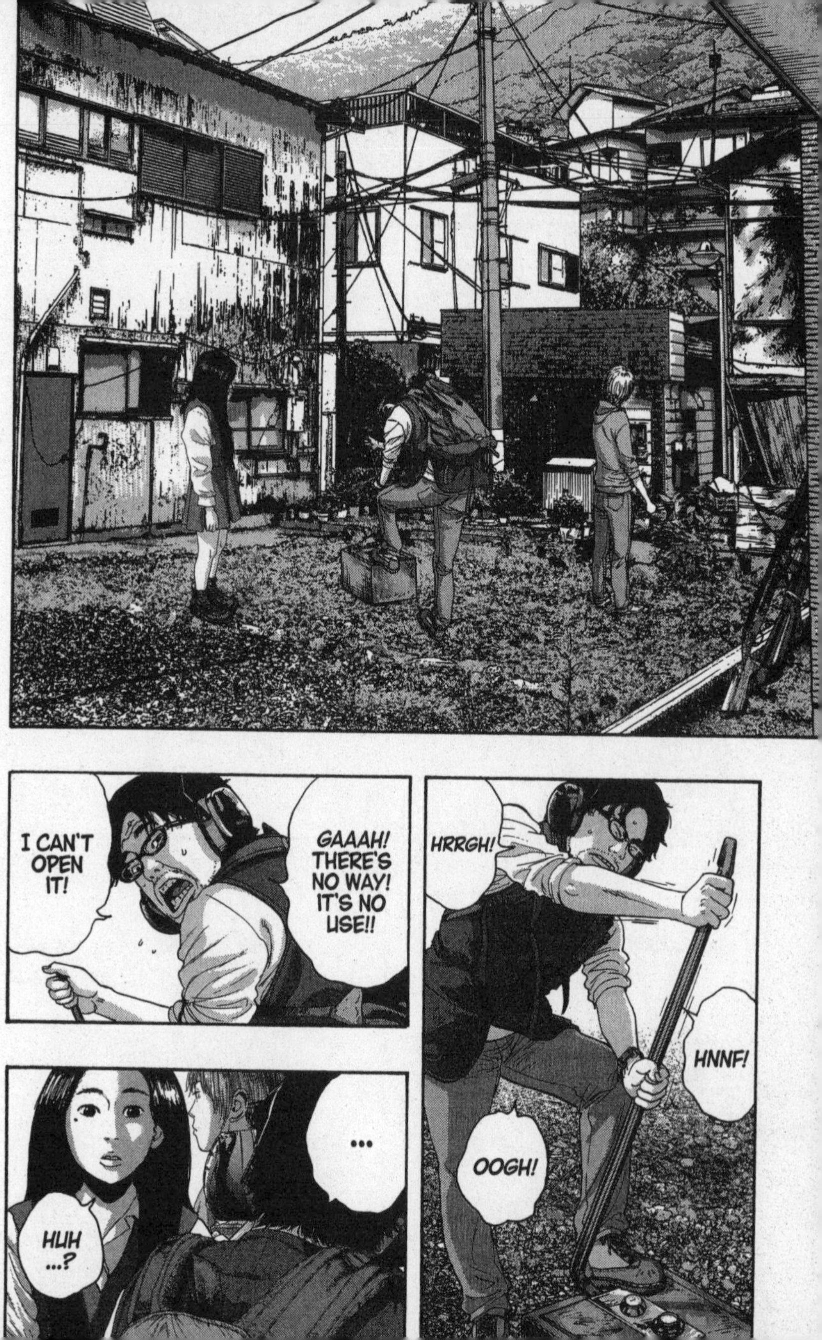
HRRGH!
HNNF!
OOGH!
GAAAH! THERE'S NO WAY! IT'S NO USE!!
I CAN'T OPEN IT!
...
HUH ...?

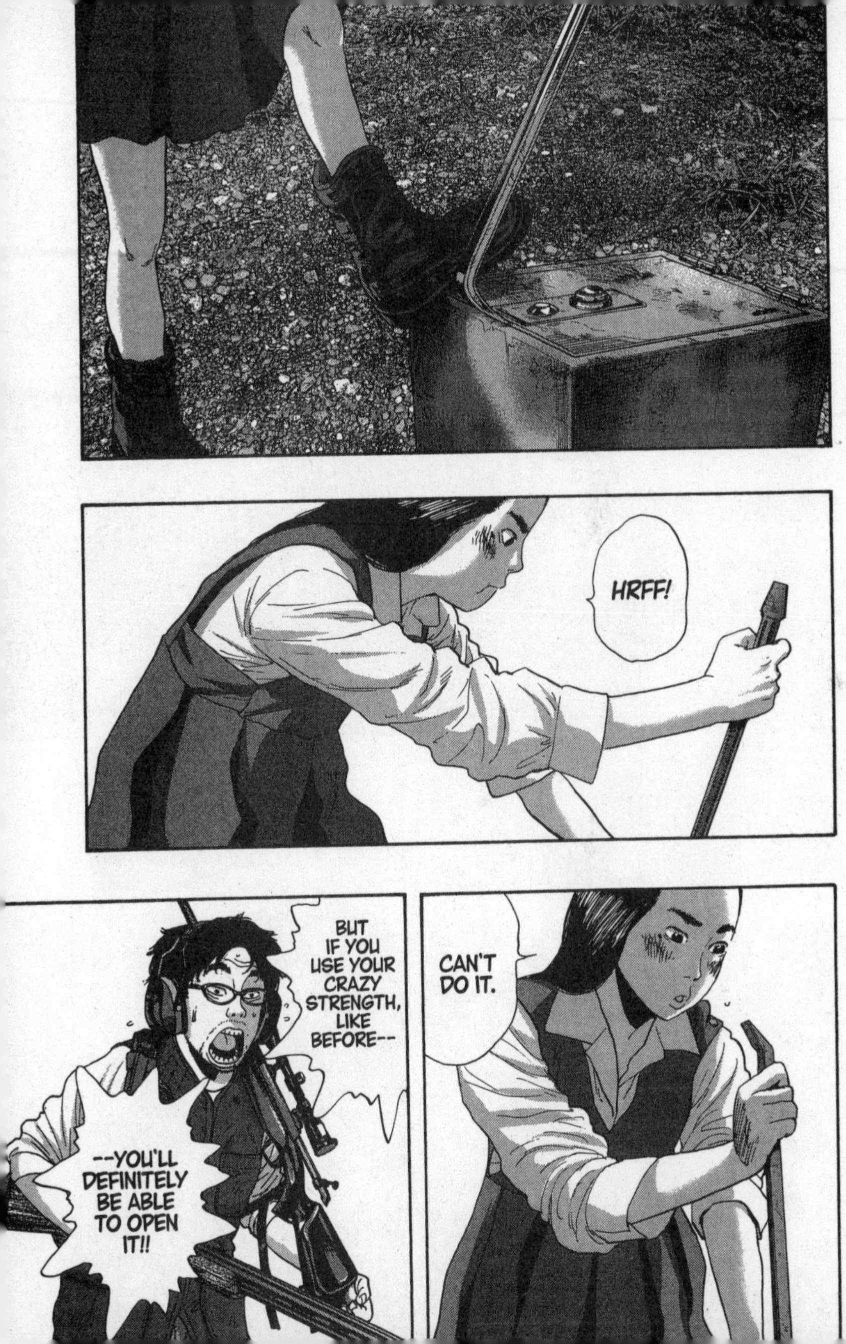
HRFF!
CAN'T DO IT.
BUT IF YOU USE YOUR CRAZY STRENGTH, LIKE BEFORE--
--YOU'LL DEFINITELY BE ABLE TO OPEN IT!!

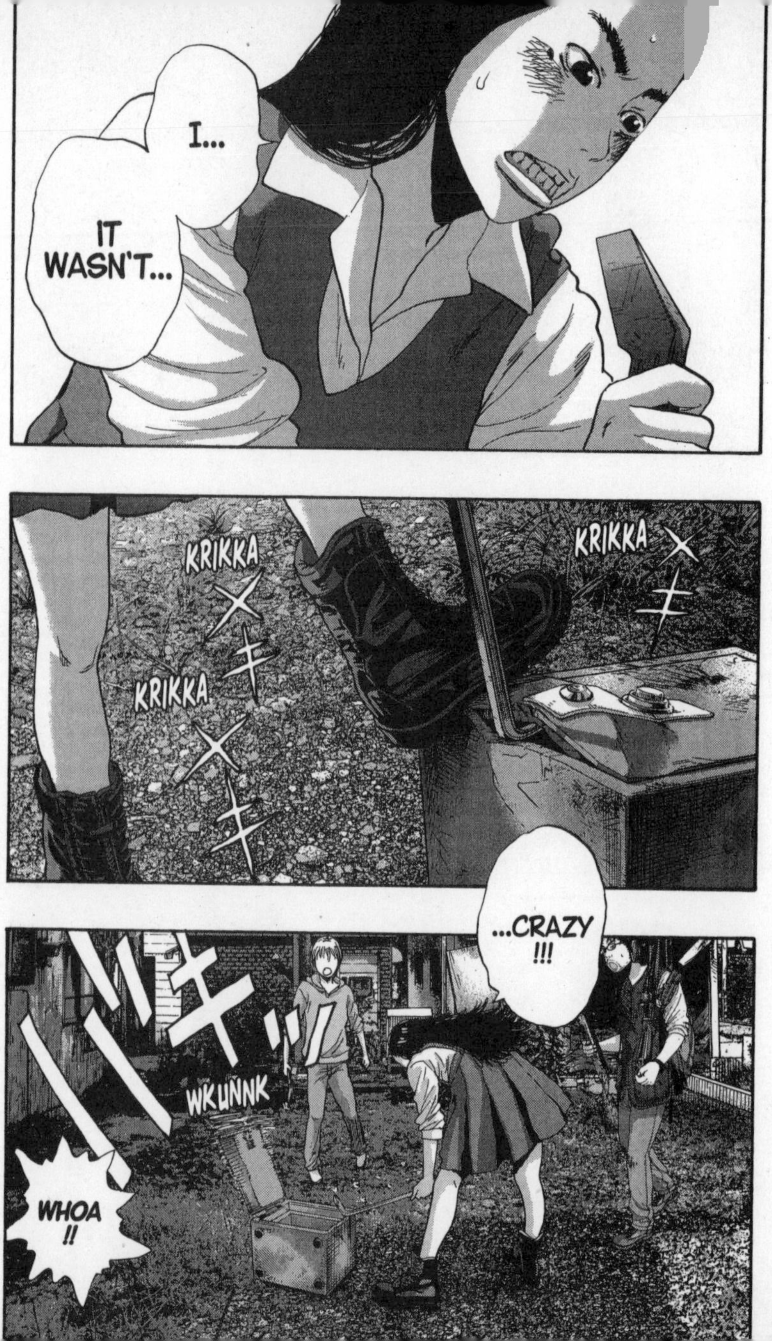
I...
IT WASN'T...
KRIKKA
KRIKKA
KRIKKA
...CRAZY !!!
WKUNNK
WHOA !!

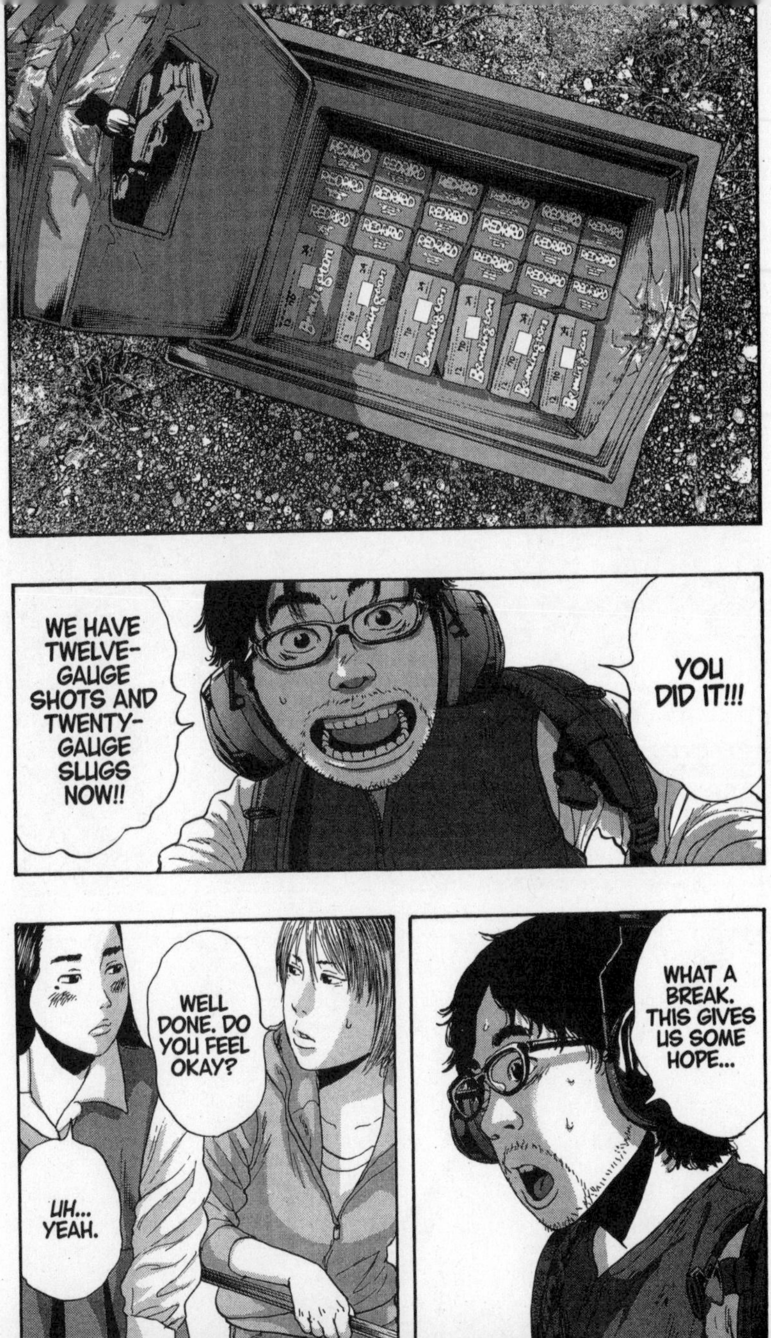
YOU DID IT!!!
WE HAVE TWELVE-GAUGE SHOTS AND TWENTY-GAUGE SLUGS NOW!!
WHAT A BREAK. THIS GIVES US SOME HOPE...
WELL DONE. DO YOU FEEL OKAY?
UH... YEAH.

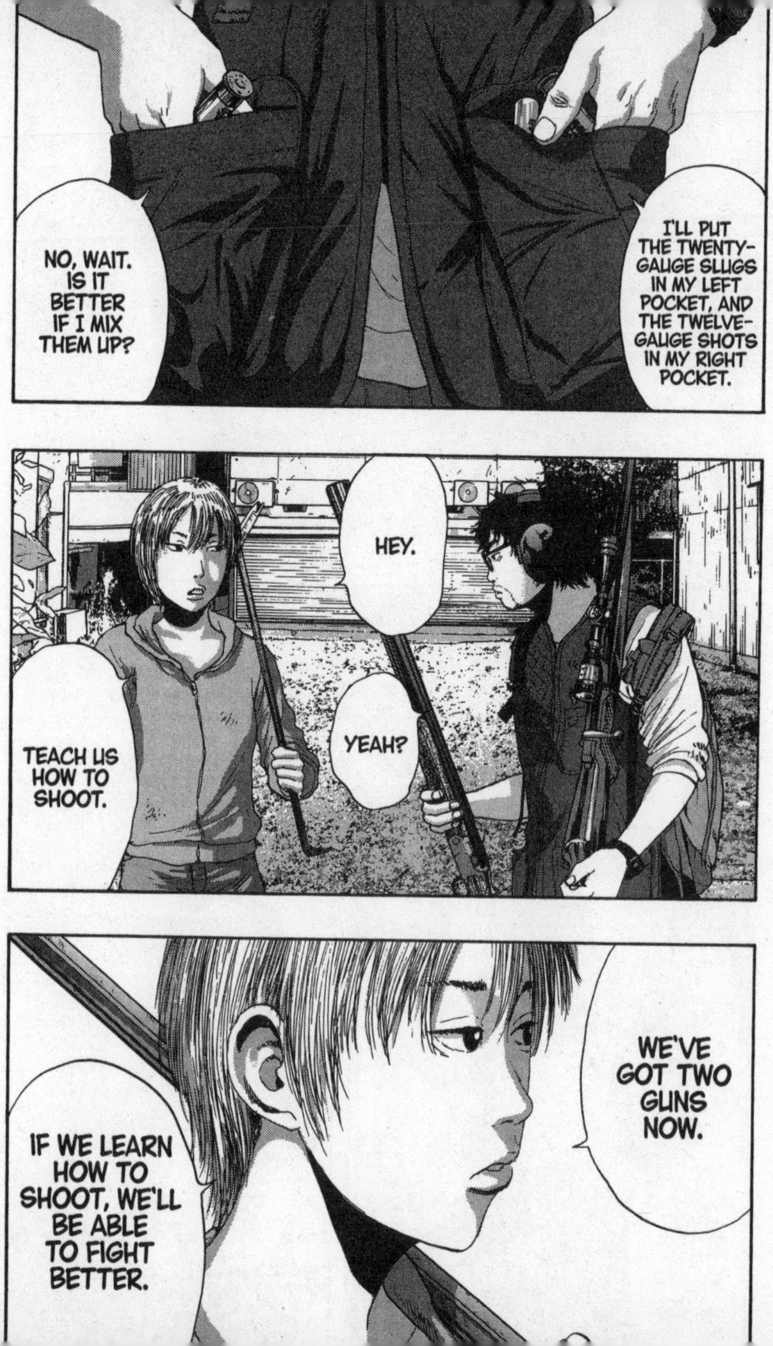
I'LL PUT THE TWENTY-GAUGE SLUGS IN MY LEFT POCKET, AND THE TWELVE-GAUGE SHOTS IN MY RIGHT POCKET.
NO, WAIT. IS IT BETTER IF I MIX THEM UP?
HEY.
YEAH?
TEACH US HOW TO SHOOT.
WE'VE GOT TWO GUNS NOW.
IF WE LEARN HOW TO SHOOT, WE'LL BE ABLE TO FIGHT BETTER.

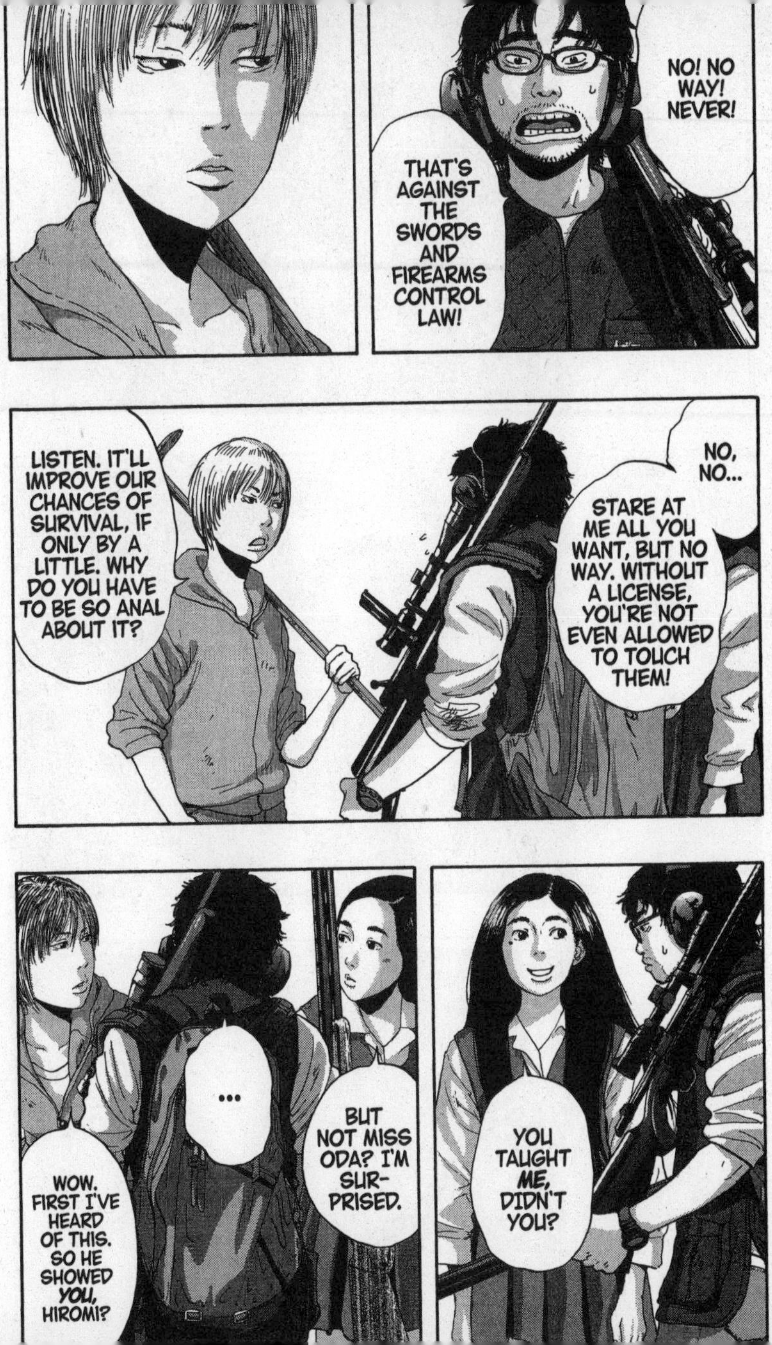
NO! NO WAY! NEVER!
THAT'S AGAINST THE SWORDS AND FIREARMS CONTROL LAW!
NO, NO...
STARE AT ME ALL YOU WANT, BUT NO WAY. WITHOUT A LICENSE, YOU'RE NOT EVEN ALLOWED TO TOUCH THEM!
LISTEN. IT'LL IMPROVE OUR CHANCES OF SURVIVAL, IF ONLY BY A LITTLE. WHY DO YOU HAVE TO BE SO ANAL ABOUT IT?
YOU TAUGHT *ME*, DIDN'T YOU?
BUT NOT MISS ODA? I'M SUR-PRISED.
...
WOW. FIRST I'VE HEARD OF THIS. SO HE SHOWED *YOU*, HIROMI?

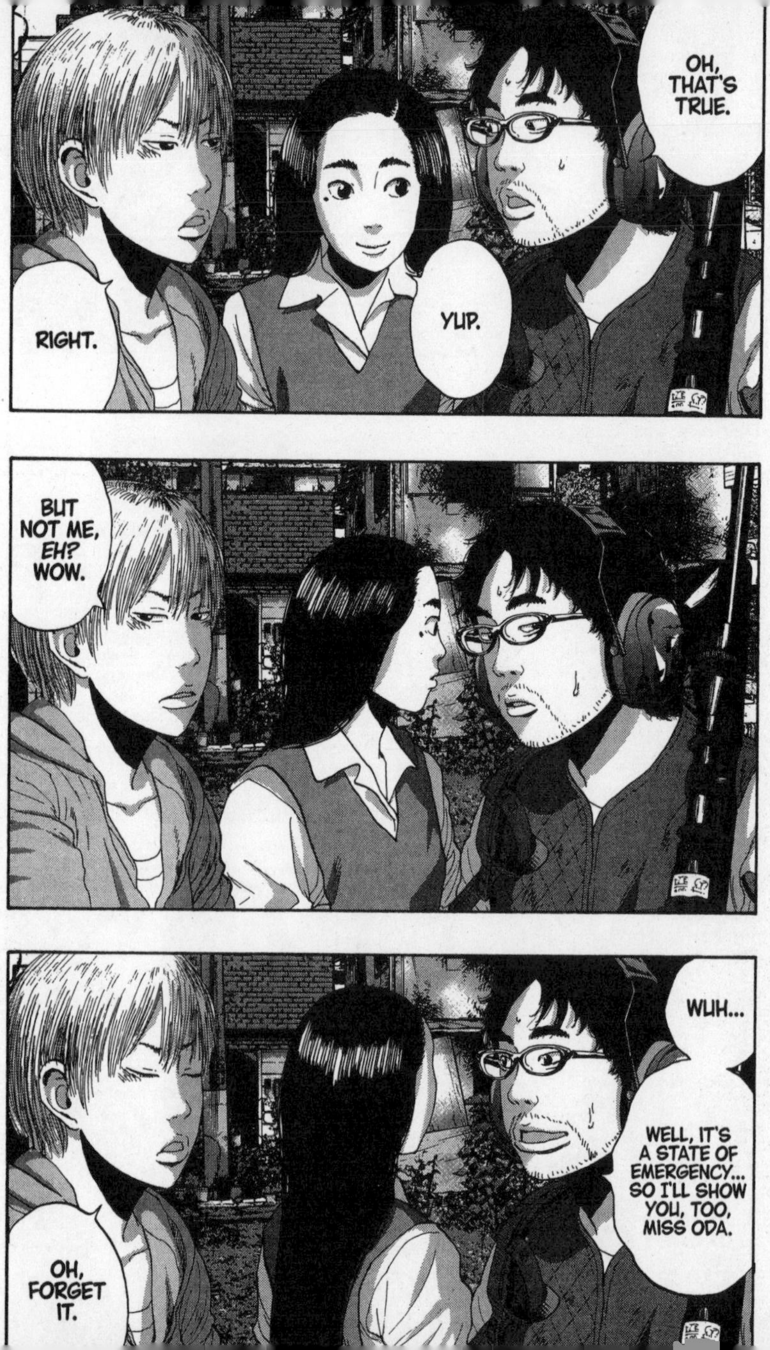
OH, THAT'S TRUE.
YUP.
RIGHT.
BUT NOT ME, EH? WOW.
WUH...
WELL, IT'S A STATE OF EMERGENCY... SO I'LL SHOW YOU, TOO, MISS ODA.
OH, FORGET IT.

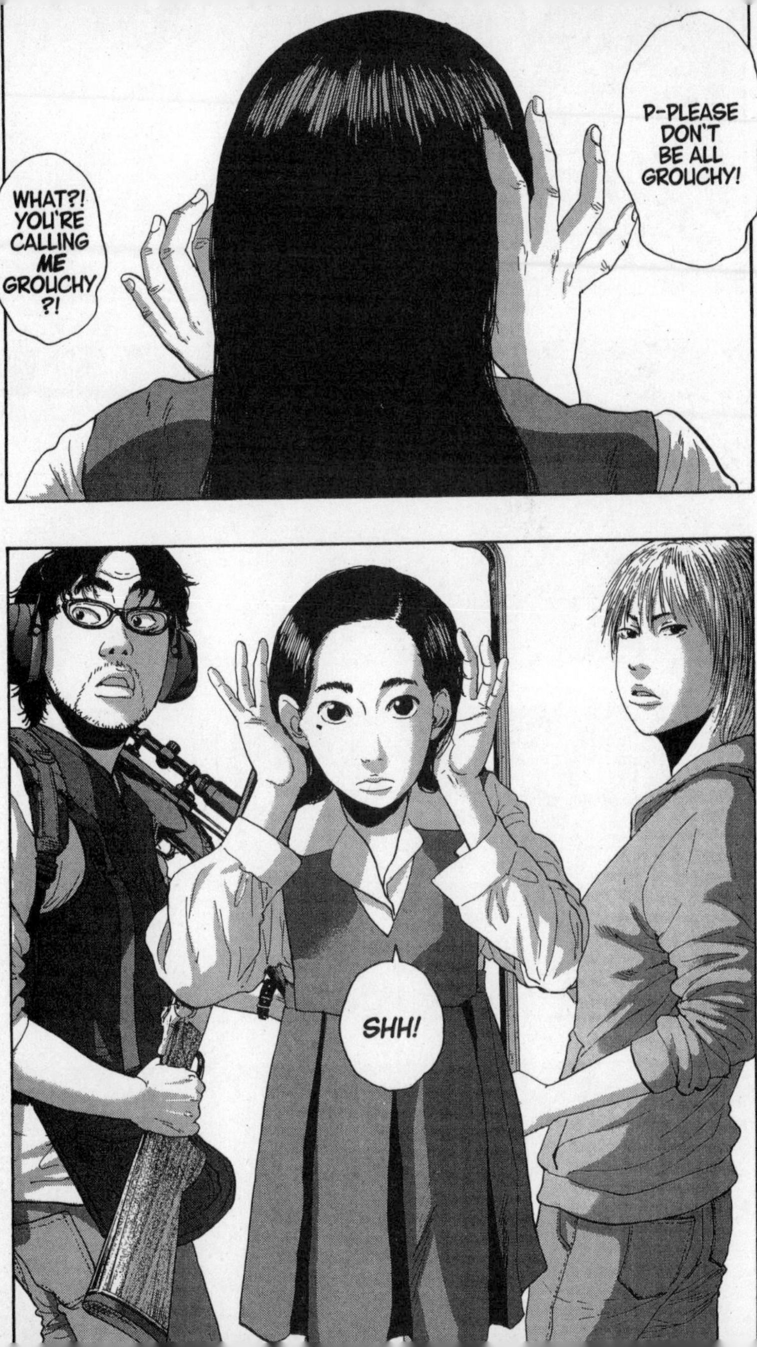
P-PLEASE DON'T BE ALL GROUCHY!
WHAT?! YOU'RE CALLING *ME* GROUCHY?!
SHH!

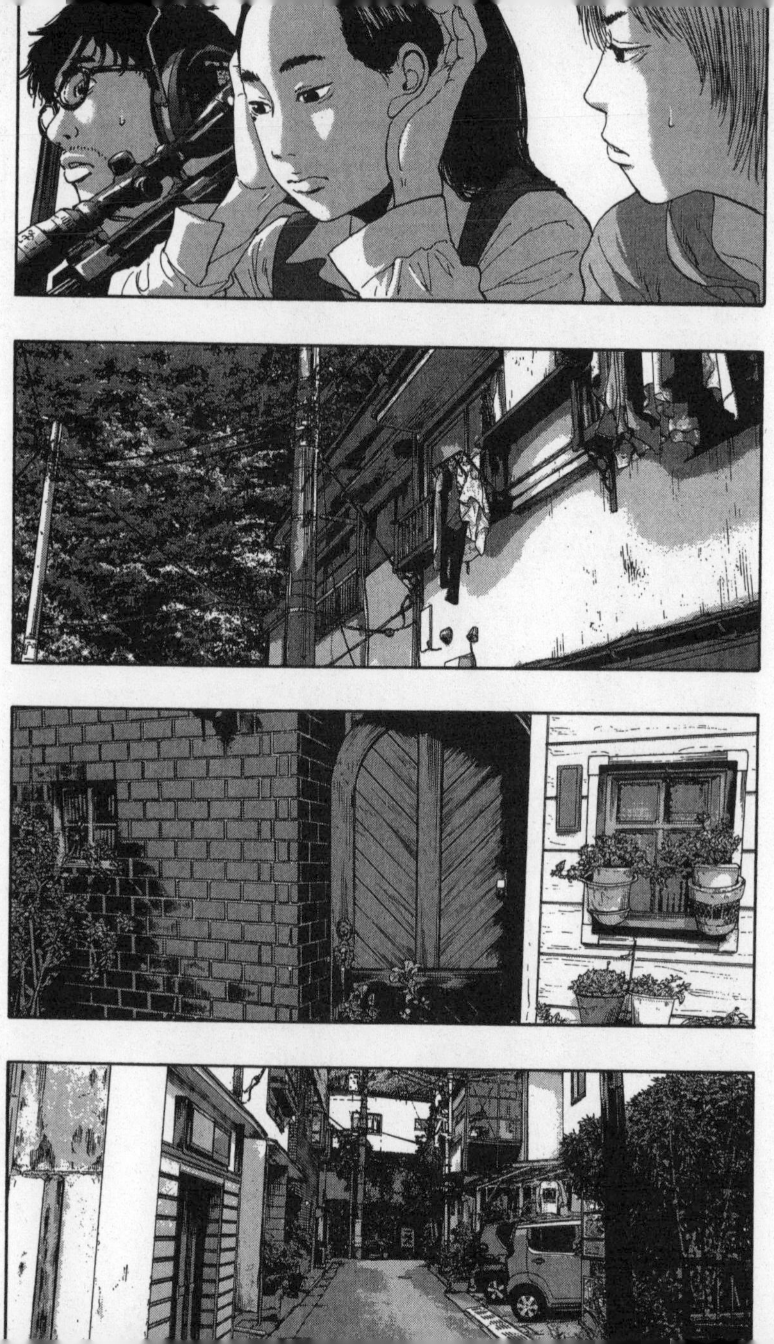

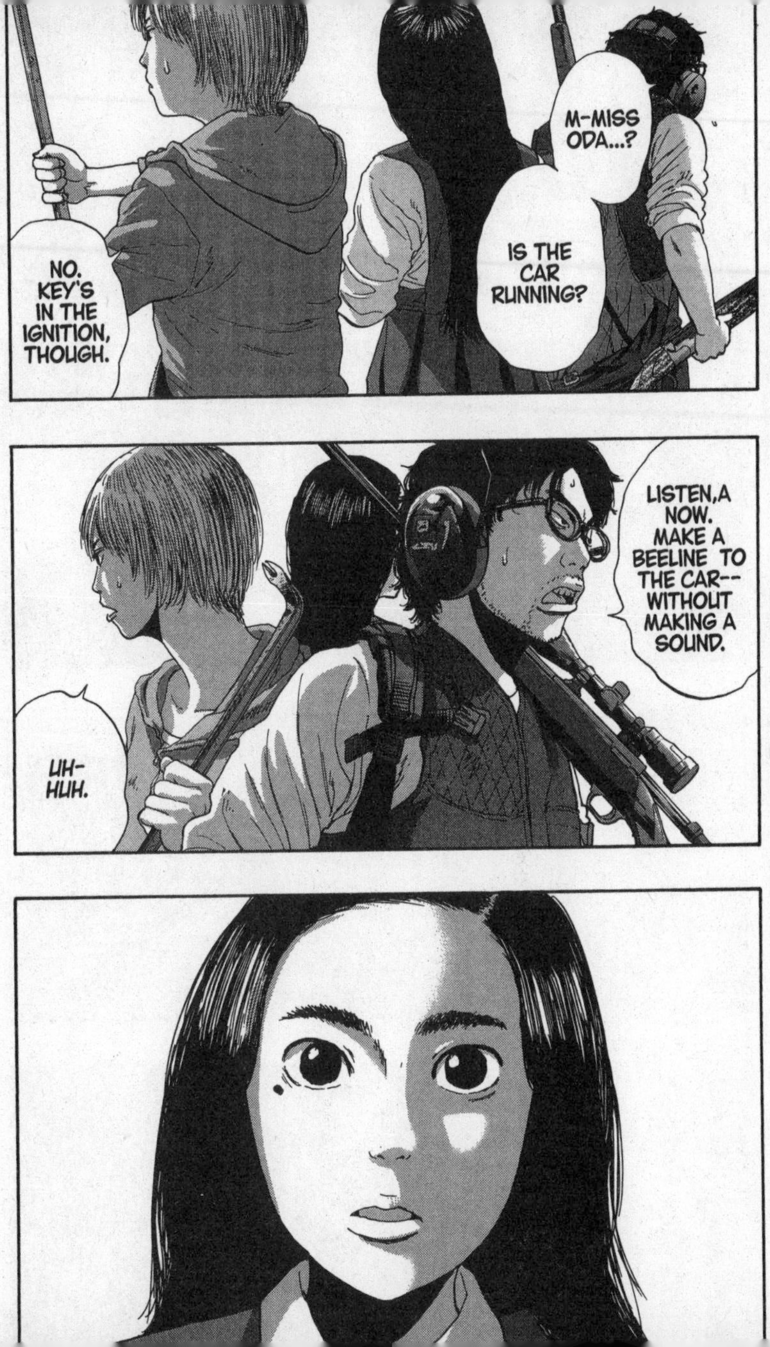
M-MISS ODA...?
IS THE CAR RUNNING?
NO. KEY'S IN THE IGNITION, THOUGH.
LISTEN,A NOW. MAKE A BEELINE TO THE CAR-- WITHOUT MAKING A SOUND.
UH-HUH.

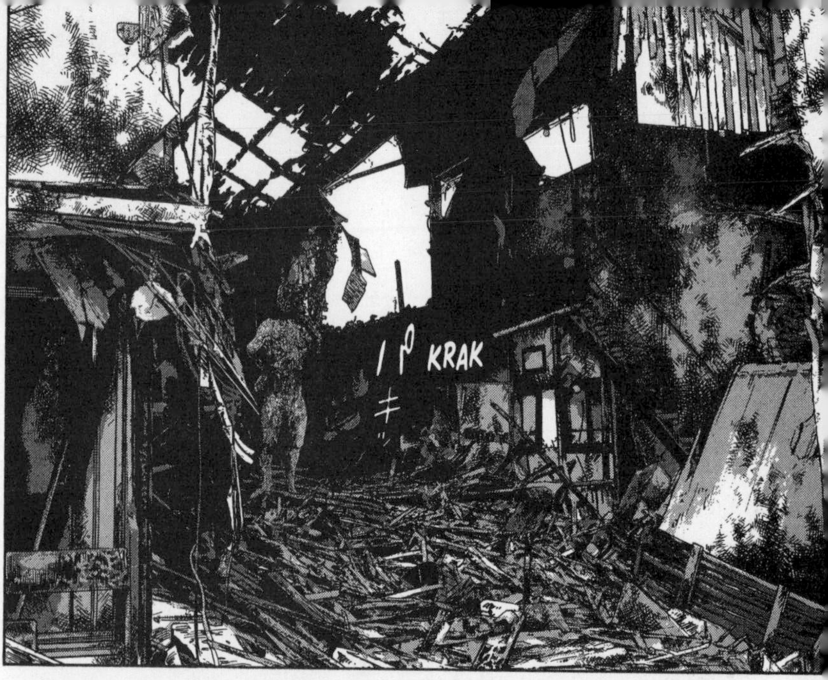

パキッ
KRAK

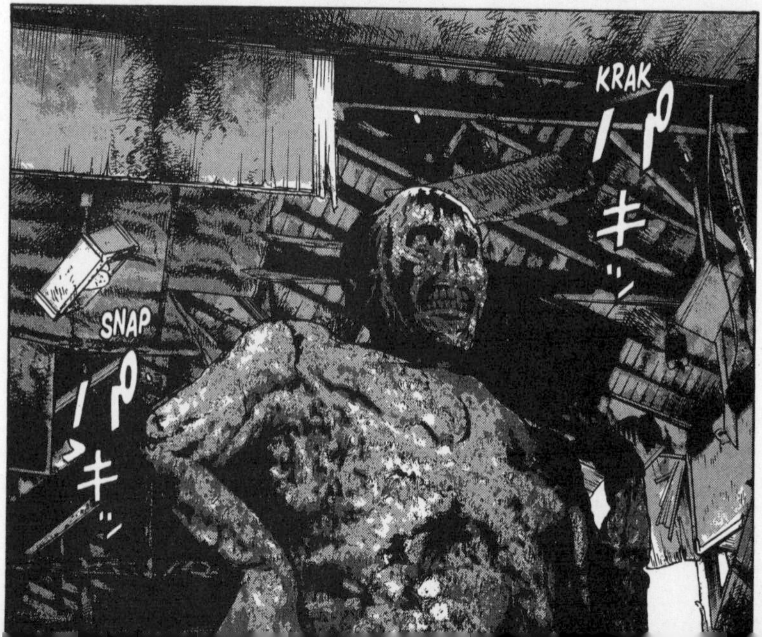

KRAK
パキッ
SNAP

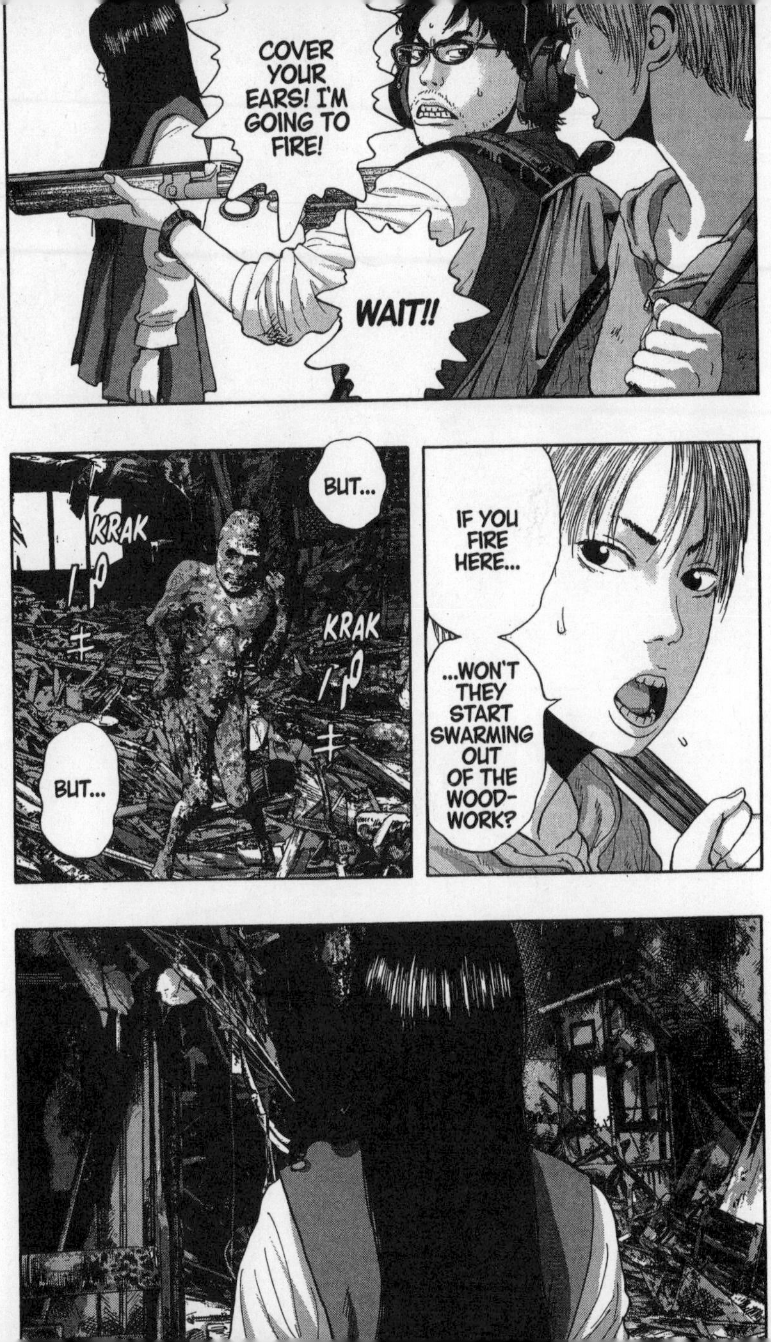
COVER YOUR EARS! I'M GOING TO FIRE!
WAIT!!
IF YOU FIRE HERE...
...WON'T THEY START SWARMING OUT OF THE WOOD-WORK?
BUT...
KRAK
KRAK
BUT...

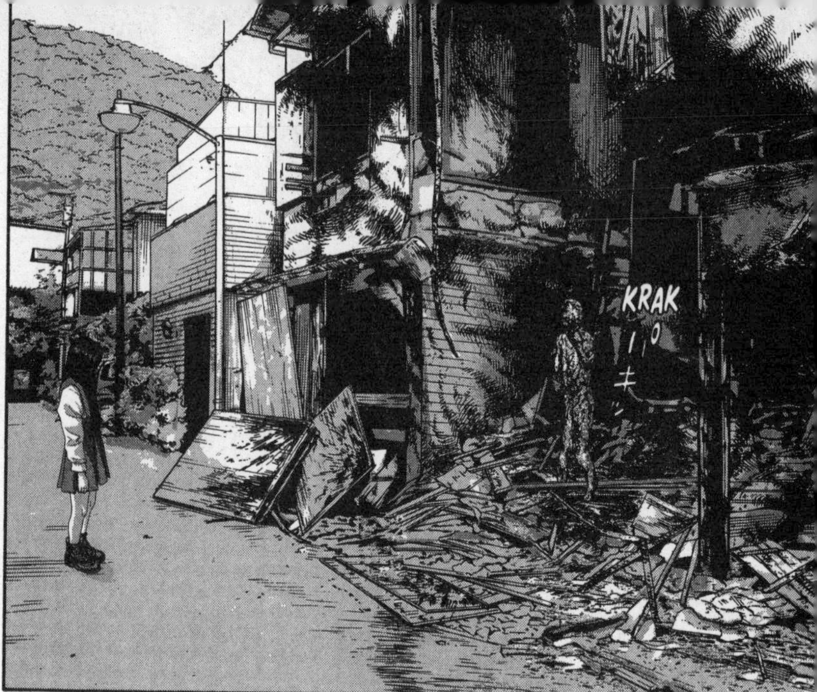
KRAK
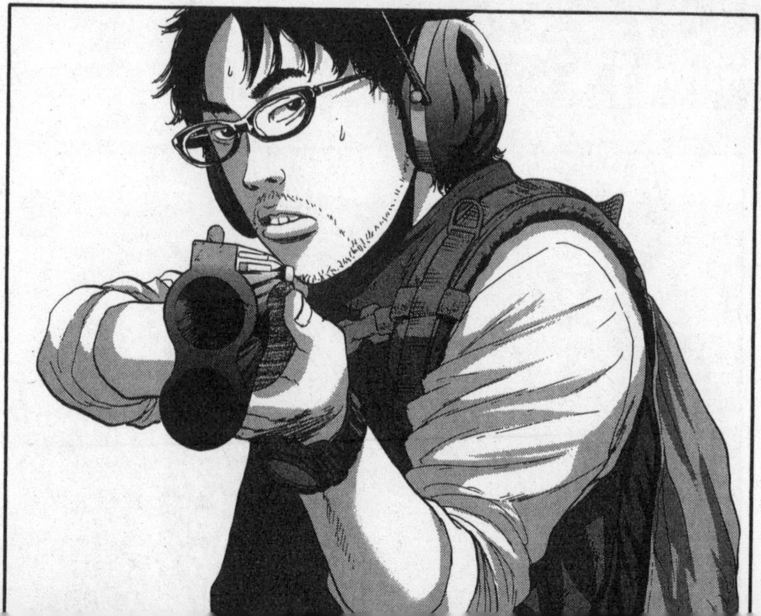

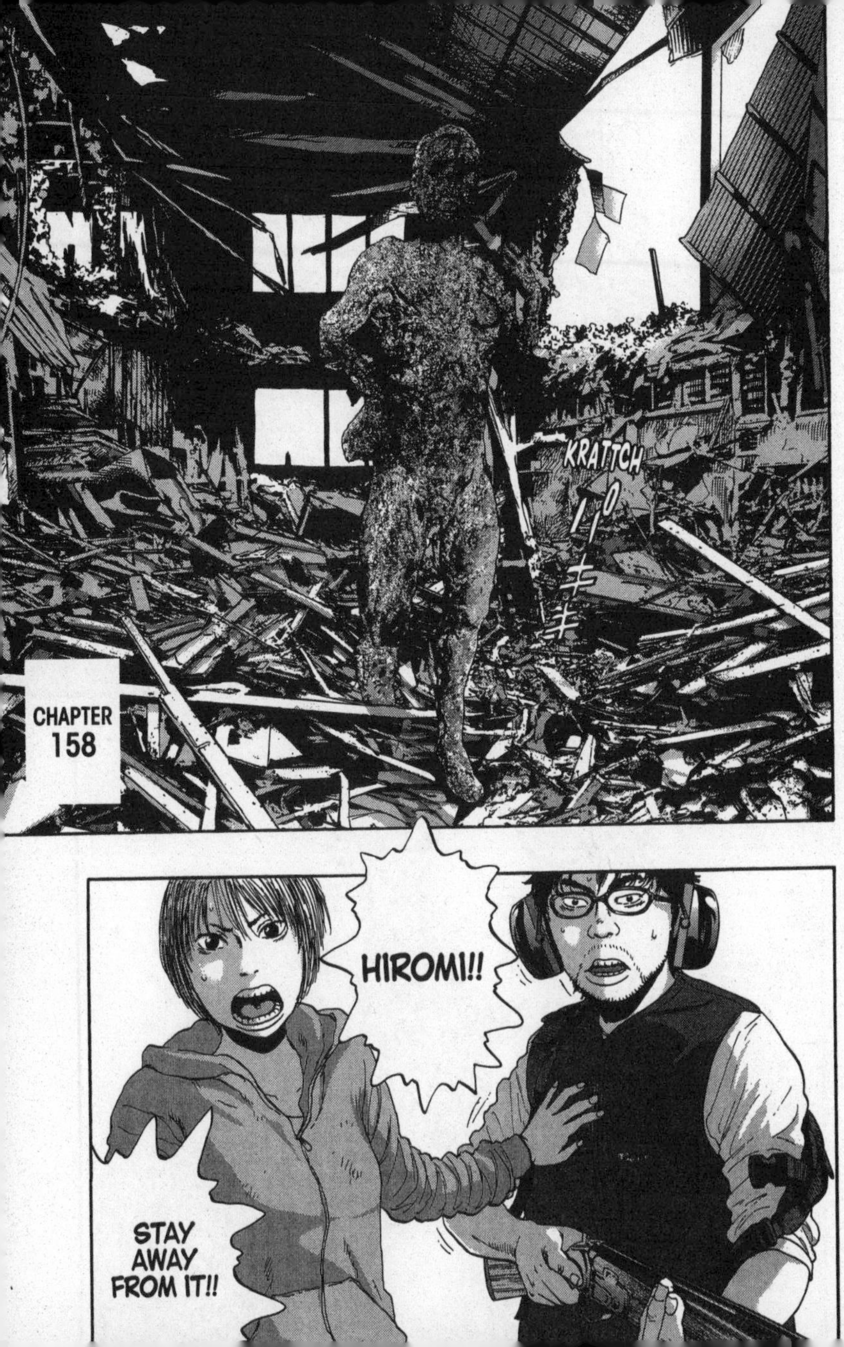
KRATTCH
CHAPTER 158
HIROMI!!
STAY AWAY FROM IT!!

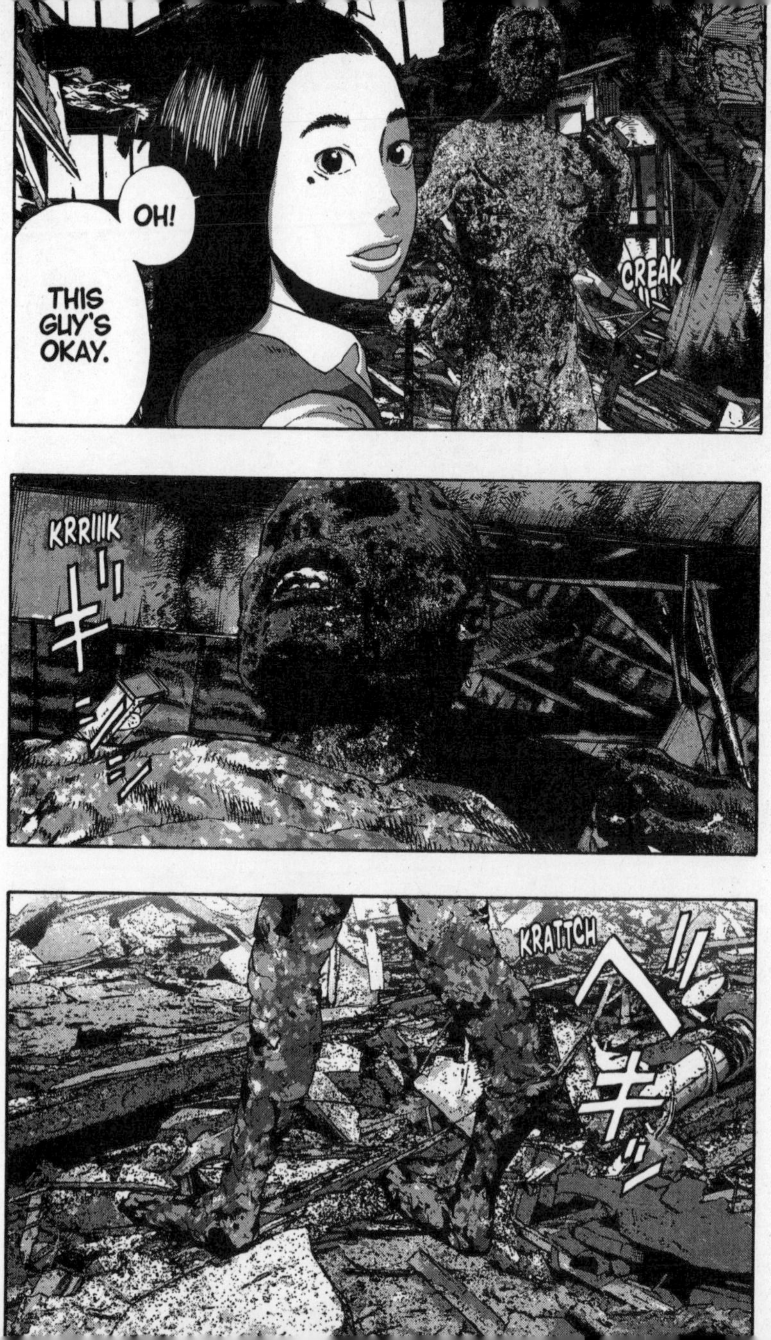
OH!
THIS GUY'S OKAY.
CREAK
KRRIIIK
KRATTCH

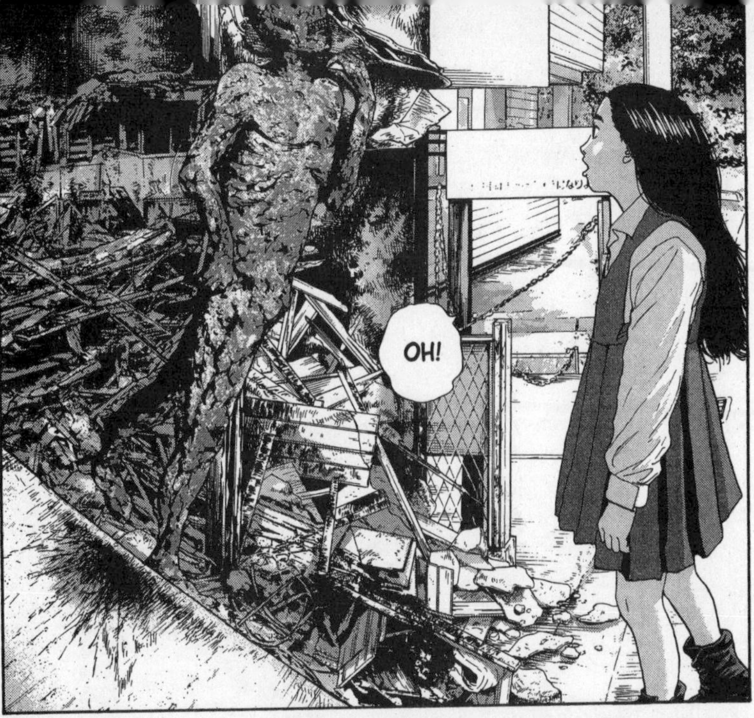
OH!

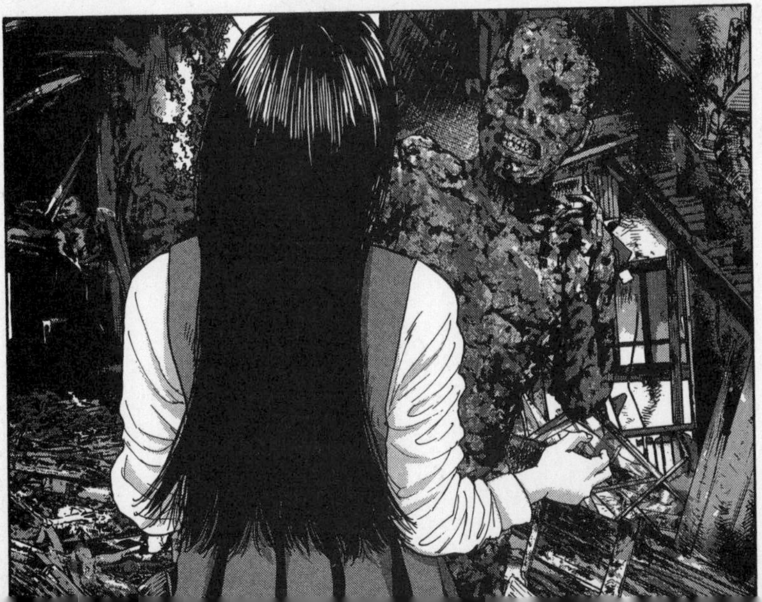

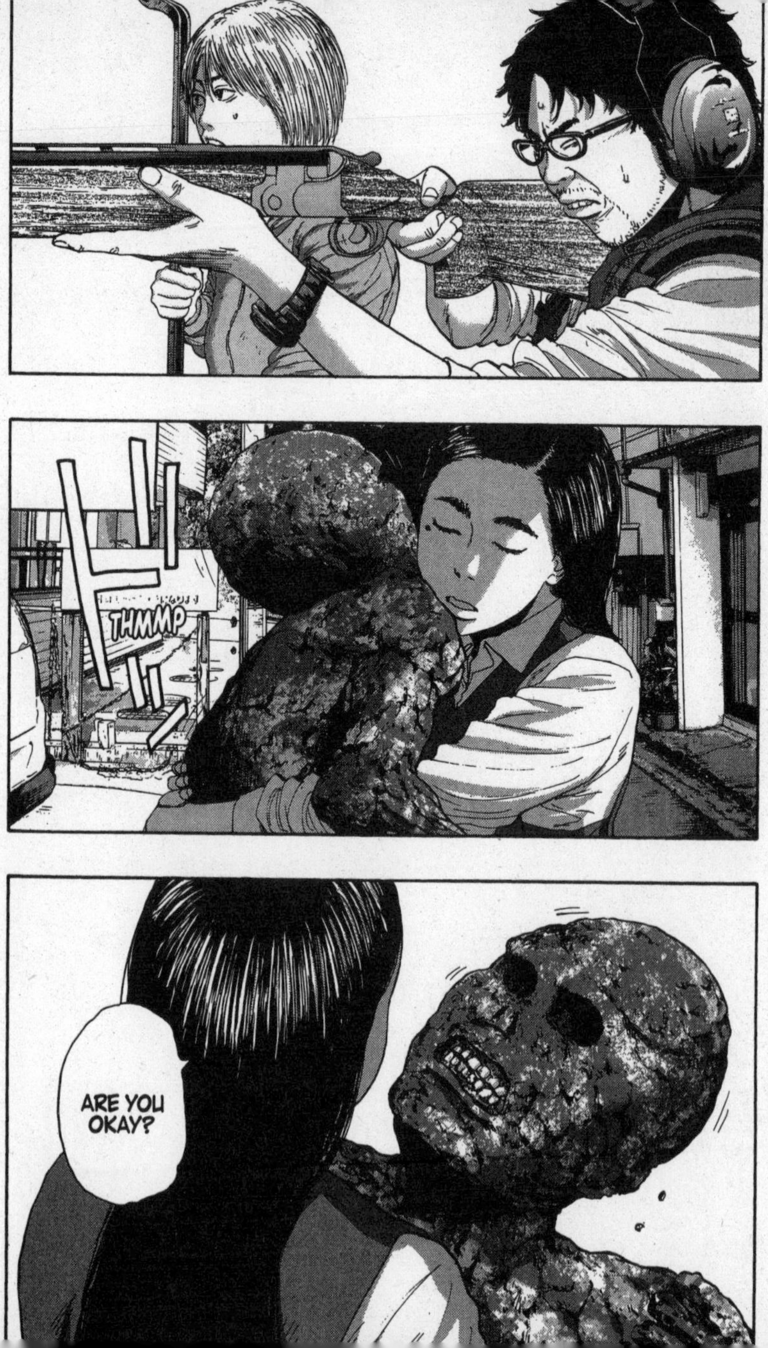
THMMP
ARE YOU OKAY?

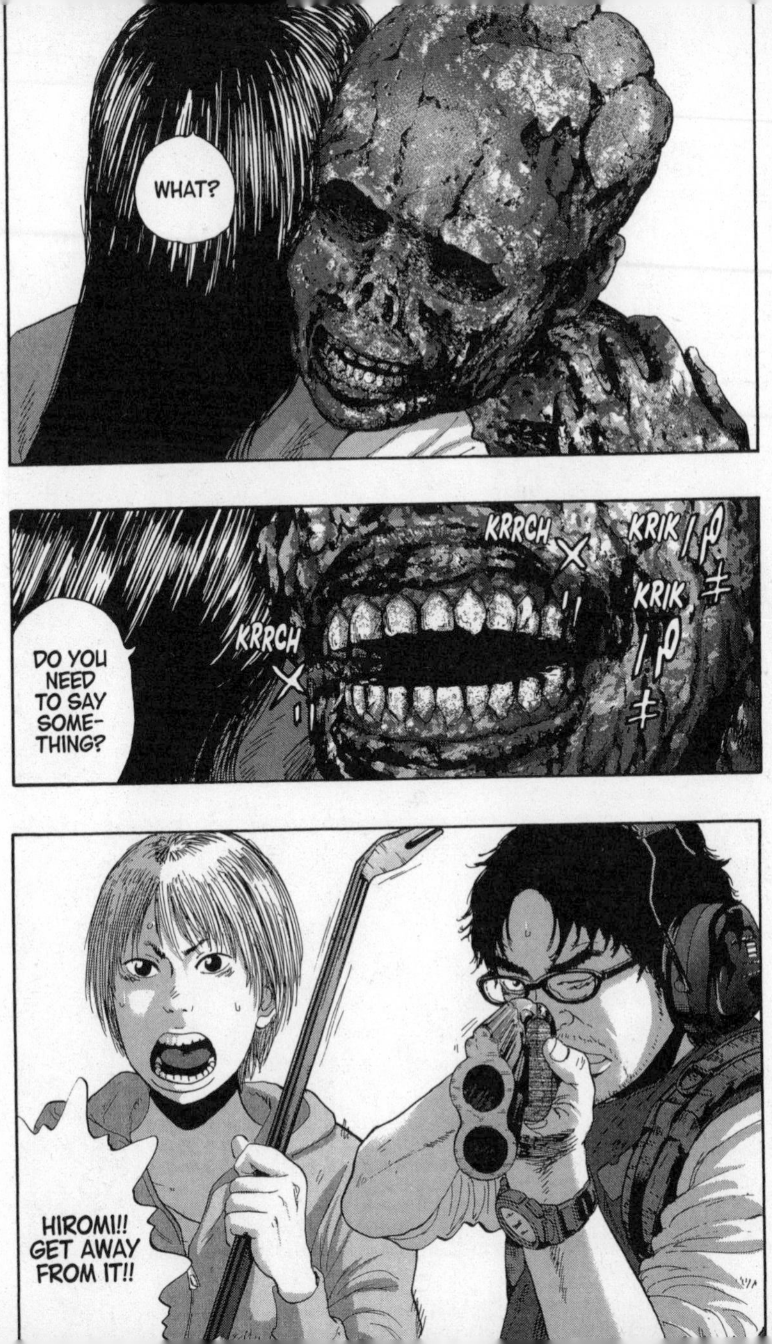
WHAT?
KRIK
KRRCH
KRIK
KRRCH
DO YOU NEED TO SAY SOME-THING?
HIROMI!! GET AWAY FROM IT!!

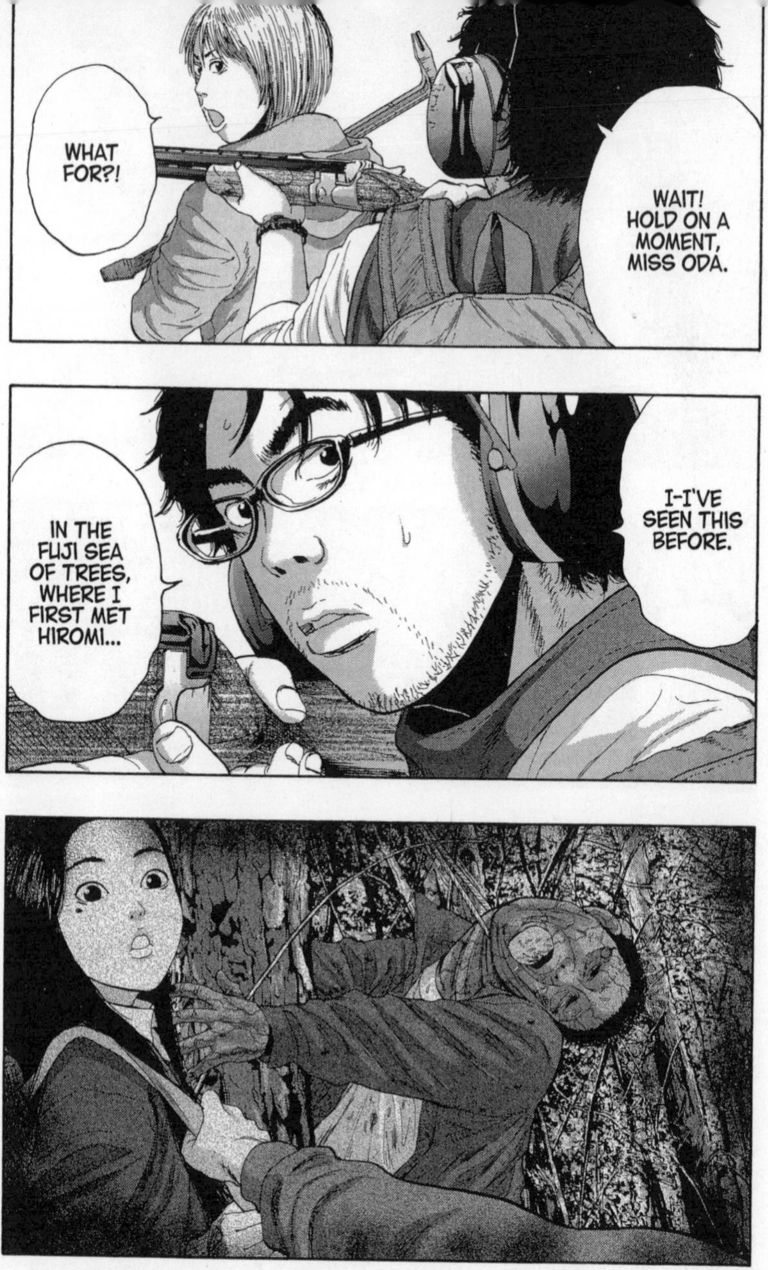
WAIT! HOLD ON A MOMENT, MISS ODA.
WHAT FOR?!
I-I'VE SEEN THIS BEFORE.
IN THE FUJI SEA OF TREES, WHERE I FIRST MET HIROMI...

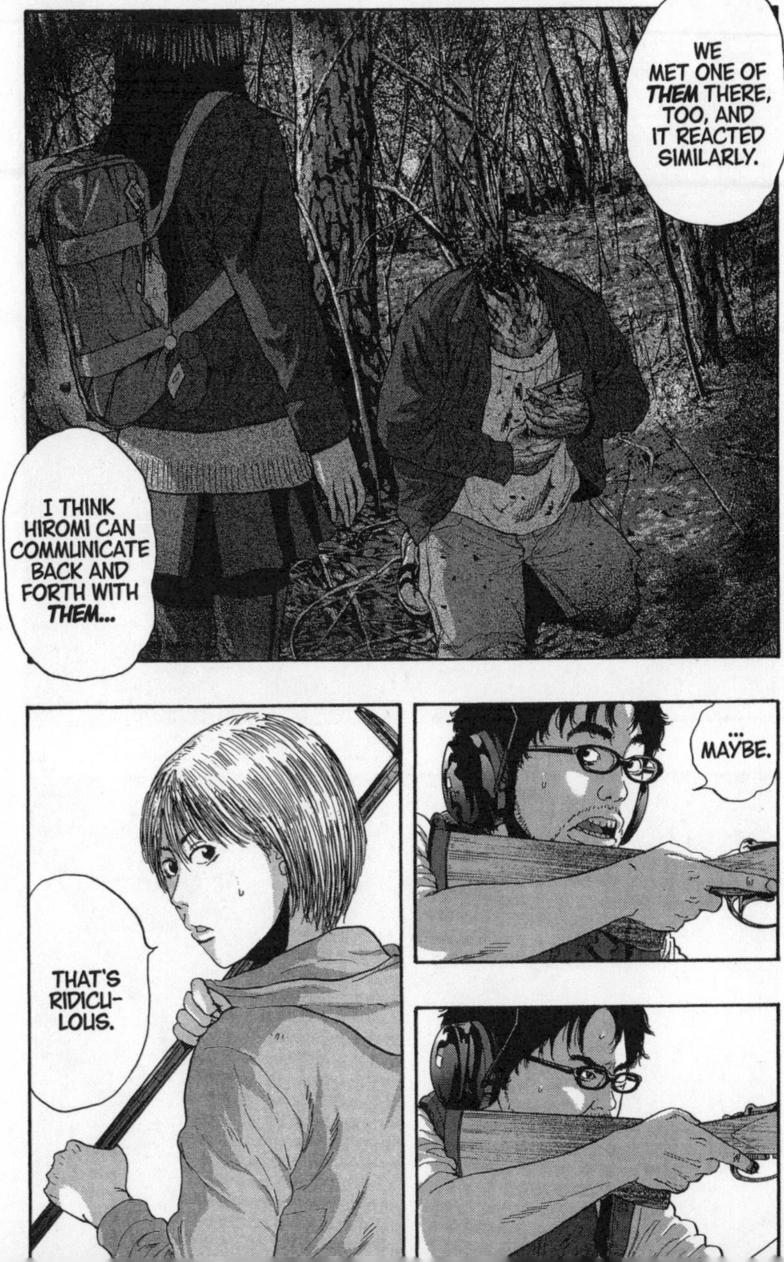
WE MET ONE OF *THEM* THERE, TOO, AND IT REACTED SIMILARLY.
I THINK HIROMI CAN COMMUNICATE BACK AND FORTH WITH *THEM*...
... MAYBE.
THAT'S RIDICU-LOUS.

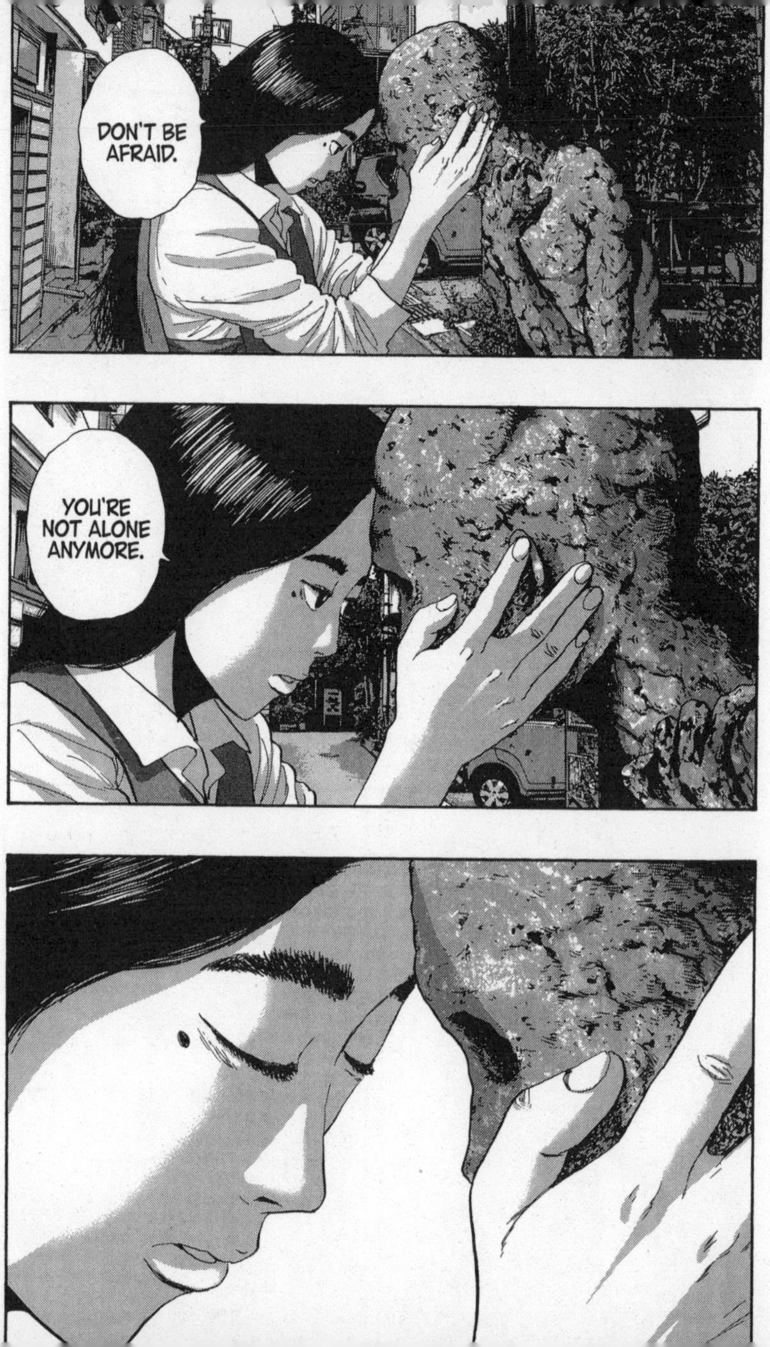
DON'T BE AFRAID.
YOU'RE NOT ALONE ANYMORE.

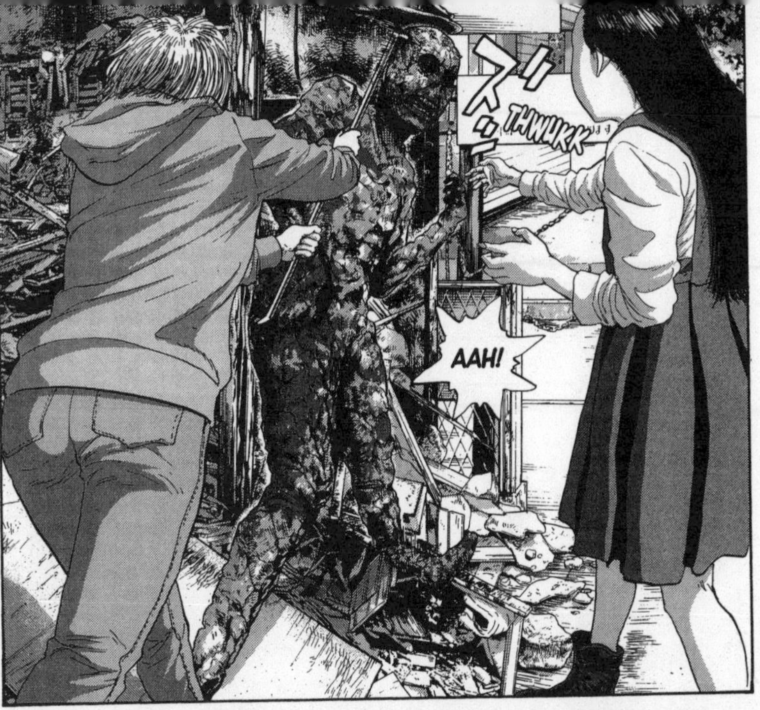
THWUKK
AAH!

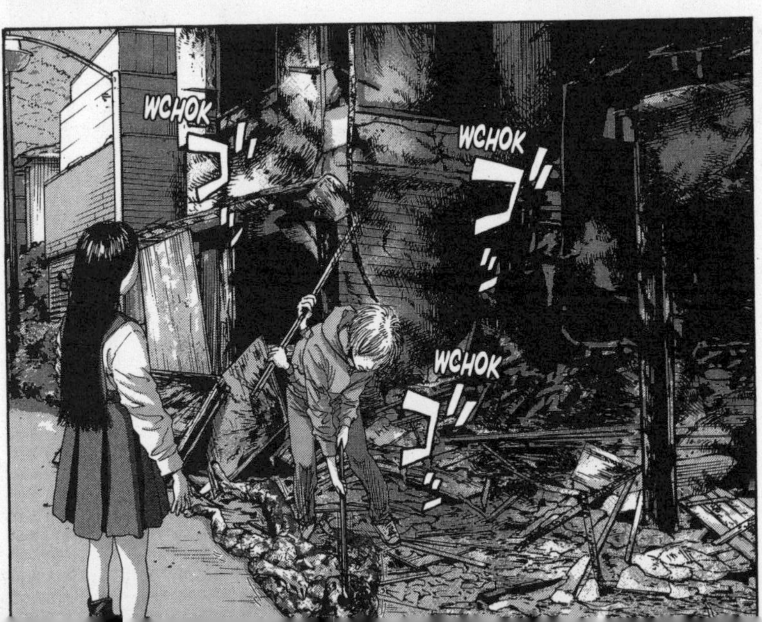
WCHOK
WCHOK
WCHOK

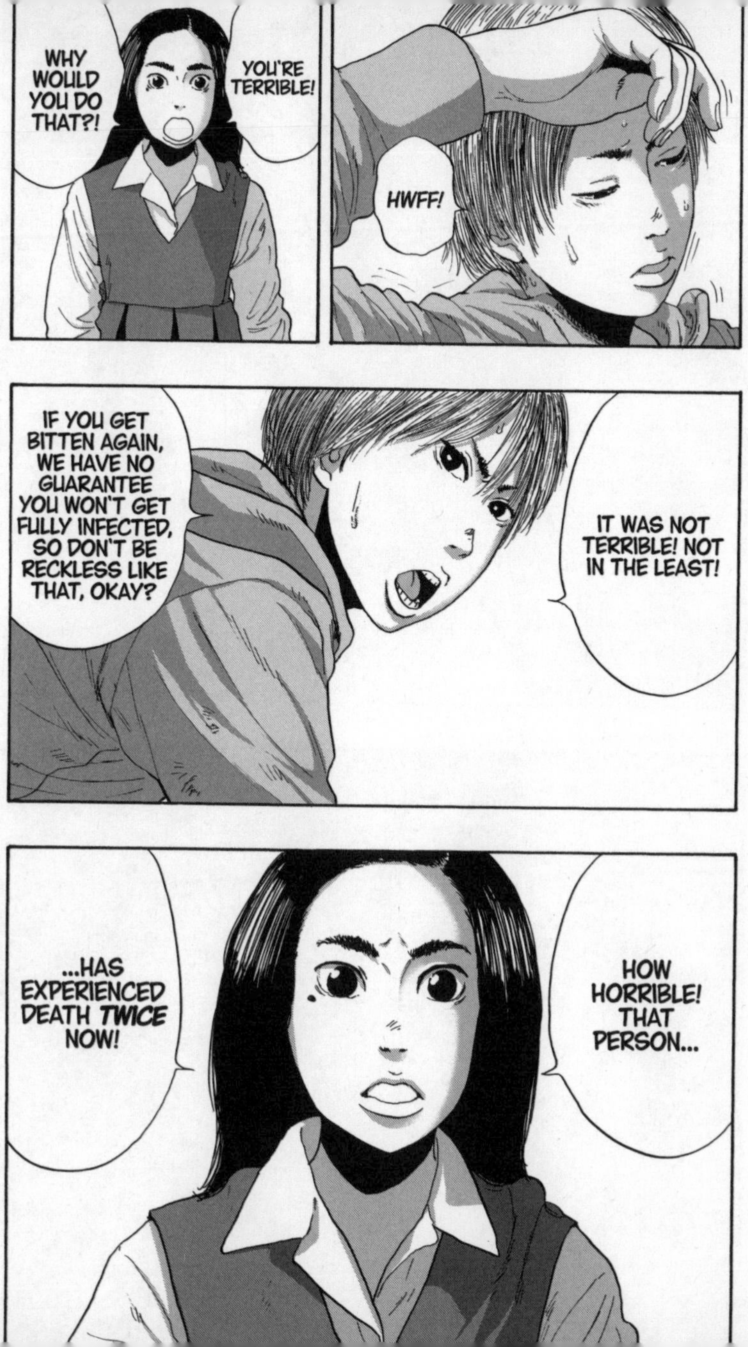
HWFF!
YOU'RE TERRIBLE!
WHY WOULD YOU DO THAT?!
IT WAS NOT TERRIBLE! NOT IN THE LEAST!
IF YOU GET BITTEN AGAIN, WE HAVE NO GUARANTEE YOU WON'T GET FULLY INFECTED, SO DON'T BE RECKLESS LIKE THAT, OKAY?
HOW HORRIBLE! THAT PERSON...
...HAS EXPERIENCED DEATH *TWICE* NOW!

MY PRIORITIES ...

...ARE WITH LIVING PEOPLE OVER DEAD ONES!

DON'T DO ANYTHING DANGER-OUS! UNDER-STAND?

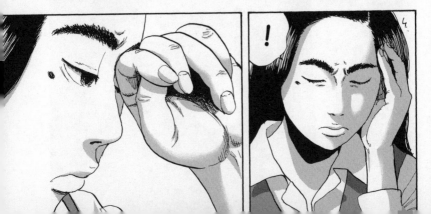

!

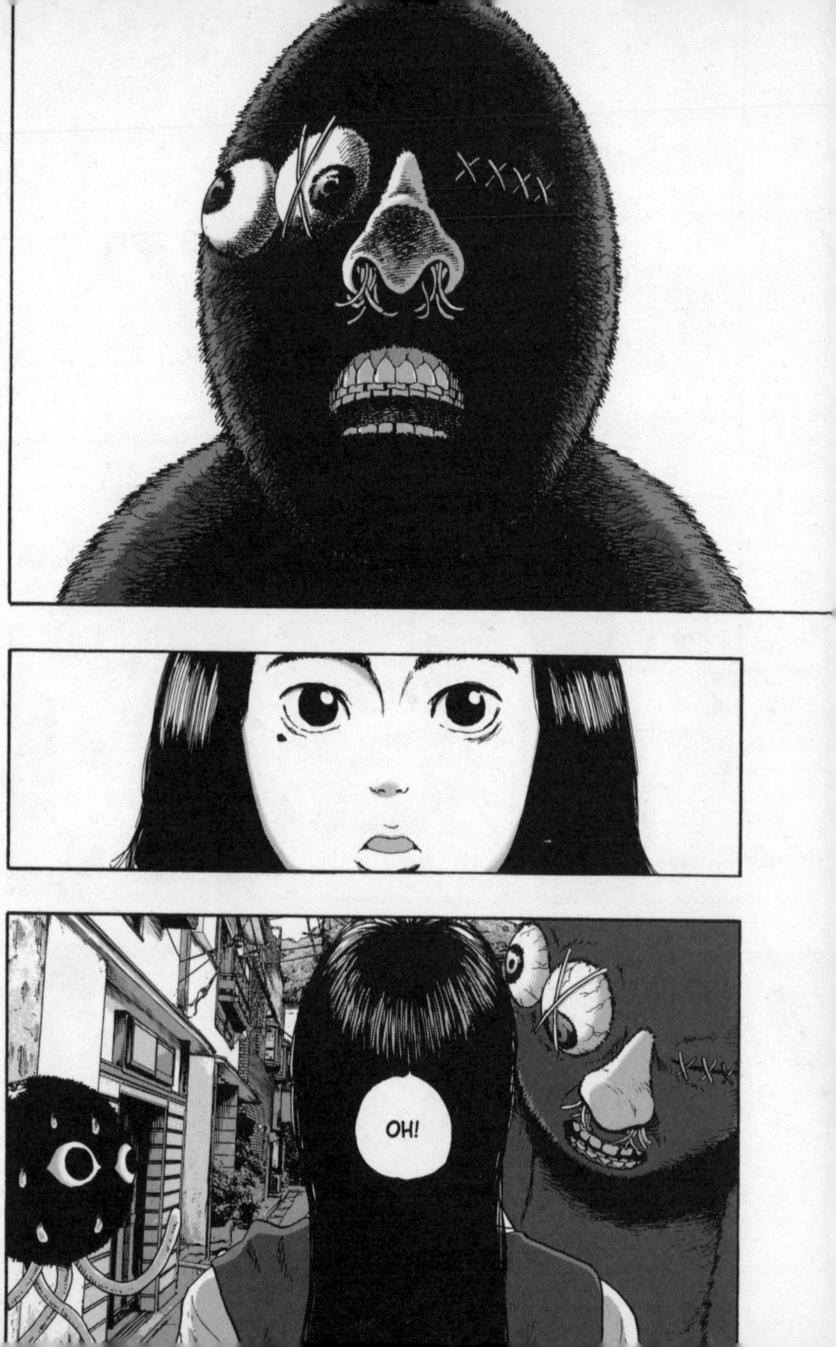
OH!

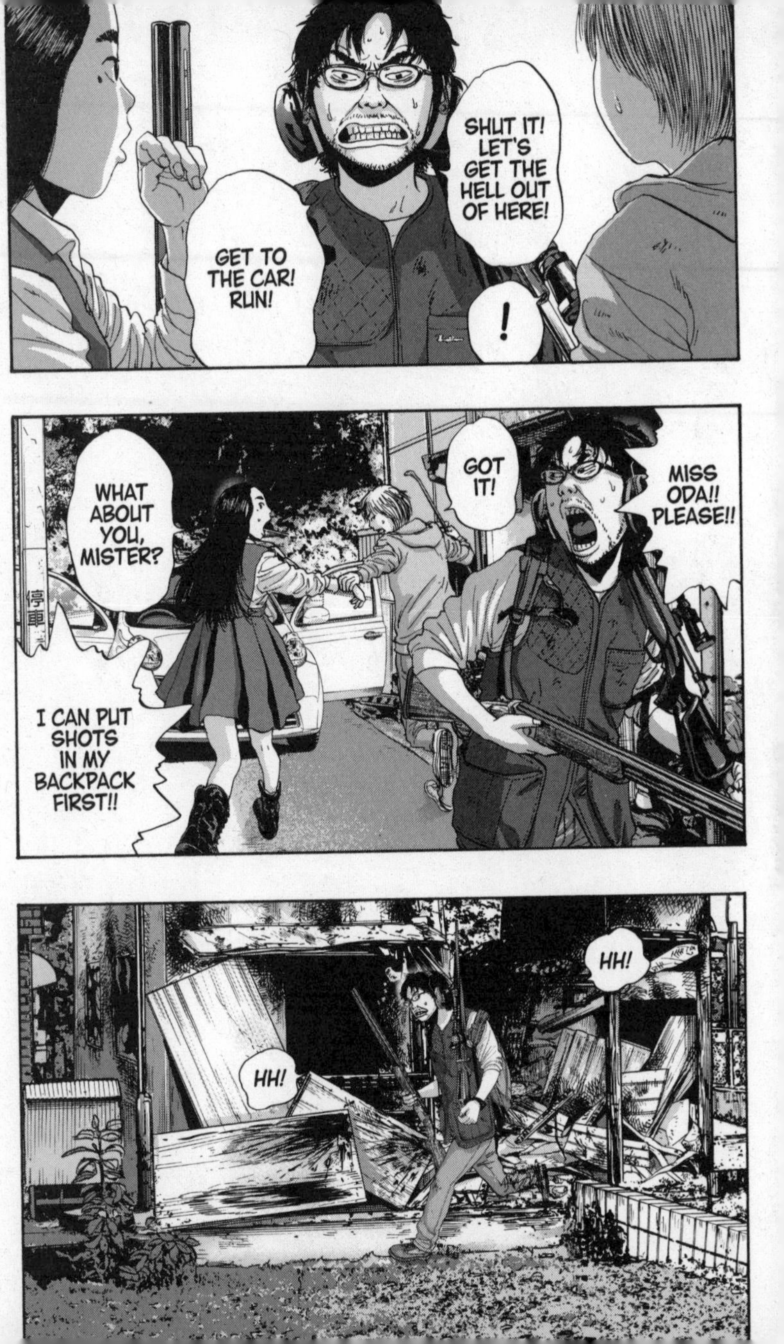
SHUT IT! LET'S GET THE HELL OUT OF HERE!
GET TO THE CAR! RUN!
!
MISS ODA!! PLEASE!!
GOT IT!
WHAT ABOUT YOU, MISTER?
停車
I CAN PUT SHOTS IN MY BACKPACK FIRST!!
HH!
HH!

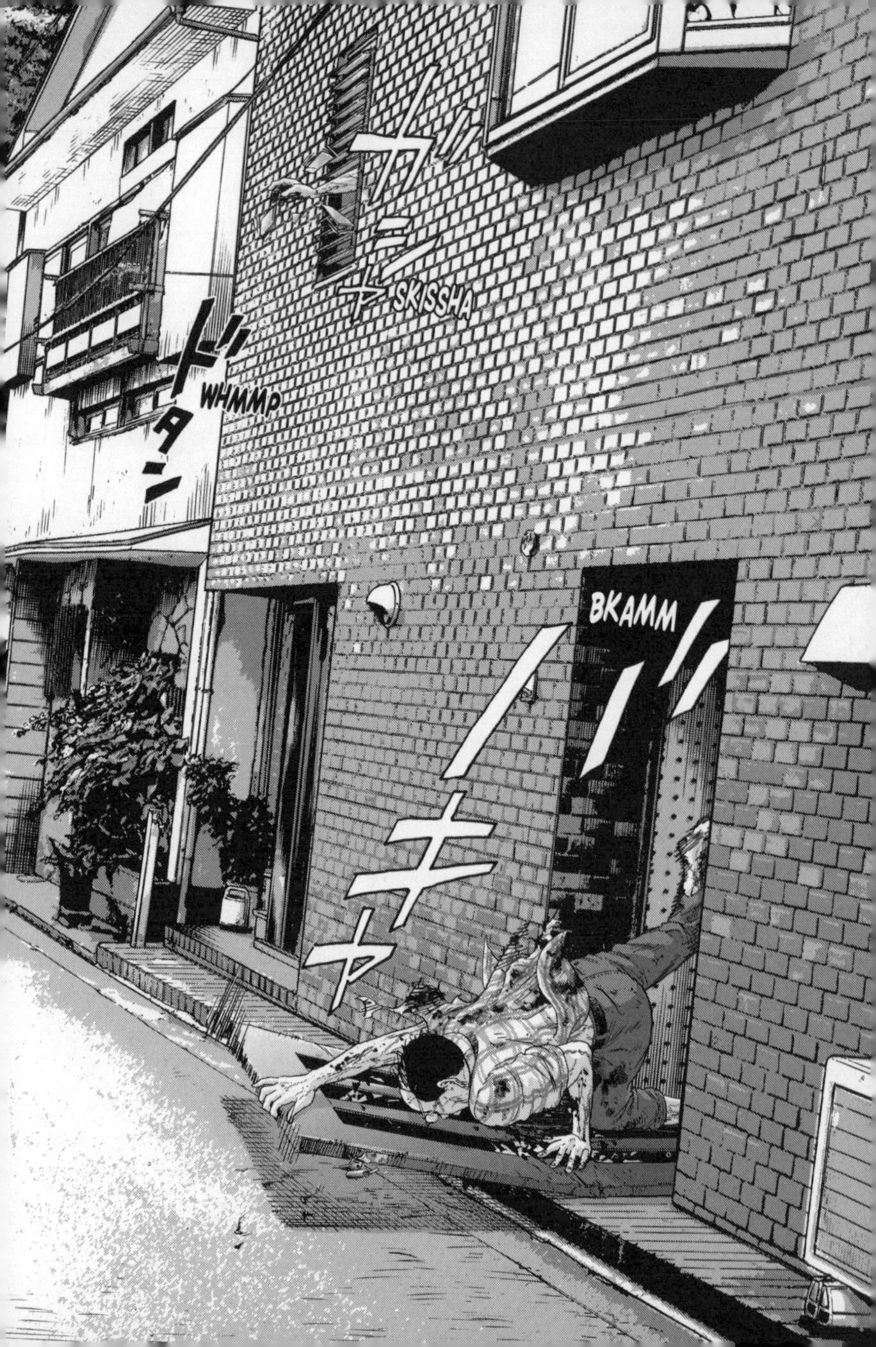
カシャ
SKISSHA
ドタン
WHMMP
バキャ
BKAMM

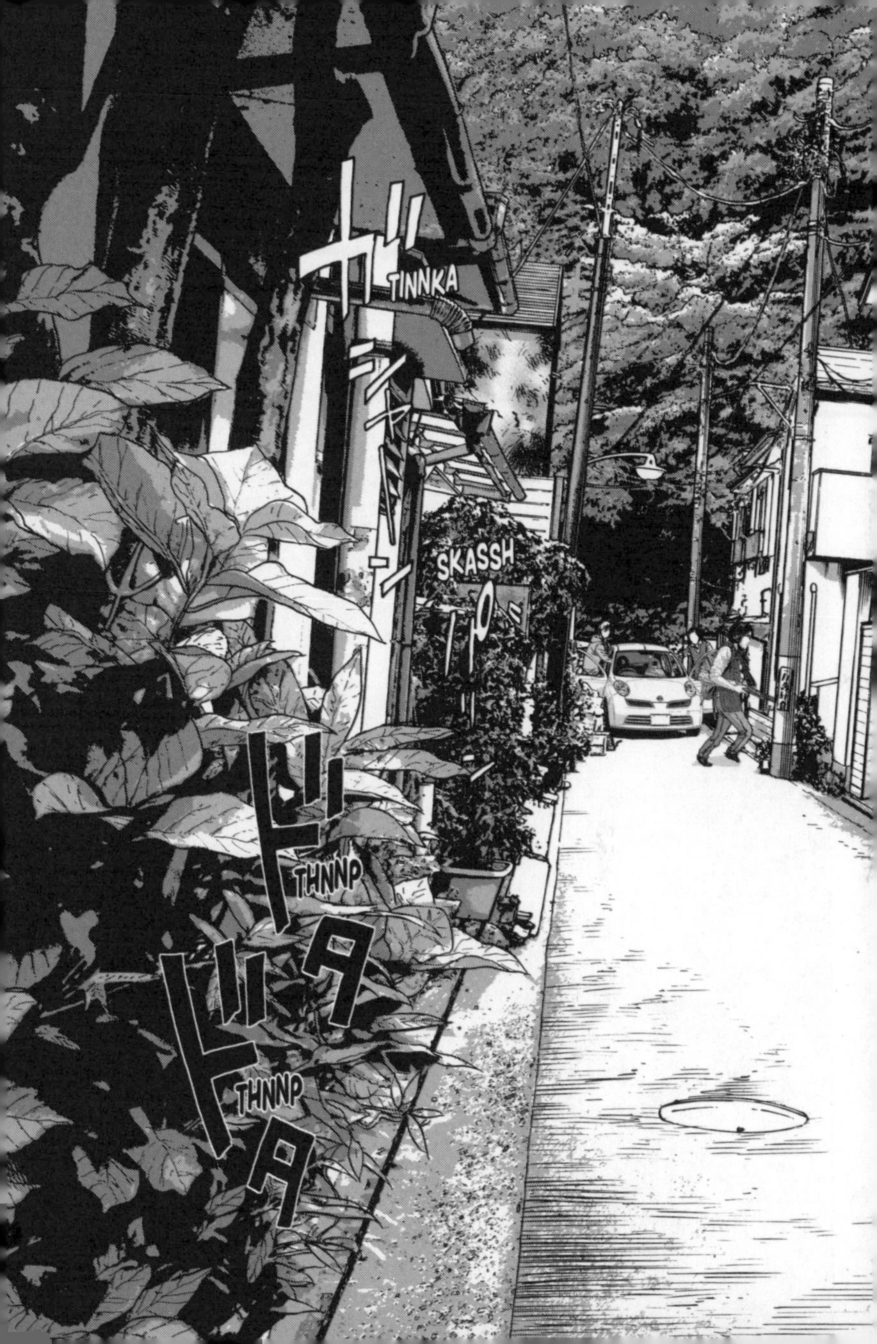
TINNKA
SKASSH
THNNP
THNNP

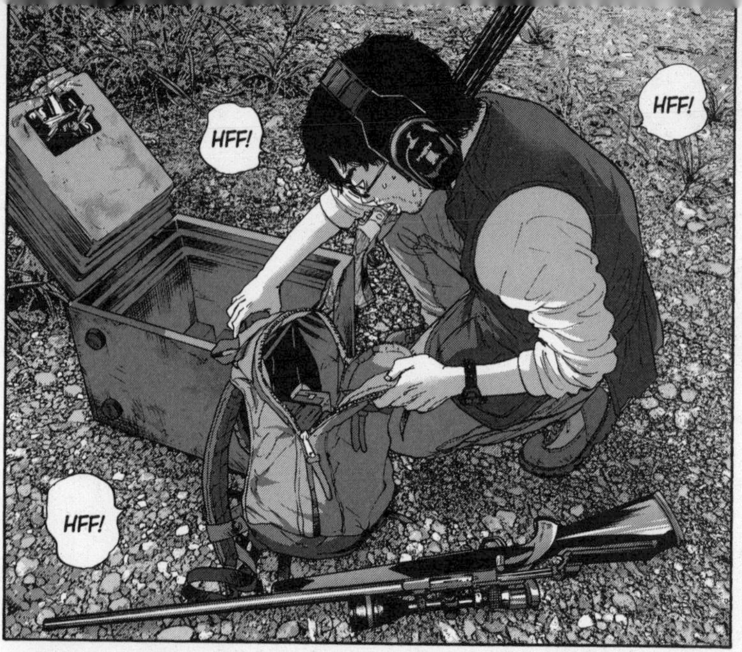
HFF!
HFF!
HFF!

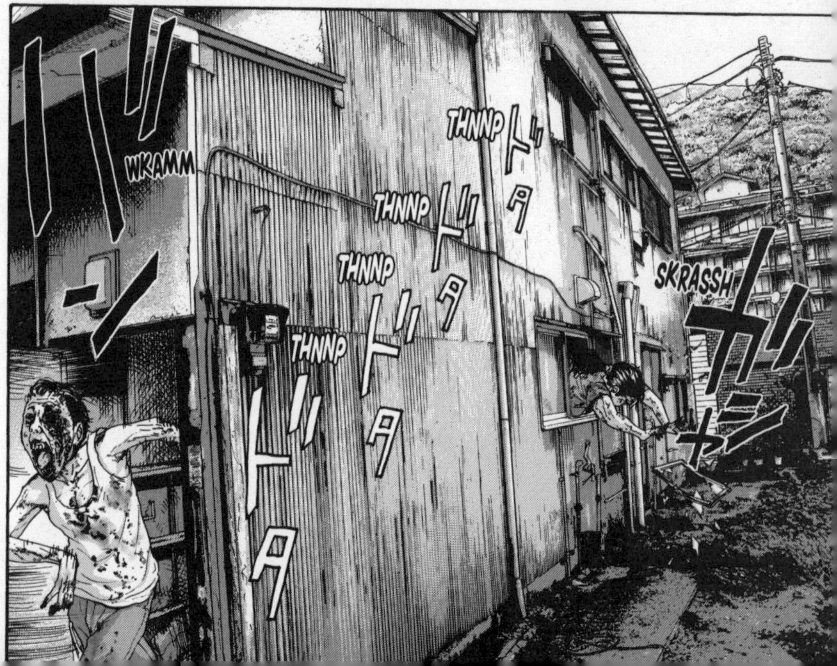
SKRASSH
THNNP
THNNP
THNNP
THNNP
WKAMM

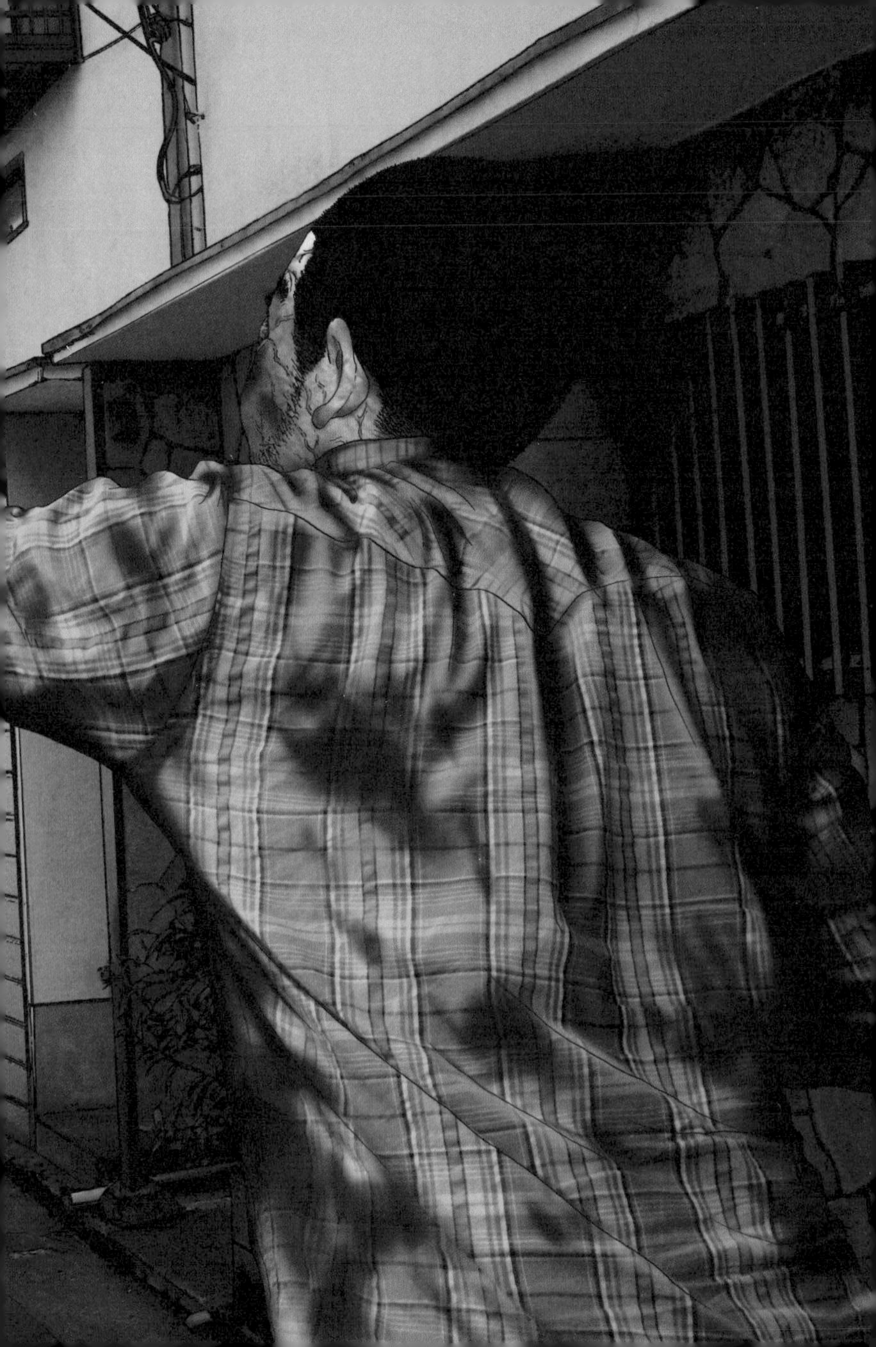

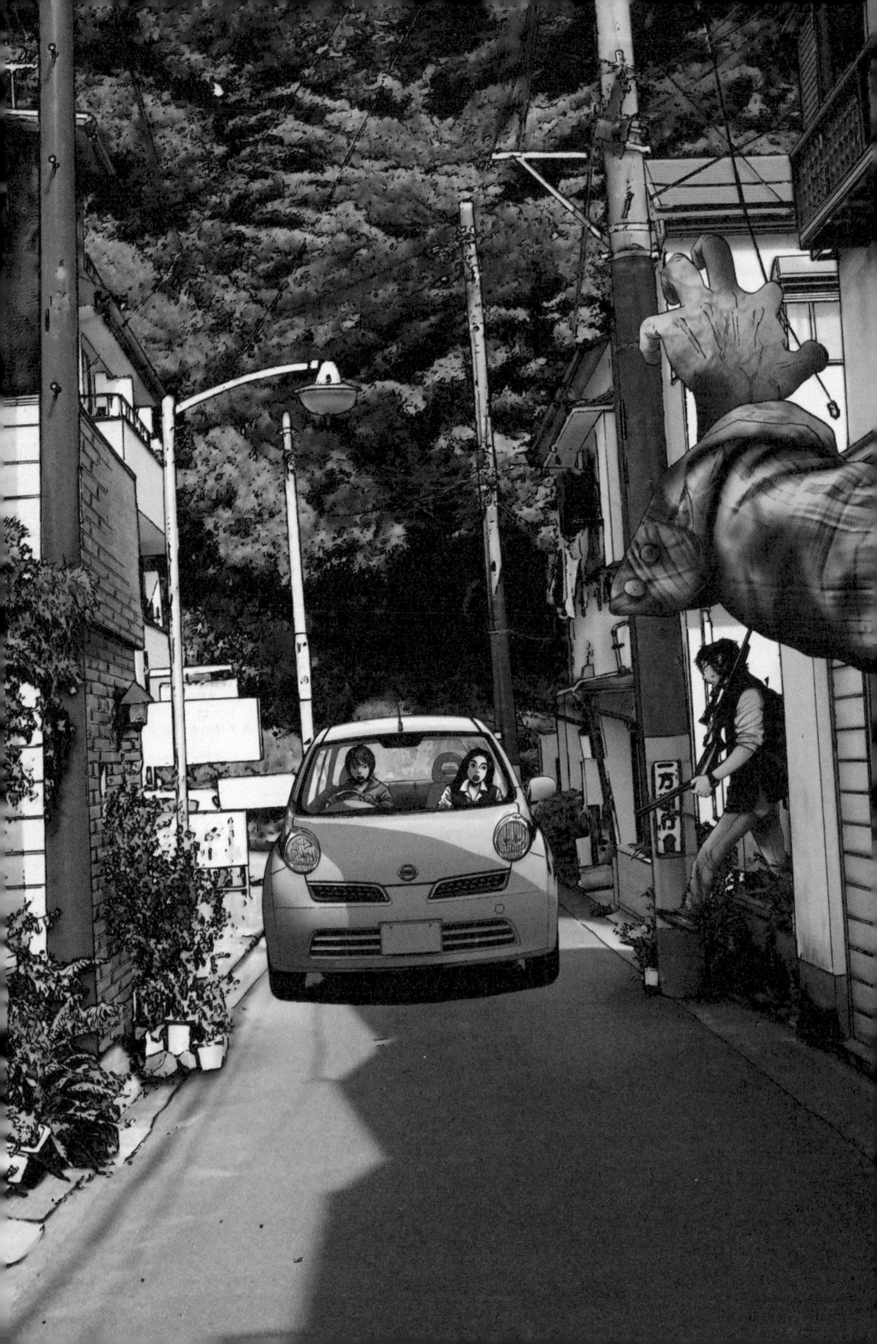

CHAPTER 159

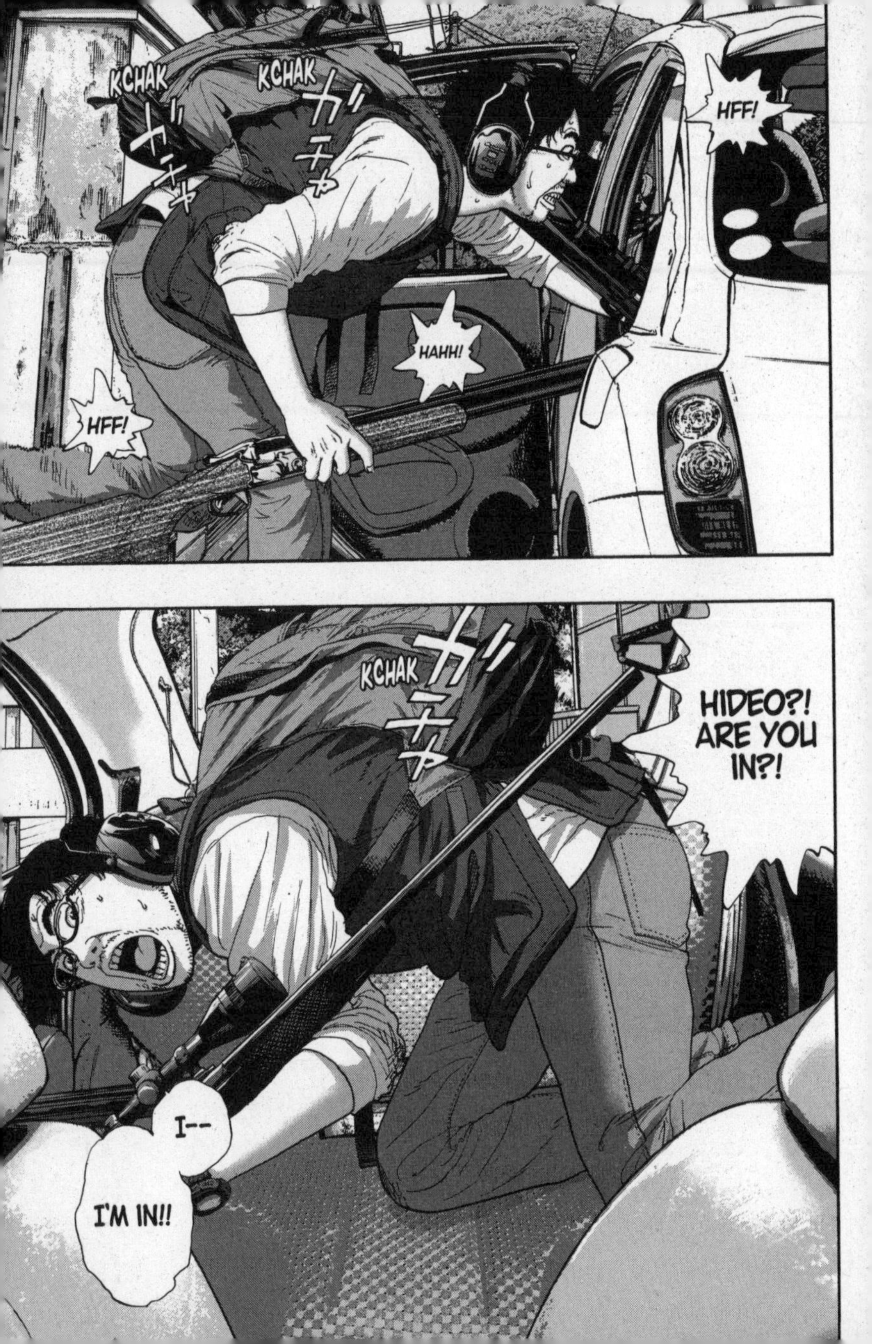
HFF!
KCHAK
ガチャ
KCHAK
ガチャ
HAHH!
HFF!
HIDEO?! ARE YOU IN?!
KCHAK
ガチャ
I--
I'M IN!!

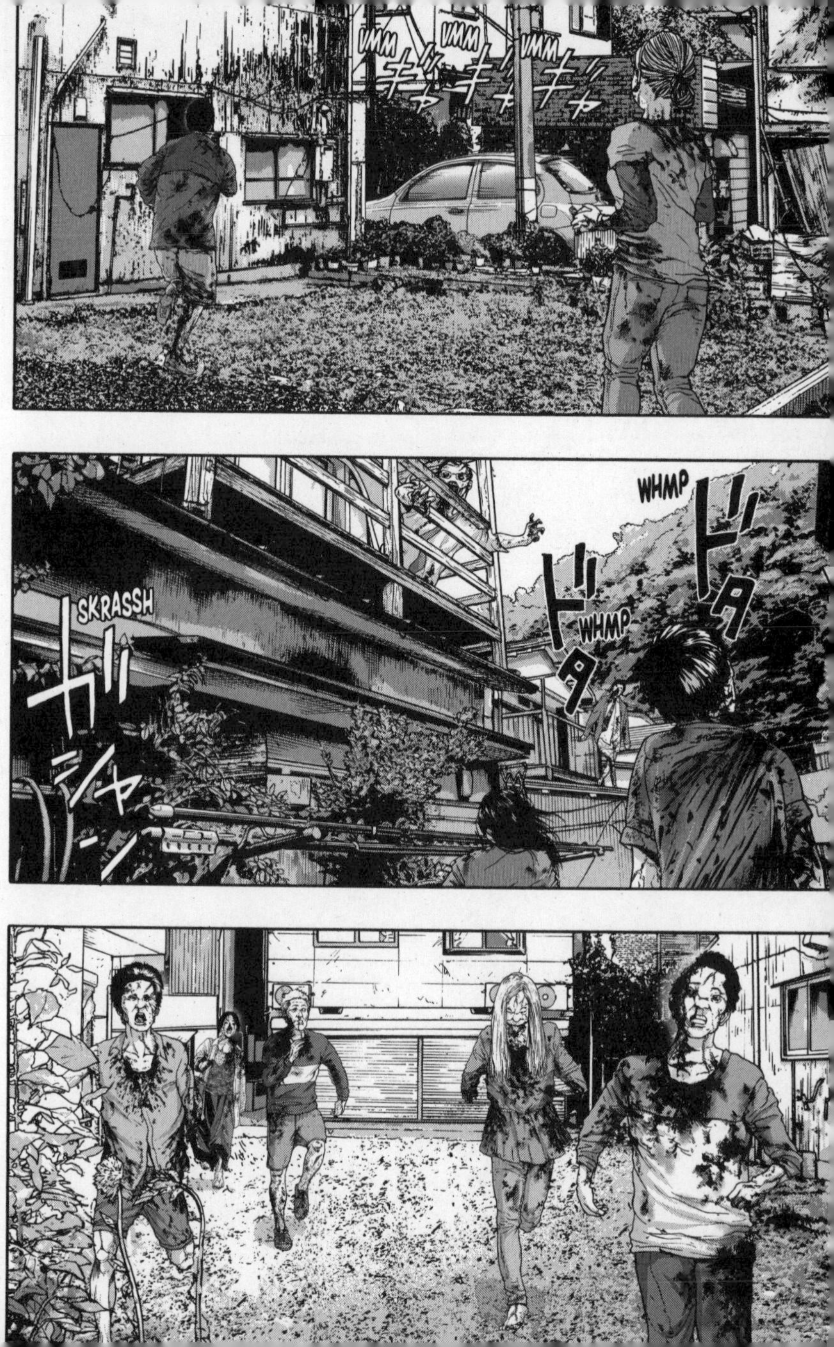
VMM
VMM
VMM
WHMP
WHMP
SKRASSH

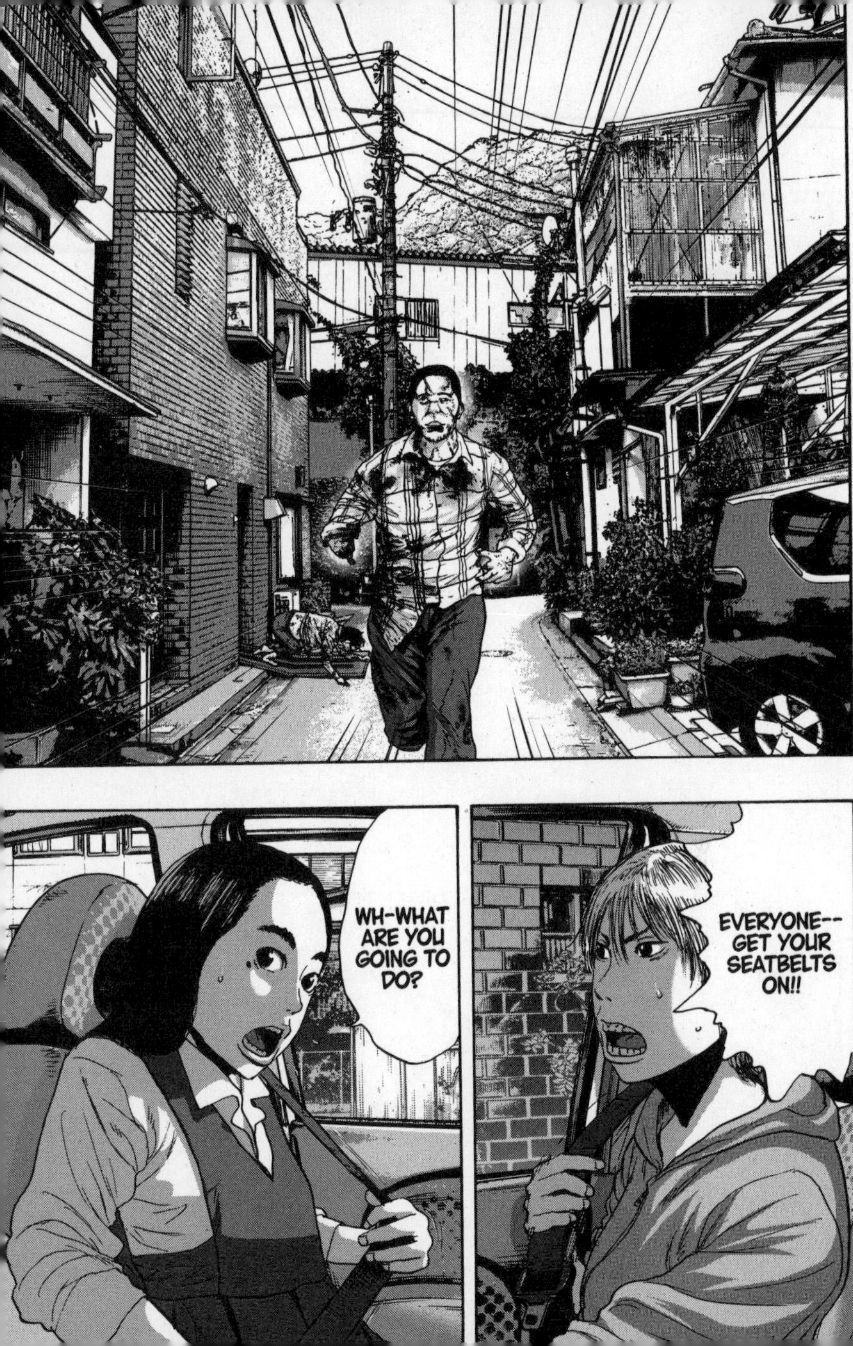
EVERYONE-- GET YOUR SEATBELTS ON!!
WH-WHAT ARE YOU GOING TO DO?

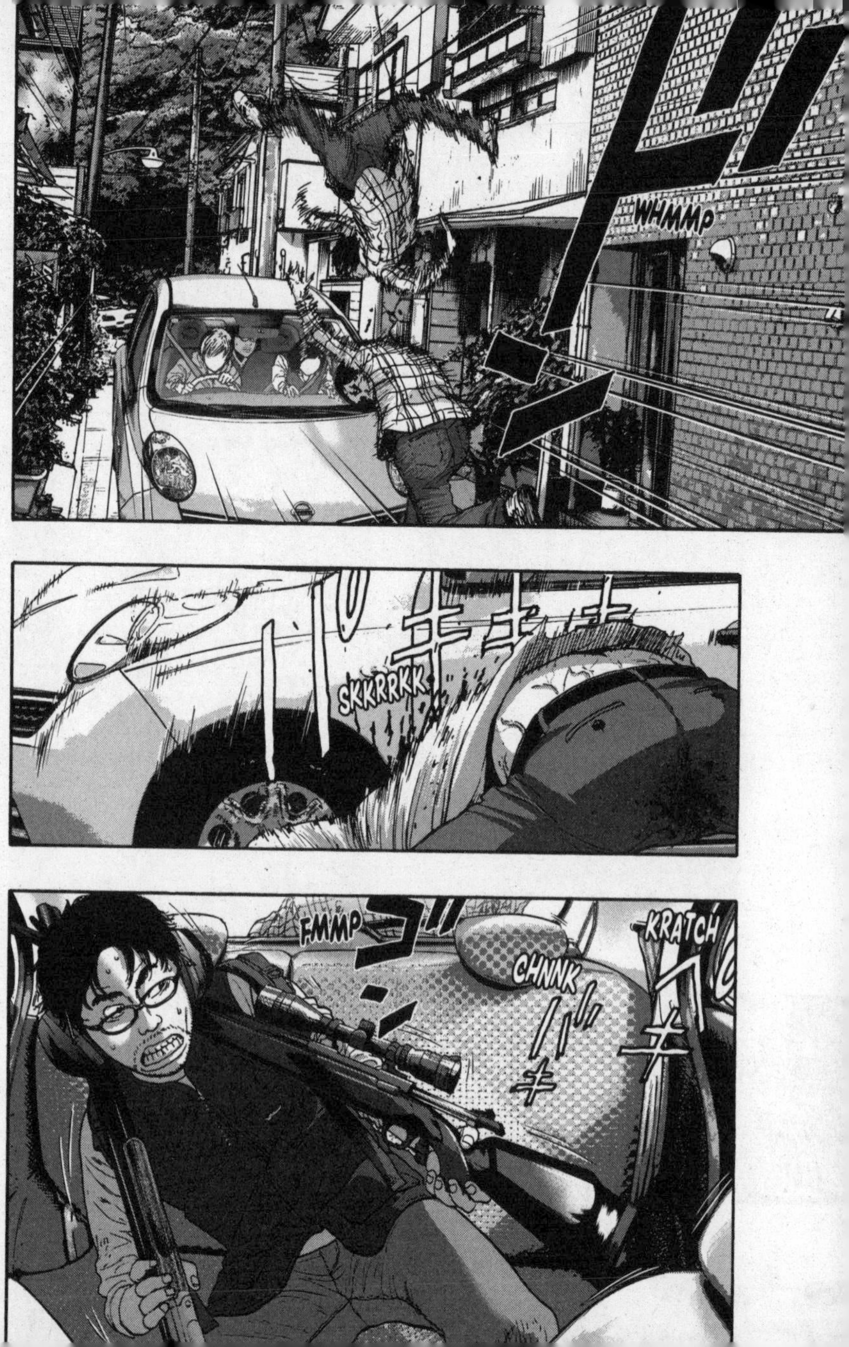
WHMMP
SKKRRKK
KRATCH
CHNNK
FMMP

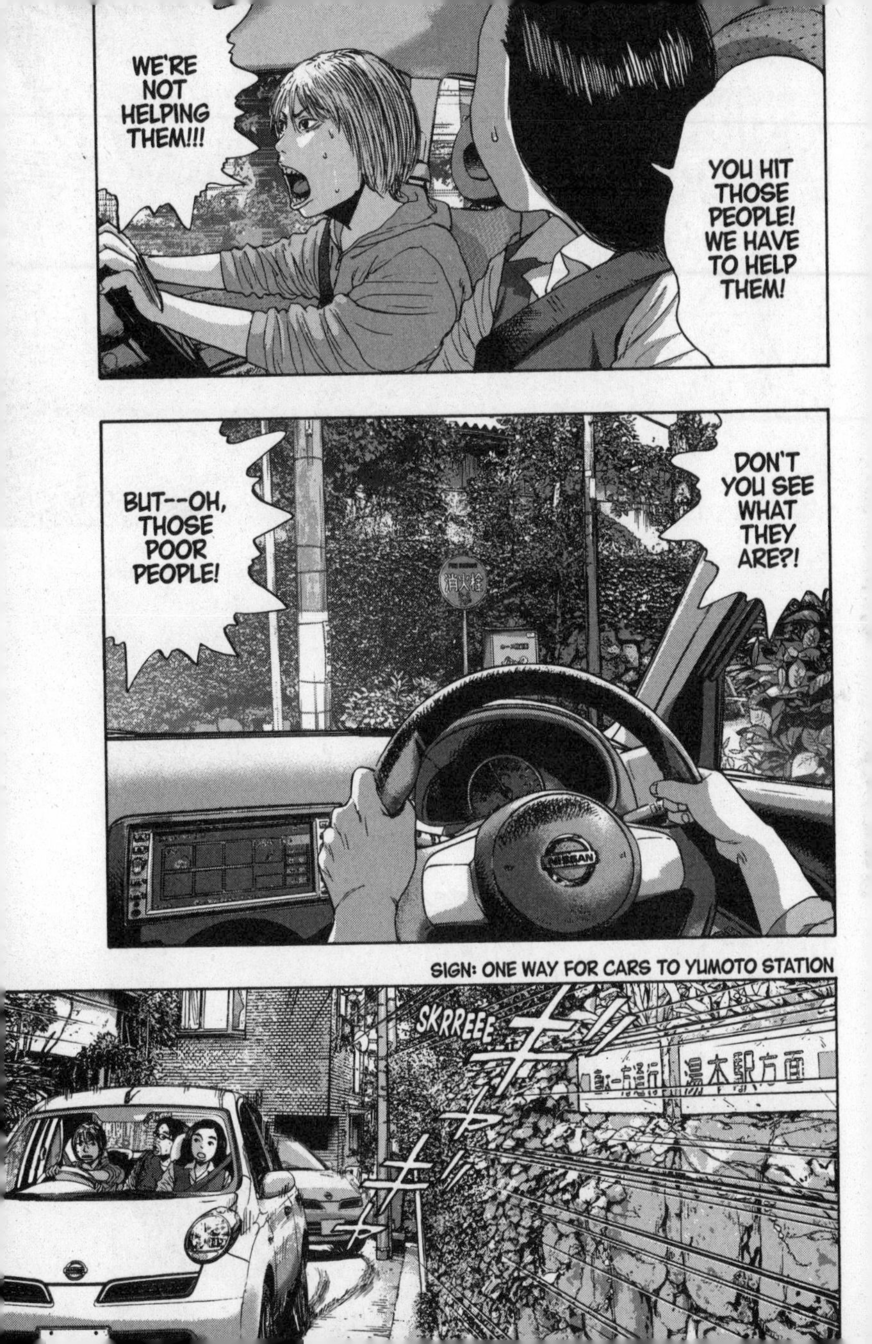
YOU HIT THOSE PEOPLE! WE HAVE TO HELP THEM!
WE'RE NOT HELPING THEM!!!
DON'T YOU SEE WHAT THEY ARE?!
BUT--OH, THOSE POOR PEOPLE!
消火栓
SIGN: ONE WAY FOR CARS TO YUMOTO STATION
SKRREEE
湯本駅方面

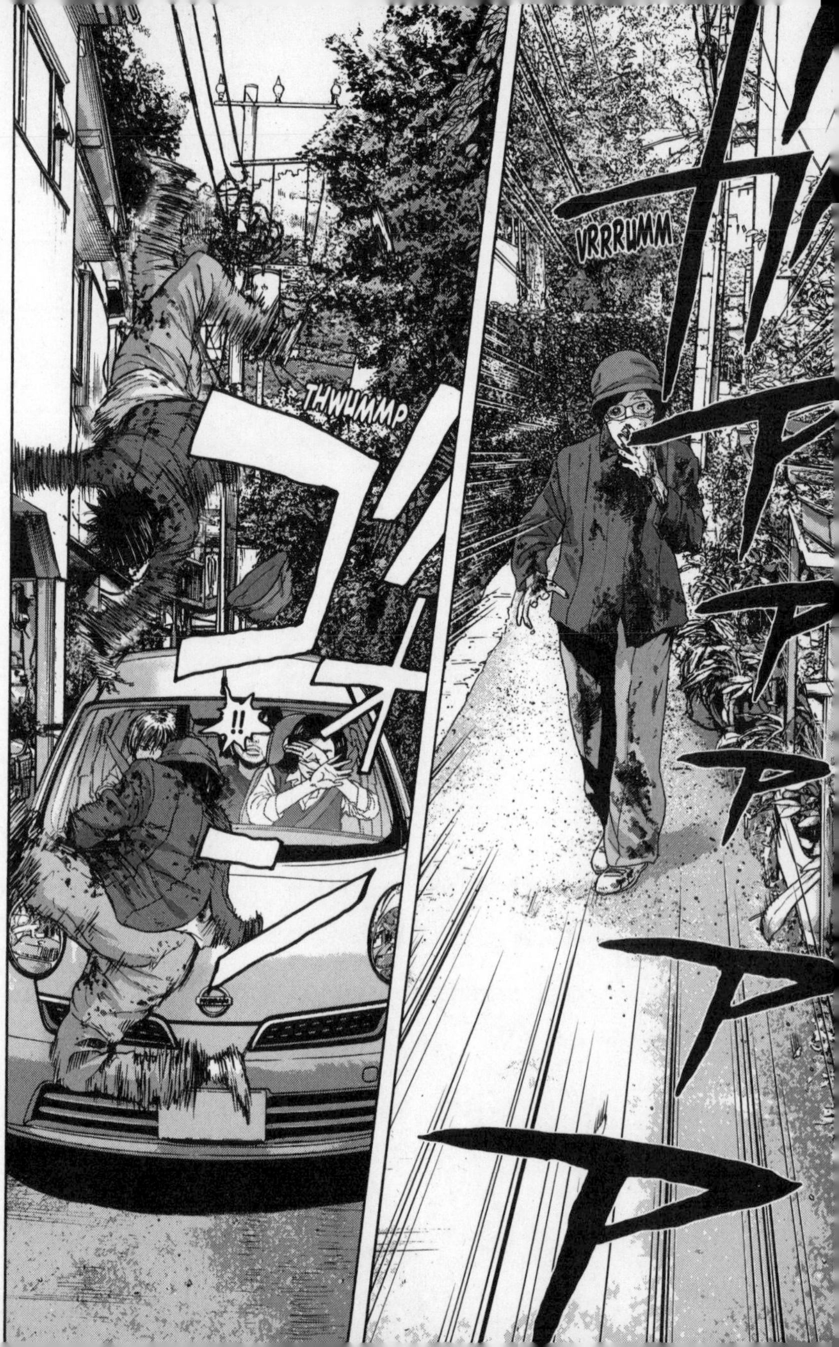

VRRRUMM
THWUMMP
!!

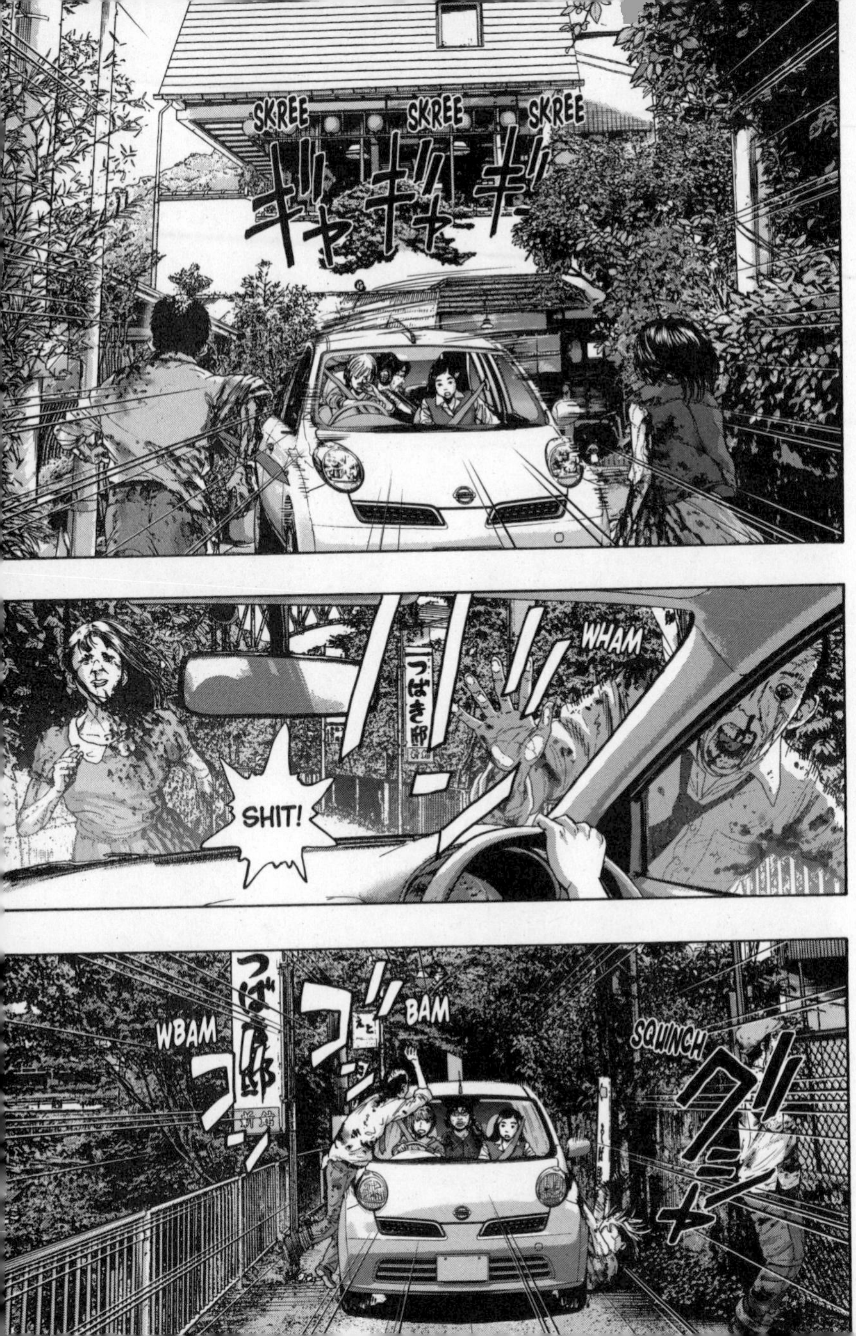
SKREE
SKREE
SKREE
WHAM
つばき邸
SHIT!
SQUINCH
BAM
WBAM
つばき邸

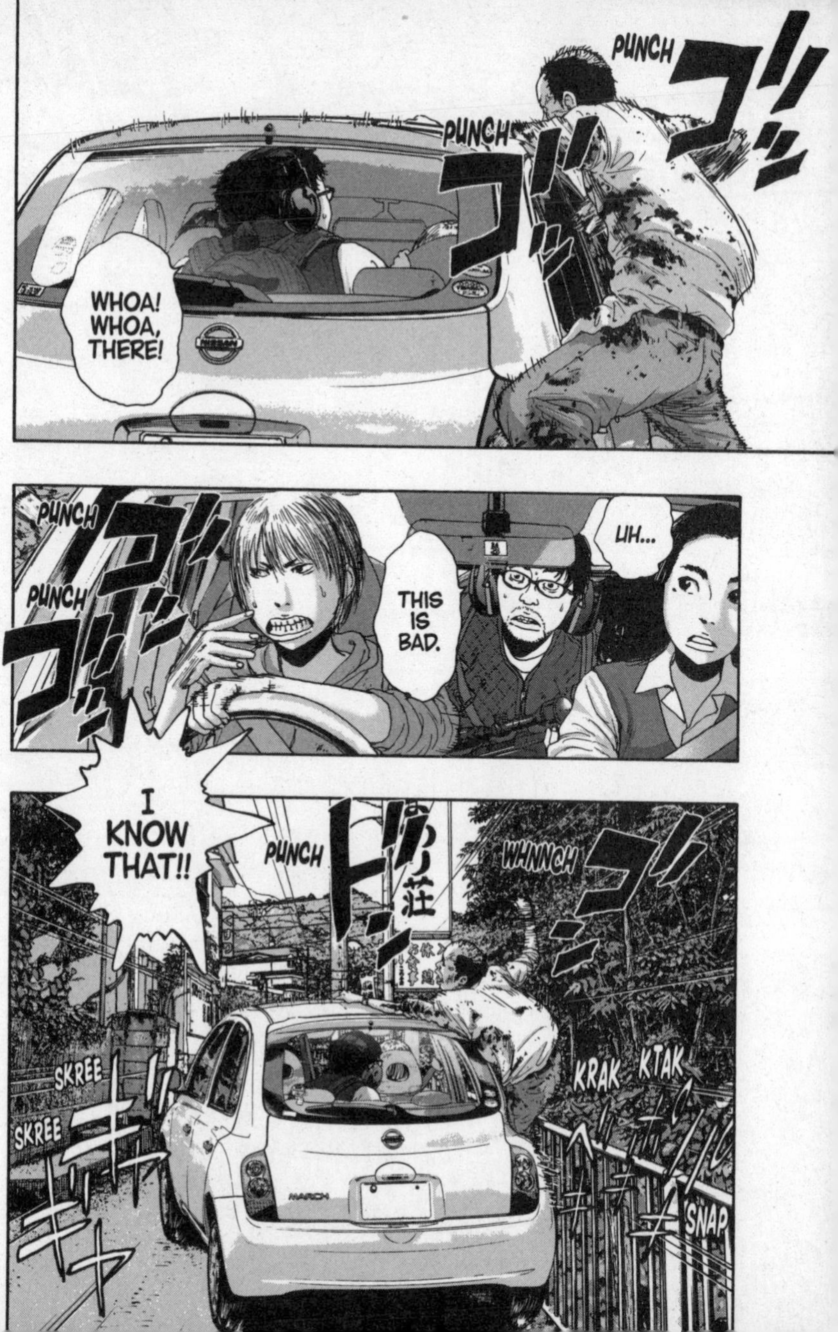
PUNCH
PUNCH
WHOA! WHOA, THERE!
UH...
THIS IS BAD.
PUNCH
PUNCH
WHNNCH
PUNCH
I KNOW THAT!!
KRAK
KTAK
SNAP
SKREE
SKREE

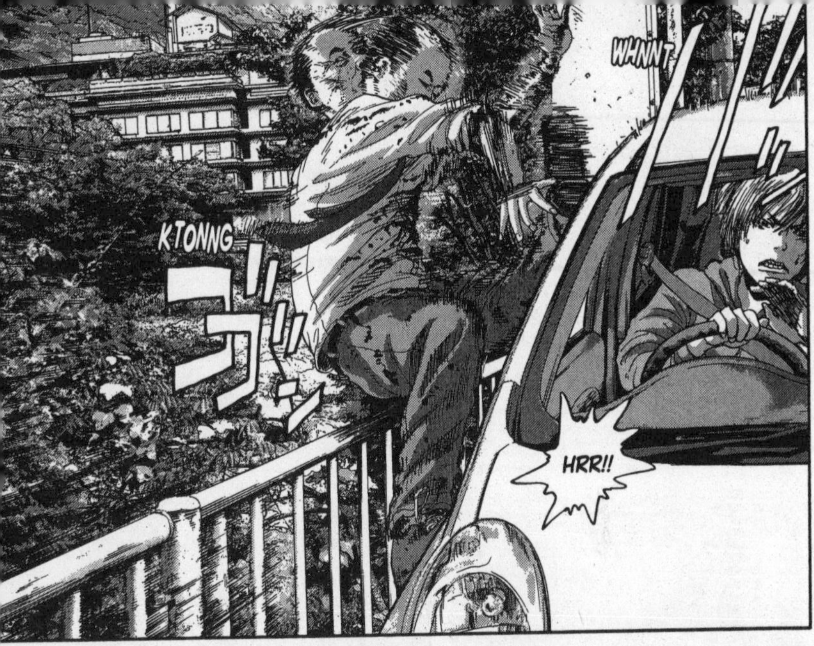
WHNNT
HRR!!
KTONNG
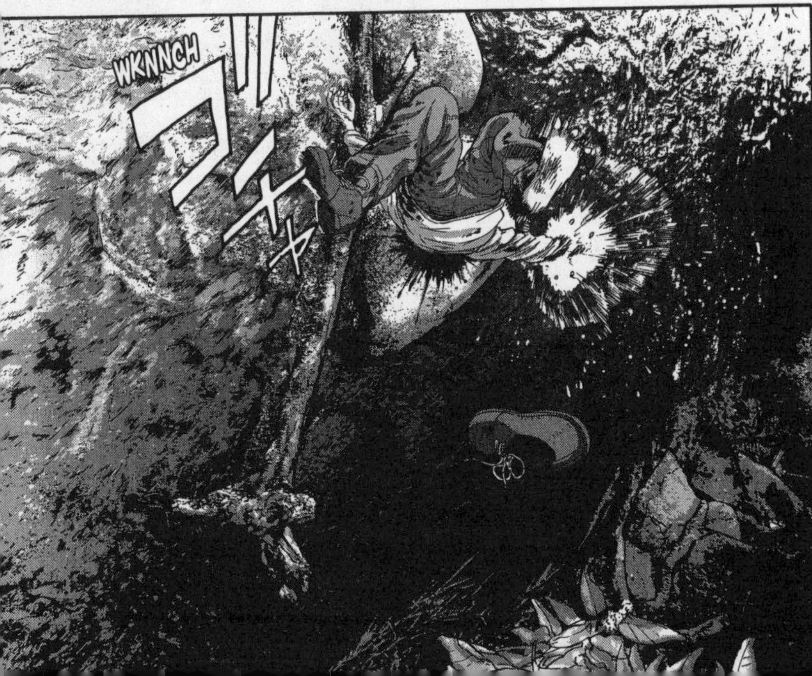
WKNNCH

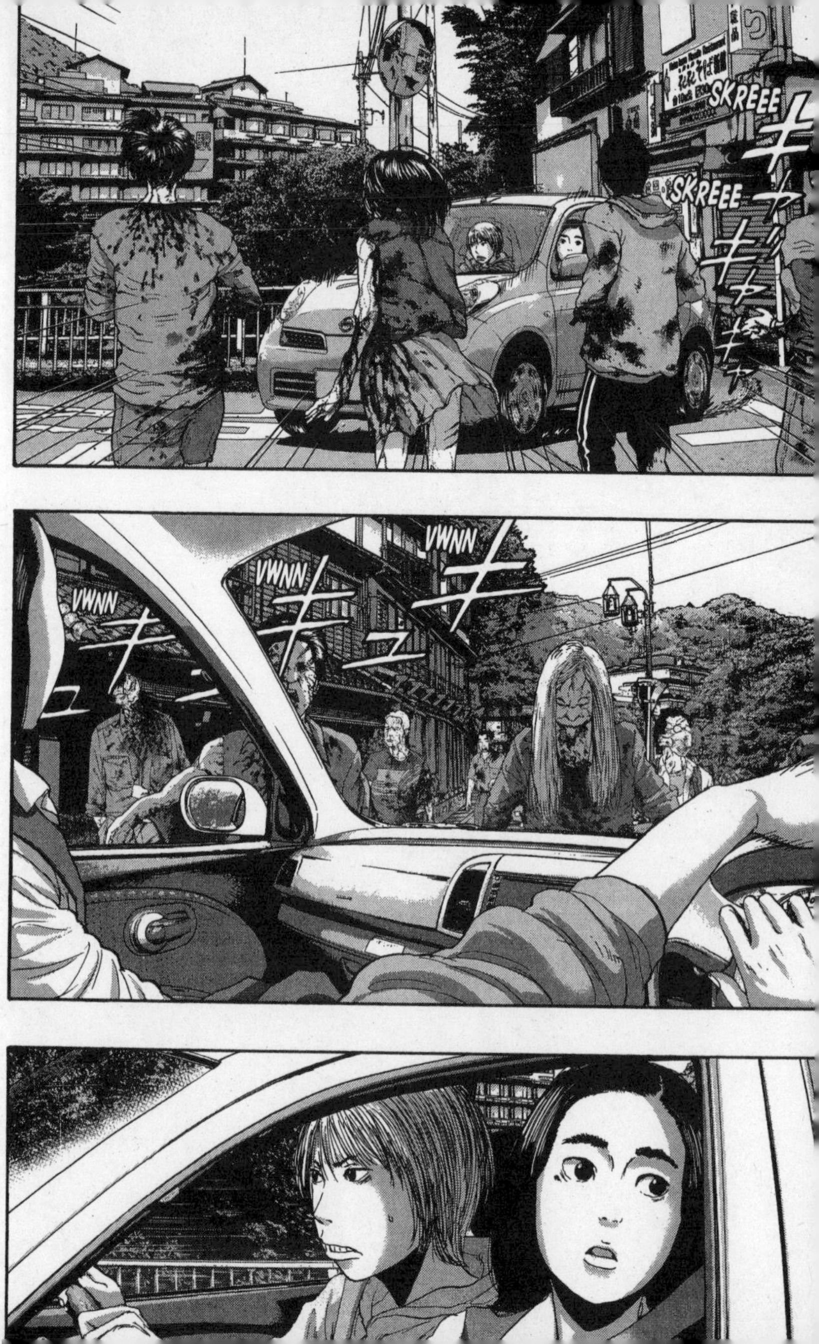
SKREEE
SKREEE
VWNN
VWNN
VWNN

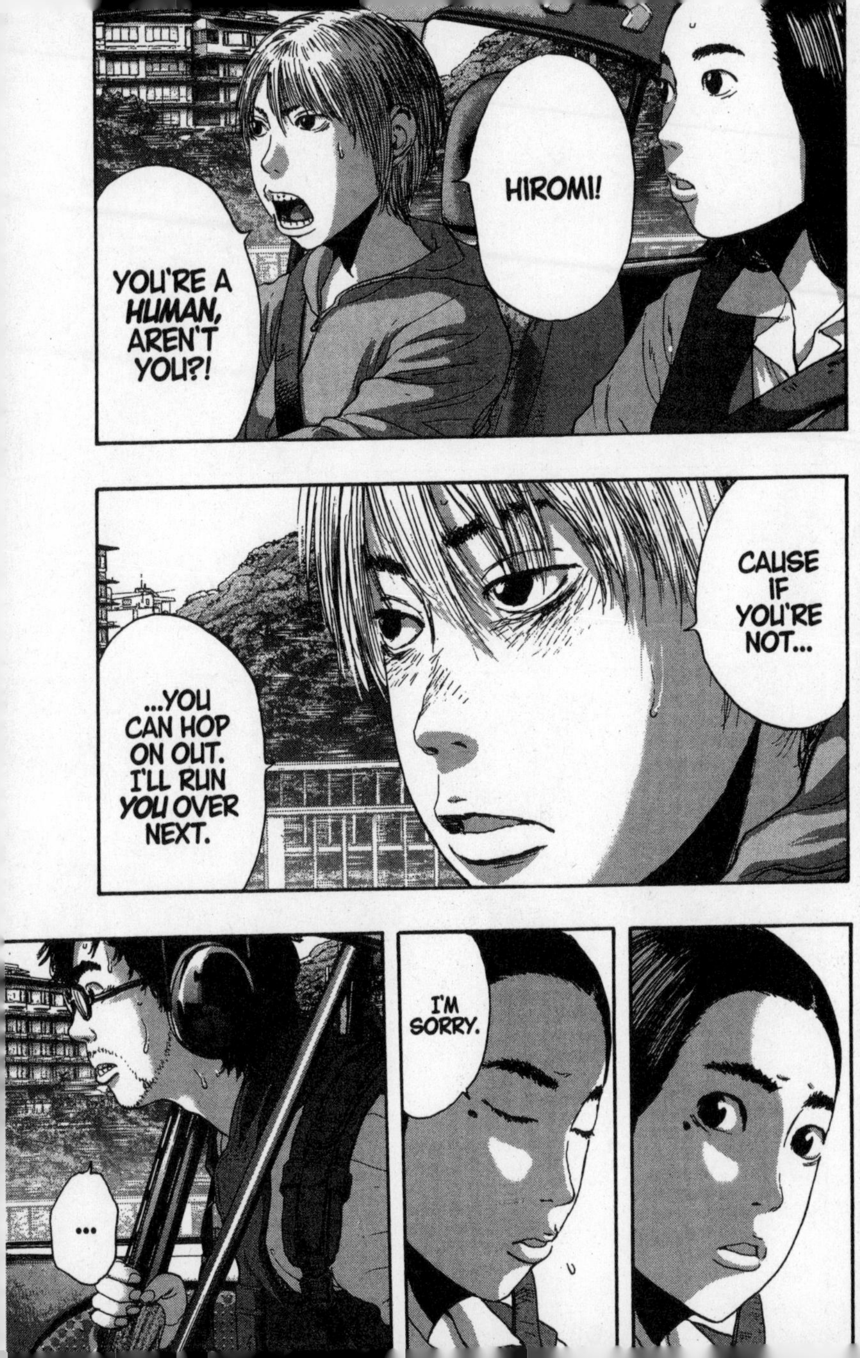
HIROMI!
YOU'RE A HUMAN, AREN'T YOU?!
CAUSE IF YOU'RE NOT...
...YOU CAN HOP ON OUT. I'LL RUN YOU OVER NEXT.
I'M SORRY.
...

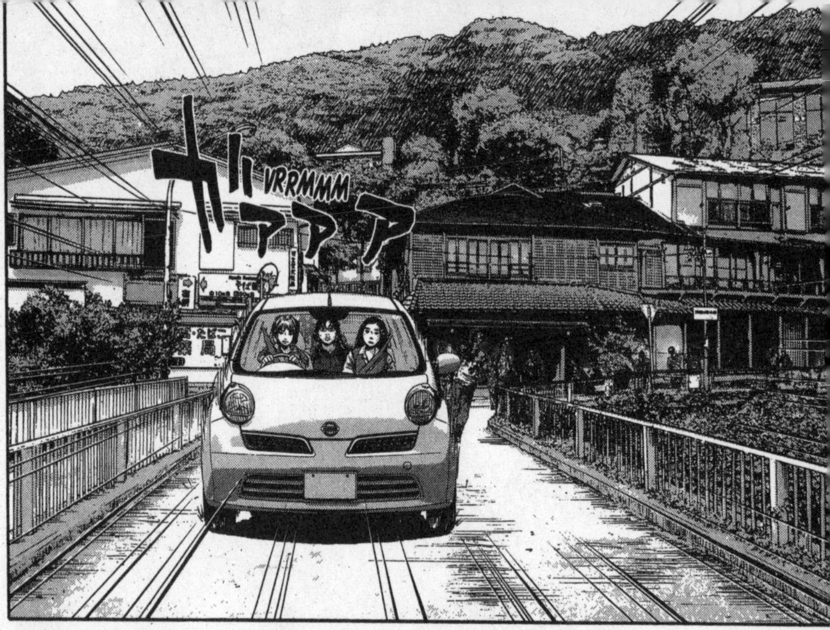
VRRMMM
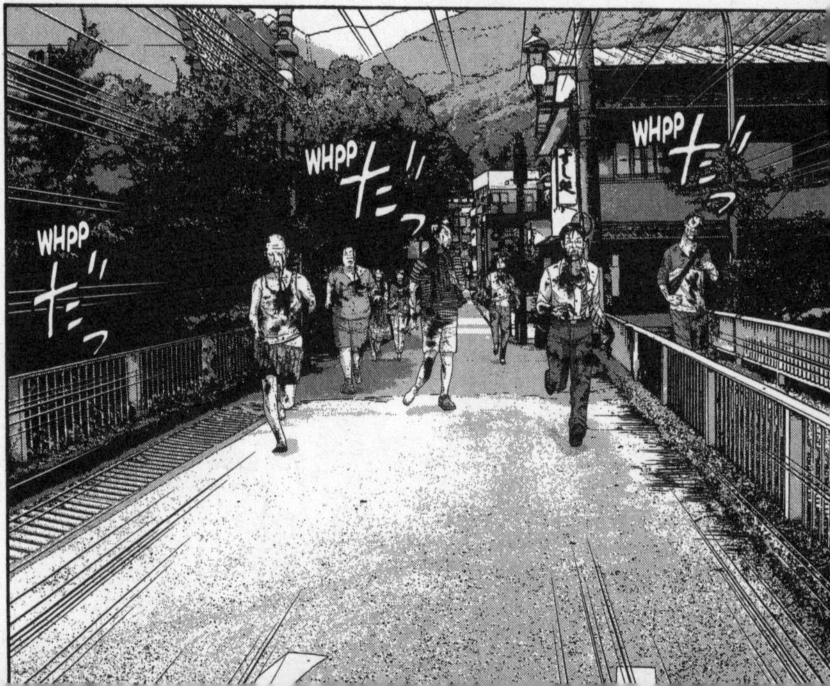
WHPP
だっ
WHPP
だっ
WHPP
だっ

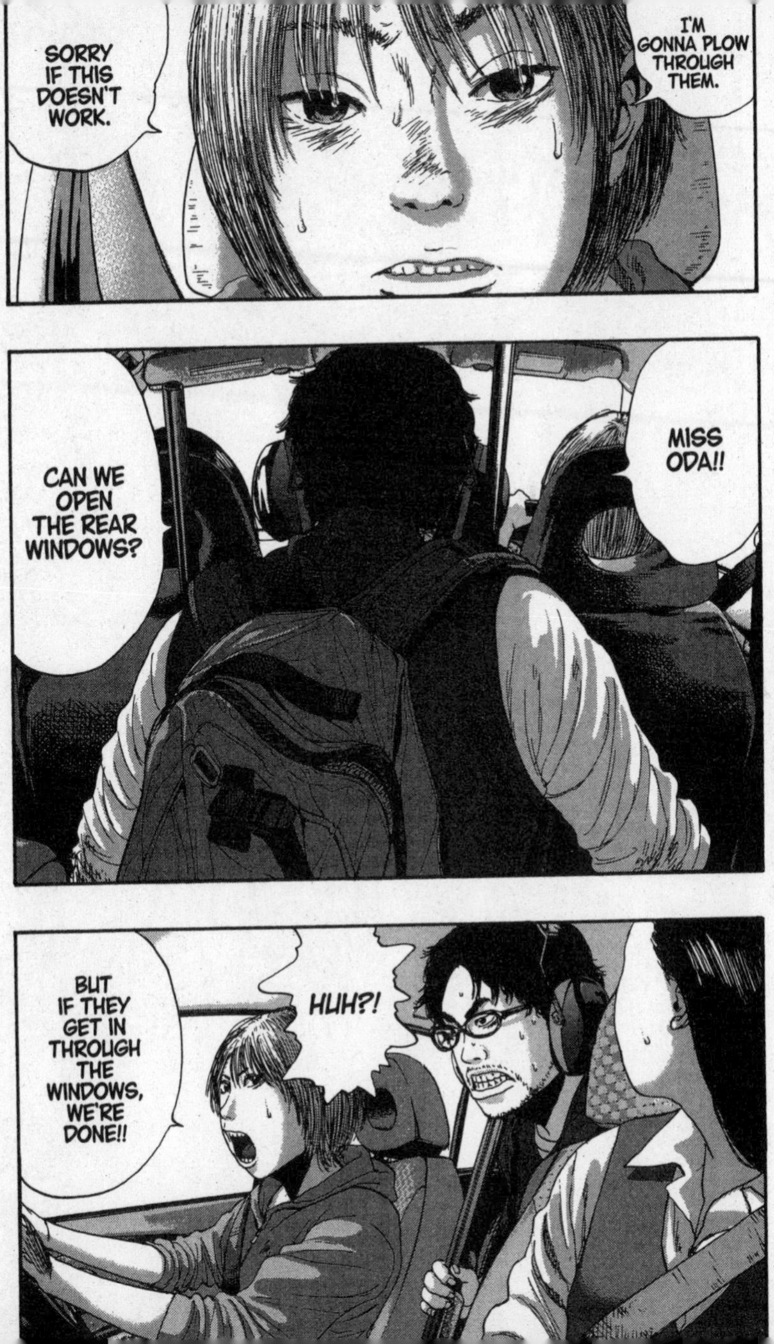
I'M GONNA PLOW THROUGH THEM.
SORRY IF THIS DOESN'T WORK.
MISS ODA!!
CAN WE OPEN THE REAR WINDOWS?
HUH?!
BUT IF THEY GET IN THROUGH THE WINDOWS, WE'RE DONE!!

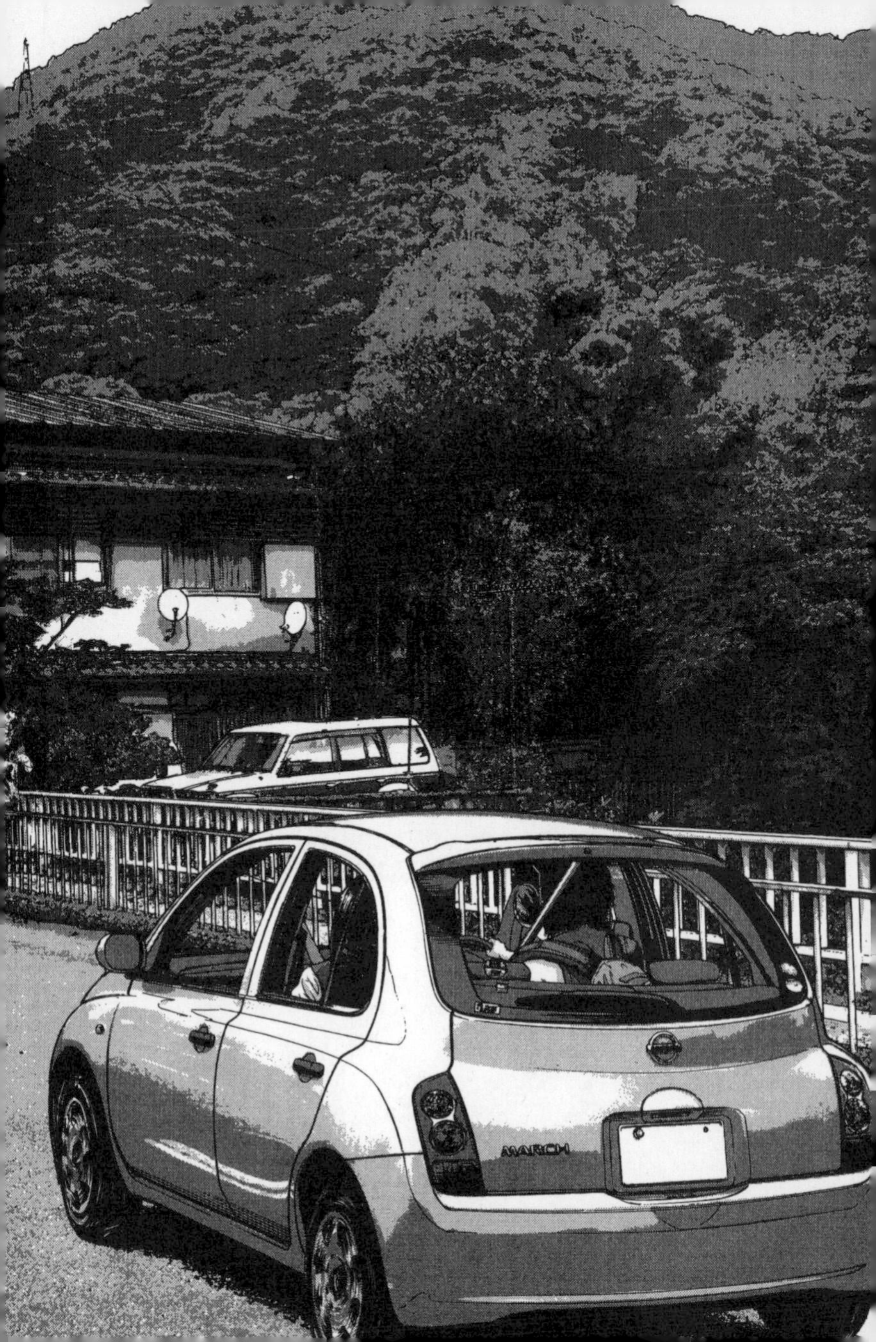
MARCH

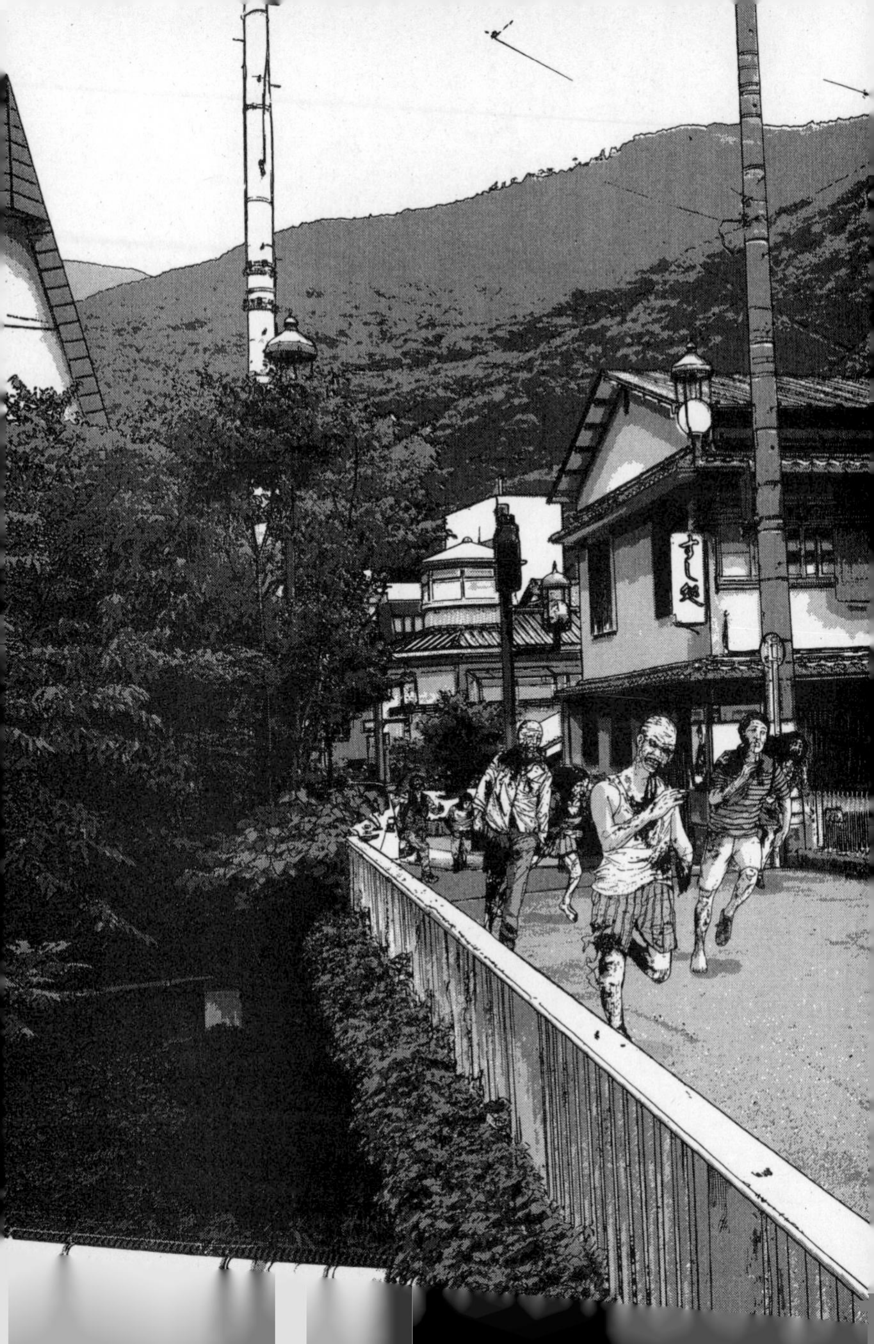
すし処

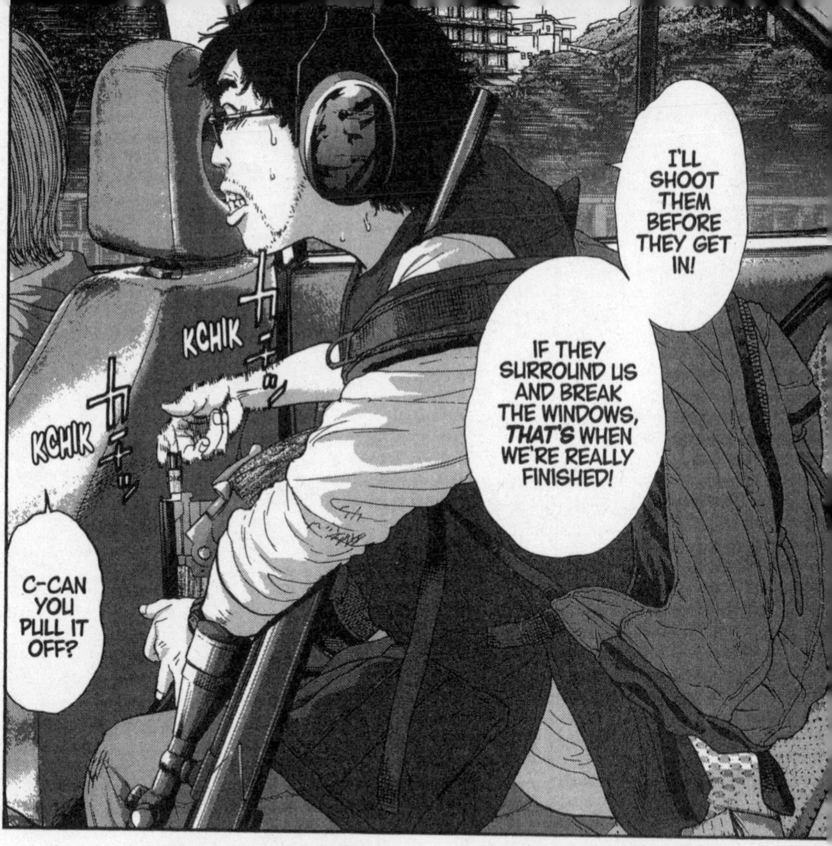
I'LL SHOOT THEM BEFORE THEY GET IN!
IF THEY SURROUND US AND BREAK THE WINDOWS, ***THAT'S*** WHEN WE'RE REALLY FINISHED!
KCHIK
KCHIK
C-CAN YOU PULL IT OFF?
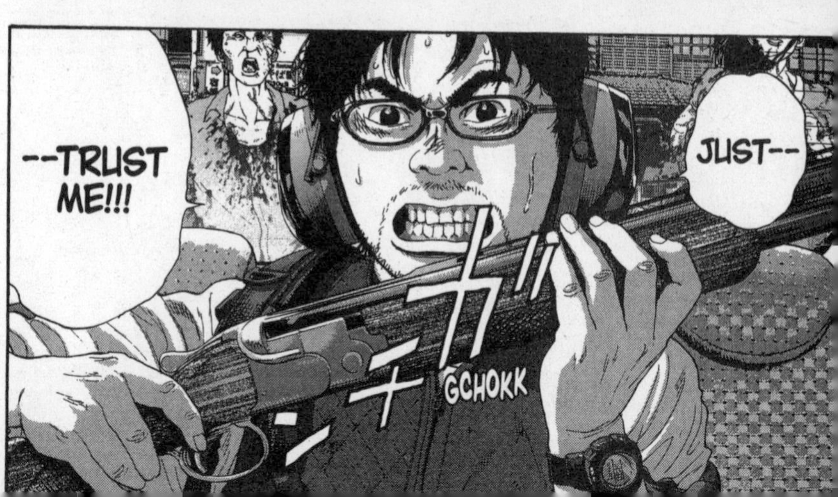
JUST--
--TRUST ME!!!
GCHOKK

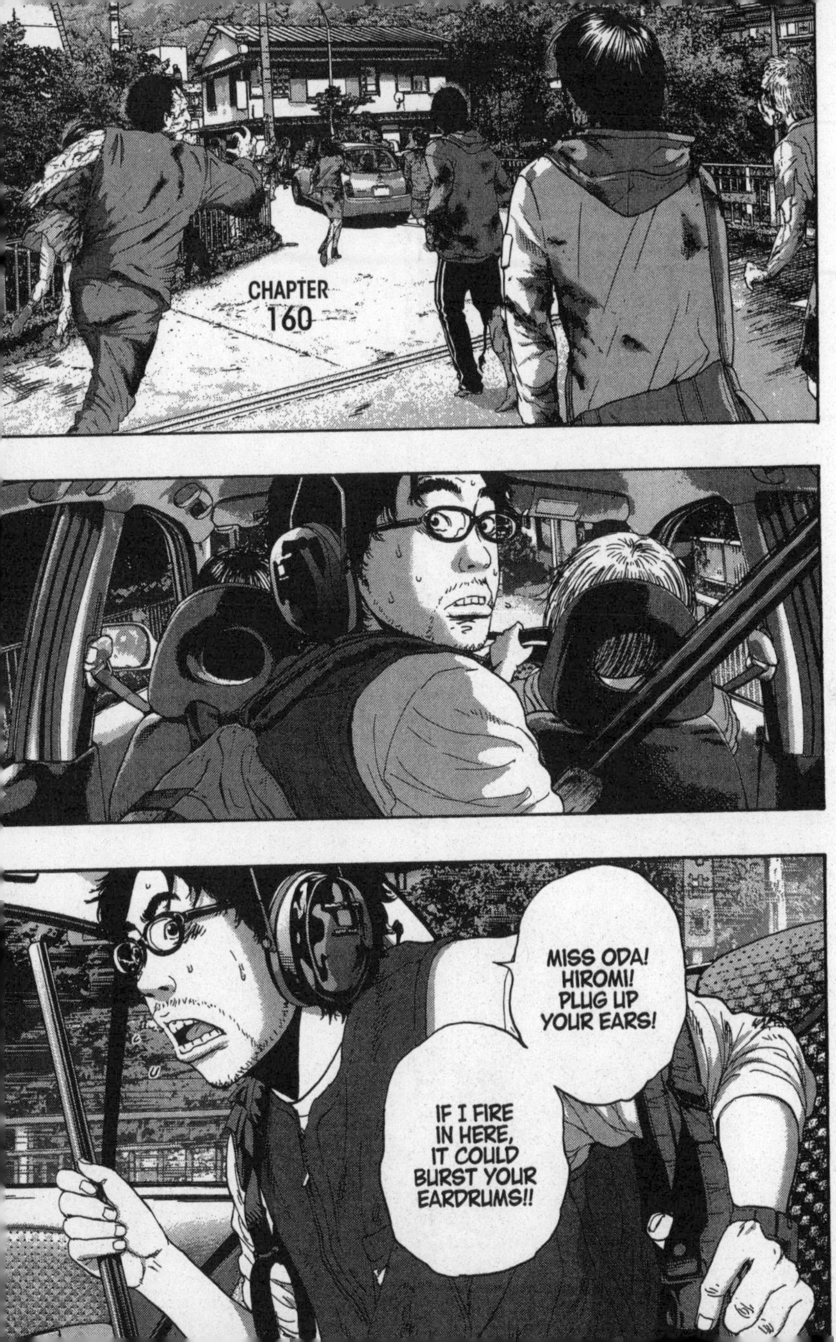
CHAPTER 160
MISS ODA! HIROMI! PLUG UP YOUR EARS!
IF I FIRE IN HERE, IT COULD BURST YOUR EARDRUMS!!

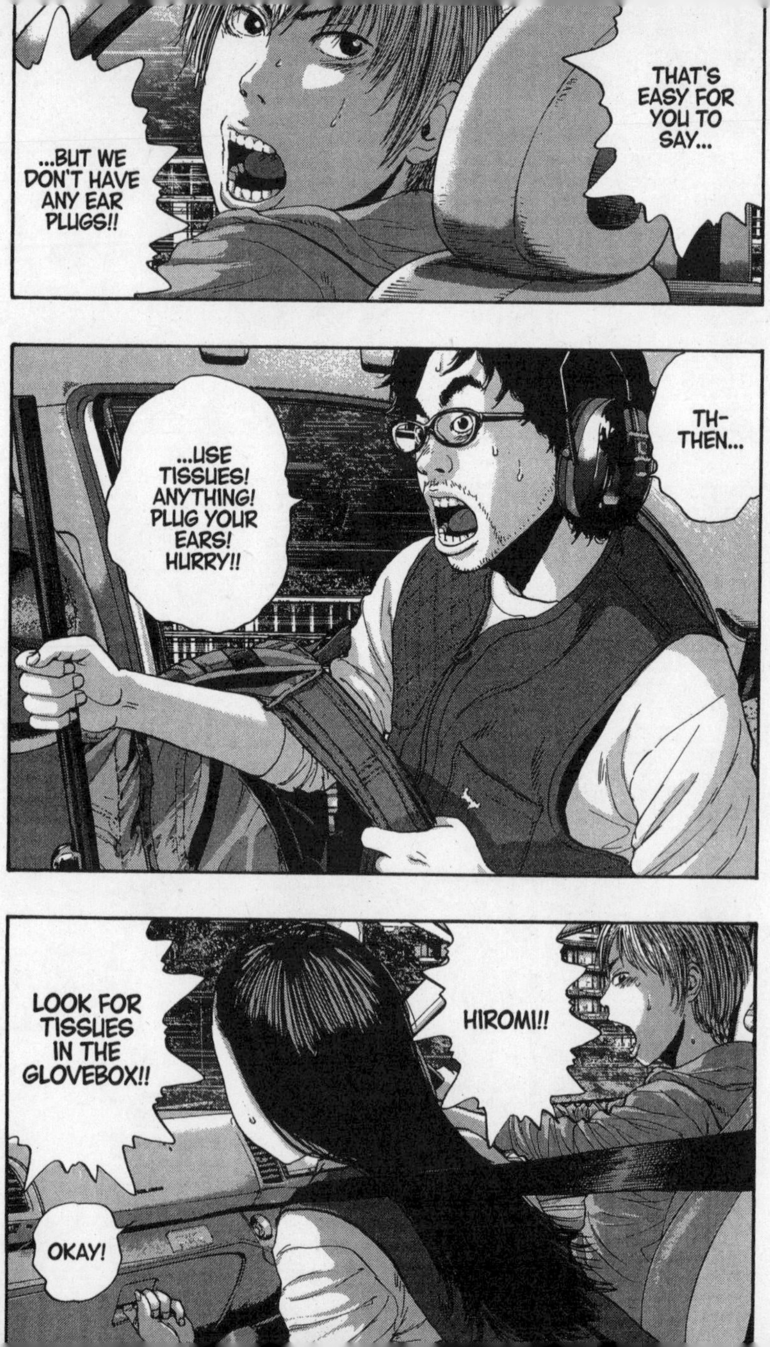
THAT'S EASY FOR YOU TO SAY...
...BUT WE DON'T HAVE ANY EAR PLUGS!!
TH-THEN...
...USE TISSUES! ANYTHING! PLUG YOUR EARS! HURRY!!
HIROMI!!
LOOK FOR TISSUES IN THE GLOVEBOX!!
OKAY!

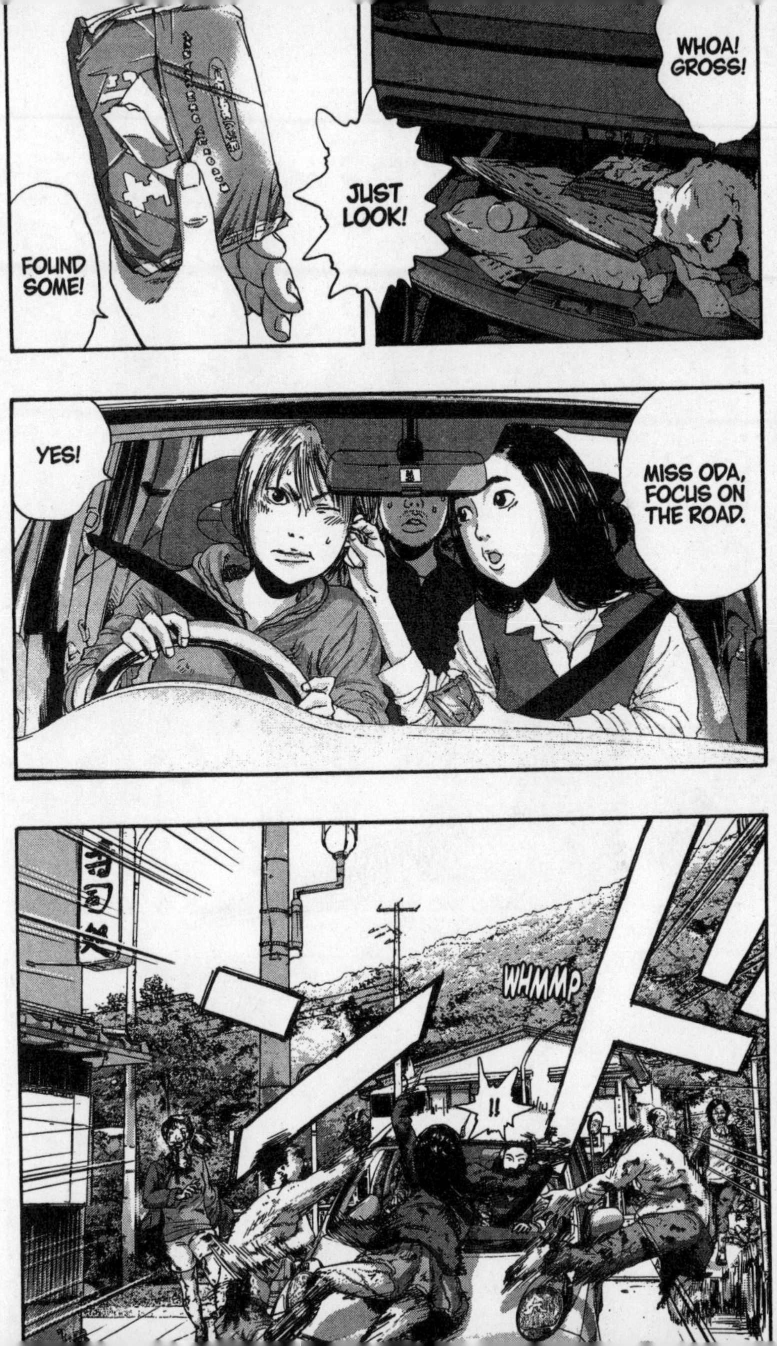
WHOA! GROSS!
JUST LOOK!
FOUND SOME!
MISS ODA, FOCUS ON THE ROAD.
YES!
WHMMP
!!

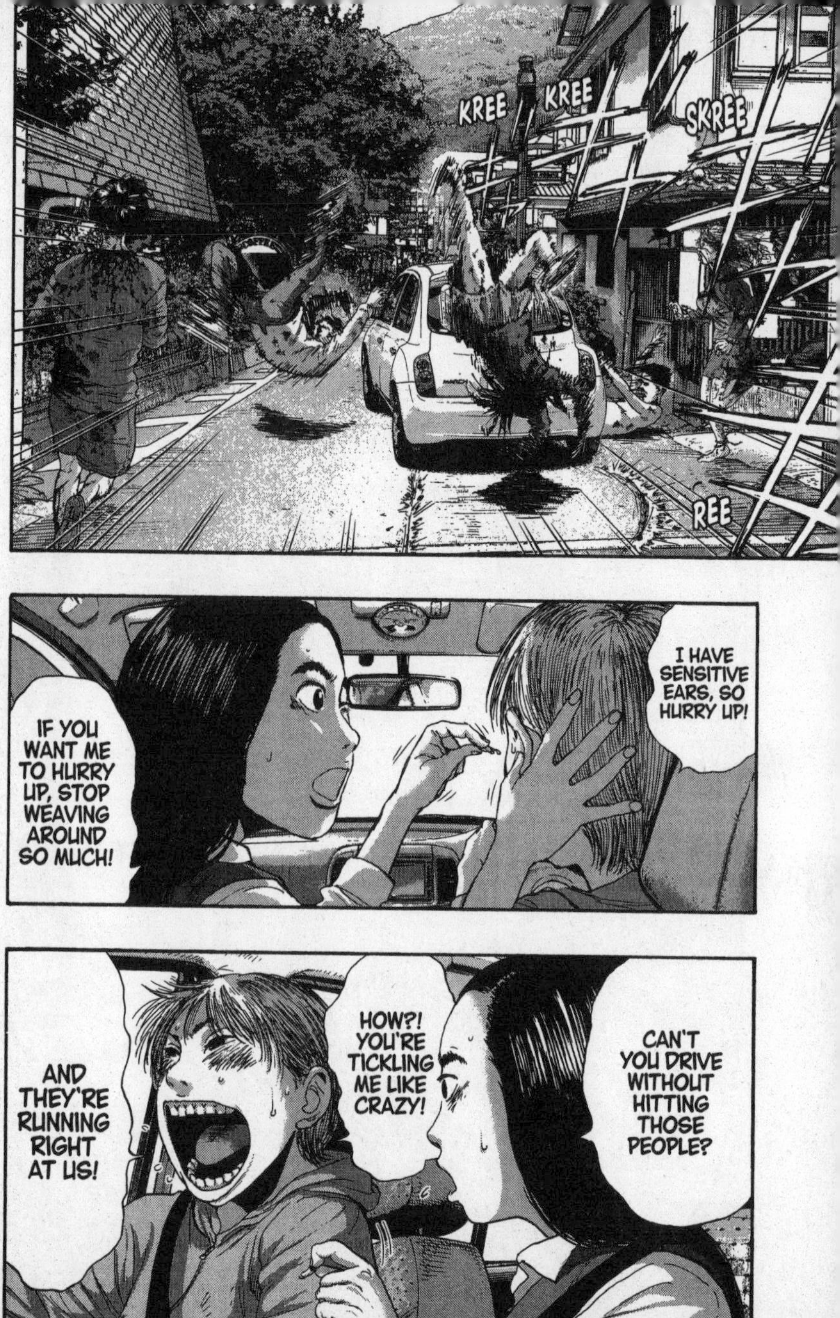
SKREE
KREE
KREE
REE
I HAVE SENSITIVE EARS, SO HURRY UP!
IF YOU WANT ME TO HURRY UP, STOP WEAVING AROUND SO MUCH!
CAN'T YOU DRIVE WITHOUT HITTING THOSE PEOPLE?
HOW?! YOU'RE TICKLING ME LIKE CRAZY!
AND THEY'RE RUNNING RIGHT AT US!

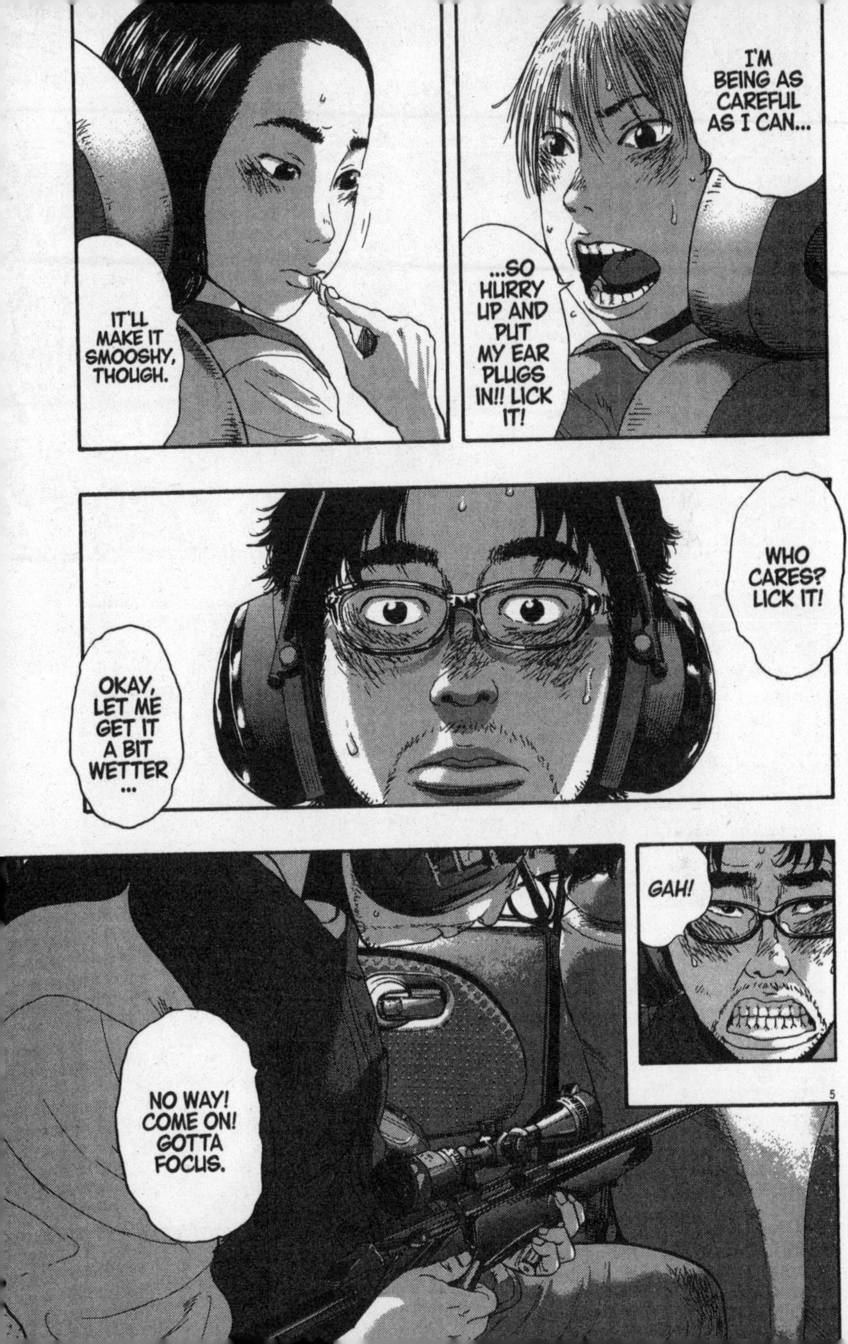
I'M BEING AS CAREFUL AS I CAN...
...SO HURRY UP AND PUT MY EAR PLUGS IN!! LICK IT!
IT'LL MAKE IT SMOOSHY, THOUGH.
WHO CARES? LICK IT!
OKAY, LET ME GET IT A BIT WETTER ...
GAH!
NO WAY! COME ON! GOTTA FOCUS.

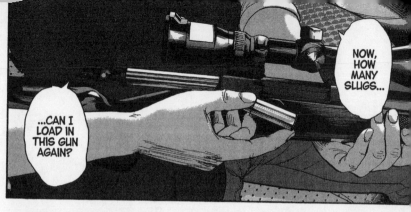

NOW, HOW MANY SLUGS...

...CAN I LOAD IN THIS GUN AGAIN?

KCHOKT

TRY A SECOND ...

OH! IT WENT IN.

KCHOKT

THAT'S ONE...

YES!

TOKK

WHHK

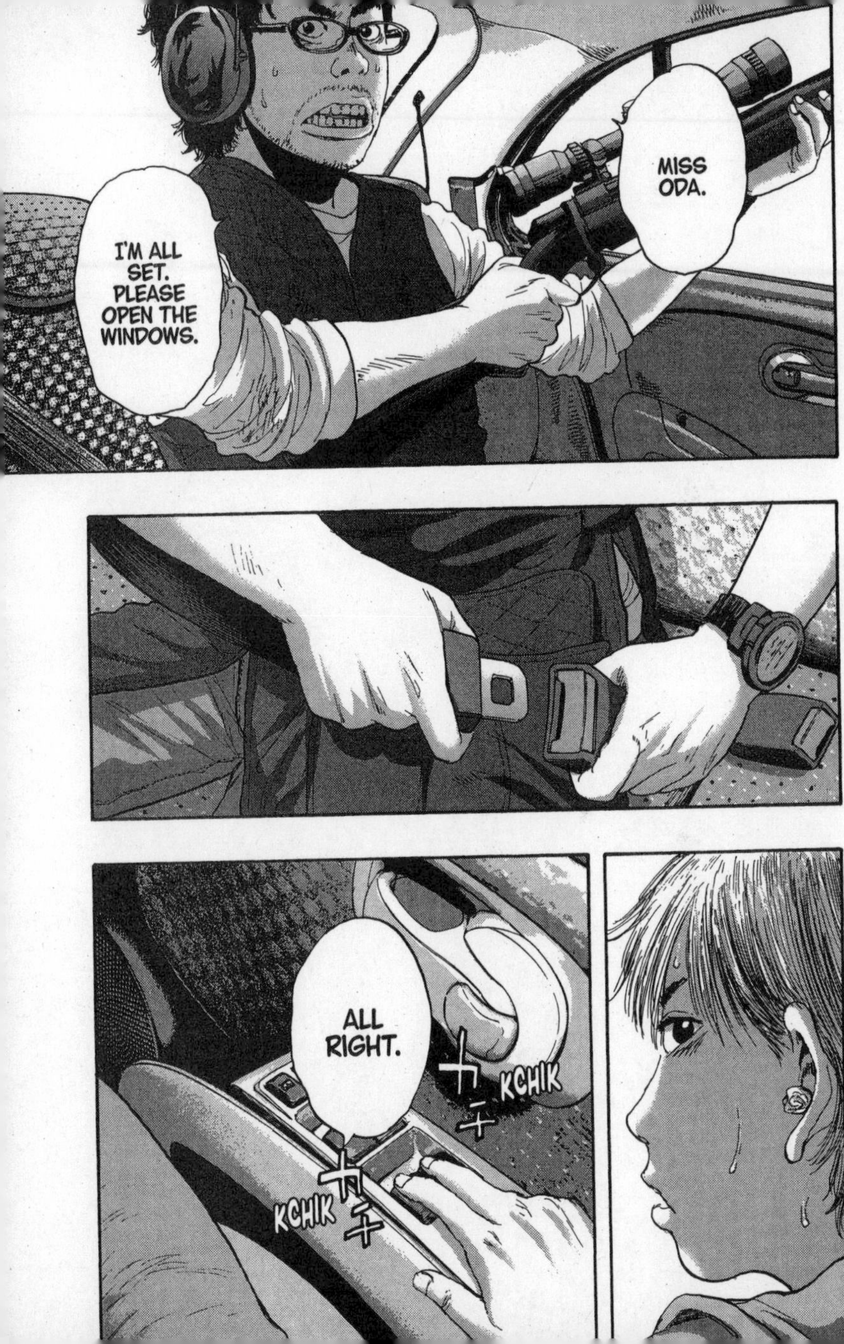
MISS ODA.
I'M ALL SET. PLEASE OPEN THE WINDOWS.
ALL RIGHT.
KCHIK
KCHIK

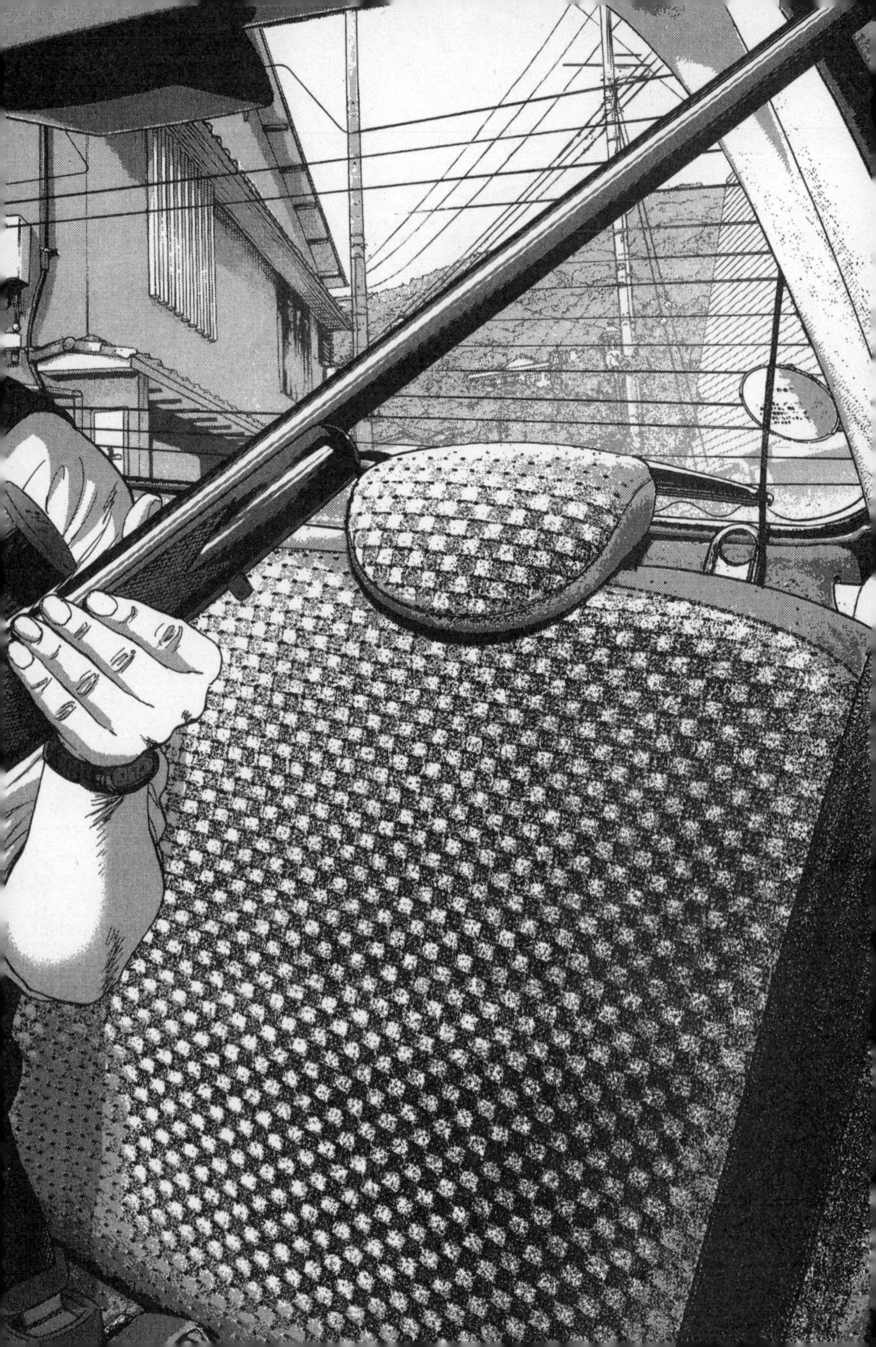

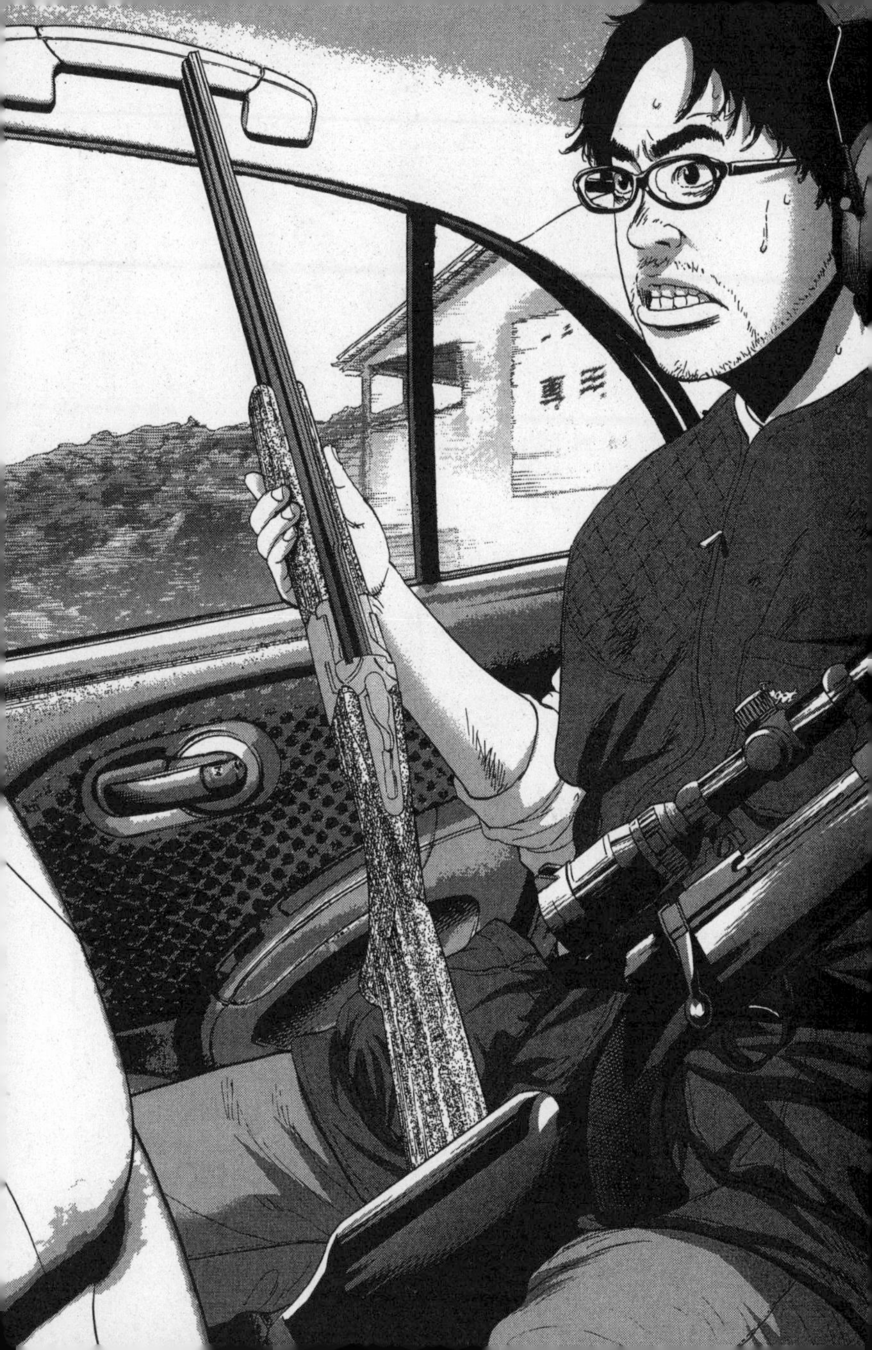

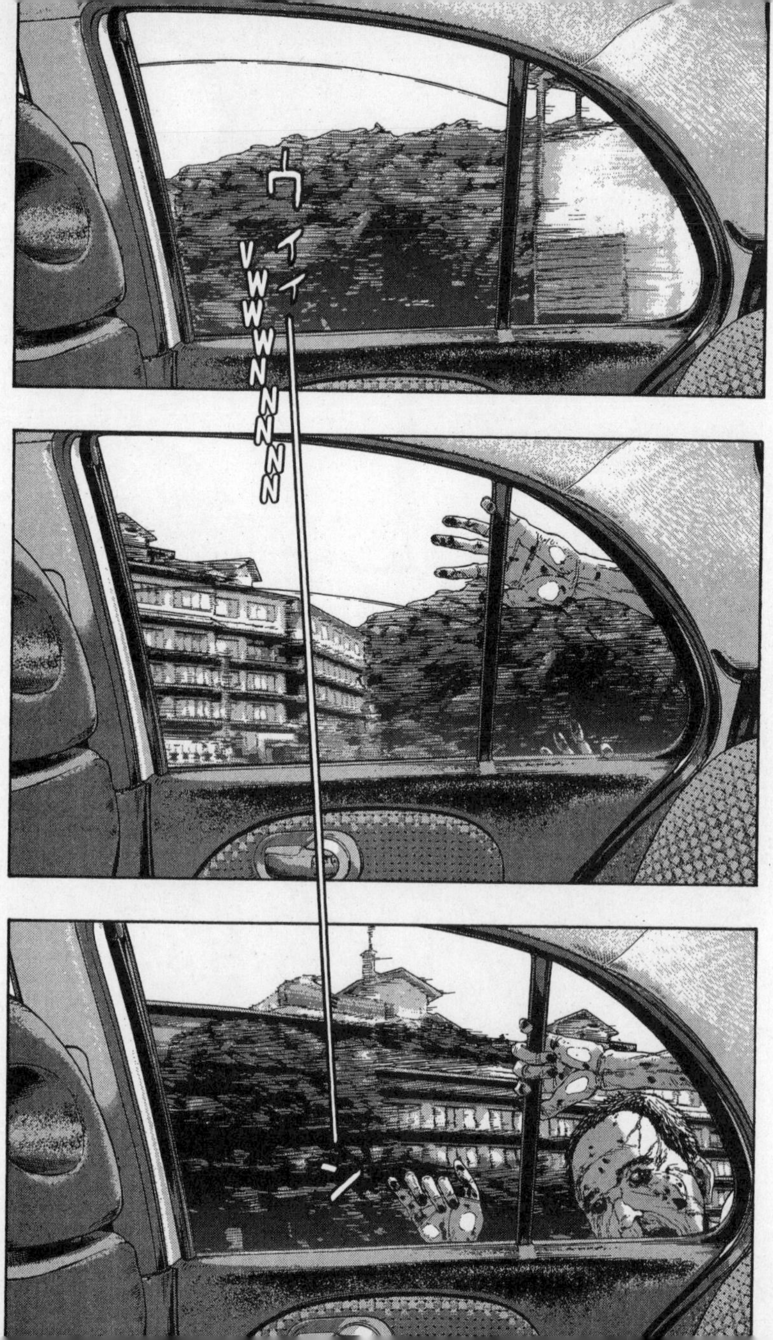
ウイイー
VWWWNNNNN

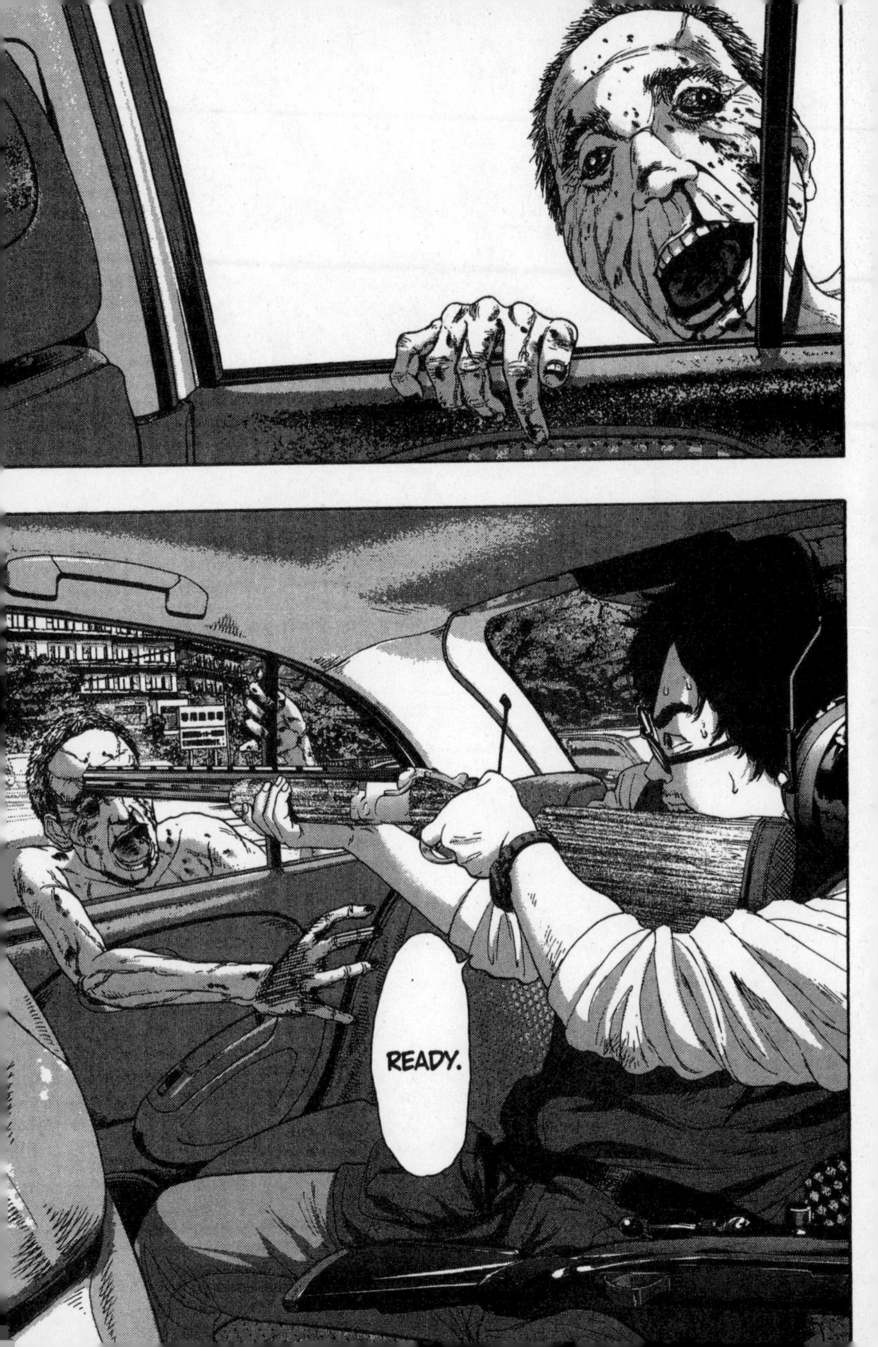
READY.

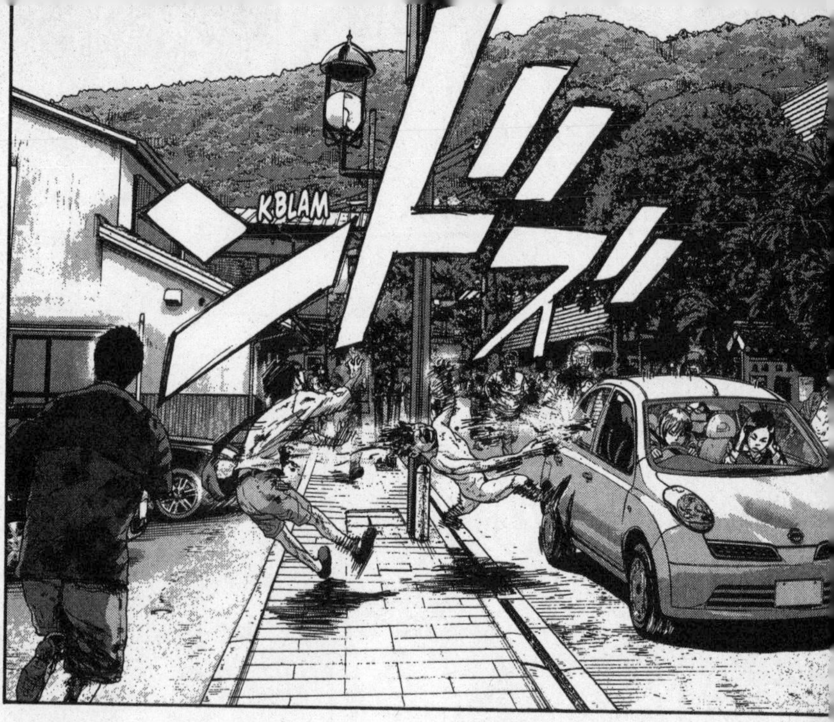
KBLAM

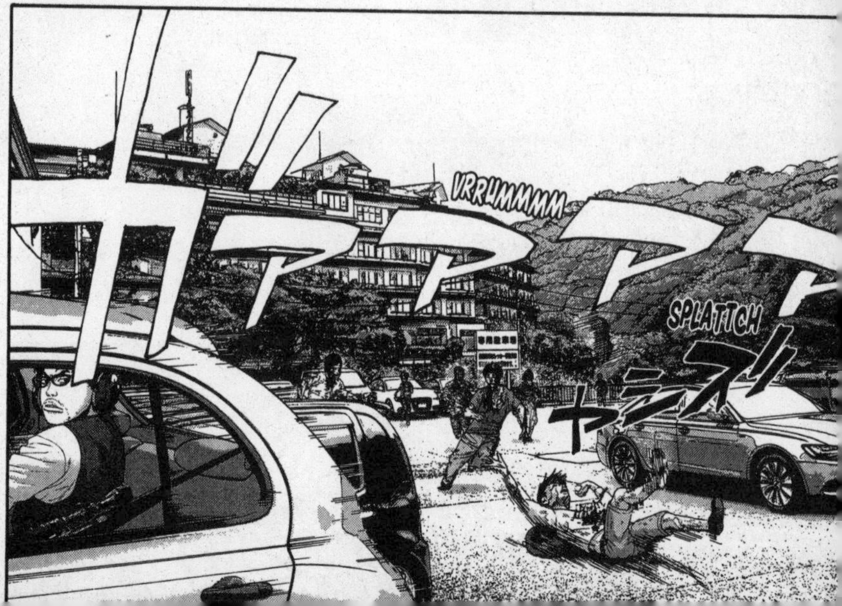
VRRUMMMM
SPLATTCH

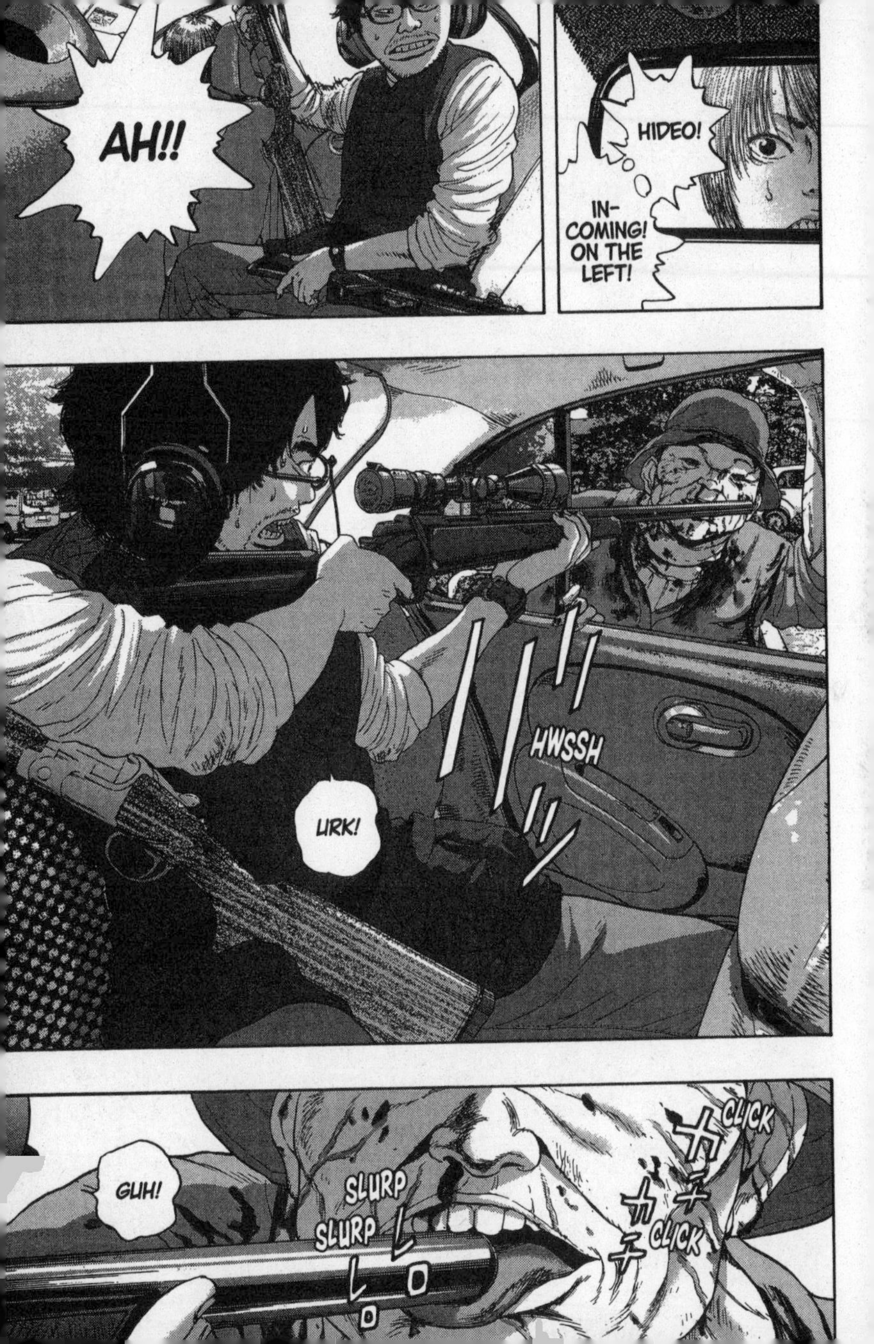
HIDEO!
IN-COMING! ON THE LEFT!
AH!!
HWSSH
URK!
CLICK
カチ
CLICK
カチ
SLURP
レロ
SLURP
レロ
GUH!

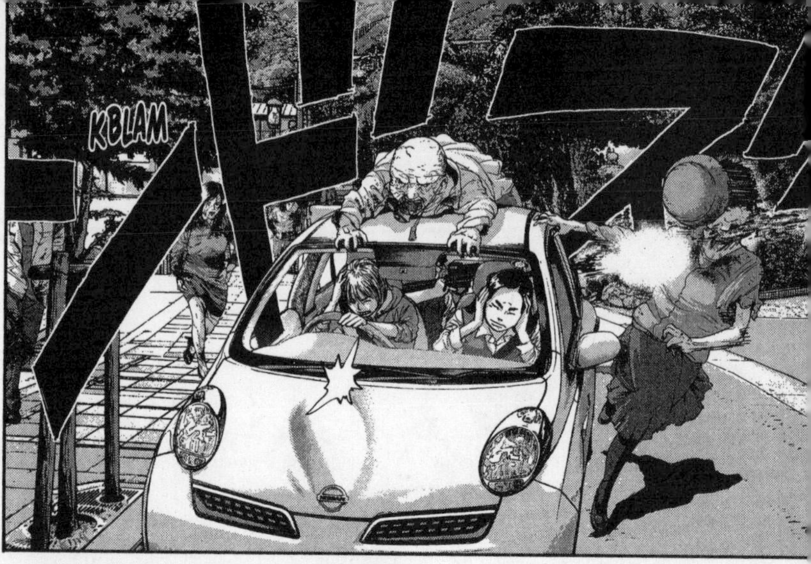
KBLAM

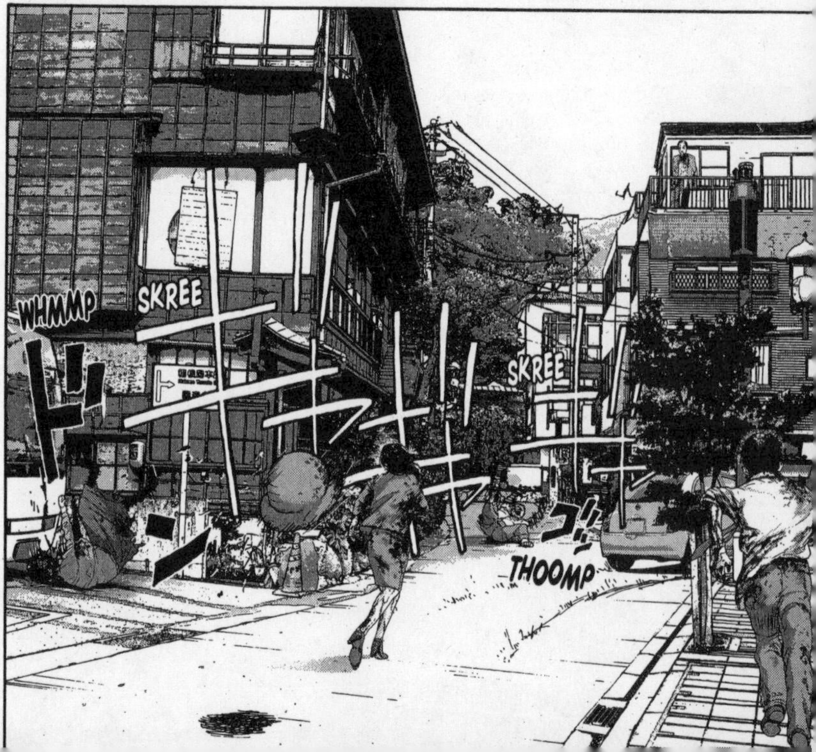
SKREE
THOOMP
SKREE
WHMMP

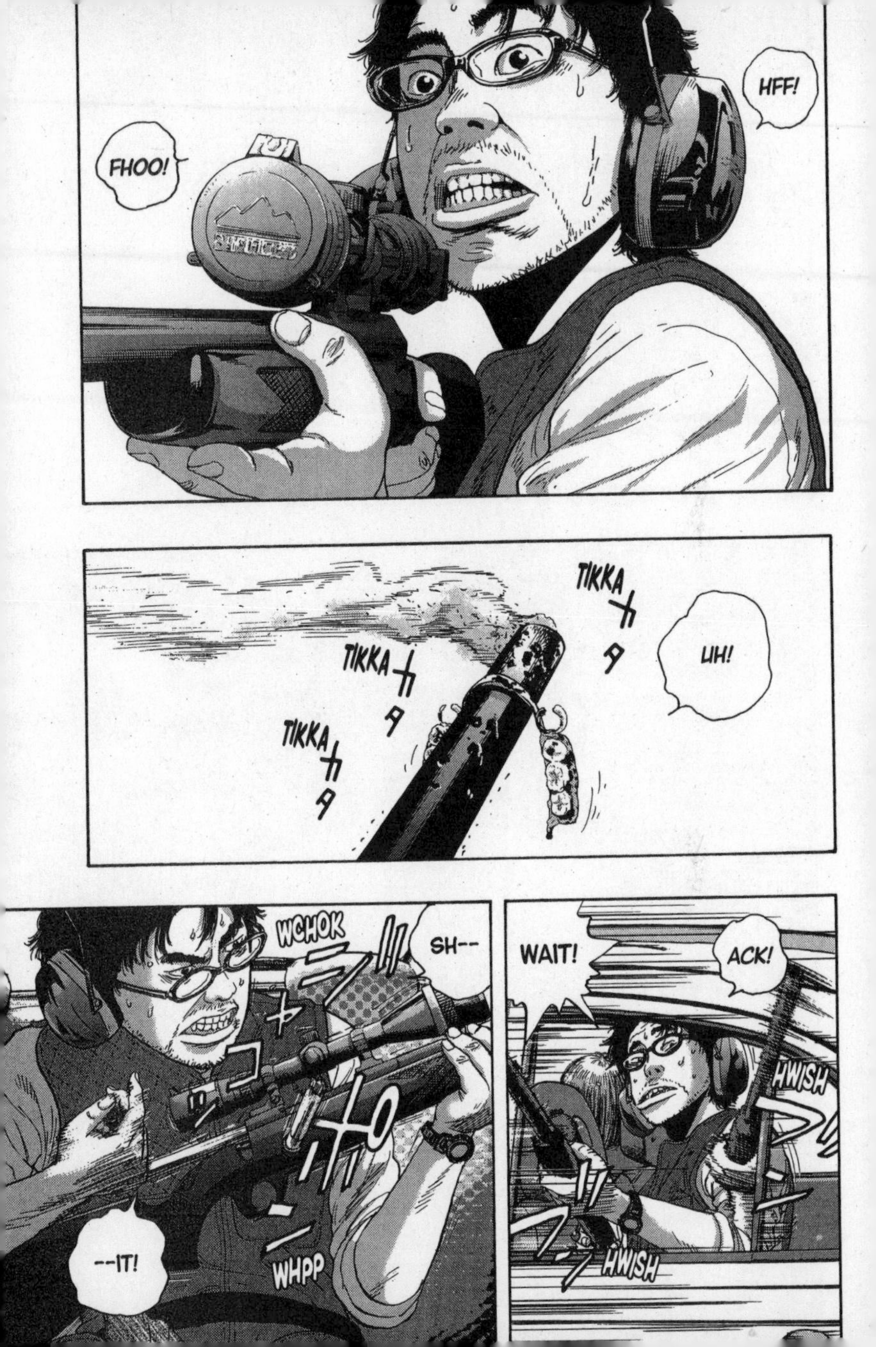
HFF!
FHOO!
UH!
TIKKA
TIKKA
TIKKA
ACK!
WAIT!
HWISH
HWISH
SH--
WCHOK
--IT!
WHPP

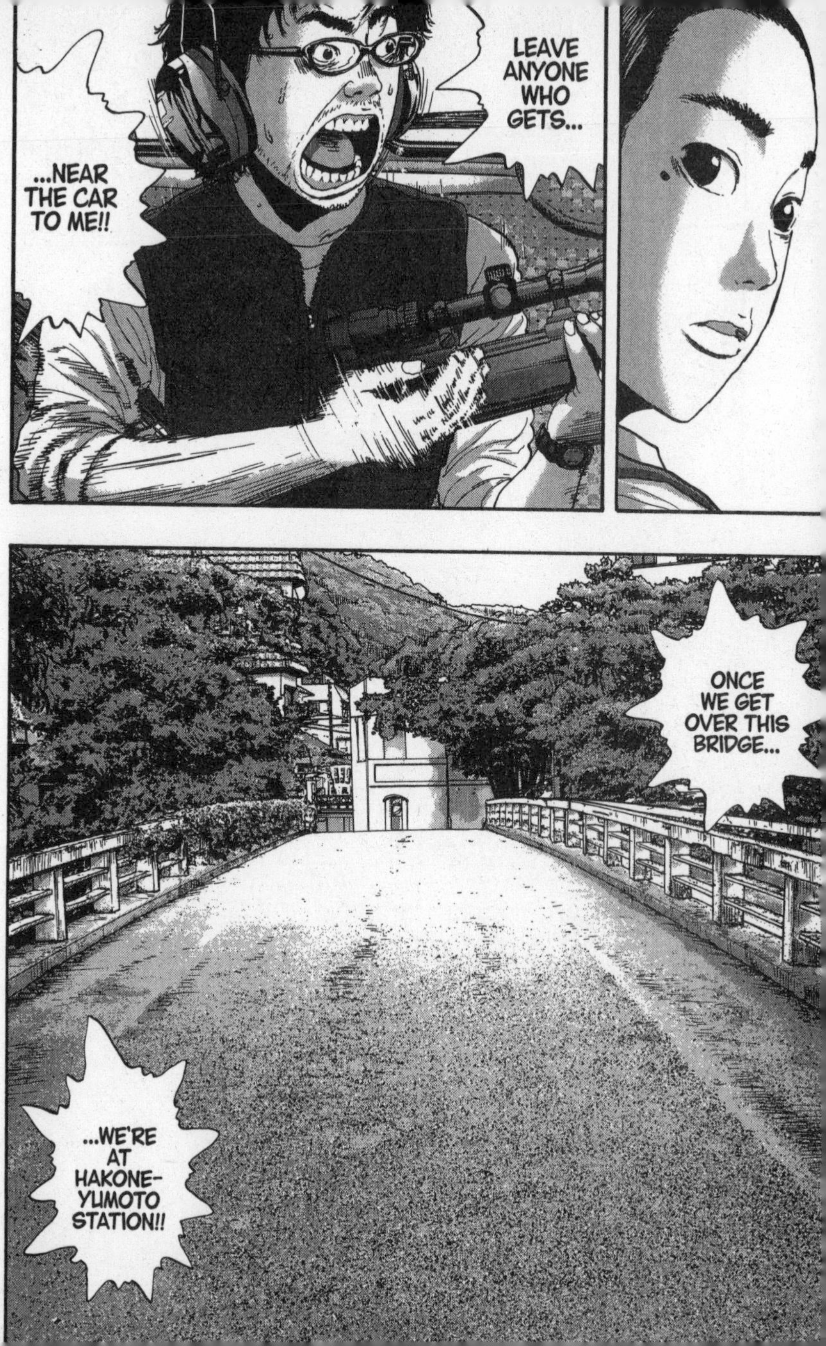
LEAVE ANYONE WHO GETS...
...NEAR THE CAR TO ME!!
ONCE WE GET OVER THIS BRIDGE...
...WE'RE AT HAKONE-YUMOTO STATION!!

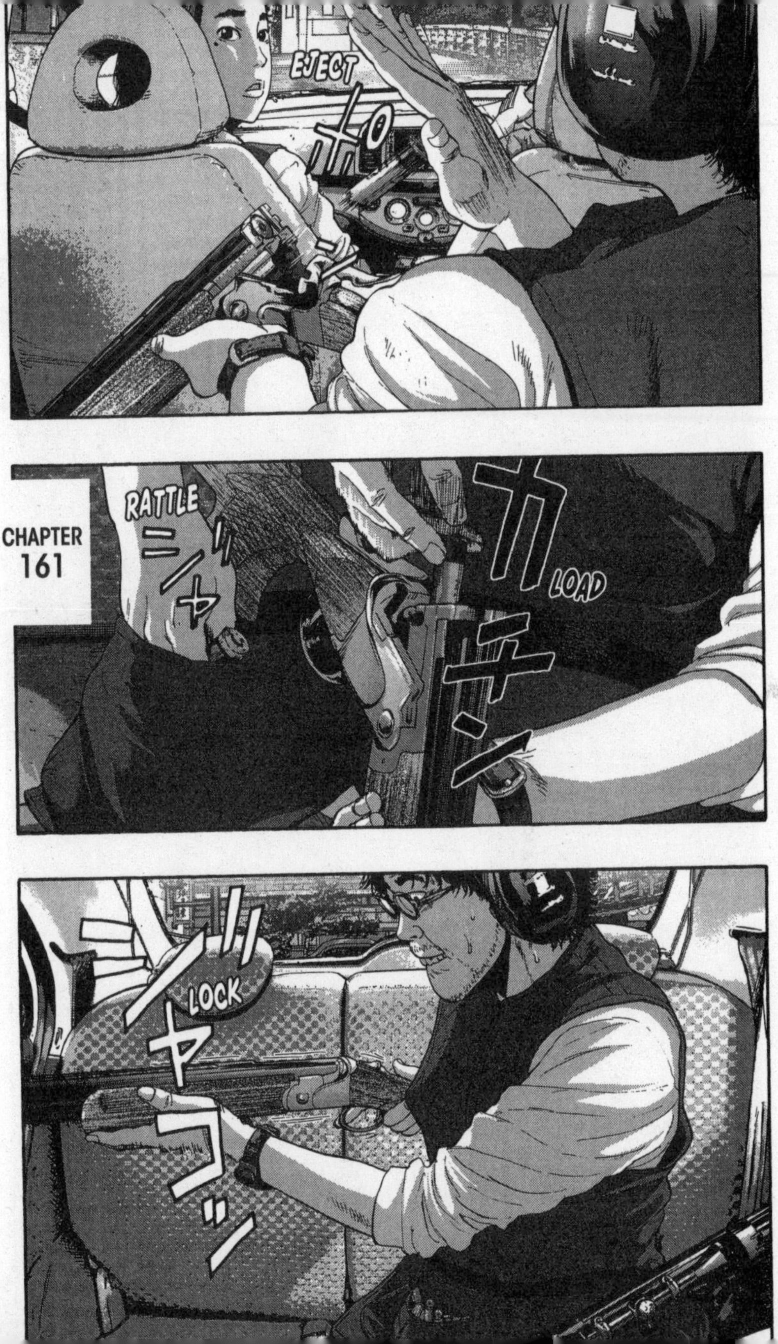
EJECT
CHAPTER 161
RATTLE
LOAD
LOCK

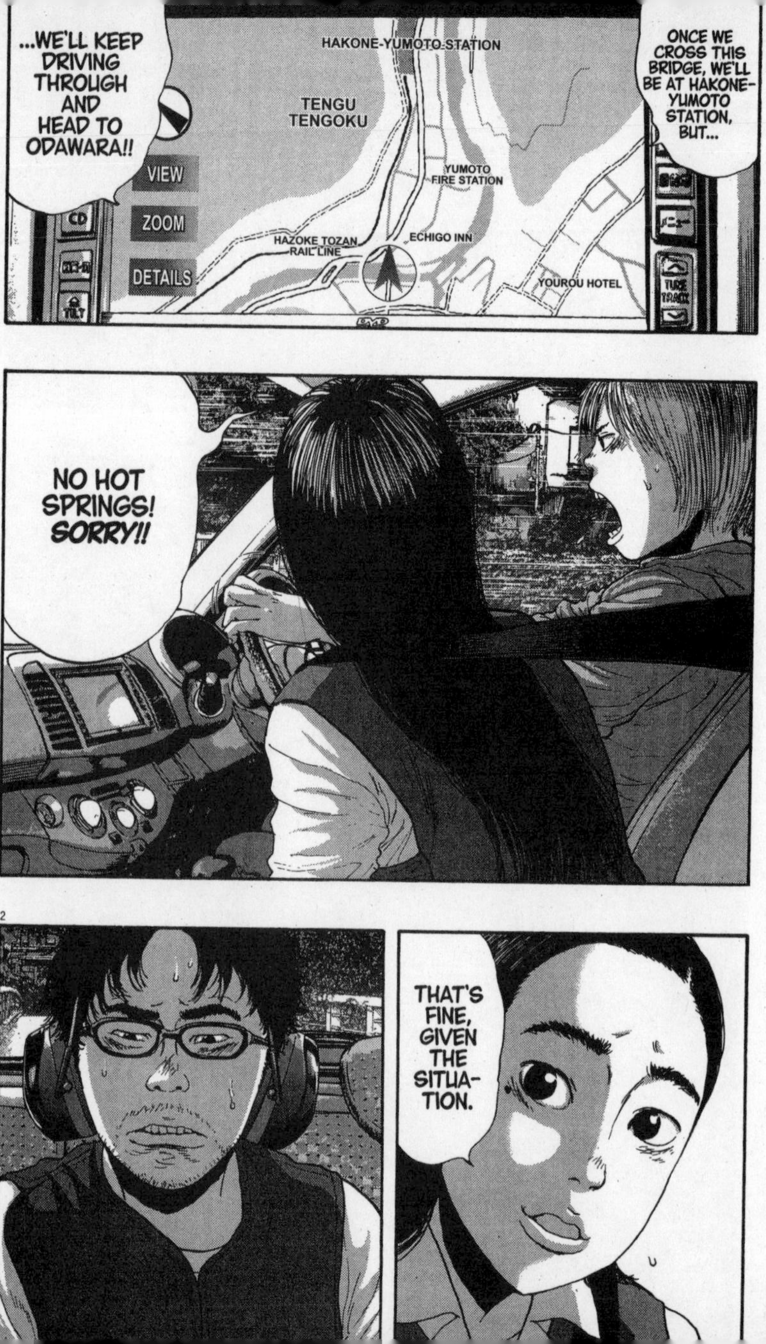
ONCE WE CROSS THIS BRIDGE, WE'LL BE AT HAKONE-YUMOTO STATION, BUT...
...WE'LL KEEP DRIVING THROUGH AND HEAD TO ODAWARA!!
HAKONE-YUMOTO STATION
TENGU TENGOKU
YUMOTO FIRE STATION
ECHIGO INN
HAZOKE TOZAN RAIL LINE
YOUROU HOTEL
VIEW
ZOOM
DETAILS
CD
NO HOT SPRINGS! SORRY!!
THAT'S FINE, GIVEN THE SITUATION.

2

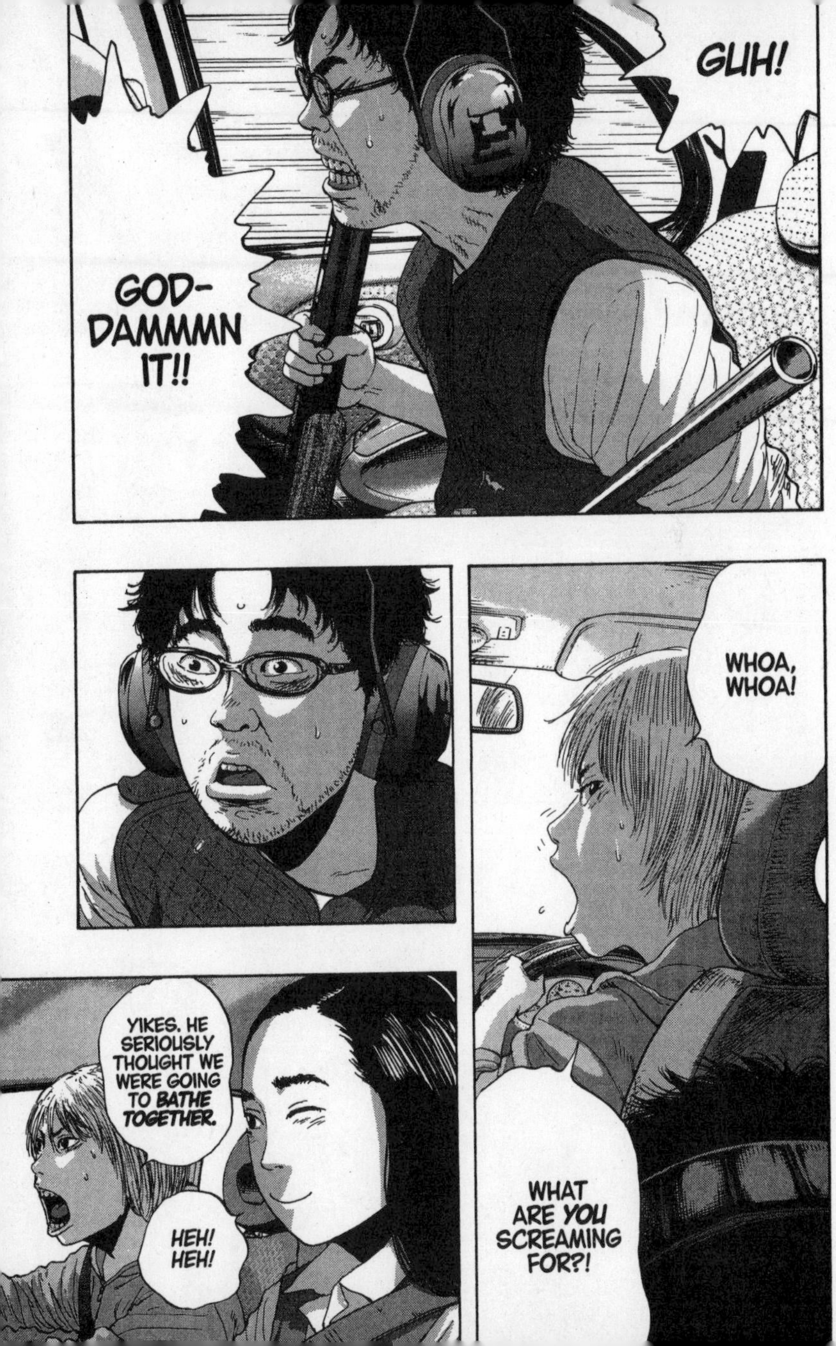
GUH!
GOD-DAMMMN IT!!
WHOA, WHOA!
WHAT ARE *YOU* SCREAMING FOR?!
YIKES. HE SERIOUSLY THOUGHT WE WERE GOING TO *BATHE TOGETHER.*
HEH! HEH!

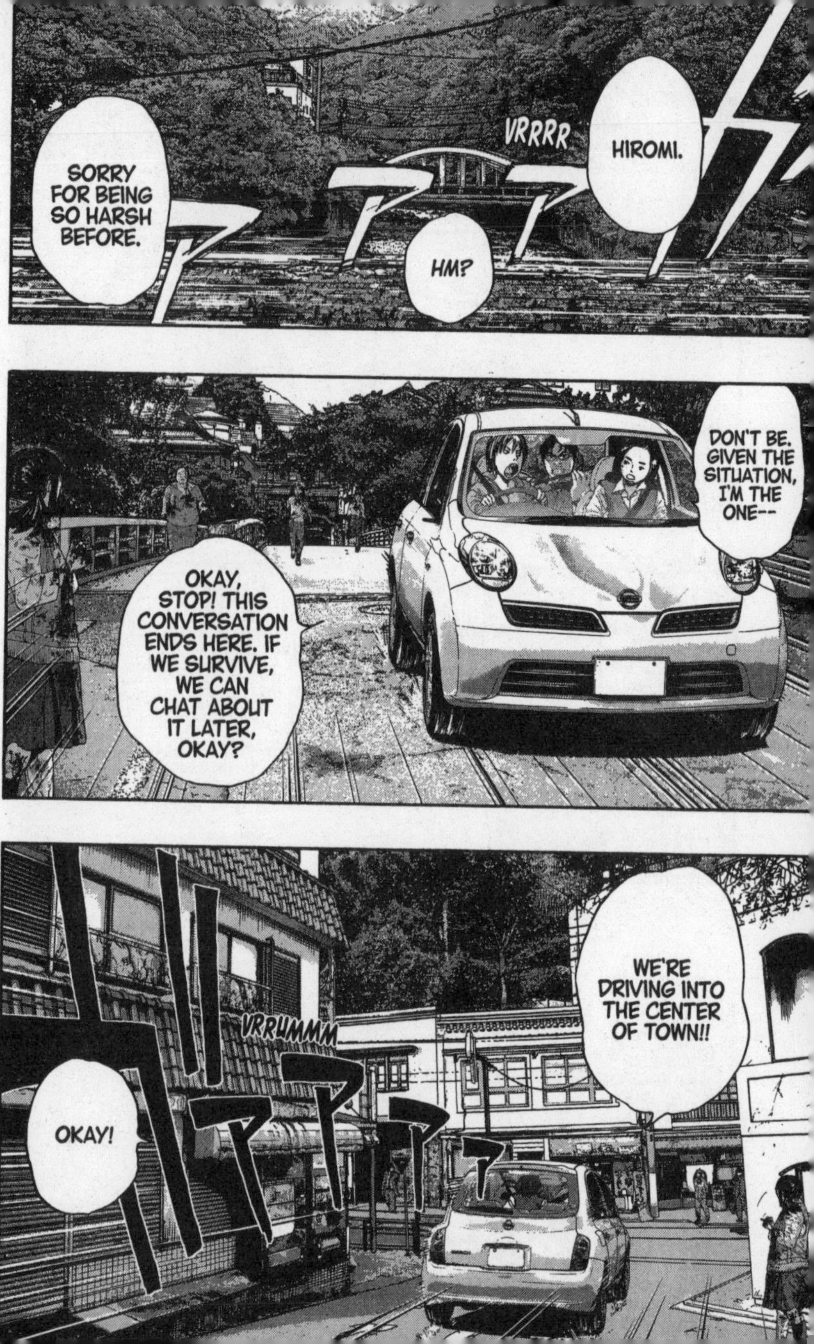
HIROMI.
VRRRR
HM?
SORRY FOR BEING SO HARSH BEFORE.
DON'T BE. GIVEN THE SITUATION, I'M THE ONE--
OKAY, STOP! THIS CONVERSATION ENDS HERE. IF WE SURVIVE, WE CAN CHAT ABOUT IT LATER, OKAY?
WE'RE DRIVING INTO THE CENTER OF TOWN!!
VRRUMMM
OKAY!

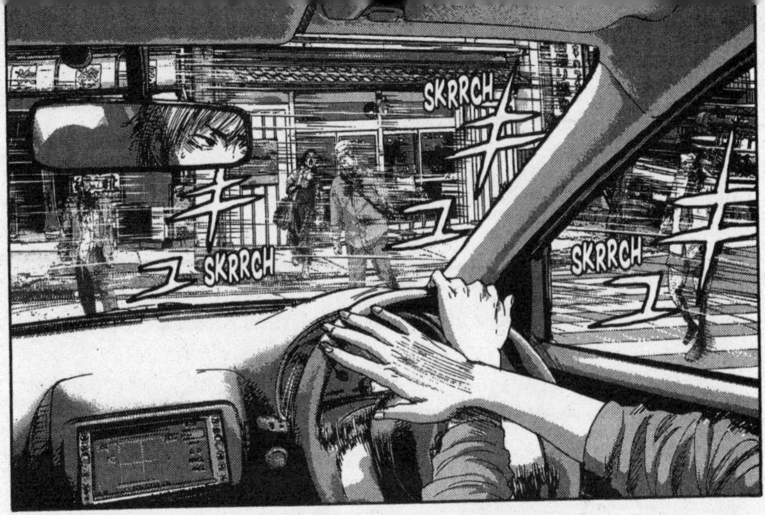
SKRRCH
SKRRCH
SKRRCH
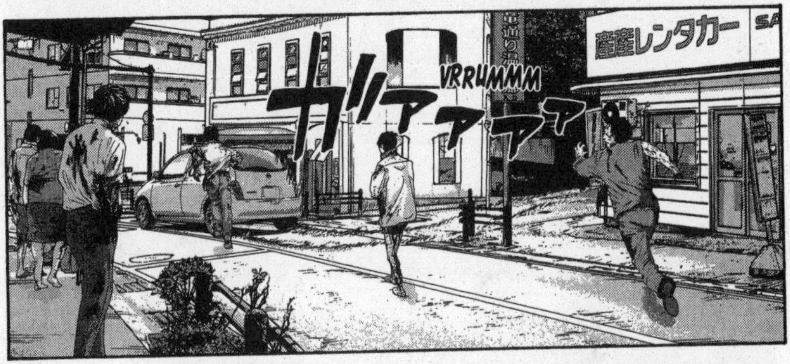
VRRUMMM
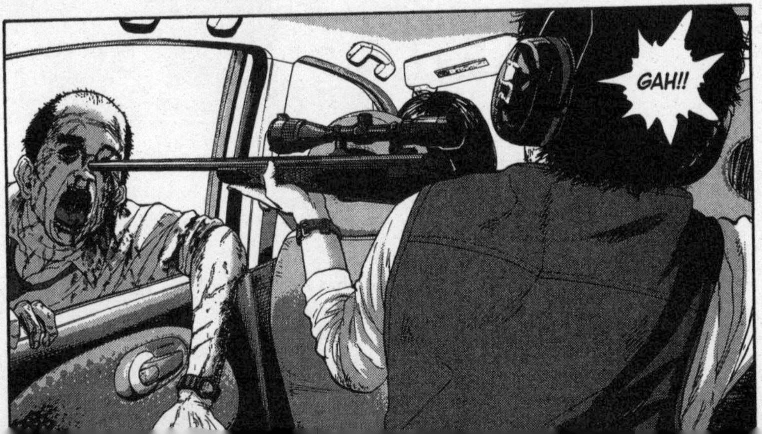
GAH!!

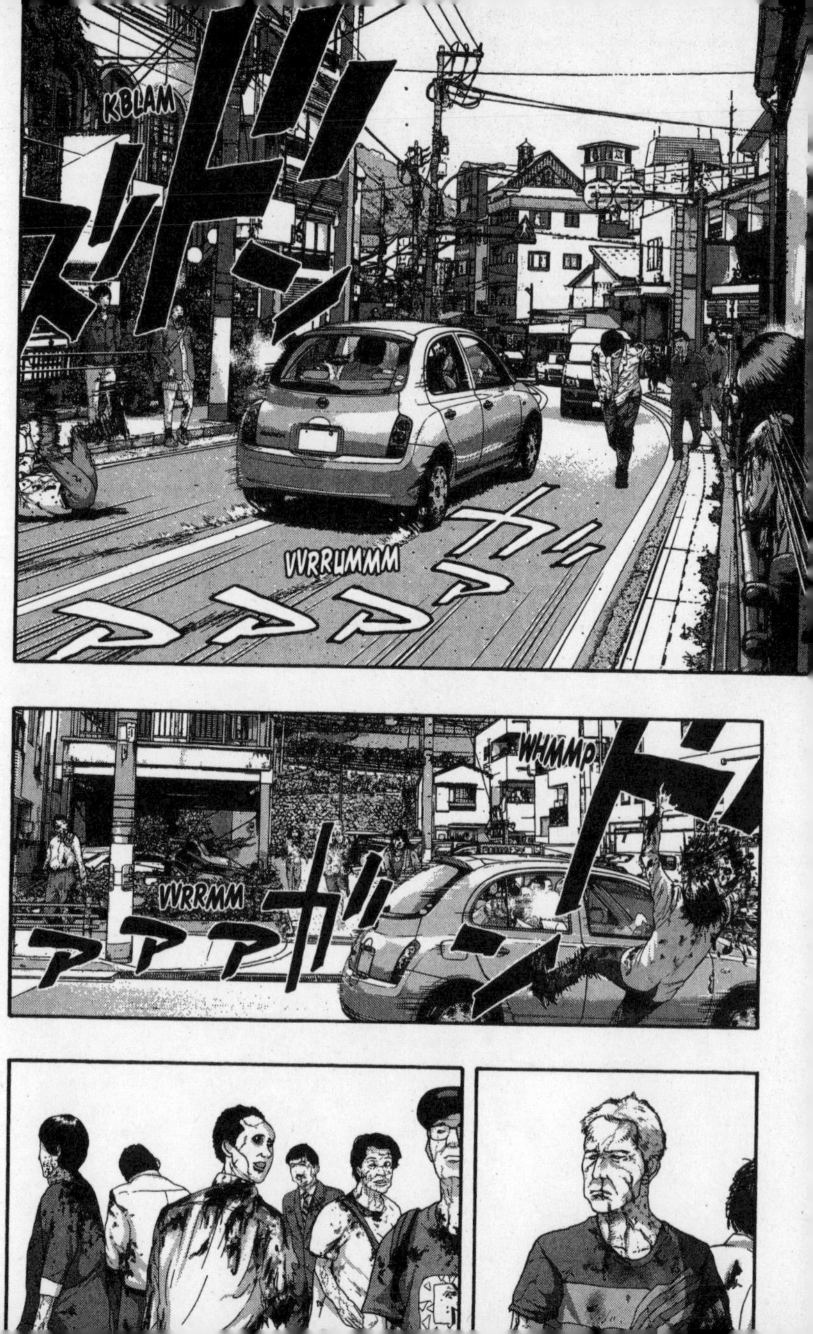
KBLAM
VVRRUMMM
WHMMP
VVRRMM

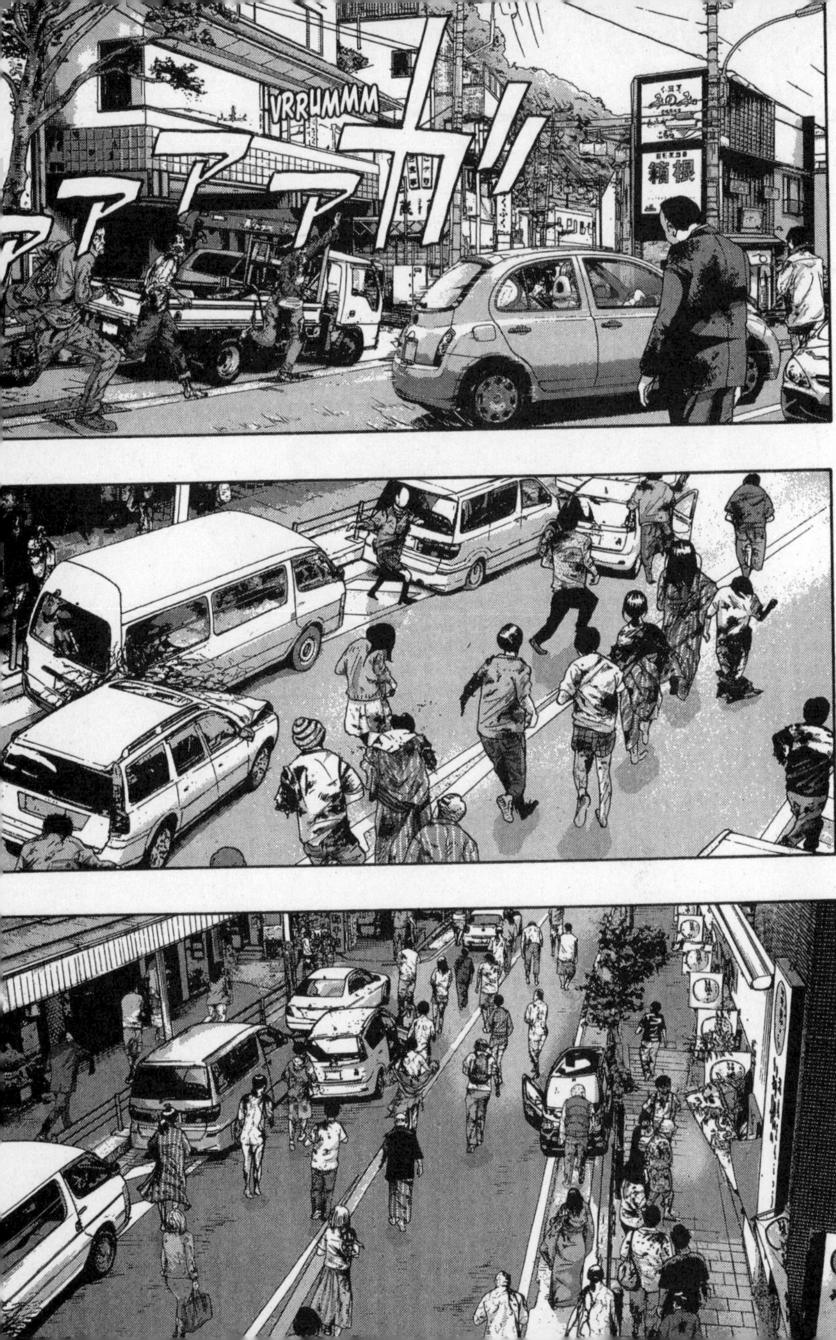
VRRUMMM

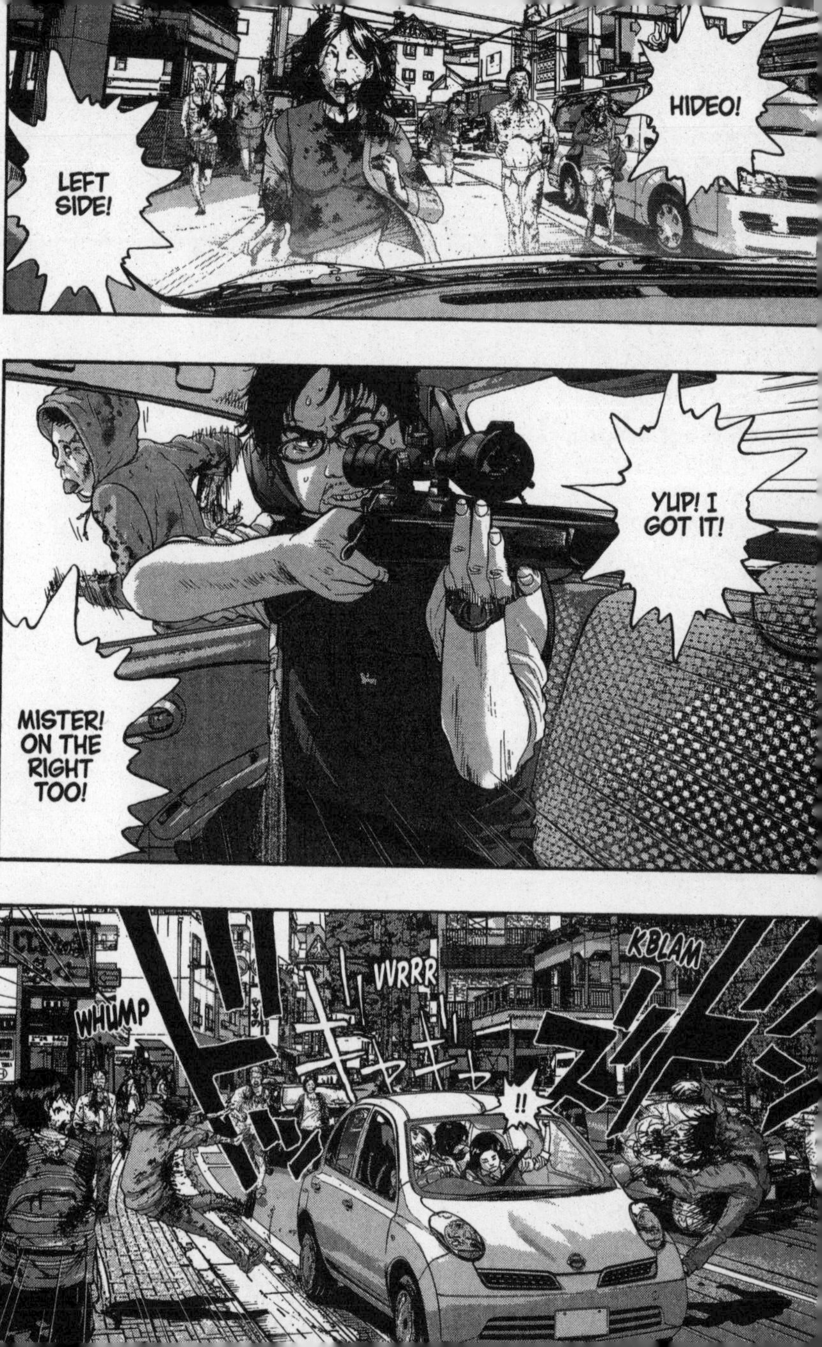
HIDEO!
LEFT SIDE!
YUP! I GOT IT!
MISTER! ON THE RIGHT TOO!
KBLAM
!!
VVRRR
WHUMP

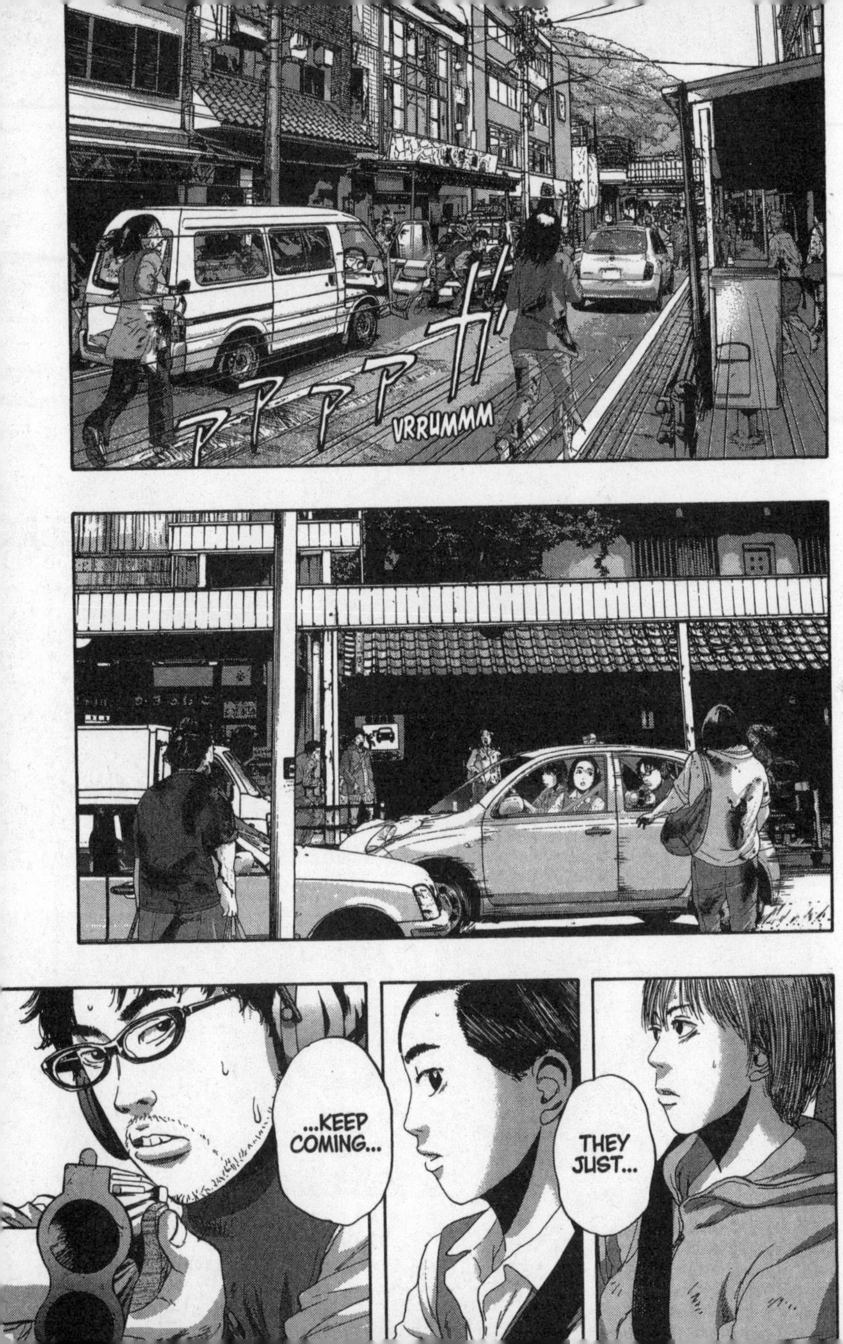
ガアアアア
VRRUMMM
THEY JUST...
...KEEP COMING...

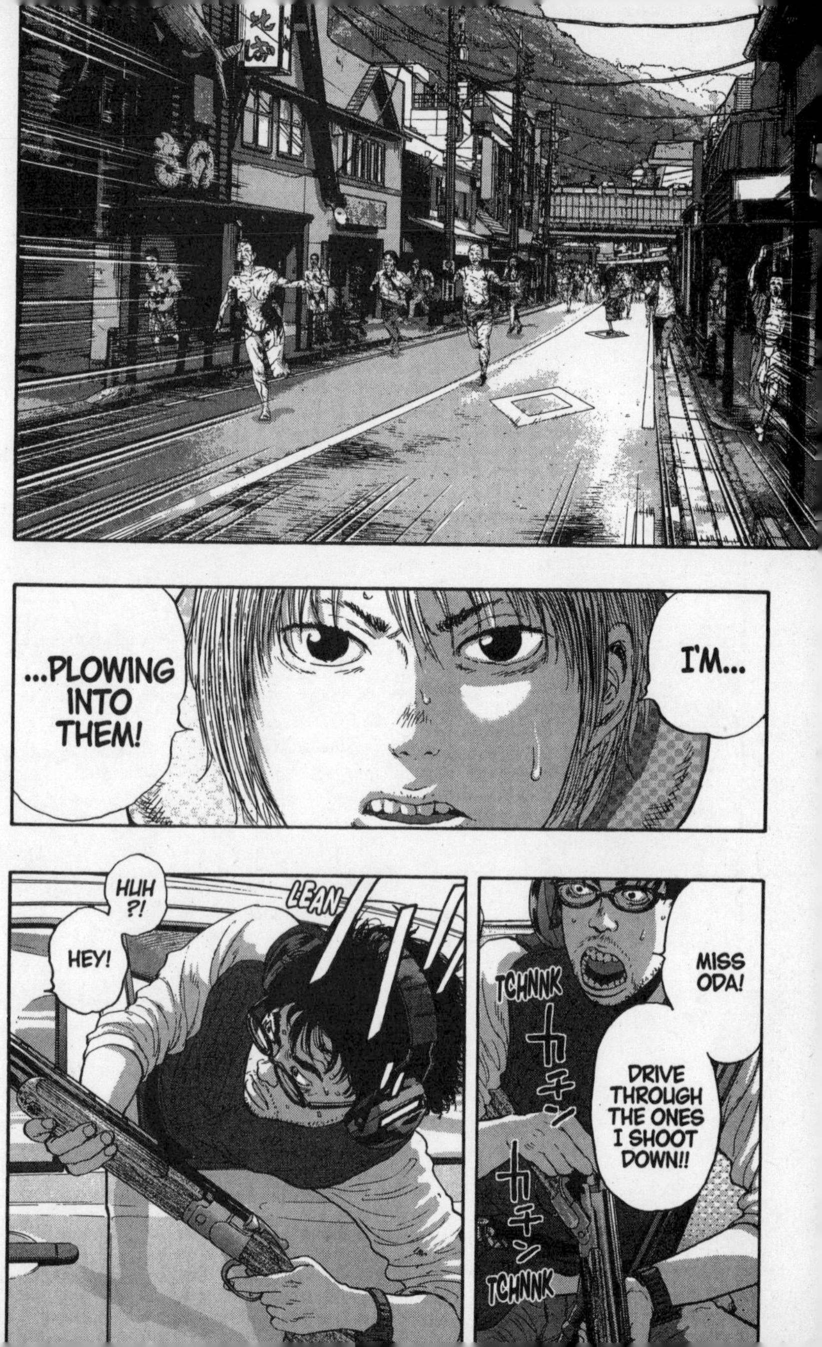
I'M...
...PLOWING INTO THEM!
MISS ODA!
DRIVE THROUGH THE ONES I SHOOT DOWN!!
TCHNNK
カチン
カチン
TCHNNK
LEAN
HUH ?!
HEY!

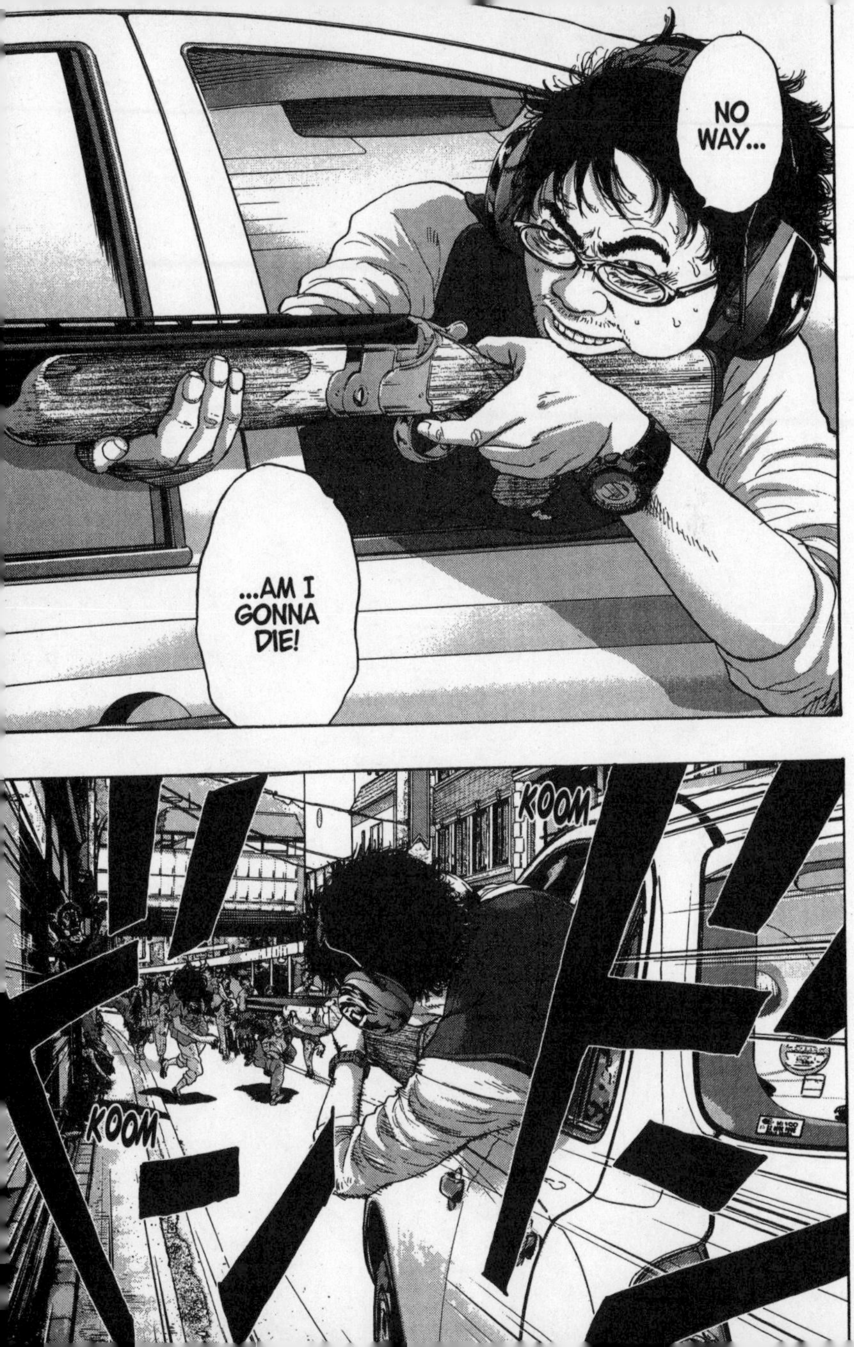
NO WAY...
...AM I GONNA DIE!
KOOM
KOOM

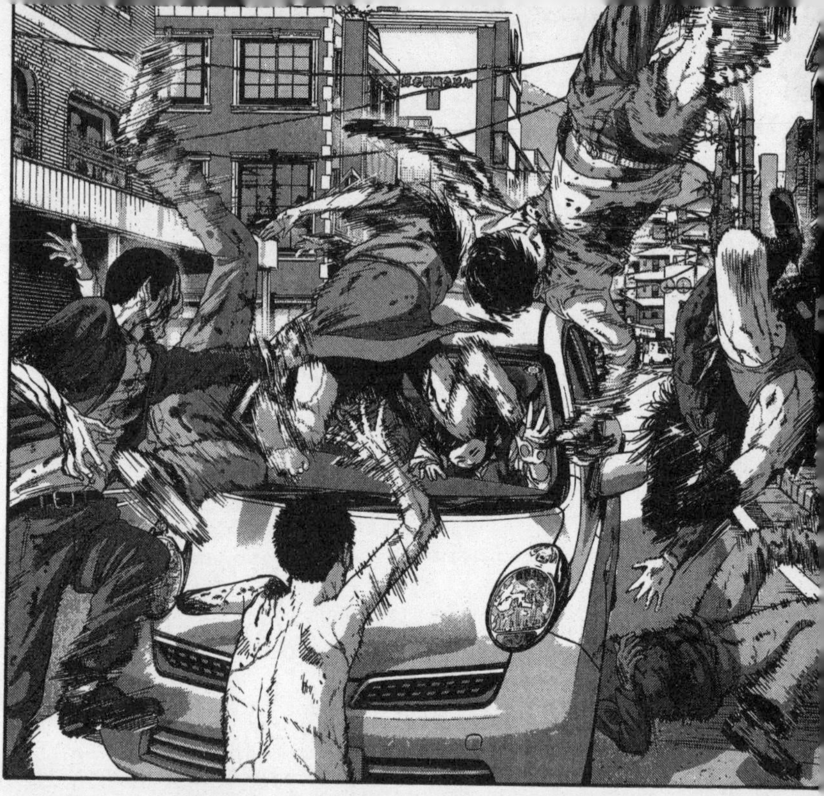

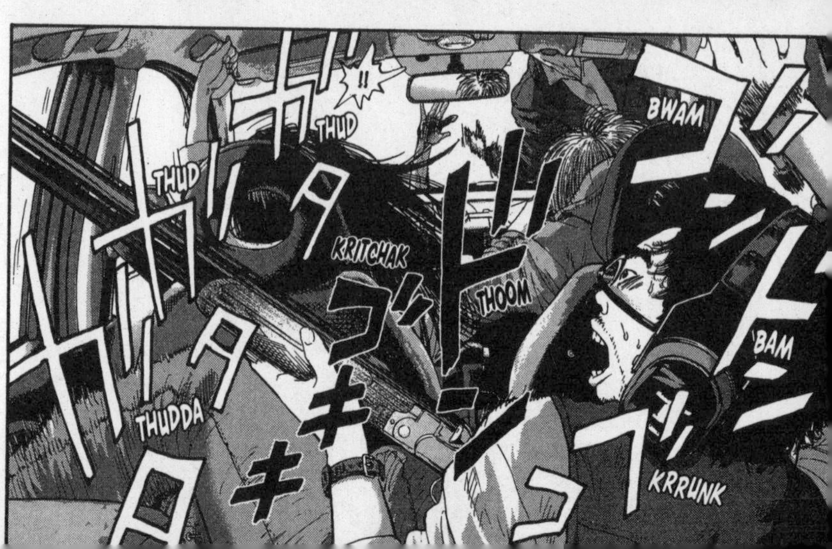

BWAM
BAM
KRRUNK
THOOM
!!
THUD
KRITCHAK
THUD
THUDDA

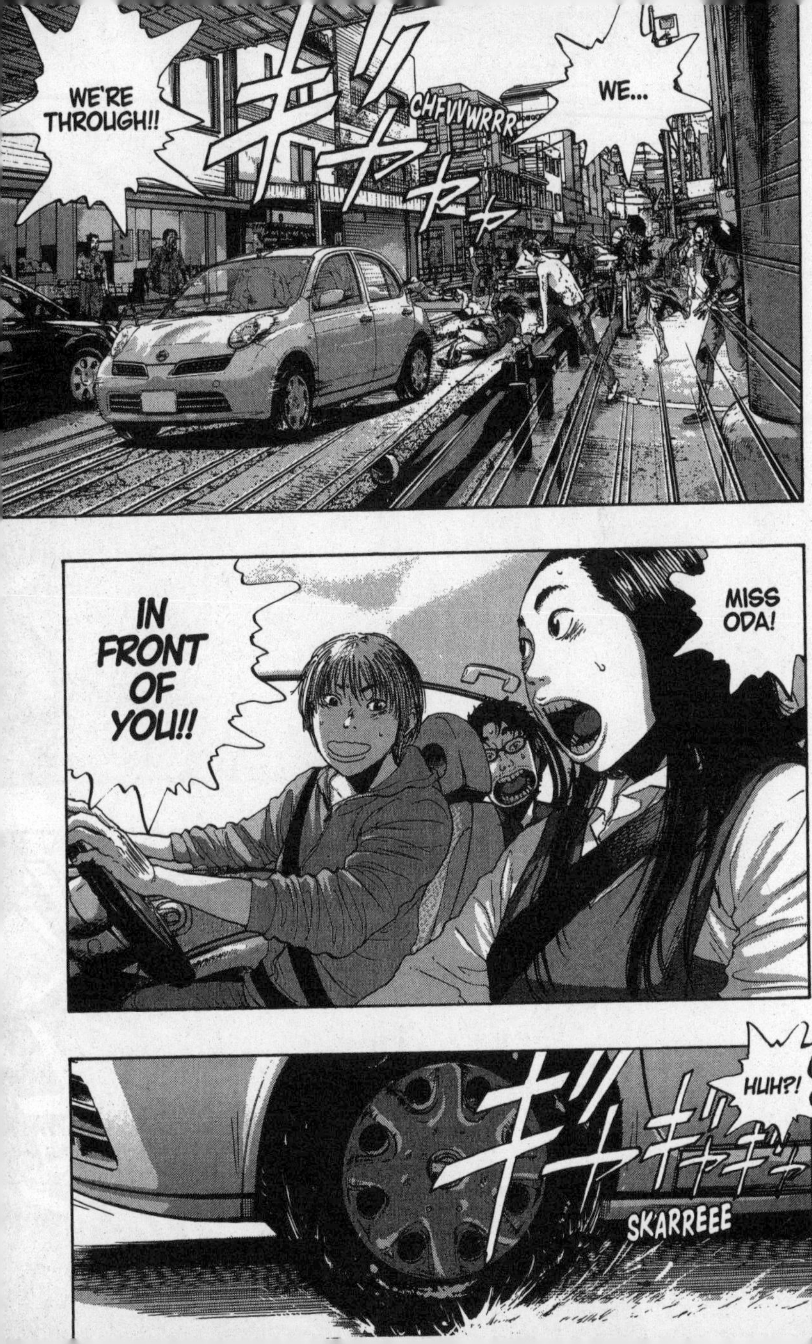
WE...
CHFVVWRRR
WE'RE THROUGH!!
MISS ODA!
IN FRONT OF YOU!!
HUH?!
SKARREEE

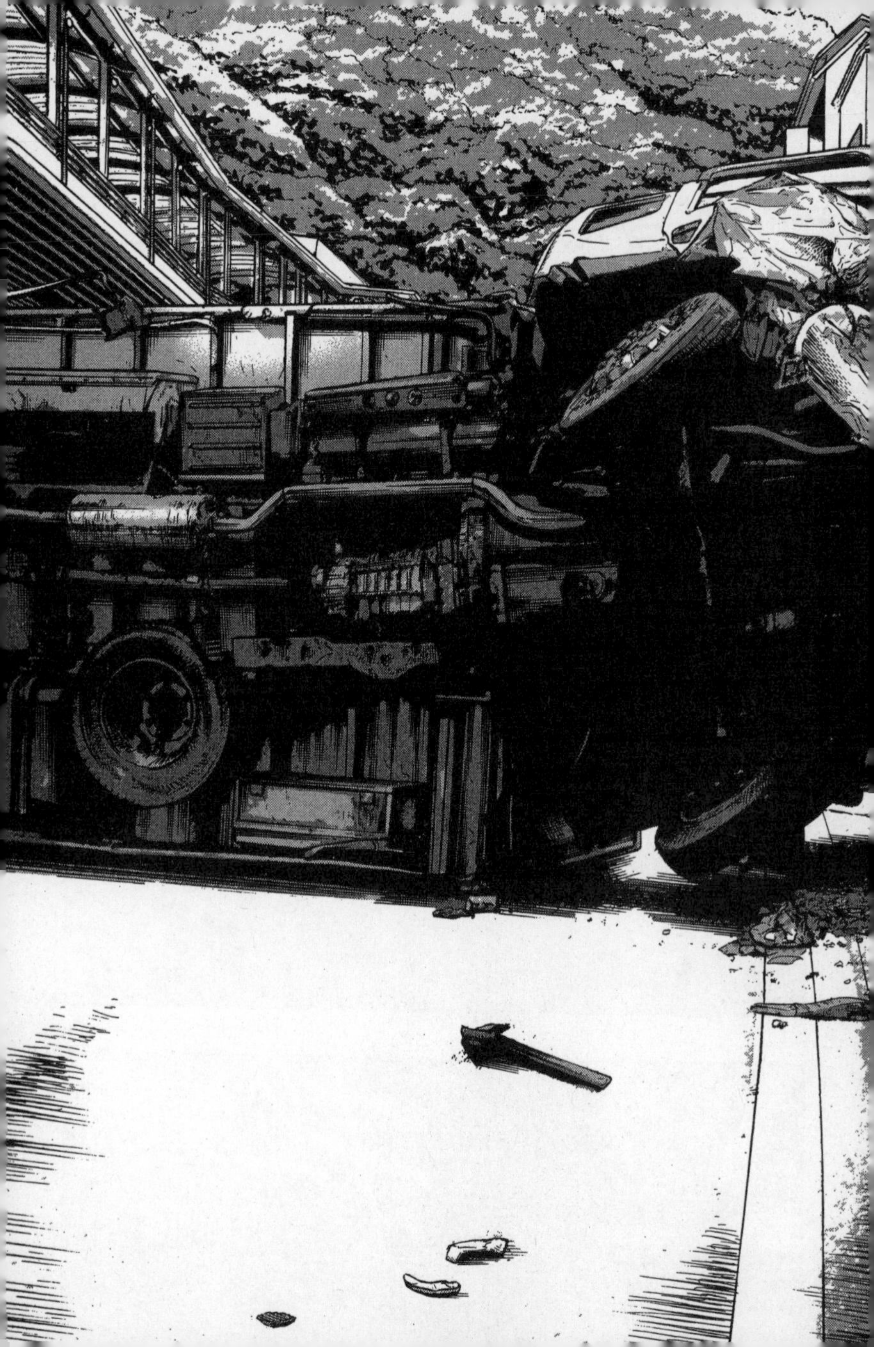

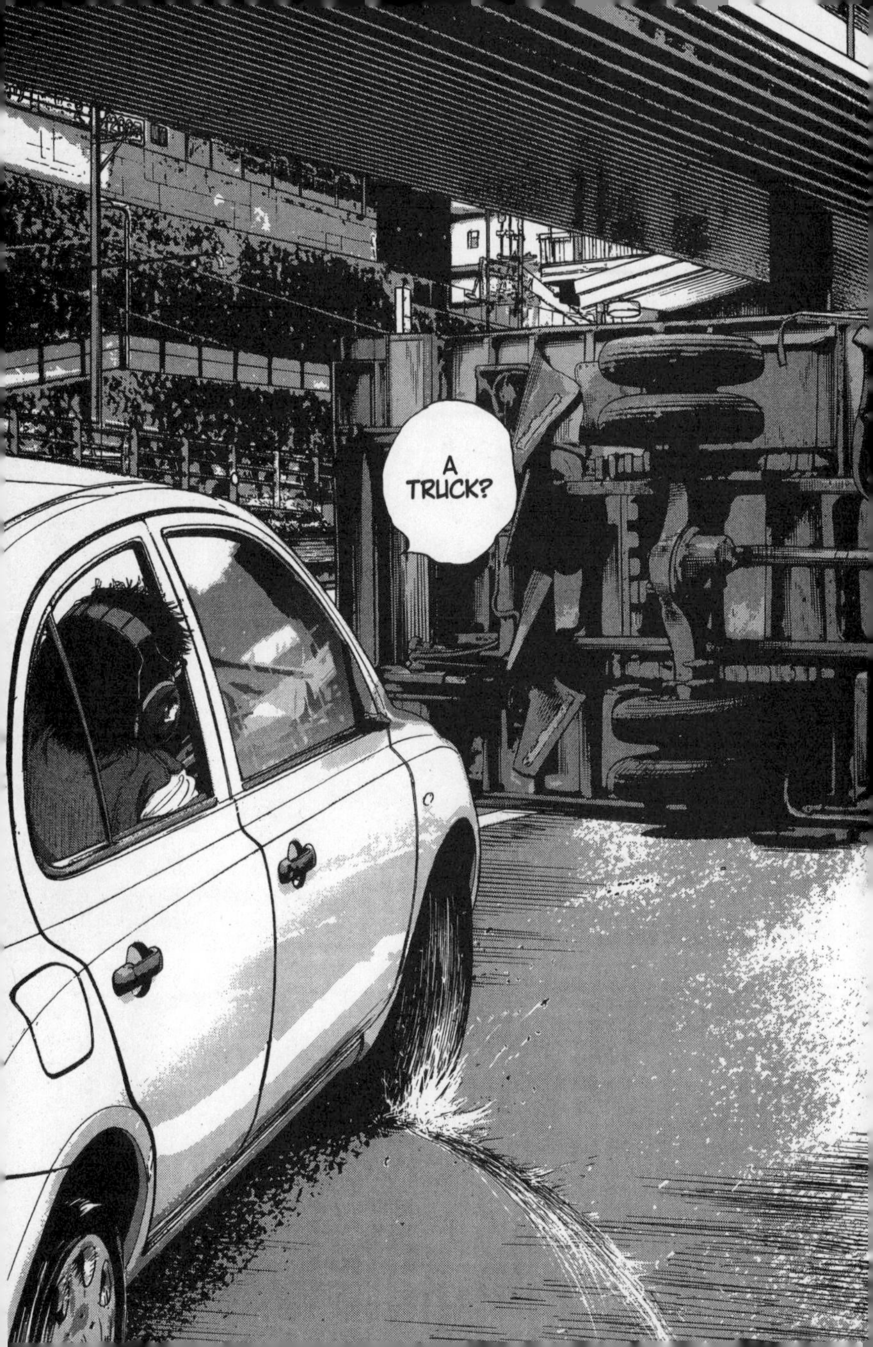
A TRUCK?

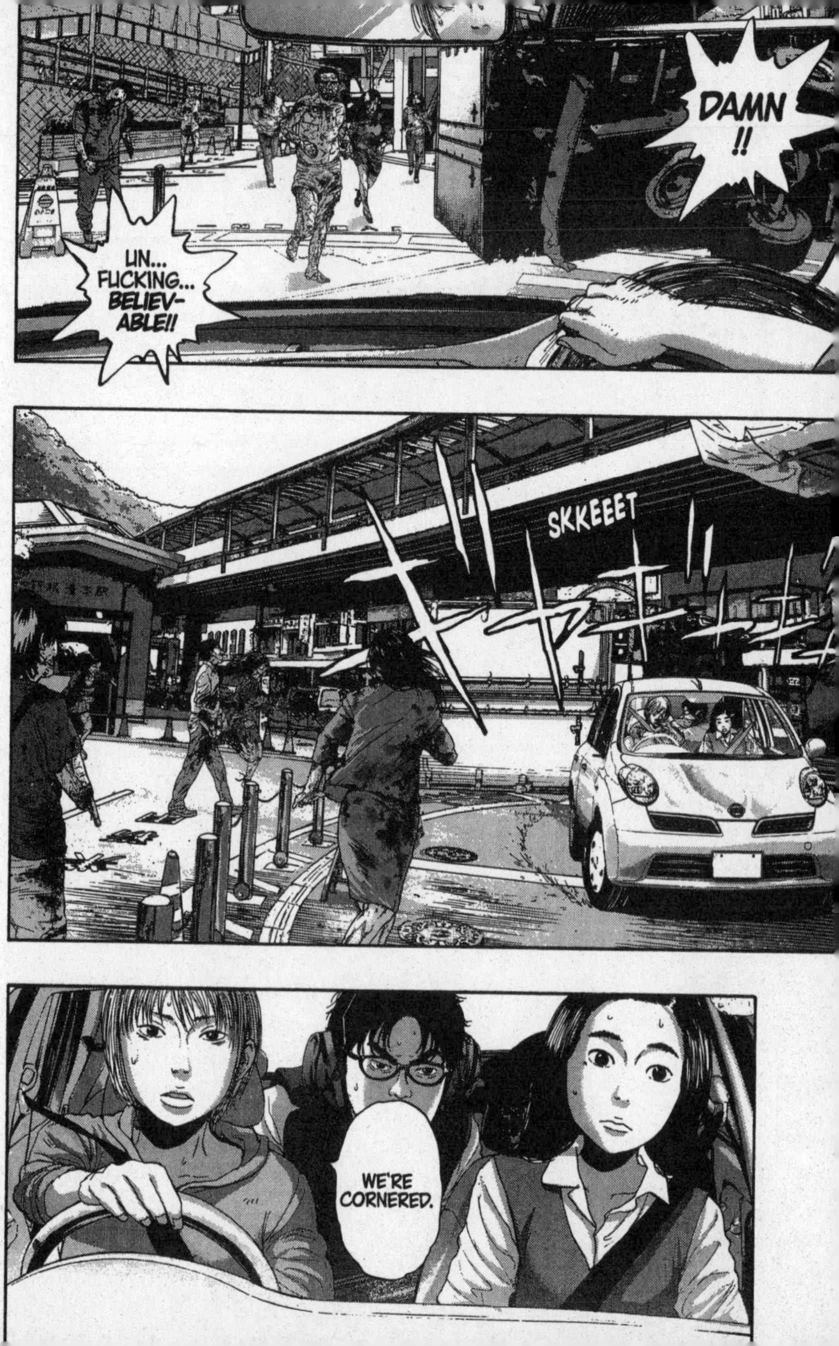
DAMN!!
UN... FUCKING... BELIEV-ABLE!!
SKKEEET
WE'RE CORNERED.

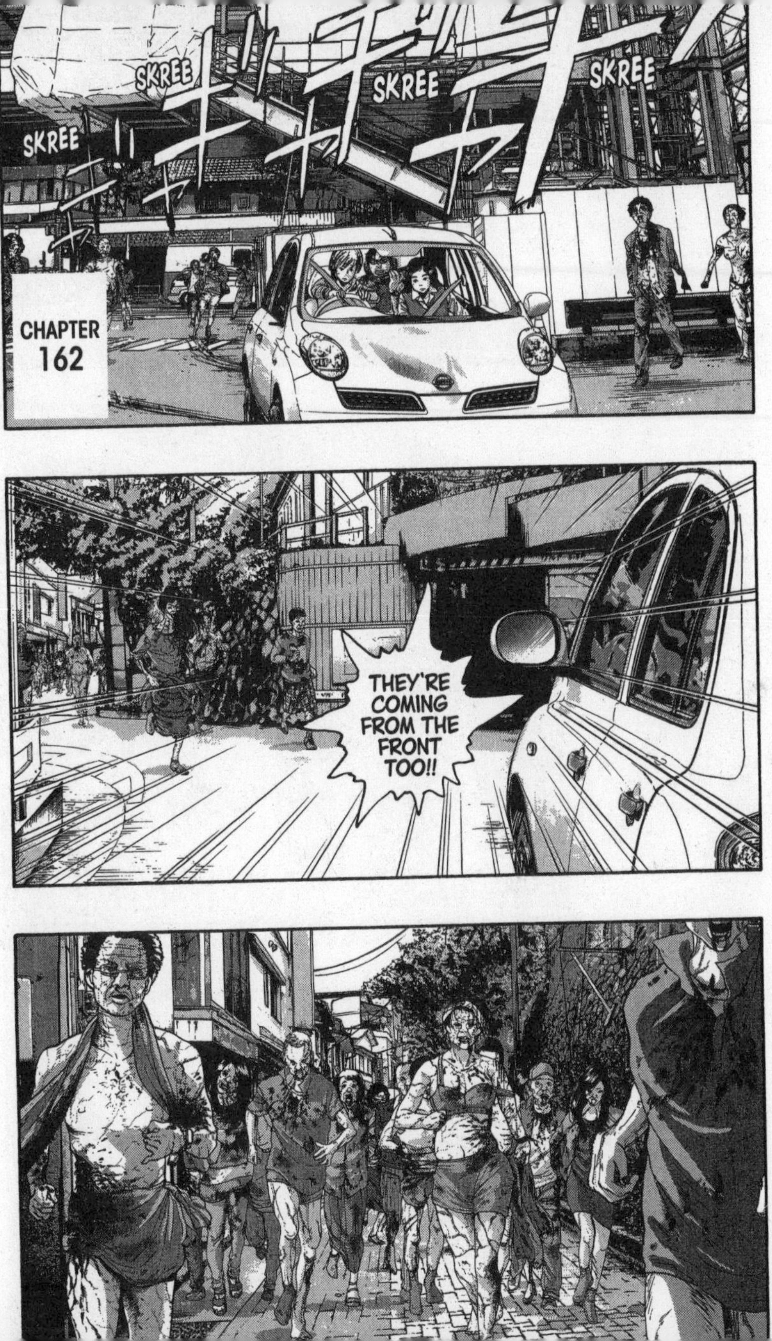
SKREE
SKREE
SKREE
SKREE
CHAPTER 162
THEY'RE COMING FROM THE FRONT TOO!!

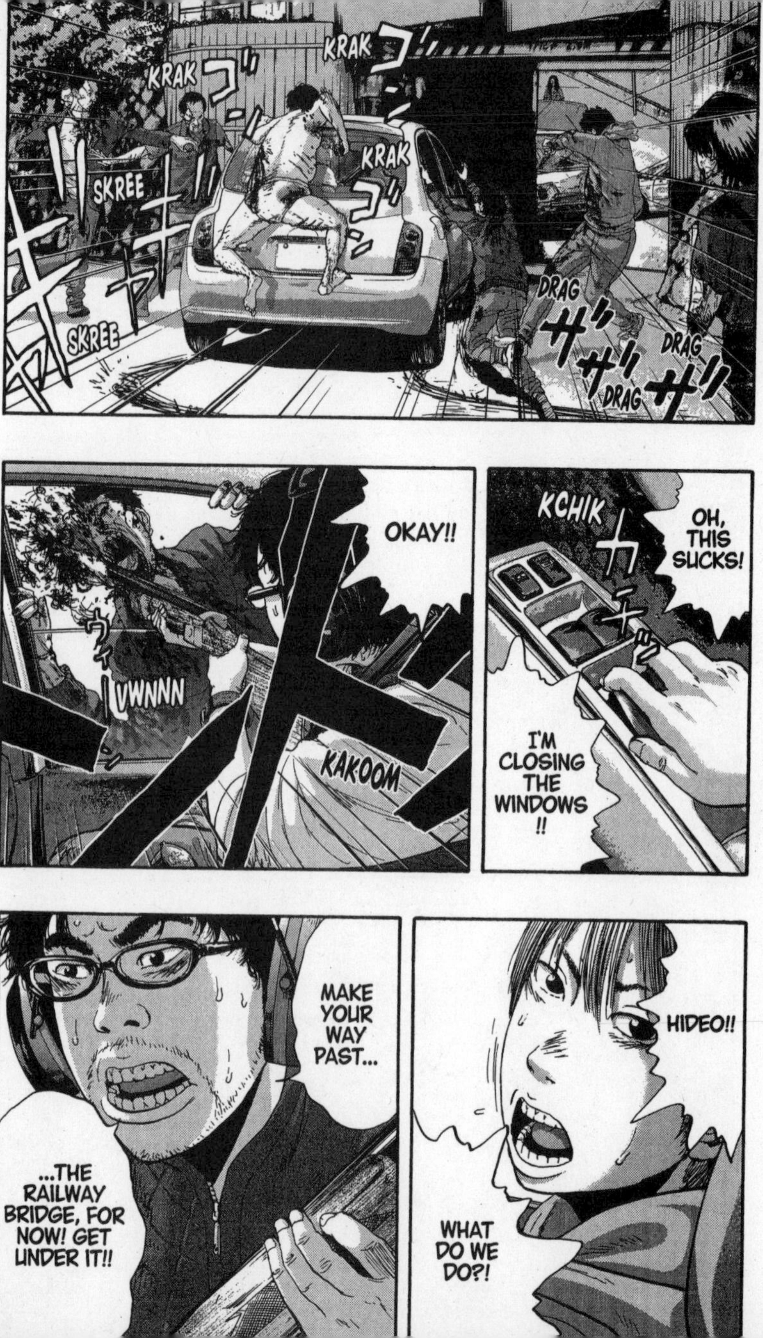
KRAK
KRAK
KRAK
SKREE
SKREE
DRAG
DRAG
DRAG
KCHIK
OH, THIS SUCKS!
I'M CLOSING THE WINDOWS!!
OKAY!!
VWNNN
KAKOOM
HIDEO!!
WHAT DO WE DO?!
MAKE YOUR WAY PAST...
...THE RAILWAY BRIDGE, FOR NOW! GET UNDER IT!!

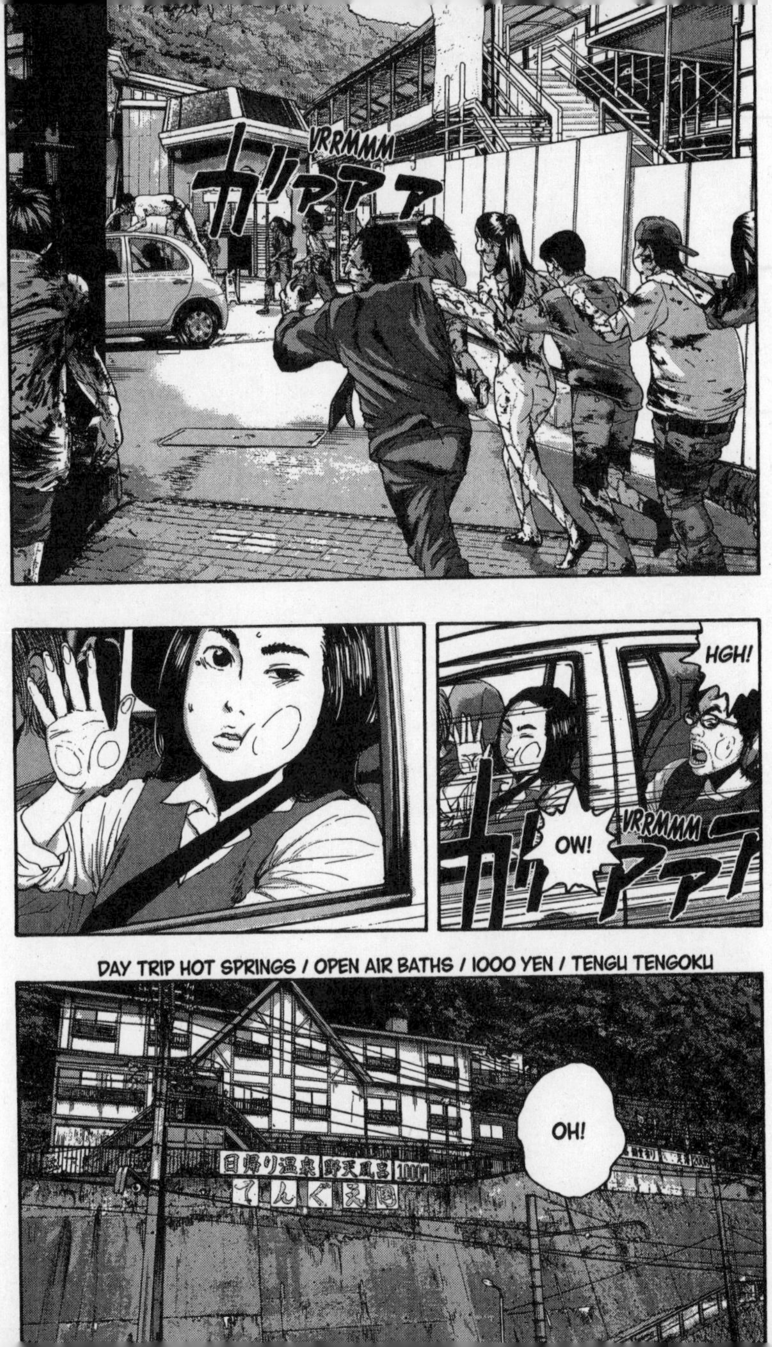
VRRMMM
HGH!
OW!
VRRMMM
DAY TRIP HOT SPRINGS / OPEN AIR BATHS / 1000 YEN / TENGU TENGOKU
日帰り温泉 野天風呂 1000円
てんぐ天国
OH!

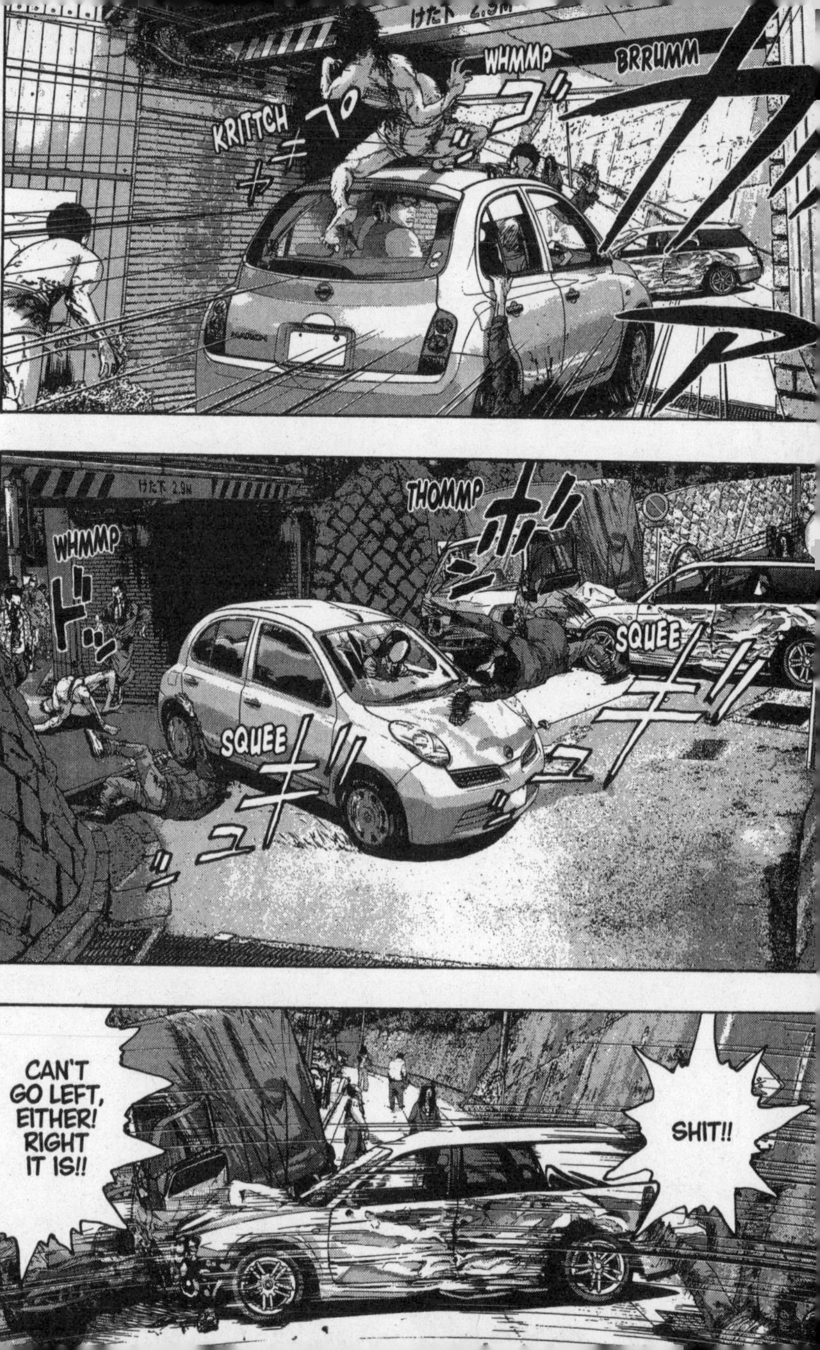
BRRUMM
WHMMP
KRITTCH
THOMMP
SQUEE
WHMMP
SQUEE
SHIT!!
CAN'T GO LEFT, EITHER! RIGHT IT IS!!

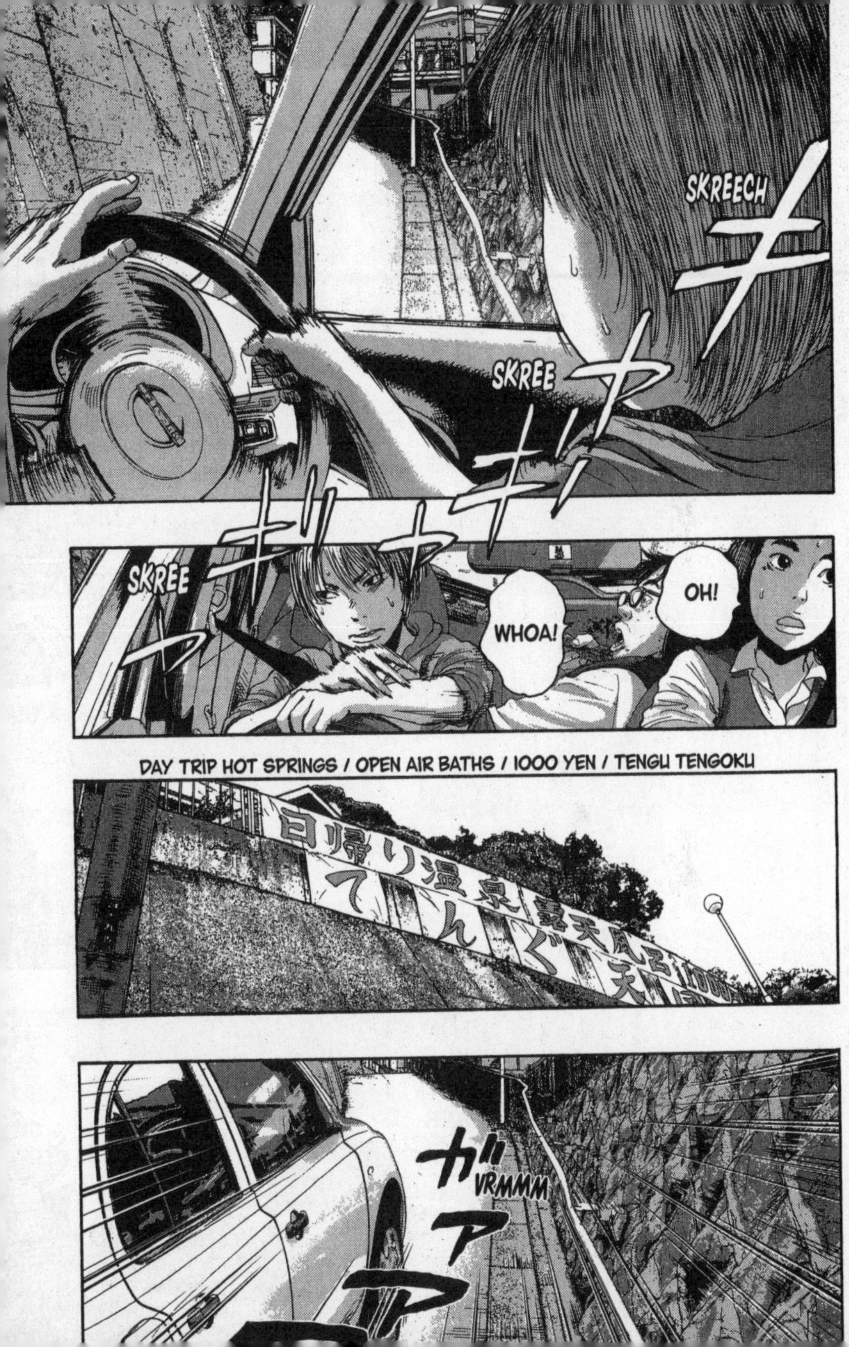
SKREECH
SKREE
OH!
WHOA!
SKREE
DAY TRIP HOT SPRINGS / OPEN AIR BATHS / 1000 YEN / TENGU TENGOKU
VRMMM

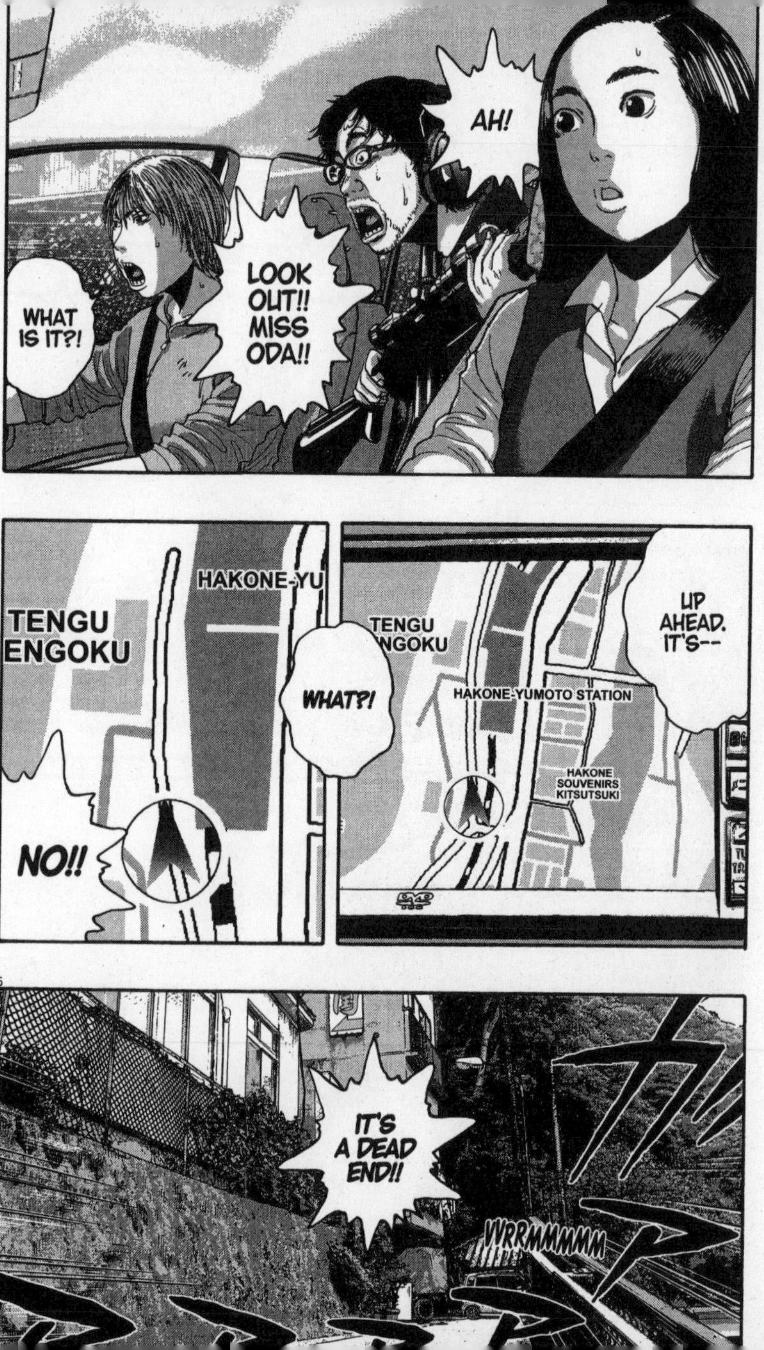
AH!
LOOK OUT!! MISS ODA!!
WHAT IS IT?!
UP AHEAD. IT'S--
WHAT?!
TENGU
NGOKU
HAKONE-YUMOTO STATION
HAKONE SOUVENIRS KITSUTSUKI
HAKONE-YU
TENGU ENGOKU
NO!!
IT'S A DEAD END!!
VVRRMMMMM

6

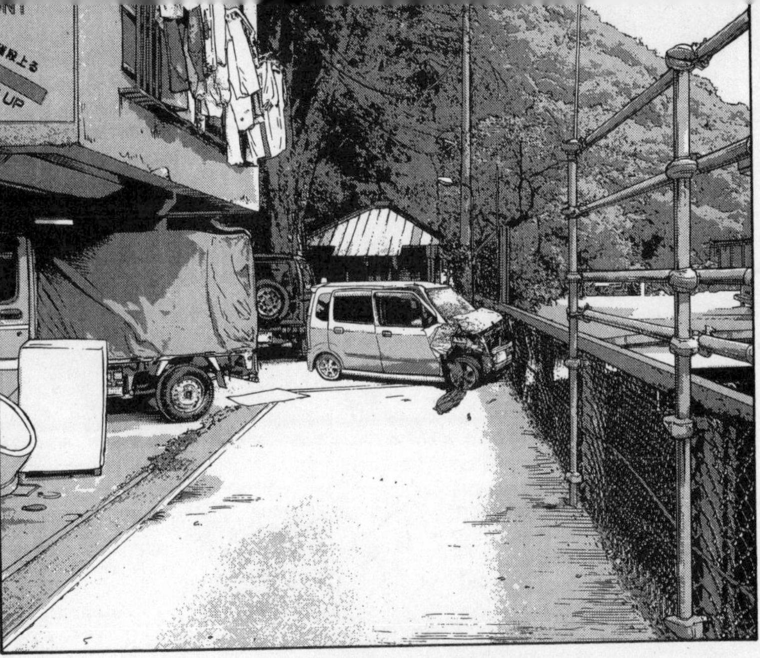

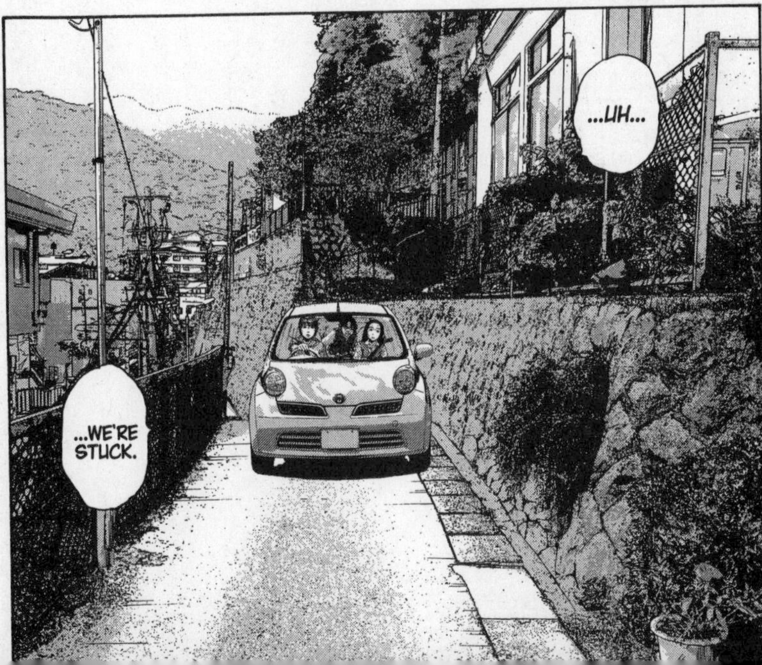
...UH...
...WE'RE STUCK.

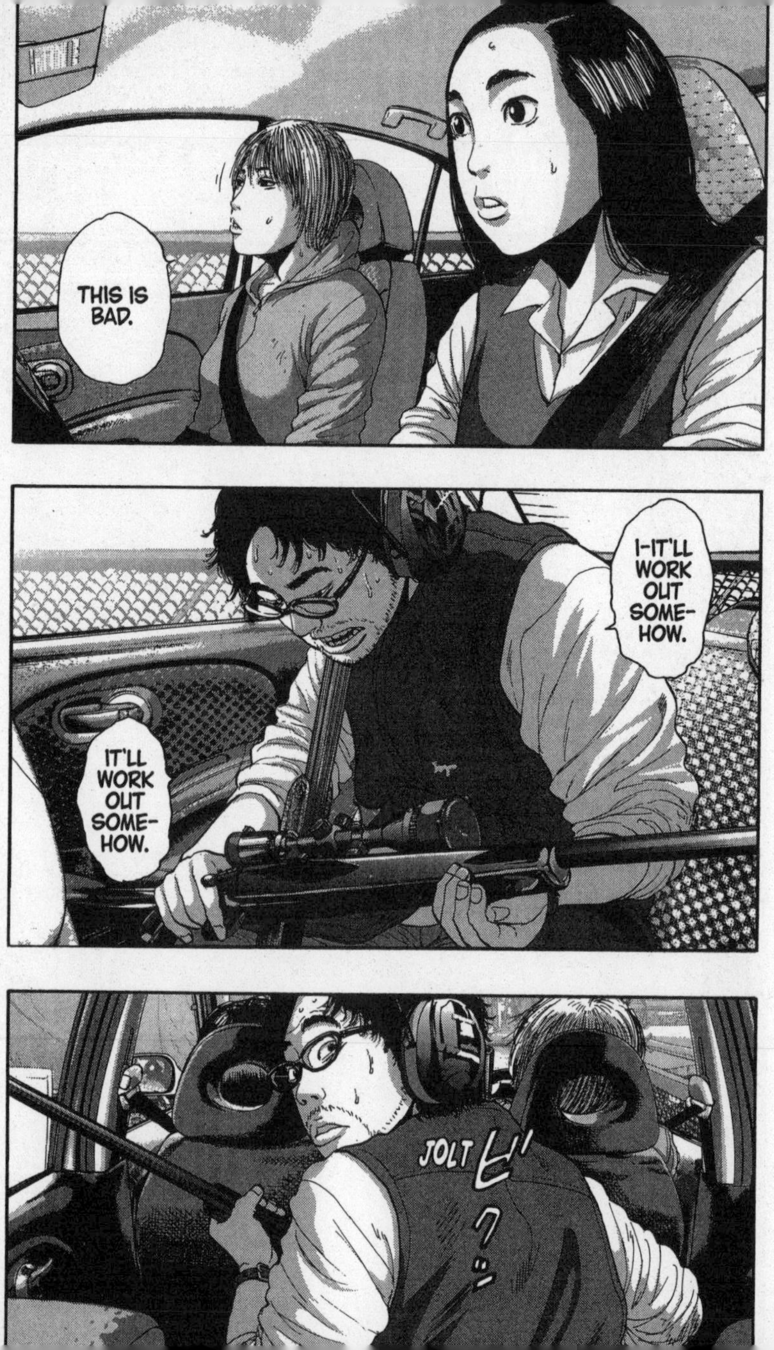
THIS IS BAD.
I-IT'LL WORK OUT SOME-HOW.
IT'LL WORK OUT SOME-HOW.
JOLT
ビクッ

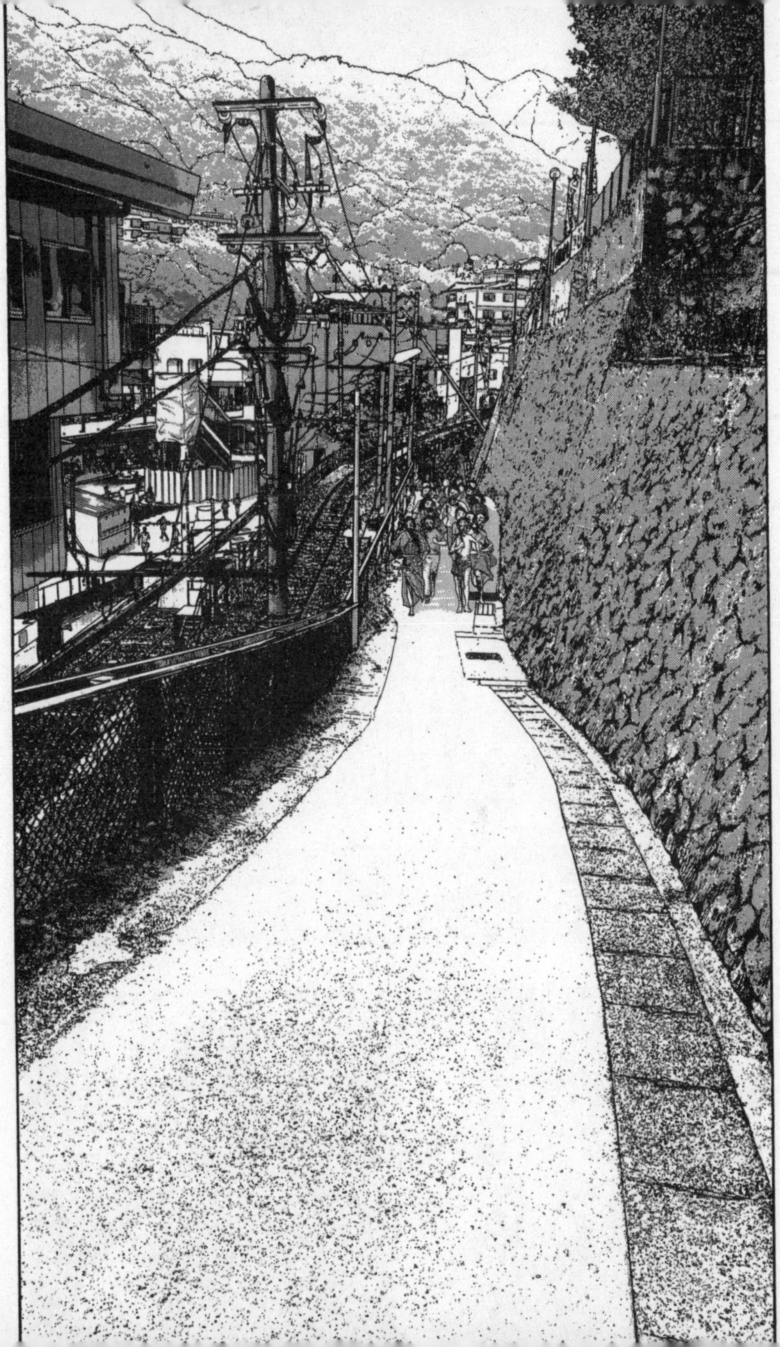

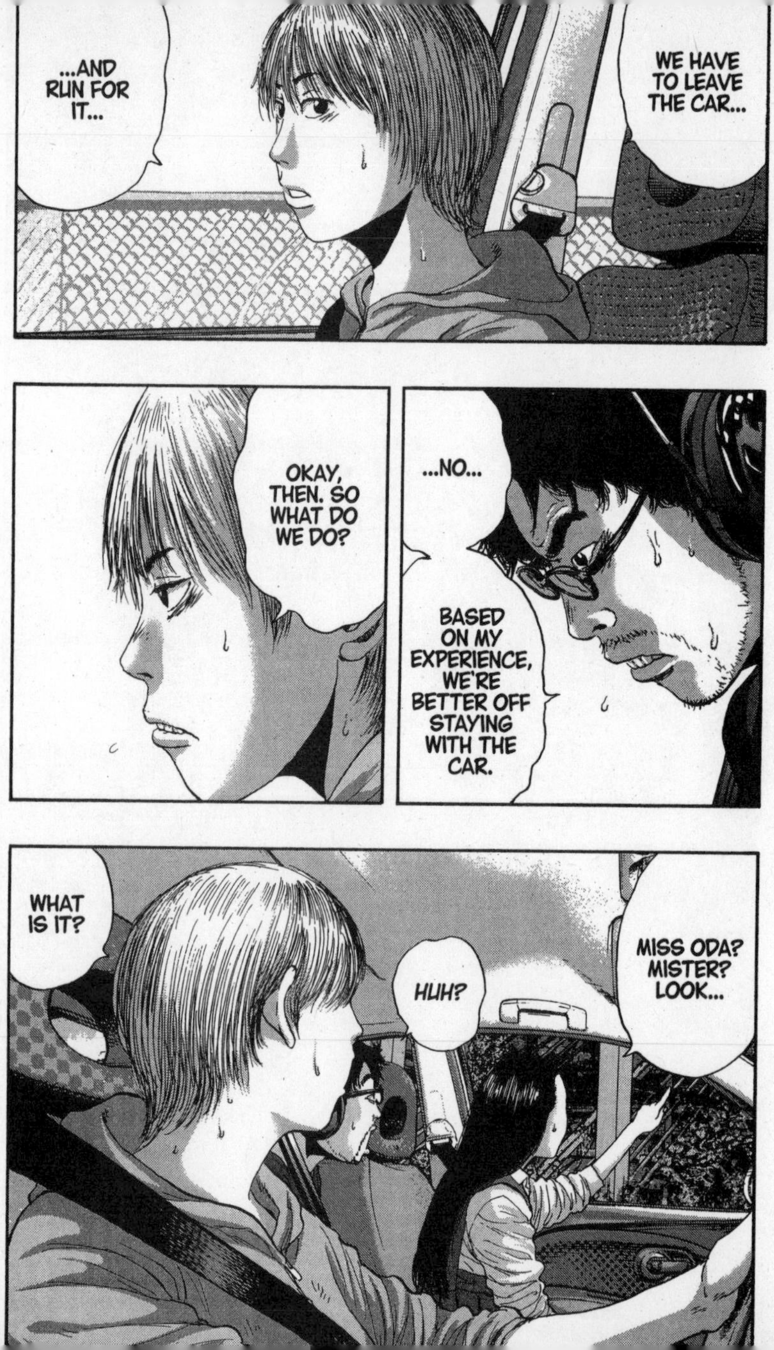
WE HAVE TO LEAVE THE CAR...
...AND RUN FOR IT...
...NO...
BASED ON MY EXPERIENCE, WE'RE BETTER OFF STAYING WITH THE CAR.
OKAY, THEN. SO WHAT DO WE DO?
MISS ODA? MISTER? LOOK...
HUH?
WHAT IS IT?

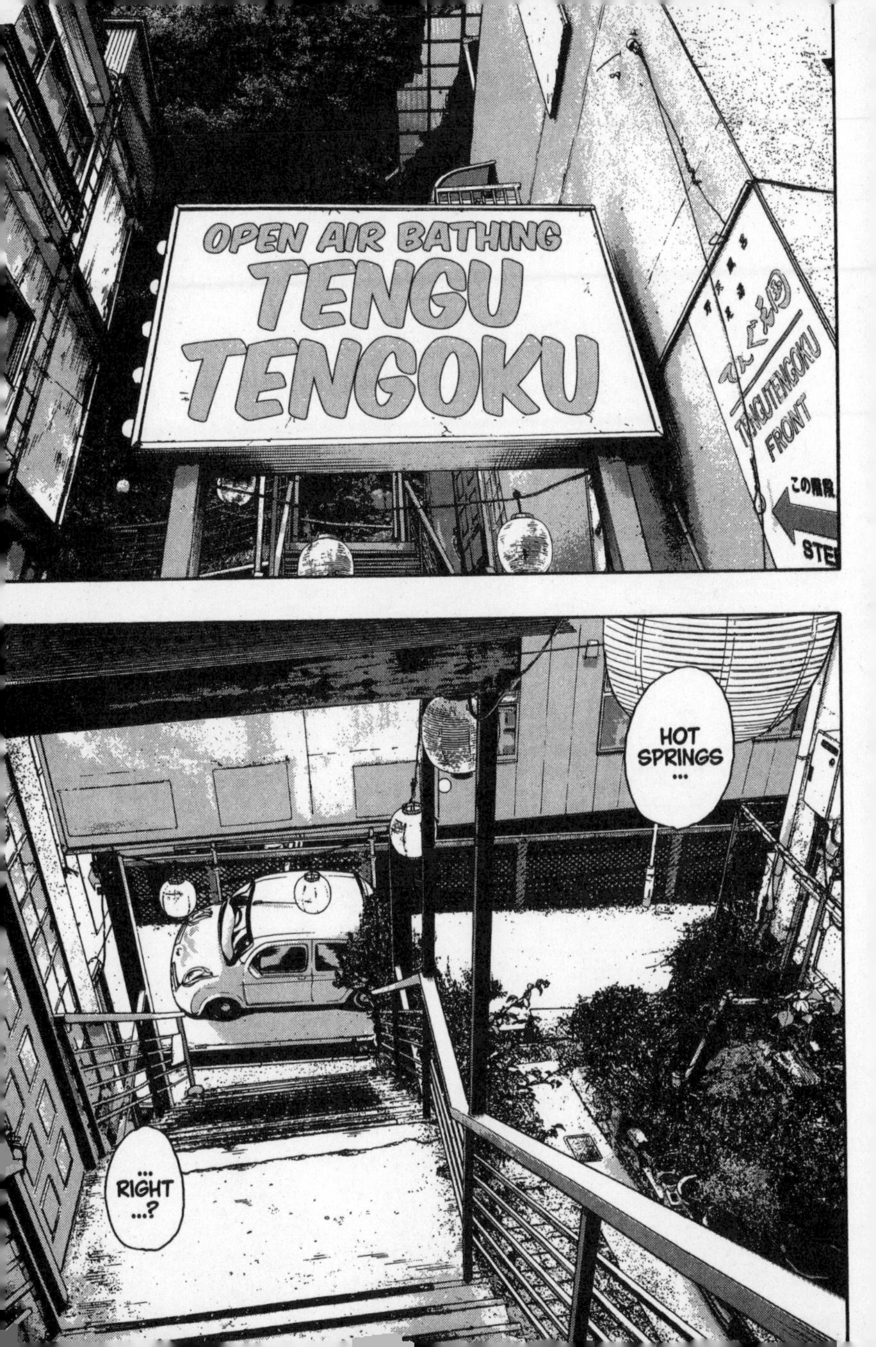
OPEN AIR BATHING
TENGU TENGOKU
TENGUTENGOKU
FRONT
この階段
HOT SPRINGS ...
... RIGHT ...?

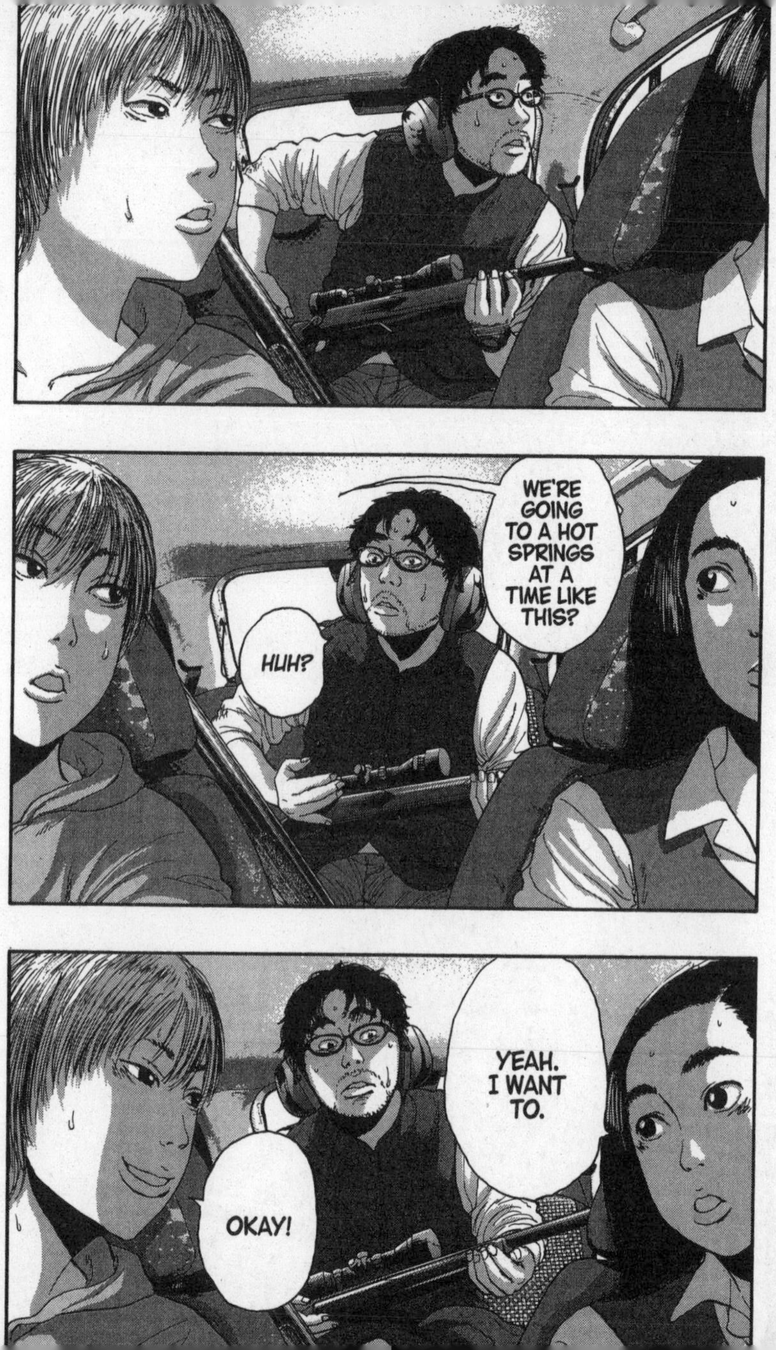
WE'RE GOING TO A HOT SPRINGS AT A TIME LIKE THIS?
HUH?
YEAH. I WANT TO.
OKAY!

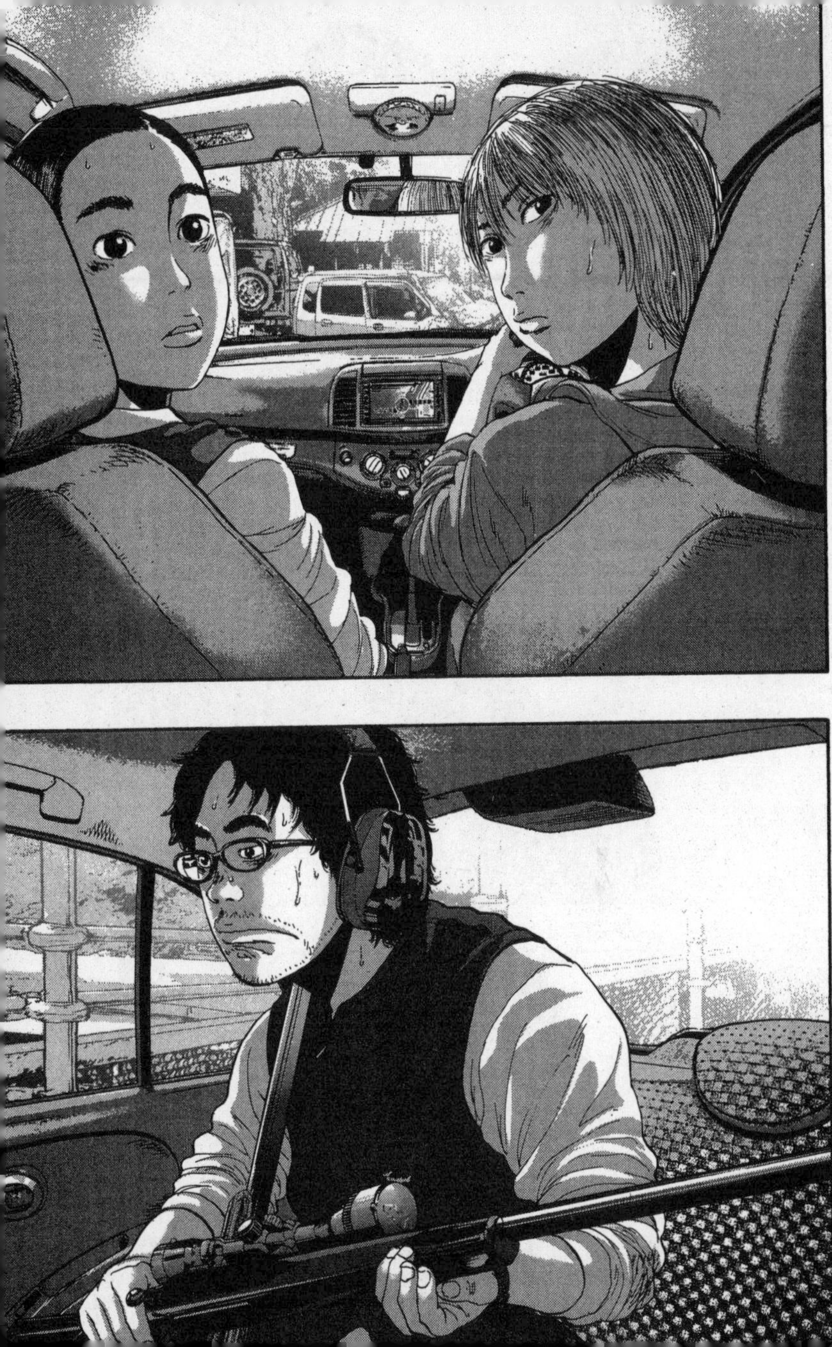

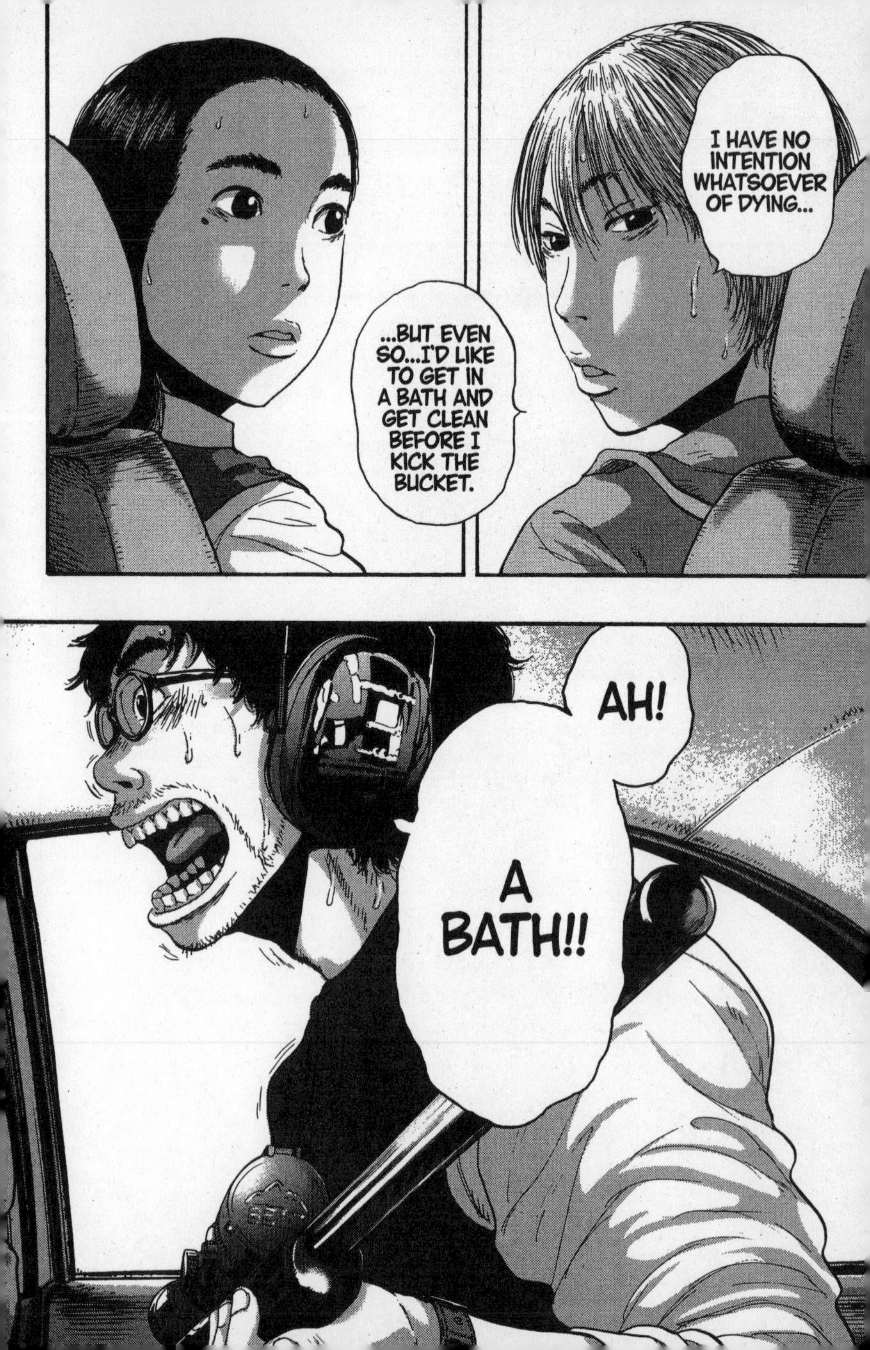
I HAVE NO INTENTION WHATSOEVER OF DYING...
...BUT EVEN SO...I'D LIKE TO GET IN A BATH AND GET CLEAN BEFORE I KICK THE BUCKET.
AH!
A BATH!!

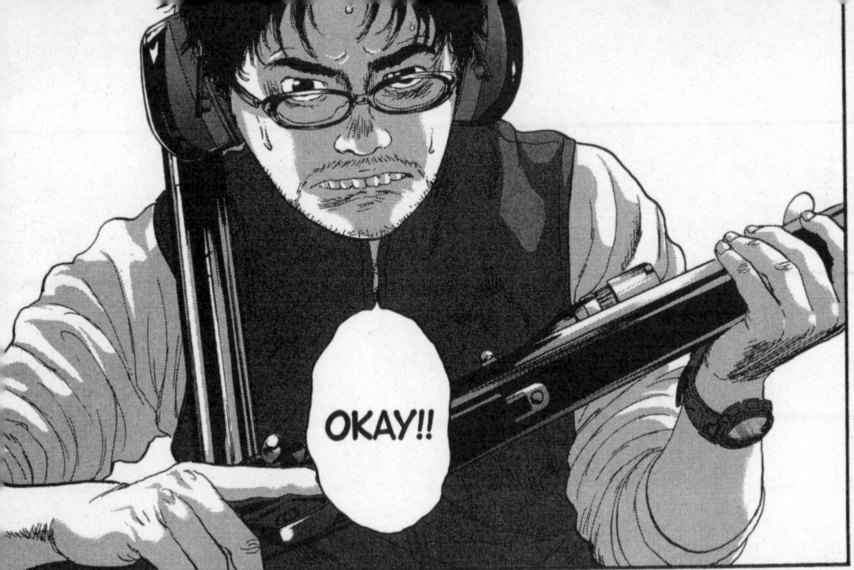
OKAY!!
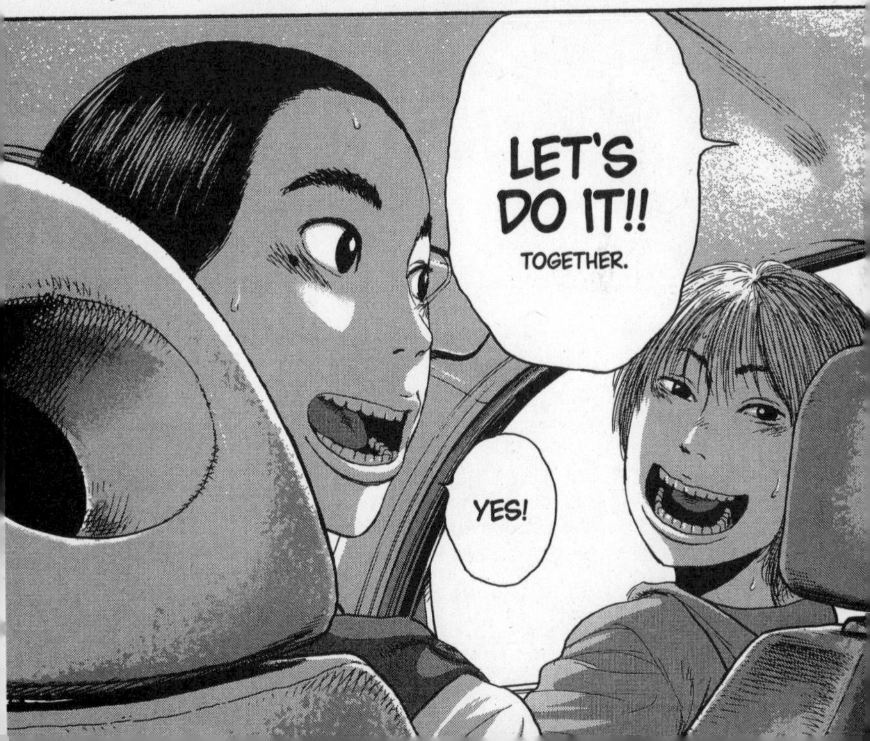
LET'S DO IT!!
TOGETHER.
YES!

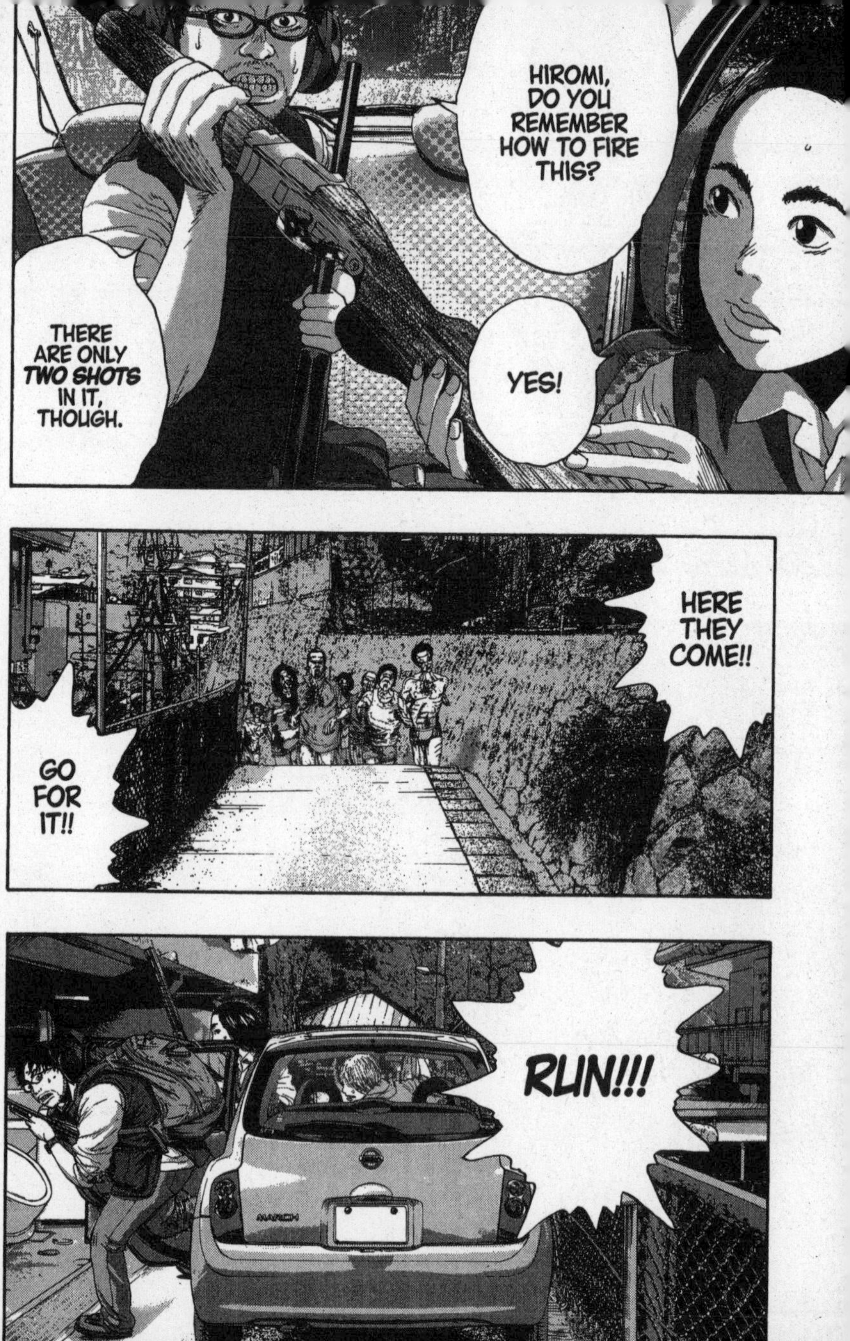
HIROMI, DO YOU REMEMBER HOW TO FIRE THIS?
YES!
THERE ARE ONLY TWO SHOTS IN IT, THOUGH.
HERE THEY COME!!
GO FOR IT!!
RUN!!!

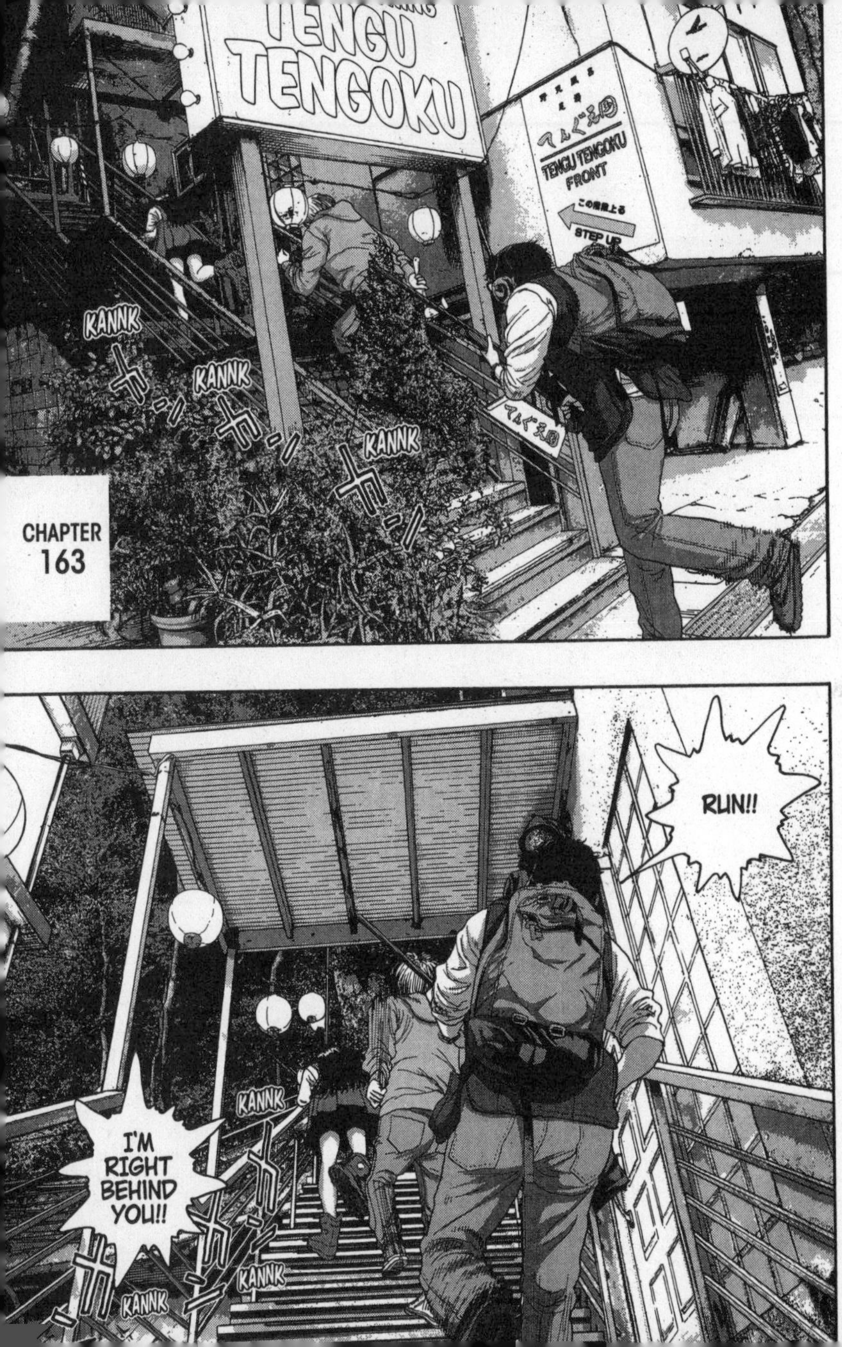
TENGU TENGOKU
TENGU TENGOKU FRONT
STEP UP
CHAPTER 163
KANNK
KANNK
KANNK
RUN!!
I'M RIGHT BEHIND YOU!!
KANNK
KANNK
KANNK

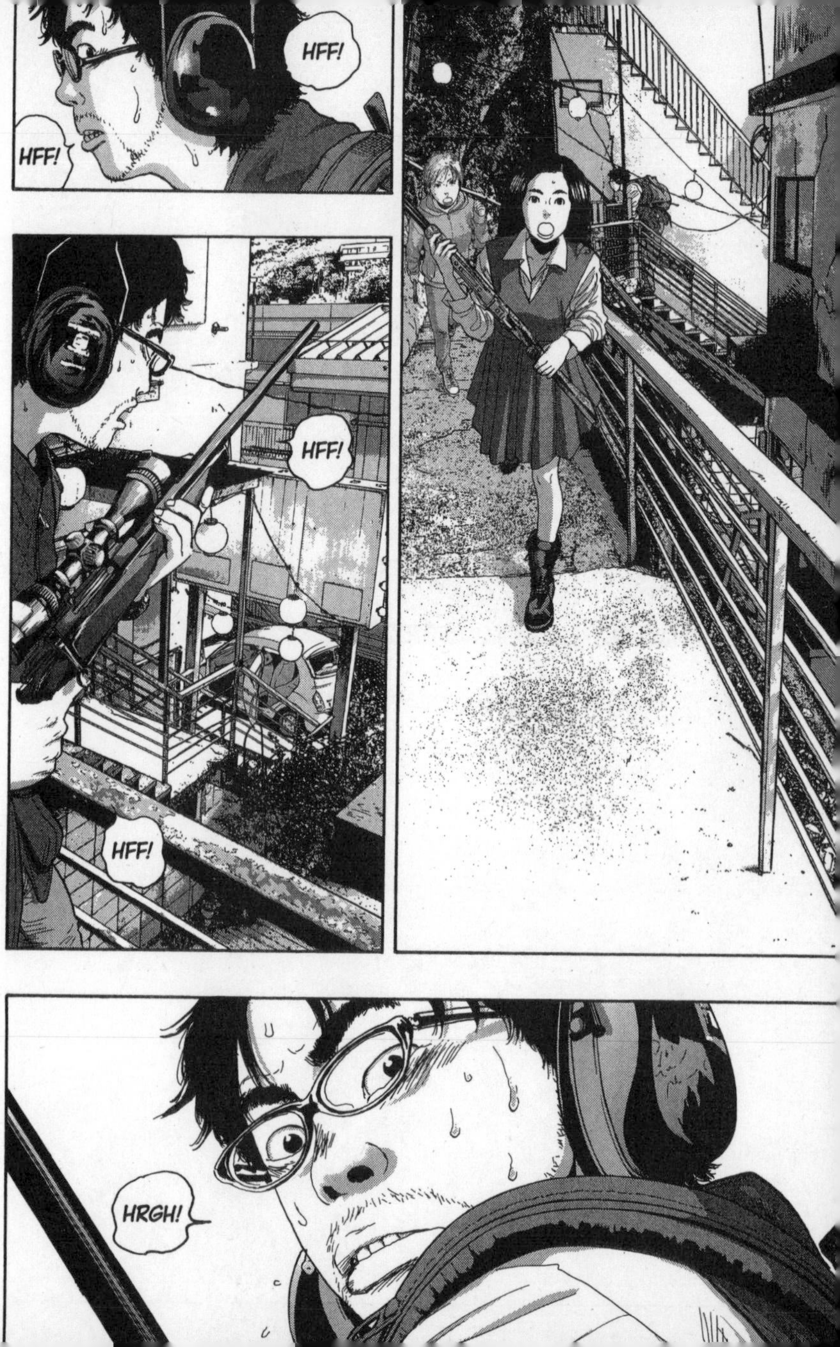
HFF!
HFF!
HFF!
HFF!
HRGH!

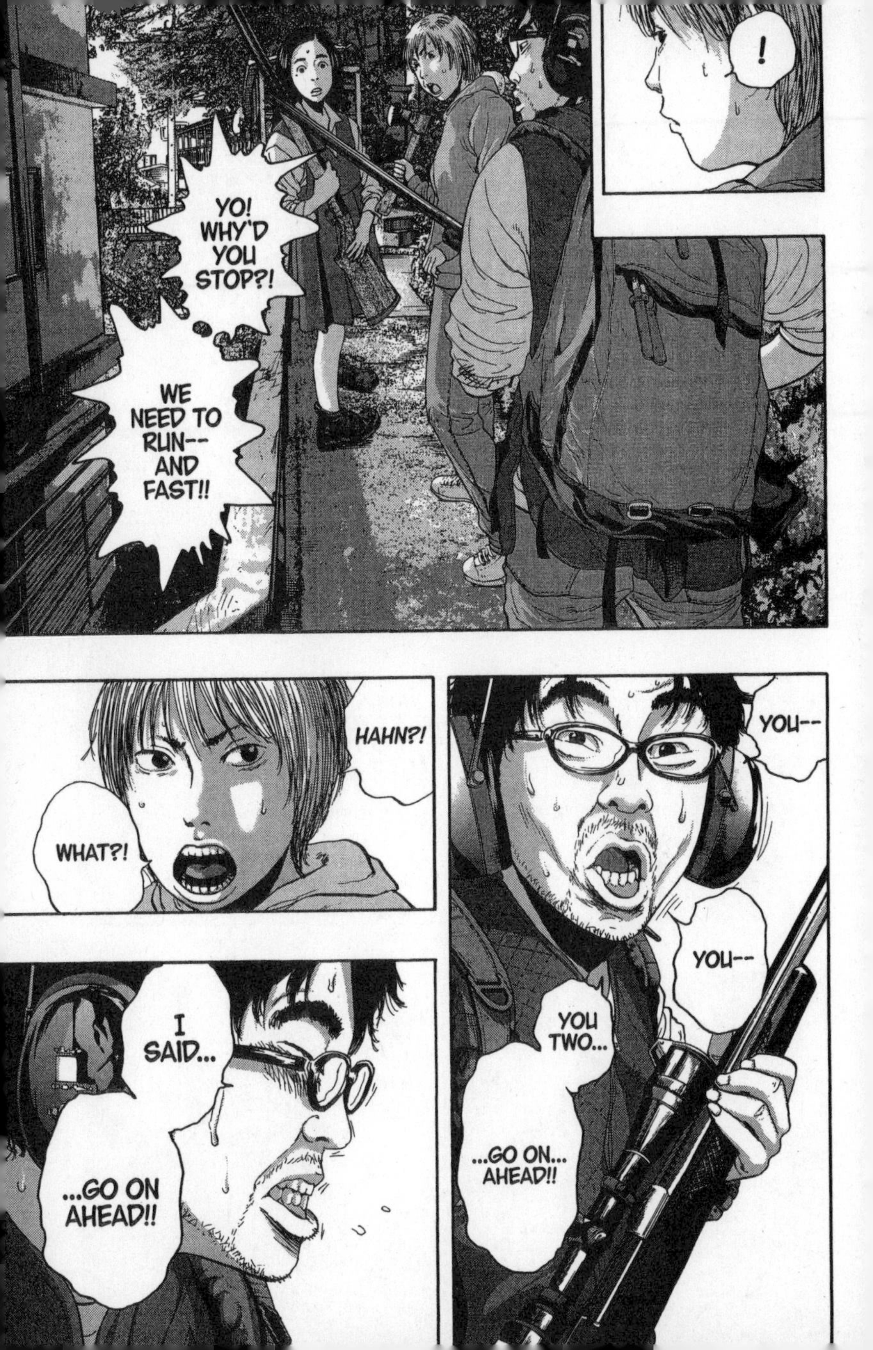
!
YO! WHY'D YOU STOP?!
WE NEED TO RUN-- AND FAST!!
YOU--
YOU--
YOU TWO...
...GO ON... AHEAD!!
HAHN?!
WHAT?!
I SAID...
...GO ON AHEAD!!

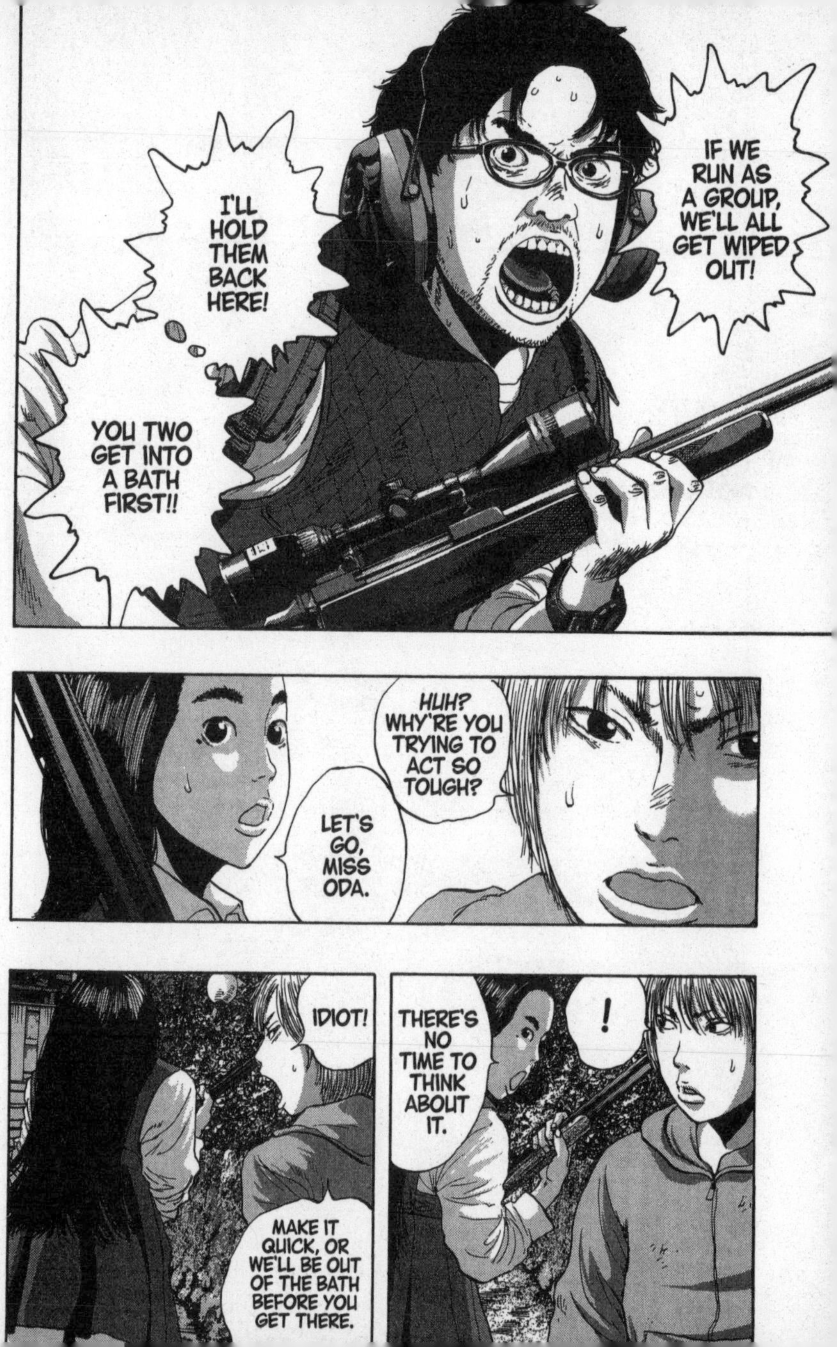
IF WE RUN AS A GROUP, WE'LL ALL GET WIPED OUT!
I'LL HOLD THEM BACK HERE!
YOU TWO GET INTO A BATH FIRST!!
HUH? WHY'RE YOU TRYING TO ACT SO TOUGH?
LET'S GO, MISS ODA.
!
THERE'S NO TIME TO THINK ABOUT IT.
IDIOT!
MAKE IT QUICK, OR WE'LL BE OUT OF THE BATH BEFORE YOU GET THERE.

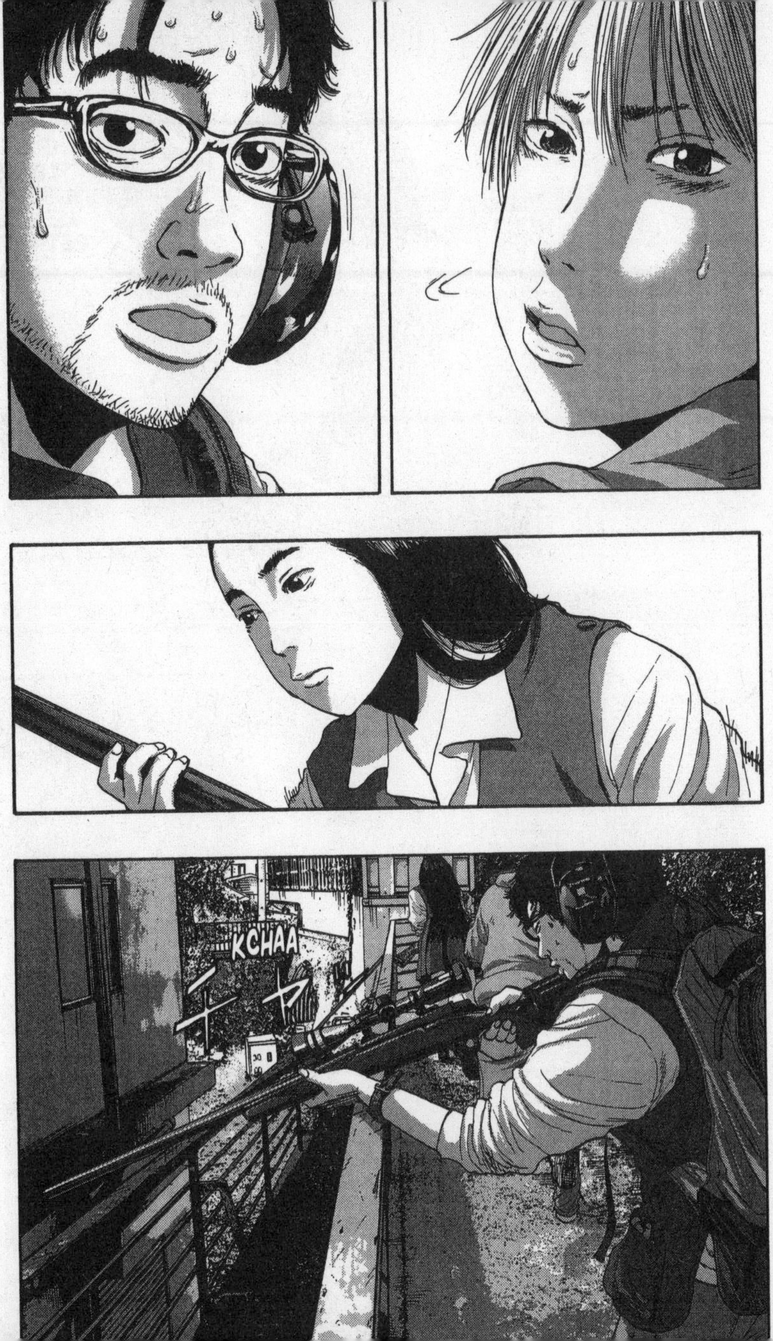
KCHAA

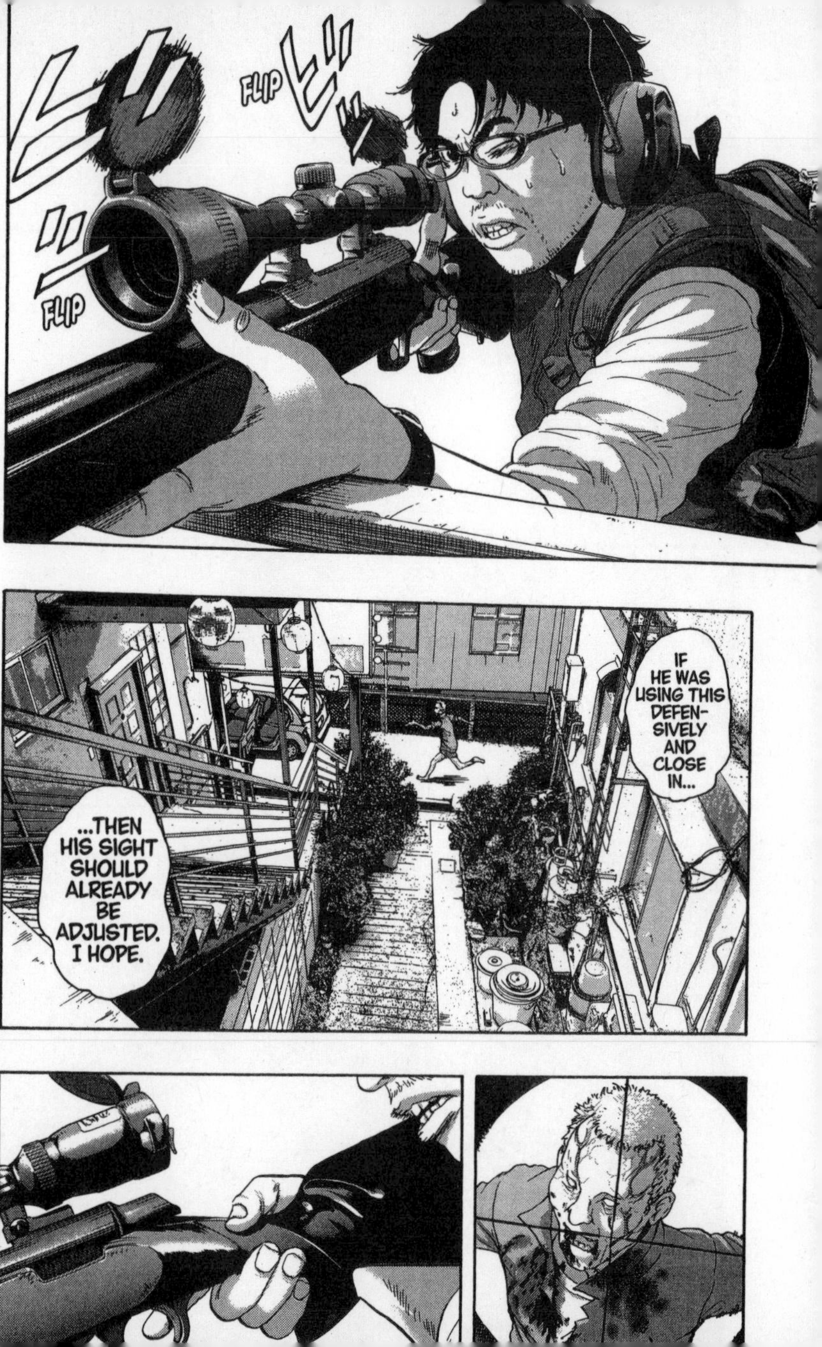
FLIP
FLIP
IF HE WAS USING THIS DEFENSIVELY AND CLOSE IN...
...THEN HIS SIGHT SHOULD ALREADY BE ADJUSTED. I HOPE.

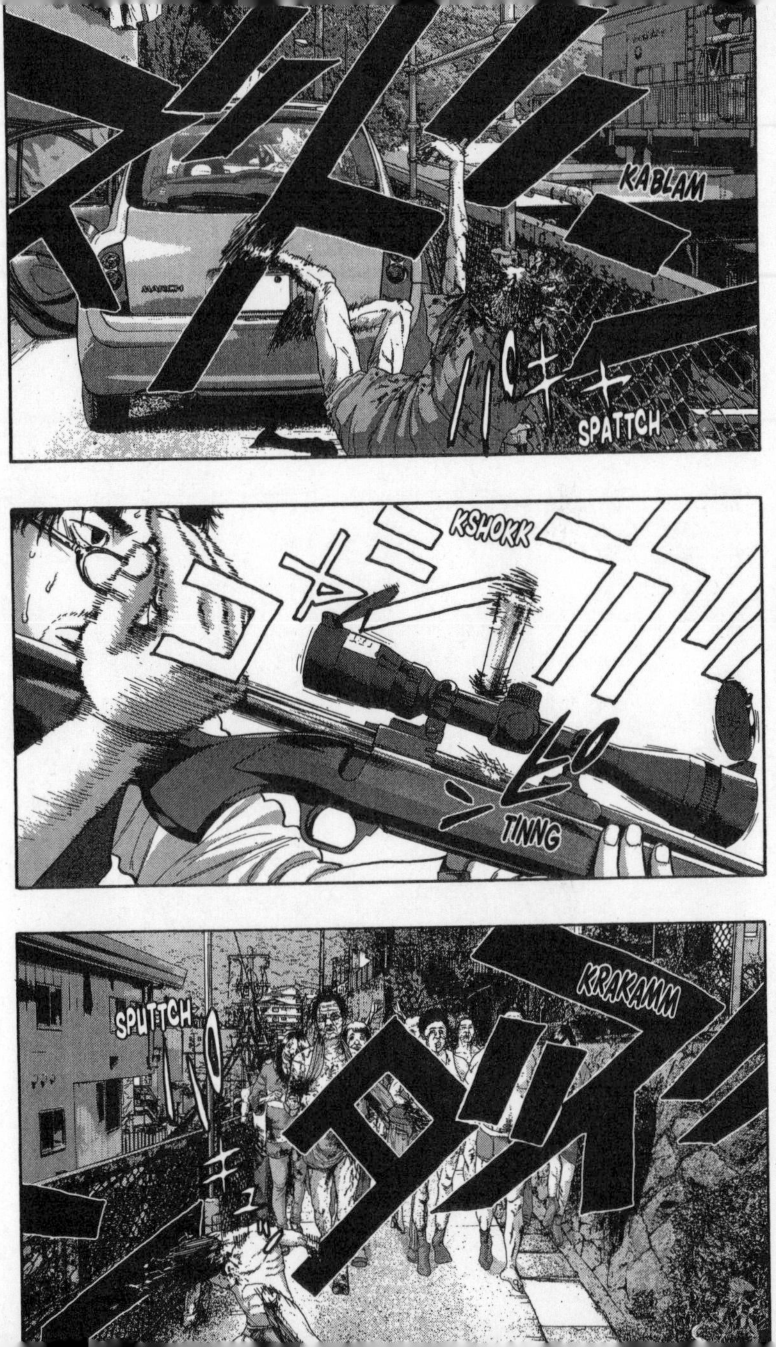
KABLAM
SPATTCH
KSHOKK
TINNG
KRAKAMM
SPUTTCH

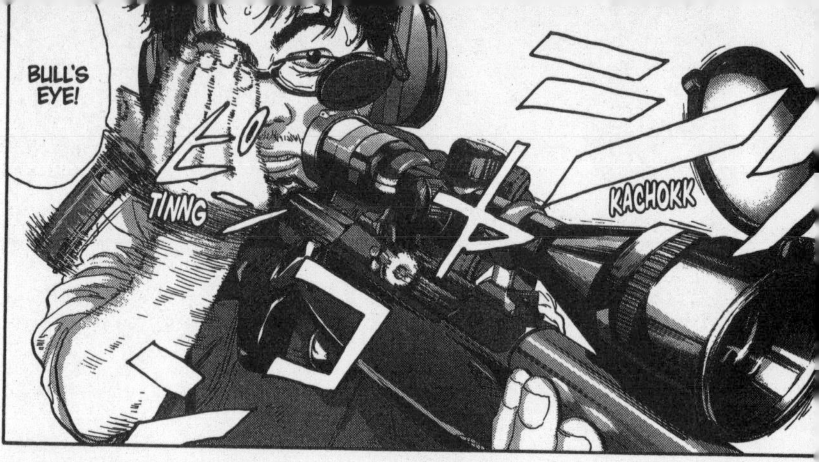
BULL'S EYE!
KACHOKK
TINNG
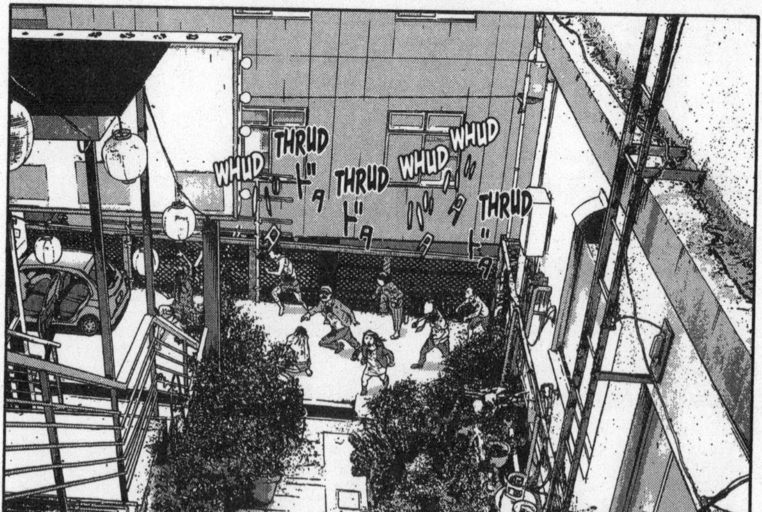
WHUD
THRUD
WHUD
THRUD
THRUD
WHUD
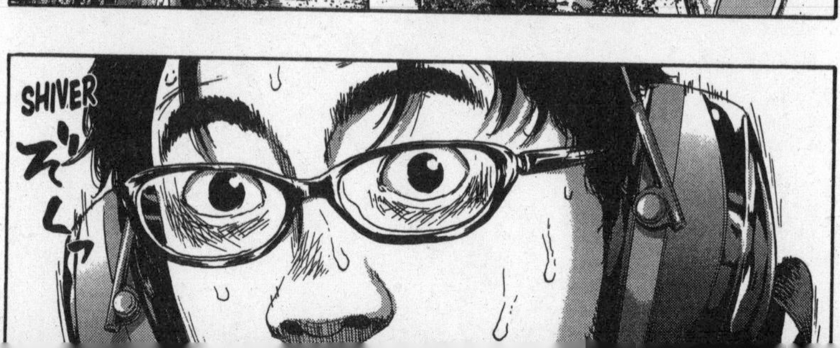
SHIVER

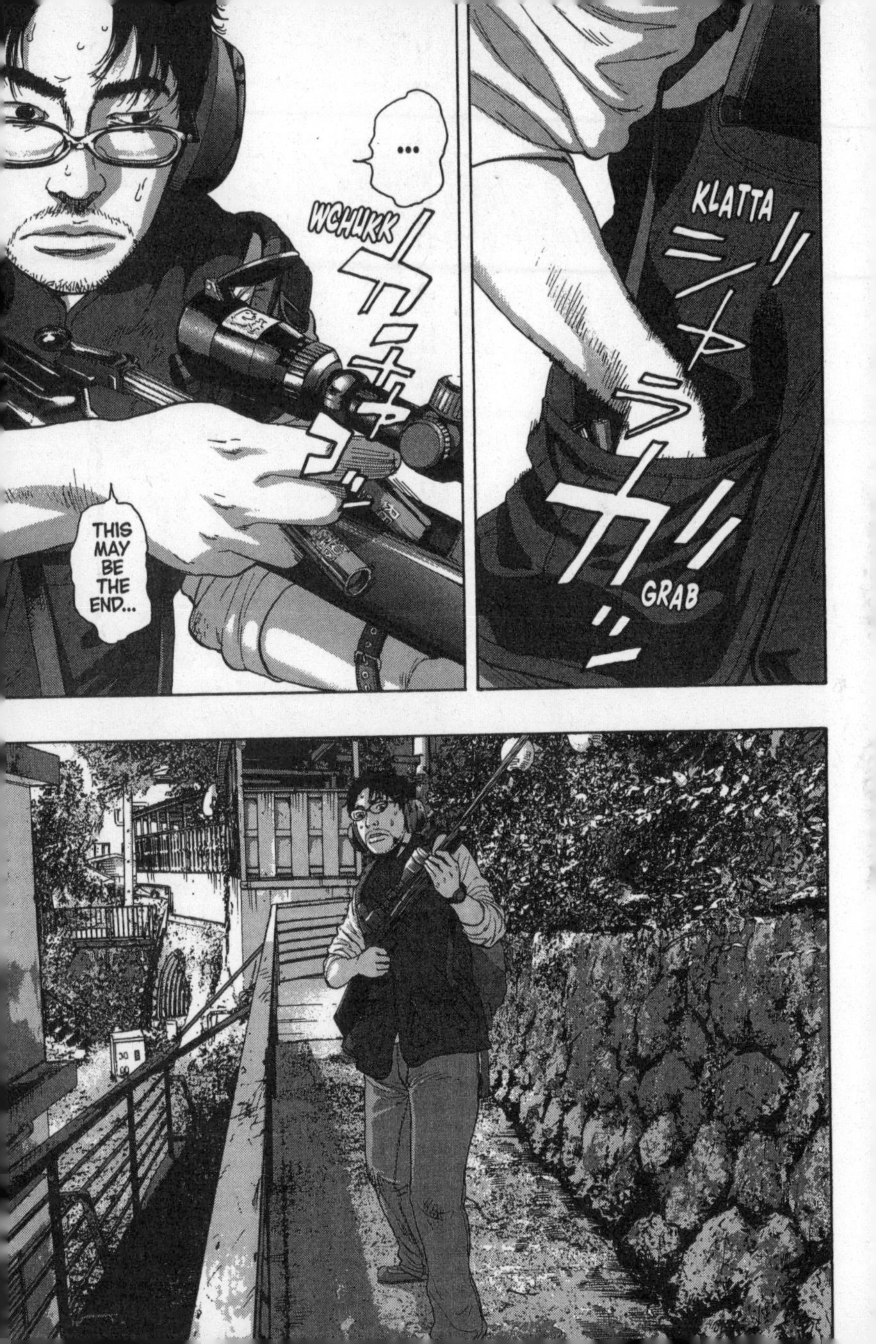
KLATTA
GRAB
...
WCHUKK
THIS MAY BE THE END...

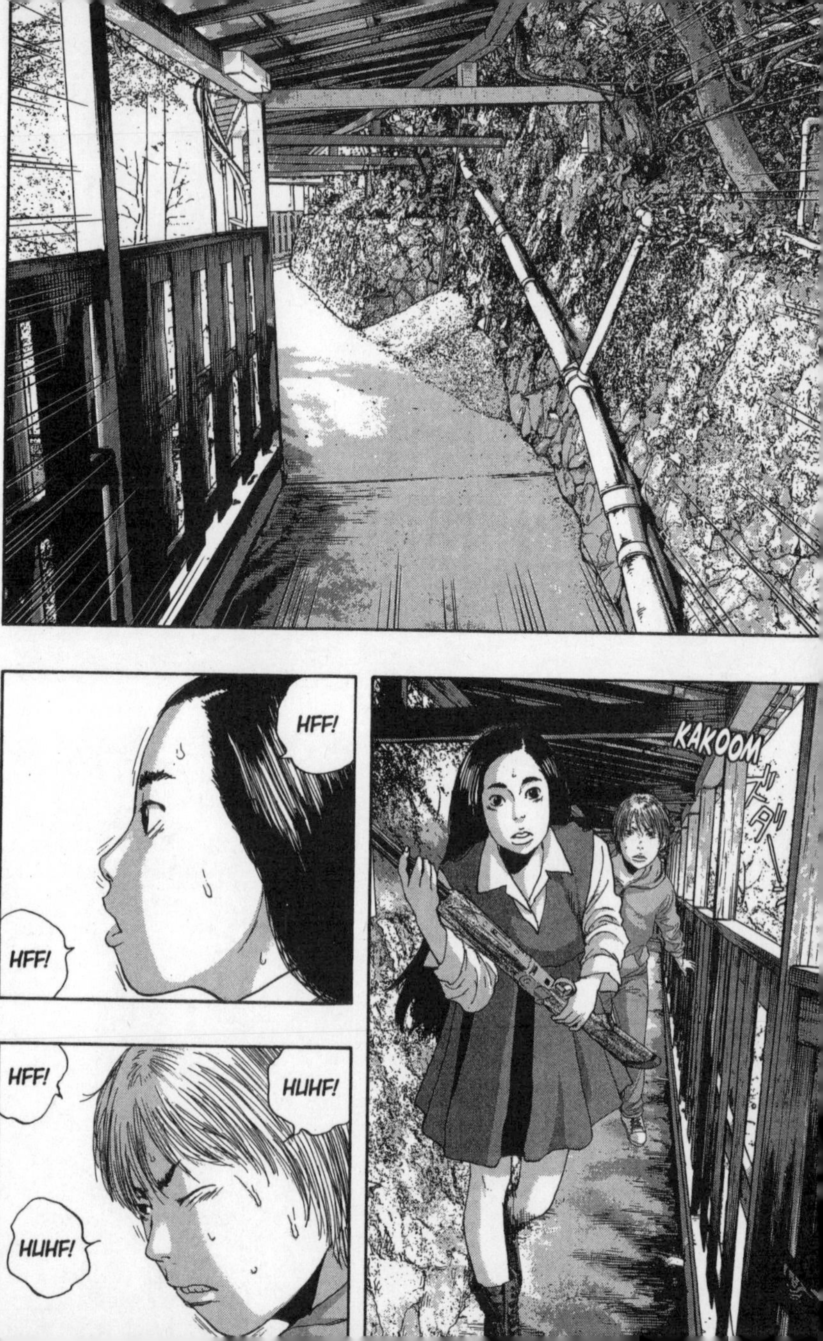
KAKOOM
HFF!
HFF!
HUHF!
HFF!
HUHF!

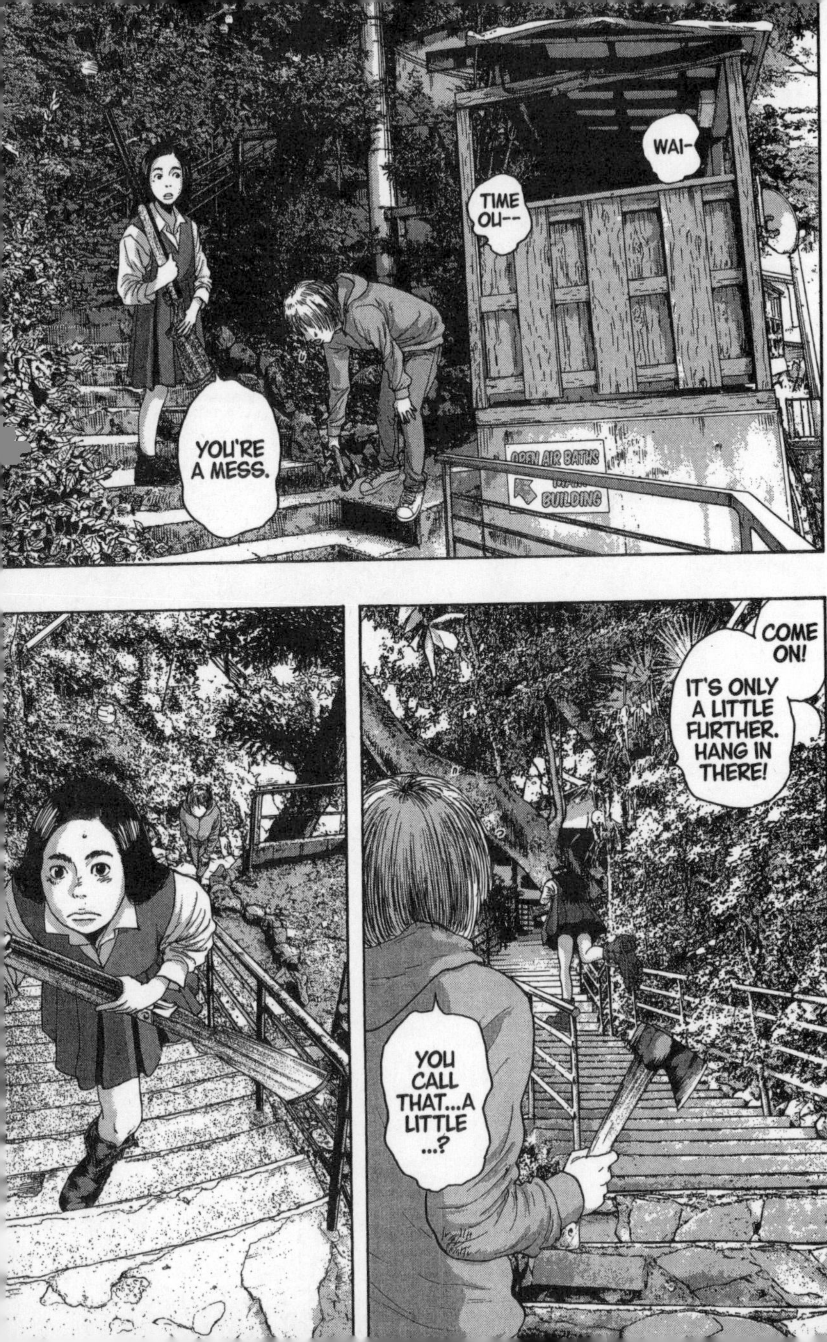
WAI-
TIME OU--
YOU'RE A MESS.
OPEN AIR BATHS
BUILDING
COME ON!
IT'S ONLY A LITTLE FURTHER. HANG IN THERE!
YOU CALL THAT...A LITTLE ...?

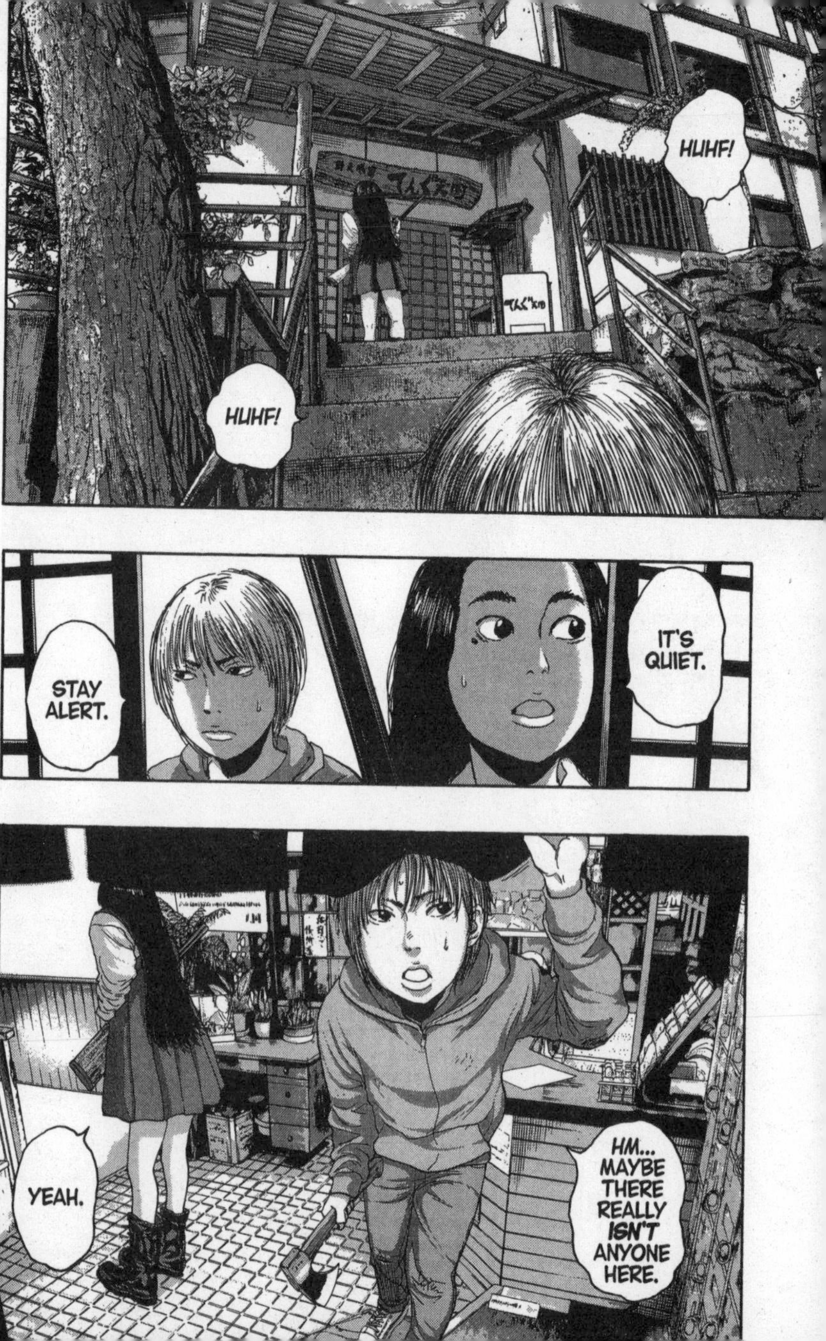
HUHF!
HUHF!
IT'S QUIET.
STAY ALERT.
HM... MAYBE THERE REALLY ***ISN'T*** ANYONE HERE.
YEAH.

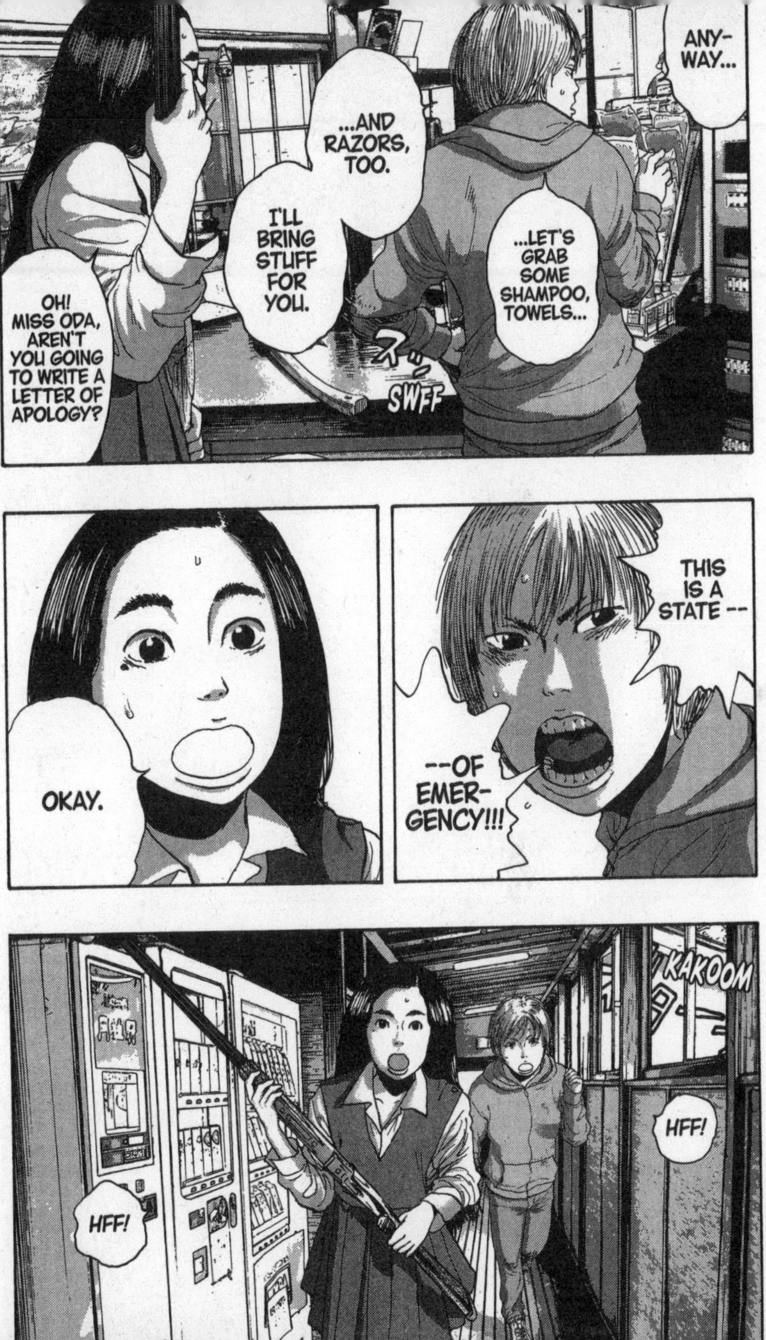
ANY-WAY...
...LET'S GRAB SOME SHAMPOO, TOWELS...
...AND RAZORS, TOO.
I'LL BRING STUFF FOR YOU.
SWFF
OH! MISS ODA, AREN'T YOU GOING TO WRITE A LETTER OF APOLOGY?
THIS IS A STATE --
--OF EMERGENCY!!!
OKAY.
KAKOOM
HFF!
HFF!

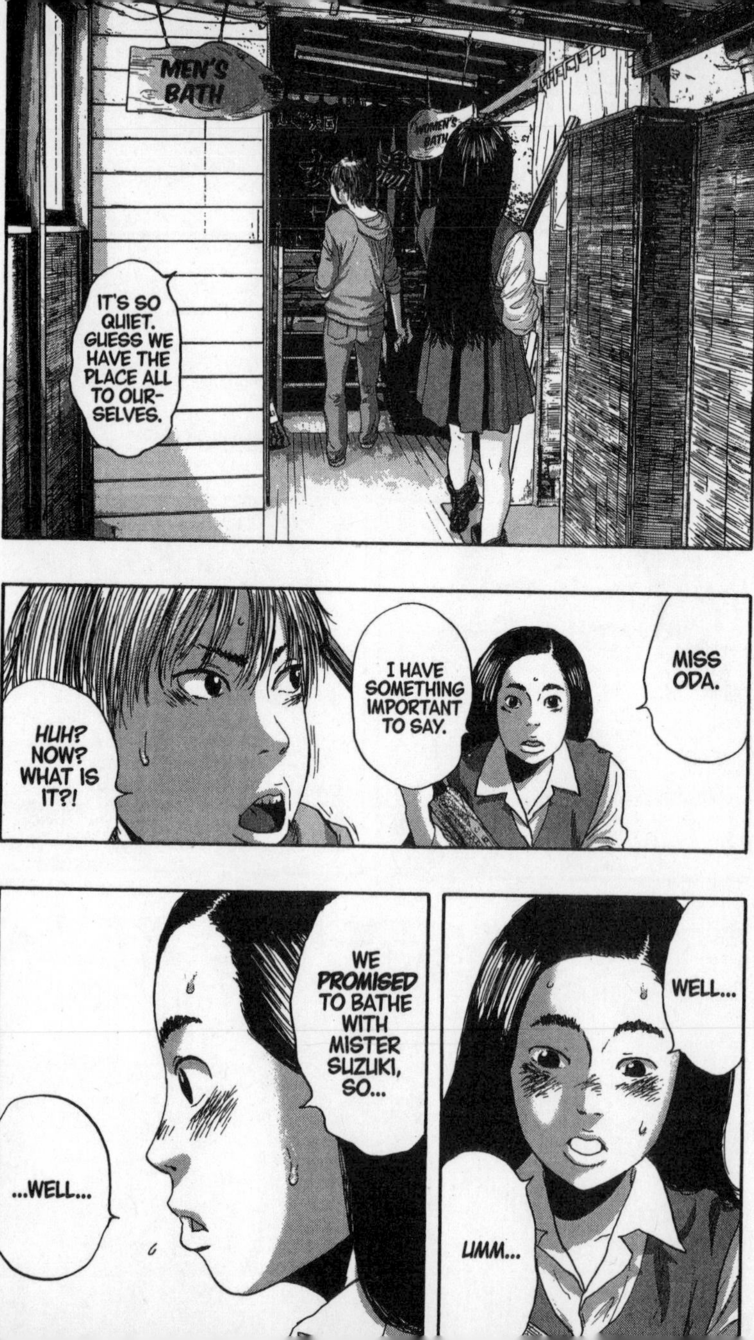
MEN'S BATH
WOMEN'S BATH
IT'S SO QUIET. GUESS WE HAVE THE PLACE ALL TO OUR-SELVES.
MISS ODA.
I HAVE SOMETHING IMPORTANT TO SAY.
HUH? NOW? WHAT IS IT?!
WELL...
UMM...
WE **PROMISED** TO BATHE WITH MISTER SUZUKI, SO...
...WELL...

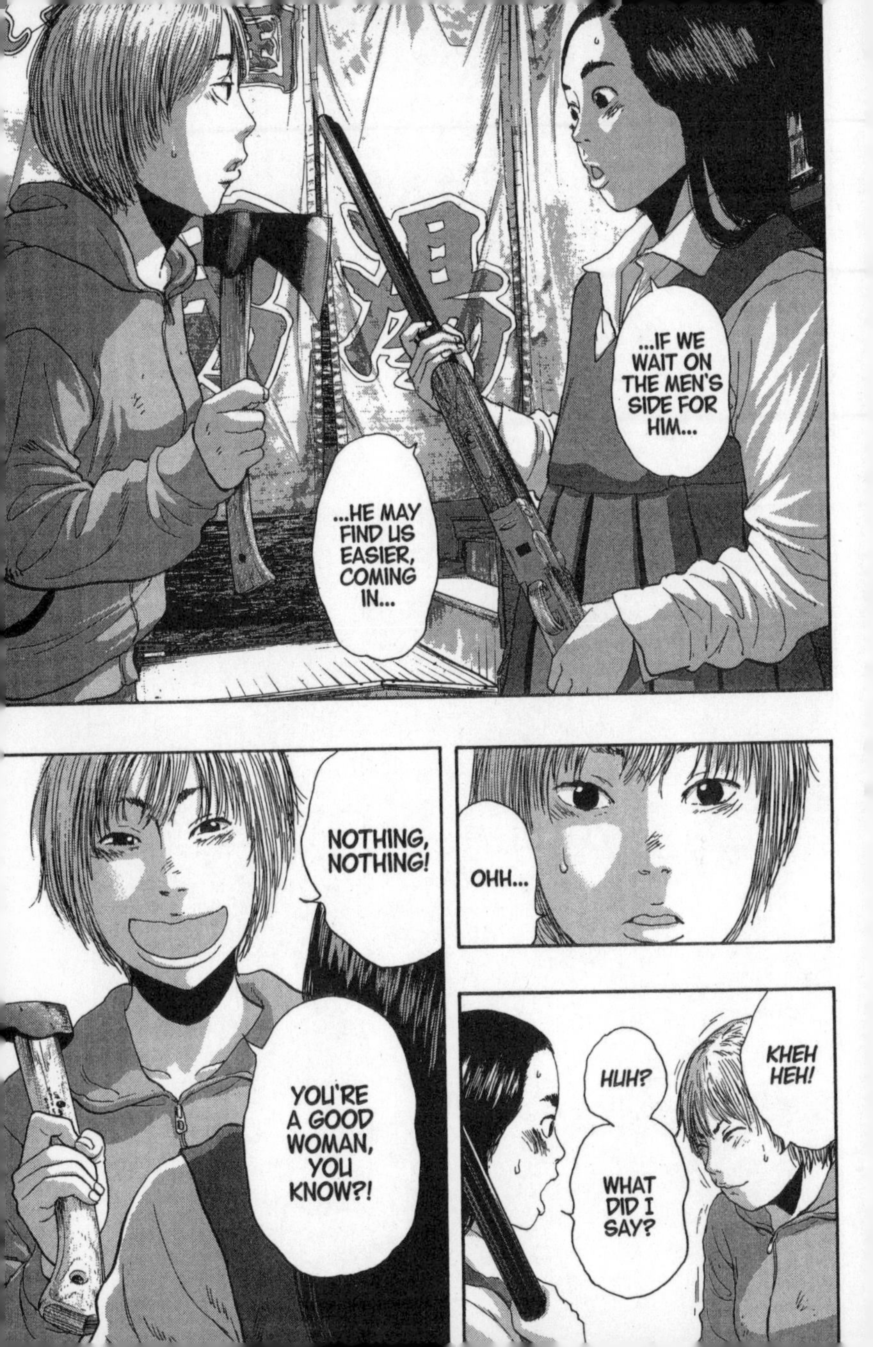
...IF WE WAIT ON THE MEN'S SIDE FOR HIM...
...HE MAY FIND US EASIER, COMING IN...
OHH...
KHEH HEH!
HUH?
WHAT DID I SAY?
NOTHING, NOTHING!
YOU'RE A GOOD WOMAN, YOU KNOW?!

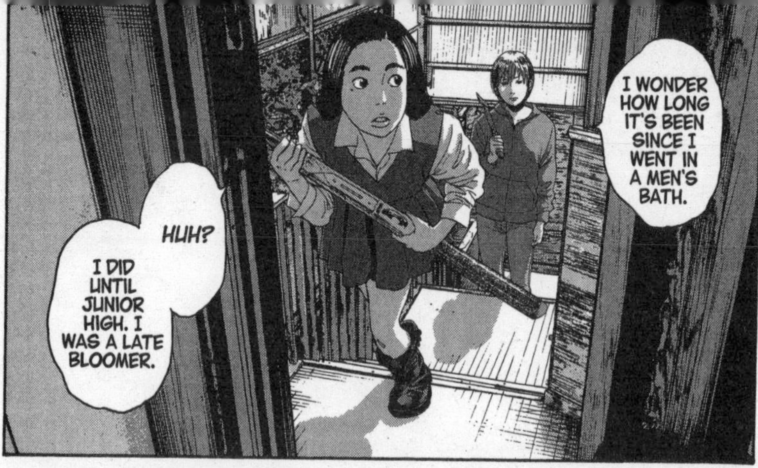
I WONDER HOW LONG IT'S BEEN SINCE I WENT IN A MEN'S BATH.
HUH?
I DID UNTIL JUNIOR HIGH. I WAS A LATE BLOOMER.
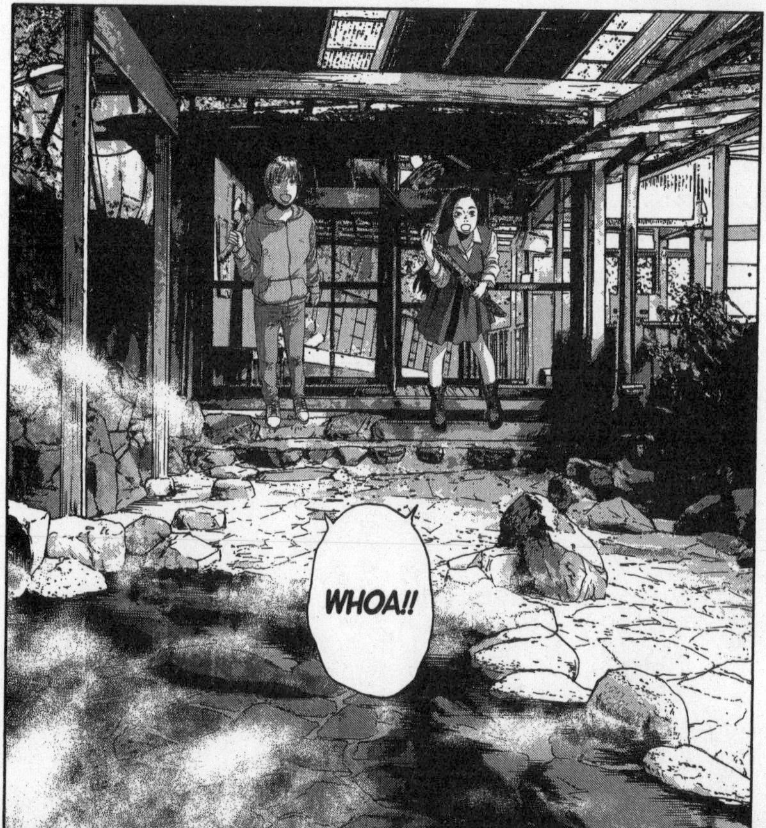
WHOA!!

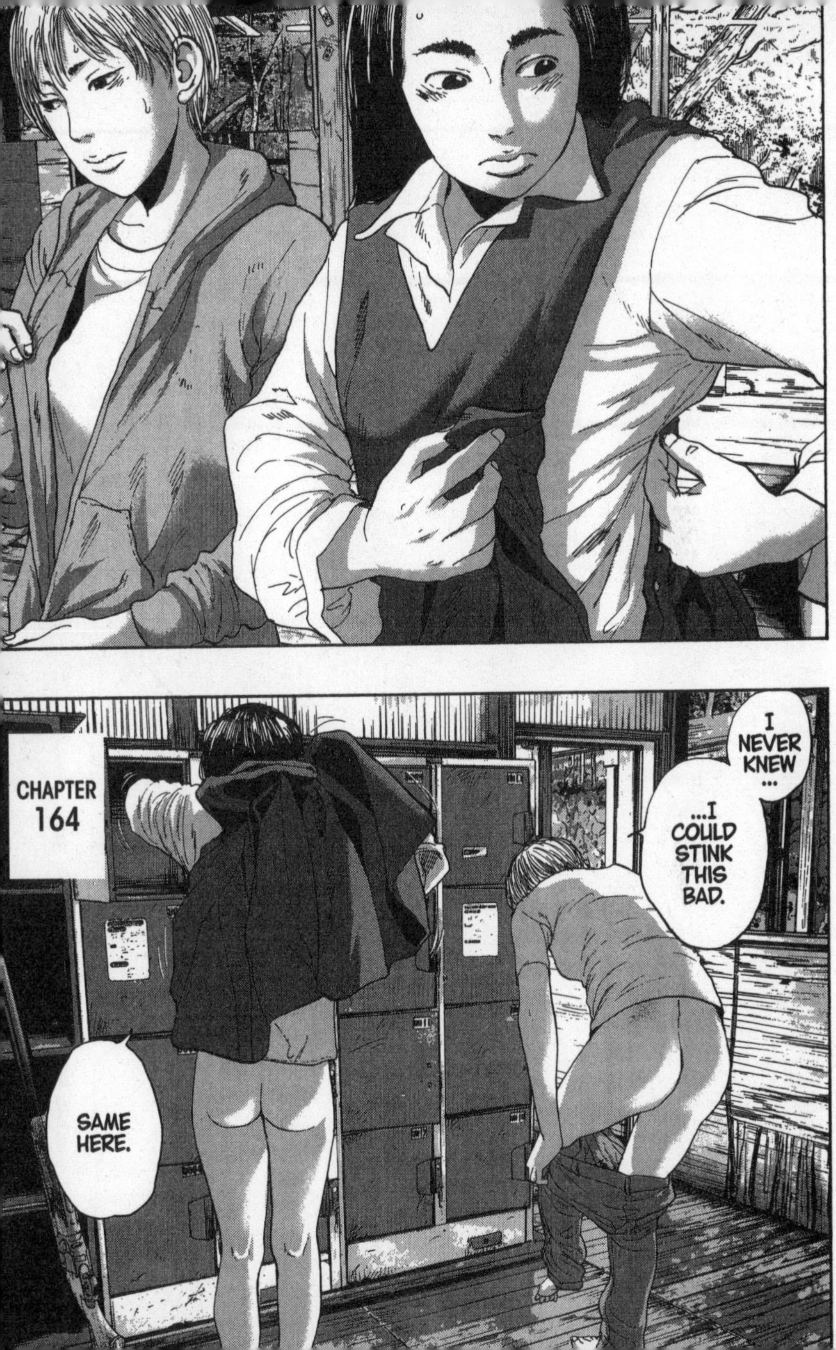

I NEVER KNEW...
...I COULD STINK THIS BAD.
CHAPTER 164
SAME HERE.

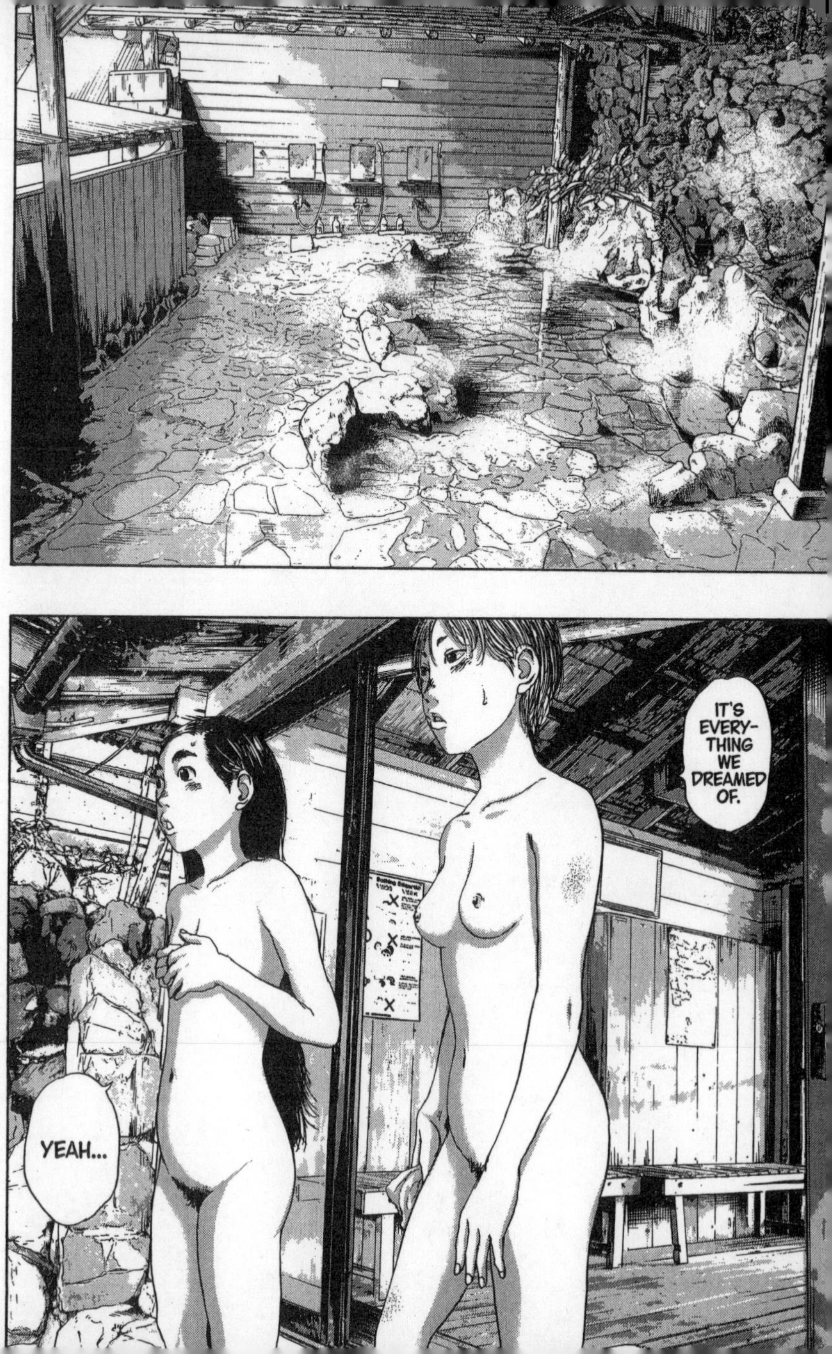
IT'S EVERY-THING WE DREAMED OF.
YEAH...

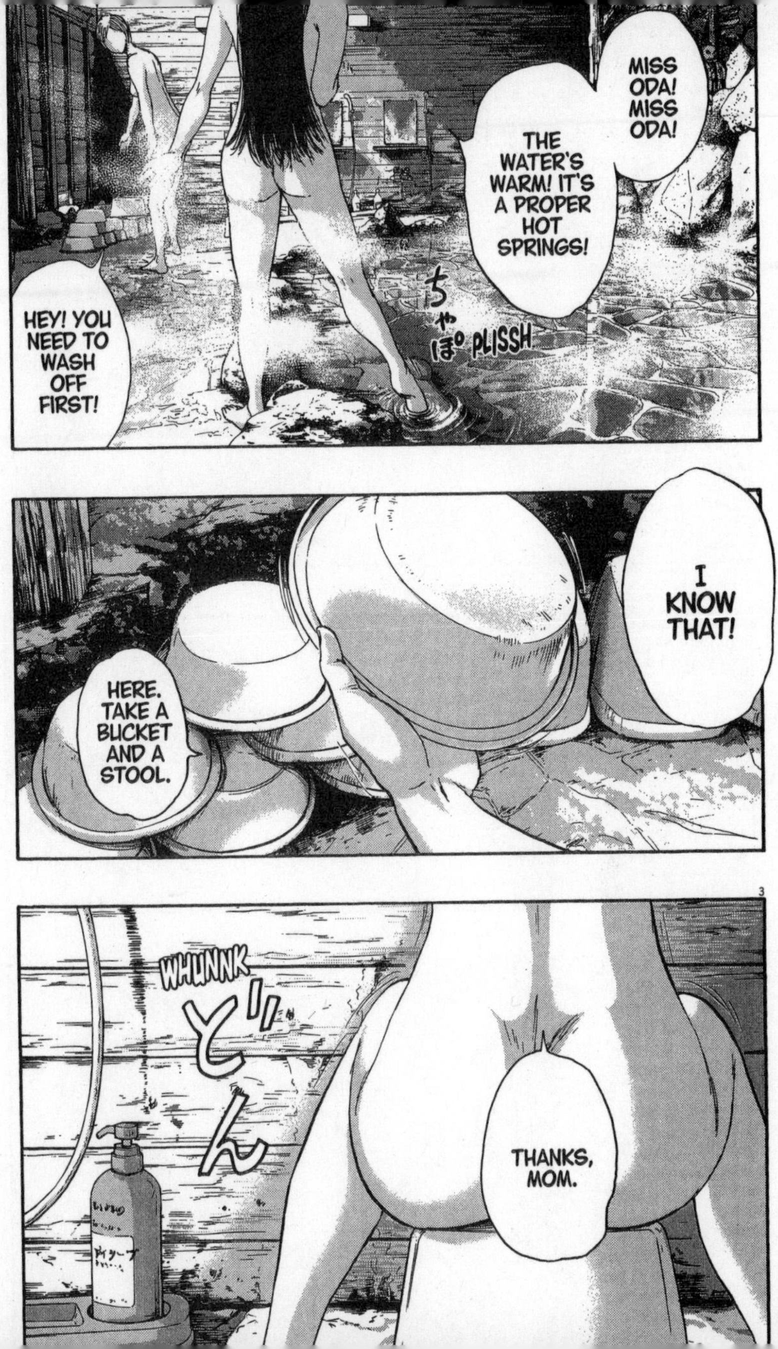
MISS ODA! MISS ODA!
THE WATER'S WARM! IT'S A PROPER HOT SPRINGS!
ちゃぽ PLISSH
HEY! YOU NEED TO WASH OFF FIRST!
I KNOW THAT!
HERE. TAKE A BUCKET AND A STOOL.
WHUNNK どん
THANKS, MOM.

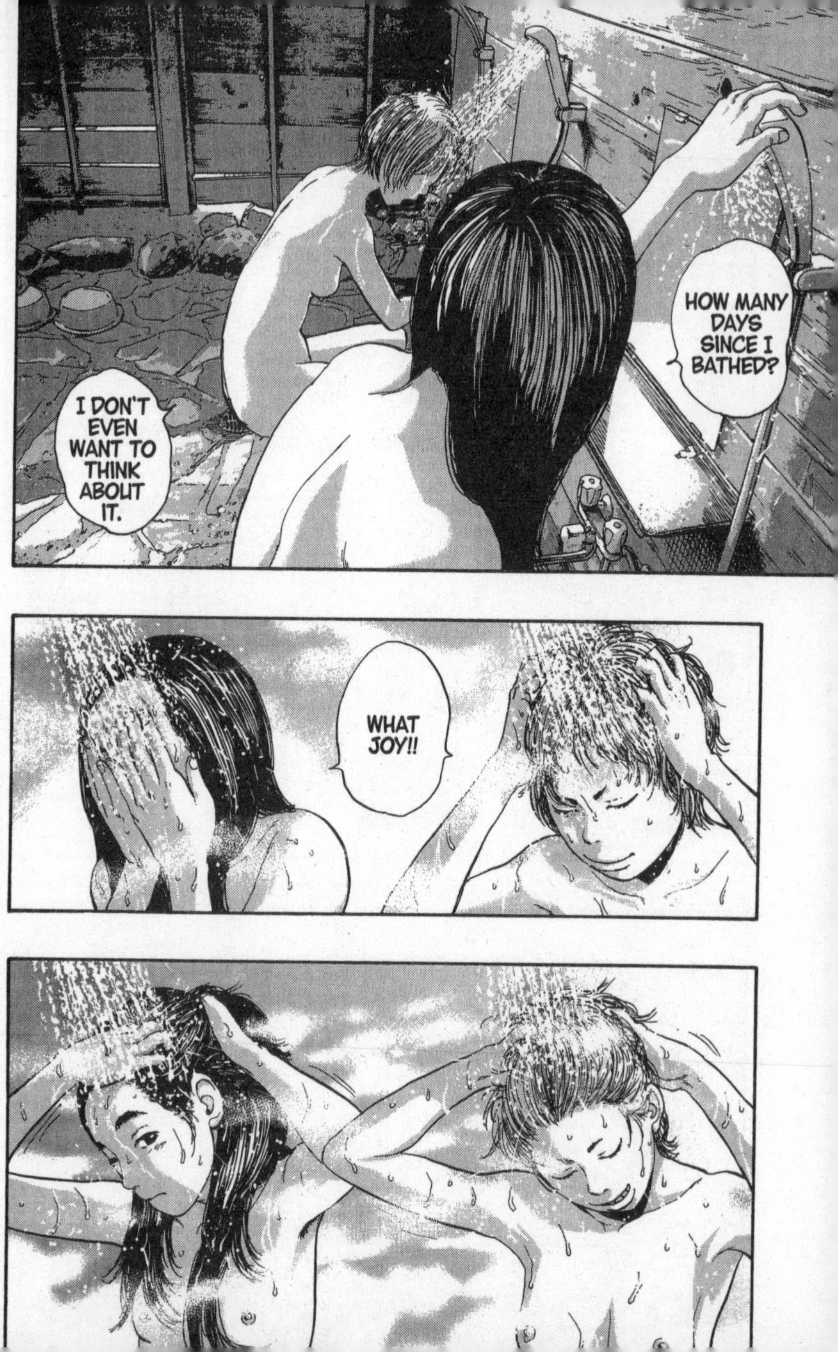
HOW MANY DAYS SINCE I BATHED?
I DON'T EVEN WANT TO THINK ABOUT IT.
WHAT JOY!!

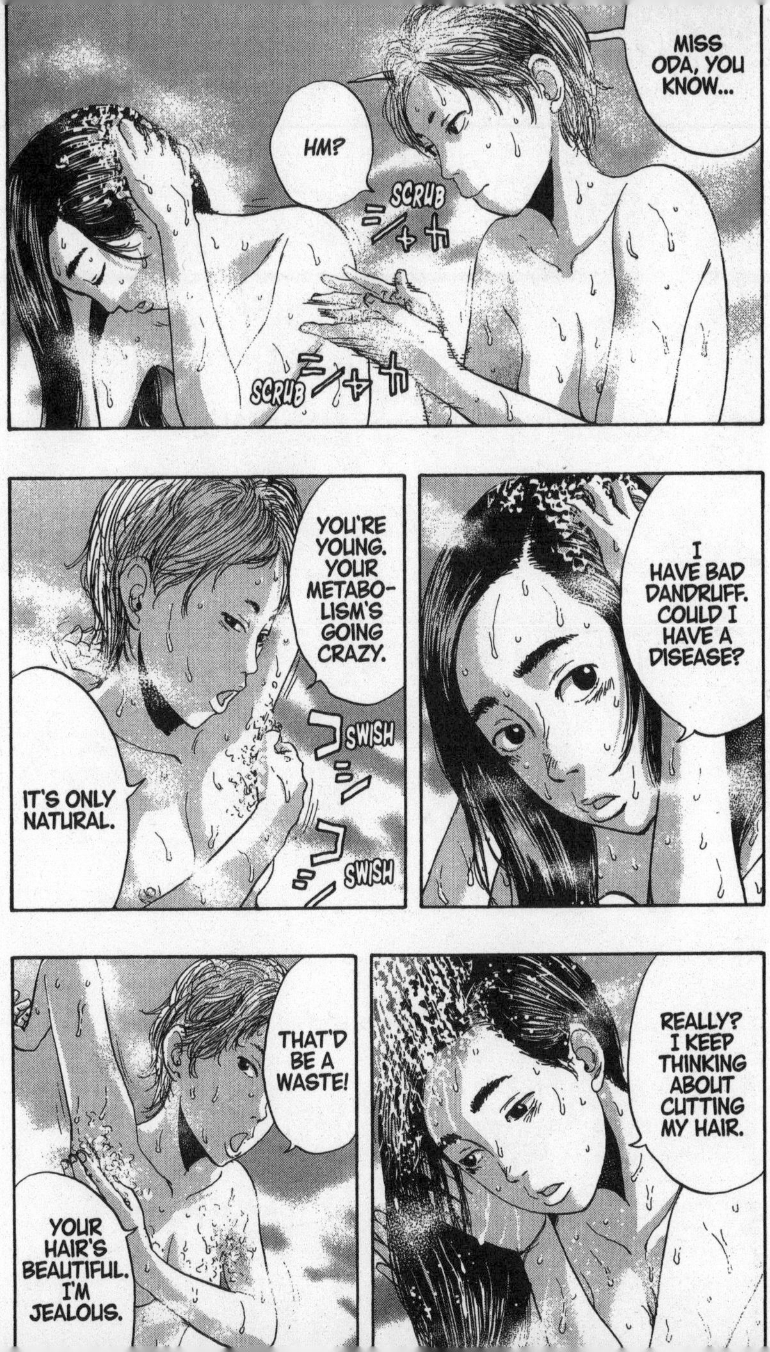
MISS ODA, YOU KNOW...
HM?
SCRUB
SCRUB
I HAVE BAD DANDRUFF. COULD I HAVE A DISEASE?
YOU'RE YOUNG. YOUR METABO-LISM'S GOING CRAZY.
SWISH
SWISH
IT'S ONLY NATURAL.
REALLY? I KEEP THINKING ABOUT CUTTING MY HAIR.
THAT'D BE A WASTE!
YOUR HAIR'S BEAUTIFUL. I'M JEALOUS.

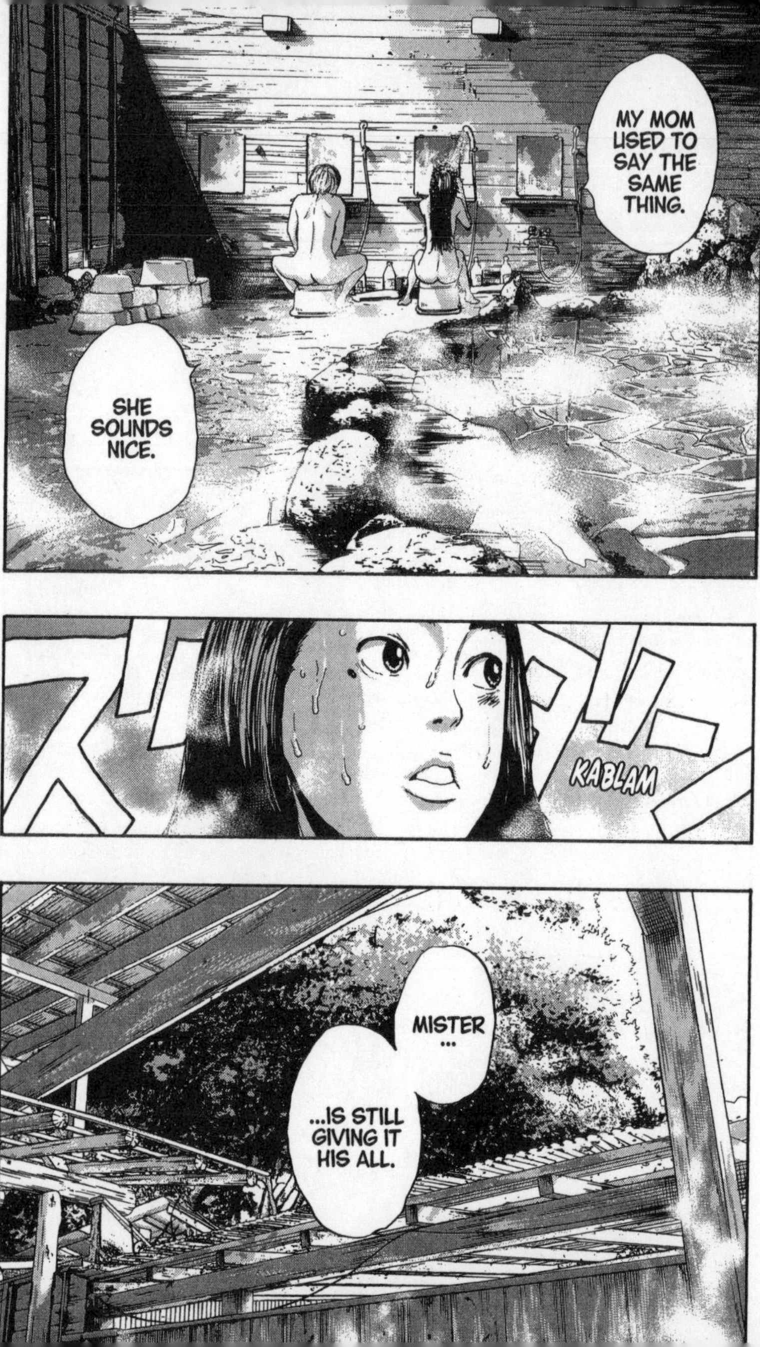
MY MOM USED TO SAY THE SAME THING.
SHE SOUNDS NICE.
KABLAM
MISTER...
...IS STILL GIVING IT HIS ALL.

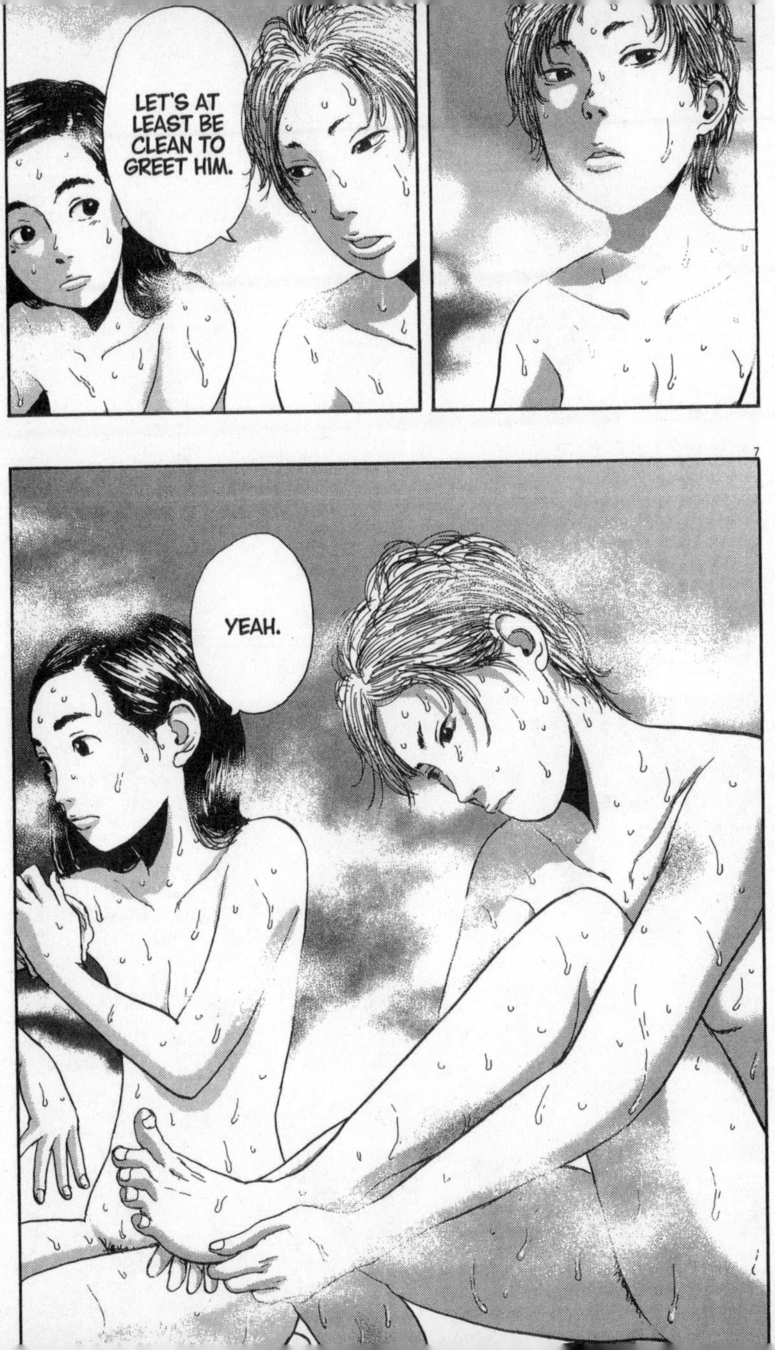
LET'S AT LEAST BE CLEAN TO GREET HIM.
YEAH.

7

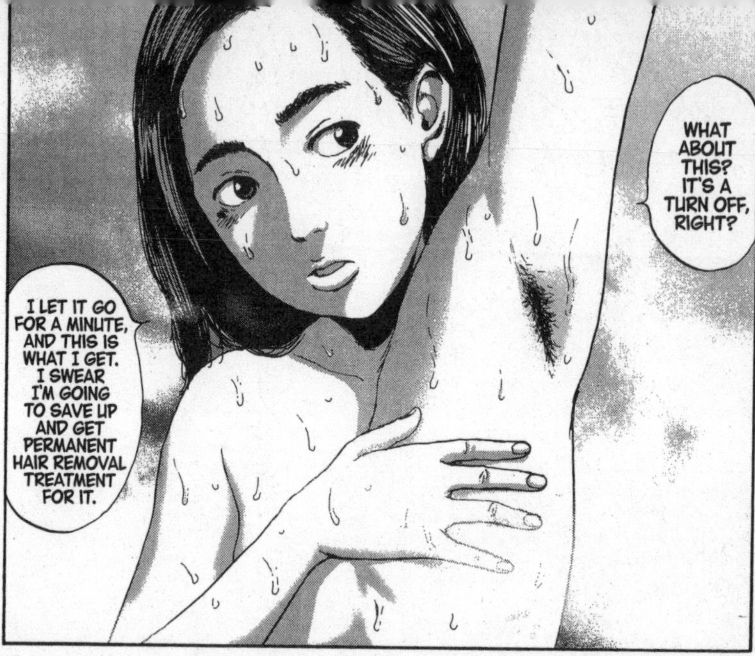
WHAT ABOUT THIS? IT'S A TURN OFF, RIGHT?
I LET IT GO FOR A MINUTE, AND THIS IS WHAT I GET. I SWEAR I'M GOING TO SAVE UP AND GET PERMANENT HAIR REMOVAL TREATMENT FOR IT.

8

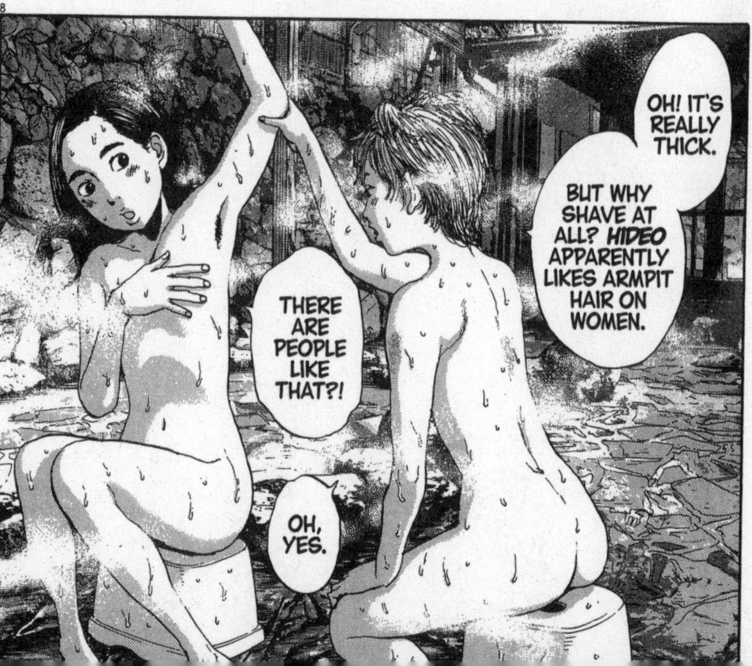
OH! IT'S REALLY THICK.
BUT WHY SHAVE AT ALL? *HIDEO* APPARENTLY LIKES ARMPIT HAIR ON WOMEN.
THERE ARE PEOPLE LIKE THAT?!
OH, YES.

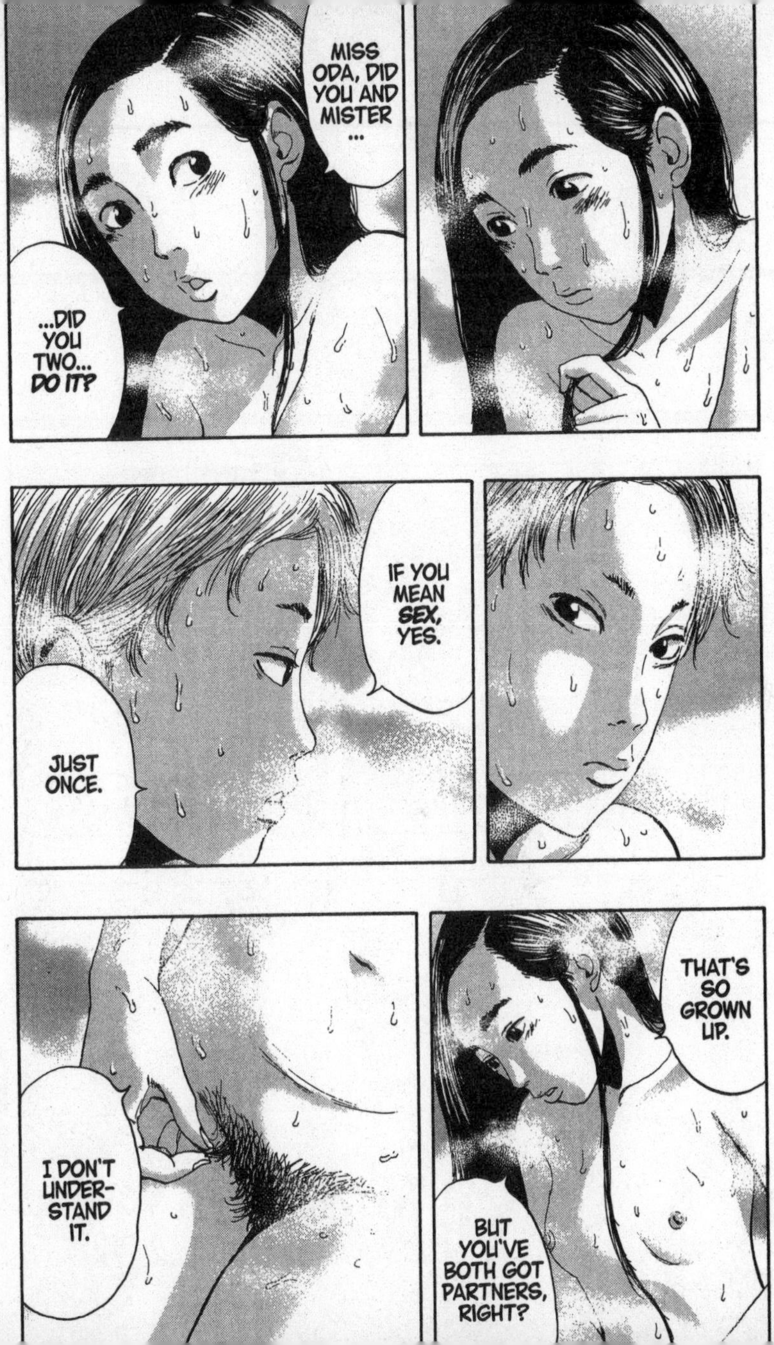
MISS ODA, DID YOU AND MISTER ...
...DID YOU TWO... DO IT?
IF YOU MEAN SEX, YES.
JUST ONCE.
THAT'S SO GROWN UP.
BUT YOU'VE BOTH GOT PARTNERS, RIGHT?
I DON'T UNDER-STAND IT.

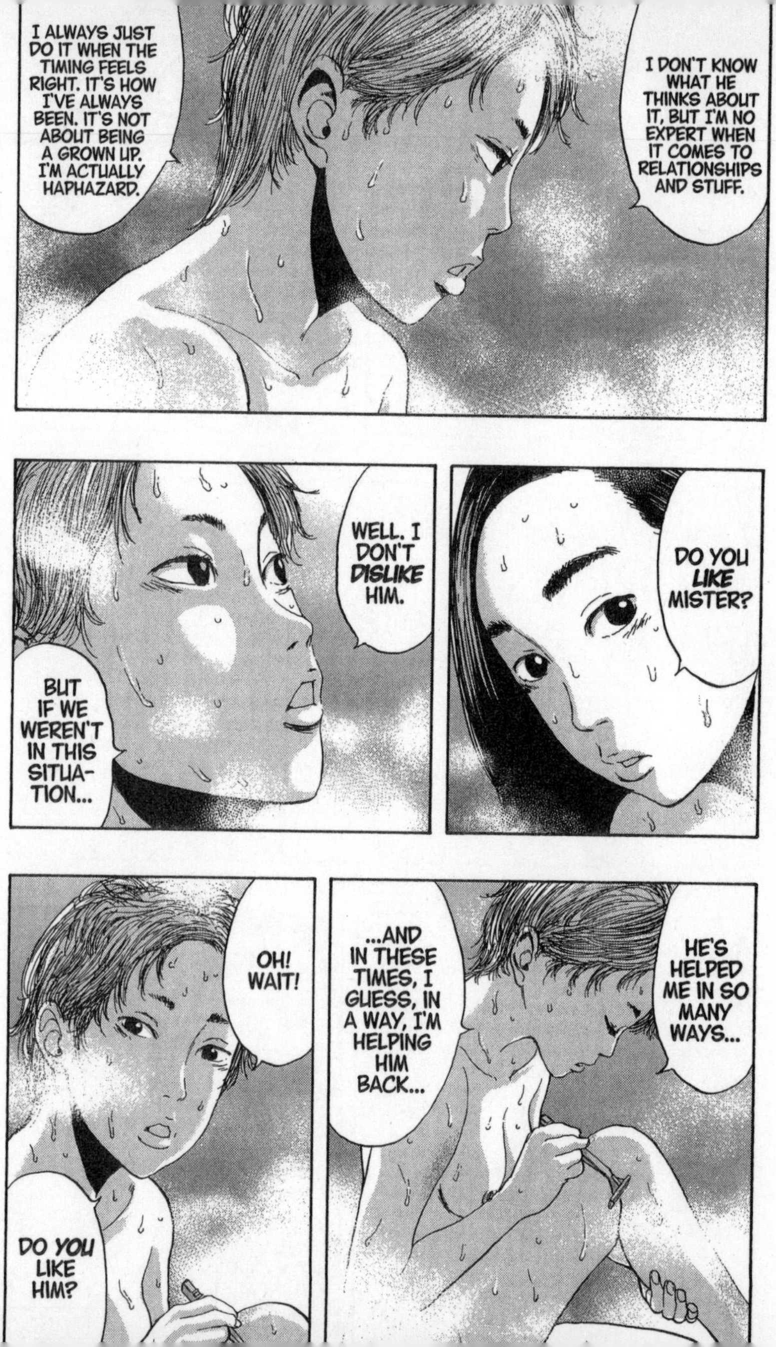
I DON'T KNOW WHAT HE THINKS ABOUT IT, BUT I'M NO EXPERT WHEN IT COMES TO RELATIONSHIPS AND STUFF.
I ALWAYS JUST DO IT WHEN THE TIMING FEELS RIGHT. IT'S HOW I'VE ALWAYS BEEN. IT'S NOT ABOUT BEING A GROWN UP. I'M ACTUALLY HAPHAZARD.
DO YOU *LIKE* MISTER?
WELL. I DON'T *DISLIKE* HIM.
BUT IF WE WEREN'T IN THIS SITUA-TION...
HE'S HELPED ME IN SO MANY WAYS...
...AND IN THESE TIMES, I GUESS, IN A WAY, I'M HELPING HIM BACK...
OH! WAIT!
DO *YOU* LIKE HIM?

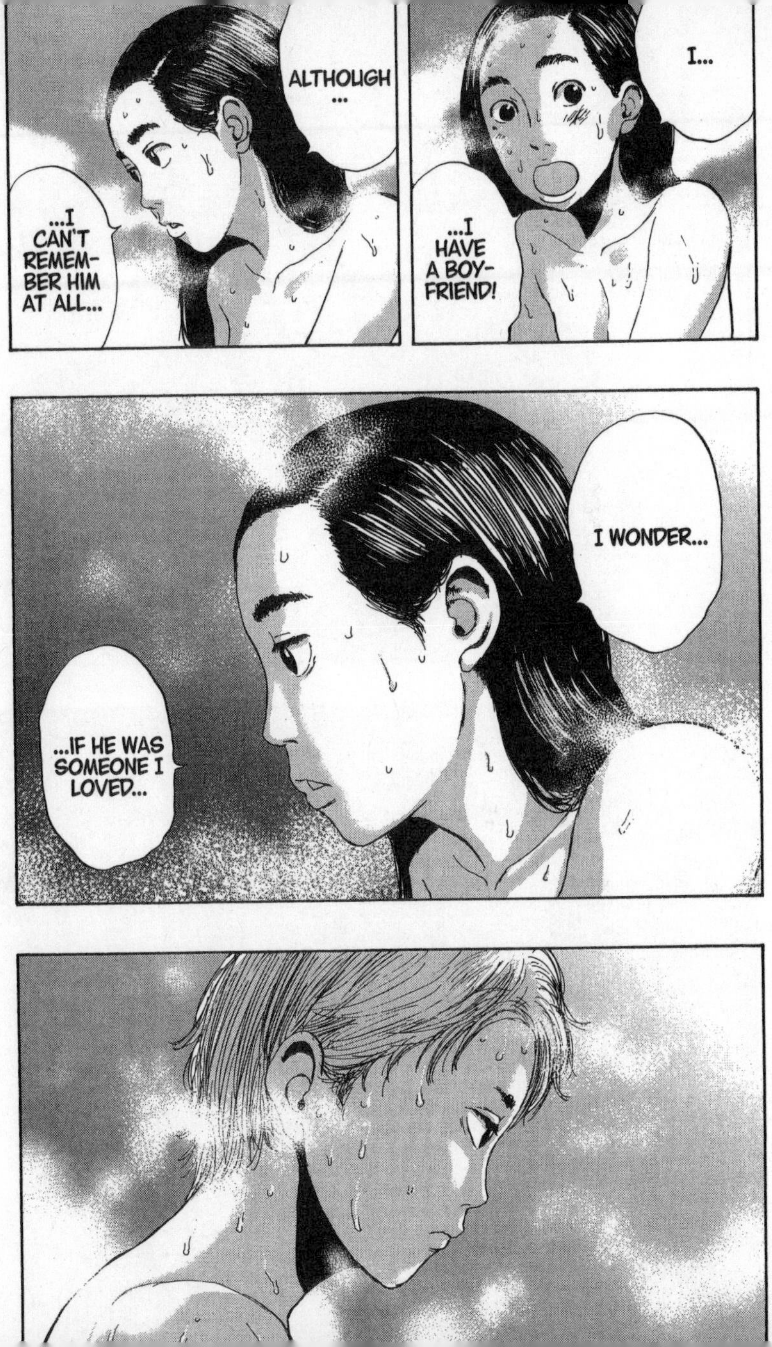
I...
...I HAVE A BOY-FRIEND!
ALTHOUGH...
...I CAN'T REMEMBER HIM AT ALL...
I WONDER...
...IF HE WAS SOMEONE I LOVED...

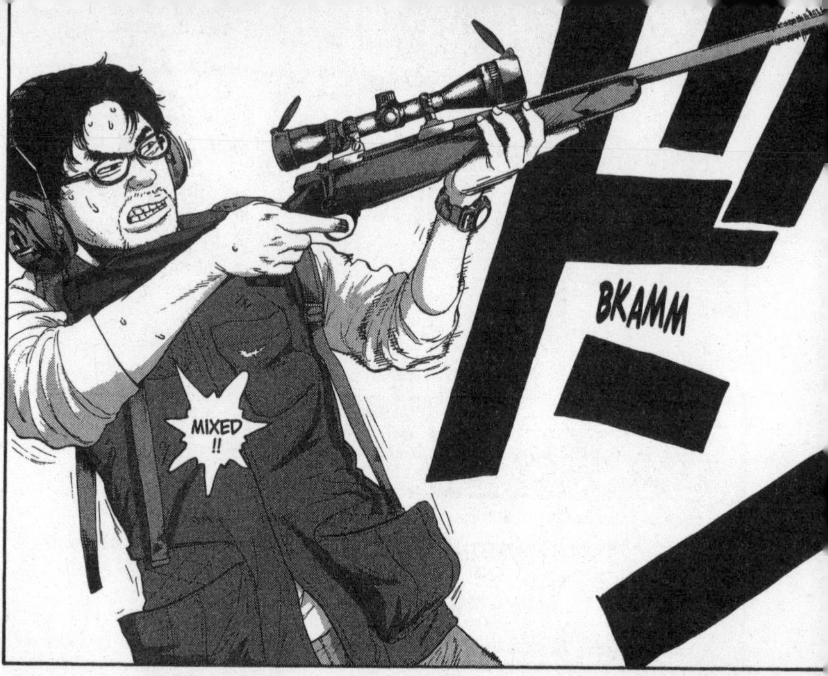
BKAMM
MIXED !!
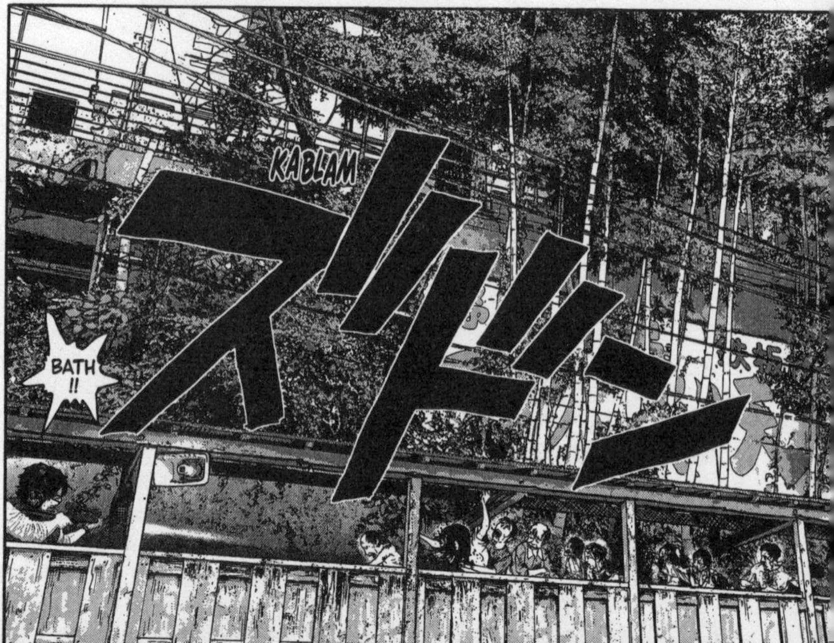
KABLAM
BATH !!

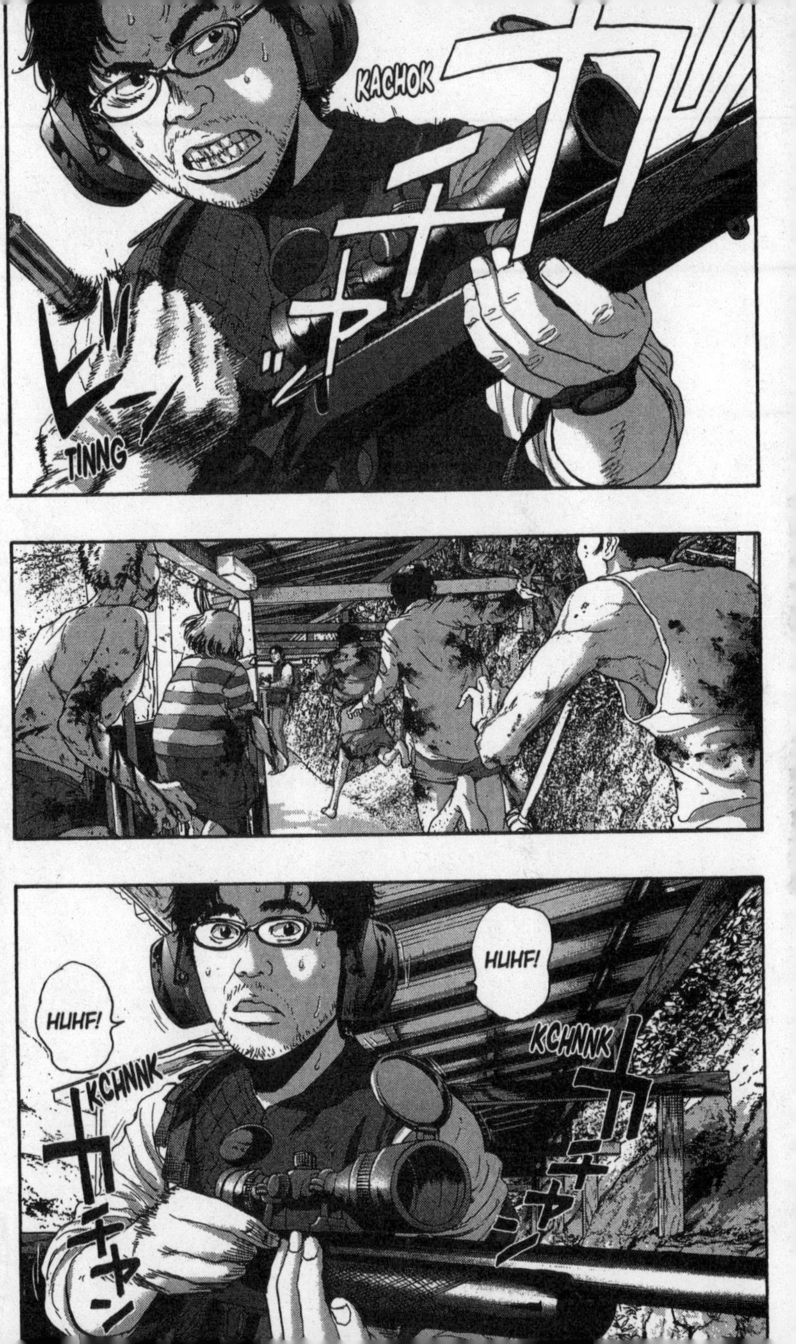
KACHOK
TINNG
HUHF!
KCHNNK
HUHF!
KCHNNK

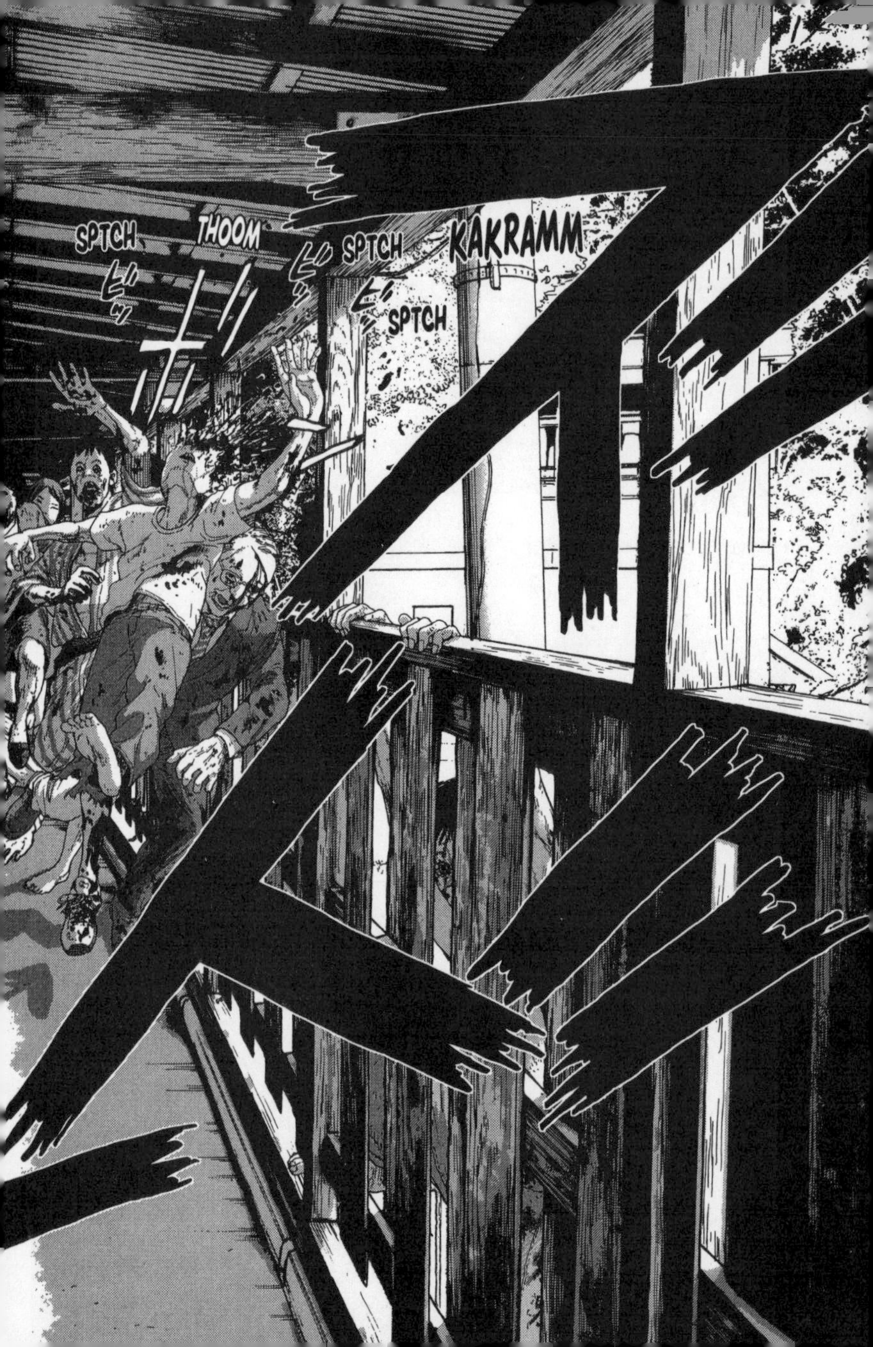
KAKRAMM
SPTCH
SPTCH
THOOM
SPTCH

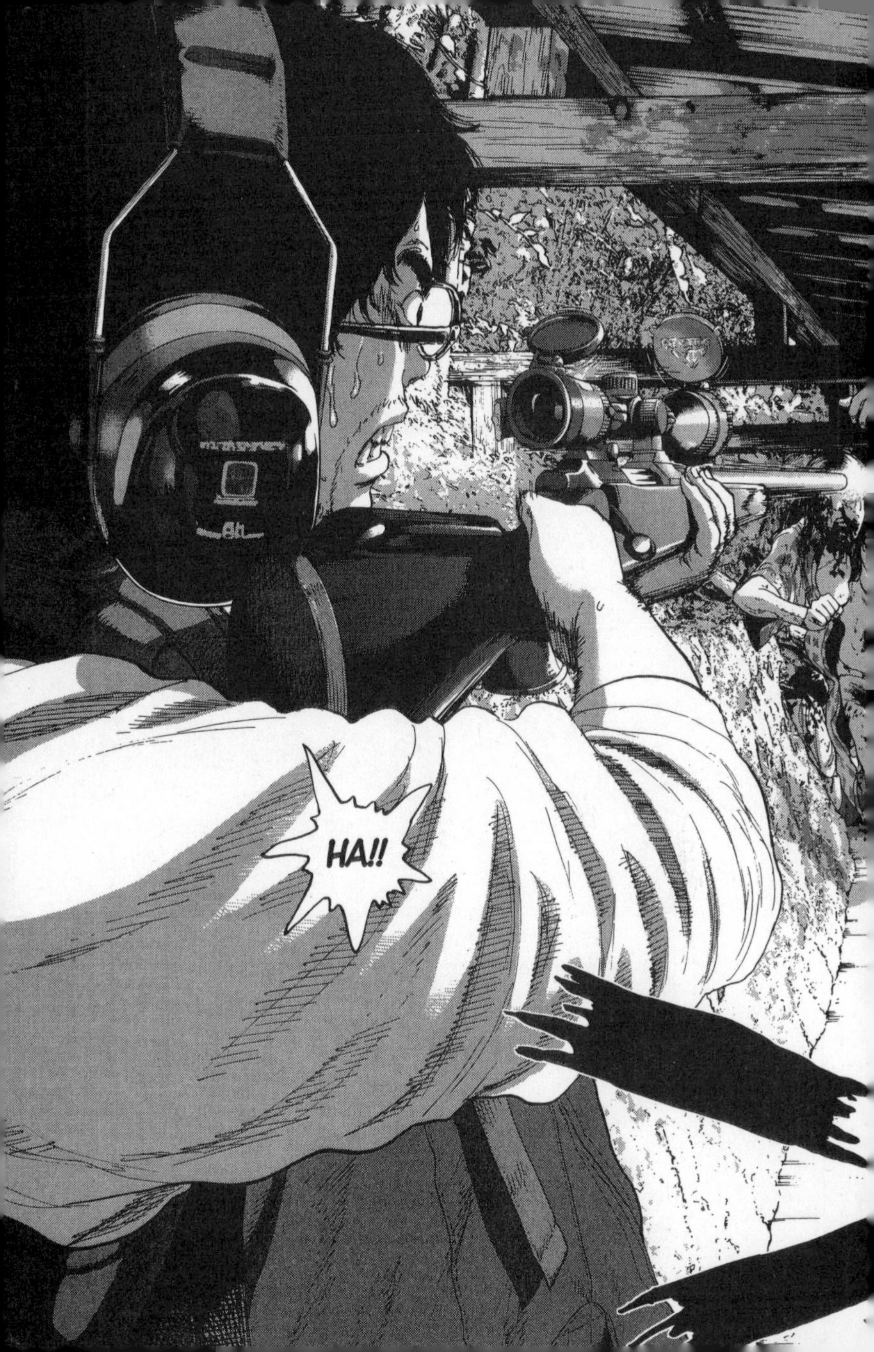
HA!!

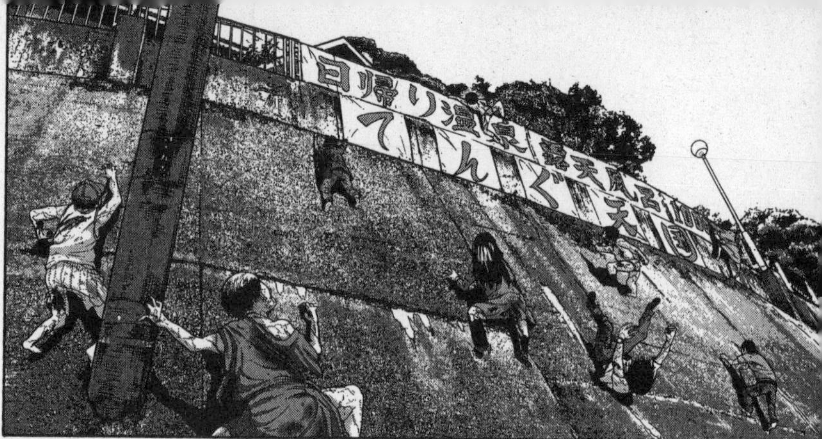
日帰り温泉
露天風呂1000円
てんぐ天国

DAY TRIP HOT SPRINGS / OPEN AIR BATHS / 1000 YEN / TENGU TENGOKU

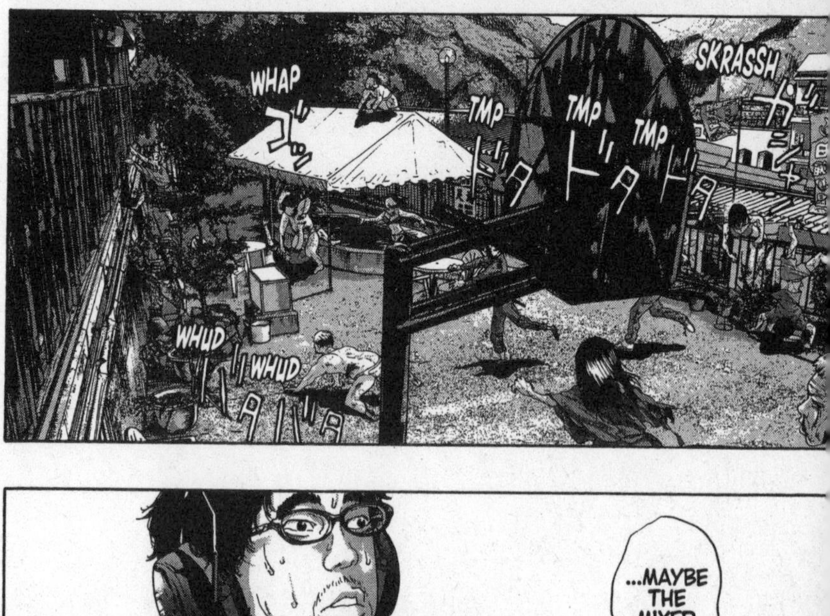
SKRASSH
TMP
TMP
TMP
WHAP
WHUD
WHUD

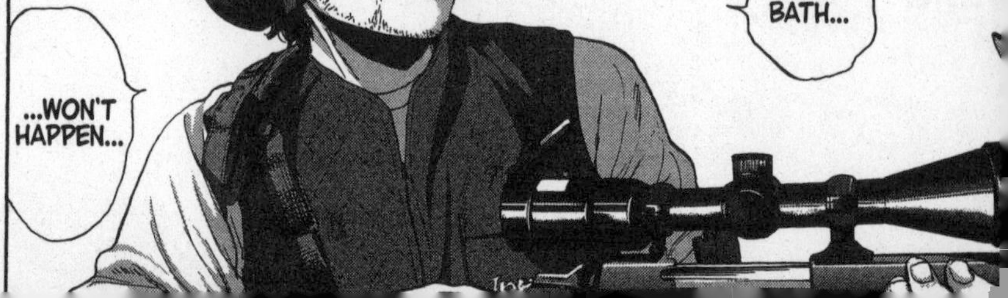
...MAYBE THE MIXED BATH...
...WON'T HAPPEN...

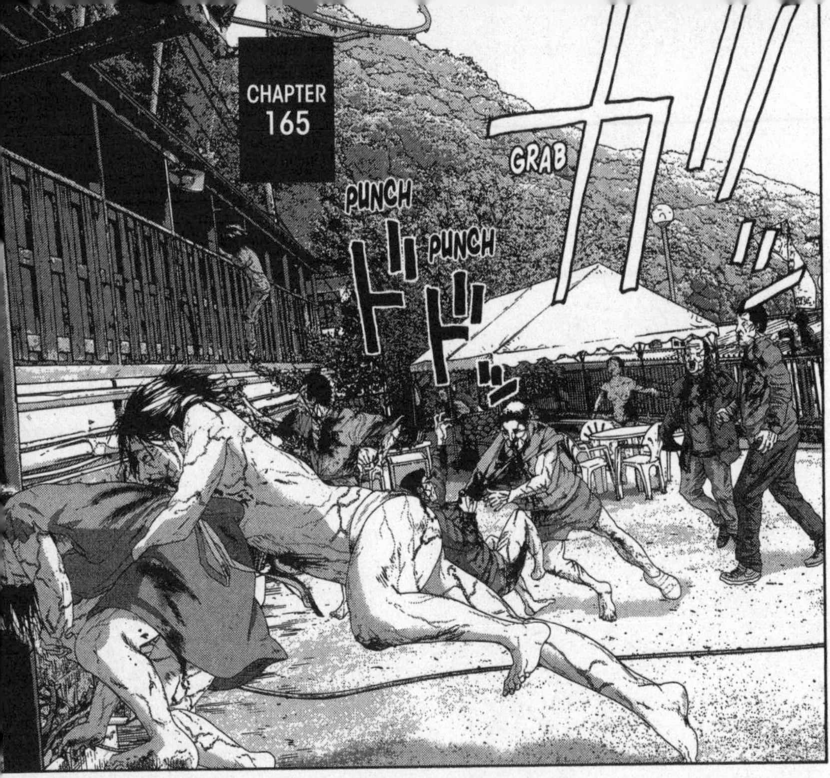
CHAPTER
165
GRAB
PUNCH
PUNCH
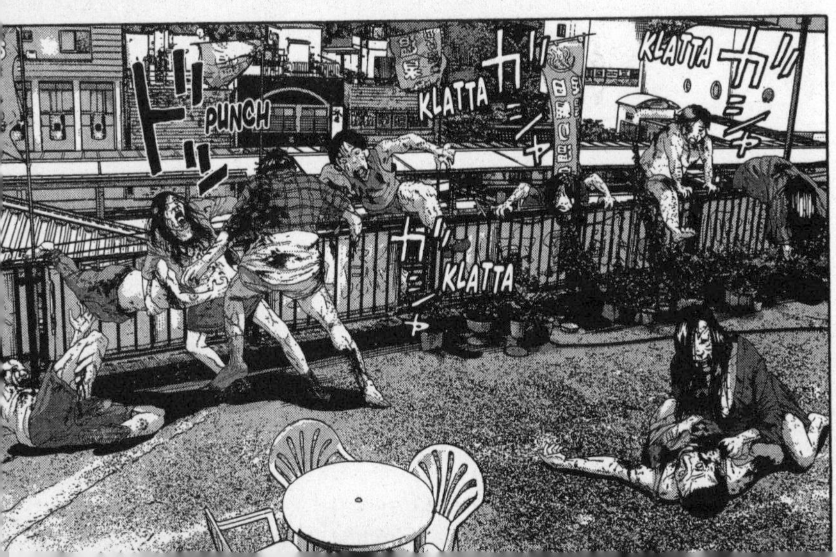
KLATTA
KLATTA
PUNCH
KLATTA

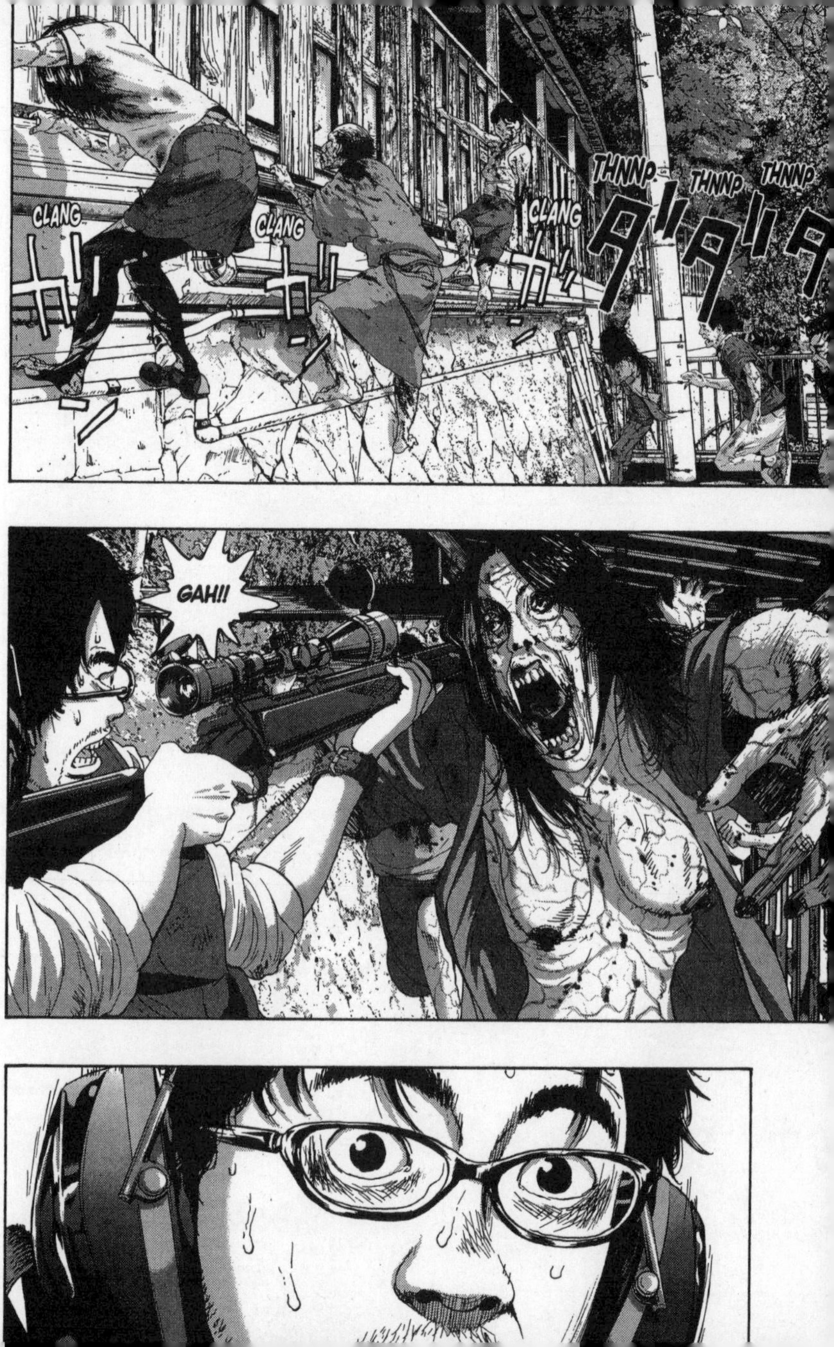
THNNP
THNNP
THNNP
CLANG
CLANG
CLANG
GAH!!

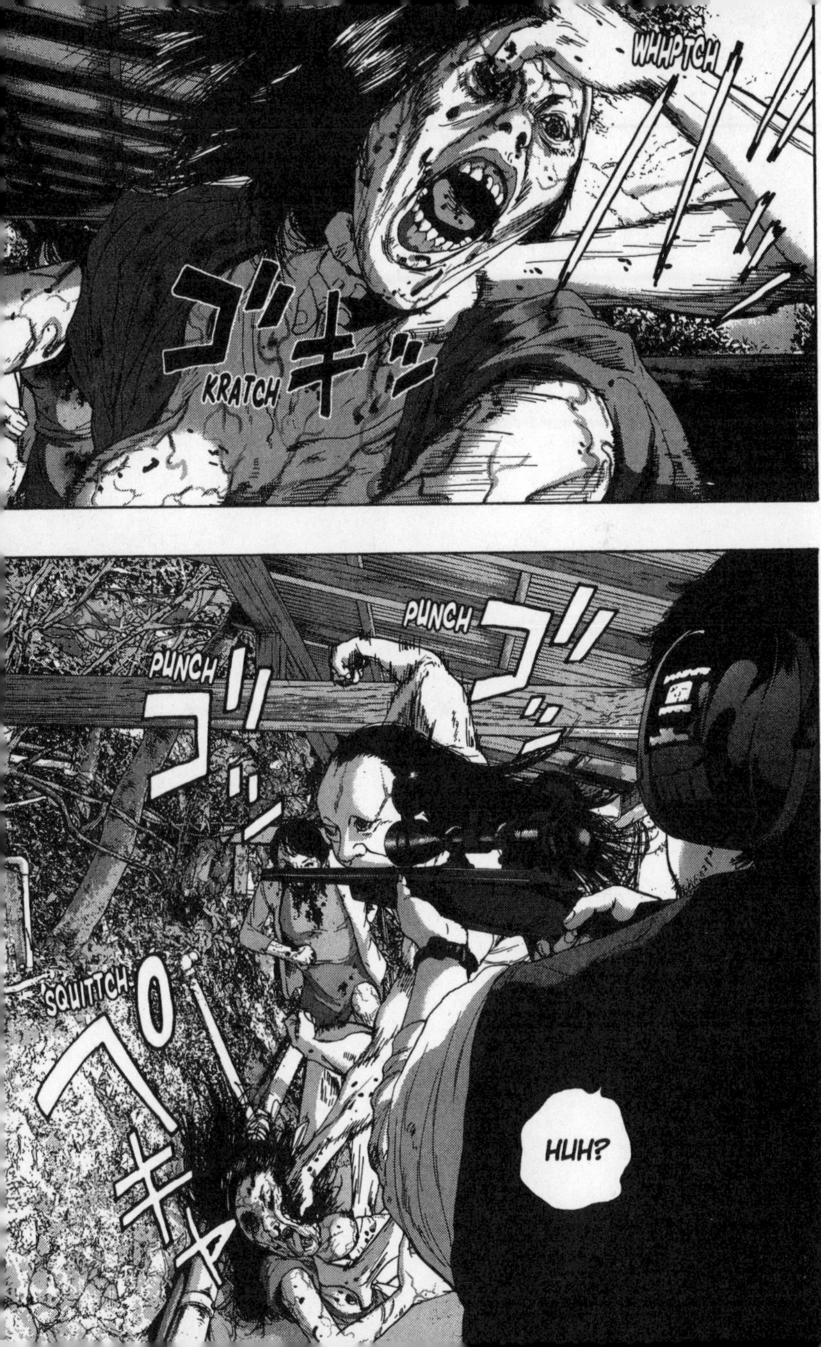
WHHPTCH
ゴキッ
KRATCH
PUNCH
ゴッ
PUNCH
ゴッ
HUH?
SQUITTCH
ヘキャ

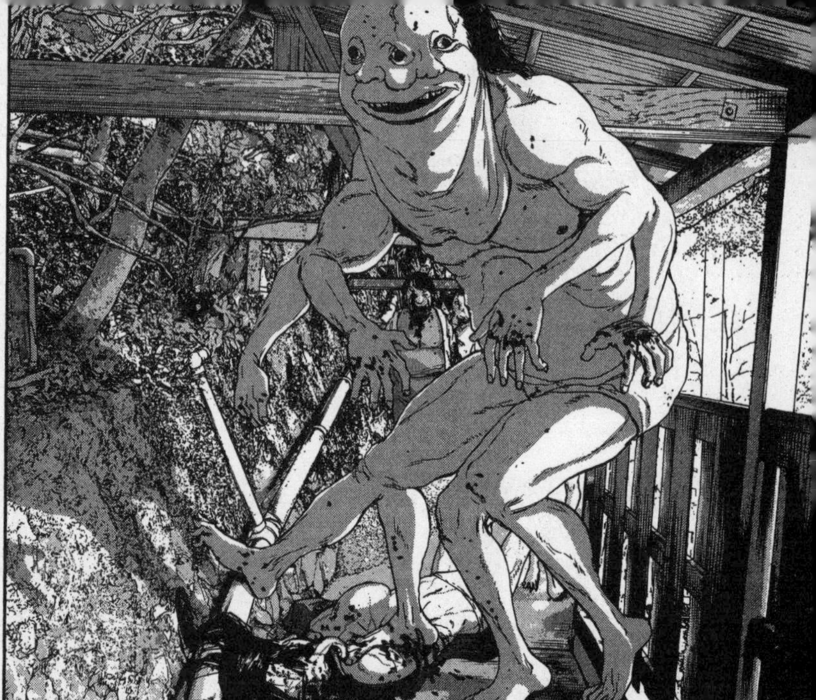
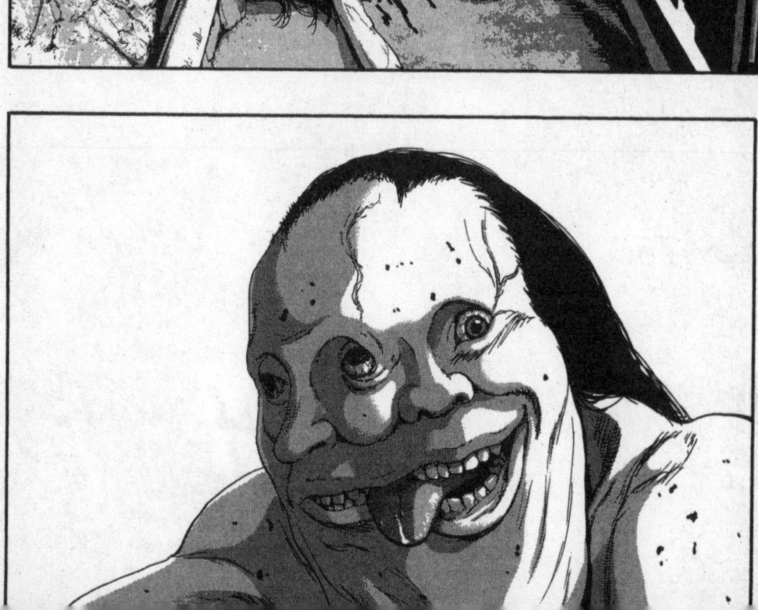

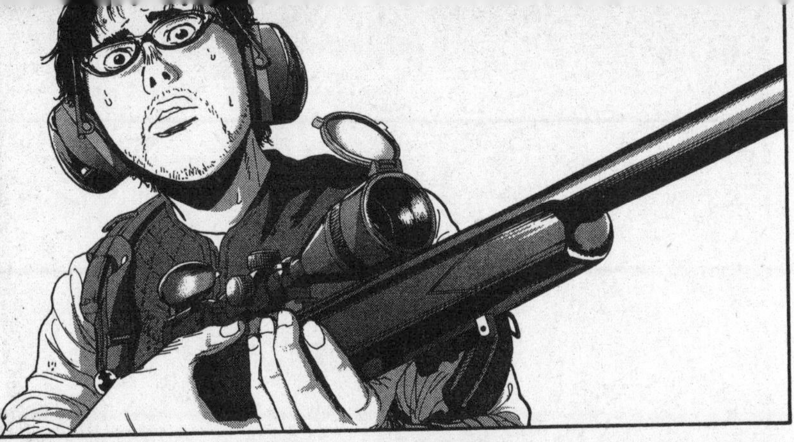

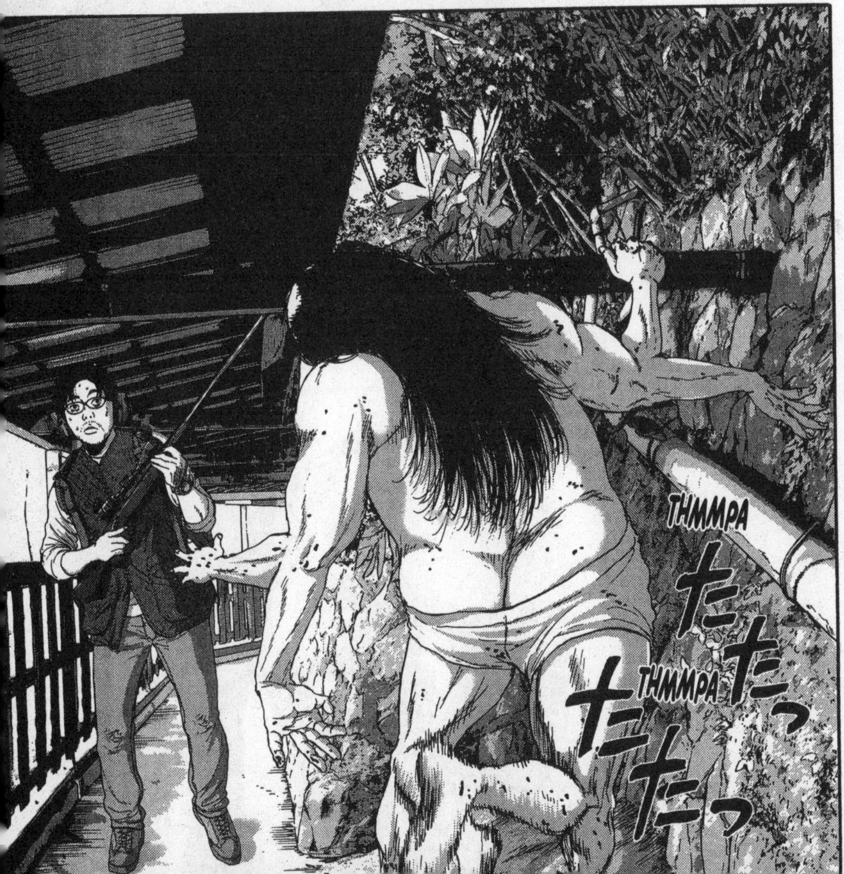
THMMPA
たたっ
THMMPA
たたっ

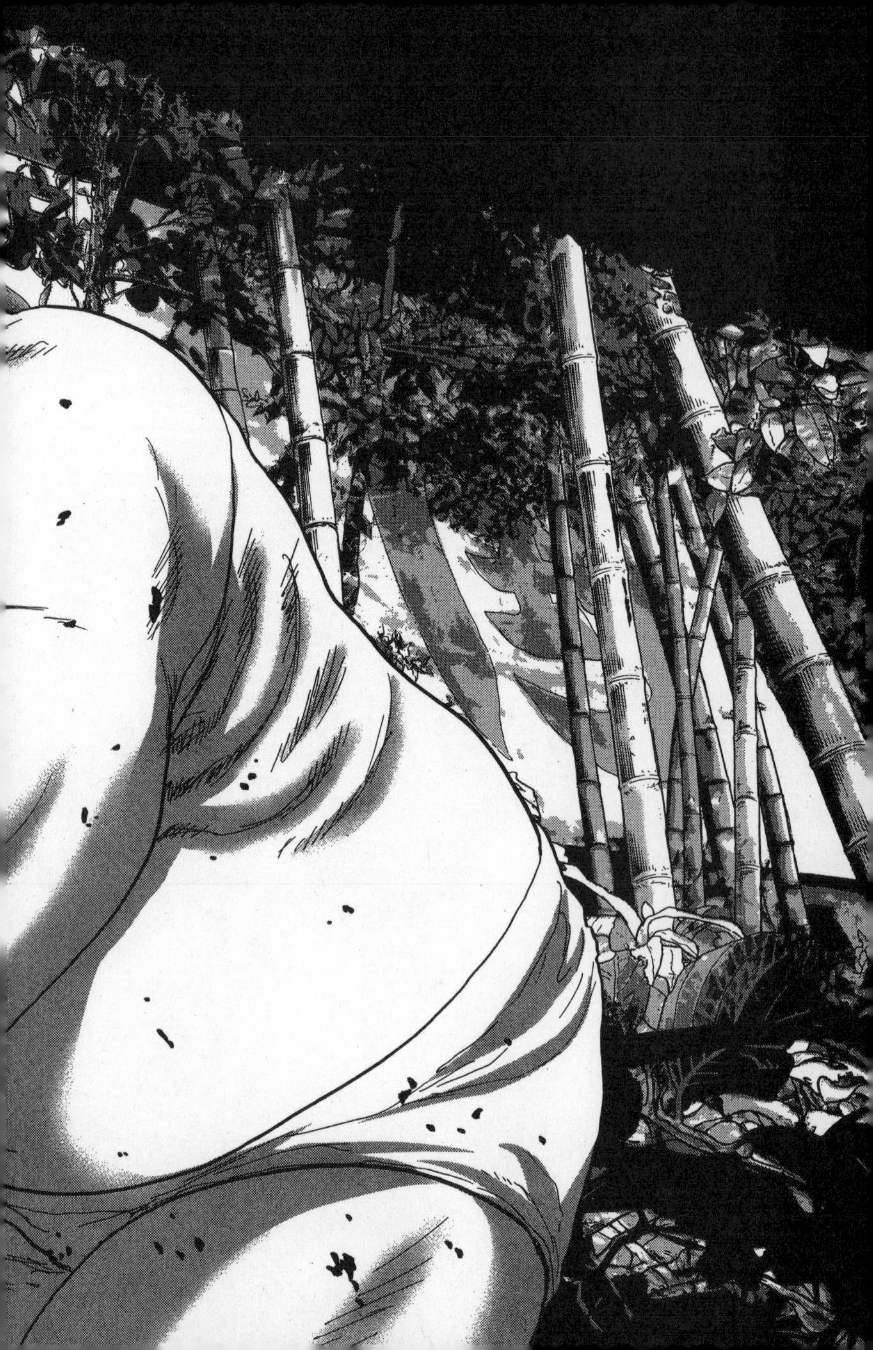

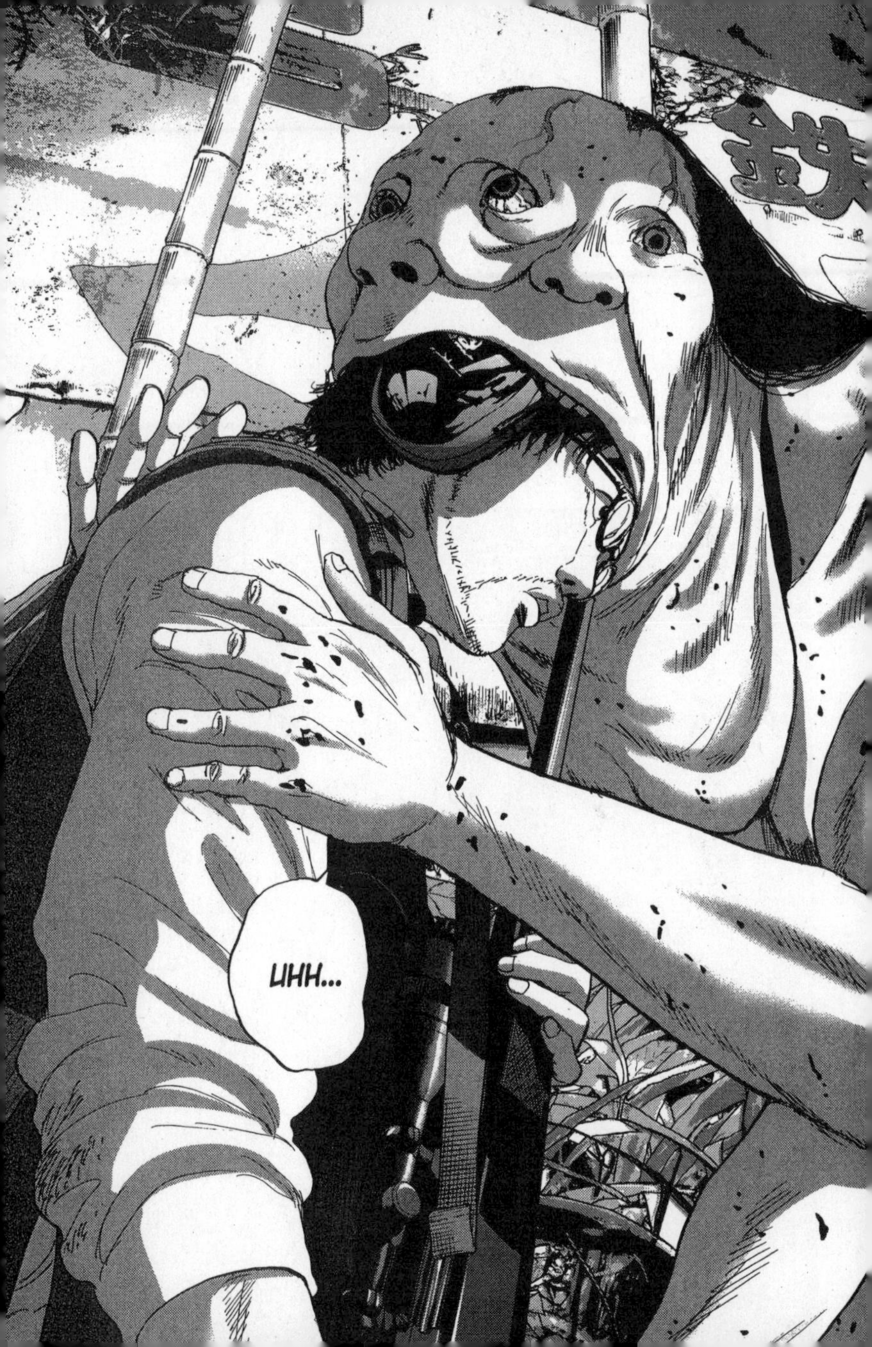
UHH...

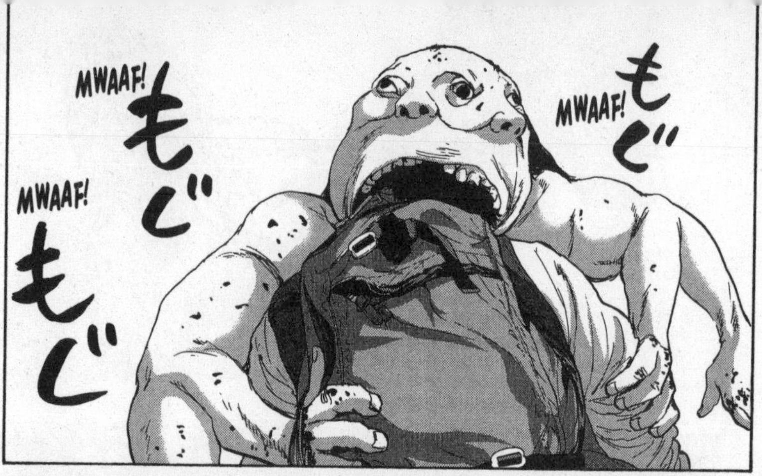
MWAAF!
もぐ
MWAAF!
もぐ
MWAAF!
もぐ
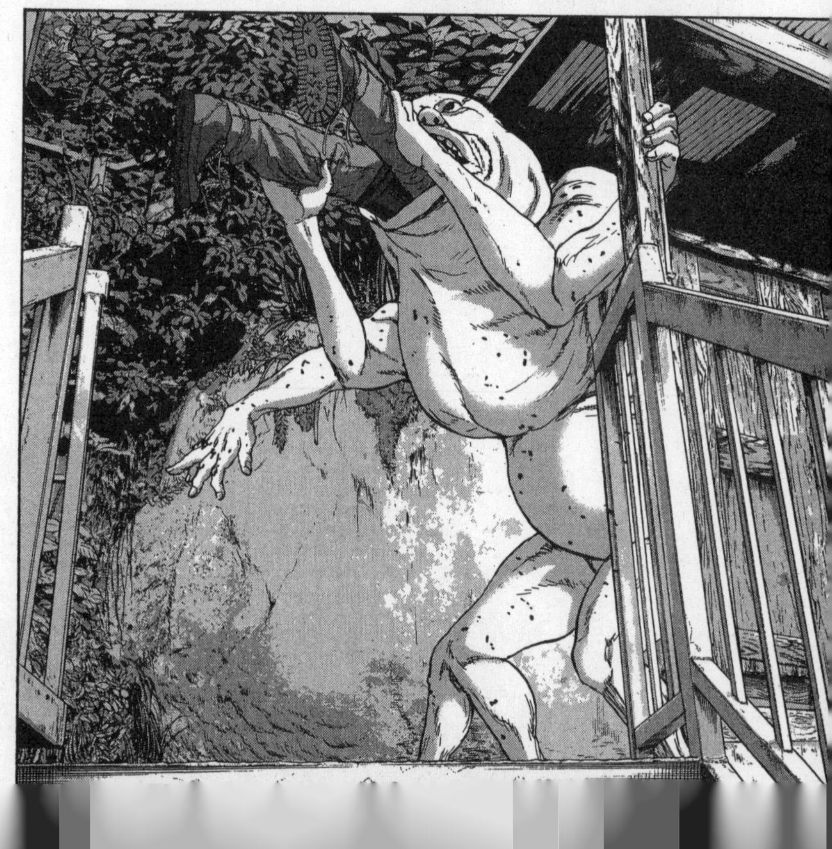

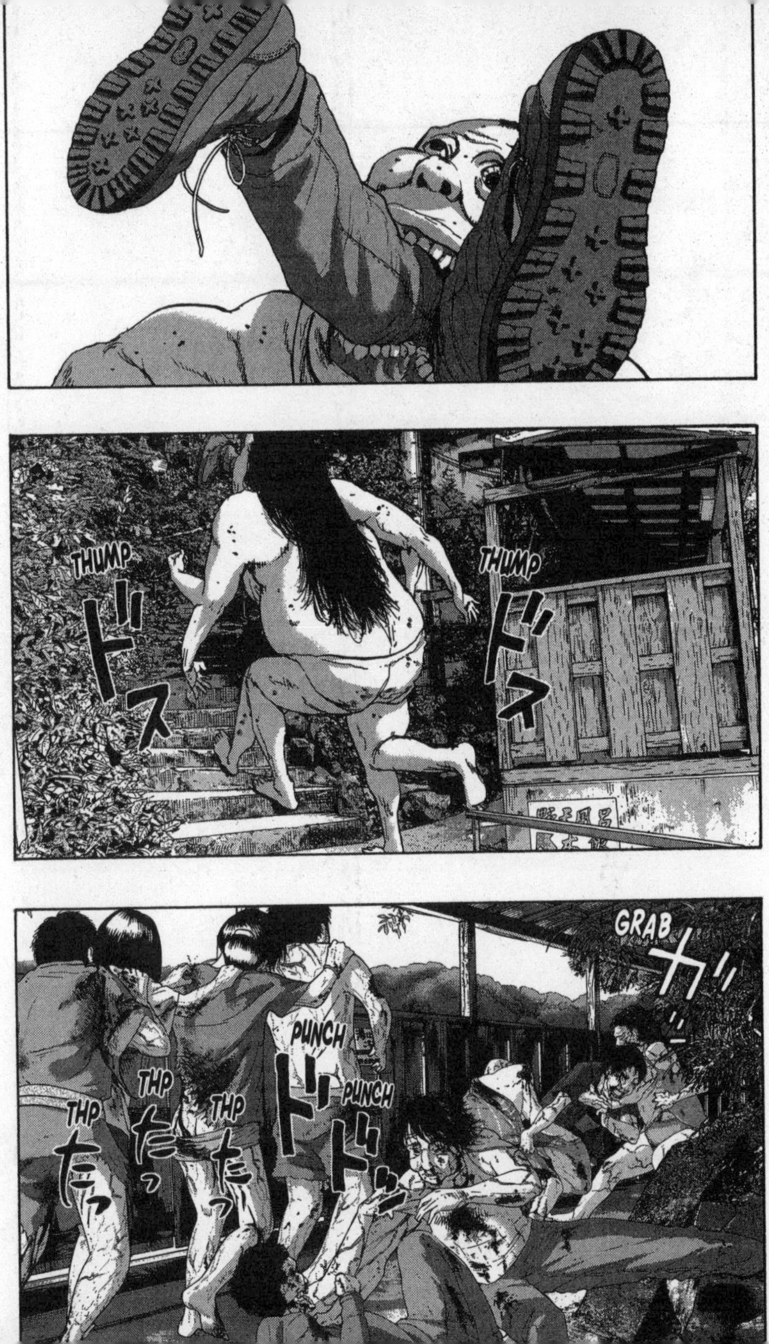
THUMP
ドス
THUMP
ドス
GRAB
ガッ
PUNCH
ドッ
PUNCH
ドッ
THP
たっ
THP
たっ
THP
たっ

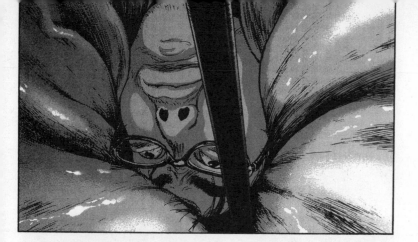

GLUBB!

GLUK

GLUB

GLUB

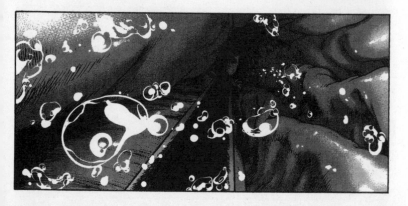

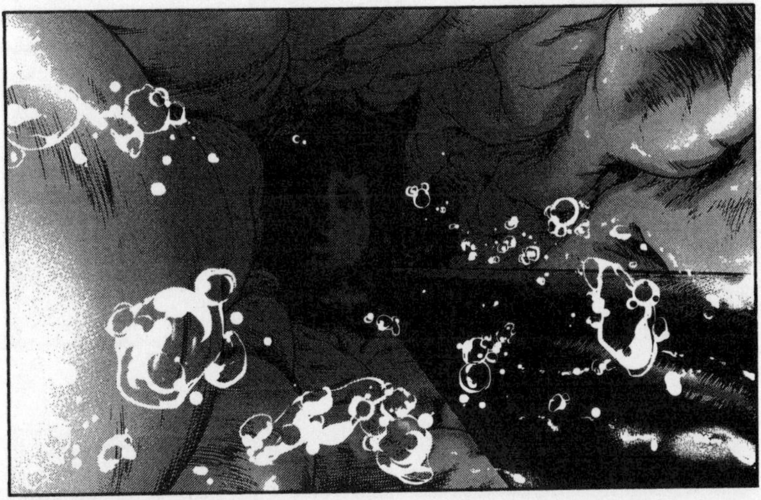
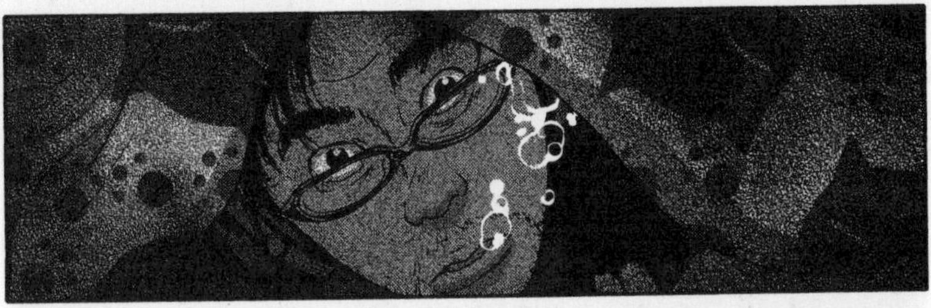
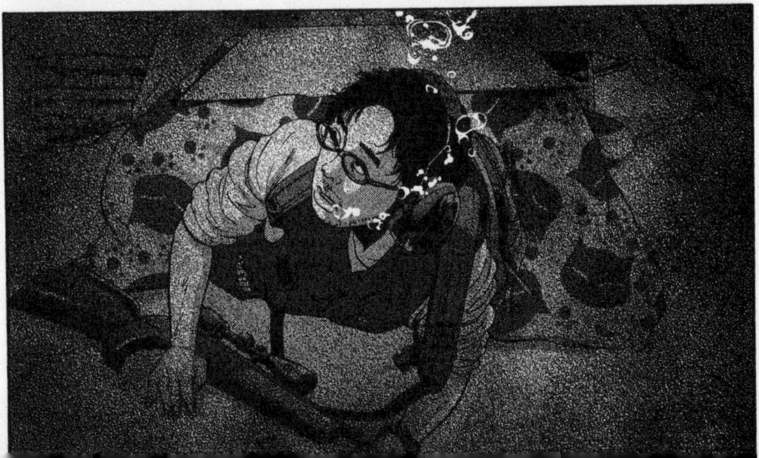

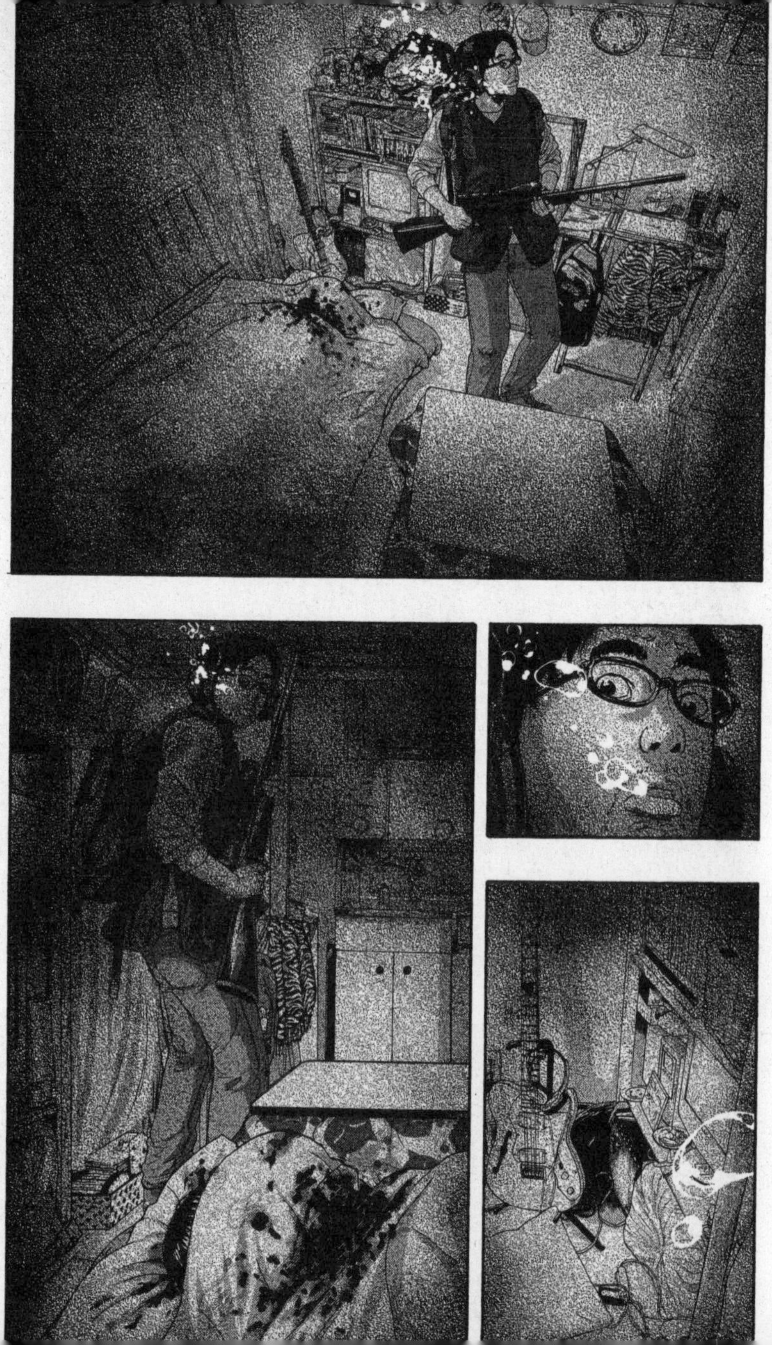

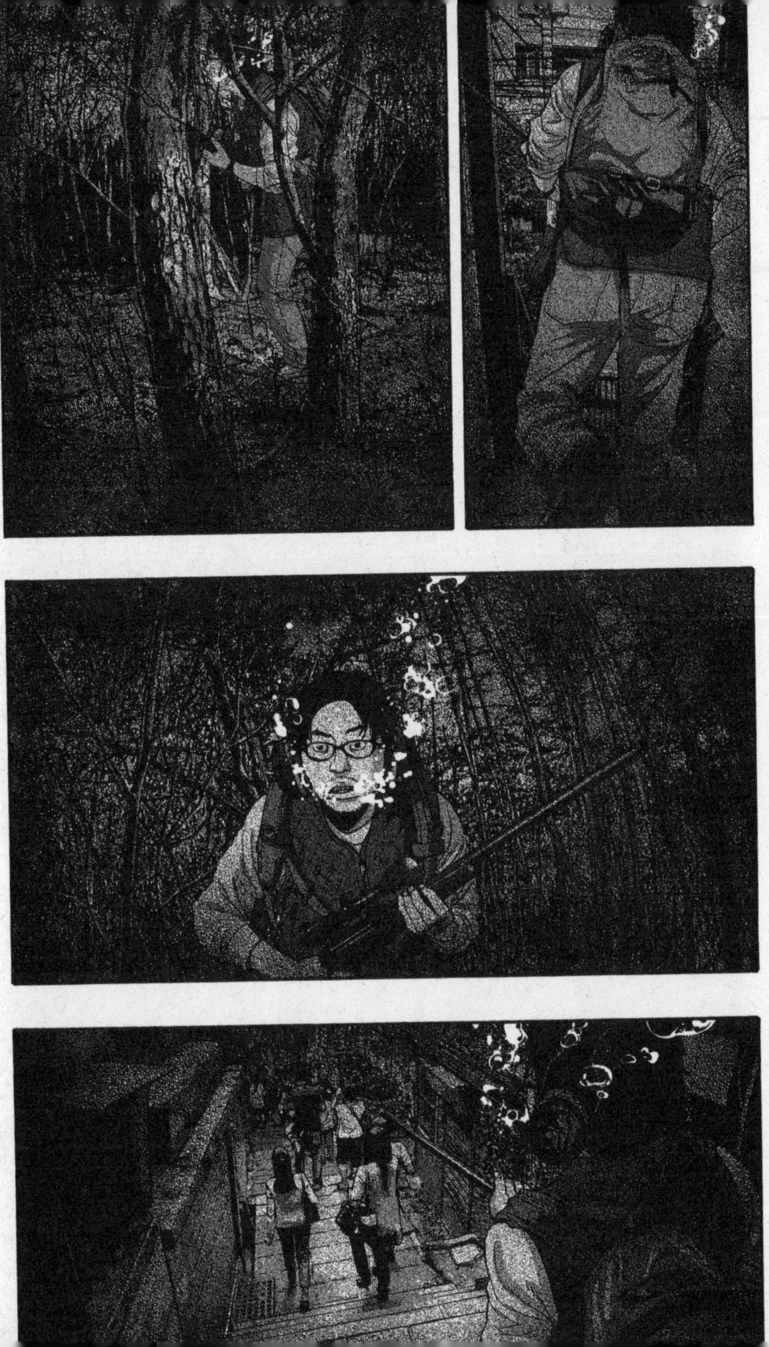

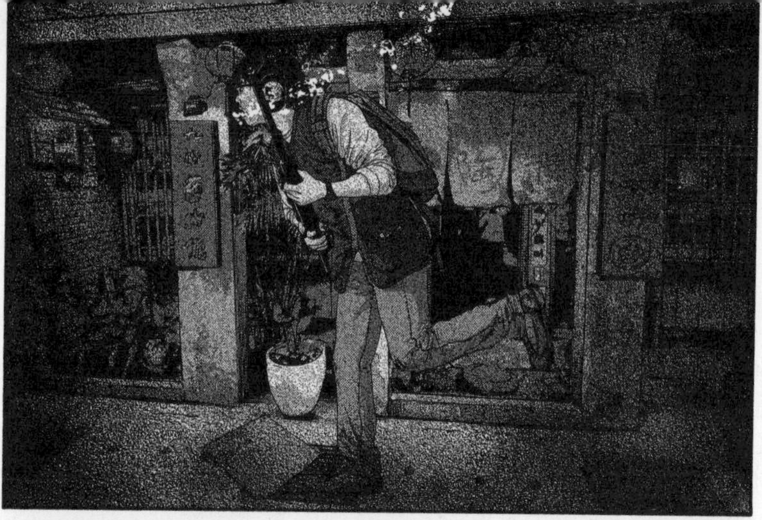

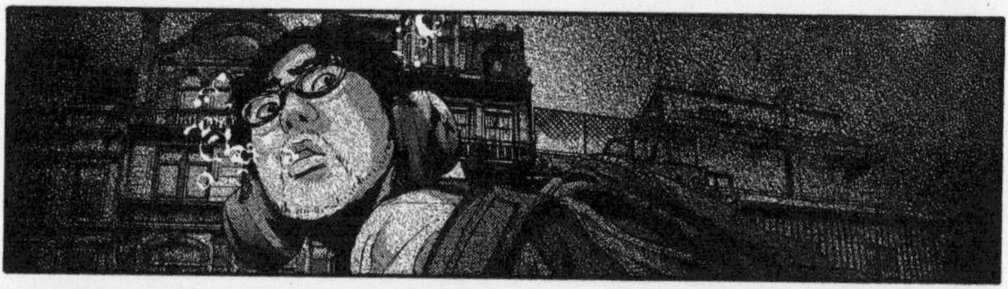

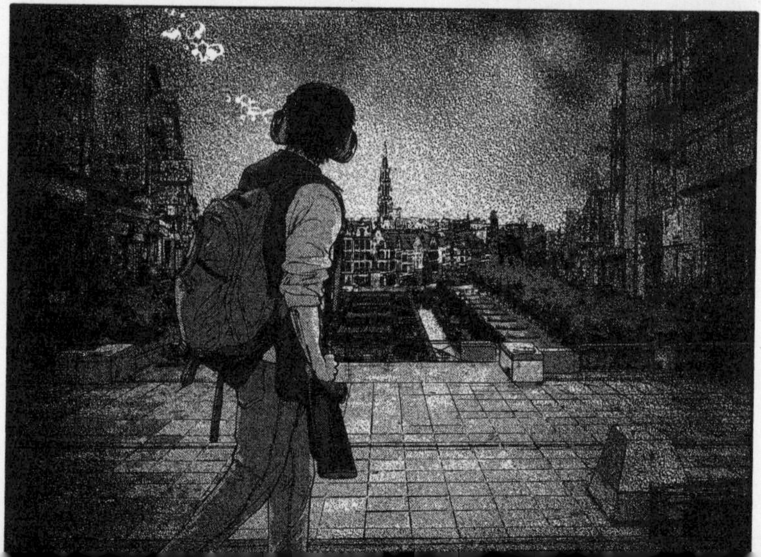

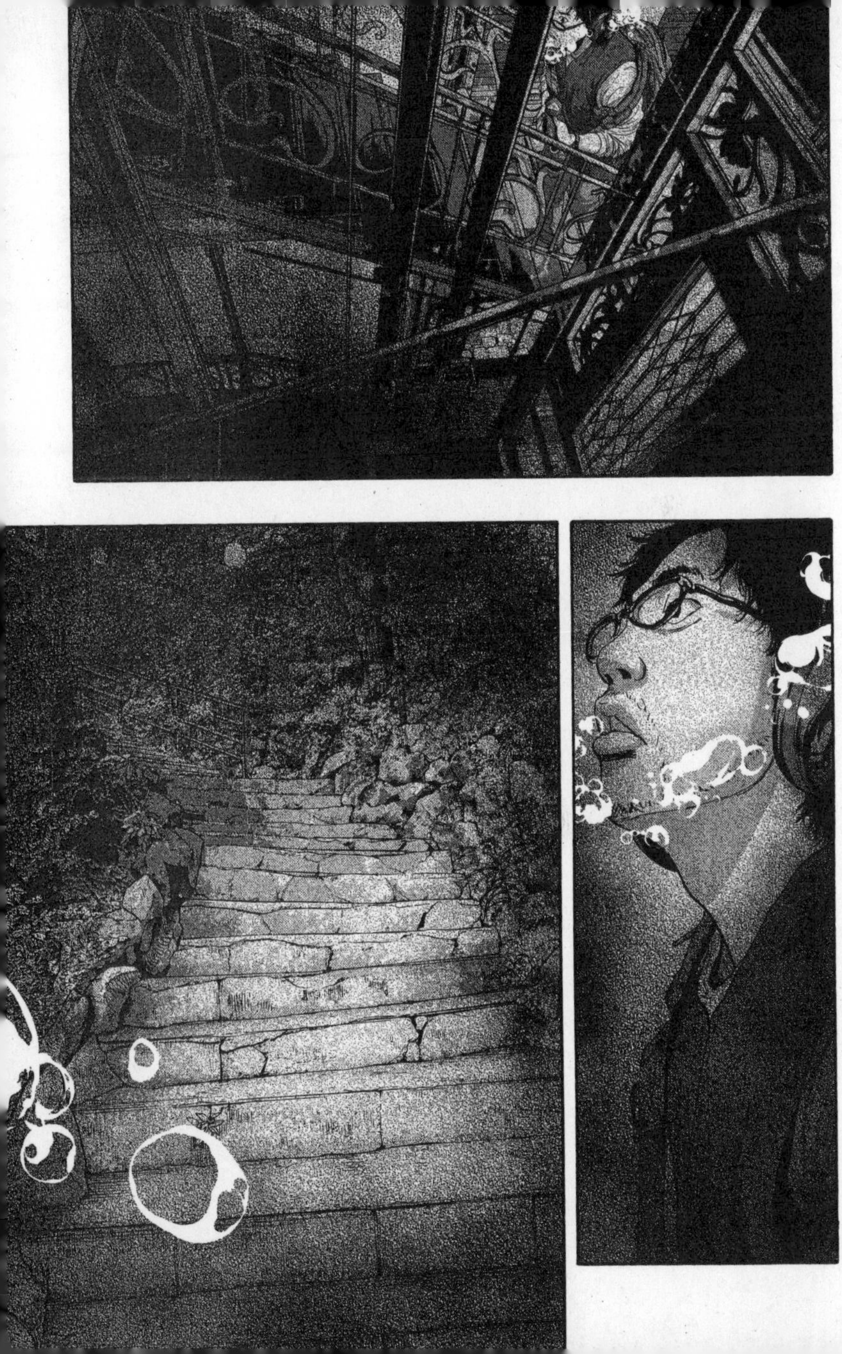

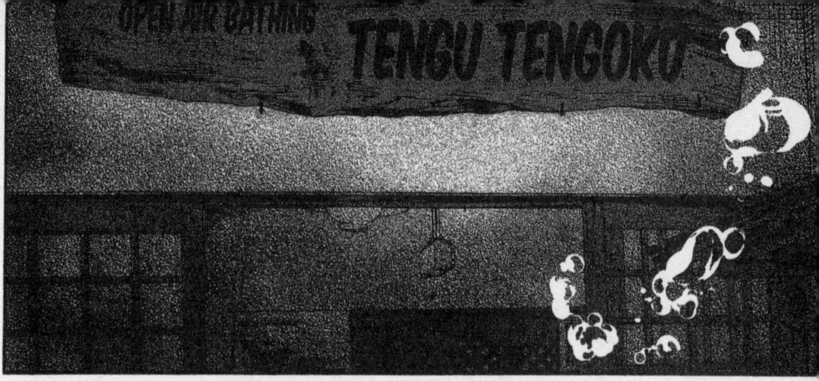
OPEN AIR BATHING
TENGU TENGOKU

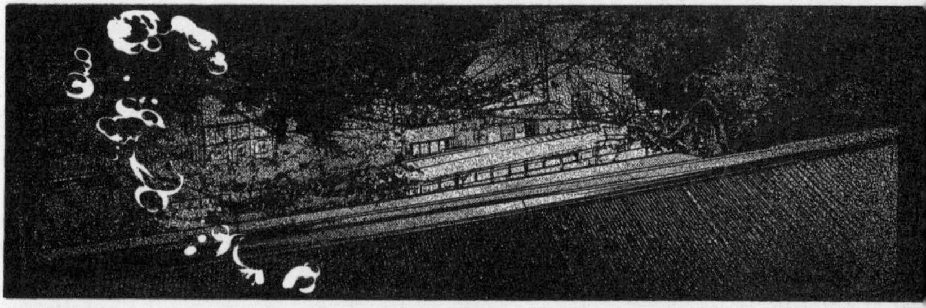

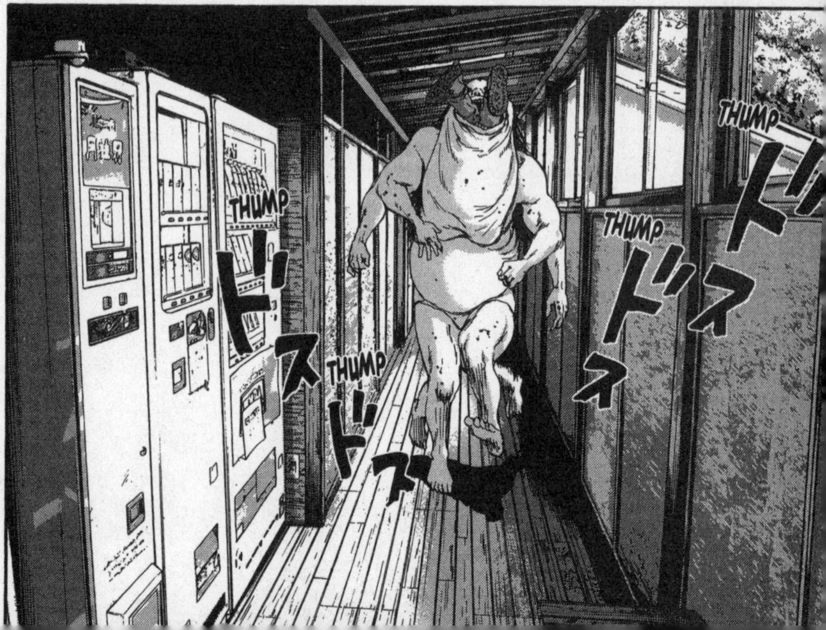
THUMP
THUMP
ドス
THUMP
ドス
THUMP
ドス

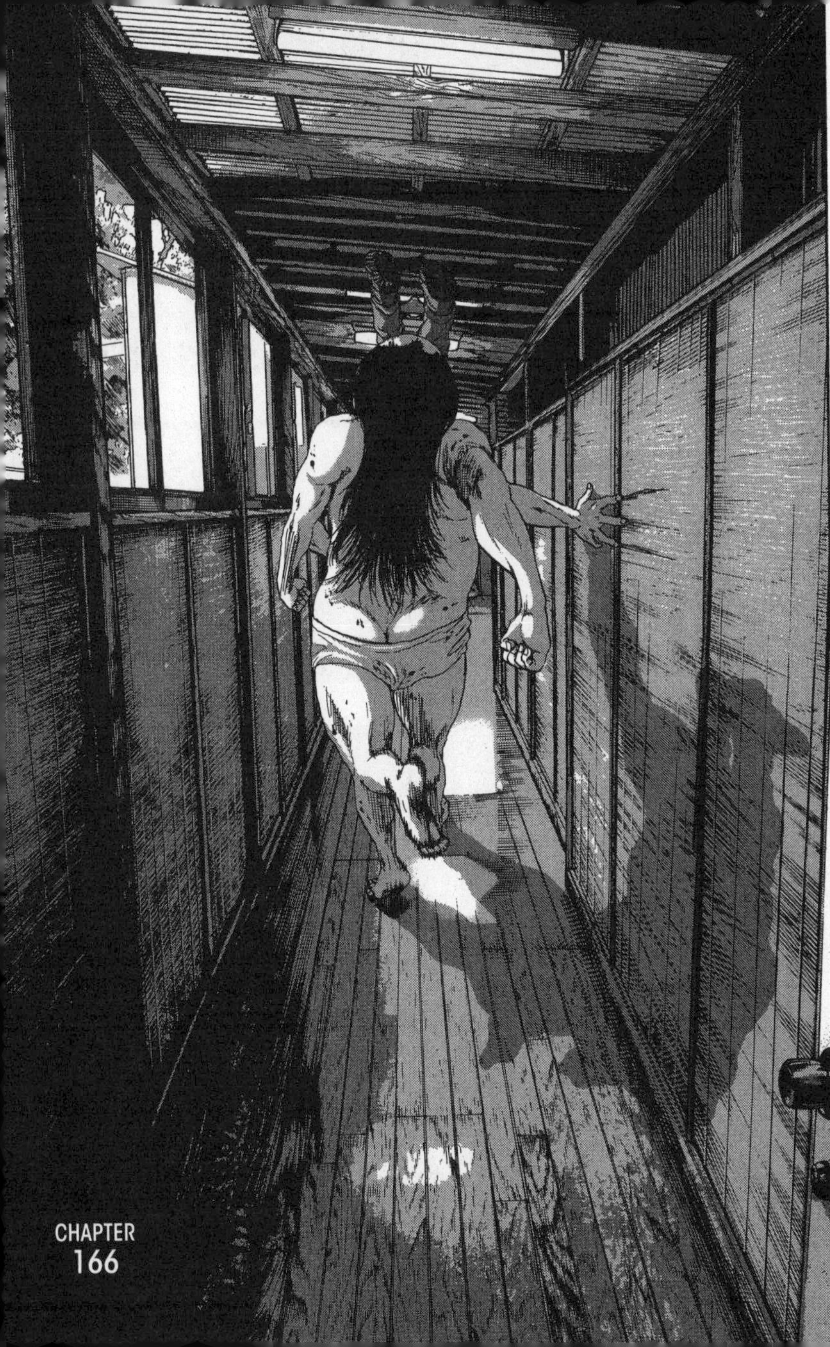

CHAPTER 166

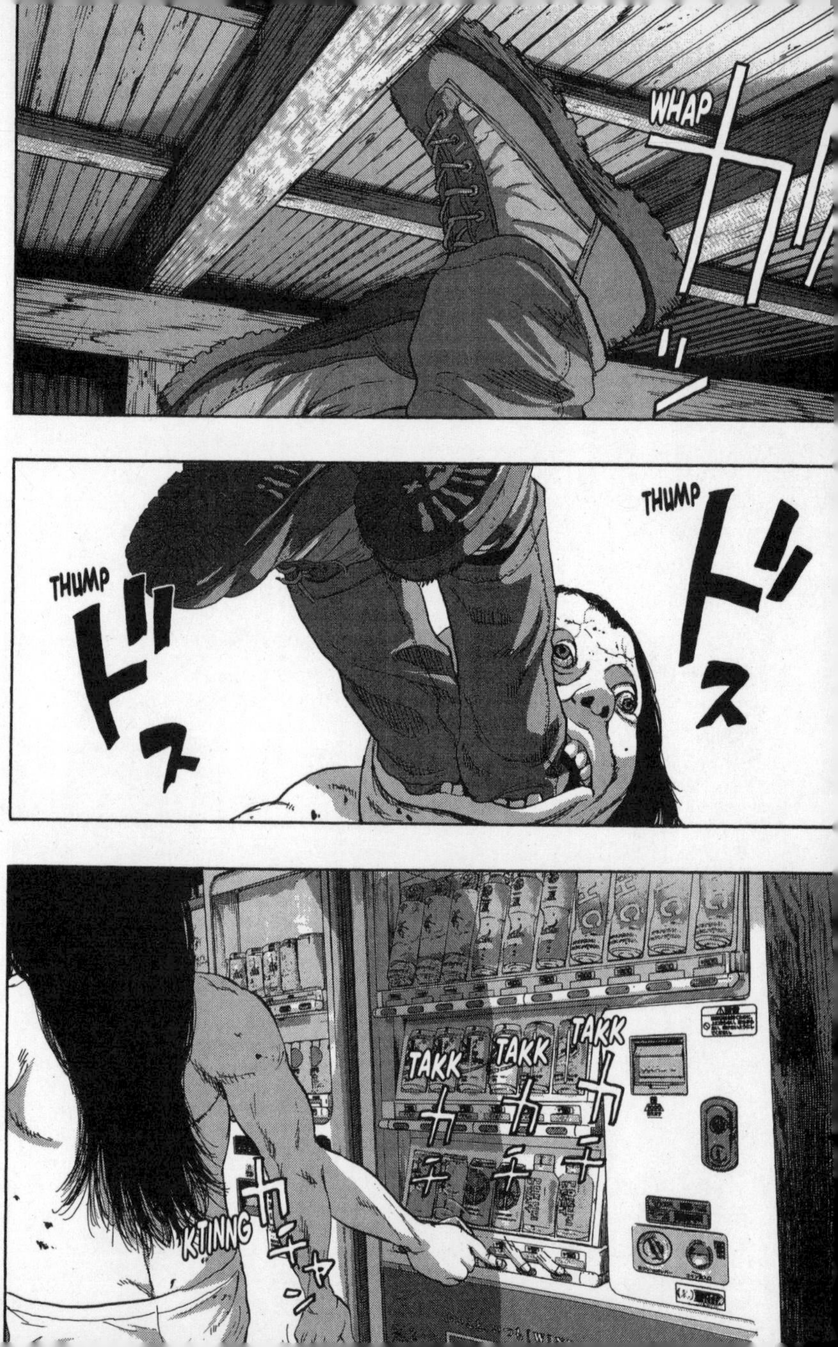

WHAP
カッ
THUMP
ドッス
THUMP
ドス
TAKK
カチ
TAKK
カチ
TAKK
カチ
KTINNG
カチャン

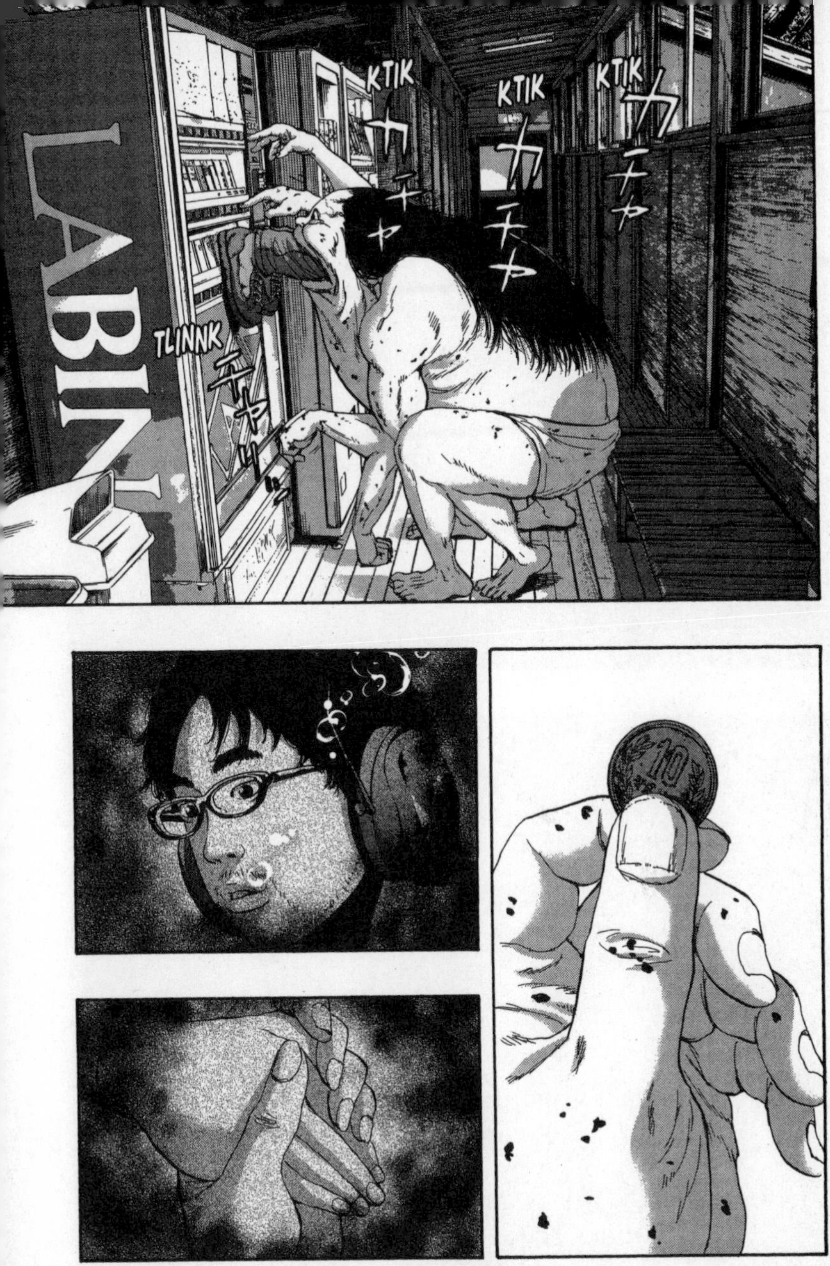
KTIK
KTIK
KTIK
TLINNK
10

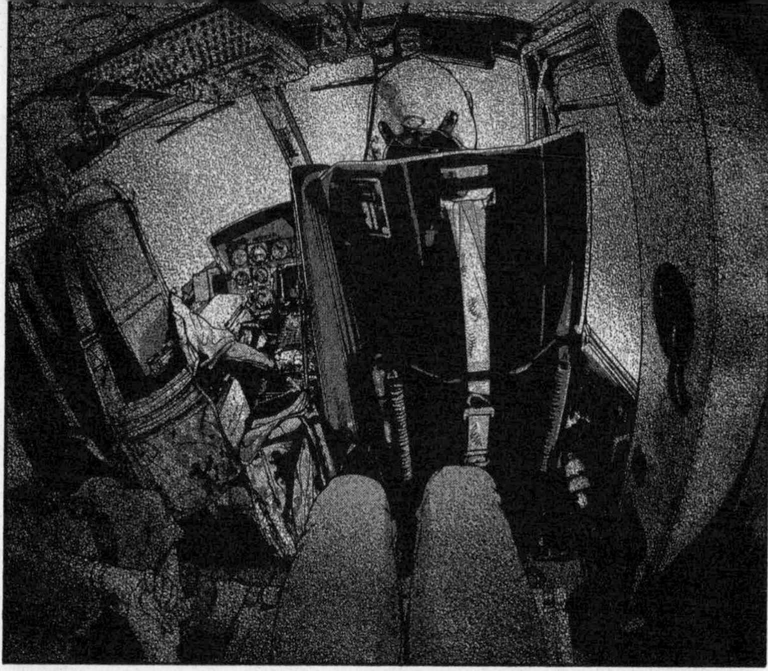

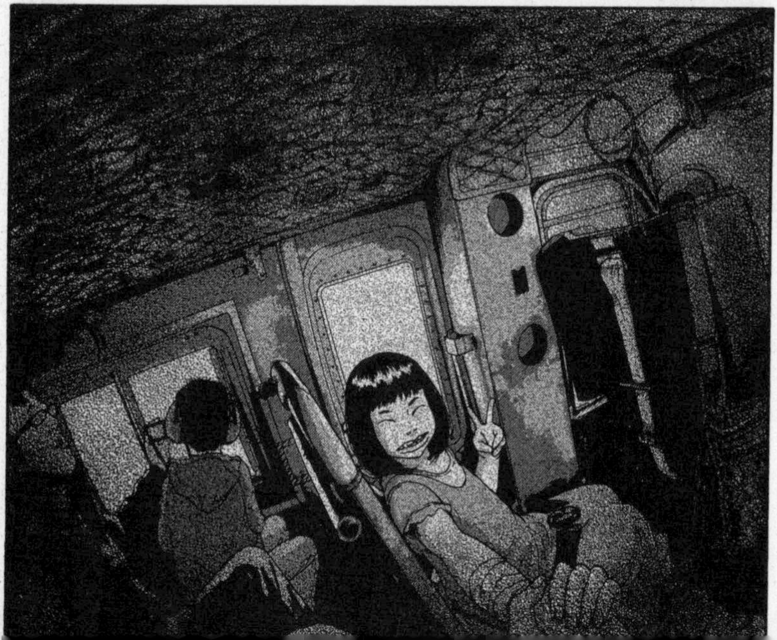

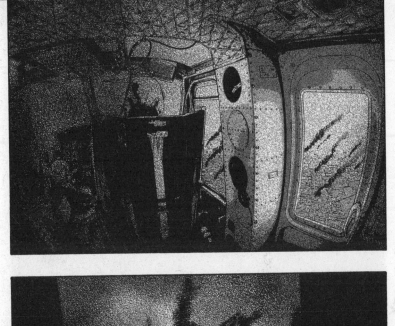

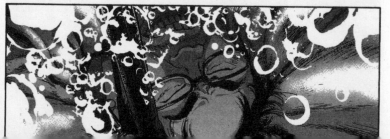

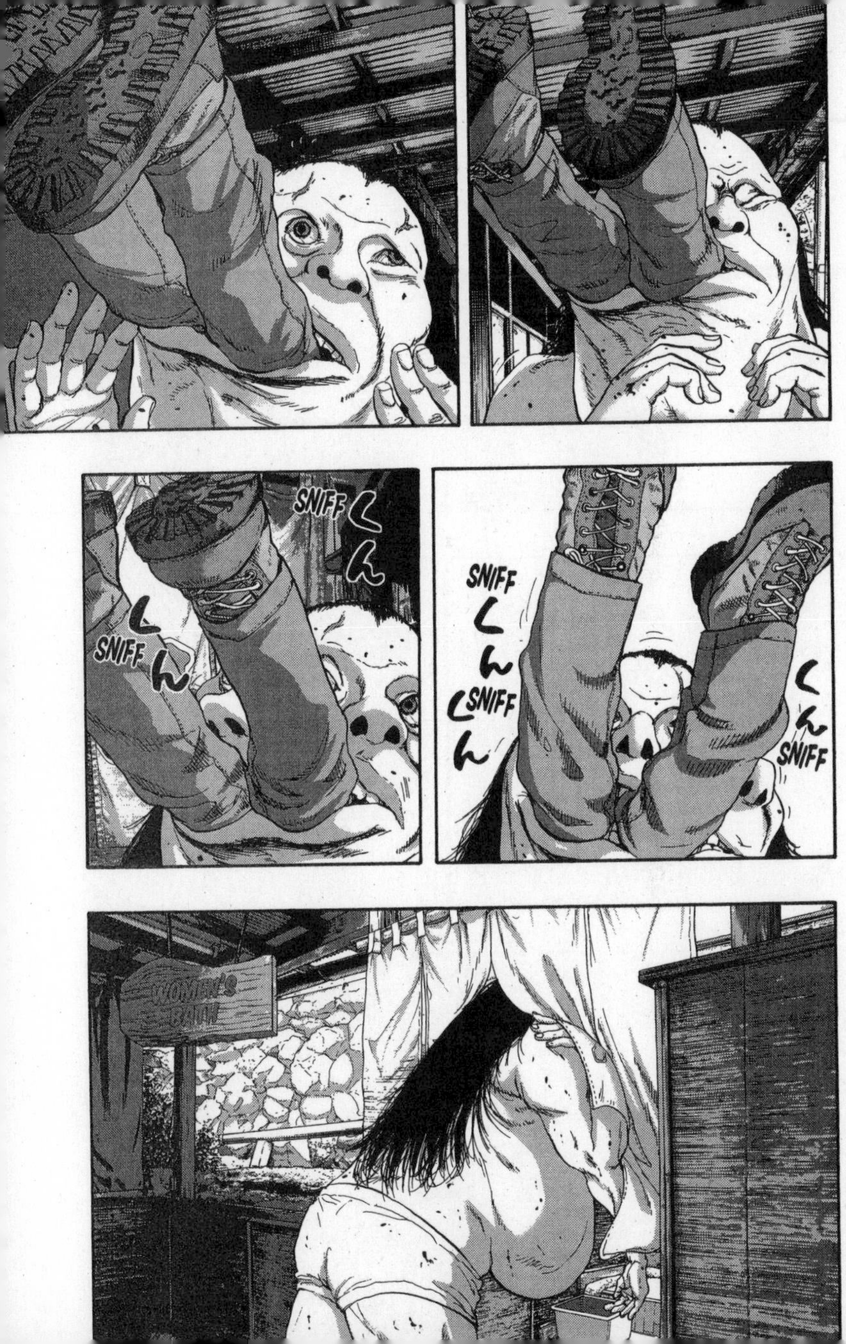

SNIFF
くん
SNIFF
くん
SNIFF
くん
SNIFF
くん
SNIFF
くん
SNIFF
くん

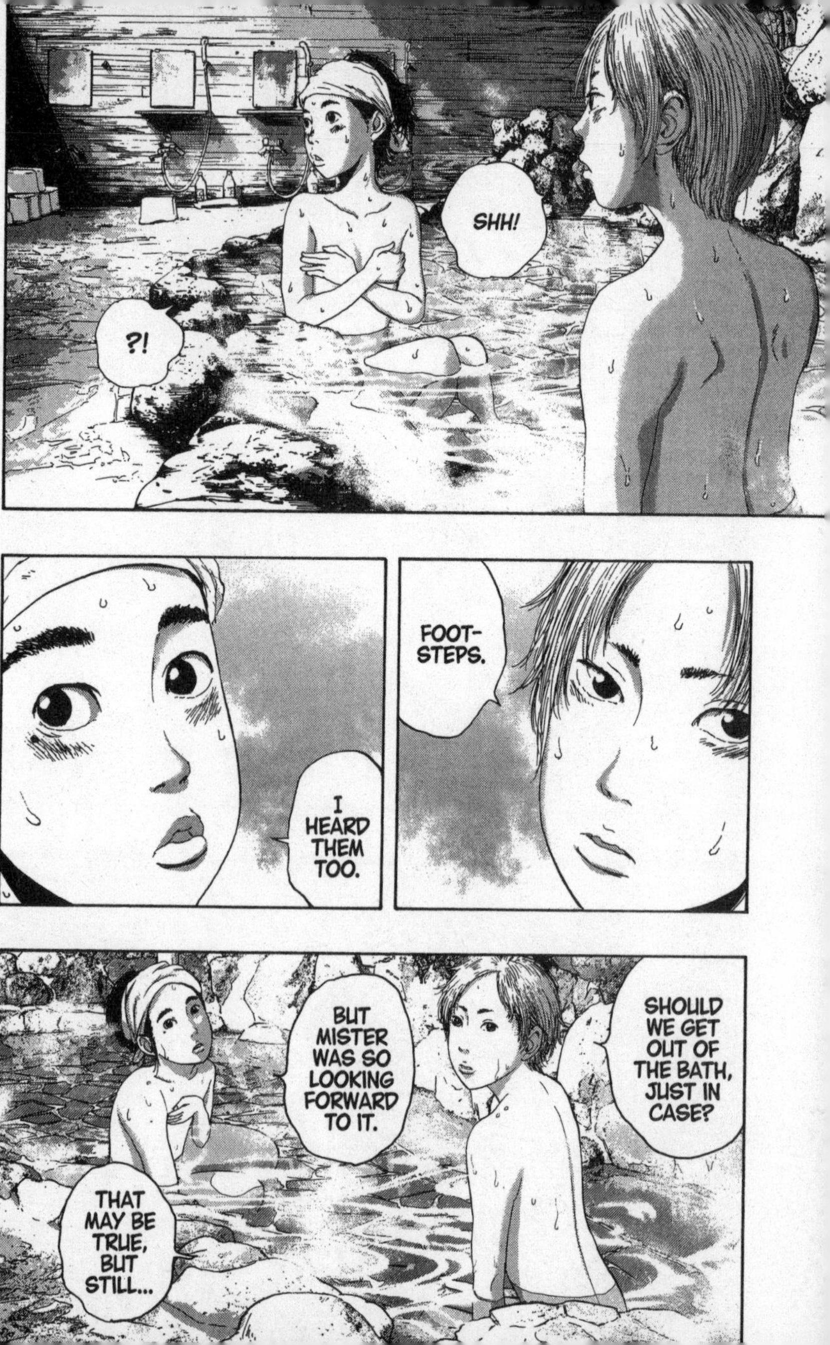
SHH!
?!
FOOT-STEPS.
I HEARD THEM TOO.
SHOULD WE GET OUT OF THE BATH, JUST IN CASE?
BUT MISTER WAS SO LOOKING FORWARD TO IT.
THAT MAY BE TRUE, BUT STILL...

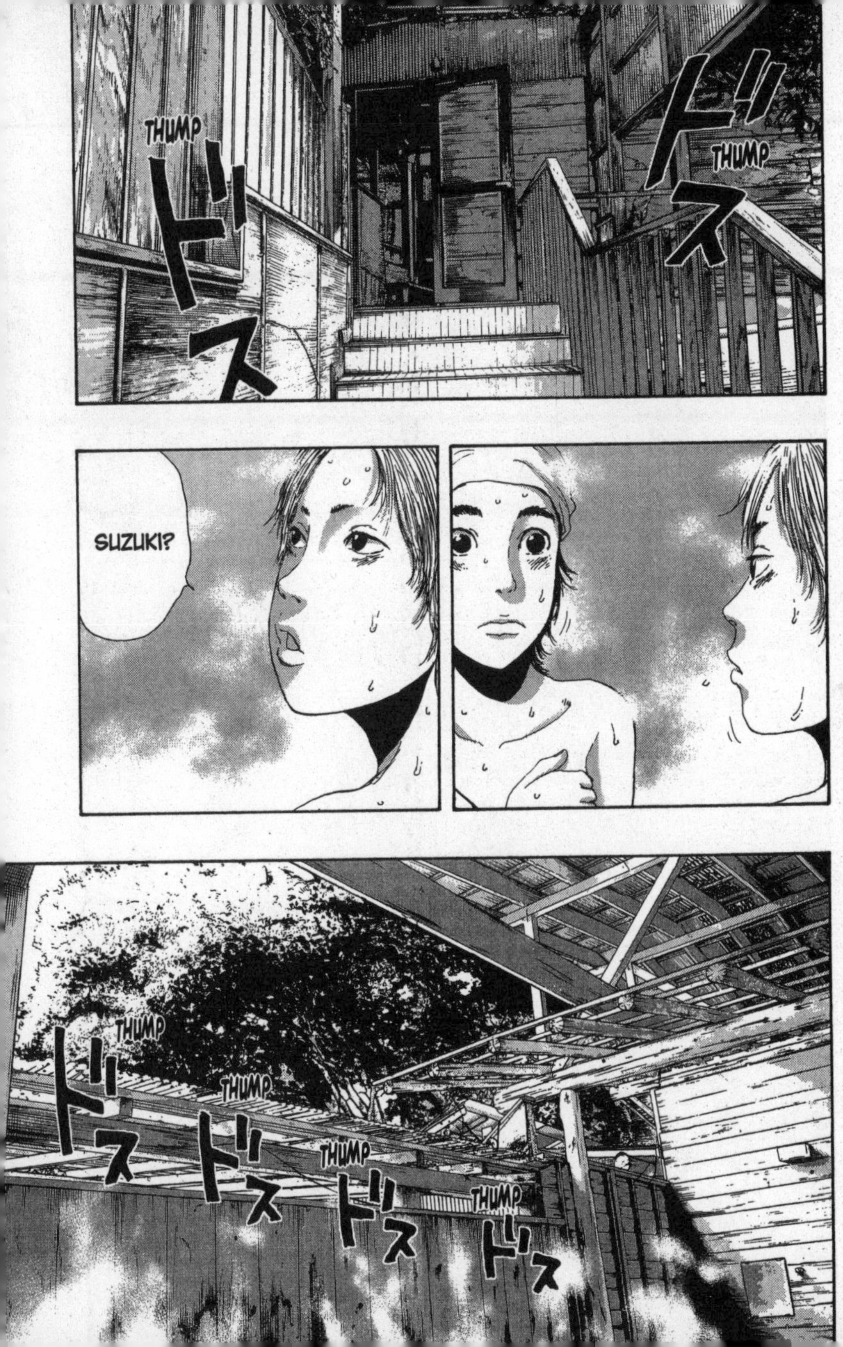
ドス
THUMP
THUMP
ドス
SUZUKI?
THUMP
ドス
THUMP
ドス
THUMP
ドス
THUMP
ドス

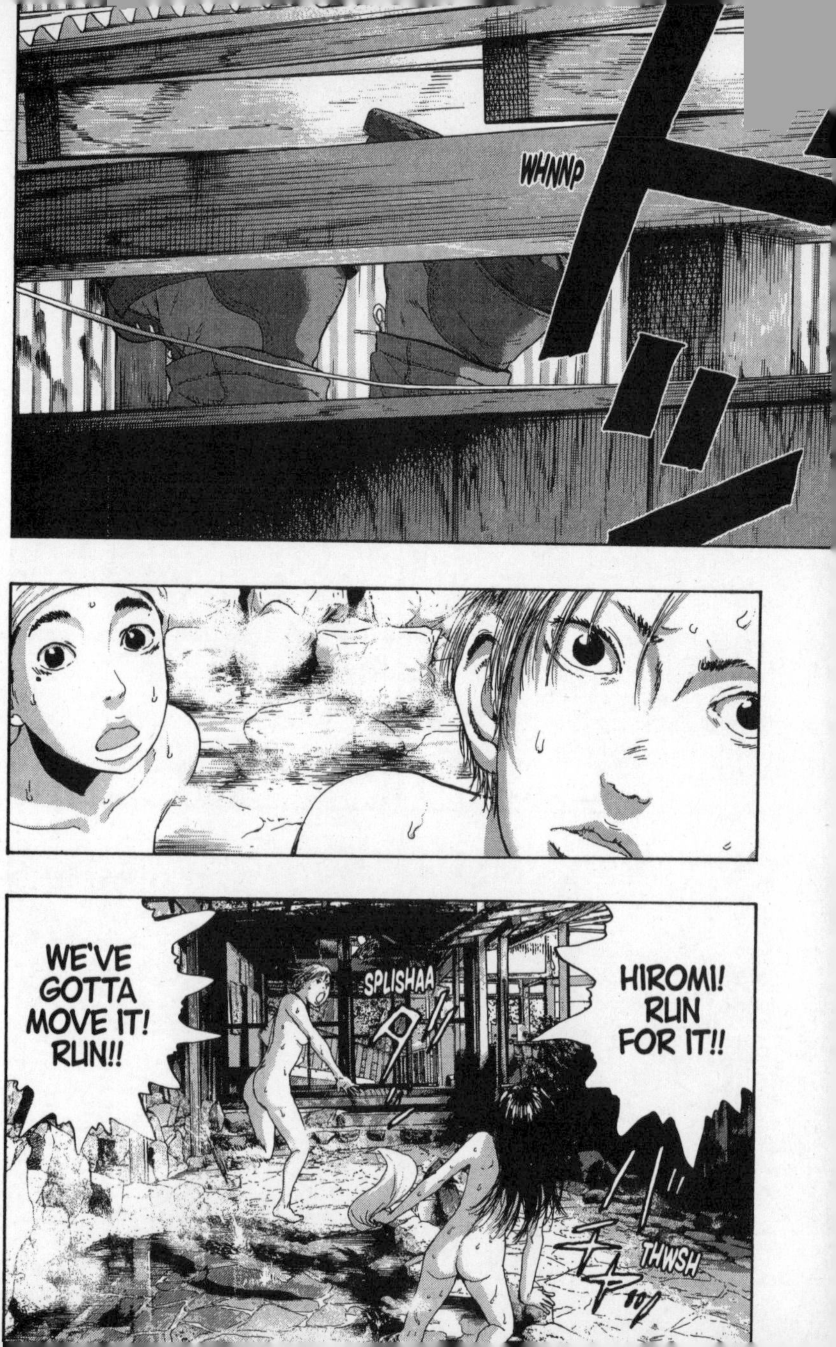
WHNNP
HIROMI! RUN FOR IT!!
SPLISHAA
WE'VE GOTTA MOVE IT! RUN!!
THWSH

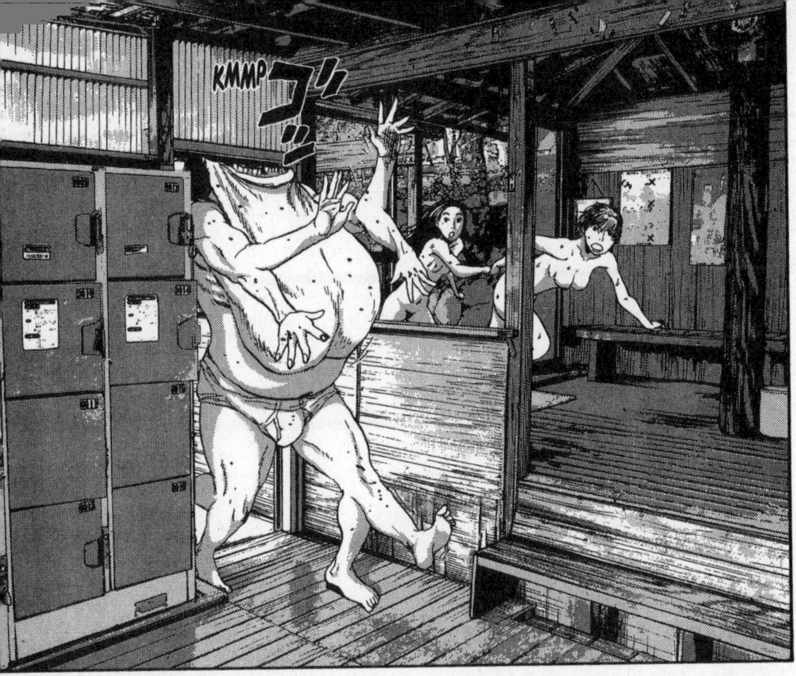
KMMP
ゴゴ
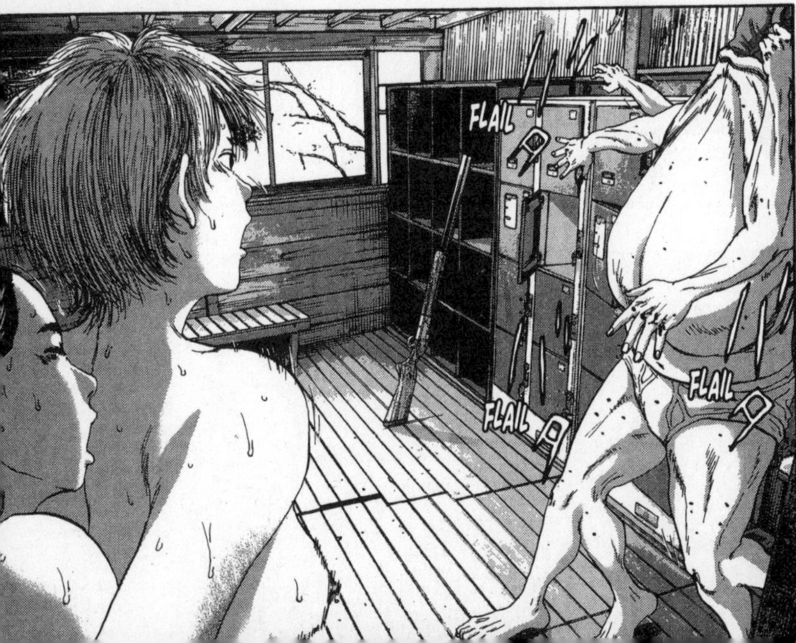
FLAIL
FLAIL
FLAIL

ギョロ
LOOK
ギョロ
LOOK
LOOK
ギョロ

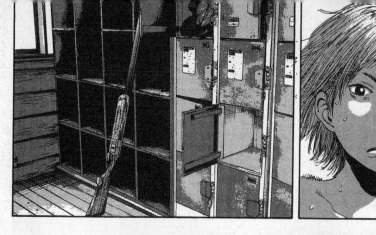

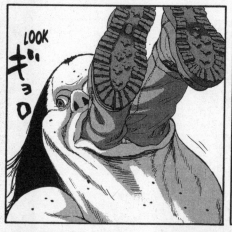

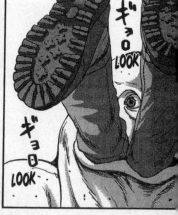

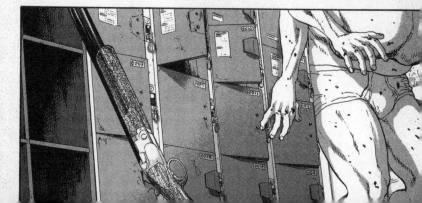

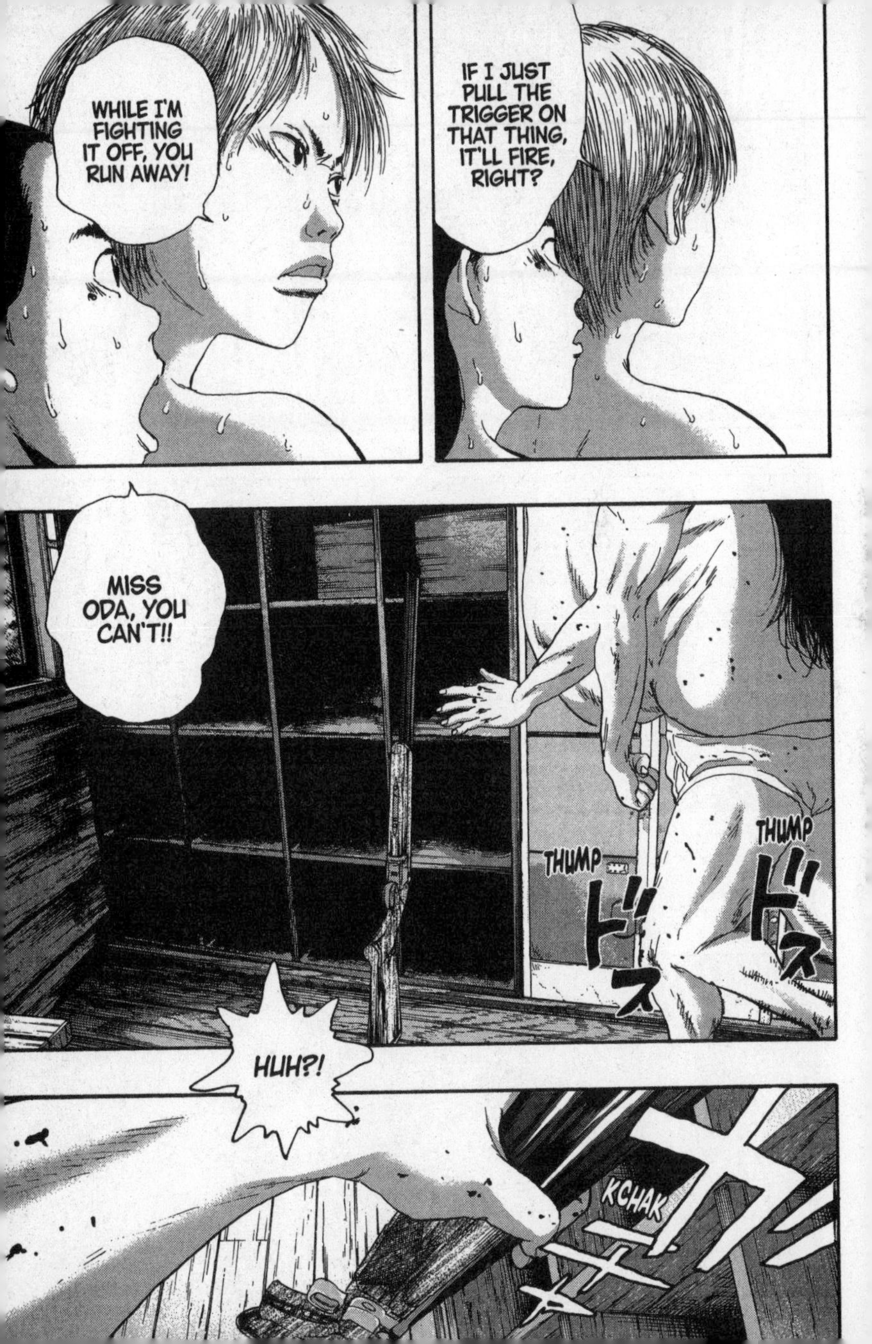
IF I JUST PULL THE TRIGGER ON THAT THING, IT'LL FIRE, RIGHT?
WHILE I'M FIGHTING IT OFF, YOU RUN AWAY!
MISS ODA, YOU CAN'T!!
THUMP
ドス
THUMP
ドス
HUH?!
KCHAK

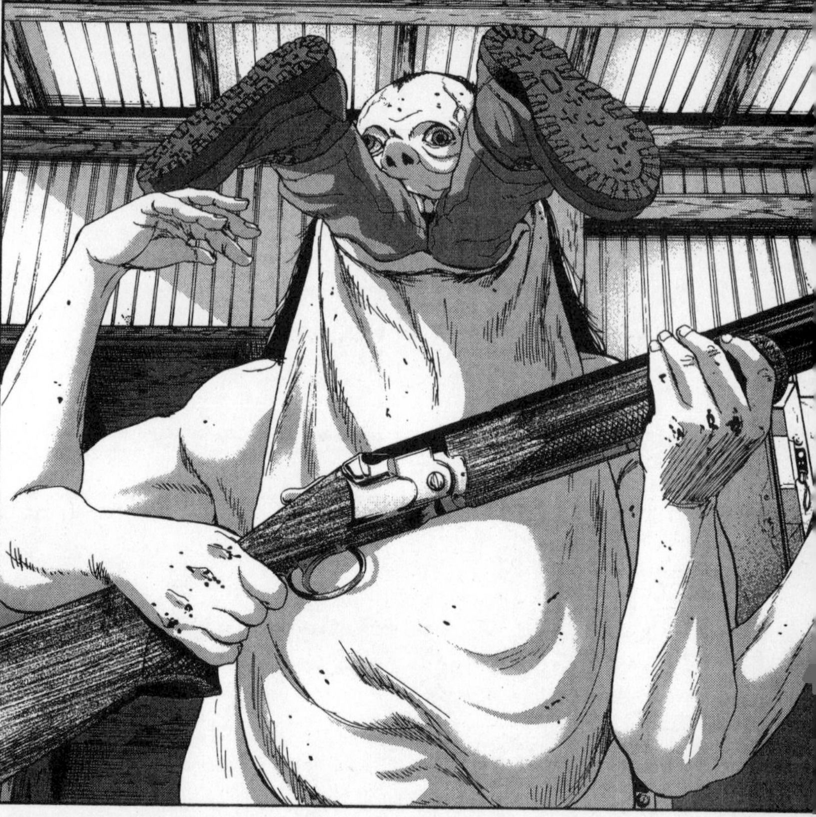
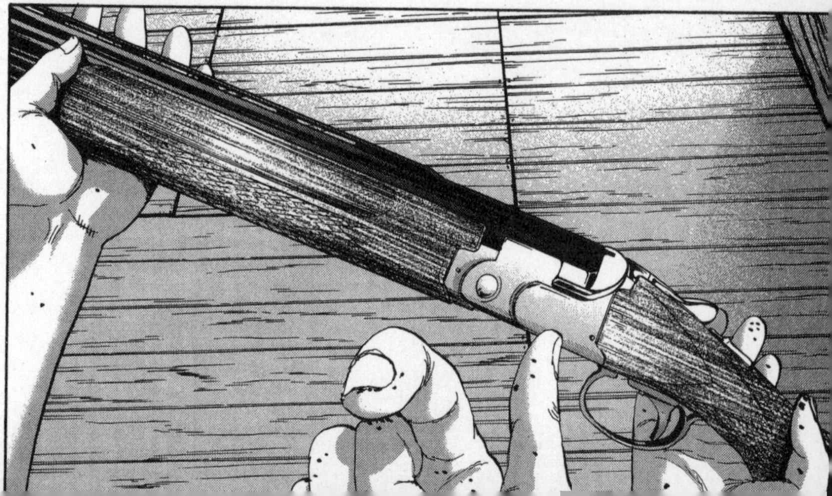

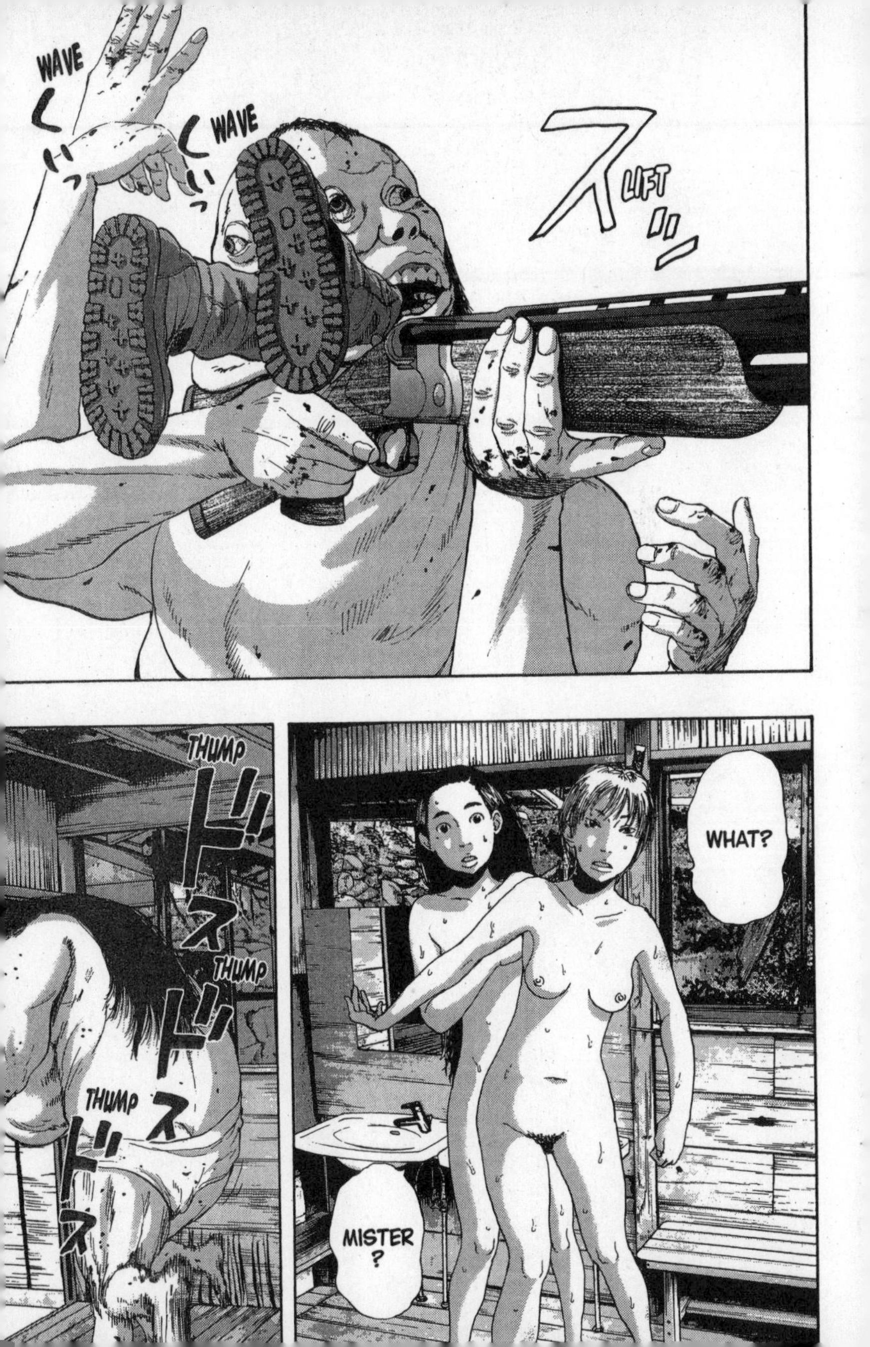
LIFT
WAVE
WAVE
WHAT?
MISTER ?
THUMP
THUMP
THUMP

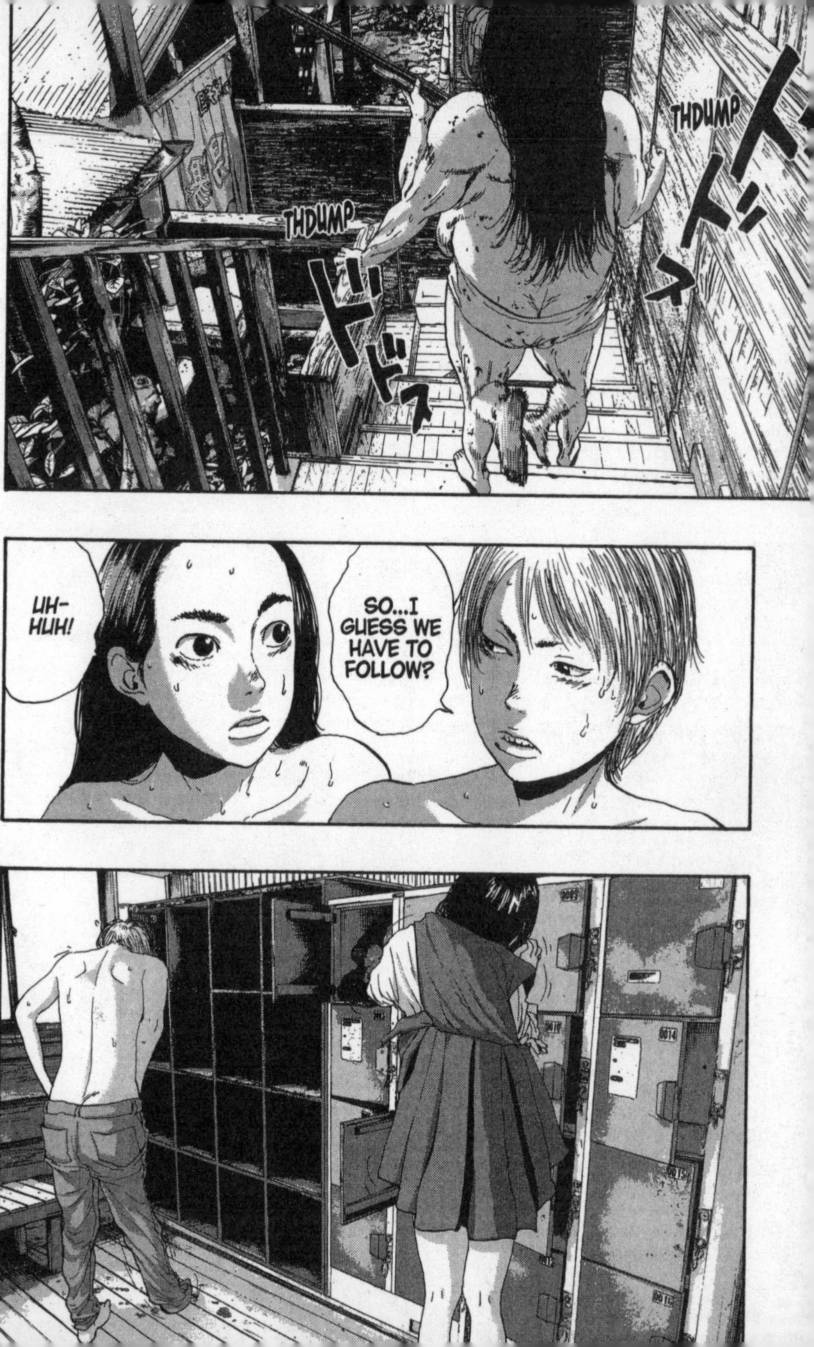
THDUMP
THDUMP
SO...I GUESS WE HAVE TO FOLLOW?
UH-HUH!

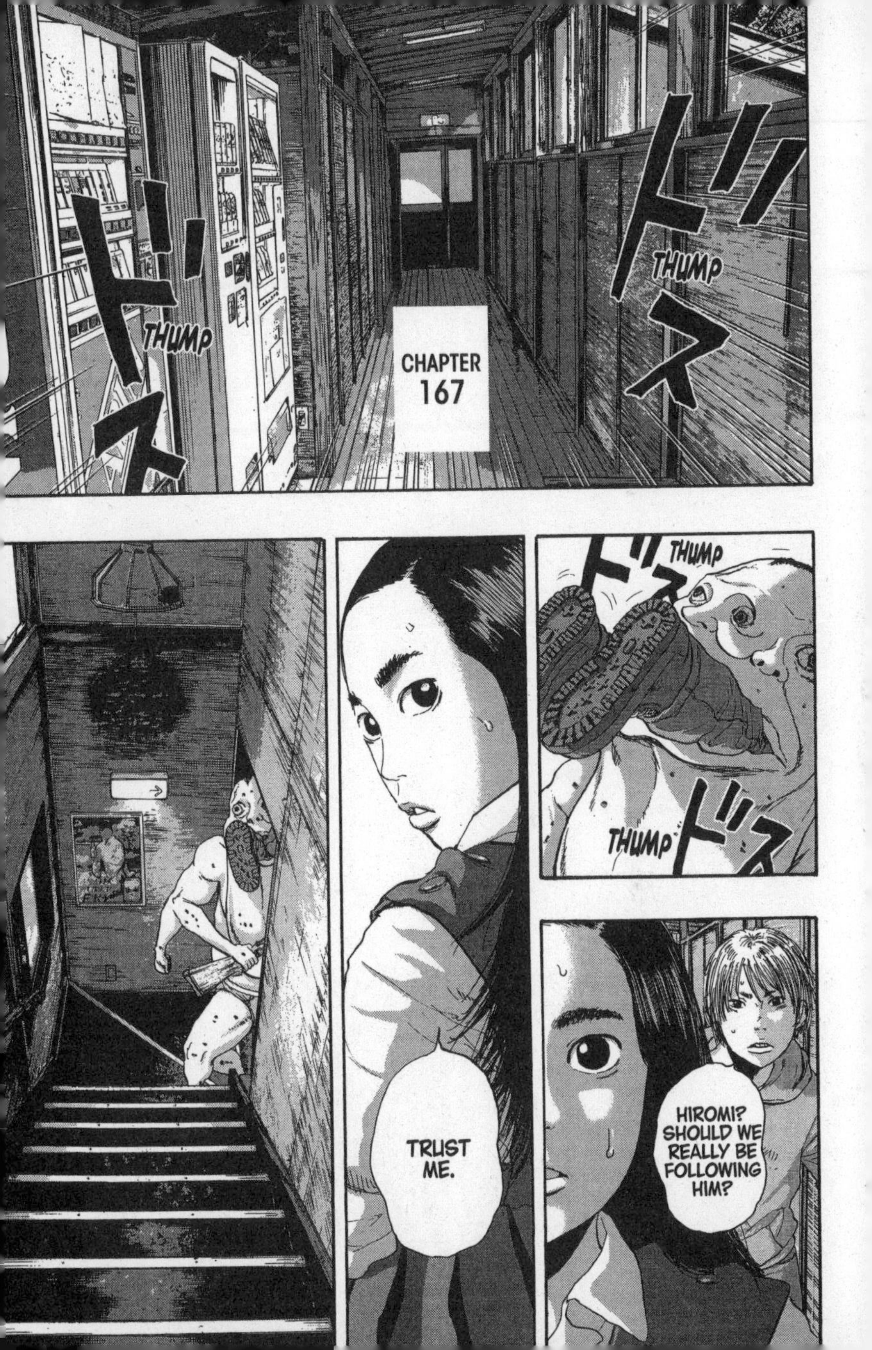
THUMP
THUMP
CHAPTER 167
THUMP
THUMP
HIROMI? SHOULD WE REALLY BE FOLLOWING HIM?
TRUST ME.

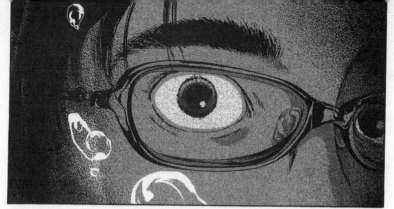

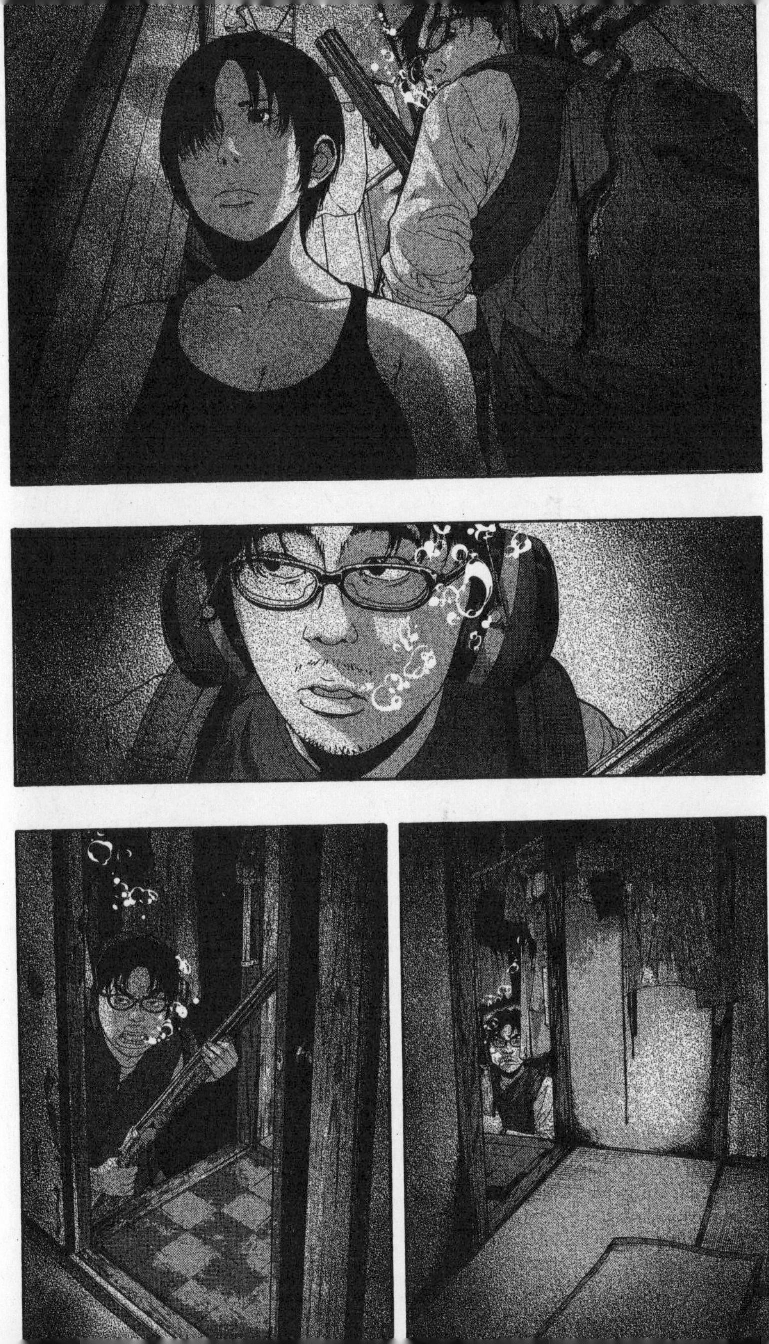

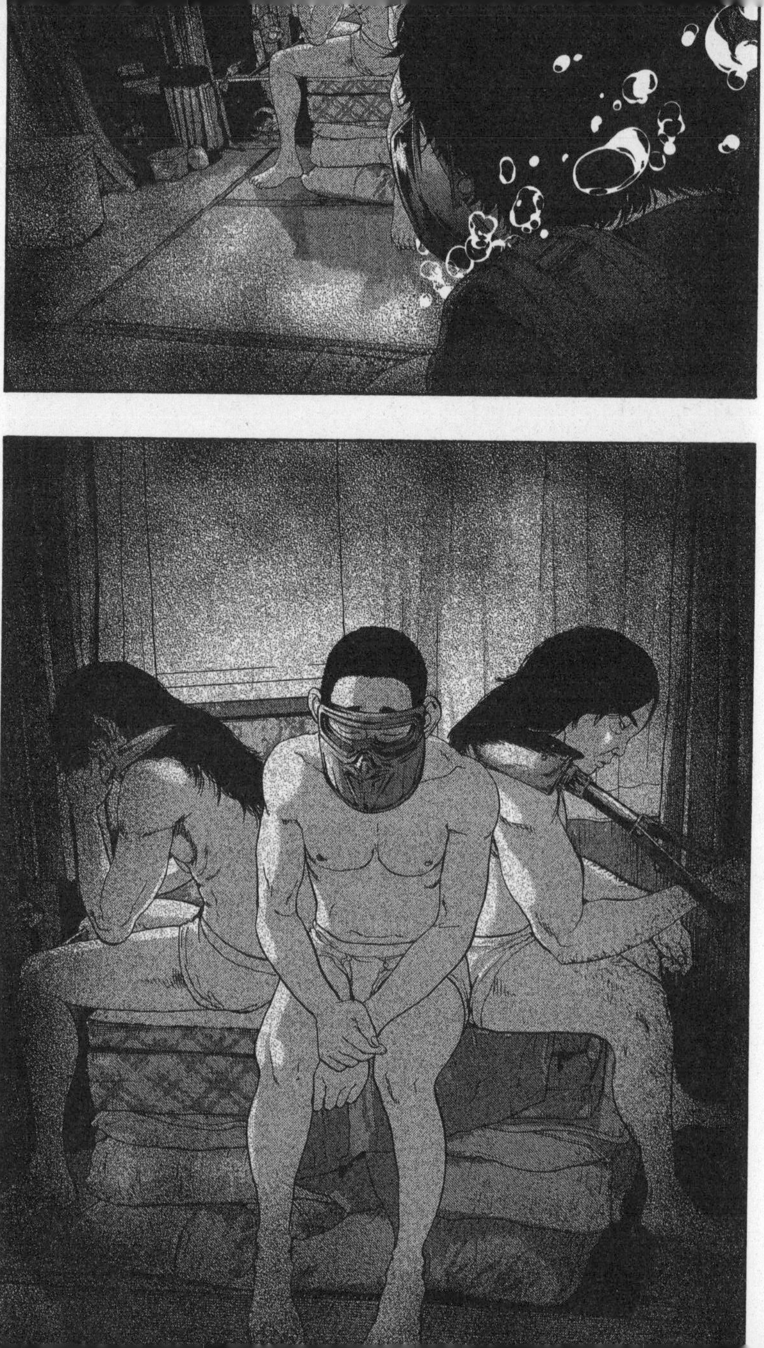

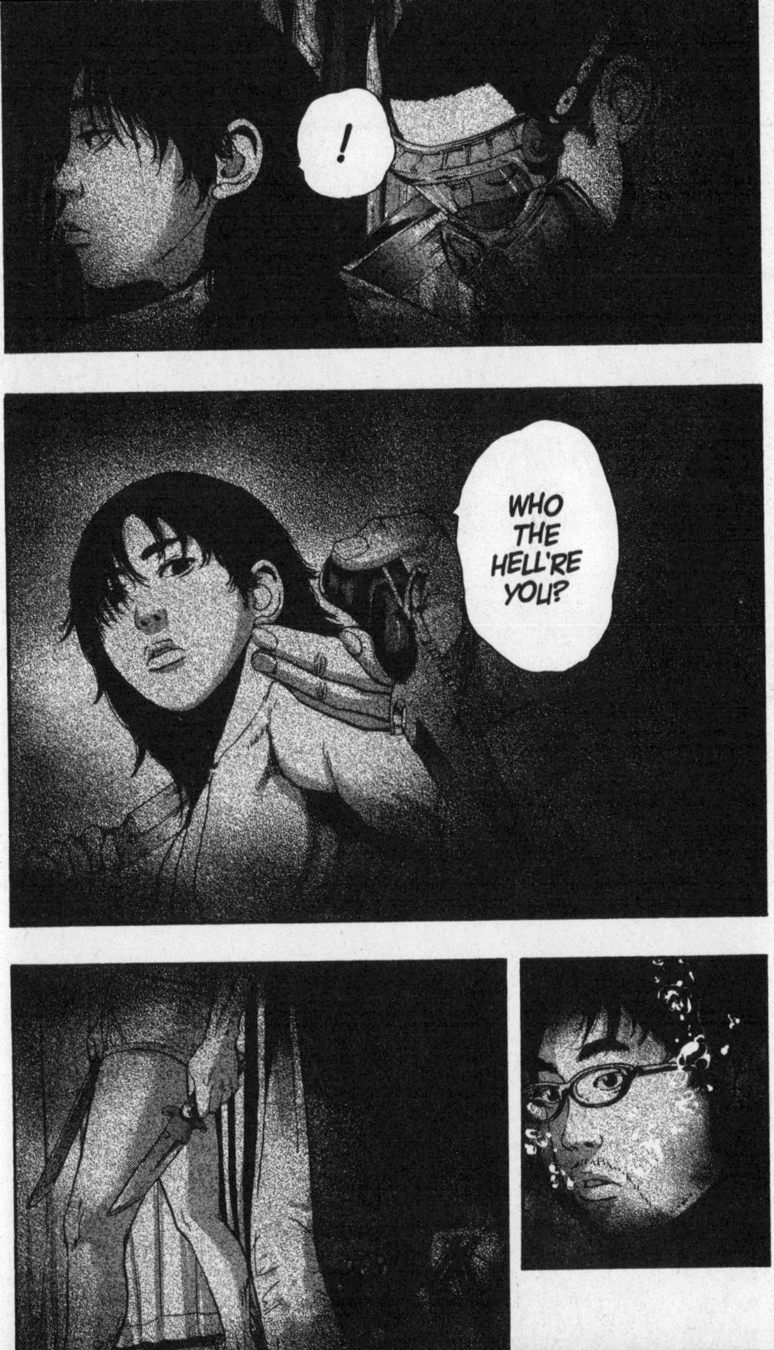
!
WHO THE HELL'RE YOU!?

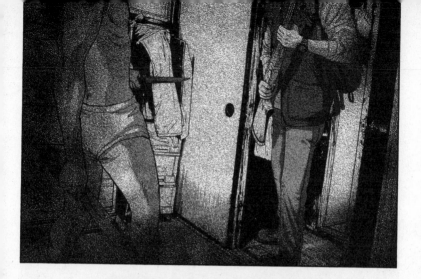

WHAT'RE YOU DOING HERE?

•••

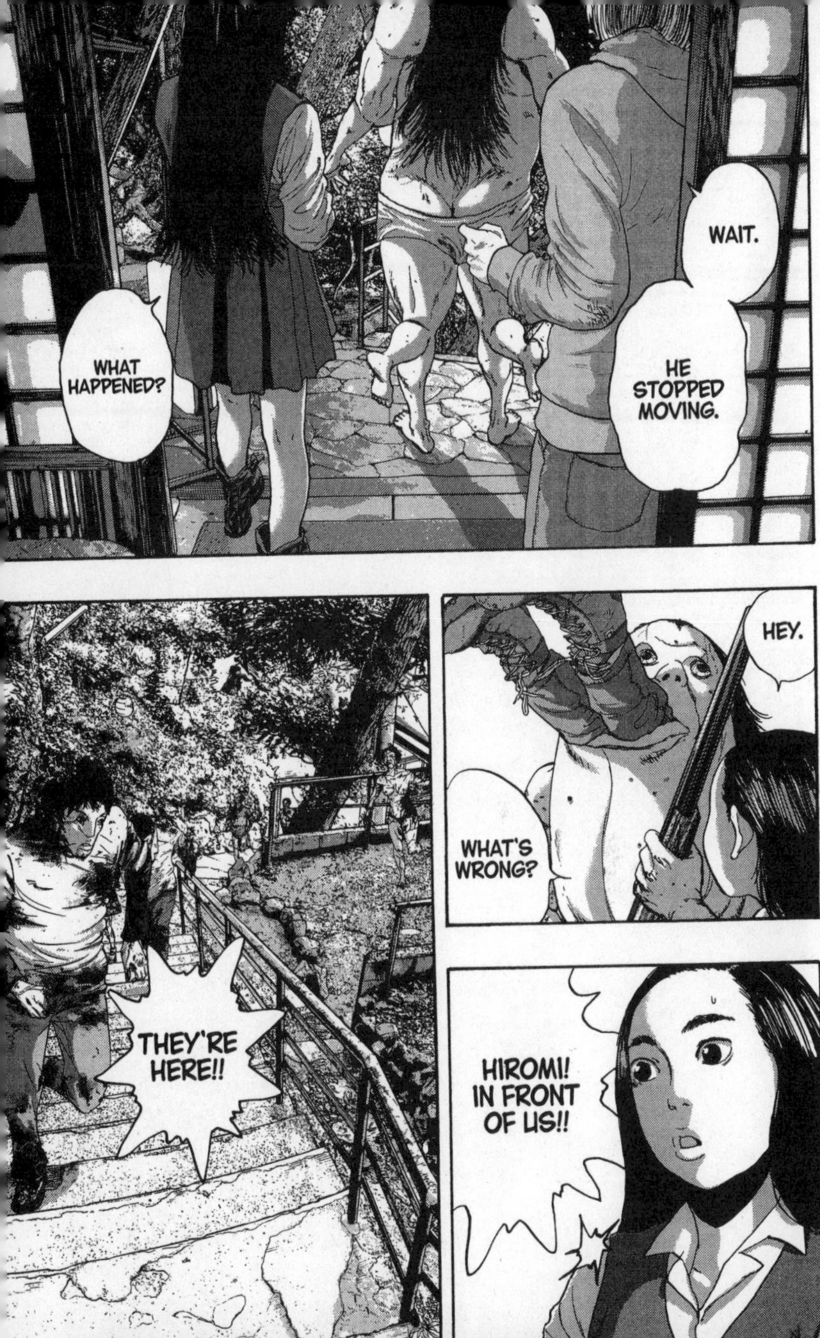
WAIT.
HE STOPPED MOVING.
WHAT HAPPENED?
HEY.
WHAT'S WRONG?
HIROMI! IN FRONT OF US!!
THEY'RE HERE!!

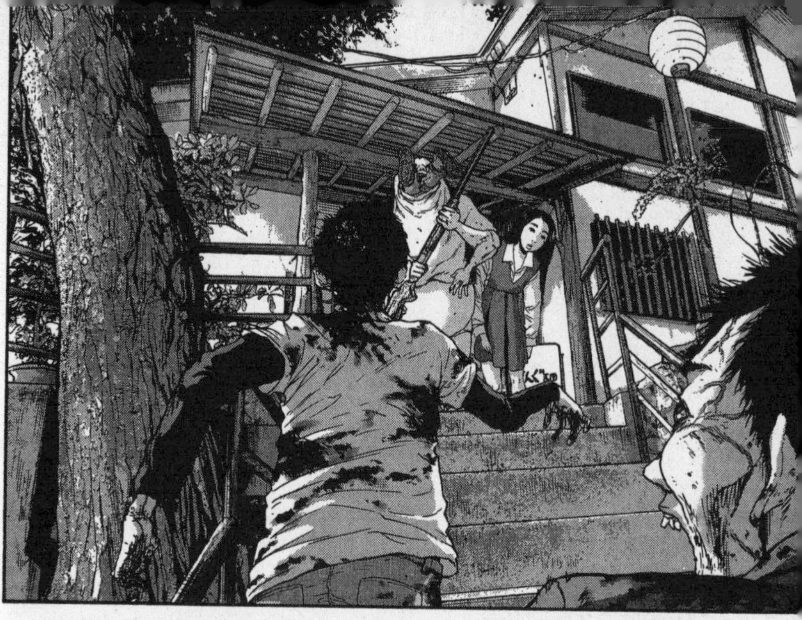

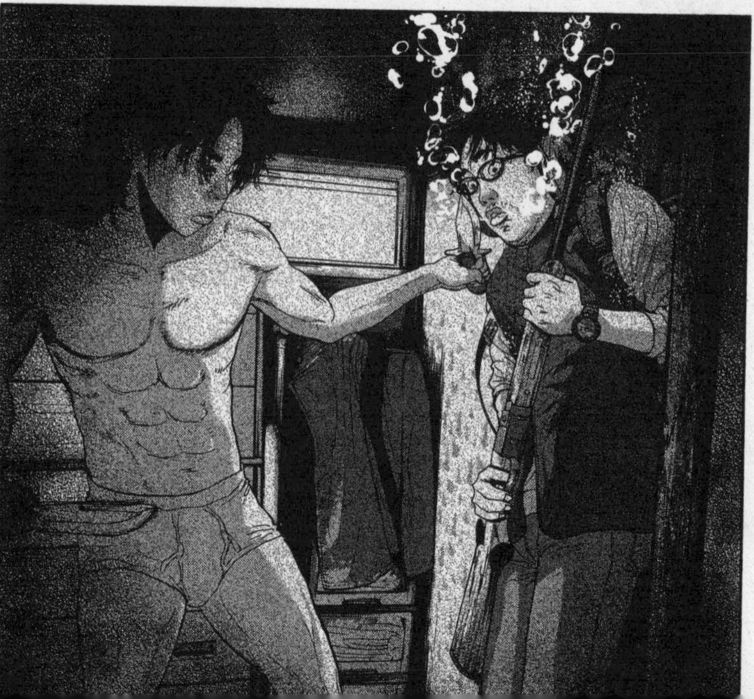

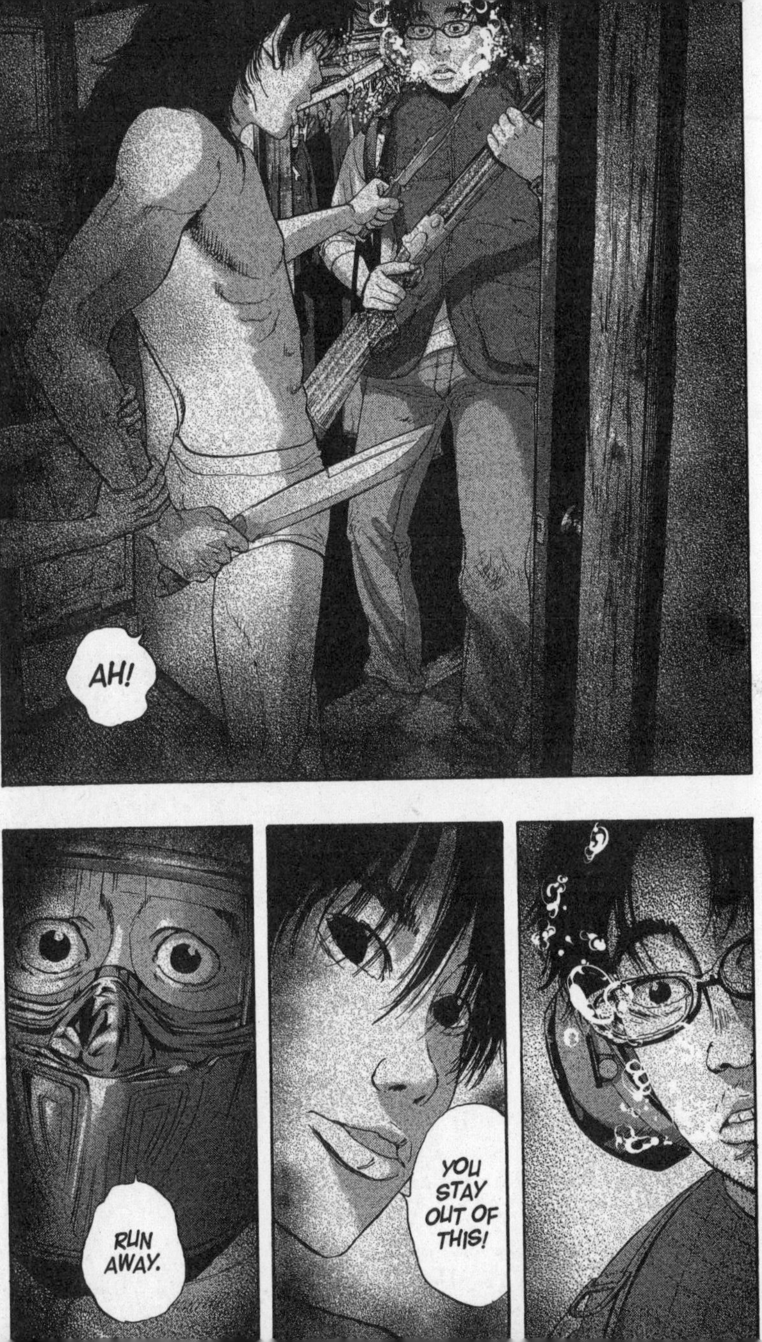
AH!
YOU STAY OUT OF THIS!
RUN AWAY.

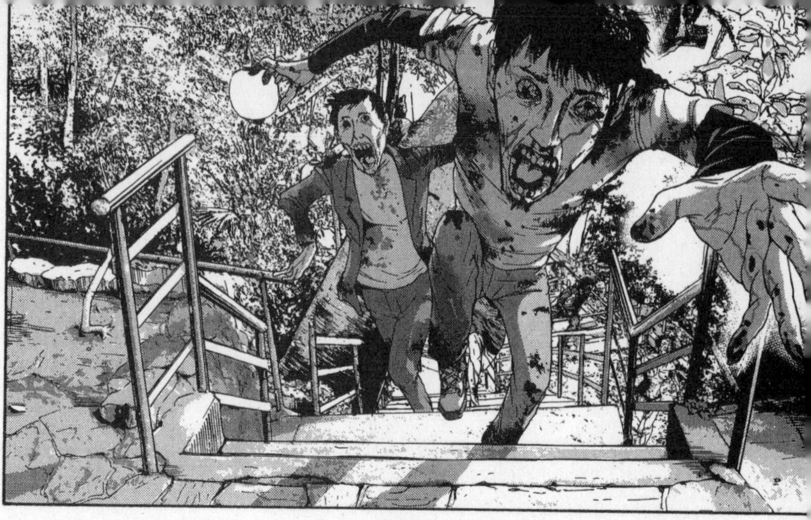

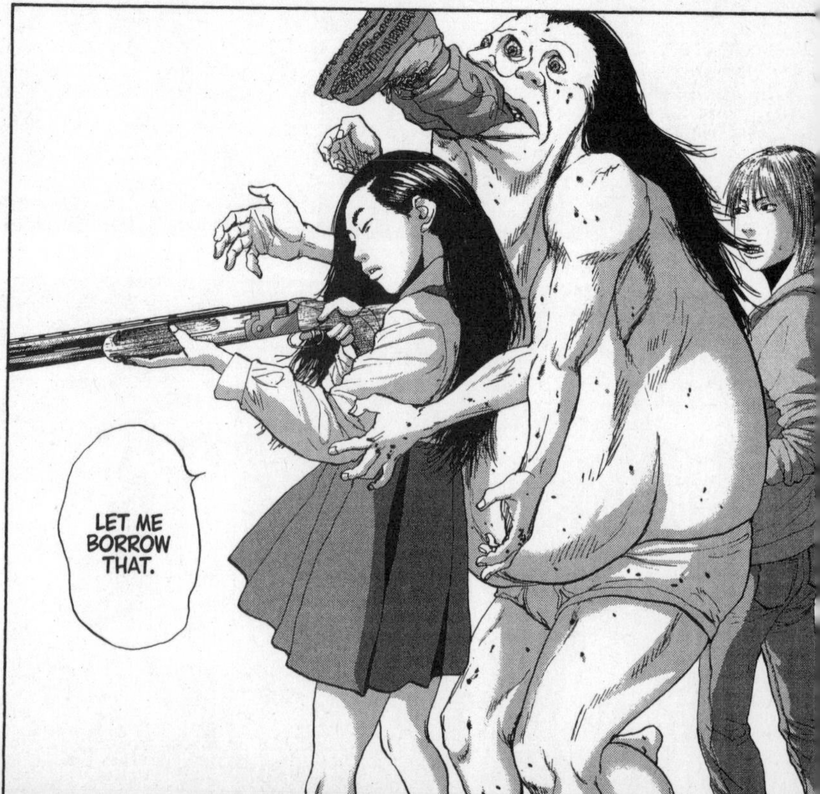
LET ME BORROW THAT.

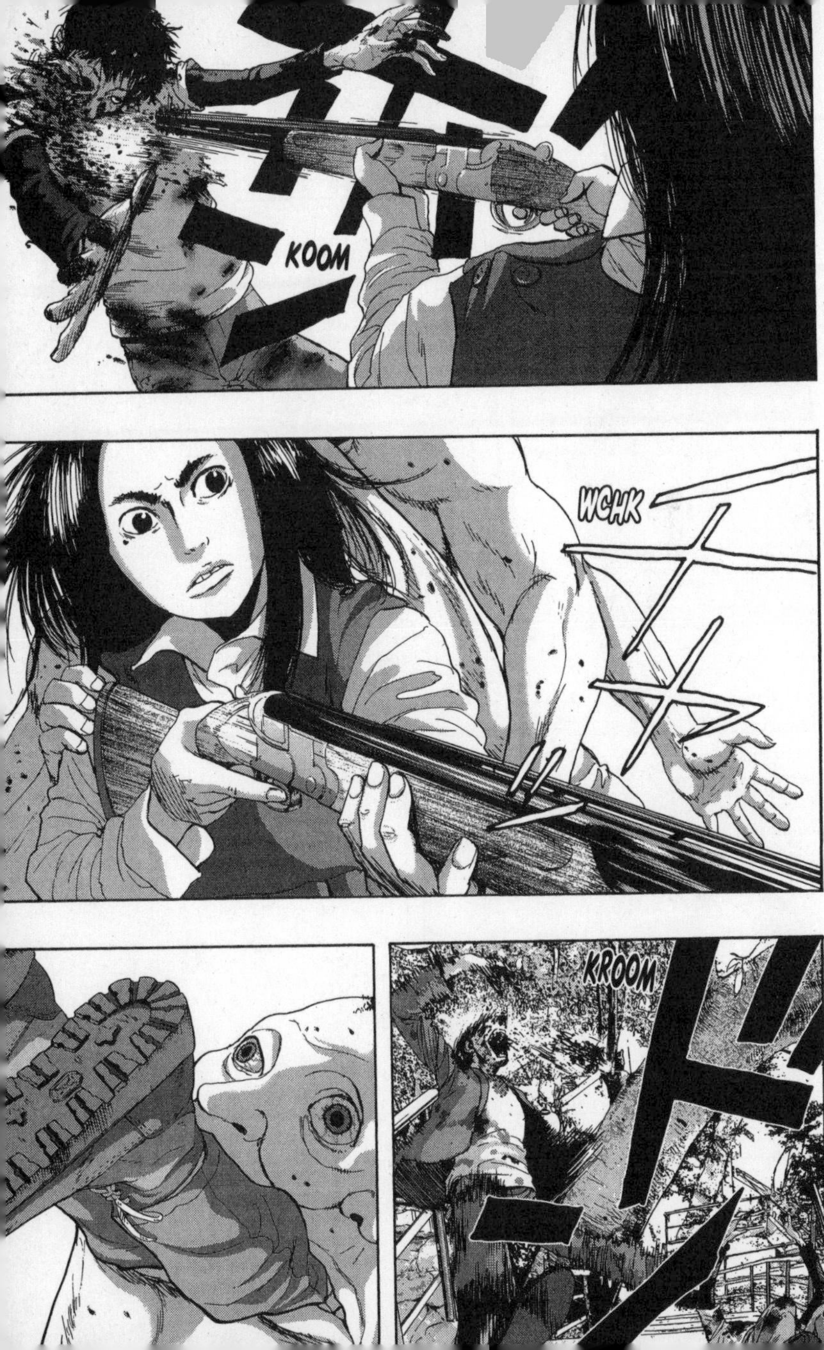
KOOM
WCHK
KROOM

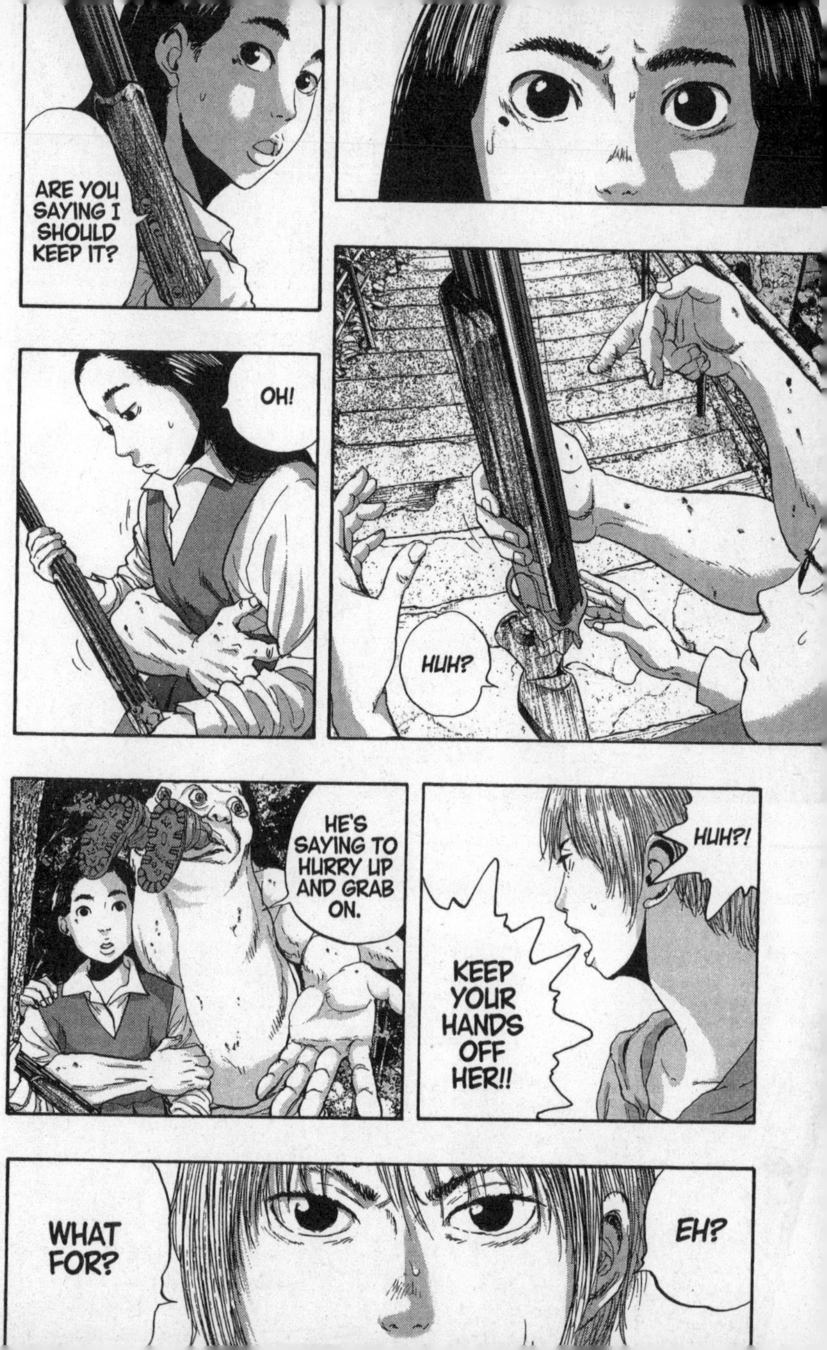
ARE YOU SAYING I SHOULD KEEP IT?
HUH?
OH!
HUH?!
KEEP YOUR HANDS OFF HER!!
HE'S SAYING TO HURRY UP AND GRAB ON.
EH?
WHAT FOR?

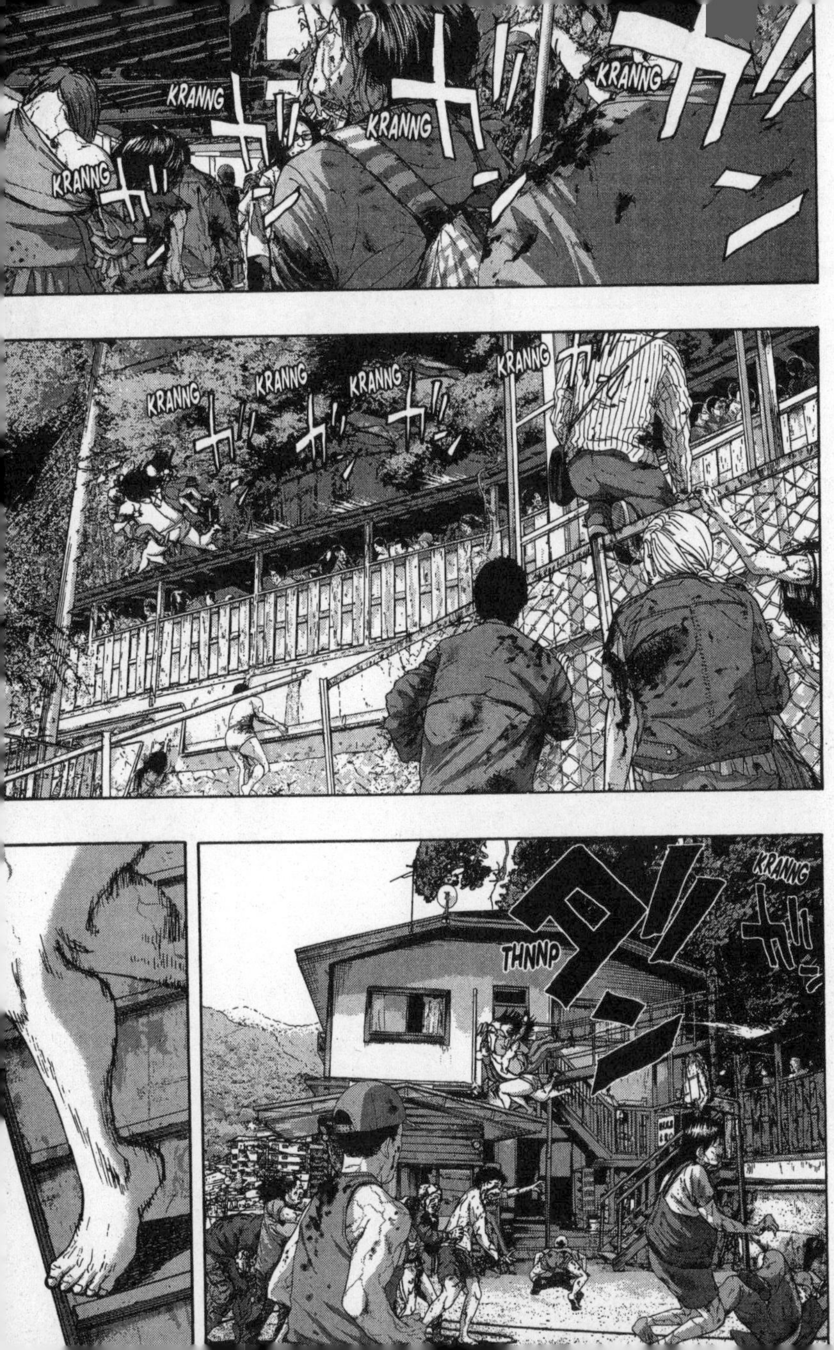
KRANNG
KRANNG
KRANNG
KRANNG
KRANNG
KRANNG
KRANNG
KRANNG
KRANNG
THNNP

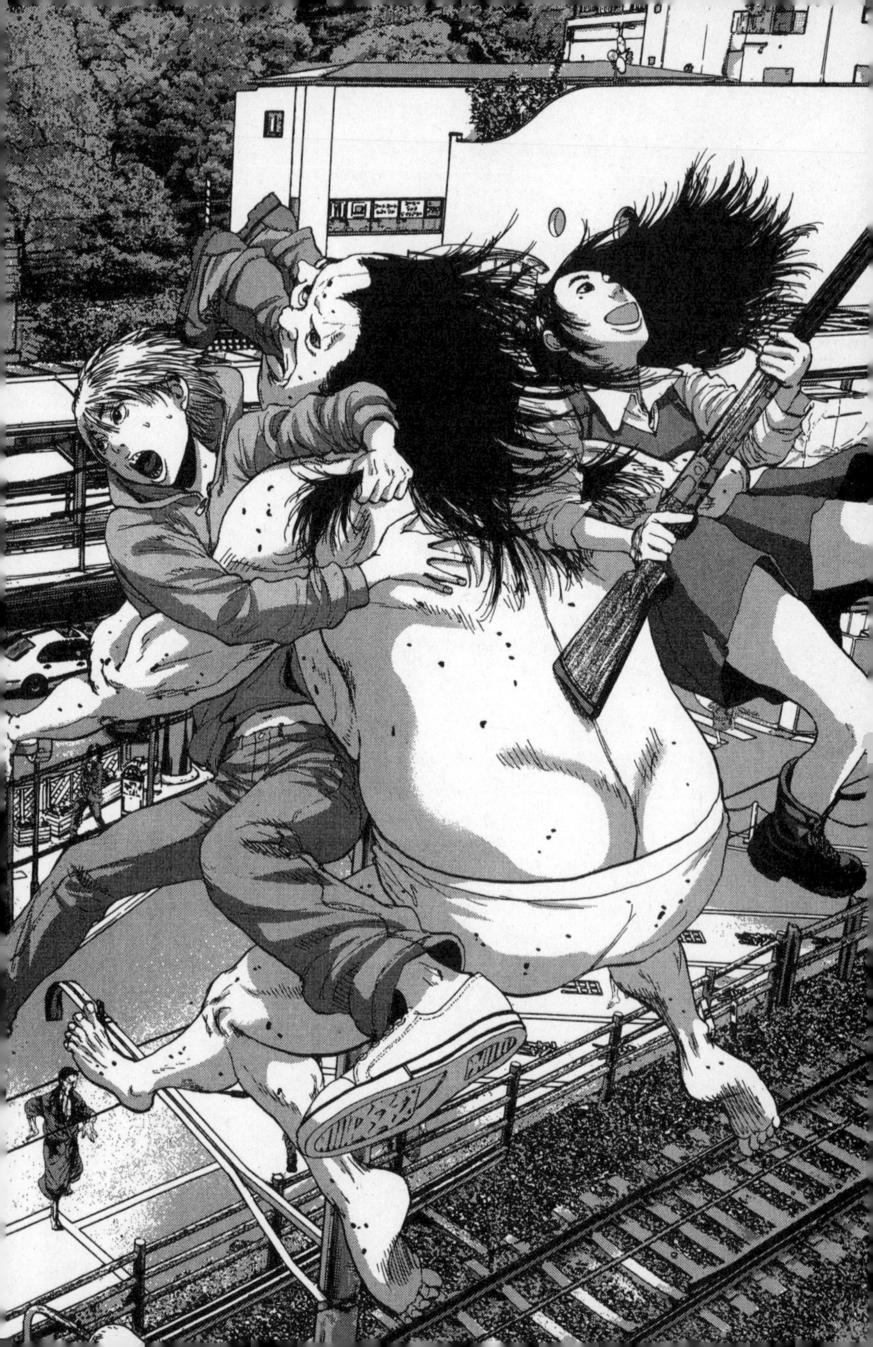

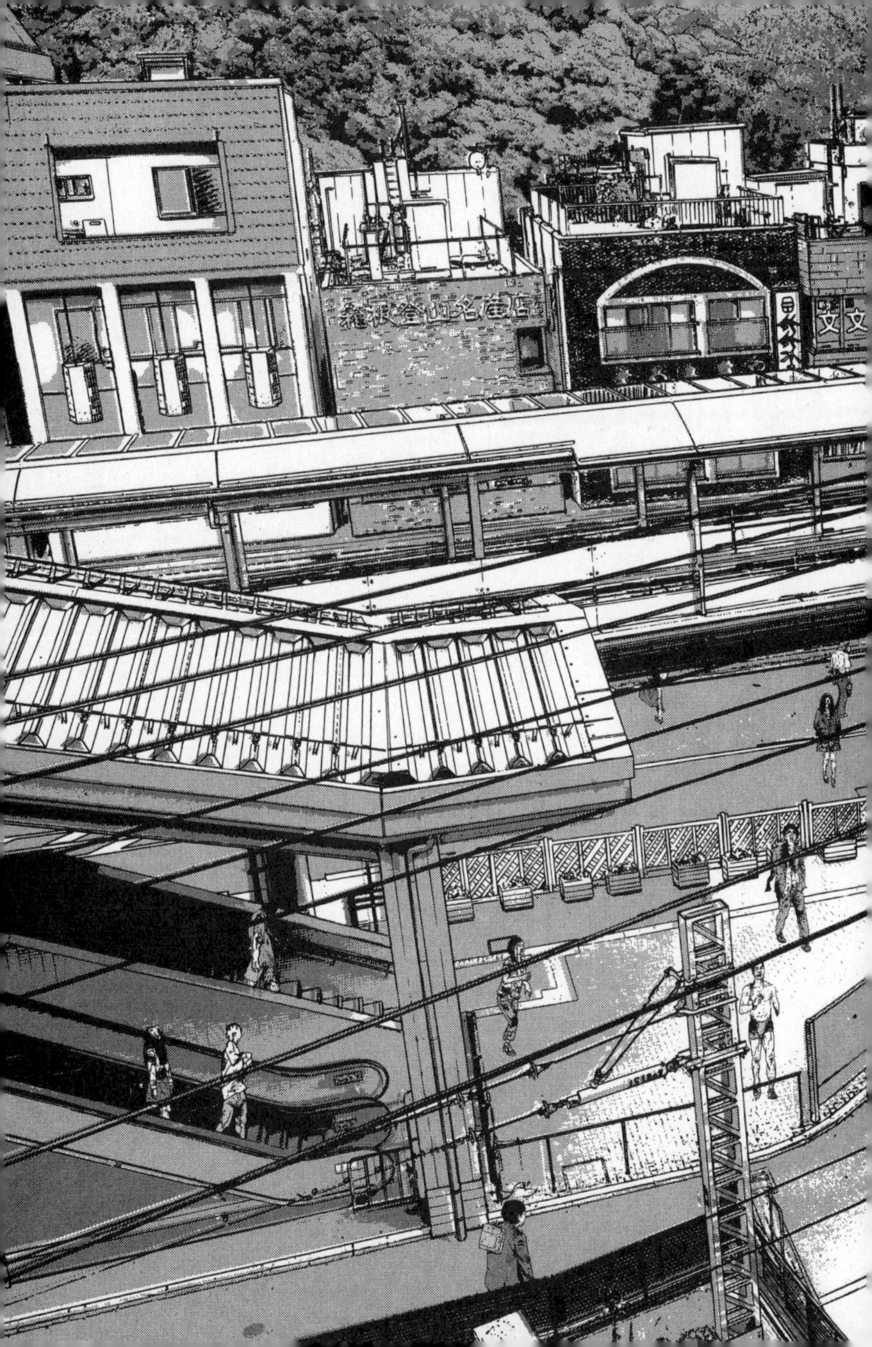

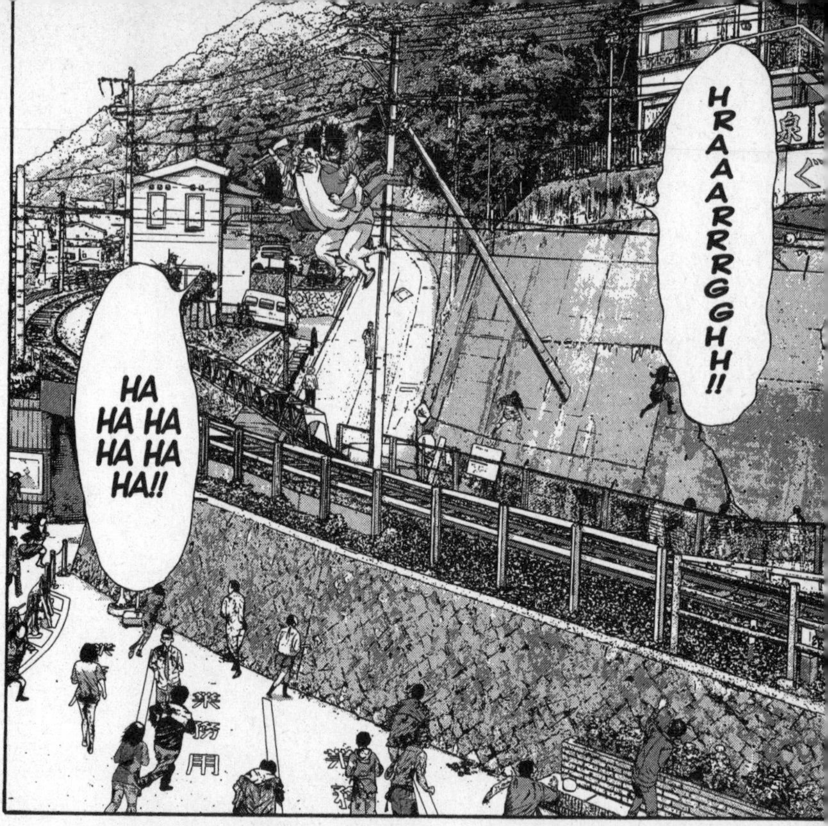
HRAAARRGGHH!!
HA HA HA HA HA HA HA!!

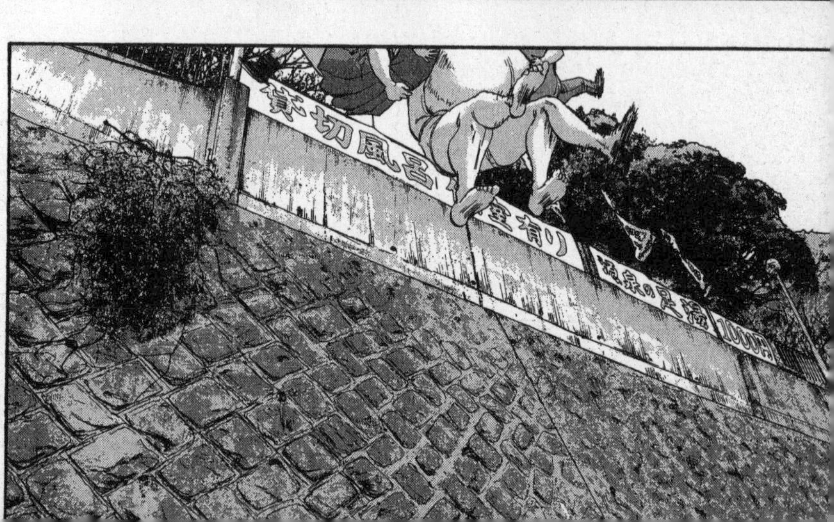
貸切風呂

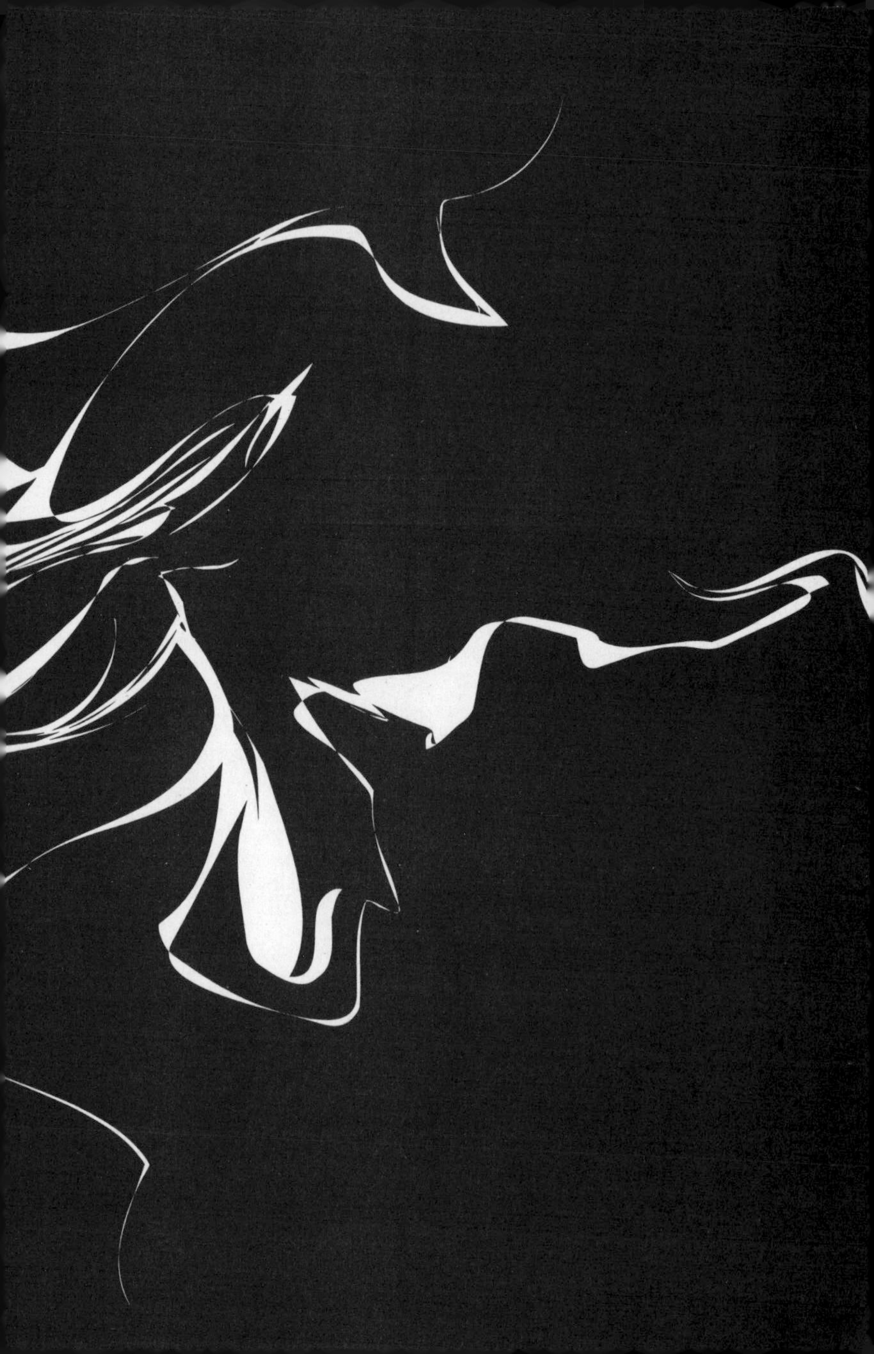

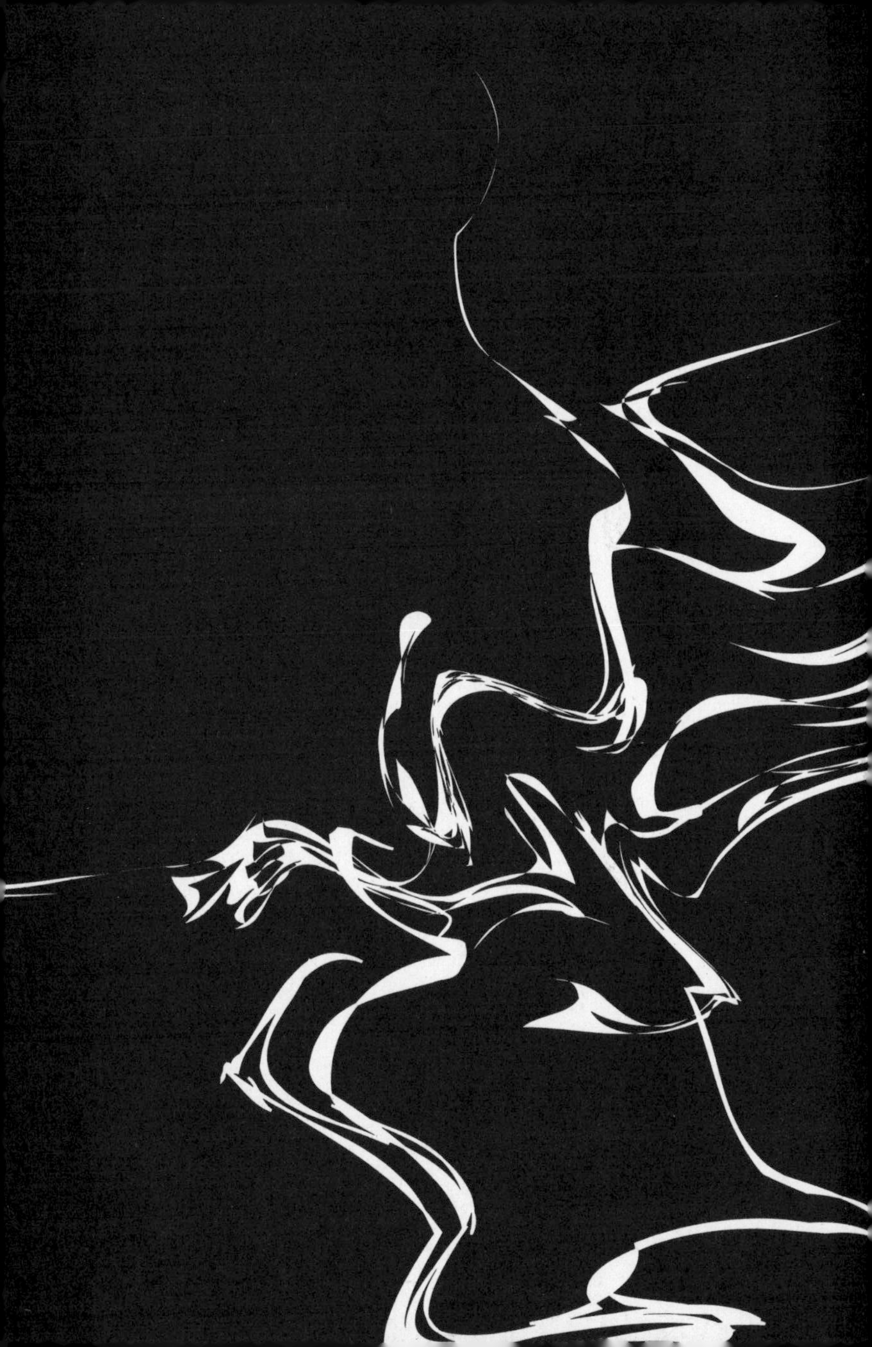

I AM A HERO

I AM A HERO

TRANSLATION NOTES

HAPTER 146

lan and Cécile talk about "Gresbaak Castle," which they visited a ong time ago. "Gresbaak" is a deliberate misspelling of and nod o Gaasbeek Castle in Belgium.

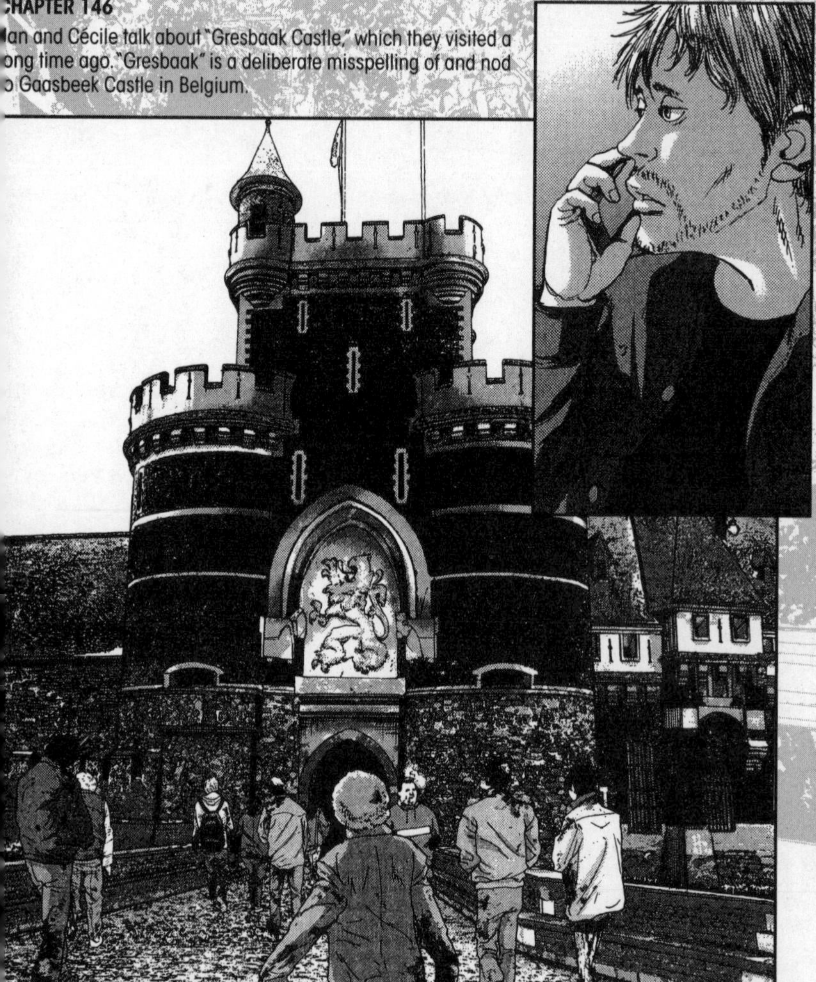

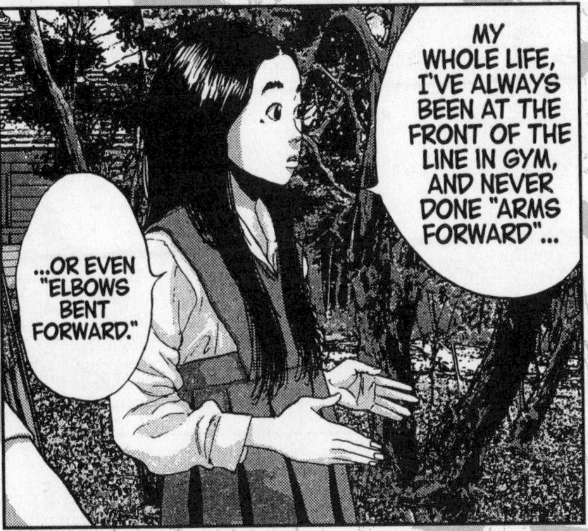
MY WHOLE LIFE, I'VE ALWAYS BEEN AT THE FRONT OF THE LINE IN GYM, AND NEVER DONE "ARMS FORWARD"...
...OR EVEN "ELBOWS BENT FORWARD."

CHAPTER 147

Hiromi remarks, "My whole life, I've always been at the front of the line in gym, and never done 'arms forward' or even 'elbows bent forward.' I only ever do 'hands on hips!'" This refers to a practice in Japanese Physical Education classes in which students line up in a single-file line (conga-line style), in order of height. The student in front puts their hands on their hips. All other students put their arms out straight to maintain an even distance between everybody. If a shorter line is needed for whatever reason, the students put their arms out with their elbows bent

CHAPTER 150

"My name's Oda. I'm a nurse." It seems that after being partially infected and then taking a crossbow bolt to the head, Hiromi has some post-coma amnesia, which is not strange given the trauma she endured. In addition to growing taller and being physically stronger than before, Hiromi doesn't seem to remember everything that happened with the doomed group of survivors living above the mall in *I Am a Hero Omnibus* Volumes 3 and 4.

Later in this chapter, Hideo mentions "Murai's bacon," referring to the food scavenged by fellow survivor Masakazu Murai when the group of mall survivors went on an ill-fated supply run in *I Am A Hero Omnibus* Volume 4.

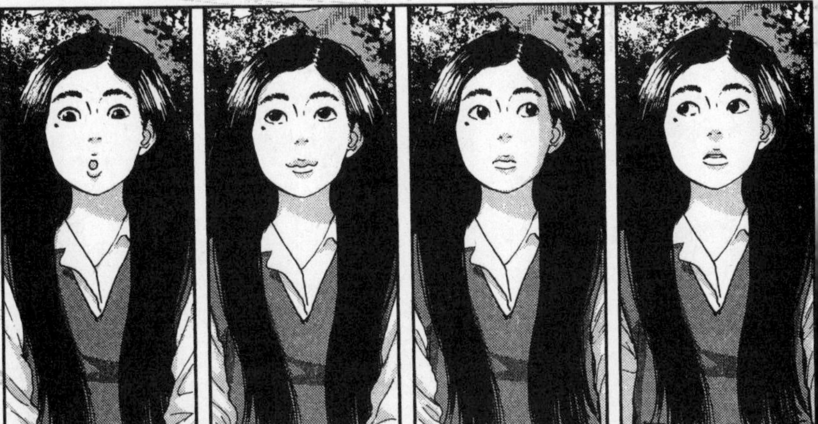

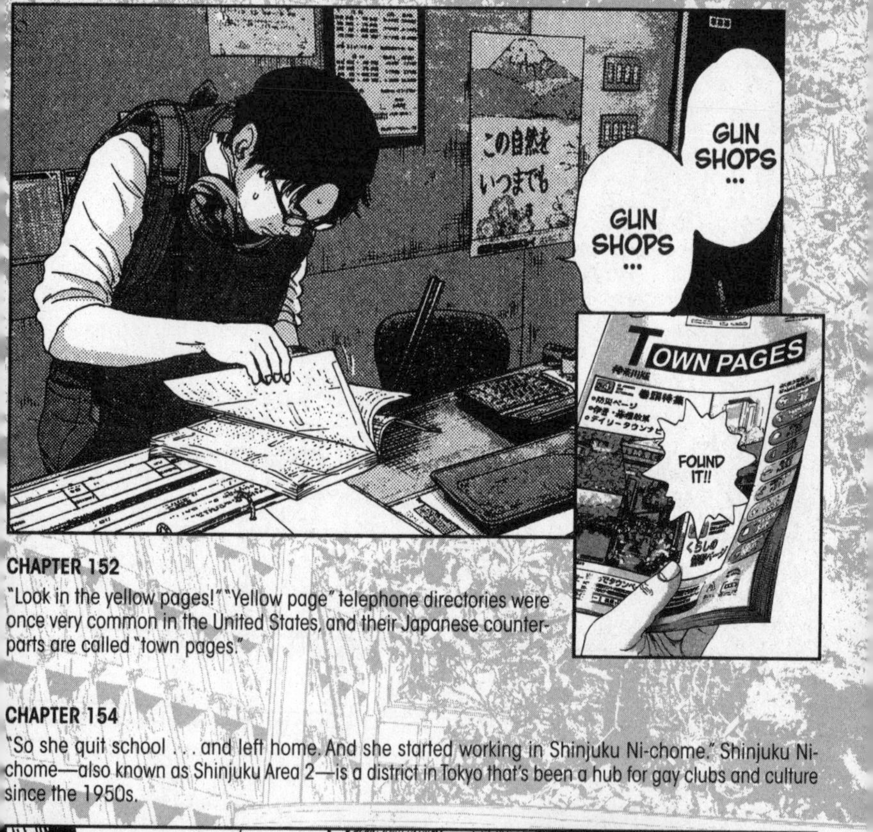
この自然を
いつまでも
GUN SHOPS...
GUN SHOPS...
TOWN PAGES
FOUND IT!!

CHAPTER 152

"Look in the yellow pages!" "Yellow page" telephone directories were once very common in the United States, and their Japanese counterparts are called "town pages."

CHAPTER 154

"So she quit school . . . and left home. And she started working in Shinjuku Ni-chome." Shinjuku Ni-chome—also known as Shinjuku Area 2—is a district in Tokyo that's been a hub for gay clubs and culture since the 1950s.

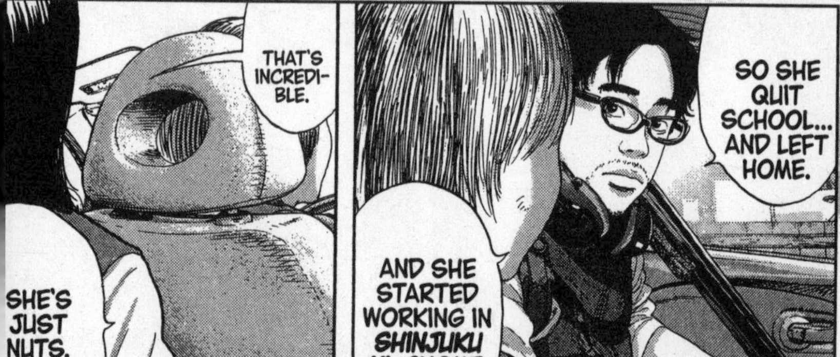
SO SHE QUIT SCHOOL... AND LEFT HOME.
AND SHE STARTED WORKING IN SHINJUKU NI-CHOME.
THAT'S INCREDIBLE.
SHE'S JUST NUTS.

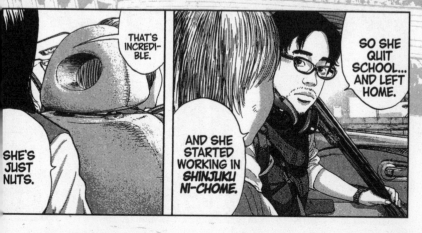

CHAPTER 159

"Hiromi! You're a *human*, aren't you?" asks Oda. At this point, Hiromi is now a human-ZQN hybrid, more akin to the multiple Kurusu creatures than the full-blown mindless zombies—but no longer completely human. ZQN is a word used for the infected that stems from the Japanese use of "DQN" on bulletin boards and in text messages to refer to someone as a "dumbass" or "delinquent." DQN itself is a play on the word "dokyun." In this case, the ZQN are fully "zombified" and tied to hive minds or "nests," while other human-ZQN hybrids retain some human independence and personal memories and benefit from superhuman strength and endurance. Some human-ZQN hybrids are known as "Kurusus." A Kurusu appears to be a higher-functioning human-ZQN hybrid with incredible strength, the ability to coexist with and quell the anger of ZQNs (making some gather in nest-like locations), and the ability to mentally communicate with other ZQNs. All Kurusu hybrids seem to be male, unpredictably violent, and tend to wear only underwear. Hiromi appears to be a hybrid—but she's not a Kurusu.

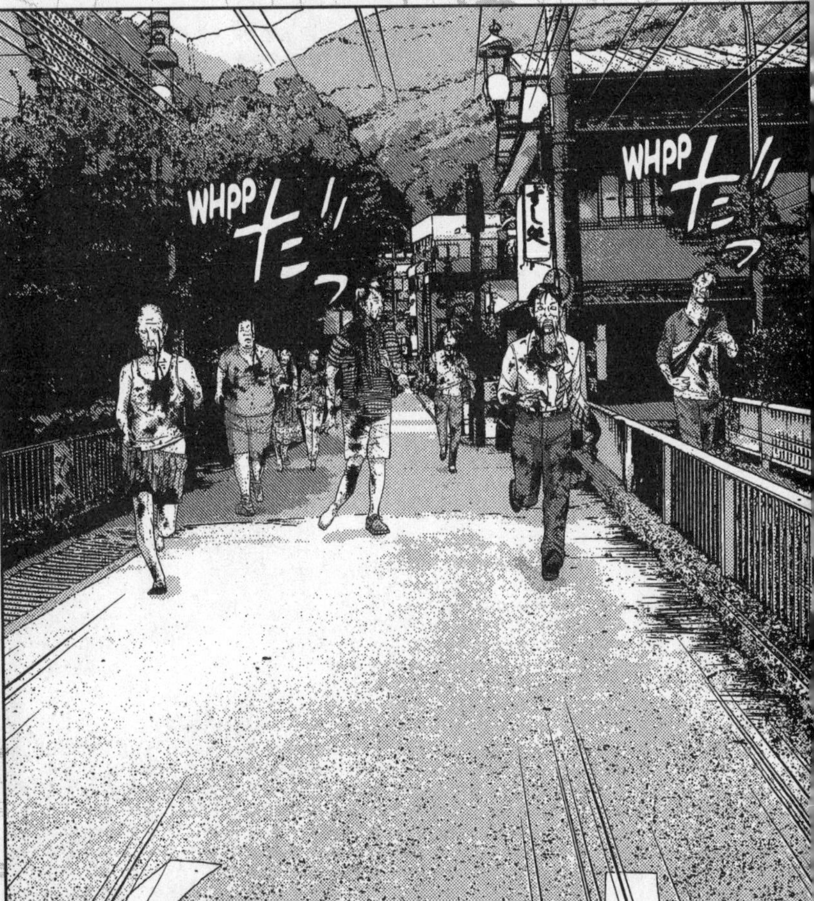
WHPP
WHPP

I AM A HERO

OMNIBUS 8—COMING SOON!

OUR ZOMBIE-SURVIVAL SAGA GETS STRANGER!

As the ZQN virus continues to mutate and alter those living and dead, Hiromi and Oda attempt to get free from a zombie swarm to find help for Hideo. Across Japan, those who are fully ZQN begin to band together in surprising ways. When another group of survivors is found, Kengo Hanazawa's epic manga series beings to steamroll over readers and zombies alike as it revs up the action and moves closer to its stunning finale! A best-selling international hit series, a major motion picture, and—according to the Anime News Network—"the greatest zombie manga ever." Collecting two of the original Japanese volumes into each value-priced Dark Horse edition, this volume ends with yet another traumatic cliffhanger that will have readers shaking the gates for more!

Hiroaki Samura's Eisner Award–winning manga epic

BLADE OF THE IMMORTAL

OMNIBUS

Volume 1
ISBN 978-1-50670-124-0
$21.99

Volume 2
ISBN 978-1-50670-132-5
$21.99

Volume 3
ISBN 978-1-50670-172-1
$21.99

Volume 4
ISBN 978-1-50670-569-9
$21.99

Volume 5
ISBN 978-1-50670-567-5
$21.99

Volume 6
ISBN 978-1-50670-568-2
$21.99

Also by Hiroaki Samura:

Hiroaki Samura's Emerald and Other Stories
ISBN 978-1-61655-065-3
$12.99

Ohikkoshi
ISBN 978-1-59307-622-1
$12.99

The Art of Blade of the Immortal
ISBN 978-1-59582-512-4
$29.99

publisher
MIKE RICHARDSON

senior editor
PHILIP R. SIMON

associate editor
MEGAN WALKER

collection designer
LIN HUANG

digital production
CHRISTINA McKENZIE

Special thanks to Michael Gombos and Carl Gustav Horn for editorial assistance and advice. Special thanks to Chitoku Teshima and Velan Sivasubramanian for translation assistance.

Art staff, original volumes 13 and 14: Jurii Okamoto, Yukihiro Kamiya, Hiroki Tomizawa, Kurao Nabe, Miki Imai, Yoshitaka Mizutani, Satomi Hayashi.

Original Cover Design: Norito INOUE Design Office

This omnibus volume collects the original *I Am a Hero* volumes 13 and 14, published in Japan.

I AM A HERO OMNIBUS 7 by Kengo HANAZAWA / TOCHKA

Dark Horse Manga | A division of Dark Horse Comics, Inc.
10956 SE Main Street, Milwaukie, OR 97222

DarkHorse.com

To find a comics shop in your area, visit the Comic Shop Locator Service at comicshoplocator.com

First edition: August 2018
ISBN 978-1-50670-702-0

10 9 8 7 6 5 4 3 2 1

Printed in the United States of America

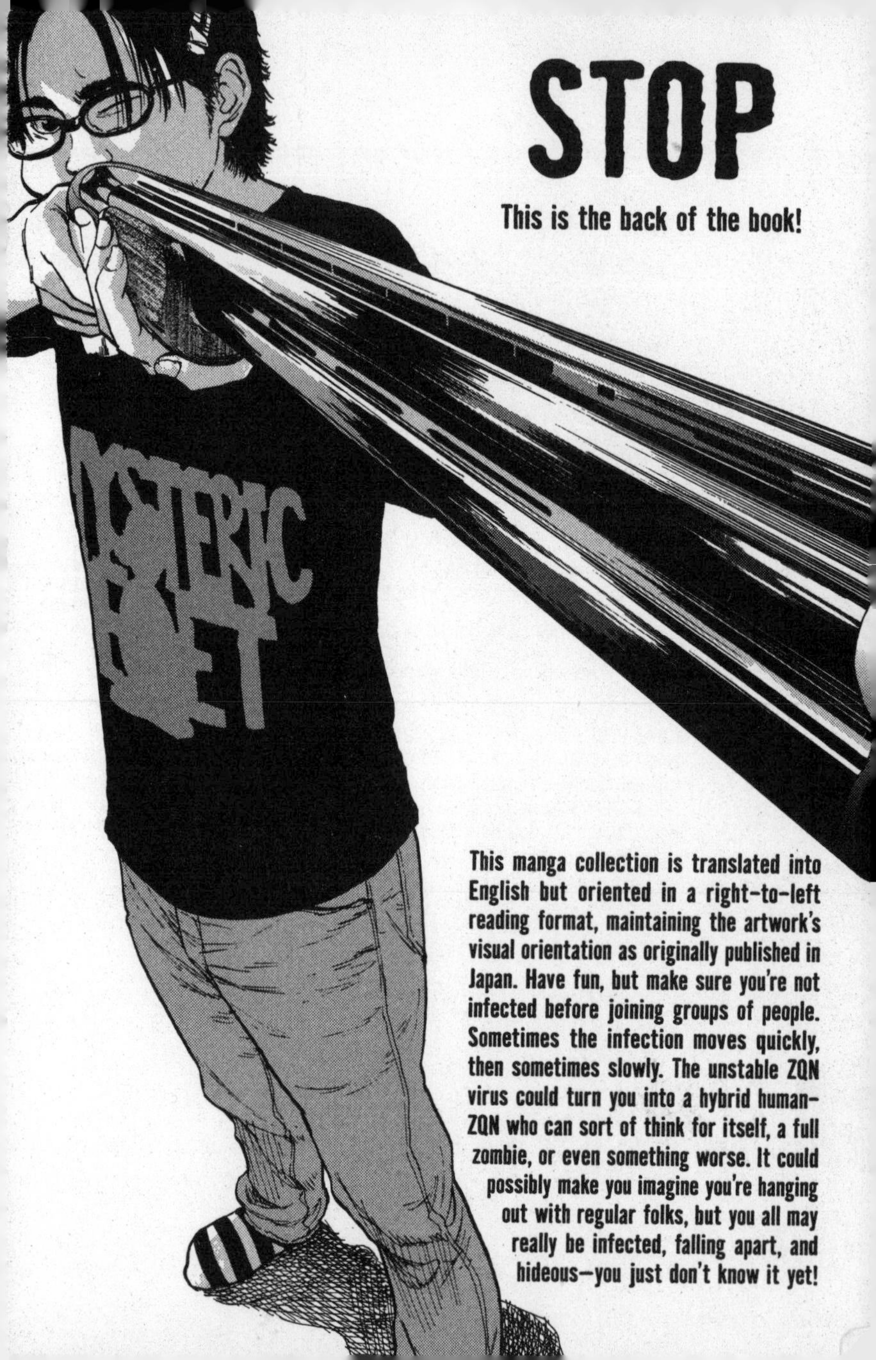

STOP

This is the back of the book!

This manga collection is translated into English but oriented in a right-to-left reading format, maintaining the artwork's visual orientation as originally published in Japan. Have fun, but make sure you're not infected before joining groups of people. Sometimes the infection moves quickly, then sometimes slowly. The unstable ZQN virus could turn you into a hybrid human-ZQN who can sort of think for itself, a full zombie, or even something worse. It could possibly make you imagine you're hanging out with regular folks, but you all may really be infected, falling apart, and hideous—you just don't know it yet!